CUSTOMER RELATIONSHIP MARKETING
Theoretical and Managerial Perspectives

CUSTOMER RELATIONSHIP MARKETING

Theoretical and Managerial Perspectives

Naresh K Malhotra
Georgia Institute of Technology, USA

James Agarwal
University of Calgary, Canada

 **World Scientific**

NEW JERSEY · LONDON · SINGAPORE · BEIJING · SHANGHAI · HONG KONG · TAIPEI · CHENNAI · TOKYO

Published by

World Scientific Publishing Co. Inc.

27 Warren Street, Suite 401-402, Hackensack, NJ 07601, USA

Head office: 5 Toh Tuck Link, Singapore 596224

UK office: 57 Shelton Street, Covent Garden, London WC2H 9HE

British Library Cataloguing-in-Publication Data
A catalogue record for this book is available from the British Library.

CUSTOMER RELATIONSHIP MARKETING
Theoretical and Managerial Perspectives

ISBN 978-1-944659-71-4 (hardcover)
ISBN 978-1-944659-74-5 (paperback)
ISBN 978-1-944659-72-1 (ebook for institutions)
ISBN 978-1-944659-73-8 (ebook for individuals)

For any available supplementary material, please visit
https://www.worldscientific.com/worldscibooks/10.1142/Y0022#t=suppl

Desk Editor: Karimah Samsudin

Typeset by Diacritech Technologies Pvt. Ltd.
Chennai - 600106, India

Printed in Singapore

With gratefulness and thankfulness to our Savior and Lord Jesus Christ, this book is dedicated to our wives: Veena Malhotra and Pritam Agarwal. Their love, encouragement, and support have been exemplary.

"Houses and wealth are inherited from parents, but a prudent wife is from the Lord." Proverbs 19:14

"For this reason a man will leave his father and mother and be united to his wife." Mark 10:7

Brief Contents

Contents

Chapter 5
Building Employee–Customer Relationship Quality and Engagement Strategies: A Stakeholder Framework 135

Chapter 11
Future of Customer Relationship
Marketing: New Directions
for Research 309

Preface

This book is about creating long-lasting, profitable, and mutually beneficial relationships with customers, businesses, institutions, as well as consumers, in the fast-changing 21st century. The field of marketing is changing dramatically, driven by several factors such as the empowerment of customers, technology, innovation, automation, social media, globalization, and the ever-changing social, economic, and political landscapes. These forces only serve to heighten the importance of building enduring relationships with customers. That, indeed, is the central focus of this book, which has both a theoretical and an applied and managerial orientation. It also emphasizes a hands-on, do-it-yourself approach, affording students several opportunities to experience customer relationship marketing (CRM) concepts through pedagogical tools such as opening vignettes, real-life examples, questions, group discussions, and Harvard Business School (HBS) and Ivey cases.

Audience

This comprehensive book is suitable for graduate (e.g., MBA, Masters in Marketing Research/Marketing Analytics) and upper-level undergraduate courses in customer relationship marketing. It is also appropriate for use in executive programs (e.g., EMBA). It presents material in a manner that is easy to read and understand, with diagrams, tables, pictures, illustrations, and examples that explain the basic concepts. The text thoroughly covers all the commonly used concepts, theories, and models encountered in customer relationship marketing.

Organization

The book is organized into 11 chapters. In Chapter 1, we provide a formal definition of marketing followed by several definitions of relationship marketing highlighting the key aspects of this concept. Customer relationship marketing evolved from traditional marketing concept and has broadened its scope today, intersecting with the following domains, namely customer buying behavior process models, customer satisfaction and loyalty, service quality, customer relationship management tools and strategies, customer centricity, and customer engagement activities. We map the evolution of customer relationship marketing and chronicle its shifting emphasis from one of value distribution and independence, i.e., short-term competition and conflict to value (co)creation and inter-dependence, i.e., long-term mutual cooperation in Chapter 2. Over the years, the foundational premises and axioms of relationship marketing have both broadened and deepened intersecting with allied marketing concepts including service dominant logic, customer-centric marketing, customer-as-assets thinking, and customer experience and engagement models. Several theories, models, and frameworks, both classic and contemporary that explain antecedents, processes, and outcomes of customer relationships with companies are briefly discussed in Chapter 2.

In Chapter 3, we primarily focus on business-to-business (B2B) relationships. First, we highlight the key differences between B2B versus business-to-consumer (B2C) marketing and set the stage for the six-market framework of relationship marketing, originally developed by Peck *et al.* (1999) with subsequent revisions by Payne *et al.* (2005). Building on this framework, we then discuss the modified and reconfigured stakeholder framework developed by Malhotra and Agarwal (2002). We discuss how firms build and sustain customer relationships by stimulating customer purchase behavior via loyalty programs in Chapter 4. Loyalty programs often tap into multiple psychological and social processes simultaneously. Here, we discuss four motivational mechanisms including: (1) instrumental benefits, (2) symbolic benefits, (3) emotional benefits, and (4) cognitive benefits. Next, we discuss how firms build and sustain customer relationships by stimulating customer non-purchase behavior via engagement strategies. Here, also, we discuss five motivational mechanisms including: (1) relationship-based motivation, (2) identification-based motivation, (3) justice-based motivation, (4) goal-based motivation, and (5) control-based motivation.

In Chapter 5, we provide a stakeholder-based framework that examines the criteria, pillars, and dimensions of relationship quality for employees and customers. In advancing this framework, we intersect the multiple views of stakeholder management and relationship quality. Next, we discuss employee–customer engagement theories, particularly the service-profit chain (SPC) paradigm (original and extended), a set of moderating factors, and finally, employee–customer engagement strategies. Analytical models and strategies are covered in Chapter 6. First, we discuss CRM-based analytical models, both for purchase and non-purchase customer behavior. Various models are discussed including traditional metrics such as recency-frequency-monetary value model, share of wallet model, and past customer value models as well as contemporary models based

on customer lifetime value (CLV) concept. CLV is an advanced forward-looking metric and several variations of the family of CLV models are briefly discussed, including model formulation, estimation, and key merits and demerits. Next, we provide models for customer engagement including customer referral value (CRV), customer influence value (CIV), and customer knowledge value (CKV). Finally, we discuss strategies for maximizing CLV, segmentation strategies, extending CLV to customer engagement value, and linking customer equity to shareholder value.

In Chapter 7, we first discuss brand equity from the firm's perspective followed by customer-based brand equity — its definition and dimensions, namely brand awareness, brand association, perceived quality, and brand loyalty. Subsequently, we present the integrative brand equity model and examine brand equity creation from the relationship marketing perspective. The linkage between customer–brand relationship and corporate reputation is discussed in Chapter 8. We then discuss the inter-relationship between corporate reputation and customer relationship marketing. Next, we discuss an identity-based symbolic–instrumental framework of customer-based reputation explaining how customer–brand congruity, brand prominence, and customer–company identification affect perceptions of corporate reputation.

In Chapter 9, we first discuss positive ethics using the popular Hunt–Vitell (1986) framework, followed by a detailed discussion of normative ethics in marketing, examining consequences-based ethical theories, duty-based ethics, contract-based morality, and virtue-based ethics. In particular, we provide detailed discussion on justice-based theories and moral foundations theories including a firm's moral authority in the marketplace. Finally, we discuss the case of digital marketing and privacy as seen from the customers' lens of ethical theories. In Chapter 10, we examine the intricate relationship between digital and social media marketing and customer–brand relationship. First, we discuss how digital technologies are changing marketing strategies by way of search engine advertising, mobile marketing, and the Internet of things (IoT), followed by a framework of digital marketing that links the five 'C's — (1) customers, (2) collaborators, (3) competitors, (4) context, and (5) the company. The next part of this chapter relates to social media marketing and customer relationship marketing. In the final chapter, Chapter 11, we discuss several important research directions that are promising as a result of big data revolution, availability of computing power, and emerging models of estimating customer lifetime value, both transaction/ engagement-based B2C activities. We also discuss some unintended consequences (dark side) of customer–brand relationships including multiple forms of disidentification and privacy-related issues in the context of normative ethics. Finally, we discuss challenges and new research opportunities in B2B relationship marketing.

Harvard Business School and Ivey Cases

To show the integration of customer relationship marketing (CRM) with marketing management decisions, the book includes three Harvard Business School (HBS) cases and one Ivey case. Relationship marketing questions geared to this book are given in each chapter. All these cases come with Teaching Notes that are accessible to instructors. Answers to all the case questions are provided in the Instructor's Manual.

Students can purchase all four cases directly from Harvard Business Publishing Case Center at https://www.thecasecentre.org/students.

The following are the cases:

- AnswerDash (9-516-106)
- Reinventing Best Buy (9-716-455)
- Chase Sapphire (9-518-024)
- Laurs & Bridz (9B18A004)

Supplements

The textbook comes with a complete set of supplements that include:

1. **Functional and Useful Web Site.** The book is supported by a Web site that is password protected, containing the following:

   - The entire instructor's manual

   - Test item file

   - PowerPoint slides containing all the main concepts, all figures, and all tables

2. **Instructor's Manual.** We personally wrote the entire *Instructor's Manual* so that it is very closely tied to the text. Each chapter contains chapter outline; and answers to all end-of-chapter review questions, group discussions, and case questions for each of the four cases.

3. **Test Item File.** This valuable resource contains a wide variety of questions for each chapter that allows you to create your own exams.

4. **PowerPoint Slides.** These slides contain the major concepts, all the figures, and all the tables for each chapter of the book. Each chapter also contains video hyperlinks pertaining to real-life CRM issues.

Acknowledgments

Many people have been extremely helpful in the writing of this textbook. We would like to acknowledge Professors Can Uslay and Ahmet Bayraktar who coauthored the first relationship marketing book (with Naresh K. Malhotra) that we published with Business Expert Press. That book laid the foundation for the present textbook. We also gratefully acknowledge research contribution made by Yizhe Lin, doctoral student at the University of Calgary, especially in the topic of brand equity and digital marketing.

The team at World Scientific Publishing provided very good support. Special thanks are due to Chua Hong Koon for commissioning this book and for his support throughout the project and to Karimah Samsudin for editorial direction and support.

I acknowledge with great respect my late parents, Mr. H.N. Malhotra and Mrs. Satya Malhotra. Their love, encouragement, support, and the sacrificial giving of themselves have been exemplary. My heartfelt love and gratitude go to my wife, Veena, and my children, Ruth and Paul, for their faith, hope, and love.

– Naresh K. Malhotra

I humbly acknowledge the unconditional love, prayers, and wisdom of my late parents, Mr. Joel Agarwal and Mrs. Sorola Agarwal, who set a Godly example to me from my early years. Words cannot express my deep love and gratitude to my wife, Pritam, for the many sacrifices she has graciously made over the years so I could achieve my dreams. I dedicate this book to her. Through the writing of this book, I also want to inspire my four boys, Joel, Joshua, Johanan, and Joseph, to set goals in life, stay focused trusting in the Lord, and to give their best in whatever they endeavor.

– James Agarwal

Above all, both of us want to acknowledge and thank our Savior and Lord, Jesus Christ, for the many miracles He has performed in our lives. This book is, truly, the result of His grace — "This is the Lord's doing; it is marvelous in our eyes" (Psalm 118:23). It is also an answer to prayers — "And whatsoever ye shall ask in my name, that will I do, that the Father may be glorified in the Son. If ye shall ask any thing in my name, I will do it" (John 14:13–14).

Naresh K. Malhotra
James Agarwal

About the Authors

Dr Naresh K Malhotra is Senior Fellow, Georgia Tech CIBER, and Regents' Professor Emeritus, Scheller College of Business, Georgia Institute of Technology, USA. In 2010, he was selected as a Marketing Legend, and his refereed journal articles were published in nine volumes by Sage with tributes by other leading scholars in the field. He is listed in Marquis Who's Who in America continuously since the 51st Edition (1997), and in Who's Who in the World since 2000. In 2017, he received the Albert Nelson Marquis Lifetime Achievement Award from Marquis Who's Who. In 2015, he received the Lifetime Achievement Award from the Prestige Institute of Management, Gwalior, India. In 2011, he received the Best Professor in Marketing Management, Asia Best B-School Award. He received the prestigious Academy of Marketing Science CUTCO/Vector Distinguished Marketing Educator Award in 2005. He has several top (number one) research rankings that have been published. His book entitled *Marketing*
Research: An Applied Orientation, seventh edition, published by Pearson Education, has been translated into several languages and is the global leader. Likewise, his books, *Basic Marketing Research: Integration of Social Media*, fourth edition, and *Essentials of Marketing Research* are widely used globally. He is the winner of numerous awards and honors for research, teaching, and service to the profession, including the Academy of Marketing Science Outstanding Marketing Teaching Excellence Award, 2003. He also has received several Best Paper awards. He has an active consulting practice. Dr. Malhotra is an ordained minister of the Gospel, a member and Deacon, First Baptist Church, Atlanta, and President of Global Evangelistic Ministries, Inc. (https://www.globalevangelisticministries.net/).

Dr James Agarwal (PhD, Georgia Tech) is Haskayne Research Professor and Full Professor of Marketing at the Haskayne School of Business, University of Calgary, Canada. He served as the CCAL Research Fellow (2013–2016), Research Director (2013–2015), and Area Chair of Marketing (2002–2005) at the Haskayne School of Business. He is listed in Canadian Who's Who, University of Toronto Press, and Marquis Who's Who in America. In 2017, he received the Albert Nelson Marquis Lifetime Achievement Award from Marquis Who's Who. His research interests are in International Marketing, Relationship Marketing, Consumer Psychology,

Ethical Issues in Marketing, and Statistical Methods. He has published 55 papers in major refereed journals, proceedings, and book chapters, and presented research papers in more than 85 national and international conferences. He has edited two books: *Research Methodology: Conjoint Analysis, Multidimensional Scaling & Related Techniques* (Sage Publication, 2011); and *Emerging Issues in Global Marketing: A Shifting Paradigm* (Springer, 2018). He has received several Best Paper awards and recognitions, including William R Darden Best Paper Award, Hans B Thorelli Best Paper Award, Temple/AIB Best Paper Award (Finalist), Most Prolific Scholar in IB Research (MSU 2005), and Best Paper Awards in Customer Relationship Management and Branding & Brand Management Tracks granted by the American Marketing Association. He is a member of the American Marketing Association, Academy of International Business, and the Academy of Marketing Science.

Commendations

Naresh Malhotra and James Agarwal have crafted a highly readable and engaging text on the creation and management of customer relationships. The book is filled with relevant tools and examples that make it immediately useful for a reader. It addresses customer relationships in both business-to-consumer (B2C) and business-to-business (B2B) contents and from the initiation of relationship building to the management of the most mature of relationships. Faculty seeking a text will find the book complete, with an instructor's manual, slide, and test bank. However, the practicing manager will also find the book a helpful source of new insights and analytical tools. The book is an outstanding addition to the literature on customer relationships.

Dr. David W. Stewart
President's Professor of Marketing and Business
Law, Loyola Marymount University
Vice President, Publications,
American Marketing Association
Past Editor, *Journal of Marketing, Journal of the
Academy of Marketing Science, Journal of Public
Policy & Marketing*

This text offers practical customer relationship marketing (CRM) guidance based on a solid theoretical foundation. An especially nice feature is the forward-looking perspective on customer engagement, customer experience, and the customer journey, big data, ethics, and other challenges facing today's managers.

Dr. Ruth N. Bolton
Professor of Marketing, Arizona State University
Past Editor, *Journal of Marketing*

This state-of-the art textbook by eminent scholars provides a much needed approach to teaching customer relationship marketing. The book integrates and synthesizes customer relationship marketing across the entire marketing system. This integrated customer contact and engagement approach recognizes all marketing elements including business-to-consumer (B2C) and business-to-business (B2B) relationships necessary to deliver value. The linkage of reputation, branding, and ethics to success provides a highly teachable framework. This is the first textbook to provide comprehensive coverage of all the domains of customer relationship marketing.

Dr. O.C. Ferrell
James T Pursell Sr. Eminent Scholar in Ethics
Director, Center for Ethical Organizational
Cultures
Department of Marketing
Raymond J. Harbert College of Business, Auburn
University
President, Academy of Marketing Science

This is by far the best and most comprehensive textbook on relationship marketing! It is very readable and full of real-world case studies and examples.

Dr. Jagdish N. Sheth
Charles H. Kellstadt Chair in Marketing,
Goizueta Business School, Emory University
Past President, Association for Consumer
Research

Put this on your bookshelf and in your classroom! This is a comprehensive guide to understanding and managing customer relationships from two top scholars and educators. Not only does it incorporate both business-to-consumer (B2C) and business-to-business (B2B) relationships, it also outlines the entire customer journey using actual examples and applications to the current marketing environment. I am looking forward to integrating this into my own classrooms.

Dr. Linda L. Price
Professor and Dick and Maggie Scarlett Chair
College of Business, University of Wyoming
Editor, *Journal of Consumer Research*
Past President, Association for Consumer
Research

01

Introduction to Customer Relationship Marketing

OVERVIEW

In Chapter 1, we provide a formal definition of marketing followed by several definitions of relationship marketing highlighting the key aspects of this concept. Customer relationship marketing (CRM) opportunities are embedded in the entire customer journey spanning several touch points across all stages including prepurchase, purchase, and postpurchase stage. Customer relationship marketing evolved from a traditional marketing concept and has broadened its scope today, intersecting with the following domains, namely customer buying behavior process models, customer satisfaction and loyalty, service quality, customer relationship management tools and strategies, customer centricity, and customer engagement activities. In this chapter, we present a structure of how the book is organized and provide a brief summary of the contents broken down by chapters (Chapters 2 to 11). At the end of each chapter, we provide key takeaways and conclude with discussion questions and HBS and Ivey cases. But first, to give a flavor of CRM, we provide some real-life vignettes.

Figure 1.1: Customer relationship marketing has a broad scope in the current business and nonbusiness environments.

OPENING VIGNETTES

Vignette 1: Despite continuous troubles and shrinking profits, there is one thing in the airline industry that has continuously grown — the customer loyalty program. The idea behind the frequent-flier programs (first launched by American Airlines in 1981, i.e., AAdvantage program) was to target passengers, especially business passengers, who tend to pay more and fly more frequently. The programs enabled the airlines to build brand loyalty in a highly competitive and somewhat undifferentiated market (see Figure 1.1). Today, airlines still have the largest loyalty program membership with more than 250 million members who enjoy different ways to earn, consolidate with partner airline programs, and redeem miles. That said, as loyalty programs have become the industry norm today and with tighter industry regulations, airlines are now focusing more on their most valuable customers using the customer lifetime value (CLV) model.

Vignette 2: In 2009, Nike partnered with the Livestrong Foundation to launch the 'Chalkbot' marketing communication initiative during the Tour de France event. Nike provided the hashtag #livestrong to enable customers who could not attend the event to contribute creative stories and messages of inspiration, hope, and encouragement to the Tour bikers. As an incentive, select messages were printed on Tour roads and on a website with a robot-captured photo of the message along with the GPS coordinates. The result — this initiative led to more than 4,000 follower gain on Twitter leading to over 36,000 participant-generated messages. It also raised over $4 million for the Livestrong cause and won several international advertising awards. Importantly, for Nike, its sales of apparel line increased by 46 percent.

Vignette 3: Starbucks has a blog, My Starbucks Idea (MSI) (mystarbucksidea.force.com), where it not only connects with customers but also co-creates the company's future with them. Customers can share ideas, vote on ideas others have suggested, discuss ideas with other customers, and view the ideas Starbucks has announced. Starbucks's Idea Partners from different departments within the company take part in answering queries and providing insights to discussions. Starbucks can then get ideas and feedback on how to improve its products to satisfy the needs of customers. The brand takes suggestions posted on the site seriously and publishes implemented suggestions for all to see. It encourages feedback from customers by providing online incentives in the form of virtual vouchers or purchase points. This enables the brand to interact with its loyal customers. In addition, Starbucks also includes qualitative and quantitative types of survey questions in the form of polls along the sidelines of the blog to solicit marketing research data. My Starbucks Idea has a significant impact — on average, one in three suggestions is implemented. All suggestions are acknowledged and commented on within an hour of uploading; an average of four suggestions is made every hour.

Starbucks's Facebook page (www.facebook.com/starbucks) has more than 37 million fans, and the number is still growing. It uses this site to promote new products and gain the feedback of customers. It also organizes events and uses Facebook's technology to invite customers to attend its events. Starbucks also uses its Facebook page to develop a target market's profile. In addition, Starbucks also uses Twitter (www.twitter.com/starbucks) to promote products and connect with customers. The firm uses Twitter to update customers about new products and services with short messages. Tools like retweets allow users to spread messages originally tweeted by Starbucks to others. Starbucks's Twitter account often directs followers to MSI for polls, surveys, or opinions casting. Starbucks also uses many other forms of social media. From the tropics of the Bahamas to the Forbidden City in Beijing, social media has helped Starbucks in establishing relationships and meeting the needs of customers (see Figure 1.2). As of 2019, the brand is represented in more than 70 countries, and continues to grow.

Figure 1.2: Starbucks has made effective use of social media to establish relationships with customers all over the globe.

INTRODUCTION

Evolving Definitions of Relationship Marketing

The American Marketing Association's definition of marketing, approved in 2017, states "marketing is the activity, set of institutions, and processes for creating, communicating, delivering, and exchanging offerings that have value for customers, clients, partners, and society at large" (AMA, 2017). Prior to this revision, AMA's 2004 definition stated that "marketing is an organizational function and a set of processes for creating, communicating, and delivering *value to customers and for managing customer relationships* in ways that benefit the organization and its stakeholders". While the new definition subsumes 'relationship marketing' (RM) implicitly, given the growing prevalence and preponderance of relationships with stakeholders, it now extends to multiple stakeholders, including society at large.

Several definitions of relationship marketing have been advanced over its evolution since its inception (Berry, 1983; Gronroos, 1997; Morgan and Hunt, 1994; Sheth and Parvatiyar, 2000). Starting chronologically, Berry (1983, p. 25) defines relationship marketing as, "Attracting, maintaining, and in multi-service organizations, enhancing customer relationships." Morgan and Hunt (1994, p. 22) define relationship marketing as "all marketing activities directed toward establishing, developing, and maintaining successful relational exchanges." Gronroos (1997, p. 407) defines it as a "[p]rocess of identifying and establishing, maintaining, enhancing, and when necessary terminating relationships with customers and other stakeholders, at a profit, so that the objectives of all parties involved are met, where this is done by a mutual giving and fulfillment of promises." Sheth and Parvatiyar (2000, p. 9) define it as "the ongoing process of engaging in cooperative and collaborative activities and programs with immediate and end-user customers to create or enhance mutual economic value at reduced cost." Finally, Palmatier (2008, p. 4) defines RM as "the process of identifying, developing, maintaining, and terminating relational exchanges with the purpose of enhancing performance."

Palmatier (2008) points out three key aspects that are fundamental to the definition of relationship marketing. These are (1) stage; (2) scope; and (3) success. The first aspect deals with relationship marketing activities and exchange characteristics that systematically vary across the four stages of RM lifecycle — (1) identifying, (2) developing, (3) maintaining, and (4) terminating. The second aspect deals with the scope or target of relationship marketing activities. Some restrict it to customer relationships, while others include relationships with stakeholders, opening its gamut to any target 'entity'. The broadened scope seems to align with today's marketplace, wherein firms often compete through their network of interfirm relationships (Rindfleisch and Moorman, 2003). Another facet of this aspect pertains to the unit of analysis or level of the relationship. Relationships can be formed and evaluated between individuals, i.e., interpersonal; between an individual and a firm, i.e., person-to-firm or firm-to-person; and between firms, i.e., interfirm. The third key aspect deals with the locus of benefits derived from relationship marketing activities. Palmatier (2008) argues that relationship marketing needs to generate benefits for both parties to achieve the implementer's long-term performance. However, relationship marketing is often initiated by one party, not for altruistic motivations, even though both parties mutually benefit. For example, firms that initiate relationship marketing evaluate program effectiveness from the returns on their investments. Customer value generated by relationship marketing efforts provides a means to increasing the firm's performance, rather than an end to itself. Profit motive is the principle business driver and so unprofitable relationships should be terminated and relationship-building investments should target optimal returns.

While Palmatier (2008) advocates the unilateral position given that firms target optimal returns and that unprofitable relationships are often terminated when such targets are not attained, we argue that long-term relationship marketing is built on mutually beneficial bilateral returns for both parties, i.e., value co-creation that underlies the tenets of the service-dominant (S-D) logic paradigm (Vargo and Lusch, 2004). In today's digital economy and social media platforms, the scope of customer relationship marketing has expanded to various types of customer engagement behaviors. We borrow from the groundbreaking work of Vargo and Lusch (2004, 2008) who laid down several fundamental premises of the S-D logic, four of which are directly relevant in explaining the conceptual foundations of customer engagement. In essence, the customer is always a co-creator of value; all social and economic actors are resource integrators which implies that value creation occurs in the context of networks; value is always uniquely and phenomenologically determined by the customer emphasizing the subjective and experiential nature of value co-creation; and that a service-centered view is inherently customer-oriented and relational (Brodie *et al.*, 2011).

Lemon and Verhoef (2016) chronicle the evolution of customer experience concept in marketing and its historical interconnections with allied marketing concepts that have taken center stage over the last five decades. They identify several themes including (1) *customer buying behavior process models* (1960s–1970s) focusing on customer decision processes and experience, including the most influential models namely, Howard and Sheth (1969) model. Many contemporary models of customer

experience owe their origins in customer decision-making process models or the path-to-purchase models; (2) *customer satisfaction and loyalty* (1970s) assessing and evaluating customer perceptions and attitudes about an experience; (3) *service quality* (1980s) identifying the specific context and elements of the customer experience and mapping the customer journey, especially the development of the SERVQUAL model (Parasuraman, Zeithaml, and Berry, 1988); (4) *relationship marketing* (1990s) broadening the scope of customer responses considered in the customer experience (e.g., Berry, 1995; Sheth and Parvatiyar, 1995) by including relational outcomes of trust, commitment, and relationship quality, as an overarching construct; (5) *customer relationship management* (2000s) identifying how specific elements of the customer experience influence each other and firm outcomes, including optimizing customer profitability and CLV (Kumar and Reinartz 2006); *customer centricity* (2000–2010s) focusing on the interdisciplinary and organizational challenges associated with successfully designing and managing customer experience (e.g., Sheth, Sisodia, and Sharma, 2000); and *customer engagement* (2010s) recognizing the customer's role in the experience, both attitudinally and behaviorally, that extend beyond purchase (e.g., Brodie *et al.*, 2011; Kumar *et al.*, 2010).

Based on the evolution of the multiple definitions of customer relationship marketing and its conceptual overlap with several marketing concepts over time, we propose the following working definition of customer relationship marketing in the context of B2C marketing: *Relationship marketing is the process of identifying, developing, maintaining, and if necessary terminating relational exchanges, including purchase and non-purchase-related exchanges, with customers as resource integrators in a networked environment, with the purpose of mutual value cocreation and enhancing firm performance.*

Engagement Marketing vs. Traditional and Relationship Marketing

Customer engagement marketing is a firm's deliberate effort to motivate, empower, and measure a customer's voluntary contribution to the firm's marketing functions beyond the core economic transaction. The firm attempts to guide the customer in ways that are beneficial to the firm, such that it is deliberately initiated and actively managed (Schmitt *et al.*, 2011). Harmeling *et al.* (2017) discuss five distinct characteristics that distinguish engagement marketing from promotional marketing and relationship marketing. These are summarized in Table 1.1.

First, engagement marketing encourages customers to actively participate and contribute to the firm's marketing functions such as word-of-mouth marketing, crowdsourcing, and social customer relationship management. Here, economic transactions with the focal customer are the key to develop future non-economic transactions to realize customer contributions to the firm. In contrast, promotion marketing is single transaction-oriented to create interest and influence the purchase of the firm's products, whereas relationship marketing is focused on future repeat transactions. Second, customer value is assessed by the resources owned by customers and their potential future

Table 1.1: Customer Engagement Marketing Theory Framework

Engagement marketing	Promotion marketing	Relationship marketing
A firm's deliberate effort to motivate, empower, and measure a customer's voluntary contribution to the firm's marketing functions beyond the core, economic transaction (i.e., customer engagement)	The use of a special offer to raise a customer's interest and influence the purchase of the focal product versus competitors' products (Wierenga and Soethoudt 2010)	"All marketing activities directed towards establishing, developing, and maintaining successful relational exchanges" (Morgan and Hunt 1994, p. 22)
1. Objective of the marketing initiative Encourage a customer's active participation in and contribution to the firm's marketing functions	Induce a single transaction with the focal firm versus a competitive firm	Retain the focal customer and motivate future, repeat transaction with the customer
2. Assesment of customer value Customer-owned resources and potential future contributions to the firm's marketing functions	Purchasing power and customer share of wallet	Customer lifetime value from past customer transactions
3. Flow of information Networked communication among the customer, other customers, and the firm	One-way communication from the firm to the customer	Bilateral communication between the customer and the firm
4. Firm-directed customer learning Training a customer how to contribute to the firm's marketing functions	Teaching the customer how to buy and use the focal product	Understanding the idiosyncratic norms of the exchange relationship
5. Customer control over value creation Customer exercises high control, which can affect outcomes relevant to the broader customer population	Customer has no control over value creation and is a receiver of marketing	Customer control is negotiated with the firm, which affects outcomes relevant to the focal customer-firm relationship

Adapted from Colleen M. Harmeling, Jordan W. Moffett, Mark J. Arnold, and Brad D. Carlson (2017), Toward a Theory of Customer Engagement Marketing, *Journal of the Academy of Marketing Science* 45, pp. 312–335.

contributions to the firm. In contrast, in promotion marketing, customer value is based on purchasing power or share of wallet, and in relationship marketing, CLV is the common metric used. Third, in engagement marketing, information flows through networked communication among customers, other customers, and the firm. In contrast, in promotion marketing, information flow is one-way from the firm to the customer, and in relationship marketing, it is bilateral. Fourth, firms direct customer learning in their new roles of pseudo-marketers, unlike promotion marketing, where the focus is on trial and usage of the product, or in relationship marketing, where the focus is on relational norms. Finally, the firm has to give up some control to the customer in engagement marketing wherein the customer influences the content and outcomes of many marketing functions that potentially influences the broader network (Hollebeek *et al.*, 2016). This is starkly different from promotion marketing, where customers are recipients of marketing functions or from relationship marketing, where value is negotiated within the customer–firm relationship and not beyond.

With a broadened scope of customer relationship marketing and deeper relational touchpoints, in this book, we have organized the chapters that emphasize the following aspects in keeping with our proposed expanded definition:

- building and sustaining relationship strategies for customer purchase and non-purchase behavior;

- customers and employees as critical stakeholders and how to build employee-customer engagement strategies;

- value co-creation and firm performance determined by CRM-based analytical models and metrics;

- brand equity and customer relationship marketing; corporate reputation and customer-brand relationship;

- perceptions of value from customers' viewpoint including ethical foundations of customer relationship marketing; and

- customer relationship marketing in a digitally networked marketplace including social media platforms.

In addition, given the importance of business-to-business (B2B) relationships and stakeholder framework to relationship marketing, we have also devoted one full chapter (Chapter 3) covering the important aspects of this relationship domain. We conclude this book by offering insights for future research for customer relationship marketing scholars. The breakdown of the chapters is as follows.

BOOK OVERVIEW

In Chapter 2, we map the evolution of customer relationship marketing examining its lifecycle stages of adoption, development, and expansion in B2C marketing over the last three decades. We start our discussion with the paradigm shift away from value distribution and independence to value co-creation and interdependence (Sheth and Parvatiyar, 2000). In particular, we discuss several theories, models, and frameworks that explain the antecedents, processes, and outcomes of customer relationships with companies. These include the:

- buyer-seller model (Dwyer, Schurr, and Oh, 1987);

- trust-commitment model (Morgan and Hunt, 1994);

- service dominant (S-D) logic (Lusch and Vargo, 2004);

- interpersonal relationship marketing (B2C) model (Palmatier, 2008);

- interfirm relationship marketing (B2B) model (Palmatier, 2008);

- reverse logic framework of relationship marketing (Kumar *et al.*, 2009);

- customer engagement behavior model (Van Doorn *et al.*, 2010);

- customer engagement marketing theory (Harmeling *et al.*, 2017);

- customer experience model (Lemon and Verhoef, 2016); and

- customer valuation model (Kumar, 2018).

In Chapter 3, we focus our attention exclusively to business-to-business (B2B) relationships. Building on Peck *et al.* (1999) and later revised by Payne *et al.* (2005), we adopt the Malhotra and Agarwal (2002) stakeholder framework of relationship marketing. This framework is reconfigured to provide special and independent status to B2B markets, B2C markets, competitor markets, and revised internal markets, all hallmarks of the market orientation concept. We also discuss the revised levels of relationship marketing — functional, structural, and strategic levels, each at the marketing unit, strategic business unit, and organizational unit level. Given the growing importance of strategic level organizational initiatives, a separate section is devoted to strategic alliances characterizing interfirm cooperation between competitors wherein each partner pools complimentary skills, resources, and knowledge, while working toward a common strategic purpose. Next, we discuss relationship dynamics in buyer–seller relationships, covering concepts such as dependence/interdependence, satisfaction, trust, commitment, and types of control in channel relationships (see Figure 1.3). In particular, we discuss two frameworks, namely, (1) the resource-based view framework of interdependence structure, and (2) the S-D logic framework in buyer-seller relationship. Finally, we end the chapter discussing in detail the importance of both upstream and downstream relationship marketing, and the importance of relationship management capability.

Figure 1.3: Relationship dynamics in buyer—seller relationships involve dependence/ interdependence, satisfaction, trust, commitment, and types of control.

In Chapter 4, we first discuss how firms build and sustain business-to-customer (B2C) relationships by stimulating customer *purchase behavior* via loyalty programs (Bijmolt *et al.*, 2018). Customer retention is the goal of loyalty programs, and herein we discuss the psychological and social mechanisms underlying customer motivations in loyalty program participation, including:

- instrumental benefits,

- symbolic benefits,

- emotional benefits, and

- cognitive benefits.

Next, we discuss how firms build and sustain customer relationships by stimulating customer *non-purchase behavior* via engagement strategies. Over the years, the foundational premises and axioms of relationship marketing have both broadened and deepened intersecting with allied marketing concepts including service dominant logic, customer-centric marketing, customer-as-assets thinking, and customer experience and engagement models. Here, we first discuss the concept of customer engagement, its conceptual intersection with the service dominant (S-D) logic (Vargo and Lusch, 2004; 2008), followed by a framework of customer engagement (Pansari and Kumar, 2017). Similar to purchase behavior, non-purchase engagement behaviors are also motivated by several underlying psychological mechanisms, including:

- relationship-based motivation,

- identification-based motivation,

- justice-based motivation,

- goal-based motivation, and

- control-based motivation.

We also discuss customer engagement through customization efforts in firm level marketing-mix strategies (Bleier, Keyser, and Verleye, 2018).

In Chapter 5, we first examine relationship quality from a stakeholder perspective. Building on three stakeholder relationship criteria, namely, descriptive, instrumental, and normative criteria (Donaldson and Preston, 1995), and focusing on the multiple facets of the relational construct of trust, namely, ability, benevolence, and integrity dimensions (Mayer, Davis, and Schoorman, 1995), we develop arguments as to which of these facets of trust form foundational bases upon which the focal firm can develop relationships with different stakeholders. In this chapter, we consider the case of two important stakeholders, (1) employees as internal stakeholders, and (2) customers as external proximal customers. In particular, we discuss stakeholder relationship criteria, pillars of stakeholder relationship quality, and dimensions of stakeholder relationship quality for both groups of stakeholders, employees, and customers. We argue that effective management of relationships is a function of understanding the appropriate stakeholder relationship criteria (i.e., descriptive, instrumental, and normative) for each stakeholder type (i.e., employees and customers) and how these influence the foundational pillars of relationship quality and, consequently, the dimensions of relationship quality. Our stakeholder framework is consistent with established theoretical perspectives on organizations. In advancing this framework, we intersect the multiple views of stakeholder management and relationship quality. Further, we highlight research on employee engagement and customer engagement, and discuss employee–customer engagement theories, particularly the original service-profit chain (SPC) paradigm (Heskett *et al.*, 1994) and the extended SPC paradigm (Hogreve *et al.*, 2017), along with a set of moderating factors. As both employee and customer engagement is linked with firm performance (Kumar and Pansari, 2016), we end the chapter discussion with employee–customer engagement strategies.

In Chapter 6, we discuss CRM-based analytical models, both for purchase and non-purchase customer behavior. Traditional metrics such as Recency-Frequency-Monetary value (RFM), Share of Wallet (SOW) and Past Customer Value (PCV), and tenure and duration are discussed. However, given their inherent limitations in not being able to link with total customer value concept, we discuss forward-looking metrics based on customer lifetime value (CLV) concept. The CLV metric, considers the future value of a customer to the firm, and aids in designing and implementing marketing strategies for the present, thus maximizing profitability (Gupta, Hanssens, Hardie, *et al.*, 2006). CLV is an advanced forward-looking metric and several variations of the family of CLV models are briefly discussed, including model formulation, estimation, and key merits and demerits. Primarily based on the work of V. Kumar and several scholars (e.g., Venkatesan and Kumar, 2004; Venkatesan, Kumar, and Bohling, 2007, Rust, Lemon, and Zeithaml, 2004; Rust, Kumar, and Venkatesan, 2011; Dreze and Bonfrer, 2009; Sunder, Kumar, and Zhao, 2016), CLV application has gained widespread popularity across all sectors and industries. Next, we provide models for customer engagement including customer referrals (CRV) (Kumar, Peterson, and Leone, 2007), customer influence (CIV) (Kumar *et al.*, 2013), and customer knowledge (CKV) (Kumar *et al.*, 2013). We next discuss strategies for maximizing CLV, segmentation strategies using CLV and Share of Unused Wallet (SUW), extending CLV to customer engagement value, and linking customer equity to shareholder value. Finally, managers are cautioned to find meaning behind the metrics and to put the 'relationship' back into CRM in truly understanding customer relationships.

In Chapter 7, we first discuss brand equity from the firm's perspective followed by customer-based brand equity — its definition and dimensions, namely brand awareness, brand association, perceived quality, and brand loyalty (Aaker, 1996; Keller, 1993; Rindova

et al., 2005; Dick and Basu, 1994). Next, we present an integrative brand equity model (Burmann, Jost-Benz, and Riley, 2009) that considers behavioral significance of a brand for internal stakeholders (i.e., employees), consisting of brand commitment and brand citizenship behavior (i.e., internal brand strength) as well as for external stakeholders (i.e., customers), consisting of knowledge, benefit, and preference oriented measures (i.e., external brand strength). Finally, we examine brand equity creation from the relationship marketing perspective. Four factors are examined: customer-based brand equity factors (Buil, de Chernatony, and Martínez, 2013), market signaling factors (Hess and Story, 2005), brand identity factors (Buil, de Chernatony, and Martínez, 2013), and consumer-brand relationship factors.

In Chapter 8, we discuss the links between corporate reputation and customer-brand relationship. Interest in corporate reputation has never been higher, and we see this renewed emphasis on protecting and enhancing reputation in the growing number of reputation rankings published in popular business press. Every firm must have three crucial qualities to sustain strong customer-brand relationships — (1) legitimacy, (2) relevancy, and (3) differentiation. While the latter two often receive their impetus from brand strategies, the former is a function of reputation. We begin our discussion by conceptualizing corporate reputation as seen from the customers' perspective, wherein reputation is positioned as an abstract construct (reputation-as-assessment, generalized favorability) consisting of first-order asset constructs (reputation-as-asset constructs denoted by perceived value, market prominence, and societal ethicality). Customers often use higher-order activations that serve to trigger perceptions of lower-order dimensions (halo effect) as quick and effortless heuristics in reputational judgments. Based on this conceptualization, we then discuss the interrelationship between corporate reputation and customer relationship marketing.

Next, we discuss an identity-based symbolic-instrumental framework of customer-based reputation explaining how customer-brand congruity, brand prominence, and customer-company identification affect perceptions of corporate reputation.

In Chapter 9, we discuss the ethical foundations of customer relationship marketing. Despite the preponderance of positive ethics approach to tackling ethical issues in marketing, firms today continue to exhibit ethical (and legal) lapses in decisions that have widespread repercussions. We emphasize the urgent and critical need for normative ethics in conjunction with positive ethics as the two are symbiotically intertwined. We start our discussion highlighting the important and influential role of positive ethics specifically using the popular Hunt-Vitell (1986) framework. The initial model was conceptualized to provide a general theory of ethical decision-making process that draws on both the deontological and teleological ethical traditions in moral philosophy. The revised model is argued to be a *general* theory of ethical decision-making, not just of *marketing* ethics, incorporating multiple ethics' perspectives and concepts. Next, we discuss normative ethics in marketing, examining consequences-based ethical theories, duty-based ethics, contract-based morality, and virtue-based ethics (Murphy, Laczniak, and Harris, 2017; Laczniak and Murphy, 2019). In particular, we provide detailed discussion on justice-based theories, namely, the social exchange model of justice (Blau, 1964), the group value model of justice (Lind and Tyler, 1988; Tyler, 1994), the instrumental model of justice (Thibaut and Walker 1975), and the heuristic model of justice (Van den Bos *et al.*, 1997; 1998). Following justice-based theories, we discuss the moral foundations theories (Haidt and Graham, 2007; Haidt and Joseph, 2004) that help explain justifying how a particular ethical standard might apply to a given marketing practice and articulating the reasons for upholding such an ideal. In the wake of growing expectations of stakeholders for firms to engage in social/political issues and motivate change, we also examine a framework of company moral authority in the marketplace (Hoppner and Vadakkepatt, 2019). Finally, we discuss the case of digital marketing and privacy as seen from the customers' lens of ethical theories (Martin and Murphy, 2017).

In Chapter 10, we examine the intricate relationship between digital and social media marketing and customer brand relationship. Digital marketing is defined as "an adaptive, technology-enabled process by which firms collaborate with customers and partners to jointly create, communicate, deliver, and sustain value for all stakeholders." First, we discuss how digital technologies are changing marketing strategies by way of search engine advertising, mobile marketing, and the internet of things (IoT), followed by a framework of digital marketing proposed by Kannan and Li (2017) that delineates how digital technologies interact with the five Cs — customers, collaborators, competitors, context, and company, as well as the interface among these elements. The next part of this chapter relates to social media marketing and relationship marketing. We discuss social media marketing followed by two frameworks of social media: (1) contingency framework of social commerce by Yadav *et al.* (2013) and (2) the functional blocks framework by Kietzmann *et al.* (2011). Yadav *et al.* (2013) organized the framework to discuss the value-creation potential of social commerce spanning the four stages of customer decision-making process:

1. Need Recognition,

2. Pre-Purchase,

3. Purchase, and

4. Post-Purchase.

Kietzmann *et al.* (2011) provides a honeycomb framework to classify different social media activities by analyzing the users' needs engaging in diverse

Figure 1.4: Customer relationship marketing makes use of social media to reach out and establish lasting relationships with customers.

social media. Specifically, the framework includes seven functional blocks:

1. Identity,

2. Conversations,

3. Sharing,

4. Presence,

5. Relationship,

6. Reputation, and

7. Groups.

We then discuss and provide an assessment of the critical issues in the implementation of social media marketing. We discuss several functions, including identity function (brand personality), conversation function (customer re-engagement), sharing function (crisis management), presence function (i.e., the 'Like' button), relationship function (social CRM), reputation function (eWOM), and group function (brand community) (see Figure 1.4). Finally, we summarize the seven steps to social media success for firms (Kumar and Mirchandani, 2012).

In Chapter 11, we discuss several important research directions that seem promising as a result of access to big data, availability of computing power, and emerging models of estimating customer lifetime value, both transaction and engagement-based activities. Specifically, we discuss the following areas worthy of future research: static versus dynamic views of relationship (Palmatier, 2008); financial vs. engagement outcomes (Palmatier, 2008); engagement strategies and relationship stages (Venkatesan *et al.*, 2018); digital and social media strategies (Yadav *et al.*, 2013); unintended consequences of relationship marketing strategies such as customer expectations and entitlement (Bijmolt *et al.*, 2018), customer heterogeneity (Steinhoff and

Palmatier, 2015), and customer reactance (White *et al.*, 2008); multiple facets of customer identification with companies including identification, disidentification, ambivalent identification, and neutral identification (Kreiner and Ashforth, 2004); role of normative ethics in relationship marketing (Murphy *et al.*, 2007); and modeling new types of costs in customer's value perception such as information privacy (Kumar and Reinartz, 2016).

KEY TAKEAWAYS

- Traditional definition of relationship marketing such as 'all marketing activities directed toward establishing, developing, and maintaining successful relational exchanges' has been broadened and customer relational touchpoints deepened. As a result, customer relationship marketing (B2C) today is best understood as a 'process of identifying, developing, maintaining, and if necessary terminating relational exchanges, including purchase and non-purchase-related exchanges, with customers as resource integrators in a networked environment, with the purpose of mutual value co-creation and enhancing firm performance'.

- Economic transactions with the focal customer are the key to develop future non-economic transactions, including engagement marketing, to realize customer contributions to the firm.

In contrast, promotion marketing is single-transaction oriented to create interest and influence the purchase of the firm's products, whereas traditional relationship marketing is focused on future repeat transactions only.

- Based on S-D logic, B2C customers are resource integrators in a networked marketplace and customer value is assessed by the resources owned by customers and their potential future contributions to the firm. The firm has to give up some control to the customer, wherein the customer influences the content and outcomes of many marketing functions that potentially influences the broader network. This is different from promotion marketing where the customer is the recipient of the marketing function and customer value is based on purchasing power or share of wallet, and in traditional relationship marketing where value is negotiated within the customer-firm relationship and not beyond, and where CLV is the common metric used.

- B2B relationships focus on value generation with a range of stakeholders at the functional, structural, and strategic levels. These key stakeholders include customer markets (channels), customer markets (end users), supplier markets, competitor markets, external influence markets, and internal markets (see Figure 1.5). The role of strategic alliances, a form of interfirm cooperation, is critical to successful relationship marketing at the B2B level.

Figure 1.5: Customer relationship marketing embraces a variety of stakeholders.

STAKEHOLDER

INVESTORS COMMUNITY TRADE UNIONS GOVERNMENT SUPPLIERS CUSTOMERS CREDITORS

- Marketers need to understand the psychological mechanisms underlying B2B relational dynamics such as buyer–seller dependence/interdependence, satisfaction, trust, commitment, and control. Similar to B2C setting, S-D logic can also be applied to B2B relationships wherein sellers cater not only to core and augmented operand resources but also operant resources, particularly the augmented operant resources. There are several opportunities for marketers to build quality relationships with, both, upstream and downstream channels.

- Firms need to understand that employee engagement is critical toward customer engagement and firm performance. As a result, effective management of relationships with these two key internal and external stakeholders is essential.

- Firms need to integrate traditional metrics with newer forward-looking CRM models that include customer purchase (CLV models) and non-purchase behavior (CRV, CIV, and CKV models). Managers are cautioned to find meaning behind the metrics and to put the 'relationship' back into CRM in truly understanding customer relationships with companies.

- Brand is a 'customer-centric' concept that focuses on what a product/service or the firm has promised to its customers, whereas corporate reputation is a 'company-centric' concept that focuses on the credibility and respect that a firm has among a broad set of stakeholders.

- There is an urgent and critical need for firms to understand and implement normative ethics in conjunction with positive ethics as the two are symbiotically intertwined. Customers' perceptions of value include ethics and morality as seen by customers, and implemented by marketers, in customer-brand relationships. The role of ethics is more pronounced in digital and social media platforms wherein protection of privacy is increasingly determining customers' assessment of value.

EXERCISES

Questions

1. Define relationship marketing. Which definition(s) of relationship marketing appeals to you the most and why?

2. The nature and essence of relationship marketing has evolved over the years. Compare promotion marketing with relationship marketing and engagement marketing.

3. Compare B2C vs. B2B relationship marketing. Explain how the tenets of the S-D logic can be applied to value creation in both B2C and B2B relationships?

4. What are some of the ways companies stimulate and build customer purchase and non-purchase behavior?

5. Why is brand strength important for both employees (internal brand strength) and customers (external brand strength)?

6. What is the relationship between (a) brand equity and customer relationship marketing and (b) corporate reputation and customer relationship marketing?

7. How important is it for marketers to uphold the highest standards of ethics and morality in building customer–company relationships?

8. Compare CRM strategies using traditional approach with digital technologies and social media platforms.

9. What are some of the limitations and unintended consequences of relationship marketing both for marketers and customers?

Group Discussion

1. As a small group, discuss the expanded role of relationship marketing with critical firm stakeholders including customers, clients, partners, and society at large. Discuss the role of marketing in fostering stakeholder-based relationships.

2. From the company's point of view, critically discuss whether marketers should only focus unilaterally on return on investment or bilaterally on mutual return for both customers and companies.

3. In the broadened scope of relationship marketing, i.e., engagement marketing, customers exercise a high degree of control over the content and outcomes of the marketing function that influences a broad network. Discuss whether or not companies should give up control to customers to gain long-term relationships.

4. While CRM-based models and metrics are important tools for marketers, managers are cautioned to find 'meaning' behind the metrics and to put the 'relationship' back into CRM. Critically discuss the merit of this statement.

5. Critically discuss the following statement: "Brand is a 'customer-centric' concept that focuses on what a product/service or the firm has promised to its customers, whereas corporate reputation is a 'company-centric' concept that focuses on the credibility and respect that a firm has among a broad set of stakeholders".

HBS and Ivey Cases

- AnswerDash (9-516-106)
- Reinventing Best Buy (9-716-455)
- Chase Sapphire (9-518-024)
- Laurs & Bridz (9B18A004)

CASE QUESTIONS

AnswerDash

1. AnswerDash, a technology startup, operates in a B2B space, specifically online customer support. What form of relationship marketing, if any, is this company practicing? How?

2. How can AnswerDash stimulate and build customer purchase and non-purchase behavior through relationship marketing?

3. How can this company practice CRM strategies using the traditional approach, and using digital technologies and social media platforms? Compare these approaches.

4. Should AnswerDash broaden the scope of relationship marketing to engagement marketing and let customers exercise a high degree of control over the content and outcomes of the marketing function? Why or why not?

Reinventing Best Buy

1. Best Buy is a leading consumer electronics retailer in the United States and is seeking to confront Amazon's disruptive online retail model. Would you say Best Buy is practicing promotion marketing, engagement marketing, or relationship marketing? Defend your reasoning.

2. Discuss the strength of the Best Buy brand from the viewpoint of employees (internal brand strength) and customers (external brand strength)

3. In the context of Best Buy, what is the relationship between (a) brand equity and customer relationship marketing and (b) corporate reputation and customer relationship marketing?

4. How can Best Buy expand the role of relationship marketing in dealing with critical firm stakeholders: customers, clients, channel partners, suppliers, and society at large?

5. Is the marketing effort of Best Buy 'customer-centric' or 'company-centric'? How can relationship marketing help in getting the right marketing focus and orientation?

Chase Sapphire

1. JPMorgan Chase, a leading bank in the United States, launched the Chase Sapphire Reserve (Reserve) credit card. How can this company stimulate and build customer purchase and non-purchase behavior related to the Reserve card through relationship marketing?

2. Discuss the strength of the JPMorgan brand from the viewpoint of employees (internal brand strength) and customers (external brand strength).

3. How can JPMorgan practice CRM strategies using the traditional approach, and using digital technologies and social media platforms? Compare these approaches.

4. How can JPMorgan expand the role of relationship marketing in dealing with critical firm stakeholders: customers, clients, channel partners, and society at large?

5. Should JPMorgan broaden the scope of relationship marketing to engagement marketing and let customers exercise a high degree of control over the content and outcomes of the marketing function? Why or why not?

Laurs & Bridz

1. Laurs & Bridz is a fast growing Indian pharmaceutical company. The company is considering several CRM solutions that have been shortlisted on the basis of features and price. Which of the CRM solutions best suits the firm?

2. How can Laurs & Bridz stimulate and build customer purchase and non-purchase behavior through relationship marketing?

3. In the context of Laurs & Bridz, discuss the relationship between (a) brand equity and customer relationship marketing and (b) corporate reputation and customer relationship marketing.

4. Should Laurs & Bridz broaden the scope of relationship marketing to engagement marketing and let customers exercise a high degree of control over the content and outcomes of the marketing function? Why or why not?

5. Is the marketing effort of Laurs & Bridz 'customer-centric' or 'company-centric'? How can relationship marketing help in getting the right marketing focus and orientation?

REFERENCES

Aaker, David A. (1996), Measuring Brand Equity Across Products and Markets, *California Management Review*, 38(3): 102–20.

American Marketing Association (AMA) (2017), *Definition of Marketing*, online at https://www.ama.org/the-definition-of-marketing-what-is-marketing/, accessed May 5, 2020.

Berry, L. (1983), Relationhip Marketing, in L.L. Berry, G.L. Shostack, and G.D. Upah (Eds.), *Emerging Perspectives of Services Marketing*, American Marketing Association, Chicago, IL: 25–28.

Berry, Leonard L. (1995), Relationship Marketing of Services: Growing Interest, Emerging perspectives, *Journal of the Academy of Marketing Science* 23(4): 236–245.

Bijmolt, Tammo H.A., Manfred Krafft, F. Javier Sese, and Vijay Viswanathan (2018), Multi-Tier Loyalty Programs to Stimulate Customer Engagement. (Eds.) Robert W. Palmatier, V. Kumar, and Colleen M. Gumme, *Customer Engagement Marketing*: 119–139, Palgrave Macmillan, Springer.

Blau, P.M. (1964), *Exchange and Power in Social Life*, New York: John Wiley and Sons.

Bleier, Alexander, A. D. Keyser, and K. Verleye (2018), Customer Engagement through Personalization and Customization, (Eds.) Robert W. Palmatier, V. Kumar, and Colleen M. Harmeling, *Customer Engagement Marketing*: 75–94, Palgrave Macmillan, Springer.

Brodie, Roderick J., Linda D. Hollebeek, Biljana Juric, and Ana Ilic (2011), Customer Engagement: Conceptual Domain, Fundamental Propositions, and Implications for Research, *Journal of Service Research* 14(3): 252–271.

Buil, I., L. de Chernatony, and E. Martínez (2013), Examining the Role of Advertising and Sales Promotions in Brand Equity Creation, *Journal of Business Research* 66(1): 115–22.

Burmann, C., M. Jost-Benz, and N. Riley (2009), Towards an Identity-Based Brand Equity Model, *Journal of Business Research* 62(3): 390–397.

Dick, A.S. and K. Basu (1994), Customer Loyalty: Toward an Integrated Conceptual Framework, *Journal of the Academy of Marketing Science* 22(2): 99–113.

Donaldson, T. and L.E. Preston (1995), The Stakeholder Theory of the Corporation: Concepts, Evidence, and Implications, *Academy of Management Review* 20(1): 65–91.

Dreze, X. and A. Bonfrer (2009), Moving from Customer Lifetime Value to Customer Equity, *Quantitative Marketing and Economics* 7(3): 289–320.

Dwyer, Robert F., Paul H. Schurr, and Sejo Oh (1987), Developing Buyer-Seller Relationships, *Journal of Marketing* 51(2): 11–27.

Gupta, S., D. Hanssens, B. Hardie, W. Kahn, V. Kumar, N. Lin *et al.* (2006), Modeling Customer Lifetime Value, *Journal of Service Research* 9(2): 139–155.

Gronroos, C. (1997), From Marketing Mix to Relationship Marketing — Towards a Paradigm Shift in Marketing, *Management Decision* 35(4): 322–339.

Haidt, J. and C. Joseph (2004), Intuitive Ethics: How Innately Prepared Intuitions Generate Culturally Variable Virtues, *Daedalus 133*(4): 55–66.

Haidt, J. and J. Graham (2007), When Morality Opposes Justice: Conservatives have Moral Intuitions that Liberals may not Recognize, *Social Justice Research 20*(1): 98–116.

Harmeling, Colleen M., Jordan W. Moffett, Mark J. Arnold, and Brad D. Carlson (2017), Toward a Theory of Customer Engagement Marketing, *Journal of the Academy of Marketing Science* 45(3): 312–335.

Heskett, J.L., T.O. Jones, G.W. Loveman, W. Earl Sasser Jr., and L.A. Schlesinger (1994), Putting the Service-Profit Chain to Work, *Harvard Business Review* 72(2): 164–174.

Hess, J. and J. Story (2005), Trust-Based Commitment: Multidimensional Consumer-Brand Relationships, *Journal of Consumer Marketing* 22(6): 313–322.

Hogreve, Jens, Anja Iseke, Klaus Derfuss, and Tonnjes, Eller (2017), The Service-Profit Chain: A Meta-Analytic Test of a Comprehensive Theoretical Framework, *Journal of Marketing* 81: 41–61.

Hollebeek, L.D., R.K. Srivastava, and T. Chen (2016), SD Logic-Informed Customer engagement: Integrative Framework, Revised Fundamental Propositions, and Applications to CRM, *Journal of the Academy of Marketing Science* September: 1–25.

Hoppner, J.J. and G.G. Vadakkepatt (2019), Examining Moral Authority in the Marketplace: A Conceptualization and Framework, *Journal of Business Research* 95: 417–427.

Howard, J.A. and J. Sheth (1969), *The Theory of Buyer Behavior.* New York: John Wiley & Sons.

Hunt, S.D. and S.J. Vitell (1986), A General Theory of Marketing Ethics, *Journal of Macromarketing* 6 (Spring): 5–15.

Kannan, P. K. and Hongshuang "Alice" Li (2017), Digital Marketing: A Framework, Review and Research Agenda, *International Journal of Research in Marketing* 34(1): 22–45.

Keller, K.L. (1993), Conceptualizing and Measuring and Managing Customer-Based Equity, *Journal of Marketing* 57(1): 1–22.

Kietzmann, Jan H., Kristopher Hermkens, Ian P. McCarthy, and Bruno S. Silvestre (2011), Social Media? Get Serious! Understanding the Functional Building Blocks of Social Media, *Business Horizons* 54(3): 241–251.

Kreiner, G.E. and B.E. Ashforth (2004), Evidence Toward an Expanded Model of Organizational Identification, *Journal of Organizational Behavior* 25: 1–27.

Kumar, V. and Anita Pansari (2016), Competitive Advantage through Engagement, *Journal of Marketing Research* 53(4): 497–514.

Kumar, V. (2018), A Theory of Customer Valuation: Concepts, Metrics, Strategy, and Implementation, *Journal of Marketing* 82: 1–19.

Kumar, V. and R. Mirchandani (2012), Increasing the ROI of Social Media Marketing, *MIT Sloan Management Review* 54(1): 55–61.

Kumar, V. and W. Reinartz (2016), Creating Enduring Customer Value, *Journal of Marketing* 80: 36–68.

Kumar, V. and Werner Reinartz (2006), *Customer Relationship Management: A Databased Approach.* New York: John Wiley & Sons.

Kumar, V. Ilaria Dalla Pozza, J. Andrew Petersen, and Denish Shah (2009), Reversing the Logic: The Path to Profitability through Relationship Marketing, *Journal of Interactive Marketing* 23: 147–156.

Kumar, V., J.A. Petersen, and R.P. Leone (2007), How Valuable is Word of Mouth? *Harvard Business Review* 85(10): 139–146.

Kumar, V., Lerzan Aksoy, Bas Donkers, Rajkumar Venkatesan, Thorsten Wiesel, and Sebastian Tillmanns (2010), Undervalued or Overvalued Customers: Capturing Total Customer Engagement Value, *Journal of Service Research* 13(3): 297–310.

Kumar, V., V. Bhaskaran, R. Mirchandani, and M. Shah (2013), Creating a Measurable Social Media Marketing Strategy: Increasing the Value and ROI of Intangibles and Tangibles for Hokey Pokey, *Marketing Science* 32(2): 194–212.

Laczniak, G.R. and P.E. Murphy (2019), The Role of Normative Marketing Ethics, *Journal of Business Research* 95: 401–407.

Lemon, Katherine N. and Peter C. Verhoef (2016), Understanding Customer Experience Throughout the Customer Journey, *Journal of Marketing* 80: 69–96.

Lind, A.E., and T.R. Tyler (1988), *The Social Psychology of Procedural Justice.* New York: Plenum.

Malhotra, N.K. and J. Agarwal (2002), A Stakeholder Perspective on Relationship Marketing: Framework and Propositions, *Journal of Relationship Marketing* 1(2): 3–37.

Martin, K.D. and P.E. Murphy (2017), The Role of Data Privacy in Marketing, *Journal of the Academy of Marketing Science* 45(2): 135–155.

Mayer, R.C., J.H. Davis, and F.D. Schoorman (1995), An Integration Model of Organizational Trust, *Academy of Management Review* 20: 709–735.

Morgan, Robert M. and Shelby D. Hunt (1994), The Commitment-Trust Theory of Relationship Marketing, *Journal of Marketing* 58 (July): 20–38.

Murphy, P.E., G.R. Laczniak, & G. Wood (2007), An Ethical Basis for Relationship Marketing: A Virtue Ethics Perspective, *European Journal of Marketing* 41(1/2): 37–57.

Murphy, P.E., G.R. Laczniak, and F. Harris (2017), *Ethics in Marketing: International Cases and Perspectives*, 2nd edition, London: Routledge.

Palmatier, Robert W. (2008), *Relationship Marketing*, Marketing Science Institute. Cambridge, MA.

Pansari, Anita and V. Kumar (2017), Customer Engagement: The construct, Antecedents, and Consequences, *Journal of the Academy of Marketing Science* 45(3): 294–311.

Parasuraman, A., A.A. Zeithaml, and L. Berry (1988), SERVQUAL: A Multiple-Item Scale for Measuring Consumer Perceptions of Service Quality, *Journal of Retailing* 64(1): 12–40.

Payne, A. D. Ballantyne, and C. Martin (2005), A Stakeholder Approach to Relationship Marketing Strategy: The Development and Use of the 'Six Markets' Model, *European Journal of Marketing* 39(7/8): 855–871.

Peck, H., A. Payne, M. Christopher, and M. Clark (1999), *Relationship Marketing: Strategy and Implementation.* Oxford, U.K.: Butterworth-Heinemann.

Rindfleisch, A. and C. Moorman (2003), Interfirm Cooperation and Customer Orientation, *Journal of Marketing Research* 40(11): 421–436.

Rindova, V.P., I.O. Williamson, A.P. Petkova, and J.M. Sever (2005), Being Good or Being Known: An Empirical Examination of the Dimensions, Antecedents, and Consequences of Organizational Reputation, *Academy of Management Journal* 48(6): 1033–1049.

Rust, R.T., K.N. Lemon, and V.A. Zeithaml (2004), Return on Marketing: Using Customer Equity to Focus Marketing Strategy, *Journal of Marketing* 68: 109–127.

Rust, R.T., V. Kumar, and R. Venkatesan (2011), Will the Frog Change into a Prince? Predicting Future Customer Profitability, *International Journal of Research in Marketing* 28(4): 281–294.

Schmitt, P., B. Skiera, and Van den Bulte (2011), Referral Programs and Customer Value, *Journal of Marketing* 75(1): 46–59.

Sheth, J.N., R.S. Sisodia, and A. Sharma (2000), The Antecedents and Consequences of Customer-Centric Marketing, *Journal of the Academy of Marketing Science* 28(1): 55–66.

Sheth, Jagdish N. and Atul Parvatiyar (1995), Relationship Marketing in Consumer Markets: Antecedents and Consequences, *Journal of the Academy of Marketing Science* 23(4): 255–271.

Sheth, Jagdish N. and Atul Parvatiyar (2000), The Evolution of Relationship Marketing, In (Eds.) Jagdish N. Sheth and Atul Parvatiyar, *Handbook of Relationship Marketing*: 119–145, Sage Publication.

Steinhoff, L. and R.W. Palmatier (2015), Understanding Loyalty Program Effectiveness: Managing Target and Bystander Effects, *Journal of the Academy of Marketing Science* 44(1): 88–107.

Sunder, S., V. Kumar, and Y. Zhao (2016), Measuring the Lifetime Value of a Customer in the Consumer Packaged goods (CPG) Industry, *Journal of Marketing Research* 53: 901–921.

Thibaut, J. and L. Walker (1975), *Procedural Justice: A Psychological Analysis.* Hillsdale, NJ: Erlbaum.

Tyler, T.R. (1994), Psychological Models of the Justice Motive: Antecedents of Distributive and Procedural Justice. *Journal of Personality and Social Psychology* 67(November): 850–863.

Van den Bos, K., H.A.M. Wilke, and E.A. Lind (1998), When do we Need Procedural Fairness? The Role of Trust in Authority, *Journal of Personality and Social Psychology* 75(6): 1,449–1,458.

Van den Bos, K., R. Vermunt, and H.A.M. Wilke (1997), Procedural and Distributive Justice: What is Fair Depends More on What Comes First than on What Comes Next, *Journal of Personality and Social Psychology* 72(January): 95–104.

Van Doorn, Jenny, Katherine N. Lemon, Vikas Mittal, Stephan Nass, Doreen Pick, Peter Pirner, and Peter C. Verhoef (2010), Customer Engagement Behavior: Theoretical Foundations and Research Directions, *Journal of Service Research* 13(3): 253–266.

Vargo, Stephen L. and Robert F. Lusch (2004), Evolving to a New Dominant Logic for Marketing, *Journal of Marketing* 68: 1–17.

Vargo, Stephen L. and Robert F. Lusch (2008), Service-Dominant Logic: Continuing the Evolution, *Journal of the Academy of Marketing Science* 36(1): 1–10.

Venkatesan and Kumar (2004), A Customer Lifetime Value Framework for Customer Selection and Resource Allocation Strategy, *Journal of Marketing* 68: 106–125.

Venkatesan, Kumar, and Bohling (2007), Optimal Customer Relationship Management using Bayesian Decision Theory: An application for Customer Selection, *Journal of Marketing Research* 44: 579–594.

Venkatesan, Rajkumar, J. Andrew Petersen, and Leandro Guissoni (2018), Measuring and Managing Customer Engagement Value through the Customer Journey, in Robert W. Palmatier, V. Kumar, and Colleen M. Harmeling (Eds.), Customer Engagement Marketing (pp. 53–74). Palgrave Macmillan, Springer Nature, London, UK

White, T.B., D.L. Zahay, H. Thorbjornsen, and S. Shavitt (2008), Getting Too Personal: Reactance to Highly Personalized Email Solicitations, *Marketing Letters* 19: 40–50.

Yadav, M.S., K. de Valck, T. Hennig-Thurau, D.L. Hoffman, and M. Spann (2013), Social Commerce: A Contingency Framework for Assessing Marketing Potential, *Journal of Interactive Marketing* 27: 311–323.

02

Customer Relationship Marketing: Theories, Models, and Frameworks

OVERVIEW

In Chapter 2, we map the evolution of customer relationship marketing (CRM) and chronicle its shifting emphasis from one of value distribution and independence, i.e., short-term competition and conflict, to value (co)creation and interdependence, i.e., long-term mutual cooperation. Over the years, the foundational premises and axioms of relationship marketing (RM) have both broadened and deepened, intersecting with allied marketing concepts including service-dominant (S-D) logic, customer-centric marketing, customer-as-assets thinking, and customer experience and engagement models.

Although the earliest concept of relationship marketing dates back to the pre-industrial era, we examine its lifecycle stages of adoption, development, and expansion in B2C marketing over the last three decades. Several theories, models, and frameworks, both classic and contemporary that explain antecedents, processes, and outcomes of customer relationships with companies are briefly discussed. In particular, we discuss the following models and frameworks:

- buyer–seller model (Dwyer *et al.*, 1987);

- trust–commitment model (Morgan and Hunt,1994);

- S-D logic (Vargo and Lusch, 2004);

- interpersonal RM (B2C) model (Palmatier, 2007a);

- interfirm RM (B2B) model (Palmatier, 2008);

- reverse logic framework (RLF) of relationship marketing (Kumar *et al.*, 2009);

- customer engagement behavior (CEB) model (Van Doorn *et al.*, 2010);

- customer engagement marketing theory (Harmeling *et al.*, 2017);

- customer experience model (Lemon and Verhoef, 2016); and

- customer valuation model (Kumar, 2018).

At the end of the chapter, we provide key takeaways and conclude with discussion questions and HBS and Ivey cases. But first, to give a flavor of CRM initiatives, we provide some real-life vignettes.

OPENING VIGNETTES

Vignette 1: Sour Patch Kids targets its core young demographics in an effort to increase brand awareness, to acquire new customers, and generate content for marketing communication. The company tapped customer creativity by assigning customers the task of writing and submitting unique love stories on Wattpad, a social media platform for up-and-coming writers, as part of the brand's "Sour Then Sweet" love story-writing contest and campaign. The company identified three Wattpad members with extensive social networks and high persuasion capital, inviting them to write and post their own love stories and encouraging others to follow their lead. Sour Patch Kids used the hashtag #SPKSAD and promised that the winning story would be turned into an animated digital film and featured across the company's social media and on Wattpad's homepage. Three stories written by popular Wattpad members were read by almost one-quarter million people and led to 1.2 million social media interactions. The initiative also received widespread coverage across a number of outlets.

Vignette 2: Disney's Magic Band technology and its online tool, MyMagicPlus, are designed to create the ultimate Disney experience. The company has invested upward of one billion dollars to remove any critical frictions in the Disney experience (e.g., wait time, frustration, and indecision) and to allow customers preplan their Disney experience that includes personalized meetings with Disney characters, lunch reservations, and rides on top attractions. The Magic Band technology (containing RFID chip, a radio, and battery and connecting to up to 100 real-time data systems in the park), bracelet-sized wristbands arrive before the planned vacation and can be used throughout the park. These bands have multiple uses including access to rides, hotel rooms, make purchases, meet and greet with a Disney character, etc. While the technology optimizes logistics, it is all about enhancing the customer experience (see Figure 2.1). The result — customers spend more and are happier.

Figure 2.1: Disney uses online tool like MyMagicPlus to enhance customer experience.

INTRODUCTION: THE PARADIGM SHIFT

In 2000, Sheth and Parvatiyar created a compendium of scholarly articles that appeared in *Handbook of Relationship Marketing*, synthesizing several position papers on relationship marketing that was in the growth stage of its lifecycle. In one of the chapters, the authors (pp. 133–138) trace the evolution of relationship marketing through the pre-industrial, industrial, and post-industrial era, wherein they argue a paradigm shift from exchange focus of the industrial era to relationship focus in the post-industrial era. They summarize fundamental shifts in axioms and foundational premises that have guided the development of relationship marketing (see Figure 2.2). First, the development of relationship marketing is characterized by a departure from competition and conflict to mutual cooperation and from choice independence to mutual interdependence. Some of the early models, for e.g., relational contract model (Dwyer *et al.*, 1987) and trust–commitment model (Morgan and Hunt, 1994), incorporated such shifts in cooperation and interdependence. Second, interdependence reduces transaction costs and generates higher quality as opposed to the transactional view of independence

that purported that independence of choice among marketing actors creates an efficient system for creating and distributing marketing value.

Sheth and Parvatiyar (2000) argued that relationship marketing enhances marketing productivity by achieving efficiency and effectiveness. Relationship marketing practices enhance efficiency through customer retention, efficient customer response, and resource sharing between marketing partners. Similarly, relationship marketing programs enhance effectiveness as customers are involved in the early stages of the marketing program development facilitating future marketing efforts. Further, through personalization and customization, relationship marketers can better address the needs and preferences of each selected customer, making marketing more effective.

In the *pre-industrial era*, producers and consumers developed strong relationships that led to the production of customized products. As a result, retaining customers, influencing repeat purchases, and fostering trust were the concerns of marketers then. In this context, branding was popular as these signified quality and trust. It was with the advent of *industrial era* that marketers adopted

Figure 2.2: Evolution of Relationship Marketing

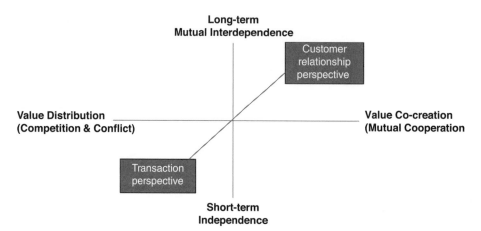

Adapted from Jagdish N. Sheth and Atul Parvatiyar (2000), The Evolution of Relationship Marketing, *Handbook of Relationship Marketing*: 119–145.

a transactional approach toward mass production and mass consumption in order to achieve economies of scale and scope. With mass production and excess inventories came the need for "hard-sell" tactics (e.g., sales, advertising, and promotion) as well as the birth of middlemen, including wholesalers, distributors, and other marketing intermediaries. The emphasis of the transactional approach was more with sales and promotion, and less with relationships. With fierce competition, firms engaged in aggressive selling and short-term orientation that focused on maximizing short-term profit. It was during this era that concepts of market segmentation and targeting became popular, as firms strived to differentiate their offerings and build brand loyalty. Vertical marketing systems also became popular as marketers wanted control over channels and to block competitors from entering these channels.

However, in the *post-industrial era*, marketers began to refocus on buyer–seller relationships. Several factors influenced its rebirth, including rapid technological advances (especially IT growth), growth of service economy, adoption of total quality programs by companies, and increase in competitive intensity that brought customer retention to the fore. For instance, some 25 years ago, marketing scientists were starting to come to grips with the new single-source scanner data sets made possible by the widespread adoption

of the Universal Product Code. Today, developments in data collection and data storage technologies mean that marketing databases have proliferated, which are being mined using sophisticated data analytic models that involve customer analysis. Today, scholars agree that the foundational premises and axioms of relationship marketing intersect with service-dominant logic; relational assets, valuing customers as assets following the customer lifetime value (CLV) concept and therefore maximizing their engagement with the firm, i.e., customer engagement value (CEV) toward maximizing firm value (see Figure 2.3). More discussion on these concepts will follow in later chapters.

In the next section, we start our discussion of several influential CRM models and frameworks, documenting their foundational premises, and how marketers are applying some of these concepts in designing and implementing marketing initiatives.

CUSTOMER RELATIONSHIP MARKETING (CRM): MODELS AND FRAMEWORKS

Dwyer et al.'s (1987) Model

The theoretical origins of relationship marketing are rooted in institutional economics, sociology, and

Figure 2.3: The various Customer Relationship Marketing (CRM): Models and Frameworks involve customer analysis

psychology. Exchanges are driven by value maximization and market efficiency. Dwyer *et al.* (1987), integrating relational contract theory (Macneil, 1980) with social exchange theory (Blau, 1964), examined exchanges lying on a continuum ranging from discrete to relational transactions. Relational exchanges transpire over time wherein each transaction is viewed in terms of its history and anticipated future collaboration. Relational actors are expected to derive complex, personal, and noneconomic satisfaction, and engage in social exchange, and the basis of future collaboration is hinged on implicit and explicit assumptions. Relational constructs include trust, commitment, norms, dependence, justice, conflict, cooperation, and communication.

Dwyer *et al.*'s (1987) framework incorporates both sellers and buyers motivational investment in a relationship (see Figure 2.4). The axes define each party's motivational investment in a relationship, i.e., the expected net benefits from a relationship, such that a party assesses costs and benefits associated with one relationship against alternatives outside the focal relationship. The model is helpful as it suggests zones in the quadrant where sellers and buyers can potentially maintain leadership roles and where a bilateral relationship maintenance role is preferred. On the low

end of the buyer and seller motivational investment, it also allows for discrete types of exchanges suggesting that relationships are not meant for all customers. Further, the model also accommodates dissolution (or disengagement) in the typical relationship building stages of awareness, exploration, expansion, and commitment. Interestingly, the authors note that discrete transactions follow the stimulus-response model, whereas relational transactions follow the capital-budgeting model where customer acquisition costs can be considered as investments offset by discounted "lifetime" customer valuation of costs and benefits.

Morgan and Hunt's Trust–Commitment Model (1994)

In the presence of market inefficiency, relational governance constructs assume critical importance and relational norms further compliment exchange performance by preventing self-seeking behaviors especially in changing conditions. In this regard, transaction cost economics (Williamson, 1975, 1985) has been a dominant theory in relationship marketing. As people are guile and serve self-interest, relationship-specific investments must be monitored and safeguarded either by internalizing assets (hierarchical capitalism)

Figure 2.4: Buyer–Seller Motivational Investment Model

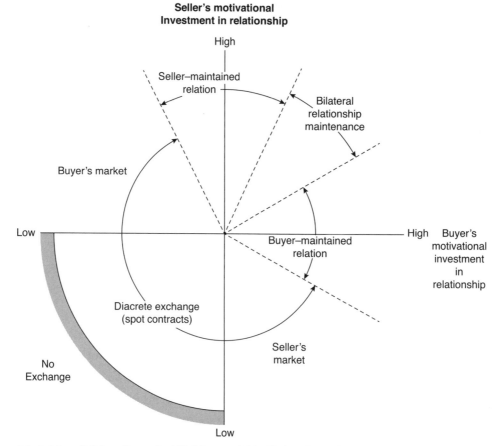

Adapted from F. Robert Dwyer, Paul H. Schurr, and Sejo Oh (1987), Developing Buyer-Seller Relationships, *Journal of Marketing* 51(2): 11–27.

or by building relational governance structures (build relationships) to avoid opportunistic behaviors by partners. Morgan and Hunt's (1994) commitment–trust theory of relationship marketing became one of the most influential papers to make a contribution in marketing thought. Morgan and Hunt (1994) define relationship marketing as "all marketing activities directed toward establishing, developing, and maintaining successful relational exchanges" (p. 22). They theorize that while there are several contextual factors that contribute to the success or failure of relationship marketing efforts, it is relationship commitment and trust that are central to successful relationship marketing. Thus, relationship commitment defined as an "enduring desire to maintain a valued relationship" and trust defined as "confidence in an exchange partner's reliability and integrity" are key elements that explain relationship

and firm performance. The benefits arising out of trust and commitment include preserving relationship investments by cooperating with exchange partners, resisting short-term alternatives in favor of long-term benefits of staying with existing partners, and viewing partners as trustworthy rather than opportunistic and accordingly acting on high-risk activities. As commitment entails vulnerability, parties will seek only trustworthy partners, and so trust influences commitment. Relationship commitment and trust are not only important variables in marketing relationships but also key mediating variables in these relationships (see Figure 2.5).

Most relationship marketing frameworks begin with an exploratory or identifying stage, marked by limited confidence in the exchange partner's ability

Figure 2.5: Trust–Commitment Model of Relationship Marketing

The KMV Model of Relationship Marketing

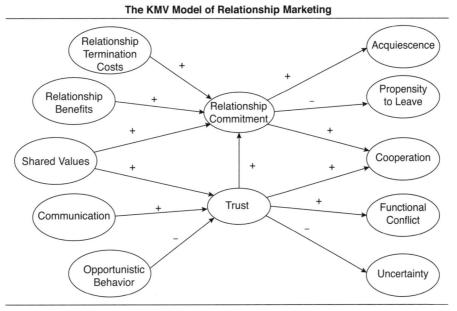

Adapted from Robert M. Morgan and Shelby D. Hunt (1994), The Commitment-Trust Theory of Relationship Marketing, *Journal of Marketing* 58 (July): 20–38.

and trustworthiness. Generally, initial levels of trust and commitment are calculative and deterrence based in nature, i.e., calculative-based trust (Lewicki and Bunker, 1996; Rousseau *et al.*, 1998). Palmatier (2008) argues that at the exploratory stage, expectations of trustworthy behavior are based on assumptions that the partner will avoid opportunistic behavior so as to protect itself from institutional enforcement mechanisms and relational investments, not to mention to shield itself from reputational damage at the minimum. The partners engage in increased communication to discover goal congruence and synergistic norms, which then leads to desired outcomes, and the relationship begins to grow. Further, Palmatier (2008) argues that the growth or expansion stage of the relationship is marked by an escalation of reciprocated transactions and mutual dependence that leads to knowledge-based trust (Lewicki and Bunker, 1996). As the relationship continues to develop into maturity stage, marked by increased benefits and interdependence, calculative/ knowledge-based trust develops into identification-

based trust (Lewicki and Bunker, 1996) (see Figure 2.6). At this stage, shared norms are well developed, and each partners' behaviors are predictable leading to a willingness to continue long-term commitments (Dwyer *et al.*, 1987). Palmatier (2008) notes that there is some evidence to support the finding that trust and commitment levels lose their predictive power during later stages of the relationship. Interestingly, new research indicates that the trajectory, i.e., velocity and acceleration of commitment (relationship dynamics), and not the initial level of commitment (relationship levels), determines exchange performance (Palmatier *et al.*, 2007a; 2013).

Service Dominant (S-D) Logic (Vargo and Lusch, 2004 with Subsequent Extensions)

The origin of the S-D logic (Vargo and Lusch, 2004) shifted the focus away from production and products to value (co)creation and process. It was instrumental in identifying commonalities in research streams in relationship marketing, services marketing, and

Figure 2.6: Trust is an important building block in the Morgan and Hunt (1994) Framework

business-to-business (B2B) marketing. The service-centered view (as opposed to product-centered view) focused on identifying and developing core competences, the fundamental knowledge and skills of an economic entity (operant resources) that represents competitive advantage and then identifying potential customers (as co-producers of service) that could benefit from such competences. The goal was cultivating relationships with customers by offering compelling value propositions to them (i.e., value-in-use) and seeking marketplace feedback to improve the value proposition so as to further improve firm performance. The eight core foundational premises (FP) of the S-D logic (Vargo and Lusch, 2004) include:

1. (FP1) — The application of specialized skills and knowledge is the fundamental unit of exchange.

2. (FP2) — Indirect exchange masks the fundamental unit of exchange.

3. (FP3) — Goods are distribution mechanisms for service provision.

4. (FP4) — Knowledge is the fundamental source of competitive advantage.

5. (FP5) — All economies are services economies.

6. (FP6) — The customer is always a co-producer.

7. (FP7) — The enterprise can only make value propositions.

8. (FP8) — A service-centered view is customer oriented and relational.

The S-D logic framework has since continued to evolve and expand in scope by moving from a dyadic orientation toward a network orientation, specifying service as a basis of exchange rather than a unit of output, and that all economic and social actors are resource integrators implying a network structure (i.e., actor-to-actor orientation) for value creation determined uniquely and phenomenologically by the beneficiary (Lusch and Vargo, 2006). In short, all actors integrate resources and engage in service exchange, all in the process of co-creating value that takes place in networks. Recently, Vargo and Lusch (2011, 2016) further broadened the systems and network view to include dynamic mechanisms that facilitate resource integration and service exchange by acknowledging the role of institutions and institutional arrangements. They use the term "service ecosystems" to denote actor–environmental interaction and critical flow of mutual service provision. Here, resource-integrating actors are connected by shared institutional arrangements within the ecosystem, which results in mutual value creation through service exchange (see Figure 2.7).

The "service ecosystem" in S-D logic emphasizes the role of institutions, i.e., rules, norms, and beliefs or "rules of the game" (North, 1990), and institutional arrangements, i.e., institutional logics. These rules can be codified laws, codes of ethics, social norms, symbolic meaning, or routinized rubrics. Institutions provide shortcuts to cognition and enable actors to accomplish service exchange and value co-creation under time and cognitive constraints. The role of institutions seems to appear in relationship marketing in the form of "relational norms". Relationship norms are shared expectations about behavior based on mutuality of expectations. For instance, Cannon *et al.* (2000) describe relational norms of flexibility, solidarity, mutuality, conflict handling, and restrain in the use of power, in safeguarding the continuity of exchanges. Institutions are instrumental in fostering

cooperation and coordination in ecosystems for providing the building blocks for increasingly complex resource integration and service exchange activities (Vargo and Lusch, 2016).

Interpersonal Relationship Marketing (B2C) Model — Palmatier (2008)

The resource-based view (Wernerfelt, 1984) states that "resources or assets that are valuable, rare, inimitable, and non-substitutable lead to sustainable competitive advantage and superior firm performance". According to this theory, relational governance constructs that build relationship bond serve as invaluable resources to enhance relational and firm performance. Palmatier *et al.* (2007a) demonstrated that while trust and commitment strengthen the relational bond, relationship-specific investments add significant firm performance-enhancing effects beyond that of trust and commitment. They identified missing relational mechanisms to explain direct effects of relationship marketing activities on firm performance and theoretically distinguished relationship marketing mechanisms between interfirm relationships (B2B) and interpersonal relationships (B2C). They also added a dynamic view of relationship. In this book our focus will be on B2C relationships.

The model describes relationship marketing as a dynamic process entailing cognitive-based relational factors of trust and commitment and emotional/social-based micro-foundational processes of gratitude and norms of reciprocity that affect short- versus long-term performance (see Figure 2.8). Palmatier (2008) argues that gratitude and norms of reciprocity take a central role, in addition to trust and commitment, in interpersonal relationship marketing. The underlying psychological emotion of gratitude, which leads to a desire to repay debt, generates feelings of pleasure, whereas the failure to do so generates feelings of guilt. In addition to a well-designed psychological system that causes consumers to repay relationship marketing

Figure 2.7: Service-Dominant (S-D) Logic Model

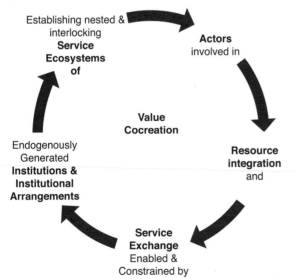

Adapted from Stephen L. Vargo and Robert F. Lusch (2016), Institutions and Axioms: An Extension and Update of Service-Dominant Logic, *Journal of the Academy of Marketing Science* 44: 5–23.

Figure 2.8: Interpersonal Relationship Marketing with Customers (B2C)

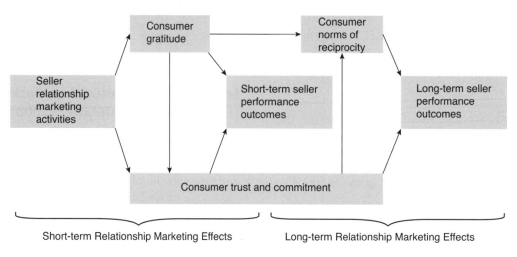

Adapted from Robert Palmatier (2008), *Relationship Marketing*, Marketing Science Institute, Cambridge, MA.

investments, these same mechanisms result in strong social norms that reinforce consumers' compliance with relationship marketing efforts.

While trust and commitment, as building blocks of social exchange theory, are important to study the effects of relationship marketing on firm performance, norms of reciprocity and gratitude likely represent critical mediators of interpersonal relationship marketing. Bagozzi (1995, p. 275) states that reciprocity sits "at the core of marketing relationships." Feelings of reciprocity and gratitude are genetically and socially hardwired into people, making their pervasiveness throughout societies reasonable; they represent the fundamental social and moral components for the functioning of stable social systems (Emmons and McCullough, 2004; Gouldner, 1960; Ostrom and Walker, 2003).

Relationship marketing assumes cyclical reciprocation. Gratitude is inseparable from reciprocity because it reflects an ingrained psychological pressure to return the favor. As gratitude entails psychological pressure that leads to *social* conformity pressures, Palmatier (2008) argues norms of reciprocity emerge and create persistent behavior cycles. That is, people engage in

reciprocation cycles because they always have and because social norms support that action. Gratitude and reciprocity also operate at the lowest level (or below) of awareness (i.e., emotions and peer pressure), but social exchange theory focuses on "higher" cognitive processing levels. Palmatier *et al.* (2007b) argue that the two constructs actually help explain the effectiveness of relationship marketing, such that including reciprocity and gratitude as mediators in the relationship marketing paradigm provides a "micro"-theoretical explanation of the underlying association between relationship marketing investments and outcomes. While interpersonal trust and commitment mediate interpersonal relationships, just as they do interfirm relationships, according to Palmatier (2008) a true micro-theoretical explanation of interpersonal relationship effectiveness involves gratitude and norms of reciprocity. As grateful people acknowledge how others have contributed to their well-being (Watkins *et al.*, 2003), customer gratitude increases in response to favors (Goei and Boster, 2005), and grateful customers reward firms for extra efforts (Morales, 2005), such as by complying with subsequent requests (Goei and Boster, 2005). According to retailing research, consumers satisfy their obligations to salespeople by purchasing (Dahl, *et al.*, 2005), which implies seller investments in relationship marketing make consumers feel grateful, which then prompts them to engage in behaviors that improve seller performance (Palmatier *et al.*, 2007b).

Cognition and emotion intertwine closely, and gratitude positively influences judgments of trust (Dunn and Schweitzer, 2005). Not only does gratitude enhance short-term consumer purchasing behaviors, it also promotes consumer trust and reciprocity norms with its longer-term effects (Palmatier *et al.*, 2007b). According to Palmatier (2008), gratitude represents a "starting mechanism" that influences prosocial behavior as long as the emotion lasts and then extends to longer-term effects, because it builds the relationship (Bartlett and DeSteno, 2006) by prompting norms of reciprocity in consumers' minds. Schwartz (1967, p. 8) highlights the gratitude–reciprocity cycle link by describing the "continuing balance of debt — now in the favor of one member, now in the favor of another," which guarantees relationship continuation, because "gratitude will always constitute a part of the bond linking them." Thus, gratitude enhances relationship marketing performance in three main ways (Palmatier *et al.*, 2007b):

1. Consumers engage in positive purchase behaviors to satisfy their feelings of obligation in response to relationship marketing-induced feelings of gratitude.

2. The increased levels of consumer trust, due to gratitude, increase consumer commitment and thus enhance relational performance outcomes.

3. Gratitude promotes the development of norms of reciprocity over the longer term and initiates a reciprocation cycle, which has long-term positive effects on consumer behaviors.

Palmatier's Interfirm Relationship Marketing (B2B) Model (2008)

The model of interfirm relationship marketing (see Figure 2.9) proposed by Palmatier (2008) integrates social network theory to develop an interfirm-specific relationship marketing framework. In addition to relationship quality, two other relational drivers are critical to understanding the impact of interfirm relationships on performance, namely, relationship breadth and composition. In addition, the model recognizes the multiplicative effects that emerge from the interactions of these drivers.

Figure 2.9: Interfirm Relationship Marketing Model (B2B)

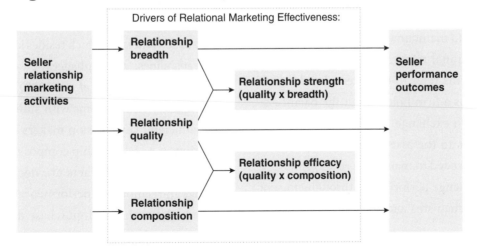

Adapted from Robert Palmatier (2008), Relationship Marketing, Marketing Science Institute, Cambridge, MA.

Business-To-Business (B2B) relationships involve multiple interactions among many people resulting in a network of relationships. Drawing from network theory developed in sociology, Palmatier (2008) makes a strong argument for the application of network perspective in interfirm relationships. A seller's relationship marketing activities in an exchange dyad influence three fundamental drivers of RM effectiveness, namely, relationship quality, relationship breadth, and relationship composition. Each of these drivers work synergistically to capture different and yet important aspects of interfirm relationships.

Relationship Quality

The strength of relational bonds with an exchange partner represents *relationship quality* and captures the concepts of relational embeddedness, closeness, and degree of reciprocity in social bond theory (e.g., Rindfleisch and Moorman, 2001). The concept of relationship quality parallels the concept of tie strength in network theory. A large scholarship in marketing exists involving relationship quality capturing varied facets of relational bond such as trust, commitment, reciprocity norms, and exchange efficiency, which in turn influence specific exchange outcomes (e.g., Crosby *et al.*, 1990; Kumar *et al.*, 1995b). Trust is an evaluation of the partner's reliability and integrity that engenders confidence in the partner's future actions without fear of opportunism. Commitment represents exchange partners' desire to maintain valued relationships and thus their relational motivation toward partners. Reciprocity norms refer to the internalized beliefs and expectations a firm holds about the balance of obligations in an exchange. Importantly, exchange efficiency refers to the assessment of time, effort, and resources needed to maintain a relationship and to enhance exchange performance through efficient governance mechanisms and structures (Palmatier, 2008).

Relationship Breadth

Relationship breadth represents the number of relational bonds and interpersonal ties with an exchange partner and parallels the network concepts of network density, i.e., level of interconnectedness among network members and degree centrality, i.e., number of direct ties between a specific member and other network members. The benefits of a broad relationship include several interpersonal ties that can uncover key information, find profit-enhancing opportunities, and withstand disruptions to individual bonds such as in cases of reorganizations and turnover (Palmatier, 2007a, 2008). For example, broad interorganizational relationships recover more easily and suffer fewer long-lasting impacts from the departure of a key contact person (Bendapudi and Leone, 2002). In addition, relationship breadth positively affects cooperation, knowledge transfer, communication efficiency, and product development performance (Rowley, 1997; Tsai, 2001; Walker *et al.*, 1997).

Relationship Composition

Relationship composition refers to the decision-making capability of relational contacts and the underlying premise is that a diverse contact portfolio of critical decision makers with authority can provide sellers the access to information from multiple buyer sources and perspectives (Palmatier, 2008). This concept is similar to the network concepts of diversity and attractiveness on which resides knowledge, skills, and capabilities, which enhances network performance and efficiency (Baum *et al.*, 2000). Merely having high-quality relationships with sufficient breadth is not sufficient; key decision makers in a portfolio of positions (i.e., relationship composition) as opposed to homogeneous contacts are necessary to effect change in relationship performance. For instance, a strong relationship with purchase department head may have little impact when the product is waiting for approval in the quality control department. Relationship composition, thus, captures the contact portfolio's aggregate ability to influence decisions understanding that various departments within customer firms make decisions.

Relationship Strength

Palmatier (2008) explains that relationship strength equals the interaction between relationship quality and relationship breadth, or relationship quality × relationship breadth. In other words, multiple high-quality relational bonds result in strong, resilient relationships. Synergies are accrued in relationship strength when both relationship quality and relationship breadth are high. For instance, greater breadth but lower quality yields many cursory contacts that may provide little protection against the stress of a service failure. Similarly, a single, high-quality contact may not be sufficient to leverage and influence group decisions (Brown, 2000). However, multiple high-quality contacts (quality × breadth) experience both relational motivation (commitment, norms of reciprocity) and confidence (trust) and therefore support the seller during a service recovery.

Relationship Efficacy

Relationship efficacy — relationship quality × relationship composition — captures the ability of interorganizational relationship to achieve desired objectives (Palmatier, 2008). For instance, sellers are advantaged when they exercise high-quality bonds in well-structured contact portfolios. If the contacts are key decision makers but the bonds are weak, the contacts will not disclose information (Crosby *et al.*, 1990); therefore, only high-quality relationships can institute change. In contrast, if the relationship quality is high but restricted to one functional area, perhaps, with limited decision-making authority, the results will be similar to the earlier case. As network theory similarly notes, "It is critical to separate the

issues of tie strength from that of network diversity," because "the most desirable ties are both *strong* and *diverse*" (Li, 2007, p. 239), and only when both exist is performance maximized.

In summary, it is the relationship quality, relationship breadth, and relationship composition, and their respective interactions yielding relationship strength and relationship efficacy that characterize the relational assets. In other words, relational assets reflect the intangible value that a firm receives from its relationships with a customer or portfolio of customers (Palmatier, 2008). Strong interfirm relationships lead to cooperative behaviors increasing customers' willingness to be flexible and adapt to the seller's requests. Trust and commitment lead to cooperation among the parties and eventually value creation. Once relational loyalty is achieved, buyers provide sellers favored status (Palmatier, 2008) often rebuying without soliciting competitive bids. Such favored status or relationship-induced loyalty is a result of strong relational bonds. Such loyalty affects financial performance of the firm often measured by metrics such as sales-based outcome measures (e.g., annual sales growth, sales diversity, sales volatility, share of wallet), performance-based outcome measures (e.g., price premiums, reduced selling costs), aggregate performance measures (e.g., CLV metrics, ROI), and knowledge-based outcome measures (e.g., patents, time to market, and new product success).

Kumar et al.'s (2009) Reverse Logic Framework to Relationship Marketing

Kumar *et al.* (2009) question the conventional path to firm profitability for firms using relationship marketing strategy. In this framework, innovation of products and services based on customer needs is believed to be the lifeblood of every firm and the cornerstone of customer acquisition. When a firm produces high-quality products and services, it will inevitably lead to higher levels of satisfaction for all customers. Higher levels of satisfaction lead to higher levels of loyalty (retention), which then lead to higher levels of profits. This satisfaction–loyalty–profitability chain has been a fundamental approach in relationship marketing. Kumar and colleagues provide three main reasons why firms should not base the foundations of their relationship marketing strategy on the satisfaction–loyalty–profitability framework. First, satisfaction and loyalty are perceptual and attitudinal in nature and also backward-looking metrics; further, the links connecting satisfaction–loyalty and loyalty–profitability are weak (see Bolton and Lemon, 1999; Capraro *et al.*, 2003). Using four different firms in different industries, Reinartz and Kumar (2002) find that the correlation between behavioral loyalty and profitability ranged from 0.20 to 0.45. Second, the traditional framework focuses only on current customers, often ignoring potential customers. This can be problematic as measures of future customer lifetime value (CLV) are important in acquisition efforts by companies. Third, the satisfaction–loyalty–profitability framework ignores competitive effects which we know is critical as many satisfied customers who are satisfied and report high intentions of repurchase get lured away by competitors (Rust *et al.*, 2004). Instead, Kumar *et al.* (2009) propose a reverse logic framework (RLF) that follows a similar path as the conventional framework but in the reverse direction (see Figure 2.10).

The starting point in the RLF approach is future customer value, or customer profitability, measured by customer lifetime value, or CLV as this metric outperforms all other metrics when selecting customers for marketing intervention (Kumar *et al.*, 2006) (see Figure 2.11). Firms need to know each customer's CLV before selectively choosing to up-sell and cross-sell. Customer loyalty strategy should be contingent upon the profit potential of each customer. This means that differential loyalty programs and customized experience for customers should be implemented based on their profitability contribution to the firm. Rewarding the most profitable customers at the expense of less profitable or unprofitable customers will increase their retention rate. Further, most profitable customers need to be profiled and their profile should be used to acquire new customers. These customers then become the bastion for new product/service innovation for future profit potential.

Figure 2.10: Reverse Logic Framework (RLF) of Relationship Marketing

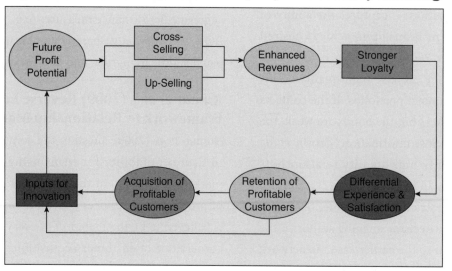

Adapted from V. Kumar, Ilaria Dalla Pozza, J. Andrew Petersen, and Denish Shah (2009), Reversing the Logic: The Path to Profitability through Relationship Marketing, *Journal of Interactive Marketing* 2: 147–156.

Figure 2.11: The starting point in the Reverse Logic Framework (RLF) is future customer value, or customer profitability, measured by customer lifetime value, or CLV.

Van Doorn et al.'s (2010) Customer Engagement Behavior (CEB) Model

In the last decade, there has been a flurry of academic research on customer engagement with firms as a new dimension of relationship marketing. Research in marketing has widely investigated customer engagement (e.g., Bowden, 2009; Brodie *et al.*, 2011, Hollebeek, 2011) and customer engagement behaviors (CEBs) (Kumar *et al.*, 2010; Pansari and Kumar, 2017; Van Doorn *et al.*, 2010). Van Doorn *et al.* (2010) examine customer engagement from the customer perspective beyond purchase behavior. The authors posit that customer engagement behaviors go beyond transactions and they define it as a customer's behavioral manifestations that have a brand or firm focus, beyond purchase, resulting from motivational drivers. These behavioral manifestations outside purchase-related behaviors can be both positive (i.e., posting a positive brand message on a blog) and negative (i.e., rallying a public protest against the firm) and may be targeted to a broader network of actors (i.e., current and potential customers,

employees, regulators, suppliers, and general public). The customer engagement behavior model is shown in Figure 2.12.

Van Doorn *et al.* (2010) identify five dimensions of CEBs, namely, valence, modality, scope, nature of impact, and customer goals. As noted earlier, CEBs can be both positive and negative and its modality can vary from in-role behaviors (e.g., complaint behavior), extra-role behaviors (e.g., offering suggestions and feedback), and elective behaviors (e.g., product improvement). Scope refers to both temporal parameters (e.g., momentary engagement vs. systematic engagement) and spatial parameters (e.g., local vs. global reach). The nature of impact of CEBs is conceptualized in terms of immediacy of impact, intensity of impact, breadth of impact, and the longevity of impact. For instance, persuading a friend to buy a brand has narrow breadth but high intensity. In an interconnected digital world, the immediacy, intensity, breadth, and longevity are expected to be higher and therefore more impactful on the firm and its constituents. Finally, customer

Figure 2.12: Customer Engagement Behavior (CEB) Model

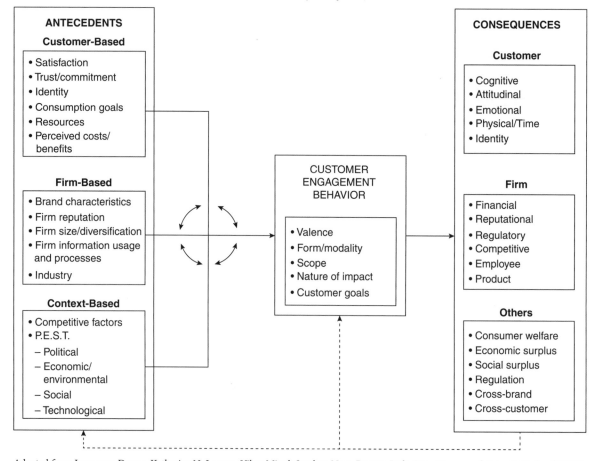

Adapted from Jenny van Doorn, Katherine N. Lemon, Vikas Mittal, Stephan Nass, Doreen Pick, Peter Pirner, and Peter C. Verhoef (2010), Customer Engagement Behavior: Theoretical Foundations and Research Directions, *Journal of Service Research* 13(3), pp. 253–266.

goals refer to the target of engagement, planned versus unplanned engagement, and goal alignment between customer-firm goals.

Van Doorn *et al.* (2010) identify several antecedents of CEBs, including customer-based, firm-based, and context-based factors. Customer-based antecedents include traditional relational factors such as satisfaction, trust, commitment, identification, and brand attachment. Customer goals and traits also determine the types of CEBs that customers engage in, for instance, customers with high moral identity (Winterich *et al.*, 2009) are more likely to engage in helping behaviors toward others in the social network, brand community, or firm employees and customers. Similarly, customer traits of self-enhancement and agentic versus communal orientation can also explain

underlying motivations (He *et al.*, 2008). Firm-based antecedents include reputation and brand equity, firm platforms and processes, and activities (e.g., incentive and loyalty programs). For instance, highly reputable firms engender higher levels of positive CEBs; however, the negative fallout may be higher as well in case of brand transgression. Finally, context-based antecedents include political, legal, economic, environmental, social, and technological factors of the society in which firms and customers exist. The role of media and competitor activities deserves closer scrutiny as they induce varying CEBs such as the role of media in publicizing competitor's product recall or a new product introduction by the competitor.

Finally, CEBs have consequences for customers and firms. Successful CEBs can create positive attitudes and reinforce behaviors including expanding the repertoire of CEBs. Customers also gain varying facets of benefits including functional benefits, hedonic benefits, experiential benefits, and relational benefits. For instance, customers reap financial benefits through loyalty and reward programs, emotional and experiential benefits through company-sponsored events, and relational benefits through company brand communities. Of course, firms benefit in several ways through CEBs including customer's direct economic value contribution, depth of the direct economic value contribution, and breadth of the indirect economic value contribution. These are explained in greater detail in the customer valuation model (Kumar, 2018) in later section of this chapter.

Harmeling et al.'s (2017) Customer Engagement Marketing Theory

Different from CEBs that are customer initiated, Harmeling *et al.* (2017) identified two primary forms of engagement marketing initiatives from the firm perspective: (1) task-based and (2) experiential-based. Task-based engagement initiatives occur outside the core, economic transaction in which customers

voluntarily contribute to marketing functions using structured tasks, i.e., work-related. In general, task-based engagement is extrinsically motivated. Customers use their resources to complete some structured task that involves mental or physical effort for which the company offers some type of reward such as discounts or points. Customers provide ratings, word-of-mouth marketing, crowdsourcing, knowledge, and other user-generated content. As task-based engagement marketing is extrinsically motivated, they tend to be short lived, prone to opportunism, and unsustainable since an enduring commitment to value creation is lacking (Verlegh *et al.*, 2013). In contrast, experiential engagement initiative is more about play than work generating emotions and enjoyment. Here, the motivation is intrinsic and the goal to create long-lasting psychological and emotional connections and attachment with the firm, brand, and other customers. These initiatives are often multisensory and interactive bringing the community together to collectively experience self-transformation through self-brand connections and integration. Engagement marketing theory is shown in Figure 2.13.

Figure 2.13: Customer Engagement Marketing Theory Framework

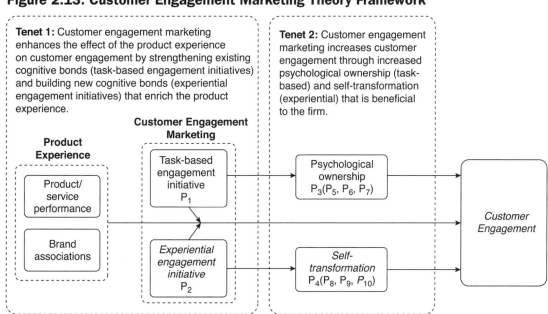

Adapted from Colleen M. Harmeling, Jordan W. Moffett, Mark J. Arnold, and Brad D. Carlson (2017), Toward a Theory of Customer engagement Marketing, *Journal of the Academy of Marketing Science* 45: 312–335.

According to the customer engagement marketing theory, engagement initiatives can affect long-term customer engagement by strengthening existing cognitive bonds and creating new cognitive bonds within knowledge structures of the core offering. Task-based engagement initiatives build on the core offering such that the same task gets repeated over time, strengthening cognitive bonds and thus its accessibility from memory networks. Further, task-based engagement initiatives create a sense of psychological ownership ("what is mine?") towards the firm that motivates customers to engage. That is, in psychological ownership the customer feels that the target of ownership is theirs and therefore it enhances the perceived value of the target (Pierce *et al.*, 2001). Experiential engagement initiatives involve more sensory, emotional, and social information, and create vivid images associated with the core offering such that when the customer experiences the core offering, it acts as retrieval cue activating such experiences. Further, experiential engagement initiatives help define the customer by incorporating distinctive and admired characteristics of the brand on the self and, thereby, creating self-transformation ("who am I?").

Lemon and Verhoef's (2016) Customer Experience Model

The customer experience model, in part, owes its origin to relationship marketing (Berry, 1995; Sheth and Parvatiyar, 1995), customer relationship management (Kumar and Reinartz, 2006), and customer engagement model (Brodie *et al.*, 2011; Kumar *et al.*, 2010). In general, scholars and practitioners agree that *total customer experience* is a multidimensional construct that involves cognitive, emotional, behavioral, sensorial, and social components (Schmitt, 1999, 2003; Verhoef *et al.*, 2009). An experience may relate to specific aspects of the offering, such as a brand or technology, and it consists of individual contacts between the firm and the customer at distinct points in the experience

called touch points. Customer experience occurs in three stages: (1) pre-purchase, (2) purchase, and (3) post-purchase (see Figure 2.14). Pre-purchase stage encompasses all customer interactions with the brand, category, and environment prior to purchase, and typical behaviors/motivations include need, goal, impulse recognition to search, and consideration of options leading to a purchase. Purchase stage encompasses customer interactions with the brand and its environment during the purchase event and includes the following behaviors: choice, ordering, and payment. At this stage, which is temporally compressed, marketers deploy marketing-mix activities to influence their brand purchase decision. In the post-purchase stage, the product itself becomes a critical touchpoint and customer interactions with the brand and its environment include several important behaviors including usage, consumption, service recovery, product return, variety-seeking, post-purchase engagement, and service requests.

Each of these behaviors across the three stages of the customer journey is facilitated by several categories of touchpoints: (1) brand-owned touch points, (2) partner-owned touch points, customer-owned touch points, and (3) social/external touch points. Brand-owned touch points are designed and managed by the firm and under the firm's control including brand-owned media such as advertising, websites, and loyalty and brand-controlled elements of the marketing-mix including product and service attributes, packaging, price, sales force, etc. Extensive research has been conducted to examine the direct and indirect effects of brand-owned and controlled activities on customer behavior across the three stages of the customer journey. Partner-owned touch points are jointly designed, managed, or controlled by the firm and one or more partners, which include marketing agencies, multichannel members, multiple vendors, and communication channel partners. Customer-owned touch points are actions within the

Figure 2.14: Customer Experience Model

Process Model for Customer Journey and Experience

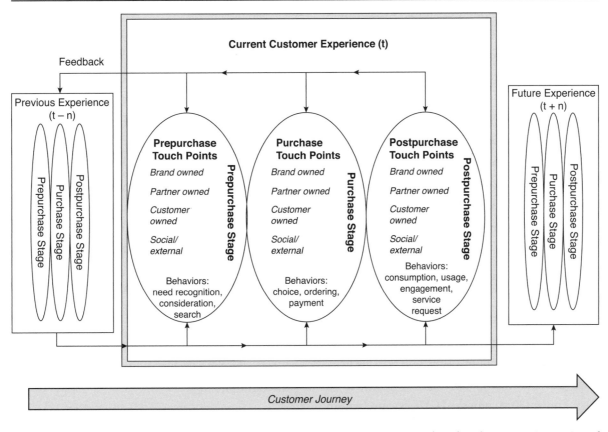

Adapted from Katherine N. Lemon and Peter C. Verhoef (2016), Understanding Customer Experience Throughout the Customer Journey, *Journal of Marketing*, AMA/MSI Special Issue 80: 69–96.

control of customers and include customers' choice of brand and payment method, consumption and usage experience, and cocreation activities. Finally, social/external touch points are influenced by other customers, peer influences, independent information sources, and the environment. Other customers and peers exert influence in all three stages of the customer journey. Third-party information sources such as review sites (e.g., TripAdvisor) and social media also exert influence on customers.

Past experiences at each stage of the customer journey may influence the customer's current journey. Past experiences influence current experience through expectation formation such as been evidenced in customer satisfaction research, at both aggregate and individual levels (Bolton and Drew, 1991; Verhoef and Van Doorn, 2008). Several dynamic influences also act on customers' responses including customer relationship with firms and the effectiveness of CRM strategies targeting customers.

From a customer engagement value (CEV) perspective, Venkatesan *et al.* (2018) provide rationale for firms employing different engagement strategies depending on the stage of the customer in the journey: prepurchase stage, purchase stage, and postpurchase stage. They argue that firms can acquire customers with higher CLV or by leveraging current customers using referrals. Once a customer is acquired, the next step by a firm is to increase value by growing the relationship through cross-selling and up-selling to customers. The next focus for firms is to keep an eye on customers that might churn. Some models have helped to predict potential customers that might defect (Neslin *et al.*, 2006) by examining the drivers of customer retention and defection and by focusing on customer duration and customer profitability (CLV). Of those that leave, the firm has to decide whether it is important to make an effort to reacquire the customer. Here some work has been done on the type of win-back offers, which should be provided to customers (Tokman *et al.*, 2009), as well as predicting the right customers to target based on their potential second customer lifetime value (SCLV) (Kumar *et al.*, 2015).

Customer Valuation Model — Kumar's (2018) Model

Recently, Kumar (2018) proposed customer valuation theory (CVT) by examining the direct and indirect economic value contribution of customers to the firm. It explains CLV based on satisfaction and engagement theories. Kumar (2018) proposed CVT as a mechanism to measure the future value of each customer on the basis of three components (see Figure 2.15). These are:

1. customer's direct economic value contribution,

2. depth of the direct economic value contribution, and

3. breadth of the indirect economic value contribution.

Direct Economic Value Contribution: At the individual level, the CLV is calculated as the sum of cumulative cash flows, discounted using the weighted average cost of capital, over the customer's entire lifetime with the company (Kumar, 2008). CLV is a function of three factors, namely, the predicted contribution margin, the propensity of the customer to continue in the relationship, and the marketing resources allocated to the customer, as expressed in the formula:

$$\text{CLV}_i = \sum_{t=1}^{T} \frac{(\text{Future Contribution Margin}_{it} - \text{Future Cost}_{it})}{(1 + d)^t},$$

where *i* is the customer index, *t* is the time index, *T* refers to the number of time periods, and *d* is the discount rate.

Kumar (2018) points out that for most CLV measures, the life cycle window is three years because future

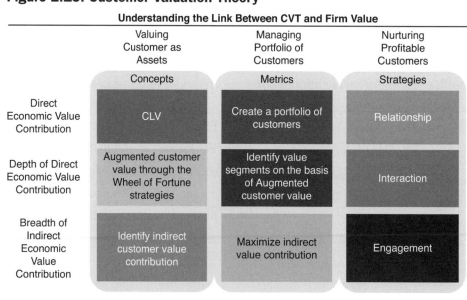

Figure 2.15: Customer Valuation Theory

Understanding the Link Between CVT and Firm Value			
	Valuing Customer as Assets	Managing Portfolio of Customers	Nurturing Profitable Customers
	Concepts	Metrics	Strategies
Direct Economic Value Contribution	CLV	Create a portfolio of customers	Relationship
Depth of Direct Economic Value Contribution	Augmented customer value through the Wheel of Fortune strategies	Identify value segments on the basis of Augmented customer value	Interaction
Breadth of Indirect Economic Value Contribution	Identify indirect customer value contribution	Maximize indirect value contribution	Engagement

Adapted V. Kumar (2018), A Theory of Customer Valuation: Concepts, Metrics, Strategy, and Implementation, *Journal of Marketing*, 82: 1–19.

cash flows are heavily discounted, and the predictive accuracy of the models declines over a longer time horizon. Further, customer needs change significantly over three years, and in response, product offerings change to match new customer needs and to leverage new technological advances. A firm can utilize the CLV concept to make optimal allocation of marketing resources in order to maximize customer value with the goal to maximize return on marketing investments. Marketing investments typically would include past, current, and future promotional costs toward customer acquisition, retention, win-back, technology upgrades, service improvements employee management, and quality control. It should be noted that CLV metric can also be computed at the aggregate level including customer cohort, segment, and firm levels.

Depth of Direct Economic Value Contribution: Here, the direct economic value of the customer in terms of intensity and inclusiveness in making significant

financial contributions to the firm is of interest. Some examples include acquisition and retention of profitable customers, customer purchase potential across multiple channels of buying, and likelihood of customers buying across product categories. For instance, how do firms decide which prospects will make better customers in the future and therefore worthwhile to acquire? Further, not all long-life customers are profitable, and firms should use CLV metrics to identify the right customers for retention (see Figure 2.16). Similarly, how can firms discern profitable versus unprofitable cross-purchase customers and how can resources (e.g., sales and service resources) be allocated across multiple channels?

Breadth of Indirect Economic Value Contribution: This refers to customers' indirect value contributions to the firm through their referral behavior, influence behavior, and their knowledge behavior. Referral behavior generally includes incentivized referral,

Figure 2.16: Customer retention enhances the efficiency of relationship marketing programs.

influence behavior includes online influence on both current and future customers' (i.e., prospects') purchases, and knowledge behavior includes offering review/feedback and knowledge on current and future products and services. The engagement value of each of these indirect behaviors is termed customer referral value (CRV), customer influence value (CIV), and customer knowledge value (CKV) (Kumar *et al.*, 2010). CRV captures the net present value of future profits of new customers who purchased the firm offerings as a result of the referral behavior of the current customer. It is important for firms to integrate CLV and CRV databases to keep track of the referral activities by current customers. CIV impacts customers to use the firm's offering and/or to adapt their purchase patterns continuously, but more importantly, to persuade and convert others into customers. CIV calculates the monetary gains/losses that are attributable to a customer as a result of her or his positive and negative message spread (net spread) and influence on others (i.e., customer influence effect). Finally, CKV refers to the monetary value attributed to a customer by a firm as a result of the profit generated by implementing an idea/suggestion/feedback from that customer. This feedback applies to current product improvements as well as future product updates and new product introductions. The relationship between CLV and CKV on firm performance, however, may be somewhat tricky: low levels of CLV may indicate also low levels of CKV (due to low familiarity), whereas high levels of CLV may also indicate low levels of CKV (due to high satisfaction) (Kumar, 2018).

Kumar (2018) propounds that the customer valuation theory (CVT) essentially is about the individual customer and is at the center of every marketing action and reaction. Customers benefit by connecting with the firm at the transactional level and by collaborating with the firm at the relational level. For the firms,

it helps them to allocate optimal resources and customize strategies for each customer. At the macro level, CVT also benefits society and the environment as firms focus only on resources that meet customer needs and that prevent wasteful usage of valuable environmental and infrastructural resources.

KEY TAKEAWAYS

- Early models of customer relationship marketing moved away from short-term competition and conflict to long-term mutual cooperation and interdependence.

- Relationship marketing programs enhance efficiency through retention and resource-sharing as well as effectiveness through participation and engagement with firm's marketing program.

- Low levels of buyer and seller motivational investment in a relationship are conducive for discrete-type transactions, whereas high levels are conducive for long-term relationships.

- Trust and commitment are central to successful relationship marketing and are not only important variables in marketing relationship but also key mediating variables as well.

- In the exploratory stage of relationship marketing, initial levels of trust and commitment are calculative and deterrence-based in nature; as the relationship grows, with increased communication and mutual dependence, calculative trust leads to knowledge-based trust; in the maturity stage of relationship marketing, with shared relational norms and mutual interdependence, knowledge-based trust leads to identification-based trust.

- Service-dominant logic emphasizes value pro-position for customers in the relationship by identifying, (co)developing, and modifying core competences (i.e., knowledge) — the fundamental unit of exchange and the source of competitive advantage. All economic and social actors are resource integrators in a service ecosystem for the purpose of value (co)creation.

- While trust and commitment are central in relationship marketing, customer gratitude and norms of reciprocity are also critical mediators in interpersonal relationship (B2C) marketing. Grateful customers reward firms by engaging in purchase behavior, increased commitment, and long-term firm performance.

- Relationship quality, relationship breadth, and relationship composition are important drivers in interfirm (B2B) relationship marketing. Relationship quality is the strength of relational bonds with an exchange partner. Relationship breadth represents the number of relational bonds and interpersonal ties with an exchange partner and parallels the network concepts of network density. Relationship composition refers to the decision-making capability of relational contacts, and the underlying premise is that a diverse contact portfolio of critical decision makers with authority can provide sellers access to information from multiple buyer sources and perspectives.

- In interfirm (B2B) relationship marketing, relationship strength (relationship quality × relationship breadth) and relationship efficacy (relationship quality × relationship composition) also synergistically capture seller performance outcomes and are important relational assets.

- While the conventional satisfaction–loyalty–profitability framework of relationship marketing has been foundational, the reverse logic framework (RLF) overcomes many inherent weaknesses of the conventional framework. In the new framework, the starting point is future customer value or customer profitability as measured by customer lifetime value (CLV). Different loyalty programs for customers should be implemented based on customer profitability.

- Customer engagement behaviors (CEB) are fast-becoming a critical pillar of relationship marketing. These go beyond purchase-related transactions into non-purchase behaviors resulting from customer motivational drivers that affect firm performance, which includes several customer-based factors (e.g., relational factors, consumption goals), firm-based factors (e.g., reputation, brand equity, loyalty programs), and context-based factors (e.g., political/legal/technological environment, external stakeholders).

- Firm-initiated customer engagement programs are often task-based engagement initiatives and/or experiential-based engagement initiatives. The former offers extrinsic motivations to customers in the form of rewards, while the latter offers intrinsic motivations often involving multisensory interactions bringing the community together.

- Opportunities for customer relationship marketing are now embedded in specific aspects of the firm offering intersecting brand-owned, customer-owned, partner-owned, and external touchpoints. Each critical touchpoint is an opportunity to build and sustain relationship with customers at each stage of the customer's journey: pre-purchase, purchase, and post-purchase stages.

- Recent models of customer relationship marketing focus on the future value of customers, which arises from three sources: (1) customer's direct economic value contribution (i.e., customer lifetime value), (2) depth of economic value contribution (i.e., purchase potential across firm's multiple channels and product categories), and (3) breadth of indirect economic contribution (i.e., customer referral value, customer influence value, and customer knowledge value).

EXERCISES

Questions

1. Discuss the critical roles of trust and commitment in relationship marketing. Explain how the nature of buyer–seller trust changes over the lifecycle stages of a relationship with specific reference to transaction cost economics.

2. While trust and commitment are cognitive-based relational factors, gratitude and norms of reciprocity that provide emotional and social-based processes are also important in B2C relationship marketing. Explain this in light of the interpersonal relationship marketing model.

3. While relationship quality is important, relationship breadth and relationship composition are important additional drivers in B2B relationship marketing. Explain this in light of the interfirm relationship marketing model.

4. Explain the process of how the synergistic effects involving relationship strength and relationship efficacy work in the interfirm relationship model.

5. Discuss the fundamental premises of the service dominant (S-D) logic. What is the role of institutional logic in fostering cooperation among relational partners?

6. Explain the satisfaction–loyalty–profitability chain inherent in relationship marketing framework. What are some of the pitfalls for companies that design and implement relationship marketing strategies based on this approach?

7. Explain the various types of customer-based, company-based, and context-based antecedents of customer engagement behavior.

8. Marketers generally engage in task-based versus experiential-based initiatives with their customers. Explain how these initiatives work in keeping customers engaged with companies.

Which initiative is more effective for companies in building a long-term relationship with customers and why?

9. Explain the total customer experience with a company at various touchpoints in each of the three stages: (1) pre-purchase, (2) purchase, and (3) post-purchase.

10. Explain the customer valuation theory (direct and indirect economic value contribution) as a mechanism to measure the future value of each customer.

11. How do marketers maximize the depth of direct economic value contribution of customers?

12. How do marketers maximize (or optimize) the breadth of indirect economic value contribution of customers?

Group Discussion

1. Critically discuss the following statement: "Relationship marketing is characterized by a departure from competition and conflict to mutual cooperation and from choice independence to mutual inter-dependence". Give some examples of companies that have embraced relationship marketing and implemented such transition over time.

2. In the transactional approach to marketing, marketers typically used "hard-sell" tactics in sales and promotion as well as market segmentation to differentiate their offerings so as to build brand loyalty. How has this changed for firms that have adopted the relational approach to marketing?

3. In the service-dominant (S-D) logic, knowledge is the source of competitive advantage, service is the basis of exchange, and all actors are resource integrators in value co-creation process. Compare the foundational premises of S-D logic with the traditional product-centered view of relationship marketing.

4. Discuss how customer gratitude toward a company enhances relationship marketing performance for companies. Give some real-life examples of how grateful customers reward companies for their extra efforts.

5. Given that customer lifetime value (CLV) is important for the acquisition of future potential customers, make a strong and compelling case why the reverse logic framework (RLF) to relationship marketing makes better sense than the traditional logic of satisfaction–loyalty–profitability chain.

6. Discuss the pros and cons of the dimensions of customer engagement behavior (CEBs) in an online versus offline setting. Think of a real-life company (e.g., Starbucks) and discuss how marketers develop strategies to monitor and control the impact of various CEBs in terms of immediacy, intensity, breadth, and longevity of impact.

HBS and Ivey Cases

- AnswerDash (9-516-106)

- Reinventing Best Buy (9-716-455)

- Chase Sapphire (9-518-024)

- Laurs & Bridz (9B18A004)

CASE QUESTIONS

AnswerDash

1. How can AnswerDash use trust and commitment to strengthen relationships with its key stakeholders?

2. Discuss the pitfalls for AnswerDash in designing and implementing relationship marketing strategies based on the satisfaction–loyalty–profitability chain approach. Should AnswerDash apply the reverse logic relationship framework starting with profitability? Why?

3. Which initiative, task-based versus experiential-based, is more effective for AnswerDash in building a long-term relationship with customers? Explain your reasoning.

4. How can AnswerDash maximize the depth of direct economic value contribution of customers?

5. How can AnswerDash maximize the breadth of indirect economic value contribution of customers?

6. How can AnswerDash make use of customer lifetime value (CLV) to improve the acquisition of potential customers?

Reinventing Best Buy

1. How would you apply the interpersonal relationship marketing model to strengthen the marketing effort of Best Buy?

2. How can Best Buy apply the service dominant (S-D) logic to improve its market share?

3. What are the antecedents of customer engagement behavior for Best Buy?

4. What is the total customer experience with Best Buy at various touchpoints in each of the three stages: (1) pre-purchase, (2) purchase, and (3) post-purchase?

5. How can Best Buy make use of the customer valuation theory (direct and indirect economic value contribution) as a mechanism to measure the future value of each customer?

6. How can Best Buy apply the foundational premises of S-D logic to improve its sales through relationship marketing?

7. Discuss the pros and cons of the dimensions of customer engagement behavior (CEBs) for Best Buy in an online versus offline setting? How can Best Buy develop strategies to monitor and control the impact of various CEBs in terms of immediacy, intensity, breadth, and longevity of impact?

Chase Sapphire

1. How can JPMorgan use trust and commitment to strengthen relationships with its key stakeholders?

2. How would you apply the interpersonal relationship marketing model to strengthen the marketing effort of JPMorgan?

3. How can JPMorgan apply the service dominant (S-D) logic to improve its market share?

4. Which initiative, task-based versus experiential-based, is more effective for JPMorgan in building a long-term relationship with customers? Explain your reasoning.

5. What is the total customer experience with JPMorgan at various touchpoints in each of the three stages: (1) pre-purchase, (2) purchase, and (3) post-purchase?

6. How can JPMorgan apply the foundational premises of S-D logic to improve its sales through relationship marketing?

7. Discuss the pros and cons of the dimensions of customer engagement behavior (CEBs) for JPMorgan in an online versus offline setting. How can JPMorgan develop strategies to monitor and control the impact of various CEBs in terms of immediacy, intensity, breadth, and longevity of impact?

Laurs & Bridz

1. Discuss the pitfalls for Laurs & Bridz in designing and implementing relationship marketing strategies based on the satisfaction–loyalty–profitability chain approach. Should Laurs & Bridz apply the reverse logic relationship framework starting with profitability? Why?

2. How would you apply the interfirm relationship marketing model to strengthen the marketing effort of Laurs & Bridz?

3. What are the antecedents of customer engagement behavior for Laurs & Bridz?

4. How can Laurs & Bridz make use of the customer valuation theory (direct and indirect economic value contribution) as a mechanism to measure the future value of each customer?

5. How can Laurs & Bridz maximize the depth of direct economic value contribution of customers?

6. How can Laurs & Bridz maximize the breadth of indirect economic value contribution of customers?

REFERENCES

Bagozzi, Richard P. (1995), Reflections on Relationship Marketing in Consumer Markets, *Journal of the Academy of Marketing Science* 23(4): 272–277.

Bartlett, Monica Y. and David DeSteno (2006), Gratitude and Prosocial Behavior, *Psychological Science* 17: 319–325.

Baum, Joel A. C., Tony C. Calabrese, and Brian S. Silverman (2000), Don't Go It Alone: Alliance Network Composition and Startups Performance in Canadian Biotechnology, Strategic Management Journal 21 (March): 267–94.

Bendapudi, Neeli, and Robert P. Leone (2002), Managing Business-to-Business Customer Relationships Following Key Contact Employee Turnover in a Vendor Firm, Journal of Marketing 66 (April): 83–101.

Berry, Leonard L. (1995), Relationship Marketing of Services: Growing Interest, Emerging perspectives, *Journal of the Academy of Marketing Science* 23(4): 236–245.

Blau, P.M. (1964), *Exchange and Power in Social Life.* New York: John Wiley & Sons.

Bolton, Ruth N. and James H. Drew (1991), A Multistage Model of Customers' Assessment of Service Quality and Value, *Journal of Consumer Research* 17(4): 375–384.

Bolton, Ruth N. and Katherine N. Lemon (1999), A Dynamic Model of Customers' Usage of Services: Usage as an Antecedent and Consequence of Satisfaction, *Journal of Marketing Research*, 36: 171–199.

Bowden, Jana lay-Hwa (2009), The Process of Customer Engagement: A Conceptual Framework, *Journal of Marketing Theory and Practice* 17(1): 63–74.

Brodie, Roderick J., Linda D. Hollebeek, Biljana Juric, and Ana Ilic (2011), Customer Engagement: Conceptual Domain, Fundamental Propositions, and Implications for Research, *Journal of Service Research* 14(3): 252–271.

Brown, Rupert (2000), Group Processes: Dynamics Within and Between Groups. Malden, Mass.: Blackwell Publishing Ltd.

Cannon, J.P., Ravi S. Achrol, G.T. Gundlach (2000), Contracts, Norms, and Plural Form Governance, *Journal of the Academy of Marketing Science* 28(2): 180–194.

Capraro, Anthony J., Susan Broniarczyk, and Rajendra Srivastava (2003), Factors Influencing the Likelihood of Customer Defection: The Role of Customer Knowledge, *Journal of the Academy of Marketing Science* 31(2): 164–176.

Crosby, Lawrence A., Kenneth R. Evans, and Deborah Cowles (1990), Relationship Quality in Services Selling: An Interpersonal Influence Perspective, *Journal of Marketing* 54 (July): 68–81.

Dahl, Darren W. Heather Honea, and Rajesh V. Manchanda (2005), Three Rs of Interpersonal Consumer Guilt: Relationship, Reciprocity, and Reparation, *Journal of Consumer Psychology* 15(4): 307–315.

Dunn, Jennifer R. and Maurice E. Schweitzer (2005), Feeling and Believing: The Influence of Emotion on Trust, *Journal of Personality and Social Psychology* 88(5): 736–748.

Dwyer, Robert F., Paul H. Schurr, and Sejo Oh (1987), Developing Buyer-Seller Relationships, *Journal of Marketing* 51(2): 11–27.

Emmons, Robert A. and Michael E. McCullough (2004), *The Psychology of Gratitude*. New York, NY: Oxford University Press.

Goei, Ryan and Franklin J. Boster (2005), The Roles of Obligation and Gratitude in Explaining the Effect of Favors on Compliance, *Communication Monographs* 72: 284–300.

Gouldner, Alvin W. (1960), The Norm of Reciprocity: A Preliminary Statement, *American Sociology Review* 25: 161–178.

Harmeling, Colleen M., Jordan W. Moffett, Mark J. Arnold, and Brad D. Carlson (2017), Toward a Theory of Customer Engagement Marketing, *Journal of the Academy of Marketing Science* 45(3): 312–335.

He, Xin, J. Jeffrey Inman, and Vikas Mittal (2008), Gender Jeopardy in Financial Risk Taking, *Journal of Marketing Research* 45: 414–424.

Hollebeek, Linda D. (2011), Exploring Customer Brand Engagement: Definition and Themes, *Journal of Strategic Marketing* 19(7): 555–573.

Kumar, Nirmalya, Lisa K. Scheer, and Jan-Benedict E. M. Steenkamp (1995a), The Effects of Perceived Interdependence on Dealer Attitudes, Journal of Marketing Research 32 (August): 348–56.

Kumar, Nirmalya, Lisa K. Scheer, and Jan-Benedict E. M. Steenkamp (1995b), The Effects of Supplier Fairness on Vulnerable Resellers, Journal of Marketing Research 32 (February): 54–65.

Kumar, V. (2008), *Managing Customers for Profit: Strategies to Increase Profit and Build Loyalty*, Upper Saddle River, NJ: Wharton School Publishing.

Kumar, V. (2018), A Theory of Customer Valuation: Concepts, Metrics, Strategy, and Implementation, *Journal of Marketing* 82: 1–19.

Kumar, V., Lerzan Aksoy, Bas Donkers, Rajkumar Venkatesan, Thorsten Wiesel, and Sebastian Tillmanns (2010), Undervalued or Overvalued Customers: Capturing Total Customer Engagement Value, *Journal of Service Research* 13(3): 297–310.

Kumar, V., Y. Bhagwat, X. Zhang (2015), Regaining "Lost" Customers: The predictive Power of First Lifetime Behavior, the Reason for Defection, and the Nature of the Winback Offer, *Journal of Marketing* 79(4): 34–55.

Kumar, V., Ilaria Dalla Pozza, J. Andrew Petersen, and Denish Shah (2009), Reversing the Logic: The Path to Profitability through Relationship Marketing, *Journal of Interactive Marketing* 23: 147–156.

Kumar, V. and Werner Reinartz (2006), *Customer Relationship Management: A Databased Approach.* New York: John Wiley & Sons.

Kumar, V., Denish Shah, and Rajkumar Venkatesan (2006), Managing Retailer Profitability — One Customer at a Time, *Journal of Retailing* 82(4): 277–294.

Lemon, Katherine N. and Peter C. Verhoef (2016), Understanding Customer Experience Throughout the Customer Journey, *Journal of Marketing* 80: 69–96.

Lewicki, Roy J. and Barbara B. Bunker (1996), *Developing and Maintaining Trust in Working Relationships.* Thousand Oaks, CA: Sage Publications.

Li, Peter Ping (2007), Social Tie, Social Capital, and Social Behavior: Toward an Integrative Model of Informal Exchange, Asia Pacific Journal of Management 24 (2): 227–46.

Lusch, Robert F. and Stephen L. Vargo (2006), Service-Dominant Logic as a Foundation for a General Theory, in R.F. Lush and S.L. Vargo (Eds.), *The Service-Dominant Logic of Marketing: Dialog, Debate, and Directions* (pp. 381–420). Armonk: ME Sharpe.

Macneil, Ian R. (1980), *The New Social Contract, An Inquiry into Modern Contractual Relations.* New Haven, CT: Yale University Press.

Morales, Andrea C. (2005), Giving Firms an 'E' for Effort: Consumer Responses to High-Effort Firms, Journal of Consumer Research 31 (March): 806–12.

Morgan, Robert M. and Shelby D. Hunt (1994), The Commitment-Trust Theory of Relationship Marketing, *Journal of Marketing* 58 (July): 20–38.

Neslin, S.A., S. Gupta, W. Kamakura, J. Lu, and C.H. Mason (2006), Defection Detection: Measuring and Understanding the Predictive Accuracy of Customer Churn Models, *Journal of Marketing Research* 43(2): 204–211.

North, D.C. (1990), *Institutions, Institutional Change, and Economic Performance.* Cambridge: Cambridge University Press.

Ostrom, Elinor and James Walker (2003), *Trust and Reciprocity: Interdisciplinary Lessons from Experimental Research.* New York, NY: Russell Sage Foundation.

Palmatier, Robert W. (2008), *Relationship Marketing*, Cambridge, MA: Marketing Science Institute.

Palmatier, Robert W., Rajiv P. Dant, Dhruv Grewal, and Mark B. Houston (2007b), *Relationship Marketing Dynamics* (pp. 1–37) Seattle WA: University of Washington Working Paper 1.

Palmatier, Robert W., Mark B. Houston, Rajiv P. Dant & Dhruv Grewal (2013), Relationship Velocity: Toward a Theory of Relationship Dynamics, *Journal of Marketing* 77: 13–30.

Palmatier, Robert W., Lisa K. Scheer, Mark B. Houston, Kenneth R. Evans, and Srinath Gopalakrishna (2007a), Use of Relationship Marketing Programs in Building Customer-Salesperson and Customer-Firm Relationships: Differential Influences on Financial Outcomes, *International Journal of Research in Marketing* 24: 210–223.

Pansari, Anita and V. Kumar (2017), Customer Engagement: The construct, Antecedents, and Consequences, *Journal of the Academy of Marketing Science* 45(3): 294–311.

Pierce, Jon L., Tatiana Kostova and Kurt T. Dirks (2001), Toward a Theory of Psychological Ownership in Organizations, *Academy of Management Review* 26(2): 298–310.

Reinartz, Werner and V. Kumar (2002), The Mismanagement of Customer Loyalty, *Harvard Business Review* 80(7): 86–94.

Rindfleisch, Aric, and Christine Moorman (2001), The Acquisition and Utilization of Information in New Product Alliances: A Strength-of-Ties Perspective, Journal of Marketing 65 (April): 1–18.

Rousseau, Denise M., Sim B. Sitkin, Ronald S. Burt, and Colin Camerer (1998), Not So Different After All: A Cross Discipline View of Trust, *Academy of Management Review* 23(3): 393–404.

Rowley, Timothy J. (1997), Moving Beyond Dyadic Ties: A Network Theory of Stakeholder Influences, Academy of Management Review 22 (4): 887–910.

Rust, Roland T., Katherine N. Lemon, and Valerie A. Zeithaml (2004), Return on Marketing Using Customer Equity to Focus Marketing Strategy, *Journal of Marketing* 68(1): 109–127.

Schmitt, Bernd H. (1999), *Experiential Marketing.* New York: The Free Press.

Schmitt, Bernd H. (2003), *Customer Experience Management: A Revolutionary Approach to Connecting with Your Customers.* New York: The Free Press.

Schwartz, Barry (1967), The Social Psychology of the Gift, *The American Journal of Sociology* 73: 1–11.

Sheth, Jagdish N. and Atul Parvatiyar (1995), Relationship Marketing in Consumer Markets: Antecedents and Consequences, *Journal of the Academy of Marketing Science* 23(4): 255–271.

Sheth, Jagdish N. and Atul Parvatiyar (2000), The Evolution of Relationship Marketing, in Jagdish N. Sheth and Atul Parvatiyar (Eds.), *Handbook of Relationship Marketing* (pp. 119–145) Sage Publication.

Tokman, M., R.E. Bucklin, and K. Pauwels (2009), Effect of Word-of-Mouth versus Traditional Marketing: Findings from an Internet Social Networking Site, *Journal of Marketing* 73: 90–102.

Tsai, Wenpin (2001), Knowledge Transfer in Interorganizational Networks: Effects of Network Position and Absorptive Capacity on Business Unit Innovation and Performance, *Academy of Management Journal* 44 (October): 996–1001.

Van Doorn, Jenny, Katherine N. Lemon, Vikas Mittal, Stephan Nass, Doreen Pick, Peter Pirner, and Peter C. Verhoef (2010), Customer Engagement Behavior: Theoretical Foundations and Research Directions, *Journal of Service Research* 13(3): 253–266.

Vargo, Stephen L. and Robert F. Lusch (2004), Evolving to a New Dominant Logic for Marketing, *Journal of Marketing* 68: 1–17.

Vargo, Stephen L. and Robert F. Lusch (2011), It's All B2B and Beyond…: Toward a Systems Perspective of the Market, *Industrial Marketing Management*, 40(2): 181–187.

Vargo, Stephen L. and Robert F. Lusch (2016), Institutions and Axioms: An Extension and Update of Service-Dominant Logic, *Journal of the Academy of Marketing Science* 44: 5–23.

Venkatesan, Rajkumar, J. Andrew Petersen, and Leandro Guissoni (2018), Measuring and Managing Customer Engagement Value through the Customer Journey, in Robert W. Palmatier, V. Kumar, and Colleen M. Harmeling (Eds.), *Customer Engagement Marketing* (pp. 53–74) Palgrave Macmillan, Springer.

Verhoef, Peter C. and Jenny Van Doorn (2008), Critical Incidents and the Impact of Satisfaction on Customer Share, *Journal of Marketing* 72: 123–142.

Verhoef, Peter C., Katherine N. Lemon, A. Parasuraman, Anne Roggeveen, Michael Tsiros, and Leonard A. Schlesinger (2009), Customer Experience Creation: Determinants, Dynamics, and Management Strategies, *Journal of Retailing* 85(1): 31–41.

Verlegh, Peter W., Gangseog Ryu, Mirjam A. Tuk, and Lawrence Feick (2013), Receiver Responses to Rewarded Referral: The Motives Inferences Framework, *Journal of the Academy of Marketing Science* 41(6): 669–682.

Walker, Gordon, Bruce Kogut, and Weijan Shan (1997), Social Capital, Structural Holes and the Formation of Industry Networks, *Organization Science* 8 (March-April): 109–25.

Watkins, Philip C., Kathrane Woodward, Tamara Stone, and Russell L. Kolts (2003), Gratitude and Happiness: Development of a Measure of Gratitude and Relationships with Subjective Well-Being, *Social Behavior and Personality: An International Journal* 31: 431–451.

Wernerfelt, Birger (1984), A Resource-Based View of the Firm, *Strategic Management Journal* 5(2): 171–180.

Williamson, Oliver E. (1975), *Markets and Hierarchies, Analysis and Antitrust Implications.* New York, NY: The Free press.

Williamson, Oliver E. (1985), *The Economic Institutions of Capitalism.* New York: The Free Press.

Winterich, Karen P., Vikas Mittal, and William T. Ross, Jr. (2009), Donation Behavior toward In-Groups and Out-Groups: The Role of Gender and Moral Identity, *Journal of Consumer Research* 36: 199–214.

03

Building Business-to-Business (B2B) Relationships

OVERVIEW

In Chapter 3, we primarily focus on business-to-business (B2B) relationships. First, we highlight the key differences between B2B versus and business-to-consumer (B2C) marketing before we set the stage for the six-markets framework of relationship marketing (RM), originally developed by Peck *et al.* (1999) with subsequent revisions by Payne *et al.* (2005). Building on this framework, the modified and reconfigured stakeholder framework developed by Malhotra and Agarwal (2002) is then discussed. This framework adopts a broadened approach to relationship marketing programs (i.e., functional–structural–strategic levels) and expands on the growing role of strategic alliances. Relationship dynamics in buyer–seller relationships covering concepts such as dependence/interdependence, satisfaction, trust, commitment, and types of control in channel relationships are discussed. In particular, two frameworks, namely, the resource-based view framework of interdependence structure and the service-dominant (S-D) logic framework in buyer–seller relationship, are discussed. Separate sections have been devoted to highlighting in detail the importance of both upstream and downstream relationship marketing. Finally, the chapter concludes with the discussion on relationship management capability. At the end of the chapter, key takeaways are provided concluding with discussion questions and HBS and Ivey cases. But first, to give a flavor of B2B relationship marketing, we provide some real-life vignettes.

OPENING VIGNETTES

Vignette 1: In the early 2000s, Mercedes-Benz (MB) cars had been sold in the UK market through a franchised network of about 138 dealerships. Although the technical quality of the product was highly regarded, customers complained that the service they received was not of the same high standard. There was an inconsistency between the communication they received and the service that was delivered. As a first step, MB adopted a new distribution model by reorganizing the market into 35 new, larger geographical areas or "market areas" (MAs) consisting of about six dealership outlets. The project management team set out to identify the key customer relationship management (CRM) processes and integrate these processes within the new structure including control structure across MB UK, the MAs, and individual dealerships; prospect management; customer communication and complaint management; and CRM marketing team–salesperson interface. Similarly, a centralized CRM relationship management capability was set up, which could be leveraged and shared across multiple entities, and a comprehensive training was designed to educate employees at every level in CRM. The result? Over a 12-year period, there was a steady improvement in customer satisfaction and customer loyalty (see Figure 3.1). Cross-selling and upselling opportunities were increased, and relationships with customers were extended and deepened.

Figure 3.1: Emphasis on customer relationship management (CRM) has helped Mercedes-Benz to improve customer satisfaction and customer loyalty.

Vignette 2: The relationship between Apple and Corning is like a marriage between two companies. Corning makes Gorilla Glass, which after strengthening with potassium ions is ideal for the screen of every iPhone, and the two companies have been together since the iPhone's introduction in 2007. Recently, Apple responded by making a $200 million research-and-development investment

in Corning and its plant in Harrodsburg, Kentucky, that specializes in making cutting-edge glass. Long-term B2B relationships like the one between Apple and Corning are paramount for the health of any business, and companies spend more than $12 billion annually on customer relationship management. Palmatier (2008) spent six years analyzing the B2B relationships of a Fortune 500 wholesaler that serves retailers around the United States. According to this study, customer relationship quality in channel management can be summarized along four dimensions — trust, commitment, dependence, and norms, each covering a different facet of a relationship.

Vignette 3: Apple and Clearwell, a leader in intelligent e-discovery, jointly developed and provided Clearwell's E-Discovery Platform on the iPad device. Clearwell for the iPad created a new paradigm in electronic discovery for an exciting and revolutionary experience. This integration helps enterprises and law firms leverage Clearwell's E-Discovery Platform for the collection, processing, analysis, review, and production of electronically stored information using the new Apple iPad. In other words, E-Discovery helps enterprises and law firms obtain documents and information in a legally defensible manner. It enables leading enterprises and law firms to do e-discovery on their own terms — anywhere, anytime. Clearwell for the iPad was approved for distribution on the App Store and made widely available for the iPad in April 2010. Clearwell Systems transforms the way enterprises and law firms perform electronic discovery (e-discovery) in response to litigation, regulatory inquiries, and internal investigations. With iPad, the Clearwell E-Discovery Platform automates the processing, analysis, review, and production phases of e-discovery via a single, integrated product. Leading organizations utilize Clearwell to accelerate early case assessments, intelligently cull-down data, increase reviewer productivity, and ensure the defensibility of their e-discovery process.

Vignette 4: eatiply™ is a good example of cause-related marketing program in which some US restaurants engage in collaborative partnership with a nonprofit organization to build and maintain relationships that would enhance the motives of the partners. It is a food donation project that was created to help the fight against world hunger. Each time someone supports an eatiply-partnered business and chooses their eatiply-featured product or service, a meal is donated and provided to someone in need (see Figure 3.2). That is, by choosing to shop at eatiply-participating businesses and purchasing an eatiply-featured product or service, a meal is donated on one's behalf. There is no need to register, apply, or give a fake name. After one chooses one of their partners' eatiply-featured products or services, he/she just needs to pay for it like he/she would do for any other time. Making the choice to purchase from an eatiply-supported business is the single most important factor. The business will have a list of all their eatiply-featured items on their eatiply profile and will also have it labeled inside their establishment. Contributors do not have to adopt a child, write a check, or even add to her or his bill. This project is 100% hands-free and designed for the convenience of one's life. Currently, eatiply is partnering with local businesses across the nation. One can locate all eatiply-supporting partners on their website, www.eatiply.com.

Figure 3.2: Many restaurants are partnering with eatiply™ to not only serve delicious meals to their customers but also to fight world hunger.

INTRODUCTION

The true beginnings of business relationship research can be traced back to the late 1970s and the 1980s (Webster, 1978) examining industrial marketing (now referred to as business-to-business (B2B) marketing) and services marketing and focusing on business relationships, constellation of sales processes, just-in-time (JIT) supply relationships, and network perspective. It became established during the 1990s with several conceptual studies (Heidi and John, 1992; Morgan and Hunt, 1994) and received an additional impetus in the first decade of the new century with the development and implementation of customer relationship management (CRM).

B2B marketing represents value-generating relationships between businesses and the full range of stakeholders. Adopting from Grewal and Lilien (2012), Lilien (2016) distinguishes B2B from business-to-consumer (B2C) by asking a simple question: Is the demand for a product or service derived (i.e., driven by the demand of some subsequent customers — B2B) or primary (i.e., driven by specific tastes and preferences of the buyer — B2C). Several differences between B2B and B2C are worth mentioning. Relative to B2C marketers, B2B marketers operate in a manufacturing/technology-driven culture (versus marketing culture); focus on value chain intermediaries (versus end consumers); develop a technical/economic value proposition (versus perceptual value proposition); incorporate economic value (versus brand value); face fewer customers (versus larger number of customers); engage in larger individual transactions (versus fewer transactions); are interlinked to buyers through production and delivery transaction processes (versus process linkage); engage in purchasing process that is highly complex (versus less complexity); and involve a wider range of stakeholders (versus fewer stakeholders). Table 3.1 summarizes the differences between B2B and B2C marketing.

Table 3.1: Key Differences between B2B and B2C Markets

Business-to-Consumer (B2C)	Business-to-Business (B2B)
Marketing culture	Manufacturing/Tech culture
Market to end of chain	Market to value chain
Perceptual proposition	Technical proposition
Value in brand relationship	Value in use, quantifiable
Large customer segments	Small number of customers
Small-unit transactions	Large-unit transactions
Transaction linkage	Process linkage
More direct purchase	Complex buying sequences
Consumer decides	Web of decision participants

Source: Adapted from Grewal, Rajdeep and Gary L. Lilien (2012), Business-to-Business Marketing: Looking Back, Looking Forward, in G.L. Lilien and R. Grewal (Eds.), *Handbook of Business to Business Marketing* (pp. 1–14): Edward Elgar Press. Reprinted in Lilien, Gary L. (2016), The B2B Knowledge Gap, *International Journal of Research in Marketing* 33: 543–556.

Given that B2B marketing involves a far wider range of stakeholders than B2C marketing, it is appropriate that we begin our discussion on B2B relationship marketing by first introducing a generalized stakeholder framework of relationship marketing wherein we discuss the original six-markets framework (Payne *et al.*, 2005), followed by the stakeholder framework of relationship marketing proposed by Malhotra and Agarwal (2002).

A GENERALIZED STAKEHOLDER FRAMEWORK OF RELATIONSHIP MARKETING

Doyle (1995) offered a general framework for relationship marketing identifying a series of dyadic relationships between the firm's central core and the types of network partners, namely, internal, external, supplier, and customer. Following Doyle (1995), Peck *et al.* (1999) proposed the six-markets model (after several rounds of revision) with customer markets as the focal point and other markets, namely, supplier and alliance markets, internal markets, referral markets, influence markets, and recruitment markets, all revolving around the customer markets.

In general, there are some obvious similarities across these frameworks both in terms of content and structure. All agree that internal markets and upstream and downstream vertical relationships are essential elements of relationship marketing. However, there are some structural differences across the frameworks in terms of comprehensiveness and categorization. For example, Kotler (1992), Morgan and Hunt (1994), and Doyle (1995) consider competitors as part of "external macro-environmental" partnerships, while Parvatiyar and Sheth (1994) and Peck *et al.* (1999) categorize it under "competitor" and "supplier and alliance" markets, respectively. A look at the various frameworks reveal that the Peck *et al.*'s six-markets relationship framework is perhaps the most comprehensive in terms of representativeness and content validity. A closer scrutiny of the Peck et al. framework is therefore warranted.

The Peck *et al.*'s (1999) six-markets framework rightly renders the customer markets domain the central importance it deserves and breaks it down to buyers, intermediaries, and end consumers. It is imperative that for effective relationship marketing to emerge, a customer-centric approach needs to be adopted

(Sheth *et al.*, 2000). The supplier and alliance markets characterize the upstream source of raw materials and services to the firm. Peck *et al.* merge the supplier and competitor markets together as one market characterized by strategic alliances. Alliance partners supply knowledge-based competencies rather than products. The referral markets consist of customer and noncustomer sources through professional services and positive word-of-mouth referrals by customers and agencies. The influence markets consist of the most diverse range of constituent groups such as shareholders, financial analysts, government, media, and consumer groups. The recruitment markets represent all potential employees who possess necessary skills to match the profile the firm wishes to portray to its customers. It also refers to third parties such as executive search consultants, commercial recruitment agencies, and management selection consultants. Finally, the internal markets involve the idea that every employee within an organization is both a supplier and a customer and that there is a positive correlation between employee satisfaction and customer satisfaction. Subsequently, the Peck *et al.*'s (1999) model has been updated with minor amendments over time by one of the original authors, Adrian Payne (Christopher *et al.*, 2002; Payne *et al.*, 2005; Payne and Frow, 2013). The revised version (Payne *et al.*, 2005) is shown in Figure 3.3.

Malhotra and Agarwal (2002) concur with the Peck *et al.*'s framework that relationship marketing involves far more constituent groups than just customers and suppliers. A broader set of stakeholders that are corporate constituencies can affect and be affected by a company's marketing program. To our knowledge, the original Peck *et al.*'s (1999) framework (with subsequent minor revisions) is by far the most comprehensive in terms of stakeholder representation. While the content of the framework is robust, Malhotra and Agarwal (2002) proposed a reconfiguration of the structure of the framework

Figure 3.3: The Six-Markets' Framework of Relationship Marketing

Adapted from Adrian Payne, David Ballantyne, and Martin Christopher (2005), A Stakeholder Approach to Relationship Marketing Strategy: The Development and Use of the 'Six Markets' Model, *European Journal of Marketing* 39(7/8): 855–871.

based on the following rationale. *First*, they proposed to breakdown the customer markets into two separate markets – distributors and ultimate users. Business-to-business (B2B) marketing is significantly different from business-to-consumer (B2C) marketing. Kotler (1992) views the two markets as totally different and advocates different marketing approaches with trade marketing for the intermediary market and the traditional consumer marketing for the end user market. *Second*, they proposed that the competitor markets deserve a prominent position in the framework rather than being tucked away inside the "Influence" markets with other macro-environmental factors. Competitor orientation is a key cornerstone of market orientation along with customer orientation and interfunctional coordination (Day and Wensley, 1988; Narver and Slater, 1999; Porter, 1980). Reconfiguring the competitor domain to a higher and independent status would help realign the customer–competitor balance so critical in market orientation. *Third*, they combined the internal markets and the recruitment markets, because both these markets deal with existing and potential employees of the firm, respectively. The recruitment market is an important constituent market in organizations characterized by skills and experiences pivotal to customer value. However, overstating its significance in the framework at the expense of other markets may not be legitimate. While, recruitment market is vital for the maintenance of organizational skills, it logically fits in at the interface of marketing and human resource management functions, which are constituents of the internal markets. *Fourth*, while they upheld the significance of the impact referrals can have, they argued that this particular market is better categorized as sub-sets of other markets. Accordingly, they proposed to eliminate the special market status given to "referral" markets, because customer referrals and staff referrals are subsumed under customer markets and internal markets, respectively. In fact, Peck *et al.* (1999) by their own admission state that referrals are in fact benefits arising from successful managed relationships with the constituent parties.

Fifth, Malhotra and Agarwal (2002) further extended the idea of strategic alliances to all constituent markets in the framework rather than just the supplier markets. Today's marketplace is rife with strategic alliances in most markets with a potential in all markets (Kandemir *et al.*, 2006; Varadarajan and Cunningham, 1995). The goals of strategic alliances are to leverage critical capabilities, increase the flow of innovation, and improve the flexibility in responding to market and technological changes.

The Malhotra and Agarwal's (2002) relationship framework identifies six stakeholder groupings or market domains, although not all stakeholders are given equal status by the focal firm. The revised six-markets model includes customer markets (channel intermediaries); customer markets (end users); supplier markets; competitor markets; external influence markets; and internal markets. Figure 3.4

Figure 3.4: Stakeholder Framework of Relationship Marketing — Malhotra and Agarwal (2002)

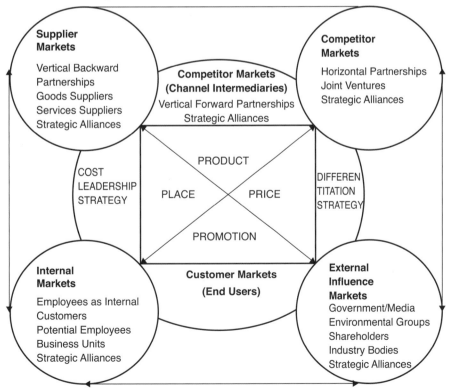

Adapted from Naresh K. Malhotra and James Agarwal (2002), A Stakeholder Perspective on Relationship Marketing: Framework and Propositions, *Journal of Relationship Marketing* 1(2): 3–37.

depicts the proposed revised framework of Malhotra and Agarwal (2002). Depending on several contextual and contingency factors, some stakeholders will be more prominent and given a higher priority by default; however, the importance weights assigned to each market domain will shift in a dynamic fashion taking into consideration key contextual/contingency factors. At the same time, the Malhotra and Agarwal's (2002) framework recognizes the multiple roles a stakeholder may play in more than one market domain. This framework adopts a broadened approach to relationship marketing programs (i.e., functional–structural–strategic levels) and expands on the growing role of strategic alliances in interfirm cooperation. We next briefly discuss each of these constituent groups in the stakeholder relationship framework.

Relationship with Customer Markets–Channel Intermediaries

The globalization of competition has increased the difficulty of getting access to end customers. This has enhanced the position of distributors who have rapidly organized themselves into powerful chains. To reach global customers, marketers are increasingly trying to build distributor partnerships where access and information about end customers are shared (Doz and Hamel, 1998; Gummesson, 1999). However, the focus of channel relationship management is shifting away from the vertical marketing system, characterized by authoritative control and centralized planning and decision-making, toward channel relationship system, characterized by contractual and normative control (Bolton *et al.*, 2003; Weitz and Jap, 1995). Norms governing channel relationships are mutually learned and accepted and become part of channel interorganizational culture over time (Deshpande and Webster, 1992). Relationships work effectively when there exist high levels of manufacturer-intermediary dependence (Frazier and Antia, 1995).

The focus on channel relationship marketing has largely been contributed by a growing disenchantment with vertical integration, the growth in power of intermediary channel firms, and the recognition of competitive advantage in relationship strategies (Gilliland and Bello, 2002; Weitz and Jap, 1995). Firms are exploring opportunities for relational channel networks and outsourcing rather than vertical integration with increasingly powerful channel members as a commitment to stick to their knitting. Ehret (2004) contributed an important discussion extending buyer's value in the relationship to value networks. Value network relationship, different from the buyer–supplier dyad, focuses on an integrated network of related companies, which jointly work on the development of new products, the integration of information infrastructures, and the coordination of the flow of goods and services. Windahl and Lakemond (2006) showed that relationships in the value network are a potential factor determining the success or failure of the development of integrated solutions. Moreover, the network configuration, the structure of the strategic network of a focal actor with regard to its patterns and intensity of relationships with other actors, as well as the focal actor's positioning and (strategic) configuring activities connect to value constellations in terms of value recipients and value outcomes (Corsaro *et al.*, 2012). The authors further revealed two elements that are relevant to the value configuration and subsequent outcomes: how the actor perceives the different network structures in which he/she is embedded and the extent to which the actor's resources combine effectively with those of other actors and thus promote the establishment of new relationships. In short, channel activities offer substantial value-added potential and channel relationship management can offer tremendous cost savings and competitive advantage (see Figure 3.5). More discussion on strategic alliances and relationship dynamics in channel relationships is provided later in this chapter.

Figure 3.5: Recognition of competitive advantage in relationship strategies has led to a focus on channel relationship marketing.

Relationship with Customer Markets– End Users

Sheth and Parvatiyar (1995a, 2000) proposed that relationship marketing has the potential to improve marketing productivity by making it more effective and efficient. Relationship marketing practices enhance efficiency through customer retention, efficient customer response, and resource sharing between marketing partners. Similarly, relationship marketing programs enhance effectiveness as customers are involved in the early stages of the marketing program development facilitating future marketing efforts. Technological advances, especially the exponential growth in digital and social media platforms, (Kannan and Li, 2017; Yadav *et al.*, 2013) have greatly facilitated long-term engagement with customers in multiple ways. Such developments mean that marketing databases have proliferated, which are being mined using sophisticated data analytic models. Today, the foundational premises and axioms of relationship marketing with end customers (i.e., B2C relationships) intersect with service-dominant (S-D) logic, relational assets, customer experience, and valuing customers as assets following the customer lifetime value (CLV) concept (Lemon and Verhoef, 2016; Vargo and Lusch, 2004; Kumar *et al.*, 2010; Van Doorn *et al.*, 2010). These concepts are elaborated in greater detail in the remaining chapters of this book, wherein our primary emphasis is on B2C relationships.

Relationship with Supplier Markets

Increased global competitiveness, industry restructuring, and rapid growth in technology have significantly influenced the procurement paradigms of firms. Supplier relationships have shifted more to a relational and global outsourcing process (Möller and Halinen, 1999; Sheth and Sharma, 1997). Supplier relationship increases cost efficiency by reducing uncertainty and controlling cost and enhances organizational effectiveness through quality and service. The future trend is to reduce the number of suppliers and enter into strategic relationships with a few who have differentiated their core competencies (Gadde and Snehota, 2000). The basis for competitive advantage comes through focusing upon that part of the value chain wherein the firm has either a distinctive cost advantage or a value advantage (Anderson, 1995; Porter, 1985). The argument has been made that firms that do not have either a cost or a value advantage in specific parts of the value chain should outsource those activities to firms that do have such an advantage. Consequently, not only are buyers outsourcing but also developing single-source suppliers because of the pressure to increase quality, reduce inventory, and develop just-in-time (JIT) systems.

Future supplier relationships would devolve around cross-functional supply teams that understand global suppliers (with its attendant cross-cultural connotations) as partners and customers to cocreate value (Sheth and Sharma, 1997). Value (co)creation has recently been trending in both academia and the business world, which emphasizes the mutual benefiting nature in the partner relationships. Supplier's capability-based value creation and the buyer's behaviors to facilitate such value creation have been established and documented (e.g., Joshi, 2009; O'Cass and Ngo, 2012). Firms and suppliers can comanage the inventories required taking into account promotional activity, competitive activities, local conditions, and so on. Firms working closely with strategic supplier(s) can benefit through supplier-led innovation in both processes and products. For example, in the auto industry, upstream suppliers have devised much of the improved technology in the finished product. Many firms have embarked upon "supplier development" programs by focusing on significant improvements in their performance with the strategic intent of improving its own product quality, lowering inventories, and providing greater operational efficiency. Similarly, continually sharing and linking information with suppliers result in cost savings, which then get passed to downstream activities (Flynn *et al.*, 2010; Stock *et al.*, 2010).

Relationship with Competitor Markets

Competitors can be involved in both cooperative and competitive relationships with each other simultaneously. Interfirm collaboration occurs when two or more firms work jointly toward a common goal (Rindfleisch and Moorman, 2001). Cooperative relationship among competitors is analyzed to be advantageous in that firm resources and capabilities can be combined and used against other (third-party) competitors (Perks and Easton, 2000). Knowledge sharing between competitors in an alliance highlights the potential to leverage the idiosyncratic resources, invisible assets and skills of each firm, and the resultant expected benefits or payoffs. Firms are increasingly opening their new product development processes to collaborate with other firms during the innovation process, and working with competing firms has become a common form of external collaboration (Laursen and Salter, 2006; Turk and Ybarra, 2011). At the same time, behavioral and environmental uncertainty in interfirm relationships especially opportunistic behavior poses a significant risk. For instance, although the primary objective may be to gain access to the partner's knowledge, loss of tacit knowledge to a competitor may dilute a firm's competitive advantage when the partner acquires or internalizes this knowledge (e.g., Mohr and Sengupta, 2002). However, interestingly, where competitive pressures are high with regard to imitation of new products (lead-time), alliance relationships offer enhanced protection against future competitors (Klien and Zif, 1994). Competitor alliance relationships offer the best alternative to circumvent global market entry barriers and to remain competitive through innovation in markets where technological and competitive uncertainty is high (Malhotra *et al.*, 2003; Sengupta and Perry, 1997).

Several configurations of relationships can be formalized with competitors within an industry. Strategic alliances between strong market leaders within a given industry are quite popular in the global market. Partnering with firms in host countries can circumvent legal, political, and other regulatory barriers to entry (Malhotra *et al.*, 2003; Varadarajan and Cunningham, 1995). In certain situations, there may be an alliance between a market leader and a market follower within the same industry. Small firms with specialized competitive strengths in specialized technology are able to enter into strategic alliances with market leaders. The small firm gains financial support, while the large firm gets access to specialized technology. Furthermore, a strategic alliance of a domestic market leader with a market follower in a foreign market shields the domestic market against attack from the market leader in the foreign market. More discussion on strategic alliances is provided later in this chapter.

Relationship with External Influence Markets

This market has the broadest and most diverse range of constituent groups. Firms compete for "space" in an "economic jungle," and that to survive in this jungle, a company must win the loyalty of the constituent groups (Campbell, 1997). Hence, there is a need for firms to rigorously use marketing techniques such as segmentation, positioning, and the development of marketing strategies to achieve strategic marketing objectives. Some of these stakeholder groups include government and the regulatory system, media, nonprofit organizations, environmental groups, and financial and investor groups.

While the role of the government in the United States is largely one of facilitating and regulating free enterprise, governments in other countries play a proactive role with corporate firms. For example, the Japanese Ministry of International Trade and Industry (MITI), later reorganized as Ministry of Economy, Trade, and Industry (METI) in 2002, established strategic alliances with companies, providing planning and technical assistance and sponsoring research. Japan has successfully used this method of creating a national competitive advantage (Porter, 1990). Of course, the role of government as a strategic stakeholder depends on the industry type. For instance, firms selling infrastructure services such as telecommunications or utilities will place governments and regulatory bodies on a high strategic priority. Similarly, the media is an

important interface between the firm and the market in today's digital economy. Firms are increasingly leveraging their offerings and value by aligning with Internet companies and broadcast media. The role of media is also context-based and becomes salient, for instance, during times of crisis management (Payne and Frow, 2013). For example, a company faced with fraud (Volkswagen in 2016) or environmental disaster (BP in 2010) will receive heightened media attention and coverage during such times relative to normal times.

Cause-Related Marketing is another example of the alignment of corporate philanthropy and enlightened business interest. It is the marketing program that strives to improve corporate performance and help worthy causes (e.g., sport, entertainment event, nonprofit organization, and social cause) by linking fund raising for the benefit of a cause to the purchase of the firm's products or services (Varadarajan and Menon, 1988). Cause-Related Marketing can, therefore, be used as a strategic marketing tool by including top management's involvement in key decisions about the program, a long-term commitment to and support of the program. These programs are designed to achieve objectives such as improving corporate reputation, brand differentiation, attracting the interest of targeted consumers, stimulating brand preference and loyalty, attracting loyal employees, and, ultimately, increasing profits and stock prices (Bloom *et al.*, 2006). At the micro-foundational level, cause-related marketing works effectively when the fit between the consumer and the cause-attributes (i.e., cause type, cause scope, and cause acuteness) is high; this congruence then impacts corporate image mediated by consumer-cause identification (Vanhamme *et al.*, 2012). Environmental influence markets represent a key group for many such as petrochemicals, mining, and manufacturing. As this constituent group becomes more vocal, organizations develop relational strategies for dealing with these groups. The Body Shop is a good example of an organization that has managed its relationship with environmentalists by forming alliances with Green peace.

The principles and approaches of relationship marketing are now being applied in the financial and investor influence market also (Payne and Frow, 2013). Financial and investor influence markets are especially crucial for organizations listed in the stock market. Tuominen (1990) has focused on several key markets including investors, stockbrokers, financial advisers, and analysts. A key issue within the investor market is the loyalty of investors. Reichheld (1990) found that without the support of loyal investors, it is very difficult for a firm to pursue long-term value-creating strategies. The challenge is to convert short-term investors into long-term investors by creating relational bonds (Malhotra and Agarwal, 2002). Research findings from customer relationship marketing (e.g., satisfaction, trust, commitment, identification) and interpersonal and interfirm relationship marketing models (Palmatier, 2008) can be effectively cross-fertilized in the realm of investor–firm relationship.

Relationship with Internal Markets

Internal Marketing is creating, developing, and maintaining an internal service culture and orientation, which in turn assists and supports the organization in the achievement of its goals (Peck *et al.*, 1999; Payne *et al.*, 2005). The development and maintenance of a customer-oriented culture in the organization is a critical determinant of long-term success in relationship marketing. Piercy and Morgan (1991) advocate the development of a marketing program aimed at the internal market that parallels the external marketplace of customers and competitors with a view to raising customer consciousness and service orientation. The internal service culture has a direct bearing on how service-oriented and customer-oriented employees will be.

Research finds support for linkages between employee satisfaction and retention and customer satisfaction and retention (Heskett *et al.*, 1994; Schlesinger and Heskett, 1991; Schneider *et al.*, 1980). The service-profit-chain (SPC) framework (Heskett *et al.*, 1994) provides an understanding of how a firm's operational investments into service quality translate into customer perceptions and behaviors and how these translate into firm profit. The idea is that satisfied employees are more productive and provide better service quality and value than less-satisfied employees, thus leading to higher customer satisfaction. Very recently, Hogreve *et al.* (2017) revisited the SPC model and tested the extended SPC model by enlarging and emphasizing the additional roles and benefits of internal service culture. (More discussion on employee–customer interface is provided in Chapter 5). In the same vein, high customer retention can also lead to higher employee satisfaction and retention as employees find their jobs easier dealing with satisfied customers rather than dissatisfied customers (Malhotra and Agarwal, 2002). Thus a reciprocal relationship between employee satisfaction and retention and customer satisfaction and retention is plausible.

There is a need to set up structures and processes across functional departments within an organization (Payne and Frow, 2013) to enable employees to transmit knowledge and generate exchange. Practices of a learning organization — needs to have a market-oriented culture and climate (structure and processes) — can be applied to internal markets (Kohli and Jaworski, 1999; Slater and Narver, 1995). This internal exchange between groups and individuals must operate effectively along the entire value chain of the organization. Srivastava *et al.* (1999) identify customer relationship management process (along with new product development and supply chain management processes) as an important organization-wide cross-functional process that creates value. Palmatier (2008) makes the point that an organization-wide strategy must consider the relative importance of organizational design such as strategy, leadership, culture, structure, and control on its ability to effectively execute relationship marketing, including internal relationship marketing. Market-facing organizations drawing from multidisciplinary teams (Piercy, 2010) are, therefore, more conducive to internal markets than the traditional hierarchical, functional organizations. There is consensus that internal marketing should not be the sole domain of marketing. Rather, an organization-wide culture of customer consciousness with boundary spanning processes and culture should be the guiding force toward internal marketing.

BROADENING RELATIONSHIP MARKETING PROGRAMS: FUNCTIONAL–STRUCTURAL–STRATEGIC LEVELS

Marketers have traditionally used relationship marketing activities to build relational assets. Three decades ago, Berry and Parasuraman (1991) and Berry (1995) distinguished among different levels of relationship marketing. Level 1 of relationship marketing relies primarily on financial bond executed through pricing incentives such as rebates, discounts, credits, etc., to secure customer loyalty. The potential for sustained competitive advantage is, however, low, because price is the most easily imitated element of the marketing mix. Level 2 of relationship marketing relies primarily on social bond, which involves personalization and customization of relationship, augmenting the core product/service, and providing continuity of service. A social environment that nurtures communication, honesty, and fair play makes a successful contribution. The power of communication is a prerequisite for trust. Level 3 of relationship marketing relies primarily on structural solutions to important customer problems that are difficult or expensive for customers to provide and

that are not readily available elsewhere. While helpful, these three levels did not fully capture RM programs at the organization-wide strategic level. Malhotra and Agarwal (2002) addressed some of the limitations and proposed a broadening of RM programs progressing from Level 1 (Functional Level) to Level 2 (Structural Level) and to Level 3 (Strategic Level). We discuss each of these three levels of RM programs next.

Functional Level (Level 1)

Malhotra and Agarwal (2002) proposed a revised framework in which they categorized Level 1 of relationship, i.e., *functional level*, to include economic content of the relationship, which includes economic benefits and costs of participating in the relationship. This level is primarily managed by marketing mix variables especially product, price, and place (channel) in the B2B context. Transaction cost theory helps the firm understand the switching cost (SC), dependence of the firm, and the attractiveness of alternatives available. High transaction cost creates dependence, which results in increased customer retention. For instance, cocreation and S-D logic are at the heart of product strategy wherein sellers and buyers cocreate value. Relationship marketing focuses beyond the core product or service to the augmented product or service. From S-D logic, sellers not only transfer the value inherent in their offering, i.e., product-centered value, but also promote the "value-in-use" for customers, i.e., use-centered value. According to DeLeon and Chatterjee (2017), this can come by way of expanding into service scope and augmenting the core product, investing in instrumental and interpersonal service, and most importantly by understanding and investing in customers' value mindset (more details in later section of this chapter). Similarly, as far as pricing strategy, firms that have implemented relationship marketing can reduce their overall marketing costs by investing up front in technology, which reduces variable or transaction costs in the future (Sheth *et al.*, 2000). This allows firms to adopt value-based pricing centered on price differentiation strategy in a way that corresponds to customer lifetime value (CLV). The control issue in channel relationship marketing is now characterized by normative and contractual control mechanisms rather than authoritative control. Normative control mechanisms are accepted and adhered to by both parties and are based on trust unlike the authoritative control mechanism where unilateral power is used to dictate the other party. Similarly, contractual control mechanisms have been introduced into relational networks wherein terms and conditions are defined either unilaterally or bilaterally via negotiations. As the relationship develops, psychological contracts replace formal legal contracts and personal relationships become more important than role relationships (Weitz and Jap, 1995). Malhotra and Agarwal's proposed Level-1 relationship consolidates Berry's (1995) financial and social bonding. The planning and implementation of these relational activities primarily come under the purview of the marketing function. While important, it is, however, limited in its impact, because the degree of customization and potential for competitive advantage is low to medium (Berry and Parasuraman, 1991).

Structural Level (Level 2)

In B2B context, as firms adapt in setting relationship boundaries, it requires structural bonds and commitment in creating and maintaining value (Wilson, 1995). Level 2 of relationship, i.e., *structural level*, is focused more on the business unit level connecting the processes and functions across the business unit. The focus at this level is on information system integration and operational efficiency of the particular business unit. It relies on providing structural solutions to important customer problems by providing value-added benefits such as electronic order-processing interface. Parties engage in ongoing relationships to secure valuable resources that they would not be able to acquire more efficiently elsewhere

(Morgan *et al.*, 2000). Malhotra and Agarwal's (2002) Level-2 relationship corresponds with Level 3 in Berry and Parasuraman's (1991) framework. While stronger than Level-1 relationship, structural relationship can lose its competitive advantage quickly in a dynamic market environment. This is because it focuses on operational processes and, therefore, can soon be imitated by competitors. Based on institutional theory (DiMaggio and Powell, 1983) firms have a tendency to model themselves after competitors within industries when faced with coercive, mimetic, or normative pressure, which bestows them legitimacy (Kostova and Zaheer, 1999). Isomorphism occurs when firms are legally required by government (coercive) or voluntarily imitate to converge to maintain competitive parity not just because of operational/cost benefits (mimetic) but also because of normative and cultural pressures (normative) imposed by informal institutions to adopt best practice standards and models (Lieberman and Asaba, 2006; North, 2005).

For customer retention programs to sustain competitive advantage, it must possess value, be rare, be imperfectly imitable, and not easily be substitutable (Barney, 1991). Hennig-Thurau and Hansen (2000) make a strong point that relationship marketing cannot be limited to tactical and operational activities but demands a wider reconsideration of the organization's values and norms by including the strategic and organizational dimensions. Therefore, while stronger than Level-1 relationship, it is limited in its impact, because the degree of customization and potential for competitive advantage is medium to high (Berry and Parasuraman, 1991). Palmatier (2008) argues that an organization-wide RM strategy should consider the relative importance of organizational design (e.g., strategy, leadership, culture, structure, and control) on its ability to execute relationship marketing effectively. Strategy is all-pervasive in that it drives other elements in the organization (e.g., strategy precedes structure) and therefore is critical in building and maintaining

Level-2 relationship. For instance, Walmart follows the cost leadership strategy (everyday low-price supplier), whereas Nordstrom follows the differentiation strategy (premium niche supplier). Accordingly differences in strategies permeate throughout the firm-level processes by influencing leadership (centralized versus distributive), structure (focus on store vs. boundary-spanner), and control (fixed versus commission-based compensation). Besides firm strategy, organizational structure is critical to ensuring Level-2 relationship effectiveness. Decisions about organizational structure and processes affect service quality, service failure resolution, effectiveness of boundary-spanners, all of which affect customer–seller relationships (Palmatier, 2008).

Strategic Level (Level 3)

Level 3 of relationship, i.e., *strategic level* in Malhotra and Agarwal's (2002) framework, is added to better reflect current forms of interfirm relationship networks (Payne *et al.*, 2005; Payne and Frow, 2013). A strategic bond is created where value-added benefits are provided by both relational partners rather than by one partner at the firm level. In other words, partners enter into a strategic alliance by pooling skills and resources to achieve one or more goals linked to the strategic objectives of the cooperative firms (Rindfleisch and Moorman, 2001). The strategic linkage binds the two firms far beyond providing structural solutions (which are often geared toward tactical and operational efficiencies) to important strategic problems and issues (Hennig-Thurau and Hansen, 2000). The resource advantage theory of competition (Hunt, 1999; Hunt and Morgan, 1996) is grounded on the premise that (a) firm resources are heterogeneous and imperfectly mobile and (2) intra-industry demand is substantially heterogeneous thereby resulting in diversity in sizes, scopes, and levels of profitability of firms. Because firm resources are heterogeneous and relatively immobile, some firms will have a comparative advantage, which

then results in competitive advantage and superior financial performance. Unlike operational benefits, strategic bonds are difficult to imitate by competition, and therefore, sustainable. This level of relationship includes interfirm cooperation such as technology licensing, joint R&D, product and technology co-development, manufacturing–marketing alliance, etc. (Varadarajan and Cunningham, 1995). Firms that particularly engage in strategic alliances can exchange, share, or co-develop products, technologies, or services.

Prior research, however, cautions that the processes involved in interfirm cooperation are not straight-forward (Bruyaka *et al.*, 2018). To be successful in cooperation, business executives need to spend significant amounts of effort and time to fully understand their partners' motivations, value systems, and goals. But more importantly, executives need to initiate value-creating relationships by developing mutual trust and respect over time. They need to embed their firms within the ongoing relationships, realize agreed-upon goals, and coevolve as synergistic partners (Koza and Lewin, 1998). These are easier said than done. Strategic partners typically possess different ways of approaching the whole cooperation-development process, with differing expectations of monitoring and control, performance measurement criteria, and dissimilar propensities of terminating the ongoing contracts (Pangarkar and Klein, 2001; Peng *et al.*, 2018). Initiating, governing, and terminating cooperative relationships become particularly complicated when partner firms originate from different institutional, cultural, or industry backgrounds and/or possess little or no previous international alliance experience or learning. That said, there is growing recognition of the mutual benefits of linking each other's value chain, in sharing resources, knowledge bases, and capabilities to achieve firm's strategic objectives. This level of relationship, therefore, has a high to very high potential for customization and competitive advantage. Palmatier (2008) agrees there is a need to further broaden and isolate the relative efficacy of antecedents across different relational constructs in the B2B context. Because of the important role of strategic alliances in B2B relationships, we devote the next section solely to it.

STRATEGIC ALLIANCES

Firms within an industry can engage in both cooperative and competitive relationships with each other simultaneously. They can achieve competitive advantage and overcome market entry barriers by combining their resources and capabilities and using them against other competitors (Malhotra and Agarwal, 2002). Cooperative relationships among competitors can be built for various purposes in addition to the typical collusion to control and subvert competition. For example, a firm can cooperate with competitors to develop product and technology standards (Ritter *et al.*, 2004). Competitor relationships are often formalized through strategic alliances, which can be either equity-based distinct corporate entity (i.e., joint ventures) or non-equity-based interorganizational entity (such as joint technology or product development center) where alliance partners commit to sharing their skills and resources. Competitor relationships are particularly important in markets where technological and competitive uncertainty is high. This kind of horizontal relationships between competitors should have well-defined boundaries in order to contain the competitive arena (Malhotra and Agarwal, 2002).

Technology-oriented alliances are very popular in B2B markets. Researchers classify these networks into two groups: R&D networks and standardization networks (Malhotra *et al.*, 2016). R&D networks are developed between companies aiming to share risks, costs, and/or competences in the development of new technologies, premarket competition, and project-like cooperation that can involve both horizontal and diagonal partners. Examples of R&D networks include Microsoft Web TV and Sematech consortium in the semiconductor research and business (Möller and Rajala, 2007). On the other hand, standardization networks are developed between horizontal and diagonal partners and often among co-opting companies aiming to set dominant technology in a product/service field and in market development. Examples of standardization networks include WAP Forum and Symbian coalition both in the mobile telephony operating systems (Möller and Rajala, 2007).

Types of Strategic Alliances

There are several types of relationships that competing firms can develop (Malhotra and Agarwal, 2002; Malhotra *et al.*, 2016):

1. A strategic alliance among strong market leaders within a given industry

2. A strategic alliance between a market leader and a market follower within the same industry

3. A strategic alliance between market leaders and small firms with specialized competitive strengths in specialized technology

4. A strategic alliance between a domestic market leader and a market follower in a foreign market

5. Partnering with firms in host countries

Although strategic alliances among strong market leaders are quite popular in the global markets, there may be an alliance between a market leader and a market follower in some situations. In addition, small firms that have competitive strengths in specialized technology are able to enter into strategic alliances with market leaders. In this kind of alliance, the small firm gets financial resources, while the large firm gets access to specialized technology. A domestic market leader can compete successfully with the market leader in a foreign market by developing a strategic alliance with a market follower in the foreign market (Malhotra and Agarwal, 2002). A firm can overcome legal, political, and other regulatory entry barriers in foreign markets by forming strategic alliances with firms in host countries (Malhotra *et al.*, 2003; Malhotra and Agarwal, 2002). This strategy is particularly important for firms that suffer from unfavorable country-of-origin image. A firm originating from a developing country with unfavorable image can overcome entry barriers in foreign markets, have strong bargaining power with channel members, and be less vulnerable to fierce global competition by forming strategic alliances with firms from countries that have favorable image.

While the existing scholarship on strategic alliances provides valuable insights, there appears to be a significant need to rethink the phenomenon in light of the changing business landscape. Today, cooperating firms may have origins in different institutional environments (i.e., developed, developing, emerging markets) that may impact how they differently plan for and enact cooperation. For instance, steady liberalization in trade and foreign direct investment in emerging economies (e.g., China, India) versus abrupt restrictive trade practices and nationalist sentiments in some developed economies (e.g., Brexit, the USA) is posing new challenges in interfirm cooperation. This is especially true when firms from varying environments desire to exploit their country-of-origin effects in order to contribute to and gain from interfirm cooperation. Research also suggests that ethnocentric customers may have a bias against foreign products and in favor of domestic ones, which has been called "domestic country bias" (Bayraktar, 2013). Consumer ethnocentrism describes the tendency of consumers to reject products from foreign countries and favor the domestic ones because of the beliefs held by consumers about the

appropriateness and morality of purchasing foreign-made products (Balabanis and Diamantopoulos, 2004; Sharma, 2011). Therefore, it can be a successful strategy to form a strategic alliance with a firm in the host country if the level of ethnocentrism or domestic country bias is high in that country.

Alliance Partnership Capabilities

The formation of alliances can be viewed as a strategic option that firms can use to pool and deploy resources of partner firms to achieve competitive advantage in the marketplace (Malhotra *et al.*, 2016). Firms need to possess unique portfolios of dynamic capabilities to manage alliance relationships effectively. Alliance management capability is a distinct dynamic capability (Eisenhardt and Martin, 2000; Schilke and Goerzen, 2010) with a "capacity to purposefully create, extend, or modify the firm's resource base, augmented to include the resources of its alliance partners" (Helfat *et al.*, 2007, p. 66). A firm's skills in configuring and deploying alliance-driven capabilities of partner firms incorporate three capabilities: (1) alliance scanning, (2) alliance coordination, and (3) alliance learning. When a firm possesses higher degrees of each of these capabilities, it is likely to successfully configure and deploy alliance-driven capabilities of partner firms, and thus outperform its rivals in many aspects of alliance management and achieve superior market performance (Kandemir *et al.*, 2006).

Alliance scanning refers to the extent to which a firm proactively monitors for and discovers partnering opportunities (Kandemir *et al.*, 2006, p. 327). When firms lose their competitive positional advantage because of the obsolescence of their existing resources and capabilities, they can reposition themselves in the marketplace and re-attain their previous advantages or develop new advantages by effective and proactive alliance scanning. To sustain the competitive advantage over time, firms must possess dynamic capabilities — the ability to build, integrate, and reconfigure available assets and capabilities to address rapidly changing environments — built on firms' capacities in sensing and seizing new opportunities to mitigate path dependence, and in managing threats through resource reconfiguration (Augier and Teece, 2009; Teece, 2007; Teece *et al.*, 1997). Firms that possess superior capabilities for alliance scanning can accomplish first-mover advantages in bringing the best candidates into relationships. Effective and proactive alliance scanning can help firms determine partners with complementary resources and strategic capabilities much more competently.

Alliance coordination refers to "the extent to which a firm systematically integrates strategies, synchronizes activities, and regularly disseminates knowledge across its alliances" (Kandemir *et al.*, 2006, p. 327). Interdependent resources are dispersed over various individuals in partner firms, which need to be harmonized. Further, alliance partners do not have all of the necessary information to align their own actions with the activities of the counterpart (Goerzen and Beamish, 2005). It helps the firm enhance its ability to share knowledge, opportunities, and activities with its partners in a channel, which will enable the firm exploit its competitive advantage more effectively. Sharing knowledge, opportunities, and activities yields mutual understanding of the alliance strategy and coordinates the firm's actions with the actions of its alliances, which in turn leads to effective planning and implementation. Firms are likely to achieve more integrated strategies, more harmonized activities, and more effective distribution of knowledge across their alliances by enhancing their coordination capabilities. This is more pronounced from a portfolio perspective, which requires comprehensive governance of a business's entire alliance portfolio (Goerzen, 2007).

Alliance learning refers to "the extent to which a firm acquires, interprets, and leverages alliance management know-how throughout its organizational network" (Kandemir *et al.*, 2006, p. 327). It is necessary because of the complexity of alliance management. Effective alliance learning requires learning capabilities that incorporate systematic information processing and transmission of learning effects across the firm's alliances (Goerzen and Beamish, 2005). It also requires the firm's internalization of its direct experiences and understandings with alliances and the appropriation of this learning across its partners. Absorptive capacity is an organization-wide capability facilitating organizational learning and built on cross-functional interfaces, formalized systems, and socialization mechanisms (Jansen *et al.*, 2005; Slater and Narver, 1995). It is not just restricted to outward-looking learning but also entails routines for inward-looking learning (Lewin *et al.*, 2011). Such a capability can result in a shared understanding of alliance experience throughout an organization that can be leveraged in response to unforeseen contingencies in alliance interactions (Kandemir *et al.*, 2006).

Knowledge Acquisition through Strategic Alliances

Strategic alliances yield distinctive learning opportunities for the partners by gathering firms with different capabilities and knowledge bases (Malhotra *et al.*, 2016). A firm's access to the partner's capabilities would probably be restricted without the formation of strategic alliances, which would limit its opportunities for alliance learning. The formation of an alliance creates sort of a laboratory for learning and an opportunity for partners to cooperate in a knowledge-sharing environment that can yield a win–win outcome for both parties. A firm that forms a strategic alliance acknowledges that the other party has useful knowledge. Otherwise, there would be no reason to form an alliance. Knowledge from an alliance that can enhance the firm's own strategy and operations is of particular importance. This knowledge is called alliance knowledge and has significance to the firm outside the specific terms of the alliance agreement. Without forming an alliance, the firm will be bereft of this valuable knowledge and of the positive outcomes that the knowledge would yield. For example, BP acquired knowledge about operating refineries and marketing lubricants from Mobil and about deep-water drilling from Shell by engaging in collaborative relationships. Although we assume that knowledge stemming from alliance formation is useful, a firm does not have to actively seek to acquire the knowledge. It depends on the firm's decision whether to devote its resources and efforts to alliance knowledge acquisition. While partners in some alliances aggressively seek to acquire alliance knowledge, partners in others choose to take a more passive approach to knowledge acquisition (Inkpen, 1998).

Learning from Cross-Sector Alliances

Cross-sector alliances are an excellent means of managing firm-specific uncertainty, which refers to unfamiliarity with new market characteristics, and policy uncertainty, which refers to ambiguous condition stemming from diverse political institutions across nations (noted earlier). In a bid to remain competitive, firms are pushed to consider introducing new products in existing markets and expanding existing products in new markets. Furthermore, many firms are considering how to develop and sustain new business models that would allow them to remain competitive through agility and innovation (Foss and Saebi, 2018; Malhotra *et al.*, 2016). In addition, to remain competitive, many firms are engaging in alliance portfolios, i.e., executing multiple simultaneously progressing alliances with different partners (Goerzen, 2007), and engaging in coopetition, i.e., simultaneous cooperation and competition between firms (Ritala, 2012). These can provide access to new mindsets and experiences that constitute the foundation for revolutionary or evolutionary changes in firms' activities.

In addition, interfirm communication through alliances enables companies to alter their ideas and establish their identity. In cross-sector alliances, the coordination of joint activities, communication with various cultures, and the negotiation of diversities enable the acquisition of new capabilities by alliance partners. Knowledge acquisition from cross-sector alliances can yield reinforced reflective decision-making and effective implementation of codes of conduct, which helps corporate ethical development. The complexity of public service requires engaging in cooperative and collaborative partnerships with diverse actors that have their own perspectives, resources, and comparative advantages. However, successful management of these cross-sector alliances requires a firm to improve its ability to leverage extant capabilities acquired from within-sector alliance and skills that consider the cultural and structural differences between cross-sector alliance partners (Arya and Salk, 2006).

Cross-sector alliances could also be likened to biological symbiotic relationships as they represent mutual dependence between unlike elements. As symbiotic species make different demands on the environment, they might supplement one another's efforts. In a sense, cross-sector alliances promote coexistence among partners with teaching intentions such as NGOs and intergovernmental agencies (the United Nations) and partners motivated by learning intentions such as private sector participants (both in developed and developing countries). This platform fosters corporate respect for the nonprofit partner's skills, helps the corporate partner establish a repository of goodwill with nonprofits, and augments partner confidence that ultimately enhances partner capability to manage these complex relationships. For example, Starbucks' prior experience with nonprofits such as the Cooperative for American Relief to Everywhere (CARE) to mount development projects in coffee-growing countries and with The Environmental Defense Fund to develop an environmentally friendly cup significantly expedited the agreement process with its next nonprofit partner, Conservation International (Arya and Salk, 2006).

Trust-Based Performance Improvement in Strategic Alliances

The extent to which partners adapt to unexpected changes in internal and external circumstances of an alliance determines whether the alliance prospers or struggles (Malhotra *et al.*, 2016). In this context, it is of vital importance for partners to predict and plan for all possible future contingencies and develop solution alternatives for possible predicaments beforehand. Therefore, partners need to develop a delicate balance between reliability and flexibility for successful adaptation to unexpected changes. Firms need flexibility to have a viable relationship in the face of changing circumstances. On the other hand, unlimited flexibility might lead partners to engage in opportunistic behaviors and provide incentive to cheat, which then reduces partners' reliance on each other. Partners encounter two types of uncertainty in their alliance partnerships: Uncertainty concerning unknown future events and uncertainty concerning

partner's responses to those future events. Emerging as a central organizing principle under the condition of double uncertainty, trust decreases complex and uncertain realities far more quickly and economically than prediction, authority, or bargaining, which in turn enhances performance of both parties (Parkhe, 1999).

By building trust in an alliance relationship, a firm tends to rely more on the capabilities of the partner and leave more space for working based on the confidence that the partner will: (a) refrain from engaging in opportunistic behaviors, (b) act in accordance with its competence, and (c) act in accordance with the contract (Silva *et al.*, 2012). This trust between the partners may act as a catalyst for engaging in right behaviors and avoiding the ones that may damage the partner's interests, which will lead to increased satisfaction with the alliance. The reciprocity of attitudes and behaviors is likely to foster this relationship and increase the possibility of enhanced performance (see Figure 3.6). Building trust between partners in an alliance relationship is likely to yield greater profits, better customer service, more adaptable organizations and satisfaction with

Figure 3.6: Strategic alliances involving trust lead to improved performance.

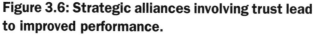

the alliance relationship, which will be reflected in their perception of performance (Silva *et al.*, 2012).

The comparison of past alliance relationships in auto industry in Japan and in the United States constitutes a good example of such trust-based performance improvement. Toyota engaged in long-standing networks of social and economic relationships characterized by higher levels of trust and lower levels of opportunism. This led Toyota and its suppliers to engage in very specialized, vulnerable exchanges confidently, which in turn enhanced efficiency while at the same time reduced the reliance on formal contracts than at General Motors. The inability to rely on social bonds in supplier relationships led GM to deal with the threat of opportunistic behaviors by reducing the level of dependence on its suppliers and increasing the number of them, by relying on detailed contractual agreements, or by engaging in vertical integration of the supply chain. Consequently, B2B relationships in Japanese auto industry were longer term and more consistent with earlier supplier involvement in product development processes than in the United States. These differences led to outstandingly different outcomes in terms of performance. The Japanese firms enjoyed a considerable advantage in various efficiency measures, such as total engineering hours spent to develop a new car and total duration required to complete and deliver a new car. Moreover, because of the higher levels of confidence in suppliers, Japanese firms usually did not inspect incoming parts, which enabled them to save on inspection labor and losses from the costs of malfunctions (Malhotra *et al.*, 2016; Parkhe, 1999).

RELATIONSHIP DYNAMICS IN BUYER–SELLER CHANNEL RELATIONSHIPS

Understanding and implementing relationship marketing effectively in the B2B context primarily requires distinguishing between the discrete transaction and relational exchange with channel members. While the former has a distinct beginning, short duration, and sharp ending by performance, the latter traces to previous agreements, has duration, and reflects an ongoing process. Before we elaborate on buyer–seller channel relationships, we first explain the social psychological mechanism underlying dependence and interdependence in channel relationships.

Dependence and Interdependence — Social Psychological Mechanism

Scheer *et al.* (2015) identify two distinct dimensions of dependence: (1) relationship value (RV) dependence and (2) switching cost (SC) dependence. RV dependence is a party's need to maintain its relationship with an exchange partner because of the irreplaceable, unique value that would be forfeited if that relationship ended. It is based on net value received from the current relationship and the extent to which that value cannot be replicated through the next best alternative. SC dependence is the need to maintain the relationship with a specific partner because of the unrealized costs that would be incurred if that relationship ended. It is based on anticipated costs of ending the current relationship and projected costs of searching, screening, evaluating, selecting, soliciting, initiating, and transitioning to the next best alternative.

Human relationships are formed by comparing costs and benefits of a relationship as well as the costs and benefits of other relationships in which they are involved (Thibaut and Kelley, 1959). In the B2B setting, a partner evaluates the results of a business relationship (i.e., RV) on the basis of two criteria. The first criterion is the comparison level (CL) based on prior experience either gained from the current business relationship or from a different one. Positive and more recent experiences increase the CL, while negative and distant experiences decrease the CL. CL is a measure of expectation and the business relationship is perceived attractive when the cost-benefit calculus is higher than the CL. The second criterion is the comparison level for alternatives (CL_{ALT}) computed as the ratio of benefits and costs in the best alternative business relationship that can be achieved. This results in attractiveness and dependency with the following cases: (a) *attractive* and *independent* relationship meaning that the current relationship (RV) is perceived as more attractive than CL and also exceeds CL_{ALT}; (b) *attractive* and *dependent* relationship meaning that RV is higher than CL making the relationship attractive but CL_{ALT} is lower than CL raising the dependency of the partner to the current relationship; and (c) *unattractive* and *dependent* meaning that RV is lower than CL making the relationship unattractive. But because the CL_{ALT} is lower than RV, switching is not an option making the current relationship dependent as well. Of course, the case of *unattractive* and *independent* relationship means that the partner will (rationally speaking) not be in the current relationship.

An investment is the acceptance of a certain disadvantage in the present in anticipation of an uncertain benefit in the future. Suppliers incur investment costs including unplanned and additional costs to secure subsequent transactions with the buyer. Both parties can benefit from substantial investments in a B2B relationship making the issue of symmetry important. It is possible that one party may have greater dependency and that the other party may choose to exploit the situation. According to TCE theory (Williamson, 1985), specific investments that can lead an economic activity to be caught up in a dependency (i.e., 'lock-in') can lead to coordination problems, especially when combined with uncertainty, bounded rationality, and opportunism. Thus, the existence of high and specific investments justifies a commitment in two ways. Resource specificity forces

the supplier to realize the planned transaction(s) so that the investment can be amortized. At the same time, specificity substantiates a dependency based on the good will of the buyer, although opportunism can dilute it. In addition to incurring loss in value of invested resources, a supplier or buyer switch can be prevented because switching cost (e.g., termination cost, search cost, setup cost) initiation and execution are costly. Thus, commitments in B2B relationships, based on Thibaut and Kelly model, are not just attributable to specific investments but also on specific contribution to the relationship, i.e., relationship success and relationship equity (Sollner, 1999).

Scheer *et al.* (2015) examined an interdependence structure resource-based view framework building on Palmatier *et al.* (2007) model of interorganizational relationship performance. In this framework, the authors use both dependence (partner dependence and own dependence) and interdependence (interdependence magnitude and asymmetry favoring the partner) to simultaneously examine their effects on two mediators, relationship quality and relationship-specific investments, and two outcomes, dyadic cooperation and performance outcomes (see Figure 3.7).

Using meta-analytic study, they find that the effects of dependence on performance flow primarily through relationship quality and cooperation; that own dependence has a direct negative effect on own performance. In contrast, interdependence magnitude and asymmetry favoring the partner does not impact relationship quality but directly impacts own performance. Further, the positive effects of own and partner dependence on dyadic cooperation are both direct and mediated by relationship quality. The study also finds (a) that interdependence magnitude promotes investment in own relationship-specific investment and in own performance and that greater asymmetry favoring the partner reduces cooperation and (b) strategic investment in own

Figure 3.7: Interdependence Structure Resource-Based View B2B Model

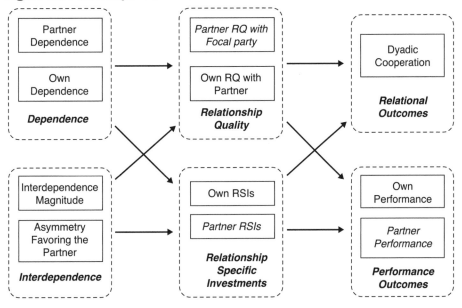

Note: Variables in boldface were examined in the structural equation model italicized variables were examined only in pairwise analyses due to insufficient number of primary studies examinig those variables and other variables in the framework
Adapted from Lisa K. Scheer, C. Fred Miao and Robert W. Palmatier (2015), Dependence and Interdependence in Marketing Relationships: Meta-Analytic Insights, *Journal of the Academy of Marketing Science* 43: 694–712.

relationship-specific investment can increase one's value to the relationship partner. Interestingly, own performance was positively impacted by asymmetry favoring the partner suggesting that, contrary to conventional belief, the powerful partner can serve the interests of both partners in the exchange.

Buyer–Seller Satisfaction in Channel Relationships

In buyer–supplier relationships, *buyer satisfaction* is considered an important antecedent of relationship continuity and relationship enhancement decisions (Selnes, 1998). Specifically, relationship continuity essentially means the buyer decides to repurchase, and customer satisfaction has critical impact on affecting the buyer's (re)purchase intention (Szymanski and Henard, 2001). Thus, customer satisfaction antecedes relationship continuity. On the other hand, relationship enhancement requires trust in the partner, because it involves more uncertainties associated with increased idiosyncratic investments. More importantly,

customer satisfaction is an important source for trust, because the latter is a generalized expectancy derived from both cultural context and experiences/ episodes within the relationship (Selnes, 1998). In their empirical study, Selnes (1998) suggested that communication, commitment, and conflict handling are antecedents of customer satisfaction following the communication theory. Focusing on social satisfaction, Sanzo *et al.* (2003) emphasized the critical role of effective communication, because it reduces conflict, increases trust, and enhances perceived value, all of which have positive impact on the buyer's satisfaction. Further, Terawatanavong *et al.* (2007) investigated the impact of five relational constructs, namely, total interdependence, trust, supplier commitment, cooperative norms, and conflict, on the buyer's satisfaction, and they also revealed that such impact might vary at different stages in the lifecycle of a relationship. Specifically, their empirical results indicate that trust and interdependence are developed at the early stages of the relationship lifecycle; that trust, commitment, and cooperative norms have more active roles when the relationship matures; and that conflicts emerge in the decline or deterioration stage of the relationship.

Besides buyer's satisfaction, *supplier satisfaction* was also explored, because it is essential to achieve supplier's full and whole-hearted support (Wong, 2000). Specifically, Wong (2000) argued that with the cooperative culture with the supplier, the buyer's commitment to supplier satisfaction and constructive controversy can lead to supplier satisfaction. Further, antecedents of supplier satisfaction were elaborated from two perspectives: business-related and communication-related (Maunu, 2003). Business-related factors include profitability, agreements, early supplier involvement, business continuity, and forecasting/planning, while communication-related factors include roles and responsibilities, openness and trust, feedback, and buying company's value. Examined from relationship quality perspective, Essig and Amann (2009) distinguished strategic, operational, and accompanying levels of a relationship, ranging from intensity of cooperation to specific aspects in operations (e.g., order process and billing-delivery) and interactions (e.g., communication, conflict management, and general view). It should be noted that supplier satisfaction is at the relationship level rather than at the transaction level, unlike buyer's satisfaction which could be at either level, because it is driven primarily by the nature of the relationship rather than by performance (Benton and Maloni, 2005).

Buyer–Seller Dependence, Trust, and Commitment in Channel Relationships

The successful development of relational exchanges among channel members requires three significant conditions: dependence, trust, and commitment. These key factors encourage firms to (1) work at preserving relationship investments by cooperating with exchange partners, (2) resist attractive short-term alternatives in favor of the expected long-term benefits of staying with existing partners, and (3) view potentially high-risk actions as being prudent because of the belief that their partners will not act opportunistically (Morgan and Hunt, 1994). Therefore, dependence, trust, and commitment lead to cooperative and collaborative activities that are conducive to relationship marketing success and to outcomes that increase efficiency, productivity, and effectiveness.

Dependence can enable a long-term channel relationship particularly when both parties have roughly the same dependence on the relationship. Interdependence is the fundamental basis of solidarity and mutuality among channel members. A channel member dependent on the performance of others in the channel is more likely to attempt to develop and maintain its relationships. Therefore, firms should seek ways to create dependence from both sides. They can do so by getting channel members to invest in transaction-specific assets. This kind of investment creates high switching costs and serves as a barrier-to-exit from the relationship. Furthermore, it encourages one party to collaborate and cooperate with the others. Besides, it increases the likelihood of relational contracts (Nevin, 1995).

On the other hand, if firm B is highly dependent on firm A, A might have substantial power over B. In followship relationships, in which a firm is highly dependent on another firm but the other is not, the nondependent firm is free to end the relationship or engage in exchange relationships with other firms and to exert considerable influence over the development of the relationship. The dependent firm has to follow the nondependent firm and adapt to its wishes and requirements, but still can influence the relationship. It faces the challenge of how to best manage and maintain its relationships with the more powerful firm. If there is no dependence between firm

A and firm B, there is likely to be no relationship to be managed, which may be the case in a perfectly competitive market in which there are numerous similar customers, suppliers, and low switching costs. For example, a small firm purchasing office supplies such as paper and pens may not be dependent on the supplier and vice versa. Another type of relationship involves mutual dependence between partners, in which no firm is clearly more powerful. This type of relationship leads the parties to depend on the other for important inputs and build a long-term exchange relationship for value cocreation. Although the relationship is mainly based on collaboration, one party may take the initiative in directing the relationship with the agreement of the other. There will be strong mutual dependence between firms when they enter into a long-term purchase agreement or establish e-procurement systems (Ritter *et al.*, 2004).

Channel relationships do not always fit neatly into an ideal form involving mutual dependence. They often involve combinations of interdependencies that can vary across issues and change over time. Moreover, interdependence between channel members can be positive or negative. Positive dependence refers to a situation in which one party's behaviors help the other party achieve its objectives. On the other hand, negative dependence refers to the situation in which one party's behaviors prevent the other party from achieving its objectives. Channel relationships typically entail a combination of both positive and negative dependencies that include cooperative, collaborative, competitive, and conflictual elements (Ritter *et al.*, 2004).

Trust is fundamental for creating long-term relationships with channel members. It is a prerequisite for collaborative and cooperative relational exchange and an essential factor for establishing long-term relationships. It is the willingness to rely on an exchange partner in whom one has confidence. In an interorganizational context, trust is the firm's belief that the other party will take actions that will lead to positive outcomes for the firm and not engage in unexpected behaviors that will lead to adverse outcomes for the firm. In other words, it helps one party in an exchange relationship to overcome the fear that the other party will engage in opportunistic behaviors. Trust exists when one party has confidence in an exchange partner's reliability and integrity, which are associated with such qualities as consistency, competence, honesty, fairness, responsibility, helpfulness, and benevolence. Doney and Cannon (1997) defined trust as the perceived credibility and benevolence of a target, the former of which reflects the expectancy that the partner's word or written statement can be relied on, while the latter stands for the genuine interest in the other partner's welfare and motivation to seek joint gain. They identified five processes by which trust can be developed: calculative, prediction, capability, intentionality, and transference process. Specifically, calculative process involves the calculation of the cost and/or rewards of another party cheating or staying in the relationship based on the economics literature. Prediction process relies on one party's ability to forecast another party's behavior based on prior interactions and courtship behavior. Capability process determines another party's ability to meet its obligations, focusing primarily on the credibility component of the trust. Intentionality process is the interpretation and assessment of the other party's motives in the relationship. Finally, transference process stands for the extension of the trust from a third party to the other party.

Trust is the cornerstone of a strategic partnership and a major determinant of relationship commitment. Channel relationships based on trust are so valuable and crucial that members will desire to commit themselves to such relationships seeking only trustworthy partners (Morgan and Hunt, 1994; Nevin, 1995). According to the principle of generalized reciprocity, "mistrust breeds mistrust and as such would also serve to decrease commitment in the relationship and shift the transaction to one of more direct short-term exchanges" (Morgan and Hunt, 1994, p. 24). Trust can substitute for hierarchical contracts in many exchange relationships and serve as an alternative governance mechanism. In strong relationships, trust becomes a low-cost substitute for contracts; marketers develop trustworthy relationships and have confidence in each other, because "they know that information about malfeasance will be disseminated quickly, good or bad deeds will be reciprocated and those who defect will be expelled from the district; in other words, trustworthy behavior is a rational choice" (Bolton *et al.*, 2003, p. 25).

Commitment refers to the belief that an ongoing relationship with one party is so important that it warrants maximum efforts and that the relationship is worth working on to ensure that it endures indefinitely. It is an enduring desire to maintain a valued relationship and exists only when both parties consider that the relationship is important. In addition to trust as a primary precursor, commitment can emerge via mechanisms like pledges (Anderson and Weitz, 1992; Gilliland and Bello, 2002), relational norms (Gundlach *et al.*, 1995; Jap and Ganesan, 2000), and social bonding (Rodríguez and Wilson, 2002; Sarkar *et al.*, 1998; Stanko *et al.*, 2007). Commitment derived from pledges follows the calculative process of trust formation, because pledges are essentially costs of the member to cheat (Doney and Cannon, 1997; Gilliland and Bello, 2002). Relational norms also stem from transactional cost paradigm and are shared expectations of the relationship governance (Gundlach *et al.*, 1995). Specifically, credible commitments of specialized resources provide an impetus for the development of relational social norms. It should be noted that the

intentionality process of trust development is applied in the formation of social norms.

Social bonding is to hold the buyer and seller closely together in personal interactivity and in feelings of personal closeness. A bond can be established at different levels and for diverse reasons. Structural bonds based on the economic and strategic benefits must be developed first in the development of a relationship, because these benefits are necessary to satisfy a minimum level of dependability and reliability before a deeper emotional investment can exist (Rodríguez and Wilson, 2002). However, economic bonds are not sufficient for the maintenance and continuation of the relationship because of the possibilities of opportunism, and thus, social bonds should work in the governance of the relationship. Stanko *et al.* (2007) elaborated the social bonds from the tie strength perspective, arguing that economic exchanges are embedded in social system where social and emotional outcomes coexist with economic utilitarian ones. As such, they investigated relationship length, emotional intensity, mutual confiding, and reciprocal service as four dimensions of social bonds that increase buyer's commitment in the relationship. Thus commitment is central to all the relational exchanges between the firm and its various partners in a channel (Morgan and Hunt, 1994). Indeed, B2B relationships include the exchange of not only economic resources (e.g. money and products) but also social resources (status, friendship, and help) (Bolton *et al.*, 2003).

Antecedents of Buyer–Seller Dependence, Trust, and Commitment in Channel Relationships

The following are considered to be the five major antecedents to dependence, trust, and relationship commitment in a channel relationship (Morgan and Hunt, 1994): These are: (1) relationship termination/switching costs; (2) relationship benefits;

(3) shared values (norms); (4) communication; and (5) opportunistic behavior.

The party that has terminated the channel relationship will need to seek an alternative relationship and have termination and switching costs, which involve all expected losses from ending the relationship and relationship dissolution expenses, and which result from the perceived lack of comparable potential alternative partners. If the relationship is a transaction-specific one, the termination and switching costs will increase further. As mentioned earlier, transaction-specific investments lead to high switching costs and serve as a barrier-to-exit from the relationship. Therefore, the firm's anticipation of high termination/switching costs enhances the firm's interest in maintaining a quality relationship. In other words, the expected high termination/switching costs will lead the parties to view an ongoing relationship as important, thus creating commitment to the relationship (Morgan and Hunt, 1994).

Firms will commit themselves to establishing, developing, and maintaining relationships with partners that deliver superior benefits. More specifically, if the firm receives superior benefits from a highly valued partner on such dimensions as profitability, product performance, product innovation, and customer satisfaction, it will be committed to the relationship and make strong efforts to maintain it (Hunt and Morgan, 1994). Indeed, there is a bilateral relationship between superior benefits and commitment. A firm will be committed to a relationship as it receives superior benefits such as receiving distinctive market information. As trust and commitment between channel members increase, the shared information will become more comprehensive, accurate, and timely.

Shared values (norms) refer to the mutual beliefs of partners about the importance, appropriateness, and accuracy of the objectives, policies, and actions.

They contribute to the development of commitment and trust among channel members. In other words, when members of an exchange relationship share values, they will be more committed to their relationship and trust each other more (Morgan and Hunt, 1994). In the early stages of the relationship, individuals may follow universal values of politeness, conflict avoidance, and the exchange of superficial information. During the subsequent stages, values of fairness and honesty can enhance and stabilize interfirm relationships such that the relationship's exchange values involve expectations of mutual interest and joint welfare (Weitz and Jap, 1995). According to the Relational Exchange Theory, relational norms serve as a distinct form of governance that stipulates commitment and disallows opportunism in exchange relationships. Shared relational norms generate a win-win exchange atmosphere by subordinating self-interests and encourage partners not to jeopardize it. They will push the partners to refrain from acting opportunistically. Relational norms can serve as an alternative to common ownership and contractual governance to resolve relational exchange problems (Bolton *et al.*, 2003).

Another antecedent to dependence, commitment, and trust is communication which refers to sharing of meaningful, valuable, and timely information among partners both formally and informally. Indeed, there is a bilateral relationship between communication and trust. Communication enhances trust by helping partners to resolve controversial issues among them in a timely manner and aligns perceptions and expectations. In turn, the consolidation of trust leads to better communication. Although a relationship's development may feature selective instances of direct communication between the partners, these instances are embedded in — and rely heavily on — a dominant pattern of indirect, or passive, communication that allows the parties to gather information in an unobtrusive manner. … Partners can indirectly communicate their attitudes and feelings with regard to the relationship's development via their actions in addition to their verbal behaviors. For example, channel members who seek to make a relationship increasingly strategic are likely to engage in extensive planning of meetings, attend a higher frequency of meetings, and use more inference, interpretation, and comparison of new information with existing information. Additionally, a partner might communicate trust by engaging in confiding behavior, keeping confidences, expressing similarity in agreement, and adapting to the other partner by keeping conversational rules and allowing the other partner to control the conversation as appropriate (Weitz and Jap, 1995, p. 314).

Finally, opportunistic behavior refers to seeking of self-interest egocentrically, as such "the essence of opportunistic behavior is deceit-oriented violation of implicit or explicit promises about one's appropriate or required role behavior" (John, 1984, p. 279). When one party in a channel relationship believes that another party engages in opportunistic behaviors, it will diminish and ultimately destroy trust. Then, such decreased trust will result in decreased relationship commitment, because the partner will believe that it can no longer trust the other partner (Morgan and Hunt, 1994).

Several factors that lead to opportunistic behaviors in B2B context can be classified into behavioral and structural factors with the presumption that the behavioral factors arouse opportunism, whereas the structural factors facilitate the opportunistic parties to pursue maximization of their self-interest. These antecedents are (Bolton *et al.*, 2003) as follows:

Behavioral Antecedents — partners' unfavorable history of collaboration; partners' expectations for the network's future (expectation about the lifetime of the relationship); partnership uncertainty; chauvinism/particularism; perceived inequity; and conflict resolution behaviors.

Structural Antecedents — the presence time bound; degree of asset specificity; mobility, transparency, and intangibility/contractibility of resources; distribution of ownership, control, and decision rights; information asymmetry; power asymmetry; inequitable incentive structure; nature of dependence or interdependence; and nature of governance mechanism.

There is a bilateral relationship between shared norms and opportunistic behaviors. Norms serve as a protective factor against opportunistic behaviors (Weitz and Jap, 1995). Opportunism can damage the relational norms that lead to long-lasting channel relationships. It decreases satisfaction and makes the parties in a relationship less likely to behave in compromising manner, which might not only destroy the relationship but also reduce firms' performance. Opportunism can be perceived as an act of betrayal and leads to retaliation that might root away the relationship perpetually. Engaging in opportunistic behaviors might initially yield favorable outcomes for the opportunistic party; however, it ultimately can limit value co-creation, increase costs, and decrease revenues, leading to lose-lose situation for both parties in an exchange relationship. In short, opportunistic behaviors not only induce lower levels of trust and commitment but also prevent the development of reciprocity (Samaha and Palmatier, 2015).

Authoritative, Contractual, and Normative Control in Channel Relationships

In today's B2B markets, the control issue in channel relationships is characterized by normative and contractual control mechanisms instead of authoritative control (Malhotra and Agarwal, 2002).

In the authoritative mechanism, one party in the channel relationship controls the activities of the other party by using its position or power through coercive influence strategies (Johnston *et al.*, 2018). In this conventional channel setting, the opportunity to control channel functions and the activities of other channel members arises from an imbalance in resources. That is, the more powerful party in the channel has greater resources that are highly valued by the less powerful party (Weitz and Jap, 1995).

Contractual control mechanism involves an agreement by the parties in a relationship on terms and conditions that are identified either unilaterally or bilaterally via negotiations and that define their responsibilities and rewards for performing channel activities. The terms and conditions can be accepted or rejected by the parties involved in the contract agreement, and also be changed during the contract period when conditions change (Bergen *et al.*, 1998; Weitz and Jap, 1995). Johnson and Sohi (2016) using a grounded approach identified types of out-of-contract alternatives for resolving contractual breaches when legal enforcement is not a viable option, which often is detrimental to the buyer–seller relationship. These relational, out-of-contract options requiring an integrative orientation set by sellers include acquisition of incremental competitive business, extending the existing contract or exempting an unrelated contract from the bid process, changing the terms of business, requiring customers to accept a dedicated resource adjustment, or the sale of excess capacity. Others requiring a compromising orientation include splitting the payment up over an extended period of time, raising prices on other business not involved in the breach, upfront payment of liquidated damages by buyer but allowed to earn it back through incentives, or quid pro quo in offsetting breaches, i.e., forbearance of enforcement of a seller's breach in exchange for the forbearance of enforcement of the buyer's breach. As the relationship between parties develops and maintains, personal relationships will become more important, which will often lead to psychological contracts to replace formal legal contracts (Malhotra and Agarwal, 2002). However, the formation and development of this relationship will be more effective when there is perceived balance, harmony, equity, mutual support, and dependence between parties, instead of coercion, conflict, and domination (Oliver, 1990).

Normative control includes a shared set of implicit principles or norms learnt from past relationships that coordinate the activities performed by the parties and that govern the relationship. In an intra-organizational context, these norms form a firm's organization culture (Macneil, 1980; Weitz and Jap, 1995). They involve various types of norms such as the fairness norm (shared interests), openness norm (exchange of proprietary information), and flexibility norm (ability to alter prior commitments). Trust is a significant prerequisite for normative control mechanisms, which are accepted and adhered to by both parties involved in a relationship (Malhotra and Agarwal, 2002). By providing formal rules and procedures to govern the relationship, normative contracts serve as deterrence against possible opportunistic behaviors, because a violation may lead to some undesirable economic and legal outcomes in addition to the loss of reputation. Particularly when a firm invests in transaction-specific assets, which serves as a barrier-to-exit from the relationship and increases the likelihood of potential value loss, the firm finds it highly appropriate to negotiate more complex contracts. These kinds of constructs serve not only as an insurance against violation and termination but also as a guidance through which such consequences or conflicts can be managed (Bolton *et al.*, 2003).

Firms limit their flexibility in channel activities when they form normative control mechanism and establish long-term channel relationships (Johnson and Sohi, 2016), which might increase uncertainty in returns. Even if one party faces a significant opportunity, it cannot end or change its relationship because of its commitment to norms that govern the channel relationships. Firms that engage in a channel relationship face two sources of uncertainty about returns. First, they might not attain a fair return on their investment. Second, even if the relationship reduces the costs and increases the benefits to end users, one party might not receive its fair share of the increased risk-adjusted returns (Weitz and Jap, 1995).

SERVICE DOMINANT (S-D) LOGIC FRAMEWORK IN BUYER–SELLER RELATIONSHIP

According to the S-D logic, value is not intrinsic to the seller's operand resources or tangible offerings, but sellers deliver value to buyers by applying operant resources such as skills and knowledge to the operand resources (Vargo and Lusch, 2004). The B2B relationship marketing has identified several factors encompassing both operand and operant resources that influence relationship satisfaction including instrumental factors established by the seller's marketing mix (Abdul-Muhmin, 2005), relational norms (Heide and John, 1992), customer value (Ulaga and Eggert, 2006), customer orientation (Homburg, 1998), and service augmentation strategies (Homburg *et al.* 2002).

DeLeon and Chatterjee (2017) discuss different types of operand and operant resources. Core operand resources fulfill basic customer expectations about a product generally in the form of compliance with functional and technical requirements, and augmented operand resources exceed customer expectations such as installation, training, and support services.

Similarly, core operant resources are instrumental service, i.e., degree of technical mastery shown by the seller, and interpersonal service, i.e., service that closely understands customer needs; whereas augmented operant resources encompasses the seller's grasp of the buyer's ability to realize maximum value, i.e., value mindset. While core operant resources meet basic customer expectations, augmented operant resources via value mindset understand buyer's enterprise-wide value-creation opportunity both from the product and the overall business perspective (see Figure 3.8). From S-D logic, sellers are not just transferring the value inherent in their offering, i.e., product-centered value, but also promoting the "value-in-use" for customers, i.e., use-centered value (Figure 3.9). Therefore, sellers can either (a) expand their operand resources of services scope to augment the core product or (b) invest in operant resource development around the core product focusing on instrumental service or interpersonal service, or (c) invest in operant resources less in core product and more in customer's value creating use of the product, i.e. value mindset. These alternative seller resource investment strategies are summarized in Figure 3.9.

DeLeon and Chatterjee (2017) propose a conceptual framework that uses seller's core and augmented resources to explain perceived value and relationship quality, specifically relationship satisfaction. Cocreation of value by both the seller and the buyer involves not just the seller's core and augmented operant resources but also the buyer's ability to assimilate new technology with support from the seller. In this conceptual framework, seller resources include core operant resources (instrumental and interpersonal service), augmented operant resource (value mindset), and augmented operand resource (services scope). These resources directly, and indirectly through assimilation constructs (see Figure 3.10), affect relationship satisfaction. In

Figure 3.8: According to the S-D logic, sellers deliver value to buyers by applying core and augmented operant resources to the operand resources.

Figure 3.9: Interdependence Structure Resource-Based View B2B Model

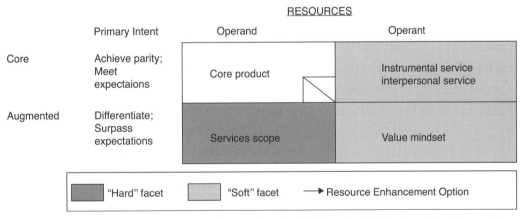

Adapted from Anthony J. deLeon and Sharmila C. Chatterjee (2017), B2B Relationship Calculus: Quantifying Resource Effects in Service-Dominant Logic, *Journal of the Academy of Marketing Science* 45: 402–427.

their empirical findings (in B2B software Business Intelligence setting), the authors demonstrate that the augmented operant resource, i.e., value mindset, has the most significant impact on realized value and relationship satisfaction. The actual scope of services provided seems to have little influence on either technology assimilation or customer relationship quality.

In short, these findings suggest that it is not the services per se that influence customer-perceived value and relationship quality in a B2B setting, but rather the service mindset manifested in customer value terms including how the product enhances the buyer's performance, how the buyer can implement the product to realize maximum value and the seller's grasp of the buyer's business context.

Figure 3.10: Relative Effects of Seller Resources — A Conceptual Model

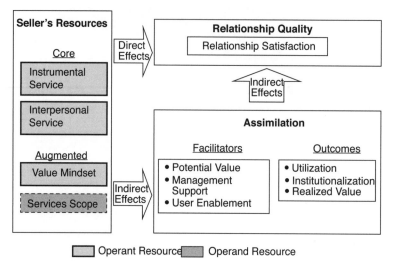

Adapted from Anthony J. deLeon and Sharmila C. Chatterjee (2017), B2B Relationship Calculus: Quantifying Resource Effects in Service-Dominant Logic, *Journal of the Academy of Marketing Science* 45: 402–427.

Value Creation in Buyer–Seller Relationship

It should be noted that value cocreation in buyer–seller relationships can be derived and measured in several ways. For instance, Terpend *et al.* (2008) categorized value derived from the relationship into operational performance-based, integration-based, supplier capability-based, and buyer financial-based values.

Operational performance-based values are the first type of values recognized and discussed in the literature, and it dominated the discussion of relationship outcomes at the very beginning of the literature (see Terpend *et al.*, 2008). Noordewier *et al.* (1990) showed that governance elements (e.g., purchase relationships, such as supplier's flexibility, supplier's assistance, and information provided to supplier, monitoring of supplier, and expectation of continuity) benefit buyer transaction performance in terms of inventory turnover, percentage of on-time delivery, and percentage of acceptable bearing delivered. Yet, this is not an exhaustive list for performance metrics in the relationship (see Daugherty *et al.*, 2006 for details).

These diverse values in operational performance are mostly based on classic transaction cost paradigm (Noordewier *et al.* 1990; Shrader, 2001). *Integration-based values* are highly associated with operational performance-based values because of the shared theoretical foundation. The shift in the study focusing from the performance-based to the integration-based value indicated a greater emphasis on long-term orientation (Terpend *et al.*, 2008) and a greater use of relational exchanges. Performance-based values are more short-term oriented where the firm relies on the efficiencies of exchanges to maximize their profits in each transaction, while integrated-based values are more long-term oriented to maximize the profit in a series of transactions (Ganesan, 1994). Knowledge transfer (i.e., technology transfer) and acquisition mentioned above is a type of integration-based values, benefiting supplier's performance and in turn buyer's profitability (Kotabe *et al.*, 2003).

Supplier's capability-based values refer to the competitive advantage that the buyer can derive from the supplier, including its continuous improvement, and its capabilities in globalization, technology, and environment. Using the resource-based theory and the internalization–externalization model, Krause *et al.* (2000) identified externalized and internalized supplier performance improvement strategies. Externalized supplier improvement strategies entail use of the external market to instigate supplier performance improvements and include activities such as the use of competitive pressure, supplier assessment, and supplier incentives. On the other hand, internalized supplier improvement strategies represent a direct investment of the buying firm's resources in the supplier through activities such as supplier site visits to guide performance improvement and investments in supplier training and development. For more research, the reader is referred to Möller and Törrönen (2003), Joshi (2009), and O'Cass and Ngo (2012). Finally, *buyer financial-based values* concern the financial performance of the buyer, including metrics like sales, return on equity, total return to shareholders, and net present value of the buying firm (Terpend *et al.*, 2008). Ehret (2004) contributed an important discussion extending buyer's value in the relationship to value networks. Value network relationship, different from the buyer–supplier dyad, focuses not only on the specific relationship with a specific supplier but also on the integration of an integrated network of actors, which jointly work on the development of new products, the integration of information infrastructures, and the coordination of the flow of goods and services. For instance, Windahl and Lakemond (2006) showed that relationships in the value network are a potential factor determining the success or failure of the development of integrated solutions and that the solution's impact on existing products, services, and production structures has critical consequences for developing integrated solutions.

UPSTREAM RELATIONSHIP MARKETING OPPORTUNITIES

Developing strong relationships with suppliers can be a vital and durable source of competitive advantage and one that is hard for the competitors to imitate or steal (Malhotra *et al.*, 2016). In other words, a firm's ability to successfully build, develop, and maintain its relationships with suppliers may be viewed as a core competence, which is difficult to imitate and which is an important source of competitive advantage. Firms operate in production networks that include various chains of suppliers specializing in different aspects of the value-creation process. The compatible and effective functioning of these networks depends heavily on not only the capabilities of the actors but also the level of relationships among them (Ritter *et al.*, 2004).

What Binds Manufacturers to Suppliers?

Today's hyper-competitiveness and advanced technology have significantly influenced the procurement paradigms of firms. Modern supplier relationships have shifted more to a relational and global outsourcing process. There are four reasons for a firm to engage in relationships with its suppliers (Malhotra *et al.*, 2016). First, developing strong relationships with suppliers can enable the firm to receive better service with reduced costs and yield more efficiency in procurement. According to Transaction Cost Theory (Williamson, 1989), properties of transactions (i.e., uncertainty and infrequency) determine control structure. When a firm has multiple suppliers, the firm and its suppliers feel a high level of uncertainty, which requires multiple controls to ensure successful transactions. The augmentation in the number of controls increases costs and decreases the efficiency of relationships. On the other hand, successful supplier relationships reduce uncertainty in transactions, which in turn reduces the number of controls, leading to increased efficiency of transactions.

Second, supplier relationships can allow the firm to be more effective in implementing marketing strategies such as quality platforms (Goffin *et al.*, 2006). Particularly, total quality management philosophy emphasizes long-term approach (e.g., relational exchange) instead of short-term approach (e.g., transaction orientation), which is also the view espoused in this book. A supplier might invest in new technologies that will allow the business purchaser to provide a quality platform, better customer service, availability of spare parts, and information exchange. As explained earlier, resource specificity forces the supplier to realize the planned transaction(s) so that the investment in quality platforms can be amortized, albeit might create dependency (Scheer *et al.*, 2015). It will be reluctant to invest in such technologies if it perceives a high level of uncertainty about the channel relationship and does not trust its partner. In other words, an increase in uncertainty and a decrease in trust will discourage the supplier to invest in assets that will enhance the value provided by purchaser.

Third, new technologies such as network computing, quick response, electronic data interchange and other computer programs have modernized the procurement methods and reorganized the purchasing philosophy, processes, and platforms. For example, electronic data interchange reduces costs for both customers and suppliers and considerably decreases cycle times. In addition, these technologies enable marketers to customize their offerings to individual customers and cater to their needs. Improved customer information and ability to customize offerings will lead to a higher level of customer selectivity. Information technology (IT) allows firms to select their best customers and suppliers such as computer programs enabling

firms to calculate profitability associated with each customer or supplier. Firms would prefer to retain the more profitable customers at a cost of losing the less profitable ones. If suppliers provide customized offerings to different purchasers, some firms may have a resource-based advantage over their competitors, which might encourage a firm to be a better customer and receive additional services. Importantly, the use of information technology has enhanced buyer–supplier relationships in terms of frequency of information shared, richness of information shared, and buyer–supplier trust (Carr and Smeltzer, 2002). Further, IT has also pronounced the strategic buyer–supplier relationship and external logistics integration (and subsequently agility) (Paulraj and Chen, 2007).

Finally, in today's hyper-competitive business environment in which we are witnessing the growth of national or international mergers, acquisitions, alliances, and outsourcing, the firm can maintain a competitive edge by developing better supplier relationships (Goffin *et al.*, 2006). This shift has reorganized the procurement function from a decentralized administrative function to a centralized strategic function. Developing strong relationships with suppliers can be an effective strategy to reduce competition's negative effect on an industry (Sheth and Sharma, 1997).

Potential Outcomes of Supplier Relationships

Successful supplier relationship management can enhance firms' cost efficiency by reducing uncertainty and control cost, and improve organizational effectiveness through quality and service (Goffin *et al.*, 2006). Firms can achieve competitive advantage by reducing the number of suppliers and entering into strategic relationships with a few who have differentiated their core competencies (Malhotra and Agarwal, 2002; Malhotra *et al.*, 2016). In this context, a manufacturer can develop exclusive relationships with its suppliers by reducing the number of suppliers and having sole-source relationships with key suppliers (Weitz and Jap, 1995). For example, when Xerox and GM reduced the number of their suppliers significantly, they found that they obtained better services and prices (Sheth and Sharma, 1997).

If a firm does not have a distinctive cost or value advantage in specific parts of the value chain, it should outsource these activities to firms that have such an advantage. Firms can increase quality, reduce inventory, and develop just-in-time (JIT) systems by outsourcing and developing single source suppliers. Firms that consider global suppliers as partners and customers to create value and work closely with them can benefit from supplier-led innovation in both processes and products. They can reduce their costs drastically by constantly sharing information with suppliers (Malhotra and Agarwal, 2002). On the contrary, it is not easy for purchasers in B2B markets to demonstrate commitment and trust, because they have been traditionally willing to change their suppliers. Even if they are happy with existing suppliers, they might engage in such an opportunistic behavior, which stems from their inclination not to reduce the supplier choices because of the fear that they will be dependent on a smaller set of suppliers. This tendency results in lack of a trusting relationship (Sheth and Sharma, 1997).

A firm can develop strong collaborative relationships with suppliers when the supplier has roughly the same dependence on the relationship. In other words, when the performance of the supplier and a firm is dependent on each other, both parties are more likely to exert greater effort to develop and maintain the relationship. Firms whose purchase decisions have long-term consequences are more likely to engage in collaborative relationships with suppliers. Investments specific to a relationship increase the level of dependence and the likelihood of long-term relational contracts. The level of dependence

is generally higher among the parties involved in a relationship under conditions of uncertainty or high rates of marketplace change (Nevin, 1995). In brief, as supply function has become more a strategic differentiator and a core competency, a firm should treat its suppliers less as vendors and more like partners. Firms that reduce the number of suppliers and invest in a few suppliers regarding training, capital, and know-how are more likely to achieve competitive advantage. Therefore, firms should develop an organizational culture where relationships with suppliers are valued.

DOWNSTREAM RELATIONSHIP MARKETING OPPORTUNITIES

In this section, we focus on marketing relationships between a company and distributors, retailers, and other intermediaries in the channel. It is important to recognize that a manufacturer can provide the kinds and levels of service that create superior value for customers and that lead to very satisfied customers through effective distribution (Malhotra *et al.*, 2016). The development of successful long-term relationships with distributors, retailers, and other intermediaries in the channel involves a set of generic relationship developmental processes including relationship initiation, maintenance, and termination (Nevin, 1995).

Today's hyper-competition has increased the difficulty of getting access to end consumers, which has led many firms to increasingly attempt to build distributor partnerships to reach global consumers where access and information about end customers are shared among the firms in the channel. In this channel, the relationship form has shifted away from the vertical marketing system toward the channel relationship system, which refers to a transition from an authoritative control and centralized planning and decision-making toward a contractual and normative control and shared planning and decision-making (Weitz and Jap, 1995). An incremental disenchantment with vertical integration, the consolidation and increasing power of intermediary firms, and the potential competitive advantage of relationship strategies have resulted in channel relationship marketing (Kumar, 2005). Effective channel relationships generate great opportunities for the parties involved and offer substantial value-added potential and tremendous cost savings and competitive advantage (Malhotra and Agarwal, 2002; Malhotra *et al.*, 2016). Manufacturers, distributors, and retailers have recognized that managing channel relationships provides great opportunities for firms to achieve strategic competitive advantage and enhance financial performance. Producers' attempts to effectively manage channel relationships are a major source of value-added benefits to end users, which helps producers to reduce their costs and differentiate their offerings (Weitz and Jap, 1995).

The relationships in B2B context are governed by the norms that are mutually learned and accepted and that become part of channel interorganizational culture after a period of time. As mentioned earlier, the efficiency of these relationships depends heavily on high levels of producer-intermediary dependence (Malhotra and Agarwal, 2002; Malhotra *et al.*, 2016). Interdependence is the fundamental basis of solidarity and mutuality among channel members and a significant condition that helps collaborative and cooperative relationships to prosper. However, when a producer uses intensive and selective distribution systems, it has chosen to provide coverage to a territory through multiple channel members, which limits its dependency on any one member in the value chain. Therefore, the producer is likely to find it difficult to develop the substantial interdependency required to foster successful long-term relationships (Nevin, 1995).

In supplier–manufacturer, manufacturer–consumer, or strategic alliance contexts, exclusive relationships can be developed commonly. Manufacturers can reduce the number of suppliers and develop sole-source relationships with key ones, and end users can develop strong loyalty to one brand in a product category. However, retailers and wholesalers usually engage in exchange relationships with multiple competitive suppliers in a product category to satisfy the needs of their customers, because they have to offer assortment, which is a key for their market success. For example, although P&G has engaged in a partnership with Walmart, the relationship has not developed to the point that Walmart only offers P&G products or that P&G only sells its products through Walmart. In addition, producers might be reluctant to sharing sensitive information that are useful in coordinating activities with wholesalers and retailers, when the wholesalers and retailers engage in multiple relationships with competitive suppliers. Therefore, developing long-term committed relationships and thus achieving strategic advantage might be limited by the channel firms' need to provide assortment (Weitz and Jap, 1995).

Firms also build relationships with many other types of firms whose functions increase the efficiency of their marketing activities and enhance the value of their own outputs. One type of this relationship is joint marketing schemes in which firms cooperate in reaching out to customers in the form of joint promotion and distribution agreements. For example, Lego cooperates with Hewlett Packard to serve the children's toy market, and P&G cooperates with various firms such as Coca Cola and Pizza Hut in promotion campaigns. Firms can also engage in innovation partnership with suppliers of complementary products and services, which will enable the partners to recombine their outputs in productive ways to develop new products (Ritter *et al.*, 2004).

There is a blurring of time, place, and transaction boundaries between producers and distributors. For example, P&G assigned its employees to live and work at Walmart's headquarters to enhance the speed of delivery and reduce the cost of supplying P&G goods to Walmart stores (Sheth and Parvatiyar, 1995b). The blurring boundaries are both a symptom and cause of increased value co-creation among partners. It is therefore hard to distinguish the elements as well as the time of occurrence of exchange. In relationship marketing, organizational boundaries are hard to distinguish as companies are more likely to be involved in shared relationship with their marketing partners. Some of these activities relate to joint planning, co-production, co-marketing, co-branding, etc. where the parties in the relationship bring their resources together for creating a greater market value (Sheth and Parvatiyar, 1995b).

What Binds Manufacturers to Distributors and Retailers?

There are two forms of attitudinal commitment explaining the factors that bind a manufacturer to certain distributors and retailers in a channel: calculative and loyalty commitment (Gilliland and Bello, 2002; Kumar, 2005; Malhotra *et al.*, 2016). Calculative commitment represents a state of attitudinal attachment cognitively experienced as an acknowledgment of the benefits to be sacrificed and the losses to be incurred when the relationship ends. It is somewhat a structural syncretization that links channel members in a relationship as a result of shared objectives and that reflects a negative motivation for maintaining the relationship (Liu *et al.*, 2010). Calculative commitment represents continuance cognitively experienced as an appraisal of forgone benefits and incurred losses should the relationship end. Thus, the antecedents of calculative commitment are circumstances that clarify the manufacturer's instrumental attachment to the distributor. These

conditions include the manufacturer's relative dependence on the distributor, the manufacturer's pledges of exclusive representation made to the distributor, and the manufacturer's pledges of investments made in the distributor (Gilliland and Bello, 2002).

Based on the calculation of the benefits sacrificed and losses incurred if the relationship ends, calculative commitment is the state of cognitive, rational, and task-oriented attachment to a distributor or a retailer. Therefore, the manufacturer engages in a continuous calculation of the profit associated with continuing the relationship and the costs associated with ending. These costs include "sacrifices associated with termination, including lost current and future benefits from existing customers; the disruption and difficulty of moving to another distributor; and the loss of sunk idiosyncratic investments." As the conceptualization suggests, calculative commitment involves opportunistic behaviors and search for alternatives. That is, although it is a kind of attachment, there is no indication that shared norms and values, or other pro-social behaviors exist between the manufacturer and the channel member. Therefore, the manufacturer might end the relationship if it receives an economically better offer from another channel member, which highlights the importance of developing relational bond (Gilliland and Bello, 2002).

Loyalty commitment represents a state of attitudinal attachment to a partner experienced as a feeling of allegiance or faithfulness. It represents a manufacturer's affection for and obligation to its distributor or retailer, which stems from a strong sense of emotional sentiment and loyalty and belongingness to the relationship, not simply from economic motivations (Gounaris, 2005). A manufacturer loyally committed to a distributor or a retailer desires to maintain the relationship because of its attachment to the purchaser and enjoyment of the partnership (Liu *et al.*, 2010). This kind of relationship exists when both parties have shared business philosophies, goals, and values.

A manufacturer loyally committed to a channel member is often willing to subordinate its own interest in favor of the partner, which will enhance the alignment of daily tasks and decrease the likelihood of disagreements and controversies between the partners. It supports its partner through difficult times and desultory situations and expects that improvement can be achieved from within the relationship. In this type of relationship, the mechanisms that govern the relationship consist of ethical, relationship-specific expectations that emphasize true behavior in a given situation and may eventually displace the formal rules of the distribution agreement. The manufacturer engages in building customized social enforcement mechanisms in tandem with its distributor partner and utilizes them to resolve problems in their day-to-day relationships. Loyalty commitment reduces a manufacturer's need for a formal agreement because of the availability of social enforcement mechanisms. In this context, the contractual agreement becomes less significant and is updated and supplemented by social norms and understandings shared by the parties as the adherence enhances. As partners develop loyalty commitment, they are governed less by their formal responsibilities and more by the social drives inherent to their relationship (Gilliland and Bello, 2002). As the exchange becomes more relational, the relationship becomes more complex and the principles and practices of behavior with the relationship also become more complex. Habits, rules of thumb, and standard operating procedures develop within the more relational exchange setting and are added to (or even replace) external societal behaviors. The result is a more intricate web of relations among the exchange parties, and that web of relations is an important facet of more relational exchange relationships (Nevin, 1995).

A manufacturer involved in a channel relationship may modify the commitment forms, calculative and loyalty commitments, in parallel with the evolution of the relationship. In the early stages of the relationship, the manufacturer is likely to invest resources to maintain the relationship, calculating the costs and benefits of the investment to determine whether to continue the relationship. That is, the manufacturer will demonstrate calculative commitment to the relationship in the early stages. When the relationship develops and reaches a certain longevity, the manufacturer will reduce its reliance on calculating immediate benefits versus costs and replace formal rules and agreements with social drives, trust, and mutual interest established by experiences and understandings accumulated during the cooperative relationship. That is, the manufacturer will demonstrate loyalty commitment in the subsequent stages of a long-term relationship. The adaptations, understanding and trust between the parties will be enhanced as time goes by. Due to enhanced understanding and trust, the manufacturer will believe that the distributor or the retailer will sincerely consider its interests and refrain from engaging in opportunistic behaviors. Enhanced understanding and trust will motivate both parties to commit to maintain the relationship from an emotional sentiment and improve the affective quality of the relationship (Liu *et al.*, 2010).

RELATIONSHIP MANAGEMENT CAPABILITY

A firm that attempts to enhance its value-adding exchanges and collaborative partnerships needs to build a well-integrated and enterprise-wide relationship management infrastructure and develop its ability to learn about managing relationships and make subsequent adjustments to the relationship structure to increase the efficiency and effectiveness of exchange relationship (Malhotra *et al.*, 2016).

A relationship management capability involves three sets of capabilities: *relationship infrastructure capability, relationship learning capability*, and *relationship behavioral capability*. These are the key dimensions of an organization's relationship management capability. Each of these dimensions consists of multiple constructs describing systems, processes, and management behavior and action. Figure 3.11 demonstrates the dimensions of relationship management capabilities and the factors that constitute these dimensions (Jarratt, 2004).

Relationship infrastructure capability refers to the relationship management system, relationship experience, and memory that enhance relationship processes and that help improve relationship learning. A relationship management system refers to processes, routines, and infrastructure of market relationships. In an effective relationship management system, these components support knowledge sharing, socio-technical interactions, evaluation of potential partners, monitoring relationship progress, and relationship management coordination. Relationship experience, knowledge regarding that experience, and the processes that facilitate the

Figure 3.11: Relationship Management Capability Framework

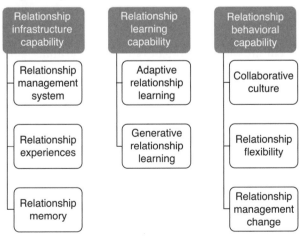

Adapted from D. Jarratt (2004), Conceptualizing a Relationship Management Capability, *Marketing Theory* 4(4): 287–309.

development of knowledge are critical infrastructure resources for an effective relationship management. In addition, information captured and interpreted, and analyses of prior behavior and outcomes are other significant infrastructure capabilities for relationship management (Jarratt, 2004).

Relationship learning capability, a unique form of the more general construct of organizational learning, refers to a joint activity between two parties in which they share knowledge, "which is then jointly interpreted and integrated into a shared relationship-domain-specific memory that changes the range or likelihood of potential relationship-domain-specific behavior" (Selnes and Sallis, 2003, p. 80). Firms can improve future behaviors in a relationship through an effective learning process. In this context, relationships vary in terms of the learning capabilities of the parties, and therefore some relationships perform better because of appropriate learning mechanisms developed by the parties. Relationship learning capability is directly linked to how the relationship is managed and to the context in which it is embedded (Selnes and Sallis, 2003). Adaptive and generative learning mechanisms are two significant sub-dimensions of a relationship learning capability. Relationship learning will enhance relationship knowledge and cognitive activity, yielding improved adjustments made to relationship management practice. A relationship learning capability will enable relationship management change and generate relationship forms and behaviors to address future relationship needs effectively (Jarratt, 2004).

Relationship behavioral capability is the third dimension of relationship management capability. This dimension reflects relationship interconnectedness and the dissemination of learning, adjusting to partner needs and market changes, and the "inter- and intra-organizational implementation of new relationship management knowledge" (Jarratt, 2004, p. 302). Collaboration allows a firm to produce intelligence with and from other organizations about new opportunities or means for building superior customer value. It has significant effects on sources of value such as product quality and new product development (Slater and Narver, 2000). Flexibility reflects a willingness to make adjustments as situations change and assures that changes can be made if a particular practice leads to unfavorable outcomes in light of changed situations. Flexibility is particularly important for long-term relationships (Dahlstrom *et al.*, 1996). The ability to modify relational exchanges and willingness to adapt to market forces promote that relationship's capability to capture opportunities as they emerge. Relationship management change proves the turning of relationship management knowledge into practice. It captures the outcomes of "the output of adaptive and generative learning, verifying both the dissemination of new relationship management knowledge and the resulting action" (Jarratt, 2004, p. 303).

KEY TAKEAWAYS

- The six-markets framework of relationship marketing (Peck *et al.*, 1999 and revised by Payne *et al.*, 2005) is by far the most comprehensive in terms of stakeholder representation. These markets include customer markets at the core, and supplier/alliance markets, internal markets, referral markets, influence markets, and recruitment markets.

- The stakeholder framework of relationship marketing (Malhotra and Agarwal, 2002) reconfigures the structure of the six-markets framework by differentiating B2B markets from B2C markets, including competitor markets, combining internal and recruitment markets, subsuming referral markets under customer/internal markets, and providing added emphasis on strategic alliances to all constituent markets.

The new structure of the six-markets model consists of customer markets (channels), customer markets (end users), supplier markets, competitors markets, internal markets, and external influence markets.

- In relationship with customers (*channel intermediaries*), firms explore opportunities for value networks relationships that provide co-development of products, integration of information infrastructures, and coordination of the flow of products/services. In relationship with customers (*end user*), firms design RM programs for maximizing customer retention, customer value, and customer engagement, which in turn maximizes marketing efficiency and effectiveness. In relationship with *competitors*, firms enter into interfirm cooperation in different facets of the value chain (e.g., R&D, new products, technology development, distribution) to leverage resources, assets, and skills for expected benefits and potential pay-off.

- In relationship with *suppliers*, firms seek cost advantage and/or value advantage (e.g., supplier-led innovation, supplier development program) in specific parts of the value chain by entering into strategic alliances with them with the net benefit of value co-creation for both partners. In relationship with *internal markets*, firms seek the development of a customer-oriented service culture within the organization with the underlying premise that satisfied employees are more satisfied/productive leading to greater customer satisfaction. An organization-wide strategy must consider leadership, culture, structure, and control to effectively execute internal relationship marketing. In relationship with *external influence markets*, firms develop meaningful relationships with governments and regulatory agencies, financial markets, not-for-profits, environmental agencies, and importantly investors.

- Functional level of RM programs focuses on the economic content of the B2B relationship and is managed by marketing-mix variables including product, price, and place (channel) strategies. TCE/S-D logic/CLV helps explain buyer–seller concept of value co-creation. Structural level builds structural bonds focusing on information system integration and operational efficiency at the business unit level. Institutional theory/RBV theory helps explain why structural-level RM programs may lose its competitive advantage. Strategic level reflects interfirm relationship networks to create firm value by way of strategic alliances (i.e., sharing of complementary skills, knowledge, and resources). TCE/RBV helps explain why (and how) firms achieve their strategic goals of value co-creation.

- Strategic alliances are cooperative interfirm arrangements, which can be equity-based or nonequity-based, wherein partners commit to sharing their unique skills and resources toward achieving their strategic objectives. Three types of alliance-based capabilities are important in the formation of alliances: (a) alliance scanning, (b) alliance coordination, and (c) alliance coordination.

- Relationship value and switching cost are distinct dimensions of dependence. Resource specificity forces the supplier to realize the planned transactions so that the investment can be amortized. At the same time, it also creates dependency based on the goodwill of the buyer. To the extent one party has greater dependency relative to the other, it creates the condition for opportunism. Interdependence is the fundamental basis of solidarity and mutuality among channel members.

- In buyer–seller relationship, both buyer satisfaction and seller satisfaction are important antecedents of relationship continuity. Communication, commitment, and conflict handling are antecedents

of *buyer satisfaction*, while business-related factors (e.g., profitability, supplier involvement) and communication-related factors (e.g., roles and responsibilities, feedback, values) are antecedents of *supplier satisfaction*. Supplier satisfaction is essentially at the relationship level, whereas buyer satisfaction could be both at the transactional and relationship levels.

- In buyer–seller relationships, trust is fundamental for creating long-term relationships with channel members. Trust is the willingness to rely on an exchange partner in whom one has confidence in terms of reliability, integrity, honesty, fairness, responsibility, helpfulness, and benevolence. Trust is developed through five mechanisms: calculative, prediction, capability, intentionality, and transference processes. It is a major determinant of commitment.

- In buyer–seller relationships, commitment refers to the belief and an enduring desire that an ongoing relationship is so important that it warrants maximum efforts to maintain it. Commitment can emerge by mechanisms such as pledges, relational norms, and social bonding. Social bond consists of four dimensions: relationship length, emotional intensity, mutual confiding, and reciprocal service.

- There are five major antecedents of buyer–seller dependence, trust, and relationship commitment in channel relationships: (a) relationship termination/switching costs; (b) relationship benefits/relationship value; (c) shared values/norms; (d) formal/informal communication; and (e) opportunistic behaviors aroused by behavioral factors and facilitated by structural factors.

- Today, control in channel relationships is characterized by normative and contractual control instead of authoritative control. Coercive influence strategies in authoritative control arise due to resource imbalance and asymmetry in power and therefore dependence.

- Based on S-D logic, sellers deliver value to buyers by applying operant resources such as skills and knowledge to operand resources. Core operand resources fulfill basic customer expectations with respect to functional/technical products and service, whereas augmented operand resources exceed customer expectation such as installation, training, and support services. Core operant resources are instrumental service such as technical mastery and interpersonal service, whereas augmented operant resources encompass the seller's understanding of buyer's ability to realize maximum value, i.e., value mindset.

- In upstream relationships, there are four reasons to bind a manufacturer to suppliers. These are: (1) buyer receives better service and higher procurement efficiency with reduced costs; (2) greater effectiveness in implementing marketing strategies such as quality platforms, customer service, and information exchange; (3) new technologies have modernized the procurement methods, customized offerings, and information exchange; and (4) centralized strategic function in hyper-competitive global markets. Outcomes include uncertainty reduction, cost control, exclusive relationships, outsourcing options, supplier-led innovation; however, opportunism and erosion of trust can also result.

- In downstream relationships, the relationship has shifted away from the vertical marketing system (i.e., authoritative control and centralized planning) toward channel relational system (i.e., contractual and normative control and shared planning). There are cost savings, value-added benefits, interdependence, greater marketing efficiency, and better value cocreation and financial performance. Calculative and loyalty commitment binds the manufacturer to distributors and retailers in downstream relationships.

- A relationship management capability involves three sets of capabilities: relationship infrastructure capability (i.e., processes, routines, and infrastructure that enhance relationship experiences and learning), relationship learning capability (i.e., adaptive and generative learning mechanisms), and relationship behavioral capability (i.e., collaborative culture, relationship flexibility, and relationship management change).

EXERCISES

Questions

1. Discuss the efficacy of the stakeholder framework of relationship marketing by Malhotra and Agarwal (2002). Does the model better reflect the marketing orientation of firms and the current shifts in relationship marketing paradigm? What changes to the stakeholder framework would you recommend in light of the growth in digital and social media technologies?

2. Discuss the three levels of relationship marketing programs: functional level, structural level, and strategic level. Explain how each level of RM programs provides benefits and competitive advantage for the focal firm? Comment on the following statement: "While stronger than functional level (Level 1), firms implementing structural relationships (Level 2) can lose its' competitive advantage quickly in a dynamic market environment."

3. What are strategic alliances and why do firms enter into such alliances? Explain the different types of strategic alliances? Explain each of the following: (a) alliance scanning, (b) alliance coordination, and (c) alliance learning. Do alliances built on trust result in better firm performance? Why?

4. Explain the social psychological mechanism underlying dependence and interdependence in buyer–seller channel relationships? Explain (giving real-life examples) how the following buyer–seller relationships work: (a) attractive and independent relationship; (b) attractive and dependent relationship; and (c) unattractive and dependent relationship; and (d) unattractive and independent relationship.

5. Discuss the roles of buyer–seller trust and commitment in channel relationships? What are the antecedents of trust and commitment? Explain the various trust building mechanisms (e.g., calculative, prediction, capability, intentionality, and transference processes) and the importance of each during the lifecycle stages of the partnership.

6. Explain the similarities and differences between contractual control and normative control mechanisms in B2B channel relationships? When can legal contracts transform into psychological contracts in channel relationships? Explain the out-of-contract alternatives for resolving contractual breaches when legal enforcement is not a viable option?

7. Explain the S-D logic of operand/operant resources in buyer–seller relationships and how can sellers adopt a value mindset that allows the buyer to realize maximum value? Explain the following ways value is derived and measured in buyer–seller relationships: (a) operational performance-based values; (b) integration-based values; (c) supplier's capability-based values; and (d) buyer financial-based values.

8. What are the reasons for a firm to engage in relationships with its suppliers? What are the potential outcomes of buyer–supplier relationships?

9. What are the reasons for a firm to engage in relationships with its distributors and retailers? What are the potential outcomes of manufacturer–distributor relationships? Explain calculative commitment and loyalty commitment in downstream relationships?

10. Explain the relationship management framework? Explain how each component, i.e., infrastructure capability, learning capability, and behavioral capability, singly and jointly, contributes to the effective implementation of the relationship management function?

Group Discussion

1. In the software industry, IT implementation projects are quite unpredictable and subject to frequent failure. Yet, global IT expenditures continue to grow exceeding $ 3.75 trillion in 2014 and forecasted to grow to about $3.92 trillion by 2020 (Gordon and Lovelock, 2014; Gartner, 2019). Services and support costs significantly outweigh the software product cost component, typically less than 10% of the total cost of ownership. Traditionally, IT companies have augmented their core product by (a) expanding into and differentiating their service scope to surpass expectations of buyers (i.e., service scope) through expansion of systems installation, systems integration, and training services; and/or (b) investing in knowledge development of the technical product or domain or service-delivery skills (i.e., instrumental/interpersonal service), typically done through staff technical training and/or service improvement initiatives.

As a small group, discuss the benefits and limitations of IT firms focusing on expanding the core product to service scope and/or instrumental/interpersonal service. Simply offering more services does little to enhance buyer–seller "relationship satisfaction" as competitive parity soon sets in negating any competitive advantage enjoyed. How can IT firms adopt a "value mindset" — i.e., develop augmented operant resources that reflect a seller's ability to see value-creation opportunities from the buyer's perspective — that is more difficult to imitate? Does it make sense for IT firms to allocate more resources on implementing "value mindset" initiatives and form third-party alliances for service delivery (i.e., service scope and instrumental/interpersonal service)?

2. Walmart has been traditionally known to exert aggressive bargaining power with its suppliers. However, Walmart is not locked in with one supplier and neither are suppliers locked-in with one buyer. For instance, while P&G has engaged in a long-standing partnership with Walmart, this relationship has not developed to the point where Walmart only offers P&G products or that P&G only sells its products through Walmart. At the same, there is a blurring of time, place, and transaction boundaries between producers and distributors. For instance, P&G assigns its employees to live and work at Walmart's headquarters to enhance the speed of delivery and reduce the cost of supplying P&G goods to Walmart stores. Further, the electronic data interchange (EDI) system binds the two companies at the structural level.

As a small group, discuss the concepts of dependence and interdependence as it applies to Walmart and P&G and how each company strategically exerts influence on the other. In your opinion, should there be power asymmetry (i.e. dependence) or power symmetry (i.e., interdependence) between channel partners and why? How is relationship satisfaction for P&G different from that for Walmart? What type of trust mechanism (i.e., calculative, predictive, capability, intentionality, and transference) predominantly characterizes the channel relationship between

P&G and Walmart and why? What type of control mechanism (i.e., authoritative, contractual, and normative) predominantly characterizes the channel relationship between P&G and Walmart and why?

HBS and Ivey Cases

AnswerDash (9-516-106)

Laurs & Bridz (9B18A004)

CASE QUESTIONS

AnswerDash

1. What changes to the Malhotra and Agarwal (2002) stakeholder framework would you recommend for AnswerDash in light of the growth in digital and social media technologies?

2. Explain, in the context of AnswerDash, how the following buyer–seller relationships work: (a) attractive and independent relationship; (b) attractive and dependent relationship; and (c) unattractive and dependent relationship; and (d) unattractive and independent relationship.

3. Explain the S-D logic of operand/operant resources in buyer–seller relationships and how can AnswerDash adopt a value mindset that allows its buyer to realize maximum value.

4. Apply the relationship management capability framework to AnswerDash. Explain how each component, i.e., infrastructure capability, learning capability, and behavioral capability, singly and jointly, contributes to the effective implementation of the relationship management function.

5. Discuss the benefits and limitations of this firm focusing on expanding the core product to service scope and/or instrumental/interpersonal service. How can AnswerDash adopt a "value mindset" —

i.e., develop augmented operant resources that reflect a seller's ability to see value-creation opportunities from the buyer's perspective — that is more difficult to imitate?

Laurs & Bridz

1. Explain how each level of RM programs, functional level, structural level, and strategic level, provides benefits and competitive advantage for Laurs & Bridz.

2. Explain the various trust building mechanisms (e.g., calculative, prediction, capability, intentionality, and transference processes) and the importance to Laurs & Bridz of each during the lifecycle stages of the partnership.

3. Explain the S-D logic of operand/operant resources in buyer–seller relationships and how can Laurs & Bridz adopt a value mindset that allows its buyer to realize maximum value.

4. What are the reasons for Laurs & Bridz to engage in relationships with its suppliers? What are the potential outcomes of buyer–supplier relationships?

5. What are the reasons for Laurs & Bridz to engage in relationships with its downstream partners? What are the potential outcomes of manufacturer–distributor relationships? Explain calculative commitment and loyalty commitment in downstream relationships?

6. Apply the relationship management capability framework to Laurs & Bridz. Explain how each component, i.e., infrastructure capability, learning capability, and behavioral capability, singly and jointly, contributes to the effective implementation of the relationship management function.

7. Discuss the concepts of dependence and interdependence as it applies to Laurs & Bridz and its channel partners and how each company strategically exerts influence on the other. In your opinion, should there be power asymmetry (i.e. dependence) or power symmetry (i.e., interdependence) between channel partners and why? What type of control mechanism (i.e., authoritative, contractual, and normative) predominantly characterizes the channel relationship between Laurs & Bridz and its channel members?

REFERENCES

Abdul-Muhmin, A.G. (2005), Instrumental and Interpersonal Determinants of Relationship Satisfaction and Commitment in Industrial Markets, *Journal of Business Research* 58(5): 619–628.

Anderson, E. and B. Weitz (1992), The Use of Pledges to Build and Sustain Commitment in Distribution Channels, *Journal of Marketing Research* 29(1), 18–34.

Anderson, J.C. (1995), Relationships in Business Markets: Exchange Episodes, Value Creation, and their Empirical Assessment [Special issue], *Journal of the Academy of Marketing Science* 23(4): 346–350.

Arya, B. and J.E. Salk (2006), Cross-Sector Alliance Learning and Effectiveness of Voluntary Codes of Corporate Social Responsibility, *Business Ethics Quarterly* 16(2): 211–34.

Augier, M. and Teece, D.J. (2009), Dynamic Capabilities and the Role of Managers in Business Strategy and Economic Performance, *Organization Science*, 20(2): 410–421.

Balabanis, G. and A. Diamantopoulos (2004), Domestic Country Bias, Country-of-Origin Effects, and Consumer Ethnocentrism: A Multidimensional Unfolding Approach, *Journal of the Academy of Marketing Science* 32(1): 80–95.

Barney, J. (1991), Firm Resources and Sustained Competitive Advantage, *Journal of Management* 17(1): 99–120.

Bayraktar, A. (2013), When Is the Country-of-Origin of a Brand a Weakness in Global Markets? *International Journal of Management Research and Review* 3(8): 3199–210.

Benton, W.C. and M. Maloni (2005), The Influence of Power Driven Buyer/Seller Relationships on Supply Chain Satisfaction, *Journal of Operations Management* 23(1): 1–22.

Bergen, M., J.B. Heidi, and S. Dutta (1998), Managing Gray Markets through Tolerance of Violations: A Transaction Cost Perspective, *Managerial and Decision Economics* 19(3): 157–165.

Berry, L.L. (1995), Relationship Marketing of Services– Growing Interest, Emerging Perspectives [Special Issue], *Journal of the Academy of Marketing Science* 23(4): 236–245.

Berry, L.L. and A. Parasuraman (1991), *Marketing Services–Competing Through Quality*. New York, NY: Free Press.

Bloom, P.N., S. Hoeffler, K.L. Keller, and C.E. B. Meza (2006), How Social-Cause Marketing Affects Consumer Perceptions, *MIT Sloan Management Review* Winter: 49–55.

Bolton, Ruth N., Amy K. Smith, and Janet Wagner (2003), Striking the Right Balance Designing Service to Enhance Business-to-Business Relationships, *Journal of Service Research,* 5(4), 271–291.

Bruyaka, O., D. Philippe, and X. Castaner (2018), Run Away or Stick Together? The Impact of Organization-Specific Adverse Events on Alliance Partner Defection, *Academy of Management Review* 43(3): 445–469.

Campbell, A. (1997), Stakeholders: The Case in Favor, *Long Range Planning* 30(3): 446–449.

Carr, A.S. and L.R. Smeltzer (2002), The Relationship between Information Technology Use and Buyer-Supplier Relationships: An Exploratory Analysis of the Buying Firm's Perspective, *IEEE Transactions on Engineering Management,* 49(3): 293–304.

Christopher, M., A. Payne, and D. Ballantyne (2002), *Relationship Marketing: Creating Stakeholder Value.* Oxford: Butterworth-Heinemann.

Corsaro, D., C. Ramos, S.C. Henneberg, and P. Naudé (2012), The Impact of Network Configurations on Value Constellations in Business Markets– The Case of an Innovation Network, *Industrial Marketing Management* 41(1): 54–67.

Dahlstrom, R., K.M. McNeilly, and T.W. Speh (1996), Buyer-Seller Relationships in the Procurement of Logistical Services, *Journal of the Academy of Marketing Science* 24(2): 110–124.

Daugherty, P.J., R.G. Richey, A.S. Roath, S. Min, H. Chen, A.D. Arndt, and S.E. Genchev (2006), Is Collaboration Paying Off for Firms?, *Business Horizons* 49(1): 61–70.

Day, G.S. and R. Wensley (1988), Assessing Advantage: A Framework for Diagnosing Competitive Superiority, *Journal of Marketing* 52(April): 1–20.

DeLeon, A.J. and S.C. Chatterjee (2017), B2B Relationship Calculus: Quantifying Resource Effects in Service-Dominant Logic, *Journal of the Academy of Marketing Science* 45: 402–427.

Deshpande, R. and F. Webster (1992), Organizational Culture and Marketing: Defining the Research Agenda, *Journal of Marketing* 53(January): 3–15.

DiMaggio, P. and Powell, D. (1983), The Iron Cage Revisited: Institutional Isomorphism and Collective Rationality in Organizational Fields. *American Sociological Review* 48: 147–160.

Doney, P.M. and J.P. Cannon (1997), An Examination of the Nature of Trust in Buyer-Seller Relationships, *Journal of Marketing* 61(2): 35–51.

Doyle, P. (1995), Marketing in the New Millennium. *European Journal of Marketing* 29(13): 23–41.

Doz, Y.L. and G. Hamel (1998), *Alliance Advantage: The Art of Creating Value through Partnering.* Boston, MA: Harvard Business School Press.

Ehret, M. (2004), Managing the Trade-off between Relationships and Value Networks. Towards a Value-Based Approach of Customer Relationship Management in Business-to-Business Markets, *Industrial Marketing Management*, 33(6): 465–473.

Eisenhardt, K.M. and J.A. Martin (2000), Dynamic Capabilities: What Are They? *Strategic Management Journal* 21: 1105–1121.

Essig, M. and M. Amann (2009), Supplier Satisfaction: Conceptual Basics and Explorative Findings, *Journal of Purchasing and Supply Management* 15(2): 103–113.

Flynn B.B., B. Huo, and X. Zhao, The Impact of Supply Chain Integration on Performance: A Contingency and Configuration Approach, *Journal of Operations Management* 2010; 28: 58–71.

Foss, N.J. and T. Saebi (2018), Business Models and Business Model Innovation: Between Wicked and Paradigmatic Problems, *Long Range Planning* 51: 9–21.

Frazier, G.L. and K.D. Antia (1995), Exchange Relationships and Interfirm Power in Channels of Distribution [Special issue], *Journal of the Academy of Marketing Science*, 23(4): 321–326.

Gadde, L.E. and I. Snehota (2000), Making the Most of Supplier Relationships, *Industrial Marketing Management* 29: 305–316.

Ganesan, S. (1994), Determinants of Long-Term Orientation in Buyer-Seller Relationships, *Journal of Marketing* 58(2): 1–19.

Gartner (2019), Gartner Says Global IT Spending to Grow 1.1 Percent in 2019, http://www.gartner.com/en/newsroom/press-release/2019-04-17-gartner-says-global-it-spending-to-grow-1-1-percent-i

Gilliland, D.I. and D.C. Bello (2002), Two Sides to Attitudinal Commitment: The Effect of Calculative and Loyalty Commitment on Enforcement Mechanisms in Distribution Channels, *Journal of the Academy of marketing Science* 30(1): 24–43.

Goerzen, A. (2007), Alliance Network and Firm Performance: The Impact of Repeated Partnerships, *Strategic Management Journal* 28: 487–509.

Goerzen, A. and P.W. Beamish (2005), The Effect of Alliance Network Diversity on Multinational Enterprise Performance, *Strategic Management Journal* 26: 333–354.

Goffin, K., F. Lemke, and M. Szwejczewski (2006), An Exploratory Study of 'Close' Supplier-Manufacturer Relationships, *Journal of Operations Management* 24: 189–209.

Gordon, R. and J. Lovelock (2014), Global IT Spending on Pace to Grow 2.1 Percent in 2014, *Forbes*, http://www.forbes.com/sites/gartnergroup/2014/07/02/global-it-spending-on-pace-to-grow-2-1-percent-in-2014/

Gounaris, S.P. (2005), Trust and Commitment Influences on Customer Retention: Insights from Business-to-Business Services, *Journal of Business Research* 58(2): 126–140.

Grewal, Rajdeep and Gary L. Lilien (2012), Business-to-Business Marketing: Looking Back, Looking Forward, in G.L. Lilien and R. Grewal (Eds.), *Handbook of Business to Business Marketing* (pp. 1–14). Edward Elgar Press.

Gummesson, E. (1999), *Total Relationship Marketing*. Oxford: Butterworth-Heinemann.

Gundlach, G.T., R.S. Achrol, and J.T. Mentzer (1995), The Structure of Commitment in Exchange, *Journal of Marketing* 59(1): 78–92.

Heide, J.B. and G. John (1992), Do Norms Matter in Marketing Relationships? *Journal of Marketing* 56(2): 32–44.

Helfat, C.E., S. Finkelstein, W. Mitchell, M.A. Peteraf, H. Singh, D.J. Teece, et al. (2007), *Dynamic Capabilities: Understanding Strategic Change in Organizations*. Malden, MA: Blackwell.

Hennig-Thurau, T. and U. Hansen (2000), Relationship Marketing–Some Reflections on the State-of-the-

Art of the Relational Concept, in T. Hennig-Thurau and U. Hansen (Eds.), *Relationship Marketing: Gaining Competitive Advantage through Customer Satisfaction and Customer Retention.* Berlin: Springer-Verlag.

Heskett, J.L., T.O. Jones, G.W. Loveman, W. Earl Sasser Jr., and L.A. Schlesinger (1994), Putting the Service-Profit Chain to Work, *Harvard Business Review* 72(2): 164–174.

Hogreve, Jens, Anja Iseke, Klaus Derfuss, and Tonnjes, Eller (2017), The Service-Profit Chain: A Meta-Analytic Test of a Comprehensive Theoretical Framework, *Journal of Marketing* 81: 41–61.

Homburg, C. (1998), On Closeness to the Customer in Industrial Markets, *Journal of Business to Business Marketing* 4(4): 35–72.

Homburg, C., W.D. Hoyer, and M. Fassnacht (2002), Service Orientation of a Retailer's Business Strategy: Dimensions, Antecedents, and Performance Outcomes, *Journal of Marketing* 66(4): 86–101.

Hunt, S.D. (1999), The Strategic Imperative and Sustainable Competitive Advantage: Public Policy Implications of Resource Advantage Theory, *Journal of the Academy of Marketing Science* 27(2): 144–159.

Hunt, S.D. and R.M. Morgan (1994), Organizational Commitment: One of Many Commitments or Key Mediating Construct? *Academy of Management Journal* 37(6): 1568–1587.

Hunt, S.D. and R.M. Morgan (1996), The Resource-Advantage Theory of Competition: Dynamics, Path Dependencies, and Evolutionary Dimensions, *Journal of Marketing* 60(October): 107–114.

Inkpen, A.C. (1998), Learning and Knowledge Acquisition through International Strategic Alliances, *Academy of Management Executive* 12(4): 69–80.

Jansen, J.J.P., F.A.J. van den Bosch, and H.W. Volberda (2005), Managing Potential and Realized Absorptive Capacity: How Do Organizational Antecedents Matter, *Academy of Management Journal* 48(6): 999–1015.

Jap, S.D. and S. Ganesan (2000), Control Mechanisms and the Relationship Life Cycle: Implications for Safeguarding Specific Investments and Developing Commitment, *Journal of Marketing Research* 37(2): 227–245.

Jarratt, D. (2004), Conceptualizing a Relationship Management Capability, *Marketing Theory* 4(4): 287–309.

John, G. (1984), An Empirical Investigation of Some Antecedents of Opportunism in a Marketing Channel. *Journal of Marketing Research* 21: 278–289.

Johnson, J.S. and R.S. Sohi (2016), Understanding and Resolving Major Contractual Breaches in Buyer-Seller Relationships: A Grounded Theory Approach, *Journal of the Academy of Marketing Science* 44: 185–205.

Johnston, W.J., A.N.H. Le, and J. M-S. Cheng (2018), A Meta-Analytic Review of Influence Strategies in Marketing Channel Relationships, *Journal of the Academy of Marketing Science* 46: 674–702.

Joshi, A.W (2009), Continuous Supplier Performance Improvement: Effects of Collaborative Communication and Control, *Journal of Marketing* 73(1): 133–150.

Kandemir, D., A. Yaprak, and S. Tamer Cavusgil (2006), Alliance Orientation: Conceptualization, Measurement, and Impact on Market Performance, *Journal of the Academy of Marketing Science* 34(3): 324–340.

Kannan, P.K. and Hongshuang "Alice" Li (2017), Digital Marketing: A Framework, Review and Research Agenda, *International Journal of Research in Marketing* 34(1): 22–45.

Klien, S. and J. Zif (1994), Global versus Local Strategic Alliance, *Journal of Global Marketing* 8(1): 51–70.

Kohli, A.K. and B.J. Jaworski (1999), Market Orientation: The Construct, Research Propositions, and Managerial Implications, in R. Deshpande (Ed.), *Developing a Market Orientation* (pp. 7–44). Thousand Oaks, CA: Marketing Science Institute, Sage Publications.

Kostova, T. and S. Zaheer (1999), Organizational Legitimacy under Conditions of Complexity: The Case of the Multinational Enterprise. *Academy of Management Review* 24: 64–81.

Kotabe, M., X. Martin, and H. Domoto (2003), Gaining from Vertical Partnerships: Knowledge Transfer, Relationship Duration, and Supplier Performance Improvement in the U.S. and Japanese Automotive Industries, *Strategic Management Journal* 24(4): 293–316.

Kotler, Philip (1992), Total marketing. Business Week Advance, *Executive Brief* 2.

Koza, M.P and A.Y. Lewin (1998), The Co-Evolution of Strategic Alliances, *Organization Science* 9(3): 255–264.

Krause, D.R., T.V. Scannell, and R.J. Calantone (2000), A Structural Analysis of the Effectiveness of Buying Firms' Strategies to Improve Supplier Performance, *Decision Sciences* 31(1): 33–55.

Kumar, N. (2005), The Power of Power in Supplier-Retailer Relationships, *Industrial Marketing Management*, 34(8): 863–866.

Kumar, V., Lerzan Aksoy, Bas Donkers, Rajkumar Venkatesan, Thorsten Wiesel, and Sebastian Tillmanns (2010), Undervalued or Overvalued Customers: Capturing Total Customer Engagement Value, *Journal of Service Research* 13(3): 297–310.

Laursen, K. and A. Salter (2006), Open for Innovation: the Role of Openness in Explaining Innovation Performance among UK Manufacturing Firms. *Strategic Management Journal* 27(2), 131–150.

Lemon, Katherine N. and Peter C. Verhoef (2016), Understanding Customer Experience Throughout the Customer Journey, *Journal of Marketing* 80: 69–96.

Lewin, A.Y., S. Massini, and C. Peeters (2011), Microfoundations of Internal and External Absorptive Capacity Routines, *Organization Science* 22(1): 81–98.

Lieberman, M. and S. Asaba (2006), Why do Firms Imitate Each Other? *Academy of Management Review* 31: 366–385.

Lilien, G.L. (2016), The B2B Knowledge Gap, *International Journal of Research in Marketing* 33: 543–556.

Liu, Y., C. Su, Y. Li, and T. Liu (2010), Managing Opportunism in a Developing Interfirm Relationship: The Interrelationship of Calculative and Loyalty Commitment, *Industrial Marketing Management* 39(5): 844–852.

Macneil, I.R. (1980), *The New Social Contract: An Inquiry into Modern Contractual Relations*. Yale University Press.

Malhotra, N.K. and J. Agarwal (2002), A Stakeholder Perspective on Relationship Marketing: Framework and Propositions, *Journal of Relationship Marketing* 1(2): 3–37.

Malhotra, N.K., J. Agarwal, and F.M. Ulgado (2003), Internationalization and Entry Modes: A Multi-Theoretical Framework and Research Propositions, *Journal of International Marketing* 11(4): 1–31.

Malhotra, N.K., C. Uslay, and A. Bayraktar (2016), *Relationship Marketing Re-Imagined: Marketing's Inevitable Shift Exchanges to Value Cocreating Relationships*. Business Expert Press.

Maunu, S. (2003), *Supplier Satisfaction: The Concept and a Measurement System: A Study to Define the Supplier Satisfaction Elements and Usage as a Management Tool*, Working Paper, University of Oulu.

Mohr, J.J. and S. Sengupta (2002), Managing the Paradox of Inter-Firm Learning: The Role of Governance Mechanisms, *Journal of Business & Industrial Marketing* 17(4): 282–301.

Möller, K.K. and A. Halinen (1999), Business Relationships and Networks: Managerial Challenge of Network Era, *Industrial Marketing Management* 28: 413–427.

Möller, K. and A. Rajala (2007), Rise of Strategic Nets—New Modes of Value Creation, *Industrial Marketing Management* 36(7): 895–908.

Möller, K.E.K. and P. Törrönen (2003), Business Suppliers' Value Creation Potential, *Industrial Marketing Management* 32(2): 109–118.

Morgan, R.M., T.N. Crutchfield, and R. Lacey (2000), Patronage and Loyalty Strategies: Understanding the Behavioral and Attitudinal Outcomes of Customer Retention Programs, in T. Hennig-Thurau and U. Hansen (Eds.), *Relationship Marketing: Gaining Competitive Advantage through Customer Satisfaction and Customer Retention*. Berlin: Springer-Verlag.

Morgan, R.M. and S.D. Hunt (1994), The Commitment-Trust Theory of Relationship Marketing, *Journal of Marketing* 58 (July): 20–38.

Narver, J.C. and S.F. Slater (1999), The Effect of Marketing Orientation on Business Profitability, in R. Deshpande (Ed.), *Developing a Market Orientation* (pp. 45–77). Thousand Oaks, CA: Marketing Science Institute, Sage Publications.

Nevin, J.R. (1995), Relationship Marketing and Distribution Channels: Exploring Fundamental Issues, *Journal of the Academy of Marketing Science* 23(4): 327–334.

Noordewier, T.G., G. John, and J.R. Nevin (1990), Performance Outcomes of Purchasing Arrangements in Industrial Buyer-Vendor Relationships, *Journal of Marketing* 54(4): 80–93.

North, D. (2005), *Understanding the Process of Economic Change*. Princeton, NJ: Princeton University Press.

O'Cass, A. and L.V. Ngo (2012), Creating Superior Customer Value for B2B Firms through Supplier Firm Capabilities, *Industrial Marketing Management* 41(1): 125–135.

Oliver, C. (1990), Determinants of Interorganizational Relationships: Integration and Future Directions, *Academy of Management Review* 15(2): 241–265.

Palmatier, Robert W. (2008), *Relationship Marketing*. Cambridge, MA: Marketing Science Institute.

Palmatier, R.W., R.P. Dant, and D. Grewal (2007), A Comparative Longitudinal Analysis of Theoretical Perspectives of Interorganizational Relationship Performance, *Journal of Marketing* 71(4): 172–194.

Pangarkar, N. and S. Klein (2001), The Impacts of Alliance Purpose and Partner Similarity on Alliance Governance, *British Journal of Management* 12: 341–353.

Parkhe, A. (1999), Building Trust in International Alliances, *Journal of World Business* 33(4): 417–437.

Parvatiyar, A. and J. Sheth (1994), Paradigm Shift in Marketing Theory and Approach: The Emergence of Relationship Marketing, in J. Sheth and A. Parvatiyar (Eds.), *Relationship Marketing: Theory, Methods, and Applications* (Section I, Session 2.1). Atlanta, GA: Center for Relationship Marketing, Emory University.

Paulraj, A. and I.J. Chen (2007), Strategic Buyer-Supplier Relationships, Information Technology and External Logistics Integration, *Journal of Supply Chain Management* 43(2): 2–14.

Payne, A., D. Ballantyne, and C. Martin (2005), A Stakeholder Approach to Relationship Marketing Strategy: The Development and Use of the 'Six Markets' Model, *European Journal of Marketing* 39(7/8): 855–871.

Payne, A. and P. Frow (2013), *Strategic Customer Management: Integrating Relationship Marketing and CRM*. Cambridge University Press.

Peck, H., A. Payne, M. Christopher, and M. Clark (1999), *Relationship Marketing: Strategy and*

Implementation. Oxford, UK: Butterworth-Heinemann.

Peng, T.A., M.-H Yen, and M. Bourne (2018), How Rival Partners Compete Based on Cooperation? *Long Range Planning* 51: 351–383.

Perks, H. and G. Easton (2000), Strategic Alliances: Partner as Customer, *Industrial Marketing Management* 29: 327–338.

Piercy, N. (2010) Improving Marketing-Operations Cross Functional Relationships, *Journal of Strategic Marketing* 18(4): 337–356.

Piercy, N. and N. Morgan (1991), Internal Marketing–The Missing Half of the Marketing Program, *Long Range Planning* 24(2): 82–93.

Porter, M.M. (1980), *Competitive Strategy*. New York, NY: Free Press.

Porter, M.M. (1985), *Competitive Advantage*. New York, NY: Free Press.

Porter, M.M. (1990). *The Competitive Advantage of Nations*. New York, NY: Free Press.

Reichheld, F.F. (1990). *The Loyalty Effect*. Boston, MA: Harvard Business School Press.

Rindfleisch, A. and C. Moorman (2001), The Acquisition and Utilization of Information in New Product Alliances: A Strength-of-Ties Perspective, *Journal of Marketing* 65: 1–18.

Ritala, Paavo (2012), Coopetition Strategy – When is it Successful? Empirical Evidence on Innovation and Market Performance, *British Journal of Management*, 23: 307–324.

Ritter, T., I.F. Wilkinson, and W.J. Johnston (2004), Managing in Complex Business Networks, *Industrial Marketing Management* 333: 175–183.

Rodríguez, C.M. and D.T. Wilson (2002), Relationship Bonding and Trust as a Foundation for Commitment in U.S.-Mexican Strategic Alliances: A Structural Equation Modeling Approach, *Journal of International Marketing* 10(4): 53–76.

Samaha, S. and R.W. Palmatier (2015), Anti-Relationship Marketing: Understanding Relationship Destroying Behaviors, in R.M. Morgan, J.T Parish, and G.D. Deitz (Eds.), *Handbook of Relationship Marketing* (pp. 268–300). London: Edward Elgar.

Sanzo, M.J., M.L. Santos, R. Vázquez, and L.I. Álvarez (2003), The Effect of Market Orientation on Buyer-Seller Relationship Satisfaction, *Industrial Marketing Management* 32(4): 327–345.

Sarkar, M.B., P.S. Aulakh, and S.T. Cavusgil (1998), The Strategic Role of Relational Bonding in Interorganizational Collaborations, *Journal of International Management* 4(2): 85–107.

Scheer, L.K., C.F. Miao, and R.W. Palmatier (2015), Dependence and Interdependence in Marketing Relationships: Meta-Analytic Insights, *Journal of the Academy of Marketing Science* 43: 694–712.

Schilke, O. and A. Goerzen (2010), Alliance Management Capability: An Investigation of the Construct and Its Measurement, *Journal of Management* 36(5): 1192–1219.

Schlesinger, L.A. and J.L. Heskett (1991), Breaking the Cycle of Failure in Services, *Sloan Management Review* (Spring): 17–28.

Schneider, B., J.J. Parkington, and V.M. Buxton (1980), Employee and Customer Perceptions of Service in Banks, *Administrative Science Quarterly* 25: 252–267.

Selnes, F. (1998), Antecedents and Consequences of Trust and Satisfaction in Buyer-Seller Relationships, *European Journal of Marketing* 32(3/4): 305–322.

Selnes, F. and J. Sallis (2003), Promoting Relationship Learning, *Journal of Marketing* 67(3): 80–95.

Sengupta, S. and M. Perry (1997), Some Antecedents of Global Strategic Alliance Formation, *Journal of International Marketing* 5(1): 31–50.

Sharma, P. (2011), Country of Origin Effects in Developed and Emerging Markets: Exploring the Contrasting Roles of Materialism and Value Consciousness, *Journal of International Business Studies* 42(2): 285–306.

Sheth, Jagdish N. and Atul Parvatiyar (1995a), Relationship Marketing in Consumer Markets: Antecedents and Consequences, *Journal of the Academy of Marketing Science* 23(4): 255–271.

Sheth, J.N. and A. Parvatiyar (1995b), The Evolution of Relationship Marketing, *International Business Review* 4(4): 397–418.

Sheth, Jagdish N. and Atul Parvatiyar (2000), The Evolution of Relationship Marketing, in Jagdish N. Sheth and Atul Parvatiyar (Eds.), *Handbook of Relationship Marketing* (pp. 119–145). Sage Publication.

Sheth, J.N. and A. Sharma (1997), Supplier Relationships: Emerging Issues and Challenges, *Industrial Marketing Management* 26: 91–100.

Sheth, J.N., R.S. Sisodia, and A. Sharma (2000). The Antecedents and Consequences of Customer-Centric Marketing, *Journal of the Academy of Marketing Science* 28(1): 55–66.

Shrader, R.C. (2001), Collaboration and Performance in Foreign Markets: The Case of Young High-Technology Manufacturing Firms, *Academy of Management Journal* 44(1): 45–60.

Silva, S.C., F. Bradley, and C.M.P. Sousa (2012), Empirical Test of the Trust–Performance Link in an International Alliances Context, *International Business Review* 21(2): 293–306.

Slater, S.F. and J.C. Narver (1995), Market Orientation and the Learning Organization, *Journal of Marketing* 59(3): 63–74.

Slater, S.F. and J.C. Narver (2000), The Positive Effect of a Market Orientation on Business Profitability: A Balanced Replication, *Journal of Business Research* 48(1): 69–73.

Sollner, A. (1999), Asymmetrical Commitment in Business Relationships, *Journal of Business Research* 46(3): 219–233.

Srivastava, R.K., T.A. Shervani, and L. Fahey (1999), Marketing, Business Processes, and Shareholder Value: An Organizationally Embedded View of Marketing Activities and the Discipline of Marketing. *Journal of Marketing* 63(Special Issue): 168–179.

Stanko, M.A., J.M. Bonner, and R.J. Calantone (2007), Building Commitment in Buyer-Seller Relationships: A Tie Strength Perspective, *Industrial Marketing Management* 36(8): 1094–1103.

Stock J., S. Boyer, and T. Harmon (2010), Research Opportunities in Supply Chain Management, *Journal of the Academy of Marketing Science* 38: 32–41.

Szymanski, D.M. and D.H. Henard (2001), Customer Satisfaction: A Meta-Analysis of the Empirical Evidence, *Journal of the Academy of Marketing Science* 29(1): 16–35.

Teece, D.J. (2007), Explicating Dynamic Capabilities: The Nature and Microfoundations of (sustainable) Enterprise Performance, *Strategic Management Journal* 28(13): 1319–1350.

Teece, D.J., G. Pisano, and A. Shuen (1997), Dynamic Capabilities and Strategic Management, *Strategic Management Journal* 18, 509–533.

Terawatanavong, C., G.J. Whitwell, and R.E. Widing (2007), Buyer Satisfaction with Relational Exchange across the Relationship Lifecycle, *European Journal of Marketing* 41(7/8): 915–938.

Terpend, R., B. Beverly, D.R. Krause, and R.B. Handfield (2008), Buyer-Supplier Relationships: Derived Value over Two Decades, *Journal of Supply Chain Management* 44(2): 28–55.

Thibaut, J. and H.H. Kelley (1959), *The Social Psychology of Groups*. New York, NY: Wiley.

Tuominen, K.M. (1990), Investor Relationship Marketing–A Theoretical Framework and Empirical Evidence. Paper presented at *26th EMAC Conference*, Warwick Business School.

Turk, T.A. and C.E. Ybarra (2011), Commitment to High-Tech Strategic Alliances: A Comparison of Direct-Competitor and Non-Competitor Alliances. *Strategic Management Review* 5(1): 1–21.

Ulaga, W. and A. Eggert (2006), Value-Based Differentiation in Business Relationships: Gaining and Sustaining Key supplier Status, *Journal of Marketing* 70(1): 119–136.

Van Doorn, Jenny, Katherine N. Lemon, Vikas Mittal, Stephan Nass, Doreen Pick, Peter Pirner, and Peter C. Verhoef (2010), Customer Engagement Behavior: Theoretical Foundations and Research Directions, *Journal of Service Research* 13(3): 253–266.

Vanhamme, J., A. Lindgreen, J. Reast and N. van Popering (2012), To Do Well by Doing Good: Improving Corporate Image Through Cause-Related Marketing, *Journal of Business Ethics* 109: 259–274.

Varadarajan, R.P. and M.H. Cunningham (1995), Strategic Alliances: A Synthesis of Conceptual Foundations [Special Issue], *Journal of the Academy of Marketing Science* 23(4): 282–296.

Varadarajan, R.P. and A. Menon (1988), Cause-Related Marketing: A Co-alignment of Marketing Strategy and Corporate Philanthropy, *Journal of Marketing* 52(July): 58–74.

Vargo, Stephen L. and Robert F. Lusch (2004), Evolving to a New Dominant Logic for Marketing, *Journal of Marketing* 68(1): 1–17.

Webster, F.E. (1978), Is Industrial Marketing Coming Off Age?, in G. Zaltman and T. Bonoma (Eds.), *Review of Marketing* (pp. 138–159). Chicago: American Marketing Association.

Weitz, B.A. and S.D. Jap (1995), Relationship Marketing and Distribution Channels, *Journal of the Academy of Marketing Science* 23(4): 305–320.

Williamson, O.E. (1985), *The Economic Institutions of Capitalism*. New York, NY: Free Press.

Williamson, O.E. (1989), Transaction Cost Economics, in R. Schmalensee and R.D. Willig (Eds.), *Handbook of Industrial Organization* (pp. 135–182). Oxford, UK: North-Holland.

Wilson, D.T. (1995), An Integrated Model of Buyer-Seller Relationships [Special Issue], *Journal of the Academy of Marketing Science* 23(4): 335–245.

Windahl, C. and N. Lakemond (2006), Developing Integrated Solutions: The Importance of Relationships within the Network, *Industrial Marketing Management* 35(7): 806–818.

Wong, A. (2000), Integrating Supplier Satisfaction with Customer Satisfaction, *Total Quality Management* 11(4–6): 427–432.

Yadav, M.S., K. de Valck, T. Hennig-Thurau, D.L. Hoffman, and M. Spann (2013), Social Commerce: A Contingency Framework for Assessing Marketing Potential, *Journal of Interactive Marketing* 27: 311–323.

Zhang, J.Z., G.F. Watson, and R.W. Palmatier (2018), Customer Relationships Evolve: So Must Your CRM Strategy, *MIT Sloan Management Review* (Summer): 1–4.

04

Building Business-to-Customer (B2C) Relationships: Purchase and Non-Purchase Behavior

OVERVIEW

In Chapter 4, first we discuss how firms build and sustain customer relationships by stimulating customer *purchase behavior* via loyalty programs. Loyalty programs often tap into multiple psychological and social processes simultaneously. Here we discuss four motivational mechanisms including (1) instrumental benefits, (2) symbolic benefits, (3) emotional benefits, and (4) cognitive benefits. Next we discuss how firms build and sustain customer relationships by stimulating customer *non-purchase behavior* via engagement strategies. Specifically, we discuss the concept of customer engagement (CE), provide a framework of customer engagement, and then discuss customer engagement behaviors (CEBs). Similar to purchase behavior, non-purchase engagement behaviors are also motivated by several underlying psychological mechanisms including relationship-based motivation, identification-based motivation, justice-based motivation, goal-based motivation, and control-based motivation. Finally, we discuss how customers engage in customizing firm level marketing-mix strategies. At the end of this chapter, we provide key takeaways and conclude with discussion questions and HBS and Ivey cases. But first, to give a flavor of customer relationship marketing (CRM) purchase and non-purchase-related initiatives, we provide some real-life vignettes.

OPENING VIGNETTES

Vignette 1: Hertz Car Rental offers three levels of loyalty rewards: (1) Gold Plus rewards, (2) Five Star, and (3) President's Circle. Gold Plus offers special offers, free additional driver, and discounts on children's seats. Five Star or President's Circle offers upgrade to next car category, 10% bonus points, and 900 bonus points after every 10th rental. President's Circle offers the guarantee of car availability or free upgrade and 25% bonus points. These multi-level loyalty programs are designed to reward customers differentially who become members (see Figure 4.1).

Figure 4.1: Hertz uses multi-tier loyalty programs in an effort to retain customers.

Vignette 2: Dove launched the "Speak Beautiful" engagement initiative on Twitter in 2015, targeting digitally savvy and socially conscious people to contribute to its marketing communication campaign. Existing and potential customers were encouraged to tweet positive body image thoughts about themselves and their friends that tapped into their creativity. Dove provided engaged participants with the hashtag #SpeakBeautiful to leverage their existing social networks and expand the initiative's reach. There were 5.9 million related tweets of which 411,000 mentioned the Dove brand name increasing the brand sentiment by 17%. Subsequently, the #SpeakBeautiful initiative was expanded to #SpeakBeautifulEffects that enabled participants to re-tweet posts from the brands social media page.

Vignette 3: Whirlpool launched the "Every Day Care Project" to connect customers with a view to contribute to the brand's acquisition, expansion, and retention efforts. Several hashtags, such as #EveryDayCare, #CareCrowd, and #ItsAllCare, were provided by Whirlpool for customers to leverage the infrastructure so that they could share in social media how they use the product and how their families care. This initiative resulted in 44,000 pieces of authentic participant-generated content, which led to 120 million social media impressions. Whirlpool's Twitter followers increased by 31%, online brand sentiment increased six-fold, and purchase intention and sales in the following six months increased by 10% and 6.6%, respectively. Further, Whirlpool leveraged their knowledge and creativity to enhance marketing communication and product innovation.

Figure 4.2: Sprite has targeted individuals with high network reach and strong persuasion capital to become a global brand.

Vignette 4: Sprite uses experiential engagement that incorporates multi-sensory events to generate content. It opened its first "Sprite Corner," a month-long pop-up venue in New York that targeted creative people who are passionate about hip-hop, comedy, art, and good food. The idea was to bring together interesting things and interesting people into multi-sensory communal events such as live concerts, movies, and cooking classes. It targets individuals with high network reach and strong persuasion capital (see Figure 4.2). It also uses its social media accounts to showcase novelty, surprise, and originality of the events using hashtags #SpriteCorner and #ObeyYourThirst for contributors to re-tweet and share content. For instance, Sprite Corner initiative led to 120 million views for participant-generated video. Further, there has been a 50% increase in mentions of the Sprite brand name in music-related conversations.

INTRODUCTION: BUILDING BUSINESS-TO-CUSTOMER (B2C) RELATIONSHIPS BY STIMULATING PURCHASE BEHAVIOR

In this section, we discuss how firms build and sustain customer relationships by stimulating customer purchase behavior via loyalty programs. The American Marketing Association defines loyalty programs as "continuity incentive programs offered by a retailer to reward customers and encourage repeat business." A loyalty program is an integrated system of structured and customized marketing actions designed to build customer loyalty among profitable customers (Bijmolt *et al.*, 2010). This means

loyalty programs are structured such that customers who become members of the program are rewarded based on purchase behavior, often supplemented with ongoing marketing efforts, with a view to foster customer loyalty and long-term relationship. Similar to the shift from a product-driven management approach to a customer-centric approach (Sheth and Parvatiyar, 1995), loyalty programs are also changing from being purely transaction-oriented to an integrated system that supports building and maintaining customer relationships (Bijmolt and Verhoef, 2017). This concept was illustrated by the loyalty rewards programs offered by Hertz in Vignette 1.

Companies are re-designing the features of the loyalty program by harnessing the power of digital and mobile technology by prioritizing customers based on their past purchase (and projected future) behavior and personalizing targeted communications to keep them incentivized and motivated. The multi-tier loyalty program is one such example to manage and to foster behavioral and attitudinal loyalty of customers with a view to improving the financial performance of the firm (Bijmolt *et al.*, 2010). The system is developed on pre-defined set of rules and procedures and designed to recognize the hierarchical structure of customer tiers based on their past purchase behavior. These rules are pre-determined and publicly available, and customers are rewarded periodically with monetary and non-monetary rewards. For instance, a customer gets rewarded by being able to collect points, acquire status, redeem rewards, and obtain other benefits. As the costs and benefits of this design are of long-term nature, companies must carefully manage each tiered customer along their journey.

Multiple Mechanisms to Stimulate Purchase Behavior

Multi-tier loyalty programs are introduced by firms with the aim to build and sustain customer relationships and thereby improve financial performance. While firms benefit from such programs financially, how do customers benefit and what motivates customers to participate in such programs? In this section, drawing from the work of Bijmolt *et al.* (2018), we discuss four such mechanisms that motivate customers to participate in loyalty programs. These benefits include instrumental benefits, symbolic benefits, emotional benefits, and cognitive benefits. Loyalty programs often tap into multiple psychological and social processes simultaneously. Henderson *et al.* (2011) provide a review of the multiple theoretical mechanisms that loyalty programs trigger in customer responses. Their review reveals that the majority of the loyalty program research rest on psychological mechanisms from three specific domains: (1) status,

(2) habit, and (3) relational. Conferring status to consumers generates favorable comparisons with others, building habits causes advantageous memory processes, and developing relationships results in favorable treatment by consumers. We discuss each of these motivations below.

Instrumental Benefits: Monetary and Non-Monetary Rewards

Multi-tier loyalty programs are designed to provide rewards to customers who become members. The rewards can be monetary (e.g., price discounts) or non-monetary (e.g., additional service) and often enhancing the economic utility of the offering (Henderson *et al.*, 2011). Customers will often change their purchase behavior to gain access to these benefits. Taylor and Neslin (2005) demonstrate that customers experience a "*points pressure*" *effect*, that is, a motivational impulse to increase purchases in the anticipation of the reward. This effect is produced by a combination of customer switching cost in the form of foregone opportunity to build up sales levels (i.e., reward points) and future orientation that impel the customer to increase spending. Here, the customer realizes that future utility is enhanced by the reward and that he/she needs to increase purchases and accumulate "points" until the reward is earned.

Taylor and Neslin (2005) also discuss a "*rewarded behavior*" *effect* which is, re-patronage is likely to persist through the cycle of behavior-reward-repeat behavior based on the behavioral learning process. From a cognitive learning perspective, a reward can increase subsequent purchase behavior if the customer develops positive feelings (i.e., affect) toward the company by way of greater recall of positive information and higher satisfaction (Tietje, 2002). Thus, the rewarded behavior is more likely to persist and be repeated in the future.

Another mechanism is the "*goal-gradient hypothesis*," which states that the tendency to approach a goal increases with proximity to the goal; that is, the achievement motivation increases with smaller goal distance and, therefore, customers accelerate and persist in their efforts as they near the program's incentive threshold. Kivetz *et al.* (2006) demonstrate that the "goal-gradient hypothesis" is present in the human psychology of rewards, particularly in the context of loyalty programs: the closer the customer gets to the reward, the stronger the effort exerted toward achieving it. Not only do customers accelerate toward rewards (in terms of timing, quantity, and persistence of effort) but their acceleration also predicts loyalty and future engagement with similar goals.

Finally, one more mechanism stems from the "*reciprocity norm*" of the social exchange theory, that is, a customer who receives a (high) reward feels the need and obligation to repay the company for the benefits received through gratitude-driven changes in purchase behavior (Palmatier *et al.*, 2009; Wetzel *et al.*, 2014). Palmatier (2008) argues that gratitude and norms of reciprocity take a central role, in addition to trust and commitment, in interpersonal relationship marketing. The underlying psychological emotion of gratitude, which leads to a desire to repay debt, generates feelings of pleasure, whereas the failure to do so generates feelings of guilt.

Symbolic Benefits: Status

Multi-tier loyalty programs provide increasing levels of symbolic benefits, such as recognition, preferential treatment, and special privileges (Drèze and Nunes, 2009), to customers in higher tiers. Receiving such symbolic benefits enhances the *perception of status* among customers in higher tiers (Brashear-Alejandro *et al.*, 2016). Henderson *et al.* (2011) provide several explanations of the multiple theoretical mechanisms that loyalty programs trigger in customer responses. One such explanation is the role of status as a loyalty-inducing mechanism in that

conferring status to consumers generates favorable comparisons with others. Status is positional in that it ranks individuals within a hierarchical structure, is a universal human motive that affects well-being, and though individually desirable, is often dependent on the social context that shapes it, in that achievements are recognized by socially accepted norms or esteem received directly from others.

Several theories such as social comparison theory (Festinger, 1954), social identity theory (Tajfel and Turner, 1979), and Schwartz's value theory (Schwartz and Bilsky, 1990) explain the motivations underlying status. People make social comparisons upward, downward, and laterally to form evaluations; upward social comparisons serve to motivate people toward greater achievement, lateral comparisons allow people to fit in with the group, and downward comparisons serve to motivate people toward self-enhancement by differentiating them from less prestigious groups. This happens because individuals are socially sensitive, and they have an intrinsic motivation to evaluate their situation by engaging in comparisons with others (social comparison theory; Festinger, 1954). In particular, customers in the top tiers perform downward comparisons that favor self-enhancement and feelings of exclusivity, by differentiating them from less prestigious groups (Drèze and Nunes, 2009). Social identity theory suggests that people's need to bolster their self-image motivates their desire to belong to or associate with a high-status group. Drèze and Nunes (2009) show that consumers prefer status when it is more exclusive and when there are more tiers below them. Also, Schwartz's value theory suggests that there is often tension between a person's desire for getting ahead (self-enhancement) and enhancing local status versus getting along (self-transcendence) and enhancing the group's global status. The downside of conferring status through tiered loyalty programs is that lower-status customers might be concerned with fairness, which will dampen the relationship. Further, lower-status consumers may feel envious of high-status customers and would want to "level-up" and achieve the same status or hope others "level-down" and lose their status (Van de Ven *et al.*, 2009).

Multi-tier loyalty programs frequently label customer tiers using status-laden tags (e.g., bronze, silver, gold, and platinum) in order to reinforce the notion of a hierarchy among customers and to provide the observable indicators of status (Drèze and Nunes, 2009; Melnyk and van Osselaer, 2012). Thus, by including this stratification, loyalty programs aim to leverage the power of status, widely recognized as a strong motivator of human behavior (McFerran and Argo, 2014). The effectiveness of the top of the tier hierarchy (e.g., Gold or Platinum) on customer behavior may depend on the size of this group. Research on customer perceptions of exclusivity suggests that the desirability of a position in society increases with its scarcity (e.g., Gierl and Huettl, 2010). Henderson *et al.* (2011) suggest that consumers prefer being conferred high status when the elite group is small. Consistent with this, Drèze and Nunes (2009) demonstrate that the attractiveness of an elite-status group decreases with an increasing number of individuals who are granted elite status. Arbore and Estes (2013) also find that perceived status in the top tier increases as the number of customers in the top tier decreases, and as the number of tiers increases. This effect is most likely to be observed in an industry with high perceived exclusivity (e.g., airlines), and not in an industry with low perceived exclusivity (e.g., supermarkets). With regard to intermediate tiers, it has been shown that customers in these tiers are more concerned about their status and more susceptible to social contagion (Hu and Van den Bulte, 2014). Finally, even low-tier members often favor programs with elite tiers despite not qualifying to becoming members of these top categories (Drèze and Nunes, 2009),

although they may resent members in higher status categories. Consistent with social comparison theory (Festinger, 1954), an individual's level of aspiration is often greater than their level of performance and, thus, customers in the multi-tier loyalty program will perform upward social comparisons that will motivate them to improve their status in the program. Therefore, symbolic benefits, such as status, are a powerful force to promote favorable behaviors among program members.

Emotional Benefits: Relational Bond

A benefit of loyalty programs is that they help initiate, grow, and maintain relationships with customers. Relationship exchanges that are reciprocal are governed by relational norms, i.e., reciprocity, mutuality, solidarity, and flexibility in which benefits are traded over extended periods without a formalized accounting, whereas negotiated exchanges are governed by contracts or formal agreements that describe the exchange of benefits and payments that occur concurrently. Loyalty programs attempt to shift customers toward a reciprocal relationship built on trust and relational norm with the hope of stronger relationships (Palmatier *et al.*, 2006). Strong relationships result in increased revenue for the firm, improved share of wallet, enhanced word of mouth (WOM), increased information sharing, and forgiveness for service failure (Henderson *et al.*, 2011). Strong relationships are tied to loyalty that is secured by customer attitudinal barriers to exit and long-term profitability for the firm. Therefore, loyalty programs need to stress the communal aspects of relationship that is benevolently motivated, which will trigger customer gratitude that leads to cycles of reciprocation, and eventually strong relational bonds (Palmatier *et al.*, 2009). However, if consumers perceive opportunistic behavior, consumers will categorize the relationship as economic-based, which will negatively affect trust and satisfaction.

Multi-tier loyalty programs, by stratifying the membership base into different customer groups, provide a sociological context, which enhances customer–company bonding in two ways and may therefore stimulate customer loyalty. First, social identity theory proposes that the groups to which an individual belongs, or aspires to be part of, are a central element to the self-concept as they provide the basis to form a *social identity* (Tajfel and Turner, 1979). Similarly, literature on group connectedness indicates that consumers tend to use brands whose images match the groups to which they belong, which enhances the association with those groups (Escalas and Bettman, 2005; Winterich *et al.*, 2009). Individuals strive to achieve a positive social identity and to bolster their self-image, which promotes aspirations to belong to elevated-status groups (Henderson *et al.*, 2011). If the rewards and benefits of the multi-tier loyalty program are visible to other customers, for example, in the form of exclusive lounge access for high-tier members, the loyalty program becomes more salient to customers and enables members to identify each other as part of the in-group (Esmark *et al.*, 2016). Thus, by creating an in-group context (e.g., gold member of Citibank) in which its members share a number of experiences and benefits, a multi-tier loyalty program helps individual customers to define who they are and enhance their self-image and self-esteem (Brashear-Alejandro *et al.*, 2016).

Second, a multi-tier loyalty program may enhance *connectedness to the firm* itself (Tanford, 2013). For example, Brashear-Alejandro *et al.* (2016) demonstrate that the symbolic benefits provided by a loyalty program promote a strong and deep identification with the company, which may be particularly strong for the high-tier groups. Drèze and Nunes (2009) further demonstrate that these programs impact a customer's perceived feelings of superiority, which are central to help individuals fulfill their self-definitional needs, including the need for self-enhancement and self-distinctiveness (Tajfel and Turner, 1979). Satisfying these self-definitional needs motivates the development of identification with the company, which becomes "the primary psychological substrate for the kind of deep, committed, and meaningful relationships" with the firm (Bhattacharya and Sen, 2003, p. 76). Clearly, firms need to utilize these findings and enable consumers to identify themselves with their brands. Digital technologies such as mobile applications can be extremely useful in this regard since there is increasing empirical evidence that such digital initiatives have a long-term effect on customers' purchase and reward redemption behaviors and vice versa (Viswanathan *et al.*, 2017a,b). Thus, multi-tier loyalty programs offer customers an important source of value through the formation of a social identity, which enhances the importance of the customer–firm relationship and promotes the development of positive attitudes, such as trust, commitment, involvement, or loyalty, that ultimately result in customer loyalty.

Cognitive Benefits: Learning and Habit

Over time, individual customers derive valuable information from a multi-tier loyalty program, which becomes the basis for acquiring, modifying, and reinforcing their knowledge, preferences, and behaviors (Kopalle *et al.*, 2012). This dynamic learning process is important, because it can have a profound impact on customer behaviors. Drèze and Nunes (2011) identify three different types of learning that can have different implications for the understanding of how customer behavior in a loyalty program evolves over time: procedural learning, learning from experience, and self-learning. A fourth type of learning, i.e., associative learning leads to the development of habits in customers.

Procedural learning refers to the process by which individuals gain knowledge about how they should proceed in order to derive benefits from the loyalty program (e.g., spend $1,000 in company products during a calendar year to become Gold member). *Learning from experience* occurs when individuals gain knowledge about something after experiencing it. For example, when a customer has been upgraded to a higher tier, he/she learns about the rewards and symbolic benefits that members of that tier receive (e.g., privileges such as lower waiting times, access to VIP areas, or special events). *Self-learning* refers to the process by which individuals gain knowledge about their abilities to perform specific activities or actions. Individual customers invest resources and direct action to yield the rewards and symbolic benefits provided by the multi-tier loyalty programs (Wang *et al.*, 2016). In principle, customers feel a drive to look up (upward comparison), which motivates them toward greater achievements in the future and being promoted to a higher tier (Henderson *et al.*, 2011). When a customer achieves or fails to achieve those goals or when a customer is successful at moving up one tier, he/she re-assess the perceptions of her or his ability to execute these actions and determines the motivation and effort needed to invest in subsequent attempts (Drèze and Nunes, 2011; Taylor and Neslin, 2005). In contrast, when a customer fails to achieve the reward-contingent goals, motivation to invest to achieve the rewards may decrease (Wang *et al.*, 2016). *Associative learning* is another type of learning that occurs in the context of multi-tier loyalty programs (Sheth and Parvatiyar, 1995), a process by which individuals learn an association between a stimulus (e.g. a reward) and a behavior (e.g., purchases). Importantly, this type of learning promotes the development of recursive customer purchases and thus may lead to the development of habits (Liu and Tam, 2013; Henderson *et al.*, 2011). Henderson *et al.* (2011) provide an explanation of habit formation using the dual process model. Based on the dual-mode model of mental processing, as behavior repeats over time, people increasingly rely on automatic decision–making strategies that are experiential, effortless, and holistic. Habit formation starts with an intention to behave, followed by repetition of behavior, and develops when provided context stability such that it gets ingrained in procedural memory. Hence, by repeatedly offering increasing levels of rewards and symbolic benefits to customers, multi-tier loyalty programs induce different customer learning processes that condition and determine future loyalty behaviors.

BUILDING B2C RELATIONSHIPS BY STIMULATING NON-PURCHASE BEHAVIOR

In this section, we discuss how firms build and sustain customer relationships by stimulating customer non-purchase behavior primarily via various types of engagement. The roots of customer engagement trace back to relationship management and service management first explored by the Nordic School (Gronroos, 1990; Gummesson, 2002). More recently, Vargo and Lusch (2004, 2008) have more formally articulated this perspective as the service-dominant (S-D) logic of marketing. Four of the 10 foundational premises of S-D logic are useful in determining the conceptual foundations underlying the concept of customer engagement (CE). These are (1) the customer is always a co-creator of value (premise 6), which highlights the interactive, co-creative nature of value creation between customers and/or other actors within service relationships; (2) all social and economic actors are resource integrators (premise 9), which implies that value creation occurs in the context of networks; (3) value is always uniquely and phenomenologically determined by the beneficiary (premise 10) emphasizing the subjective and experiential nature of value co-creation; and (4) a service-centered view is inherently customer oriented and relational (premise 8), which highlights the transcending relational nature of service and that CE stems from this expanded relationship marketing perspective (Brodie *et al.*, 2011).

There are varied definitions of CE in the literature, such as a psychological process (Bowden, 2009), a psychological state (Brodie *et al.*, 2011), activities including purchase (Kumar *et al.*, 2010) and activities excluding purchase (Van Doorn *et al.*, 2010). Brodie *et al.* (2011) identified five fundamental propositions (FPs) that characterize the conceptual domain of CE. These are *FP1*: CE reflects a psychological state, which occurs by virtue of interactive customer experiences with a focal agent/object within specific service relationships; *FP2*: CE states occur within a dynamic, iterative process of service relationships that co-create value; *FP3*: CE plays central role within a nomological network of service relationships; *FP4*: CE is a multi-dimensional concept subject to a context- and/or stakeholder-specific expression of relevant cognitive, emotional, and behavioral dimensions; and *FP5*: CE occurs within a specific set of situational conditions generating differing CE levels.

Based on the five preceding FPs, Brodie *et al.* (2011) define customer engagement as "...a *psychological state* that occurs by virtue of *interactive, co-creative customer experiences* with a *focal agent/object* (e.g., a brand) in focal service relationships. It occurs under a specific set of context-dependent conditions generating differing CE levels; and exists as a *dynamic, iterative process* within service relationships that *co-create value*. CE plays a *central role* in a nomological network governing service relationships in which other relational concepts (e.g., involvement, loyalty) are antecedents and/or consequences in iterative CE processes. It is a *multidimensional concept* subject to a context- and/or stakeholder-specific expression of relevant cognitive, emotional, and/or behavioral dimensions".

Despite a lack of definitional consensus, previous research predominantly portrays CE as a reflection of "a focal individual's psychologically based willingness to invest in the undertaking of focal interactions with particular engagement objects (e.g., a brand or a firm), often beyond purchase" (Hollebeek *et al.*, 2016, p. 393; see also Groeger, Moroko, and Hollebeek, 2016; Harmeling *et al.*, 2017; Vivek, Beatty, and Morgan, 2012). One line of research argues that CE is non-transactional in nature and should include activities beyond economic transactions (Harmeling *et al.*, 2017; Jaakkola and Alexander, 2014; Van Doorn *et al.*, 2010) that does not include customer purchase or repurchase behavior. Another line of research, represented by Kumar and colleagues (e.g., Kumar *et al.*, 2010; Pansari and Kumar, 2017), argues that customer engagement should include customer purchases that form direct contributions toward firm value. Figure 4.3 illustrates the Pansari and Kumar's (2017) framework.

The tenet of the customer engagement theory (Pansari and Kumar, 2017) lies in the evolution of customer management from transaction approach (recency, frequency, and monetary value) to relationship approach (trust and commitment) to engagement approach (satisfaction and emotion). They argue that it is not enough to simply satisfy the customer to make her or him loyal and profitable. Profitable loyalty and satisfaction need to be evolved to a higher level by engaging customers in all possible ways. The quality of customer–company relationship depends on the level of satisfaction derived from the relationship and the level of emotional connectedness of the customer towards this relationship. As the tenets of relationship marketing are subsumed in engagement theory (engagement occurs only after trust and commitment), both transaction and non-transaction behaviors are included. The focus of the firm in the Pansari and Kumar's (2017) framework is to maximize the profitability from each customer over the long-term using metrics such as Customer Lifetime Value (CLV).

Figure 4.3: Framework of Customer Engagement Theory

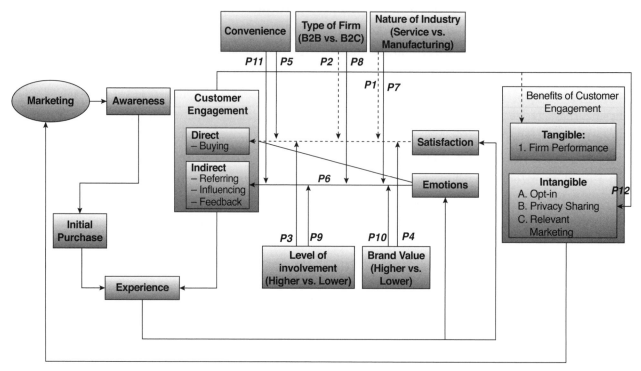

Adapted from Anita Pansari and V. Kumar (2017), Customer Engagement: The Construct, Antecedents, and Consequences, *Journal of the Academy of Marketing Science* 45: 294–311.

In this chapter, we adhere to the former approach (non-transactional) circumscribing the domain of CE beyond economic purchase behavior (i.e., referral behavior, influence behavior, and knowledge behavior) as it nicely fits within the framework of relationship marketing (Vivek *et al.*, 2012) and the foundational premises of the S-D logic (Jaakkola and Alexander, 2014). Further, different from commitment and trust, CE is interactive and co-creative (Brodie *et al.*, 2011). This concept is consistent with the service-dominant (S-D) logic of value co-creation (see Lusch *et al.*, 2010). S-D logic shifts the focus from selling tangible products to selling "the continuous flow of value," and this value is uniquely defined by consumers (Vargo and Lusch, 2004, p. 13). The foundational proposition of S-D logic is that "organizations, markets, and society are fundamentally concerned with the exchange of service — the applications of competencies (knowledge and skills) for the benefit of a party." The term "service" in S-D logic differs from *services*. Services involve intangible market offerings, whereas service refers to

the central process for value creation, during which one party employ resources (e.g., competencies) to benefit other parties (Vargo and Lusch, 2004, 2008). S-D logic emphasizes the pivotal role of *resources* (Vargo and Lusch, 2011), especially knowledge and skills.

Using the S-D logic framework, resources are distinguished between operand and operant resources; however, operant (rather than operand) resources are treated as more important resources in value co-creation (Constantin and Lusch, 1994; Vargo and Lusch, 2004). Focusing on operant resources also has substantial managerial implications. Operant resources "determine which firm resources customers are going to draw on," and hence highlighting customer operant resources enables companies "to anticipate customers' desired values and help them create value in use" (Arnould *et al.*, 2006, p. 93). Arnould *et al.* (2006, p. 92) further decompose operant resources into three sub-categories: (1) physical resources, such as physical and mental endowments, energy, and emotion, (2) cultural resources, such as specialized knowledge and skills, and (3) social resources, such as family relationships and brand communities. It is the careful blend of customer and company resource investment and resource utilization, i.e., resource integration that becomes the crucial means of value co-creation (Vargo and Lusch, 2004).

Peters *et al.* (2014) explore different ontological and epistemological perspectives that drive two different approaches to understanding resource integration, that of resource integration as emergence and resource integration as interaction-based dynamics. Emergence refers to the process of constituting a new entity with its own particular characteristics through the interactive combination of other, different entities that are necessary to create the new entity, but that does not contain the characteristics present in the new entity. The interaction perspective assumes a set of specific interactions occur between key actors (or entities) and particular resources rendering them resource status. Resources are dynamic functional concepts, i.e., they are not, they become, but also, they can cease to act as resources when they are no longer utilized in value-creating processes (Löbler, 2013; Vargo and Lusch, 2004).

Resource integration from a subject-oriented perspective focuses on subjective experience, which differs across individuals participating in specific resource-integrating processes. Here, customers as constructivists, in contrast to critical rationalists, do not believe in real, measurable phenomena, rather, believe in multiple realities that are subjectively felt and experienced. Here, the focus is on how feelings and experiences of the connected people emerged (Peters *et al.*, 2014) and is consistent with the experiential benefits of hedonistic pleasure and sensory experiences sought by customers. This also includes the self-generated risks of psychological discomfort resulting from both psychological and social risks surrounding customer engagement activities. In contrast, resource integration from an object-oriented perspective focuses on new emergent properties that represent potentially objective and measurable phenomena (Peters *et al.*, 2014). In a rigid sense, this perspective is outcome-related; however, it may also operate at the interaction level (or process level) as long as these interactions are observable and measurable (Ballantyne and Varey, 2006). This position is consistent with the positivist or critical rationalist perspective and ties in with the functional benefits of utilitarian and instrumental value sought by customers in the resource-integration process.

According to Peters *et al.* (2014), resource integration from a sign or signifier orientation focuses on the emergent new properties nothing more than signs or signifiers reflecting the nature of those specific objects. In addition, these signs are also viewed to coordinate focal interactive processes between resource-integrative stakeholders. This perspective is in keeping with what Venkatesh *et al.* (2006) calls "market as a sign system," and is consistent with the symbolic benefits of personal expression and social approval. Finally, resource integration from an inter-subjective orientation focuses not on any single actor in an objective sense; rather, resource integration either emerges or is the result of specific interactive forms when people gather either with others or with other objects and entities (Löbler, 2011), which become resources when utilized. This perspective is commensurate with both subjective and objective perspectives in that both can be socially reconstructed by individuals within service systems and is consistent with relational benefits of developing interpersonal bonds and social networks sought by customers. However, this also includes the dark side of relationships that emanate from cultural resources provided by companies by way of data-capturing technologies and policies surrounding data privacy and security.

Definition and Characteristics of Customer Engagement Behavior (CEBs)

Customer Engagement Behaviors (CEBs) are the behavioral aspect of customer engagement (CE).

Along with the research theme above (i.e., emphasis on the non-transactional nature of CE) and through the lens of resource investment, the authors define CEB as a positive online or offline activity chosen by a customer that goes above purchases, involving an interactive and co-creative process, and reflecting the customer's proactively investing resources (e.g., time, attention, competence, and knowledge) and sustaining the investment into interactions with companies and other customers (including prospects) (see Figures 4.4 and 4.5). This investment can be physical, affective, emotional, and cognitive. CEBs should create value for companies in a constructive way, even though its valence may be negative (e.g., genuine negative feedback). This value is far more than the value merely generated from transactions.

Figure 4.4: CEB is positive online (or offline) activity chosen by a customer that goes above and beyond purchases.

Figure 4.5: CEB is positive (online or) offline activity chosen by a customer that goes above and beyond purchases.

Consistent with the previous research about engagement (see Chandler and Lusch, 2015), CEBs are independent on specific moments, and does not refer to a momentary (but persistent) state. CEBs represent customer relationships enriched and strengthened through ongoing interactions between a focal company and its customers and prospects. Besides, CEBs are the behavioral representation of the CE state. Consistent with CE research (see Jaakkola and Alexander, 2014), CEBs also have a brand or firm focus. However, CEBs conceptually differ from brand engagement. Brand engagement relates to individual characteristics, which are dispositional. It refers to "an individual difference representing consumers' propensity to include important brands as part of how they view themselves" (Sprott *et al.*, 2009, p. 92).

The CEB definition connotes interactive, experiential, co-creative, self-motivational, and iterative characteristics. The *interactive* nature suggests customers proactively interact with various engagement objects, which Lemon and Verhoef (2016) refer to interactional touch points. These touch points include not only companies' market offerings (e.g., products, ads, platforms, and donating proposals) but also peer customers. Recently, marketing scholars suggest "the examination of engagement from a broader network-based or service system-based perspective" (Hollebeek *et al.*, 2016, p. 588). Through various interactional touch points, CE forms overall customer experience (Lemon and Verhoef, 2016). This interpretation bridges customer resources with what consumers experience during CEBs, and hence the *experiential* component is an important element of CEBs. The *co-creative* nature differentiates CEB from other relational concepts such as involvement and participation (Brodie *et al.*, 2011). When performing CEBs, customers are the co-creators of value.

The *self-motivational* property means that customers actively and voluntarily invest their resources in a sustainable manner. Self-motivated customers are "driven by their own unique purposes and intentions instead of those originating from the firm" (Jaakkola and Alexander, 2014, p. 248). This characteristic of CEBs is aligned with the work of Higgins (2006), which proposes that engagement results from a motivational force of attraction to or repulsion from a target. As for the *iterative* characteristic, CEBs develop in an iterative process, which denotes that a specific engagement activity can be an antecedent of one CEB process and the outcome of another level of engagement activity (Brodie *et al.*, 2011). The level of CEBs can be understood with regard to the strength, intensity, and duration of resource investment. Specific engagement activities are nested within broader engagement processes. As future research agenda, the diversity of CEBs necessitates: (1) a unified framework to explore their antecedents and consequences, (2) a typology to pinpoint the nuances of engagement activities, and (3) using this framework to analyze different types of CEBs.

Multiple Motivations to Stimulate Customer Engagement

Various CEBs have been extensively explored in previous consumer research, albeit isolated from each other. As discussed earlier, resources (resource investment and resource utilization) are common ingredients underlying CEBs, and customers play the role of resource integrators. In this section, we examine the following motivations underlying customers' engagement with several CEBs: relationship-based motivation, identification-based motivation, justice-based motivation, goal-based motivation, and control-based motivation. We discuss each of these motivations below.

Relationship-Based Motivation

Traditional models of relationship marketing focused on trust and commitment (Morgan and Hunt, 1994) as the foundational pillars of relationship marketing. However, unlike B2B relationships that focused on maximizing benefits and minimizing costs resulting from subjective cost–benefit analysis (i.e., social exchange theory), B2C relationships examined the interpersonal dyadic process operating at the cognitive/emotional levels. Palmatier (2008) described interpersonal relationship marketing as a dynamic process entailing cognitive-based relational factors of trust and commitment, and emotional- or social-based micro-foundational processes of gratitude and norms of reciprocity, which affect both short- versus long-term performance. Gratitude is inseparable from reciprocity because it reflects an ingrained psychological pressure to return the favor. As gratitude entails psychological pressure that leads to *social* conformity pressures, norms of reciprocity emerge and create persistent behavior cycles. Therefore, while trust and commitment are the building blocks of social exchange theory focusing on "higher" cognitive processing levels, gratitude and reciprocity also operate at the emotional level. Cognition and emotion intertwine closely, and gratitude positively influences judgments of trust (Dunn and Schweitzer, 2005). Not only does gratitude enhance short-term consumer purchasing behaviors, it also promotes consumer trust and reciprocity norms with its longer-term effects (Palmatier *et al.*, 2007).

Similar to Palmatier's (2008) dual cognitive/emotional processes, Pansari and Kumar (2017) advance a theory of customer engagement in which the two tenets of engagement hinge on satisfaction and emotion. Engagement occurs only after a relationship is formed and therefore subsumes the tenets of relationship marketing, i.e., trust, commitment, and satisfaction, but also includes emotional attachment. While customer satisfaction has a direct contribution to firm performance and is an essential indicator of a company's past, current, and future performance, it is the emotional attachment that indirectly contributes to various engagement behaviors including,

customer referrals, customer influence, and customer knowledge. This relationship between the customer and the firm evolves into engagement behaviors only if the customer is satisfied with her or his relationship with the firm and is also emotionally connected with the firm.

Identification-Based Motivation

Customer resources refer to "those objects, personal characteristics, conditions, or energies that are valued by the individual or the means for attainment of those objects, personal characteristics, conditions, or energies" (Hobfoll, 1988, p. 26), and have symbolic value that can help people define themselves (Hobfoll, 1989). Since resources are valued assets, and investment of these assets means much to customers, they are more likely to invest resources when such investment can help define their self-concept. Put differently, the desire for safeguarding a stable sense of self can motivate customers to invest their valuable resources and perform CEBs. According to social identity theory, "the self-concept is comprised of a personal identity, encompassing idiosyncratic characteristics (e.g., bodily attributes, abilities, psychological traits, interests), and a social identity encompassing salient group classifications" (Ashforth and Mael, 1989, p. 21; Tajfel and Turner, 1985). In short, people not only need personal identity (i.e., "I") to distinguish themselves from other members in social categories, but also seek social identity (i.e., "We") to identify themselves as a member of certain social categories, and to attach value to it. Despite non-formal members of companies, customers identify with the companies that enhance their personal and social identity (Ahearne *et al.*, 2005; Bhattacharya and Sen, 2003).

Driven by the need for maintaining and enhancing stable self-concept, customers are willing to expend their resources that help define their selves. They tend to perform certain engagement behaviors to communicate their affiliation with companies, and to retain or protect their identity (Ashforth and Mael, 1989). It is unsurprising that consumer–company identification has been identified as a powerful motivator of engagement behavior. For instance, employees' identification with their work generates greater employee engagement. By the same token, customers' identification with companies, or C–C identification, may induce customers to perform CEBs. This argument has been evidenced in previous research about specific engagement activities, such as transmitting word of mouth (WOM), recruiting new customers for companies, and providing suggestions and feedback to companies (Ahearne *et al.*, 2005; Bettencourt, 1997; Bhattacharya and Sen, 2003; Brown *et al.*, 2005). In addition to consumer–company identification, customers may develop identification with their peers, i.e., other customers in common-bond groups (Fombelle *et al.*, 2012). Peer customers are important in shaping the relationship between the individual customer and the focal company (Algesheimer *et al.*, 2005; Muniz and O'Guinn, 2001). Peer identification is defined as "the extent of an individual's identification with others of the same type of individuals associated with the organization (Fombelle *et al.*, 2012, p. 590)." This identification does not necessarily occur in formal groups, and "peers" are not limited to loyal customers but include any type of customers (Bhattacharya and Sen, 2003; Fombelle *et al.*, 2012). A customer's identification with a company provides the organizational contextual support for peer identification (Fombelle *et al.*, 2012), which in turn motivates the individual to be more devoted to the focal company (Fournier *et al.*, 2001).

Justice-Based Motivation

In the interpersonal context, resources involve the objects that can be transmitted from an individual to another (Foa, 1976). This viewpoint discusses resources in social exchanges, and accentuates the investibility of resources. People invest resources with the aim of gaining new resources and safeguarding and offsetting losses (Halbesleben, 2006; Halbesleben and Buckley, 2004; Hobfoll, 1988, 2001). An agent of resource investment expects fair return on her or his resource exchange with other agents; otherwise, this agent cannot offset her or his loss in resources. In this sense, the justice-related perspective can be employed to examine engagement activities. Indeed, previous research about employee engagement has adopted this perspective, and found that employee engagement is driven by actual or expected gains in resources (Gorgievski and Hobfoll, 2008).

Justice theorists often focus on three major issues: (1) how people respond to the outcomes they receive, (2) how they react to the procedures with which these outcomes are obtained, and (3) how they react to treatment received as procedures are enacted. The first issue involves *distributive justice* or the perceived fairness of the outcomes an exchange partner receives (Adams, 1965; Tyler, 1994). Distributive justice is based on the principles of equity and equality, in which a favorable evaluation depends on the perceived equality between inputs and outcomes compared to a point of past reference. The second issue involves *procedural justice* — which refers to the fairness and the quality of the decision-making process. Individuals view procedures as fair when control of the procedures is vested in them and when they can exercise process control thereby influencing changes in organizational policies they find objectionable (Leventhal, 1980; Tyler, 1994). The third issue, related to procedural justice is *interactional justice* — which refers to the treatment people receive as procedures are enacted, including the disclosure of information and provision of explanations of decisions taken by authorities (Cohen-Charash and Spector, 2001).

Perceived justice influences people's perceived worthiness of their resource investment, and allows them to believe that it is worthwhile to perform engagement behavior. With regard to CEBs, distributive justice involves the balance between resources invested by customers and benefits obtained or expected by customers from companies and other customers. The benefits can be related to both outcomes and processes of CEBs. Specifically, outcome-related benefits may encompass self-designed products that tailor to one's functional and aesthetic preferences, while process-related benefits are derived from engagement activities, and consist of psychological (e.g., entertainment, presentation of mastery, and pride in creation) and social (e.g., making congenial friends) benefits.

Compared to outcome-related benefits, it appears that CEBs are more driven by process-related benefits, which customers do not easily calculate. So, distributive justice may play a little role in motivating CEBs. This argument is also supported by the fact that distributive justice is exchange-related and thus contrarian to the non-transactional nature of CEBs. In terms of procedural justice, it involves appropriate rules, means, norms, principles, and procedures that companies adopt to govern CEBs. Leventhal (1980) identified six rules that govern people's evaluation of allocative procedures: (1) consistency, i.e., equality of opportunity across people and over time, (2) bias suppression, i.e., restraint of personal self-interest and blind allegiance, (3) accuracy, i.e., collection of sufficient information, (4) correctability, i.e., opportunities to change decisions, (5) representativeness, i.e., reflection of the basic values of representative individuals, and (6) ethicality, i.e., consistency with fundamental ethical values. Applying these rules to the context of CEBs, customers perceive procedural justice of CEBs if companies (a) provide equal engagement opportunities for all customers, (b) avoid overly "exploiting" customers and treating them as free employees, (c) offer transparent information disclosure and necessary interactive aids, and (d) incorporate fundamental human values (e.g., Do-It-

Yourself ethic). As for interactional justice, it refers to the fairness of communication and treatment in interpersonal interactions (Lind and Tyler, 1988; Skarlicki and Folger, 1997; Thibaut and Walker, 1975). Individuals perceive interactional justice if they are treated by other people with their politeness, courtesy, non-prejudicial statements, and justification for their decisions (Bies and Moag, 1986). For customers who perform CEBs, their interpersonal relationships involve their interactions with other customers and therefore, interactional justice may be more likely to exist between customers, i.e., peer-to-peer than between customers and companies.

Goal-Based Motivation

Deriving from the characteristics of resources, the first two perspectives above discuss the antecedents of CEBs. As noted earlier, the iterative nature of CEBs implies that CEBs have different levels. Higher levels of CEBs mean sustainable, intensive, and vigorous investment of resources, and may be more beneficial to companies. So, it is also of significance to identify the factors that prompt customers to increase their levels of CEBs. Resources are instrumental and serve as means to goal pursuits (Hobfoll, 1988). The value of resources is influenced by their contribution to the attainment of personal goals (Halbesleben *et al.*, 2014). Thus, undertaking CEBs, or the investment of resources, entails the process of achieving goals. In this sense, goal-related perspective could be another perspective to researching CEBs, and may help understand the dynamics of resource investment.

If customers derive value or a great sense of meaning from the process of goal pursuits, they may have a stronger motivation to achieve goals and, therefore, are more likely to perform higher levels of CEBs. Prior research about effort (as one type of resources) touches on the relationship between resource investment and the value of goal objects (wherein resources are invested into). The valence of this relationship can be either positive or negative, largely depending on whether the process of expending effort is perceived as gaining or taxing (Buechel and Janiszewski, 2014). Autonomy is one factor affecting how individuals perceive this process, with goal pursuits autonomously chosen leading to increased goal value and subsequent motivation. According to self-determination theory (SDT; Deci and Ryan, 1980), autonomy is also found as one of the determinants of people's engagement in activities. These previous studies may be extendable to other resources involved in performing CEBs. As CEBs involve discretionary investment of resources wherein customers have autonomy in performing them, customers are likely motivated to perform higher levels of CEBS (e.g., new product co-creation).

In addition to the autonomy (implicit in CEBs) in choosing goals, the fit between goal orientation and goal-pursuing manner also matters. Goals have motivational consequences by providing incentives for one's performance (Bandura, 1986). Engagement is a component of customers' motivational experience. Motivational experience refers to "the experience of the motivational force to make something happen… or make something not happen…" (Higgins, 2006, p. 441). Individuals pursue their goals starting with motivational orientation, which includes approach versus avoidance, or the motivated movement toward a satisfied state versus away from an unsatisfied state. Goal-pursuing manner involves vigilant or eager strategies. Promotion (prevention)-focused individuals use an eager (vigilant) goal-pursuit means (Crowe and Higgins, 1997). Promotion-oriented customers interpret goals as aspirations and accomplishments, whereas prevention-oriented customers perceive goals as responsibilities and safety maintenance (Higgins, 1997). When experiencing the fit between goal orientation and goal-pursuing manner, people "feel right" about their behaviors, and subsequently magnify their motivation and increase the strength of engagement in tasks (Higgins, 2006).

Control-Based Motivation

Goal-based perspective posits that due to the autonomous nature of CEBs, customers are likely to interpret their investment of resources as gaining (rather than losing). Researchers about personal resources, such as Halbesleben, 2006, Halbesleben and Buckley, 2004 and Hobfoll, 1988, 2001, propose that individuals who access resources are capable of gaining more resources, which then engenders even more plentiful resources. Along with this positive gain spiral, individuals may generate an "I-can-do-it" feeling. This felt competence and mastery over the environment speaks to the idea of control. Perceived control can be generated from people's efforts to attain goals. In the context of CEBs, perceived control involves beliefs regarding one's ability to influence companies' practices and policies by certain behaviors such as giving advice and product reviews. Companies employ empowerment strategies, allowing customers to "connect and collaborate with each other by sharing information; praise; criticism; suggestions; and ideas about its products, services, and policies" (Ramani and Kumar, 2008, p. 29). CEBs with experiential, co-creative, and interactive features may increase customer empowerment (Brodie *et al.*, 2011), whereby a sense of control is implicit (Fuchs *et al.*, 2010).

The level of CEBs does not only involve the strength of engagement but also the duration of engagement (i.e., long-term engagement). The former is driven by perceived value of engagement as analyzed in the goal-based perspective. Psychological ownership, which refers to "the state in which individuals feel as though the target of ownership or a piece of that target is 'theirs'" (Pierce *et al.*, 2001, p. 86), is crucial to the latter (Harmeling *et al.*, 2017). Psychological ownership may boost one's perceived value of objects (Thaler, 1980) and positively relate to voluntary citizenship behaviors toward entities such as nations and organizations (Pierce *et al.*, 2001). CEBs are one type of citizenship behaviors (toward companies). As such, it may be reasonable to infer that psychological ownership is positively associated with CEBs. Harmeling *et al.* (2017) also indirectly support this inference by delineating the contribution of psychological ownership to customer engagement marketing. Through altering one's mental self-image, psychological ownership motivates customers to go beyond economic transactions with companies and employ their resources to help the companies that they psychologically own (Harmeling *et al.*, 2017). Perceived control, generated from CEBs, is one of the most effective routes to psychological ownership (Pierce *et al.*, 2001). That is, CEBs that imply perceived control may generate psychological ownership of companies, which then increase the level of CEBs.

The key in this proposition is the role of perceived control (that is implied in CEBs). This type of control is similar to Bandura's (1977) "feelings of efficacy" and Averill's (1973) "behavioral control." In addition to behavioral control, Averill (1973) also identify two other types of control: (1) cognitive control, involving prediction and interpretation of events, and (2) decisional control, referring to choice in selecting goals, outcomes, and courses of actions. Factors, which affect the amount of overall perceived control, may moderate the effect of CEBs on a higher level of CEBs. According to Averill (1973), it seems that autonomy in choosing CEBs to pursue goals represents decisional control. That is, along with behavioral control, decisional control has also been implied in CEBs. So, from the control-related perspective, cognitive control may be a moderator of the relationship between CEBs at different levels. Customers' perceived control may evolve with the cognitive facet of control. Cognitive control involves cognitive strategies to influence how individuals interpret and experience situations (Skinner, 1996). These strategies can be providing sufficient information to reduce uncertainty and enhance the predictability of events (Averill, 1973). This implies that companies can play a role in

magnifying the positive impact of CEBs, even when CEBs are customer-initialized. By giving timely response during CEBs, companies add information to inform customers of how their engagement activities make a difference.

Customer Engagement: Opportunities for Marketing-Mix Customization

Customization is a process by which customers adapt offerings and marketing-mix to their own preferences. The degree of customization largely depends on the level of control that customers exercise, which is granted by the firm (Jimenez *et al.*, 2013). Under high autonomy, customers get quasi to full control to determine their own marketing-mix; however, under low autonomy, customization occurs within pre-determined boundaries. Here we briefly discuss different customization options surrounding different elements of the marketing-mix (Bleier *et al.*, 2018).

At high levels of autonomy, customers get the opportunity to fully customize their product and service offerings. For instance, using three-dimensional (3D) printing technology Shapeways (www.shapeways.com) can fully customize the product. Customized products and services increase customers' willingness to pay by 20% and likelihood to recommend the brand by 50% (Spaulding and Perry, 2013). In the pricing domain, price customization is getting more popular through participative pricing mechanisms. With high levels of autonomy, one such pricing strategy is Pay-What-You-Want (PWYW) pricing, where customers can pay any price they feel is appropriate, including nothing at all, which the seller has to accept. For instance, Radiohead, a British rock band, sold its album *In Rainbows* online and allowed the fans to decide how much to pay. Although there were more customers who downloaded the album for free than those who paid for it, it was before its later physical release more successful than the previous album (Lewis, 2008).

With digitization and mobile technology, firms are promoting and communicating their products and services using mobile technology using permission-based approach. For instance, Kruidvat (www.kruidvat.nl), a Dutch drug store chain has an app that allows customers to communicate how often they want special promotion offers and to be able to activate it when they are interested. Similarly, customization of place is now easily available with omni-channel retailing, including customization of channel usage such as with Nike's mobile app Nike+, where customers can set individual categories of interest as "shop favorites."

At low levels of autonomy, customers get the opportunity to partly customize their product and services depending on the degree of control. For product strategy, by-attribute customization allows customers to select components from a pre-defined set of options, such as at Spreadshirt (www.spreadshirt.com) where customers can design custom T-shirts by choosing fittings and colors. Then there is customization via starting solutions where customers start from a pre-defined product, i.e., the starting solution, and then modify specific attributes. For instance, Mix My Own (www.mixmyown.com) offers an array of breakfast cereal mixes that customers can customize by adding or removing certain ingredients. There is also by-alternative customization where relatively little control is given to customers such that they select their preferred option from a set of fully determined products. In the area of pricing, Name-Your-Own-Price (NYOP) allows less autonomy over the price compared to PWYW pricing. Customers submit a bid that is accepted if it surpasses a threshold price set by the firm and unknown to customers in advance. Priceline (www.priceline.com) uses NYOP pricing successfully. In low autonomy, customers can opt-in/opt-out from company promotions but not have the flexibility to customize promotional offers. Finally, customization of place is now easily available

with omni-channel retailing, with options ranging from online, offline, and mixed retail options.

KEY TAKEAWAYS

- A loyalty program is an integrated system of structured and customized marketing actions designed to build customer loyalty and long-term relationship among profitable customers. Based on past (and future) purchase behavior, firms target communications to customers with personalized incentive initiatives.

- Firms offer instrumental benefits to customers in the form of monetary (e.g., price discount) and/or non-monetary rewards (e.g., additional service) to keep customers motivated and loyal. Customers experience "points pressure" effect, "rewarded behavior" effect, and "goal gradient" effect, which motivate them to accumulate points, accelerate points, and persist in realizing reward points, thus enhancing customer loyalty.

- Multi-tier loyalty programs offer symbolic benefits to customers in the form of recognition, preferential treatment, and special privileges. Status serves as a loyalty-inducing mechanism as customers make social comparisons, namely, upward, lateral, and downward comparisons. Status also motivates customers to identify with high-tier groups to bolster their self-image and sense of exclusivity (see Figure 4.6).

- Multi-tier loyalty programs offer emotional benefits by shifting customers toward a reciprocal relationship built on trust and relational norm, which in turn strengthens the relational bond. These programs help define customers' self and social identity as well as enhance their connectedness to the firm

- Customers learn through multi-tier loyalty programs in various ways: procedural learning, learning from experience, and self-learning.

Figure 4.6: Multi-tier loyalty programs offer symbolic and emotional benefits and customers learn in various ways.

Associative learning in the context of loyalty reward program promotes the development of habits and automatic decision-making.

- Customer engagement with firms is fundamentally rooted in some of the foundational pillars of the S-D logic. These include customer is always a co-creator in an interactive and iterative process, a resource integrator, and that customer value is subjective and unique.

- Resources are both operand and operant, and operant resources consisting of physical, cultural, and social resources determine which firm resources customers will utilize.

- Customer engagement behaviors (CEBs) are positive online or offline activities voluntarily chosen by customers that go beyond purchases, involving an iterative and co-creative process with firms wherein customers integrate their own resources with that of firms and other current and future customers.

- Relationship-based motivation underlying customer engagement behavior operates at the interpersonal level involving micro-foundational processes of gratitude and reciprocal norms. While trust and commitment focus on higher cognitive processing, gratitude and reciprocity operate at the emotional level.

- Identification-based motivation underlying customer engagement behavior safeguards customers' sense of stable selves motivating them to invest their valuable resources and perform CEBs. Customer–company identification is a powerful motivator of engagement behavior.

- Justice-based motivation underlying customer engagement behavior creates expectations for customers as resource investors to expect fair returns in the resource exchange. Distributive justice involves the balance between resources invested by customers and benefits obtained or expected from firms. Customers perceive procedural justice and interactional justice when firms provide equal engagement opportunities, avoid exploiting customers, provide information transparency, and incorporate fundamental human values.

- Goal-based motivation underlying customer engagement behavior assumes that resources are instrumental to goal pursuits. Higher levels of resources are invested for higher levels of CEBs. Higher levels of CEBs are determined by levels of customer autonomy and fit between goal-orientation and goal-pursuit.

- Control-based motivation underlying customer engagement behavior assumes that customers who have access to more resources feel highly competent in attaining goals, and therefore sense high perceived control. Perceived control in CEBs, aided by firm empowerment, allows customers to believe they can influence firm practices and policies and is an effective route to psychological ownership.

- The degree of marketing-mix customization depends on the level of control given to customers by firms. At high levels of autonomy, customers get to fully (or largely) customize the marketing-mix, whereas at low levels customers get to partly customize.

EXERCISES

Questions

1. Loyalty programs are designed to reward customer purchase behavior. Discuss how companies are moving away from transaction-oriented loyalty programs to an integrated system to build long-term customer relationship.

2. Explain how companies design multi-tier loyalty programs to make it work. Why are customers motivated to participate in multi-tier loyalty programs?

3. Explain the following: (a) points pressure effect, (b) rewarded-behavior effect, (c) goal-gradient hypothesis, and (d) reciprocity norm present in instrumental benefits sought by customers.

4. Explain the following: (a) upward social comparison, (b) downward social comparison, and (c) lateral social comparison present in symbolic benefits sought by customers.

5. Explain the following: (a) relational norms, (b) customer gratitude, (c) social identity, and (d) customer-company identification present in emotional benefits sought by customers.

6. Explain the following: (a) procedural learning, (b) experiential learning, (c) self-learning, and (d) associative learning and habit formation present in cognitive benefits sought by customers.

7. Explain the concept of customer engagement. What are the fundamental tenets of customer engagement and how are they conceptually similar to (a) the foundational premises of the S-D logic and (b) concept of resource integration?

8. Explain the following: (a) trust and commitment and (b) gratitude and norms of reciprocity present in relationship-based motivation underlying customer engagement behavior (CEBs) with companies.

9. Explain the following: (a) customer-company identification and (b) customer-peer identification present in identification-based motivation underlying customer engagement behavior (CEBs) with companies.

10. Explain the following: (a) process-related benefits as in procedural justice and interactional justice and (b) outcome-related benefits as in distributive justice present in justice-based motivation underlying customer engagement behavior (CEBs) with companies.

11. Explain the following: (a) value of goal-object, (b) customer autonomy, and (c) customer goal orientation present in goal-based motivation underlying customer engagement behavior (CEBs) with companies.

12. Explain the following: (a) customer perceived control, (b) customer empowerment, and (c) customer psychological ownership present in control-based motivation underlying customer engagement behavior (CEBs) with companies.

Group Discussion

1. Air Canada is launching a new multi-tier loyalty program in 2020: Aeroplan Silver (25,000 miles), Aeroplan Black (50,000 miles), and Aeroplan Diamond (100,000 miles). Status members in the Aeroplan program are recognized with three exclusive benefits: *flight reward benefits* (e.g., up to 20% off, up to 25% off, and up to 35% off); *bonus miles* (e.g., up to 2 status bonus miles/$1 spent; up to 2 status bonus miles/$1 spent Plus 250 bonus miles per stay in Marriott; and up to 4 status bonus miles/$1 spent Plus 250 bonus miles per stay in Marriott). In addition, members receive other *privileges* (e.g., hotels and resorts room upgrade, priority access, preferential rate) depending on the specific plan. The higher your status in the Aeroplan program, the greater the benefits you will enjoy.

   As a small group, discuss the following benefits (along with their psychological motivation and mechanism) that loyal customers seek to obtain from Air Canada: (a) instrumental benefits, (b) symbolic benefits, (c) emotional benefits, and (d) cognitive benefits. If these multiple benefits could be prioritized into a hierarchy, which benefit(s) are customers motivated by the most and which are they motivated by the least in the context of Air Canada? Why?

2. Nikon launched the "The Warner Sound Captured by Nikon" experiential engagement initiative at the 2013 South by Southwest (SXSW) Interactive Film and Music Conference and Festival. The purpose was to generate customer contributions to the brand's marketing communication that would increase brand awareness and excitement for its key products. Nikon gave participants cameras to capture live performance and enabled them to share their live-streamed captured content automatically by providing the hashtag #NikonWarnerSound. Nikon also set up on-site Wi-Fi-enabled booths to allow participants to share captured images with their social networks. Nikon also invited select artists to participate allowing them to capture and share their own personal experiences.

   As a small group, discuss the following motivations (along with their psychological mechanism) that customers seek in *engaging* with Nikon: (a) relationship-based motivation, (b) identification-based motivation, (c) justice-based motivation, (d) goal-based motivation, and (e) control-based motivation. If these multiple engagement motivations could be prioritized into a hierarchy, which motivation(s) drive customers' engagement the most and which drive the least in the context of Nikon? Why?

HBS and Ivey Cases

- AnswerDash (9-516-106)
- Reinventing Best Buy (9-716-455)
- Chase Sapphire (9-518-024)
- Laurs & Bridz (9B18A004)

CASE QUESTIONS

AnswerDash

1. Discuss how AnswerDash can develop an integrated system of loyalty program to build long-term customer relationship.

2. Explain the following with respect to AnswerDash: (a) points pressure effect, (b) rewarded-behavior effect, (c) goal-gradient hypothesis, and (d) reciprocity norm present in instrumental benefits sought by customers.

3. Explain how AnswerDash can implement the concept of customer engagement. How can it implement the foundational premises of the S-D logic?

4. Explain the gratitude and norms of reciprocity present in relationship-based motivation underlying customer engagement behavior (CEBs) with AnswerDash.

5. Explain the following: (a) value of goal-object, (b) customer autonomy, and (c) customer goal orientation present in goal-based motivation underlying customer engagement behavior (CEBs) with AnswerDash.

6. Discuss the following motivations (along with their psychological mechanism) that customers seek in engaging with AnswerDash: (a) relationship-based motivation, (b) identification-based motivation, (c) justice-based motivation, (d) goal-based motivation, and (e) control-based motivation. If these multiple engagement motivations could be prioritized into a hierarchy, which motivation(s) drive customers' engagement the most and which drive the least in the context of AnswerDash.? Why?

Reinventing Best Buy

1. Explain how Best Buy can design multi-tier loyalty programs that work. Why would its customers be motivated to participate in such loyalty programs?

2. Explain the following with respect to Best Buy: (a) upward social comparison, (b) downward social comparison, and (c) lateral social comparison present in symbolic benefits sought by customers.

3. Explain the following: (a) procedural learning, (b) experiential learning, (c) self-learning, and (d) associative learning and habit formation present in cognitive benefits sought by customers of Best Buy.

4. Explain customer–company identification and customer–peer identification present in identification-based motivation underlying customer engagement behavior (CEBs) with Best Buy.

5. Explain the following: (a) process-related benefits as in procedural justice and interactional justice and (b) outcome-related benefits as in distributive justice present in justice-based motivation underlying customer engagement behavior (CEBs) with Best Buy.

6. How can Best Buy make use of customer psychological ownership present in control-based motivation to enhance customer engagement behavior (CEBs)?

7. Discuss the following benefits (along with their psychological motivation and mechanism) that loyal customers seek to obtain from Best Buy: (a) instrumental benefits, (b) symbolic benefits, (c) emotional benefits, and (d) cognitive benefits. If these multiple benefits could be prioritized into a hierarchy, which benefit(s) are customers motivated by the most and which are they motivated by the least in the context of Best Buy? Why?

Chase Sapphire

1. Explain how JPMorgan can design multi-tier loyalty programs that work. Why would its customers be motivated to participate in such loyalty programs?

2. Explain the following with respect to JPMorgan: (a) points pressure effect, (b) rewarded-behavior effect, (c) goal-gradient hypothesis, and (d) reciprocity norm present in instrumental benefits sought by customers.

3. Explain the following: (a) procedural learning, (b) experiential learning, (c) self-learning, and (d) associative learning and habit formation present in cognitive benefits sought by customers of JPMorgan.

4. Explain the gratitude and norms of reciprocity present in relationship-based motivation

underlying customer engagement behavior (CEBs) with JPMorgan.

5. Explain the following: (a) value of goal-object, (b) customer autonomy, and (c) customer goal orientation present in goal-based motivation underlying customer engagement behavior (CEBs) with JPMorgan.

6. How can JPMorgan make use of customer psychological ownership present in control-based motivation to enhance customer engagement behavior (CEBs)?

7. Discuss the following benefits (along with their psychological motivation and mechanism) that loyal customers seek to obtain from JPMorgan: (a) instrumental benefits, (b) symbolic benefits, (c) emotional benefits, and (d) cognitive benefits. If these multiple benefits could be prioritized into a hierarchy, which benefit(s) are customers motivated by the most and which are they motivated by the least in the context of JPMorgan? Why?

Laurs & Bridz

1. Discuss how Laurs & Bridz can move away from transaction-oriented loyalty programs to an integrated system of loyalty program to build long-term customer relationship.

2. Explain how Laurs & Bridz can design multi-tier loyalty programs that work. Why would its customers be motivated to participate in such loyalty programs?

3. Explain the following: (a) value of goal-object, (b) customer autonomy, and (c) customer goal orientation present in goal-based motivation underlying customer engagement behavior (CEBs) with Laurs & Bridz.

4. Explain how Laurs & Bridz can implement the concept of customer engagement. How can it implement the foundational premises of the S-D logic?

5. Explain customer–company identification present in identification-based motivation underlying customer engagement behavior (CEBs) with Laurs & Bridz.

6. Explain the following: (a) process-related benefits as in procedural justice and interactional justice and (b) outcome-related benefits as in distributive justice present in justice-based motivation underlying customer engagement behavior (CEBs) with Laurs & Bridz.

7. Discuss the following motivations (along with their psychological mechanism) that customers seek in engaging with Laurs & Bridz: (a) relationship-based motivation, (b) identification-based motivation, (c) justice-based motivation, (d) goal-based motivation, and (e) control-based motivation. If these multiple engagement motivations could be prioritized into a hierarchy, which motivation(s) drive customers' engagement the most and which drive the least in the context of Laurs & Bridz.? Why?

REFERENCES

Adams, J.S. (1965), Inequity in social exchange, in L. Berkowitz (Ed.), *Advances in Experimental Social Psychology* (Vol. 2, pp. 267–299). New York, NY: Academic Press.

Ahearne, M.C., C.B. Bhattacharya, and T. Gruen (2005), Antecedents and Consequences of Customer-Company Identification: Expanding the Role of Relationship Marketing, *Journal of Applied Psychology* 90: 574–585.

Algesheimer René, Utpal M. Dholakia, and Hermann Andreas (2005), The Social Influence of Brand Community: Evidence from European Car Clubs, *Journal of Marketing* 69(July): 19–34.

Arbore, A. and Z. Estes (2013), Loyalty Program Structure and Consumers' Perceptions of Status: Feeling Special in a Grocery Store? *Journal of Retailing and Consumer Services* 20: 439–444.

Arnould, Eric J., Linda L. Price, and Avinash Malshe (2006), Toward a Cultural Resource-Based Theory of the Customer, in Robert F. Lusch and Stephen L. Vargo (Eds.), *The New Dominant Logic in Marketing: Dialog, Debate and Directions* (pp. 91–104). Armonk, NY: M.E. Sharpe.

Ashforth, Blake E. and Fred Mael (1989), Social Identity Theory and the Organization, *Academy of Management Review* 14(1): 20–39.

Averill, James R. (1973), Personal Control Over Aversive Stimuli and its Relationship to Stress, *Psychological Bulletin* 80(4), 286–303.

Ballantyne, D. and R.J. Varey (2006), Creating Value-in-Use through Marketing Interaction: The Exchange Logic of Retailing, Communicating and Knowing, *Marketing Theory* 6: 335–348.

Bandura, Albert (1977), Self-Efficacy: Toward a Unifying Theory of Behavioral Change, *Psychological Review* 84(2): 191–215

Bandura, Albert (1986), *Social Foundations of Thought and Action: A Social Cognitive Theory*. Englewood Cliffs, NJ: Prentice-Hall.

Bettencourt, Lance A. (1997), Customer Voluntary Performance: Customers as Partners in Service Delivery, *Journal of Retailing* 73(3), 383–406.

Bhattacharya, C.B. and S. Sen (2003), Consumer-Company Identification: A Framework for Understanding Consumers' Relationships with Companies, *Journal of Marketing* 67(2): 76–88.

Bies, R. and R. Moag (1986), Interactional Justice: Communication Criteria of Fairness, in R.J. Lewicki, B.H. Sheppard, and M.H. Bazerman (Eds.), *Research on Negotiations in Organizations* (pp. 43–55). Stanford, CA: Stanford University Press.

Bijmolt, Tammo H.A., M. Dorotic, and P.C. Verhoef (2010), Loyalty Programs: Generalizations on their Adoption, Effectiveness and Design. *Foundations and Trends in Marketing* 5(4): 197–258.

Bijmolt, Tammo H.A., Manfred Krafft, F. Javier Sese, and Vijay Viswanathan (2018), Multi-Tier Loyalty Programs to Stimulate Customer Engagement, in Robert W. Palmatier, V. Kumar, and Colleen M. Gumme (Eds.), *Customer Engagement Marketing* (pp. 119–139). Palgrave Macmillan, Springer.

Bijmolt, Tammo H.A. and P.C. Verhoef (2017), Loyalty Programs: Current Insights, Recent Challenges, and Emerging Developments, in B. Wierenga and R. van der Lans (Eds.), *Marketing Decision Models*. New York, NY: Springer.

Bleier, Alexander, A. D. Keyser, and K. Verleye (2018), Customer Engagement through Personalization and Customization, in Robert W. Palmatier, V. Kumar, and Colleen M. Harmeling (Eds.), *Customer Engagement Marketing* (pp. 75–94). Palgrave Macmillan, Springer.

Bowden, Jana lay-Hwa (2009), The Process of Customer Engagement: A Conceptual Framework, *Journal of Marketing Theory and Practice* 17(1): 63–74.

Brashear-Alejandro, T., J. Kang, and M.D. Groza (2016), Leveraging Loyalty Programs to Build Customer-Company Identification, *Journal of Business Research* 69(3): 1190–1198.

Brodie, Roderick J., Linda D. Hollebeek, Biljana Juric, and Ana Ilic (2011), Customer Engagement: Conceptual Domain, Fundamental Propositions, and Implications for Research, *Journal of Service Research* 14(3): 252–271.

Brown, Tom J., Thomas E. Barry, Peter A. Dacin, and Richard F. Gunst (2005), Spreading the word: Investigating Antecedents of Consumers' Positive Word-of-Mouth Intentions and Behaviors in a Retailing Context, *Journal of the Academy of Marketing Science* 33(2): 123–138.

Buechel, Eva C. and Chris Janiszewski (2014), A Lot of Work or a Work of Art: How the Structure of a Customized Assembly Task Determines the Utility Derived from Assembly Effort, *Journal of Consumer Research* 40(5): 960–972.

Chandler, Jennifer D. and Robert F. Lusch (2015), Service Systems a Broadened Framework and Research Agenda on Value Propositions, Engagement, and Service Experience, *Journal of Service Research* 18(1): 6–22.

Cohen-Charash, Y. and Spector, P.E. (2001). The role of justice in organizations: A meta-analysis. *Organizational Behavior and Human Decision Processes*, 86: 278–321.

Constantin, James A. and Robert F. Lusch (1994), *Understanding Resource Management*. Oxford, OH: The Planning Forum.

Crowe, E. and E.T. Higgins (1997), Regulatory Focus and Strategic Inclinations: Promotion and Prevention in Decision-Making, *Organizational Behavior and Human Decision Processes* 69: 117–132.

Deci, Edward L. and Richard M. Ryan (1980), The Empirical Exploration of Intrinsic Motivational Processes, in Leonard Berkowitz (Ed), *Advances in Experimental Social Psychology* (Vol. 13, pp. 39–80). New York, NY: Academic Press.

Drèze, X. and J.C. Nunes (2009), Feeling Superior: The Impact of Loyalty Program Structures on Consumer's Perceptions of Status, *Journal of Consumer Research* 35(6): 890–905.

Drèze, X. and J.C. Nunes (2011), Recurring Goals and Learning: The Impact of Successful Reward Attainment on Purchase Behavior, *Journal of Marketing Research* 48(2): 268–281.

Dunn, Jennifer R. and Maurice E. Schweitzer (2005), Feeling and Believing: The Influence of Emotion on Trust, *Journal of Personality and Social Psychology* 88(5): 736–748.

Escalas, J.E. and J.R. Bettman (2005), Self-Construal, Reference Groups, and Brand Meaning, *Journal of Consumer Research* 32(3): 378–389.

Esmark, C.L., S.M. Noble, and J.E. Bell (2016), Open versus Selective Customer Loyalty Programs, *European Journal of Marketing* 50(5/6): 770–795.

Festinger, L. (1954), A Theory of Social Comparison Processes, *Human Relations* 7(2): 117–140.

Foa, Uriel (1976), Resource Theory of Social Exchanges, in John S. Thibaut, Janet Spence, and Rachel Carson (Eds.), *Contemporary Topics in Social Psychology*. Morristown, NJ: General Learning Press.

Fombelle, Paul W., Cheryl Burke Jarvis, James Ward, and Lonnie Ostrom (2012), Leveraging Customers' Multiple Identities: Identity Synergy as a Driver of Organizational Identification, *Journal of the Academy of Marketing Science* 40(4): 587–604.

Fournier, Susan, Sylvia Sensiper, James H. McAlexander, and John W. Schouten (2001), *Building Brand Community on the Harley Davidson Posse Ride*, Harvard Business School Case, Reprint No. 501009, Milwaukee.

Fuchs, Christoph, Emanuela Prandelli, and Martin Schreier (2010), The Psychological Effects of Empowerment Strategies on Consumers' Product Demand," *Journal of Marketing* 74(1): 65–79.

Gierl, H. and V. Huettl (2010), Are Scarce Products Always More Attractive? The Interaction of Different Types of Scarcity Signals with Products' suitability for Conspicuous Consumption, *International Journal of Research in Marketing* 27(3): 225–235.

Gorgievski, Marjan J., and Stevan E. Hobfoll (2008), Work Can Burn us Out or Fire Us Up: Conservation of Resources in Burnout and Engagement, in J.R.B. Halbesleben (Ed.), *Handbook of Stress and Burnout in Health Care* (pp. 7–22). Hauppauge, NY: Nova Science.

Groeger, L., L. Moroko, and L.D. Hollebeek (2016), Capturing Value from Non-Paying Consumers' Engagement Behaviors: Field Evidence and Development of a Theoretical Model, *Journal of Strategic Marketing* 24(3–4): 190–209.

Gronroos, C. (1990), Marketing Redefined. *Management Decision* 28(8): 5–9.

Gummesson, Evert (2002), *Total Relationship Marketing*. Boston, MA: Butterworth Heinemann.

Halbesleben, Jonathon R.B. (2006), Sources of Social Support and Burnout: A Meta-Analytic Test of the Conservation of Resources Model, *Journal of Applied Psychology* 91(5): 1134–1145.

Halbesleben, Jonathan R.B. and M. Ronald Buckley (2004). Burnout in Organizational Life. *Journal of Management* 30(6): 859–879.

Halbesleben, Jonathan R.B., Jean-Pierre Neveu, Samantha C. Paustian-Underdahl, and Mina Westman (2014), Getting to the 'COR': Understanding the Role of Resources in Conservation of Resources Theory, *Journal of Management*, 40(July): 1334–1364.

Harmeling, Colleen M., Jordan W. Moffett, Mark J. Arnold, and Brad D. Carlson (2017), Toward a Theory of Customer Engagement Marketing, *Journal of the Academy of Marketing Science* 45(3): 312–335.

Henderson, C.M., J.T. Beck, and Robert W. Palmatier (2011), Review of the Theoretical Underpinning of Loyalty Programs, *Journal of Consumer Psychology* 21(3): 256–276.

Higgins, E. Tory (1997), Beyond Pleasure and Pain, *American Psychologist*, 52 (12): 1280–1300.

Higgins, E. Tory (2006), Value from Hedonic Experience and Engagement, *Psychological Review* 113(3): 439–460.

Hobfoll, Stevan E. (1988), *The Ecology of Stress*. New York, NY: Hemisphere.

Hobfoll, Stevan E. (1989), Conservation of Resources: A New Attempt at Conceptualizing Stress, *American Psychologist* 44(3): 513–524.

Hobfoll, Stevan E. (2001), The Influence of Culture, Community, and the Nested-Self in the Stress Process: Advancing Conservation of Resources Theory, *Applied Psychology* 50(3), 337–421.

Hollebeek, L.D., J. Conduit, G. Soutar, J. Sweeney, I.O. Karpen, W. Jarvis, and T. Chen (2016), Epilogue to the Special Issue and Reflections on the Future of Engagement Research, *Journal of Marketing Management* 32(5–6): 586–594.

Hu, Y. and C. Van den Bulte (2014), Nonmonotonic Status Effects in New Product Adoption, *Marketing Science* 33(4): 509–533.

Jaakkola, E. and M. Alexander (2014), The Role of Customer Engagement Behavior in Value Co-Creation: A Service System Perspective, *Journal of Service Research* 17(3): 247–261.

Jimenez, F.R., K.E. Voss, and G.L. Frankwick (2013), A Classification Schema of Co-Production of Goods: An Open-Systems Perspective, *European Journal of Marketing* 47(11–12): 1841–1858.

Kivetz, R., O. Urminsky, and Y. Zheng (2006), The Goal-Gradient Hypothesis Resurrected: Purchase Acceleration, Illusionary Goal Progress, and Customer Retention, *Journal of Marketing Research* 43(1): 39–58.

Kopalle, P.K., Y. Sun, S.A. Neslin, B. Sun, V. Swaminathan (2012), The Joint Sales Impact of Frequency Reward and Customer Tier Components of Loyalty Programs, *Marketing Science* 31(2): 216–235.

Kumar, V., Lerzan Aksoy, Bas Donkers, Rajkumar Venkatesan, Thorsten Wiesel, and Sebastian Tillmanns (2010), Undervalued or Overvalued Customers: Capturing Total Customer Engagement Value, *Journal of Service Research* 13(3): 297–310.

Lemon, Katherine N. and Peter C. Verhoef (2016), Understanding Customer Experience Throughout the Customer Journey, *Journal of Marketing* 80: 69–96.

Leventhal, G.S. (1980). What Should Be Done with Equity Theory? New Approaches to The Study of Fairness in Social Relationships, in K. Gergen, M. Greenberg and R. Willis (Eds.), *Social Exchange: Advances in Theory and Research* (pp. 27–55). New York, NY: Plenum Press.

Lewis, H. (2008), http://www.businessinsider.com/2008/10/radiohead-s-innovative-approach-paid-off-or-did-it-?IR=T. accessed 10 January 2017.

Lind, A.E. and T.R. Tyler (1988), *The Social Psychology of Procedural Justice*. New York, NY: Plenum.

Liu-Thompkins, Y. and L. Tam (2013), Not All Repeat Customers are the Same: Designing Effective Cross-Selling Promotion on the Basis of Attitudinal Loyalty and Habit, *Journal of Marketing* 77(5): 21–36.

Löbler, Helge (2011), Position and Potential of Service-Dominant Logic–Evaluated in an 'Ism Frame' for Further Development, *Marketing Theory* 11(1): 51–73.

Löbler, H. (2013), Service-Dominant Networks: An Evolution from the Service Dominant Logic Perspective, *Journal of Service Management* 24(4): 420–434.

Lusch, R.F., S.L. Vargo, and M. Tanniru (2010), Service, Value Networks, and Learning, *Journal of the Academy of Marketing Science* 38(1): 19–31.

McFerran, B. and J.J. Argo (2014), The Entourage Effect, *Journal of Consumer Research* 40(5): 871–884.

Melnyk, V. and S.M.J. van Osselaer (2012), Make Me Special: Gender Differences in Consumers' Responses to Loyalty Programs, *Marketing Letters* 23(3): 545–559.

Morgan, Robert M. and Shelby D. Hunt (1994), The Commitment-Trust Theory of Relationship Marketing, *Journal of Marketing* 58(July): 20–38.

Muniz, Albert M. and Thomas C. O'Guinn (2001), Brand Community, *Journal of Consumer Research* 27: 412–432.

Palmatier, Robert W. (2008), *Relationship Marketing*. Cambridge, MA: Marketing Science Institute.

Palmatier, Robert W., Rajiv P. Dant, Dhruv Grewal, and Kenneth R. Evans (2006), Factors Influencing the Effectiveness of Relationship Marketing: A Meta-Analysis, *Journal of Marketing* 70: 136–153.

Palmatier, Robert W., Rajiv P. Dant, Dhruv Grewal, and Mark B. Houston (2007), *Relationship Marketing Dynamics* (pp. 1–37). Seattle WA: University of Washington Working Paper 1.

Palmatier, Robert W., C. Burke Jarvis, J.R. Bechkoff, and F.R. Kardes (2009), The Role of Customer Gratitude in Relationship Marketing, *Journal of Marketing* 73(5): 1–18.

Pansari, Anita and V. Kumar (2017), Customer Engagement: The Construct, Antecedents, and Consequences, *Journal of the Academy of Marketing Science* 45(3):294–311.

Peters, Linda D., Helge Löbler, Roderick J. Brodie, Christoph F. Breidbach, Linda D. Hollebeek, Sandra D. Smith, David Sorhammar, and Richard J. Varey (2014), Theorizing about Resource Integration through Service-Dominant Logic, *Marketing Theory* 14(3), 249–268.

Pierce, Jon L., Tatiana Kostova, and Kurt T. Dirks (2001), Toward a Theory of Psychological Ownership in Organizations, *Academy of Management Review* 26(2), 298–310.

Ramani, G. and V. Kumar (2008), Interaction Orientation and Firm Performance, *Journal of Marketing* 72: 27–45.

Schwartz, S.H. and W. Bilsky (1990), Toward a Theory of the Universal Content and Structure of Values: Extensions and Cross-Cultural Replications, *Journal of Personality and Social Psychology* 58(5): 878–891.

Sheth, Jagdish N. and Atul Parvatiyar (1995), Relationship Marketing in Consumer Markets: Antecedents and Consequences, *Journal of the Academy of Marketing Science* 23(4): 255–271.

Skarlicki, Daniel P., and Robert Folger (1997), Retaliation in the Workplace: The Roles of Distributive, Procedural, and Interactional Justice, *Journal of Applied Psychology* 82(3), 434–443.

Skinner, Ellen A. (1996), A Guide to Constructs of Control, *Journal of Personality and Social Psychology* 71(September): 549–570.

Spaulding, E. and C. Perry (2013), http://www.bain.com/publications/articles/making-it-personal-rules-for-success-in-product-customization.aspx. accessed 10 January 2017.

Sprott, David, Sandor Czellar, and Eric Spangenberg (2009), The Importance of a General Measure of Brand Engagement on Market Behavior: Development and Validation of a Scale, *Journal of Marketing Research* 46(1): 92–104.

Tajfel, H. and J. Turner (1979), An Integrative Theory of Intergroup Conflict, in W.G. Austin and S. Worchel (Eds.), *The Social Psychology of Intergroup Relations* (pp. 138–182). Monterey: Wadsworth.

Tajfel, Henri and John C. Turner (1985), The Social Identity Theory of Intergroup Behaviour, in S. Worchel and W. G. Austin (Eds.), *Psychology of Intergroup Relations* (pp. 7–24). Chicago, IL: Nelson-Hall.

Tanford, S. (2013), The Impact of Tier Level on Attitudinal and Behavioral Loyalty of Hotel Reward Member Members, *International Journal of Hospitality Management* 34: 285–294.

Taylor, G.A. and S.A. Neslin (2005), The Current and Future Sales Impact of a Retail Frequency Reward Program, *Journal of Retailing* 81(4): 293–305.

Thaler, Richard (1980), Toward a Positive Theory of Consumer Choice, *Journal of Economic Behavior & Organization,* 1(1) March: 39–60.

Thibaut, J. and Walker, L. (1975). *Procedural Justice: A Psychological Analysis.* Hillsdale, NJ: Erlbaum.

Tietje, Brian C. (2002), When Do Rewards Have Enhancement Effects? An Availability Valence Approach, *Journal of Consumer Psychology* 12(4): 363–373.

Tyler, T.R. (1994). Psychological Models of the Justice Motive: Antecedents of Distributive and Procedural Justice, *Journal of Personality and Social Psychology* 67(November): 850–863.

Van de Ven, N., M. Zeelenberg, and R. Pieters (2009), Leveling Up and Down: The Experiences of Benign and Malicious Envy, *Emotion* 9(3): 419–429.

Van Doorn, Jenny, Katherine N. Lemon, Vikas Mittal, Stephan Nass, Doreen Pick, Peter Pirner, and Peter C. Verhoef (2010), Customer Engagement Behavior: Theoretical Foundations and Research Directions, *Journal of Service Research* 13(3): 253–266.

Vargo, Stephen L. and Robert F. Lusch (2004), Evolving to a New Dominant Logic for Marketing, *Journal of Marketing* 68: 1–17.

Vargo, Stephen L. and Robert F. Lusch (2008), Service-Dominant Logic: Continuing the Evolution, *Journal of the Academy of Marketing Science* 36(1): 1–10.

Vargo, Stephen L. and Robert F. Lusch (2011), It's all B2B… and Beyond: Toward a Systems Perspective of the Market, *Industrial Marketing Management* 40(2), 181–187.

Venkatesh, Alladi, Lisa Penaloza, and A. Fuat Firat (2006), The Market as a Sign System and the Logic of the Market, in Robert F. Lusch and Stephen L. Vargo (Eds.), *The New Dominant Logic in Marketing: Dialog, Debate and Directions* (pp. 251–265). Armonk, NY: M.E. Sharpe.

Viswanathan, V., S. Tillmanns, M. Krafft, and D. Asselmann (2017a), *Counting on Recommendations" The Roles of Extroversion and Opinion Leadership in Customer Engagement,* Working Paper.

Viswanathan, V., F.J. Sese, M. Krafft (2017b), *The Role of Elite Members in Influencing Loyalty Program Adoption,* Working Paper.

Vivek, S.D., S.E. Beatty, R.M. Morgan (2012), Customer Engagement: Exploring Customer Relationships beyond Purchase, *Journal of Marketing Theory and Practice* 20(2): 122–146.

Wang, Y., M. Lewis, C. Cryder, and J. Sprigg (2016), Enduring Effects of Goal Achievement and failure Within Customer Loyalty Programs: A Large Scale Field Experiment, *Marketing Science* 35(4): 565–575.

Wetzel, H.A., M. Hammerschmidt, and A.R. Zablah (2014), Gratitude versus Entitlement: A Dual Process Model of the Profitability Implications of Customer Prioritization, *Journal of Marketing* 78(2): 1–19.

Winterich, Karen P., Vikas Mittal, and William T. Ross, Jr. (2009), Donation Behavior Toward In-Groups and Out-Groups: The Role of Gender and Moral Identity, *Journal of Consumer Research* 36: 199–214.

Building Employee–Customer Relationship Quality and Engagement Strategies: A Stakeholder Framework

OVERVIEW

In Chapter 5, we first provide a stakeholder-based framework that examines the criteria, pillars, and dimensions of relationship quality for employees and customers. Our stakeholder framework is consistent with established theoretical perspectives on organizations. In advancing this framework, we intersect the multiple views of stakeholder management and relationship quality. We argue that effective management of relationships is a function of understanding the appropriate stakeholder relationship criteria (i.e., descriptive, instrumental, and normative) for each stakeholder type (i.e., employees and customers) and how these influence the foundational pillars of relationship quality and, consequently, the dimensions of relationship quality. Next, we discuss employee–customer engagement theories, particularly the service-profit chain (SPC) paradigm, a set of moderating factors, and finally employee–customer engagement strategies. At the end of the chapter, we provide key takeaways and conclude with HBS and Ivey cases. But first, to give a flavor of customer relationship marketing (CRM) employee–customer relationship and engagement strategies, we provide some real-life vignettes.

OPENING VIGNETTES

Vignette 1: Walmart's recent decision to employ computerized scheduling to staff its stores dynamically according to the number of shoppers in the store is predicated on the assumption that customer satisfaction will increase as a result of having the optimal number of employees on hand, while, at the same time, the move may decrease employee satisfaction by making work schedules and pay less predictable (Brown and Lam, 2008). How does employee satisfaction carryover to customer satisfaction?

Vignette 2: Google has been placed first in Fortune's 2015 "Best Companies to Work For" list (http://fortune.com/best-companies/) and has been lauded for creating innovative products for consumers. In contrast, Walmart has been praised for its activities that positively affect customers, such as selling concentrated laundry detergent, but it has been criticized for engaging in activities that can negatively affect its employees, including allegations of gender discrimination and sourcing products from suppliers with unsafe working conditions for employees. Does consistency in a firm's activities directed at customers and employees matter?

Vignette 3: American Express began an internal program in 2006 focusing on training and incentivizing staff to engage more actively in customer purchase (e.g., airline tickets) and customer care (e.g., discussions about billing questions) (see Figure 5.1). Instead of continuing with its ineffective outbound calls, the company scrapped it in favor of a new system that invited service representatives to decide for themselves how long they wanted to spend on each call. The results were remarkable: customers increased their spending on Amex products by 8%–10% (Kumar and Pansari, 2015) and the overall profits on services also increased.

Figure 5.1: American Express launched a program to focus on training and incentivizing staff to engage more actively in customer purchase and customer care and reaped big dividends.

INTRODUCTION: A STAKEHOLDER FRAMEWORK

Stakeholder Relationship Criteria

Stakeholders are identified through actual or potential benefits or harms that they experience or anticipate as a result of the firm's actions or inactions, and vice-versa. The stakeholder model of the firm is based on three central criteria: (1) descriptive, (2) instrumental, and (3) normative (Donaldson and Preston, 1995). The *descriptive* criterion of the stakeholder framework describes, and sometimes explains, specific firm characteristics and behaviors. It is meant to outline a participant's view of what the firm actually *is* vis-à-vis stakeholders as well as the mechanisms through which different views come into being (Donaldson and Preston, 1995; Jones and Wicks, 1999). Hence, descriptive justification mirrors the observed reality of firms and reveals what firms *actually* do.

The *instrumental* criterion identifies connections between actions taken to manage stakeholders and firm objectives (Jones and Wicks, 1999). The view that stakeholder management and favorable performance go hand in hand has become commonplace in management literature. While several studies have established a connection between social and financial performance (e.g., Choi and Wang, 2009; Hillman and Keim, 2001; Waddock and Graves, 1997), there is still a lack of compelling empirical evidence (Berman *et al.*, 1999; Preston and Sapienza, 1990). However, the lack of empirical verification can be offset by analytical arguments of stakeholder–agency theory where managers are seen as agents of [all] other stakeholders and stakeholder–agent relationships are developed to accomplish organizational tasks with maximum efficiency and generate maximum value (Donaldson and Preston, 1995).

Finally, the *normative* criterion interprets the moral guidelines and obligations of the firm toward stakeholders (Evan and Freeman, 1984). While opportunistic behavior of managers as agents may be curbed through monitoring and enforcement, the ultimate success of stakeholder–agency theory requires normative considerations. The normative justification elevates the principle of fairness to a higher level and moves away from the "economic contracts" as captured under instrumental justification to "social contracts", though in the pursuit of value creation (Freeman, 1999). Normative justification, thus conceptualized, aligns with what Friedman and Miles refer to as the *third kind*, i.e., "identify to whom and for what managers are responsible given the contemporary legal and institutional context" (2006, p. 41).

We need the help of all three criteria to capture the full gamut of stakeholder relationships proposed in our framework (see Figure 5.2). For instance, the separation thesis where business decisions have no moral content and moral decisions have no business content is not defensible any longer as firms enacting moral norms are likely generating economic value as a result of it (Jones and Wicks, 1999; Freeman, 1999; Freeman *et al.*, 2010). Primary relationship criterion refers to the central criterion used by the focal firm (i.e., descriptive, instrumental, or normative) to evaluate its relationships with a given stakeholder, and therefore the focus of managerial attention. Secondary relationship criterion on the other hand is not the central focus of managerial attention but may be instrumental in influencing the primary criterion, directly or indirectly, and thus deemed to be important.

Stakeholder Relationship Quality

The concept of relationship quality is rooted in the relationship marketing literature espoused as a fundamental shift in marketing strategy and has been heralded as the impetus for a shifting marketing paradigm (Sheth and Parvatiyar, 1995). As noted earlier,

Figure 5.2: The stakeholder model of the firm is based on three central criteria: descriptive, instrumental, and normative.

relationship marketing is defined as "all marketing activities directed toward establishing, developing, and maintaining successful relational exchanges" (Morgan and Hunt, 1994, p. 22). Relationship quality refers to the overall assessment of the strength of a relationship, conceptualized as a multi-dimensional construct capturing the different but related facets of a relationship (Palmatier *et al.*, 2007). It is a complex phenomenon, and extant literature in marketing has acknowledged that it is a higher-order construct involving several facets. Despite little consensus on its conceptualization (Kumar *et al.*, 1995; Hennig-Thurau *et al.*, 2002; Roberts *et al.*, 2003), scholars overwhelmingly agree that relationship quality is characterized mainly by trust, commitment, satisfaction, and organizational identification (De Wulf *et al.*, 2001; Hennig-Thurau *et al.*, 2002; Garbarino and Johnson, 1999; Bhattacharya and Sen, 2003; Roberts *et al.*, 2003).

In our stakeholder framework, since we focus on employee and customer stakeholders, we do not include satisfaction and commitment as the bases for relationship quality for several reasons. First, the norm of satisfaction, defined as perceived equity between inputs and outcomes (Adams, 1965), is appropriate whenever stakeholders enter into a transactional

exchange with the organization and, therefore, may not be valid for all stakeholder types included in our study. Second, while satisfaction, through appropriate value creation and distribution (Clarkson, 1995), is necessary for establishing relationships, it is not a sufficient condition for developing and maintaining stakeholder relationships. For example, research in customer relationships indicates that while satisfaction is necessary in exchanges that are of transactional nature, it is not a sufficient condition for relational exchanges. Rather, it is trust that differentiates transactional from relational exchanges (Garbarino and Johnson, 1999; Morgan and Hunt, 1994). In the same vein, while commitment (i.e., affective and normative commitment) is an enduring desire to maintain a valued relationship (Meyer *et al.*, 1993; Moorman *et al.*, 1992), it is a consequence of a trusting relationship that anticipates future value (see discussion on CLV). Furthermore, while commitment in a relationship may be profitable for an organization in relation to some stakeholder types (e.g., customers, employees), such an assumption is not equally valid for all stakeholder types. For instance, external distal stakeholders that are non-supportive, i.e., pressure groups (Fassin, 2009), may be perceived as a potential threat and the focal firm may not be interested in relationship commitment. Thus, we focus solely on organizational trust and examine its multi-faceted nature as the foundation for building relationship quality.

In keeping with the literature on trust, we conceptualize trust as including the element of risk or vulnerability and define it as the psychological willingness of a party (individual or organization) to be vulnerable to the actions of another based on positive expectations regarding the other party's motivations and/or behavior (Mayer *et al.*, 1995; Rousseau *et al.*, 1998). Even though stakeholders are classified within certain groups (i.e., stakeholder categories), the origin of stakeholder trust in the focal firm is grounded in an individual perspective and is directed toward the organization by accepting vulnerability to the actions of the focal firm based on positive expectations (Zaheer *et al.*, 1998). In the current stakeholder context, we examine trust at the organizational level (i.e., organizational trust) as in a reputational umbrella although we recognize attributions can be made at the organizational actor level as well (i.e., interpersonal trust). Given that our stakeholder framework involves multiple stakeholder domains, we argue for the need to identify several bases of trust that are relevant to different stakeholders (Rousseau *et al.*, 1998; Lewicki and Bunker, 1996).

While studies on trust have identified several antecedents, three characteristics of the trustee that explain a large portion of trustworthiness are: (1) *ability*, (2) *benevolence*, and (3) *integrity* (Mayer *et al.*, 1995). Ability refers to the set of skills, competencies, and characteristics that enables a firm to effectively perform in a specific domain. Benevolence is the extent to which a trustee is believed to want to do good to the trustor, aside from an egocentric motive. Integrity refers to the trustor's perception that the trustee adheres to a set of principles — personal and moral integrity that is deemed acceptable to

the trustor. As a modification to the Mayer *et al.* (1995) dimensions of trustworthiness, Madhavan and Grover (1998) distinguish between two types of ability, namely, (1) *managerial competence* and (2) *technical competence*. Whereas, managerial competence is implicated in the focal firm's ability to make decisions and manage stakeholder relationships that reflect process efficiency, technical competence reflects operational efficiency and is the focal firm's ability to deliver high-quality products and services (Verona, 1999). Recent studies have utilized this nuanced distinction in the ability dimension of trustworthiness as different stakeholders may attribute a firm's ability to different bases of competence (Hodson, 2004; Pirson and Malhotra, 2011). Further, in our stakeholder framework since the focal firm forms the trust referent, we add *identification-based trust* (Lewicki and Bunker, 1996; Tajfel and Turner, 1986), which reflects perceived value congruence between a particular stakeholder and the focal firm. While the Mayer *et al.*'s (1995) framework subsumes identification as part of integrity (as single scale item), they admit that identification-based trust should be a separate construct in research in organizational trust especially where strong relational ties exist.

We develop arguments as to which of these facets of trust form foundational bases upon which the focal firm can develop relationships with different stakeholders. The position of the stakeholder relative to the focal firm will likely influence stakeholder trust because different stakeholders face different types of vulnerabilities (Brickson, 2005; Pirson and Malhotra, 2011). Accordingly, there are different capabilities that the organization must develop and signal to build trust with stakeholders. With this as background, we now build arguments that connect stakeholder relationship criteria and relationship quality for each of the two stakeholder types.

EMPLOYEES AS INTERNAL STAKEHOLDERS

Stakeholder Relationship Criteria

The internal stakeholders of an organization exist to create and deliver value to other stakeholders through efficiency and division of labor. Relationships with internal stakeholders are therefore process-based. We argue that the primary relationship criterion useful for internal stakeholders is analytic (i.e., descriptive and instrumental). The analytic criterion for internal stakeholders is justified on the basis of agency theory where managers (agents) are hired to fulfill certain obligations for the owners (principals) by virtue of the economic relationship. Agency theory (Jensen and Meckling, 1976; Hill and Jones, 1992) explains firm governance and is based on the notion that the interests between two actors, the principal and the agent, have inherent potential for misalignment thus creating potential for the agent to not act in the best interest of the principal (i.e., opportunistic behavior). Although it was originally developed to explain the relationship between managers and owners (stockholders), agency theory has also been applied to multiple other stakeholder contexts, such as those between different managers within the same firm, between employees and customers, and between employees and different groups of stockholders and debt holders (Barney and Hesterly, 1996).

The descriptive justification can be best explained by institutional theory. While institutional theory (DiMaggio and Powell, 1983; North, 1990, 2005) is generally applicable to the firm in relation to the institutions it interacts with, its application is not necessarily confined to the boundaries of the organization field. Rather the elements of the theory (i.e., formal and informal rules and norms) can be applied to internal stakeholders within the firm, especially in the global context of multi-national enterprises (MNEs). Subsidiaries of MNEs often follow the mimetic processes of headquarters and other subsidiaries within the global network to reduce uncertainty and leverage the transfer of knowledge and institutional practices (DiMaggio and Powell, 1983). They have a tendency to model themselves after headquarters, which bestows legitimacy both in the eyes of the parent companies and within the context of the institutions of the host countries (Kostova and Zaheer, 1999). Further, given the scope and speed of globalization and institutional convergence across global markets (Griffith, 2010), MNEs are attempting to standardize aspects of firm strategies in relation to internal stakeholders across global markets.

While we have argued that the primary relationship criterion useful for internal stakeholders is analytic, we also contend that the secondary relationship criterion useful for internal stakeholders is normative. Shankman (1999) makes the argument that agency theory must include recognition of all stakeholders and requires a minimum moral standard. In this respect, stakeholder theory is much broader than agency theory and assumes both instrumental and normative criteria. Stakeholder theory, by encouraging a richer and more accurate perception and appreciation of diverse stakeholder interests, helps firms to maintain institutional legitimacy. The normative capacity to accurately perceive internal stakeholder needs, engage in ethical deliberations, and then appropriately respond in a timely manner, is a critical capability (Litz, 1996) for value creation and long-term success of the firm (i.e., means to an end).

Pillars of Stakeholder Relationship Quality

We argue that the foundation for relationships with internal stakeholders (employees), i.e., process-focused, is based on three facets of trust: (1) *managerial competence-based trust*, (2) *identification-based trust*, and (3) *benevolence-based trust*. Internal stakeholders are in a better position to care about and evaluate managerial competence of the focal firm. Based on the knowledge-based view (KBV) theory of the firm (Kogut and Zander, 1992), managerial competence is the organizations' collective "embedded knowledge," which results from individual members' stores of tacit knowledge and their interactions with internal and external environments (Kogut and Zander, 1992; Madhavan and Grover, 1998). Managerial competence absorbs critical knowledge from both internal and external sources and integrates them with various "technical competencies" within the firm (i.e., technological capabilities and marketing capabilities, Day, 1994; Verona, 1999). The goal is to successfully integrate competencies internal to the firm and leverage them efficiently through processes, systems, and structures so as to maximize process efficiency (Verona, 1999). Internal integration requires capturing tacit knowledge and even though it is difficult to explicate and transfer due to causal ambiguity, employees as internal stakeholders due to their expertise and close involvement with management function are able to process tacit information efficiently (i.e., learning by doing and through information exchange). Thus, they tend to rely on managerial competence-based trust. Some studies have shown that employees evaluate organizations on their ability to survive, compete, and perform in the marketplace thus incorporating the instrumental relationship criterion (Hodson, 2004).

Most research examining organizational identification has focused specifically on employees' identification with the organizations they work for and about what their organization *is*, thus lending itself to the mandate of descriptive criterion of stakeholder theory (Dutton *et al.*, 1994). We extend the employee domain to include all internal stakeholders and posit that relationship quality with internal stakeholders should be built on strong organizational identification. Along the lines of the KBV theory of the firm (Kogut and Zander, 1992), identification-based trust can be linked

with the "need to belong" where groups of individuals develop firm-specific shared identities that support greater communication and coordination, restrain self-interest, and generate embedded knowledge within the firm. Internal stakeholders who have frequent interactions of longer durations with the organization tend to develop closer ties and with it the inherent identity risks (Sitkin and Roth, 1993; Rousseau *et al.*, 1998). Such close relationships entail a higher need and capacity for information exchange since the stakeholder's vulnerability is likely to increase. These stakeholders evaluate whether their own values are congruent with those of the organization and stronger relations emerge when there is value congruence and cognitive overlap (i.e., identification-based trust). Because of such vulnerability and closeness, employees as internal stakeholders will also look at the organization's concern for their well-being and whether they genuinely care for them — i.e., benevolence-based trust. Benevolence-based trust becomes salient when psychological contracts shift from primarily transactional to relational in nature and when closer ties are developed (Brickson, 2007; Mayer *et al.*, 1995).

Dimensions of Stakeholder Relationship Quality

The two dimensions of relationship quality for employees as internal stakeholders namely, *management activities* and *communication effectiveness* (Kogut and Zander, 1992; Sirgy, 2002), incorporate the instrumental, descriptive, and normative perspectives in the stakeholder relationship. Management activities are designed to play an instrumental role in enhancing the efficiency and value creation of the firm thus serving the instrumental criteria of stakeholder theory (as explained by agency theory and KBV theory). Management activities are also rendered effective through formal and informal rules, processes, and structures within the organization thus serving the descriptive criteria (as explained by institutional theory). Furthermore, we argue that management activities are successful when organizational embedded knowledge is effectively leveraged by internal stakeholders (e.g., team members, project leaders, senior managers) and this happens when they can process tacit knowledge efficiently arising out of a strong sense of managerial competence-based trust (Kogut and Zander, 1992; Madhavan and Grover, 1998). The other dimension, communication effectiveness, includes the intensity and frequency of communication through the organization-wide circulation of information, need recognition, and conflict resolution (Sirgy, 2002). Learning takes place when internal stakeholders embed in frequent interactions, especially in conditions of uncertainty, complexity, and conflict to convert tacit knowledge into management activities.

We argue that both management activities and communication effectiveness within an organization are largely based on the time-sensitive nature of information as well as the critical nature of inter-functional consultation and decision-making. Urgency is the time-sensitive "stakeholder's claim" or "manager relationship" that is viewed by the internal stakeholder as "critical or highly important" (Mitchell *et al.*, 1997, p. 867). Organizational successes requires information to be processed efficiently under the assumption that internal stakeholders primarily act on benevolence-based and identification-based trust rather than opportunism, particularly when the firm invests in managing knowledge flows for greater cognitive alignment and relationship building (Madhok, 2006, p. 112) across functional boundaries. It is the knowledge dynamics across functional boundaries through communication and coordination that gives the firm sustainable competitive advantage (Kogut and Zander, 1992). Applied to employees as internal stakeholders, this leads to the institutionalization of norms and efficient flow of communication

within the entire organization. Communication effectiveness, therefore, serves the normative criteria of stakeholder theory.

CUSTOMERS AS EXTERNAL (PROXIMAL) STAKEHOLDERS

Stakeholder Relationship Criteria

External proximal stakeholder groups are external to the focal firm and yet proximal in the exchange relationship — usually typified by their stakes in the firm's activities. Relationships with external proximal stakeholders are therefore performance-based. Economic exchange to facilitate performance is the underlying motivation in exchange relationships and we believe that the external proximal stakeholders form the raison d'être for the firm's existence. We argue that the primary criterion useful for external proximal stakeholders is analytic albeit driven by instrumental motivations. The instrumental justification can be explained by several theories that focus on *cost reduction objectives*. Transaction cost economics (TCE) (Williamson, 1991) argues that firms exist to provide products and services at lower transaction costs than would be faced in the market. As the transaction characteristics (i.e., asset specificity, uncertainty, and frequency) increase, so does the likelihood that the transaction will be internalized in a firm (or hierarchy) rather than outsourced to the market. In outsourcing situations, given agency costs, outcome-based incentives may be more appropriate for the principal in the short term than behavior-based contracts as explained by agency theory (Jensen and Meckling, 1976; Hill and Jones, 1992).

The instrumental justification for external proximal stakeholders can also be explained by several theories that focus on *asset augmenting objectives*. The basic premise of the resource dependence theory (Pfeffer and Salancik, 1978) is that a firm is dependent on resources in its environment for its survival. We argue that the focal firm's performance is dependent upon resources in its proximal environment to the extent (a) the resource is important and (b) the stakeholders possessing the resource have control and discretionary power (Pfeffer and Salancik, 1978; Mitchell *et al.*, 1997). Frooman (1999), among others, notes the importance of resource dependence theory in explaining stakeholder relationships, and more specifically power differentials due to dependencies, and subsequent influence strategies of various stakeholders. Power accrues to those who control resources needed by the organization, creating power differentials. According to network theory the less central the focal firm's position in the stakeholder network, the more relative power the stakeholders wield (Rowley, 1997). The focal firm will therefore pay more attention to stakeholders who possess and control critical resources to ensure its continued survival, which may sometimes lead to inter-firm collaborations and alliances.

While cost-benefit calculus is the basis of instrumental-based theories, Freeman and Evan (1990) emphasize the notion of fairness (a normative concept) in governance rules toward managing firm performance in value creation. Hence, with external proximal stakeholders, while instrumental relationship criterion in stakeholder management offers compelling justification, the need to incorporate normative relationship criterion becomes obvious in mature relationships (especially toward building organizational resilience). The synthesis of instrumental and normative theories leads to a convergence in shared values including a belief in the intrinsic worth of the claims of all legitimate stakeholders; the rejection of egoism as a normative standard; concern for others as opposed to self-interest; and consistency of morality and capitalism (Jones and Wicks, 1999). As relationships deepen, behavior-based contracts based on principled and deontological reasoning becomes more appropriate

for the focal firm in its relationships with external proximal stakeholders (Vermillion *et al.*, 2002).

Pillars of Stakeholder Relationship Quality

We argue that the foundation for relationships with external proximal stakeholders is based on two dimensions of trust: (1) *technical competence-based trust* and (2) *benevolence-based trust*. External proximal stakeholders can easily assess the focal firm on its technical competence and are directly impacted by it, more so than its managerial competence, since economic exchange is the raison d'être for the firm's existence (i.e., instrumental justification). Technical competence is the organizations' collective store of "explicit knowledge" more than tacit knowledge and is easily codified and transferable. It includes technological and marketing capabilities that jointly impact product effectiveness — i.e., performance-based parameters of product/service quality and fit with market needs (Day, 1994; Verona, 1999). It reflects operational efficiency and denotes how well a firm can perform a certain set of tasks by which a new product or service can be developed and marketed. Such competence can be observed and assessed much more readily through objective measures. Decision rules and protocols that form the bases of firms' performance can be spelled out and evaluated explicitly (Kogut and Zander, 1992; Madhavan and Grover, 1998). For instance, the degree to which suppliers trust the focal firm depends upon the technical competence of the buying organization (Pirson and Malhotra, 2011). Similarly, customers trust the technical competence when the firm utilizes changing market knowledge to develop higher-order routines that allow it to successfully leverage a stream of profitable products and services (i.e., firm demonstrates technical and ecological fitness).

For relationships with external proximal stakeholders that are shallow in nature wherein the interactions are sparse and durations are short, attributions of integrity are likely important for trust-building (Pirson and Malhotra, 2011). Mayer *et al.* (1995, p. 722) comment that the "effect of integrity on trust will be most salient early in the relationships prior to the development of meaningful benevolence data." However, as the relationship with external proximal stakeholders deepens, integrity-based trust would be relatively less important and the need for information that the focal firm genuinely cares for them, i.e., the need for perceived organizational benevolence, increases, thus contributing to the normative justification (Schoorman *et al.*, 2007). External proximal stakeholders perceive benevolence when the focal firm expresses concern and well-being for them beyond simply distributive and procedural justice in relational exchanges (Colquitt *et al.*, 2001). Acts of benevolence are even more pronounced in building inter-organizational trust in the form of partnerships and cooperative agreements with external proximal stakeholders (Schoorman *et al.*, 2007).

Dimensions of Stakeholder Relationship Quality

The five dimensions of relationship quality for external proximal stakeholders are borrowed from service quality literature in marketing and proposed in the broader context of proximal stakeholder relationship quality (Parasuraman *et al.*, 1991, 1995; Sirgy, 2002). The dimensions are (1) tangibility, (2) reliability, (3) responsiveness, (4) assurance, and (5) empathy.[1] They incorporate both instrumental and normative functions in external proximal stakeholder relationships. We argue that the *tangibility* and *reliability* dimensions of relationship quality can be linked to the "technical competence" basis of trust as they pertain to the

competent performance of obligations and delivery of economic value to external proximal stakeholders. There is a contractual component embedded in the technical competence dimension of trust that reflects the instrumental function of risk reduction and asset augmentation within the stakeholder relationship. This means that all parties have a fair contract and its full implementation is essential to successful firm performance (Freeman and Evan, 1990). This viewpoint of trust is what Lewis and Weigert (1985) calls "calculative rational prediction," and is consistent with reducing risks and enhancing preferred economic outcomes. The other three dimensions of relationship quality, namely (1) *responsiveness*, (2) *assurance*, and (3) *empathy* are linked to the "benevolence-based" foundation of trust and reflect the normative criterion of stakeholder theory. Benevolence implies that one partner is genuinely interested in the other partner's welfare and is motivated to seek joint gain rather than an egocentric motive (Mayer *et al.*, 1995). The focal firm projects a relational organizational identity with strong dyadic ties in meeting its obligations of delivering benevolence-based value (Brickson, 2007). This viewpoint of trust is consistent with Lewis and Weigert's (1985) "leap of faith" wherein trust consists of an emotional bond and a sense of moral and ethical "goodwill" between parties — thus satisfying the normative criterion of a trusting relationship.

EMPLOYEE-CUSTOMER ENGAGEMENT RESEARCH

Employee Engagement

Employee (or job) engagement, as the positive antithesis of job burnout (Maslach *et al.*, 2001), is largely discussed in the fields of psychology and

---

1 In the service quality literature (e.g., Parasuraman *et al.*, 1991, 1995), tangibility refers to technical quality of outcomes (i.e., products and services) including tangible elements of the service-scape. Reliability means performing the service dependably, consistently, and accurately. Responsiveness is demonstrated by employees' willingness to provide prompt service and to help customers substantively. Assurance refers to the knowledge and courtesy of employees and their abilities to inspire trust and confidence, especially in a service crisis situation. Empathy refers to the caring and individualized attention that a firm's employees provide to their customers.

human resource management. Research in these fields has demonstrated that job resources are positively associated with employee engagement (Bakker and Demerouti, 2007; Maslach *et al.*, 2001). Presence of rich job resources encourages employees to increase their engagement at work. Job resources may be located at three levels: (1) the individual level, such as job skills, (2) the interpersonal level, such as supervisory and collegial support, or (3) the organizational level, such as career opportunities and job security (Bakker and Demerouti, 2007; Maslach *et al.*, 2001). These resources include the resources owned by employees and those provided by organizations. In order to engage well at work, employees need to *invest* their personal resources and *utilize* organization-provided resources.

A large number of organizational behavior research focus on employee (or work) engagement. Similar to civic engagement, the definitions of employee engagement are not agreed upon among researchers. Some attempt to find two common characteristics of employee engagement from various definitions: (1) self-investment and simultaneous investment of physical, emotional, and cognitive resources and (2) psychological attachment that relates to the work role (Christian *et al.*, 2011; Eldor and Harpaz, 2016; Kahn, 1990). Between the two characteristics, self- and resource-investment is a trigger, leading individuals to generate psychological connection to their work. The resource perspective is also reflected in Schaufeli *et al.*'s (2002) discussion about three characteristics of employee engagement: (1) vigor, (2) dedication, and (3) absorption. Employees engage with work by expending behavioral, affective, and cognitive resources. *Vigor* represents high levels of energy and self-motivated effort investment and persistence in work (i.e., behavioral in nature), *dedication* involves "a sense of significance, enthusiasm, inspiration, pride, and challenge" (i.e., affective in nature), and *absorption* is characterized by full concentration

on and deep engrossment in work (i.e., cognitive in nature) (Schaufeli *et al.*, 2002, p. 74).

Job resources have a motivational potential to help fulfill employees' basic intrinsic needs for personal growth, learning and development, and extrinsic needs for attaining work-related goals (Bakker and Demerouti, 2007). Employee engagement is thus treated as a motivational state, wherein one's self is brought in and her or his resources (e.g., energies) are actively allocated to job tasks (Kahn, 1990). Due to the motivational nature of employee engagement, engaged employees experience an emotional connection to their work role, and hence improve their work and corporate performance. In short, employee engagement implies a positive impact on both employees (e.g., better performance and more promotion opportunities) and organizations (e.g., lower turnover and higher productivity).

To summarize employee engagement shares two conceptual themes. First, a close association is required between resources and engagement. To effectively perform employee engagement, employees *invest* their own personal resources, such as energies and skill sets, and *utilize* resources furnished by organizations, such as interpersonal support (Bakker and Demerouti, 2007; Maslach *et al.*, 2001). Second, employee engagement entails positive implications, such as improved job and corporate performance. In addition to personal goal fulfillment, engaged employees also help reach the collective community's or company's goals (see Figure 5.3). The positivity of engagement is related to the nature of resources. As Bakker and his colleagues note, resources have a motivational potential and help achieve goals (Bakker and Demerouti, 2007). The active investment of resources during the engagement process implies the motivational forces that foster and intensify one's emotional bond to engagement objects (e.g., social causes or job tasks).

Figure 5.3: In addition to personal goal fulfillment, engaged employees also help reach the collective community's or company's goals.

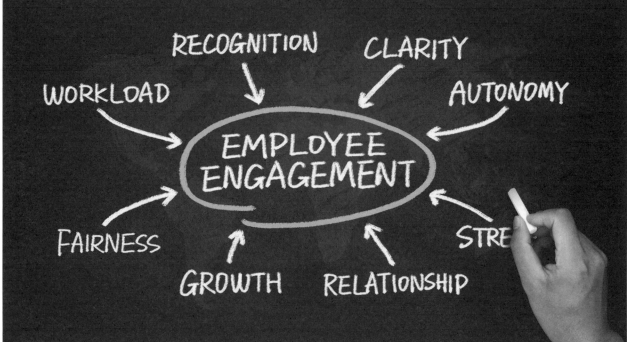

Customer Engagement

The customer engagement topic has been widely investigated in the marketing area. Some researchers, such as Bowden (2009), Brodie *et al.* (2011), Hollebeek *et al.* (2016), and Vivek *et al.* (2012), examine generic customer engagement; while others, such as Kumar *et al.* (2010), Pansari and Kumar (2017), and Van Doorn *et al.* (2010), focus on specific engagement behaviors. Recent research, such as Harmeling *et al.* (2017), Hollebeek *et al.* (2016), and Jaakkola and Alexander (2014), incorporate the notion of resources. Some aspects of resources, such as resource contribution and resource investment, are documented in the conceptualization of customer engagement.

Resource contribution reflects the value customers add to the focal company through engagement behaviors. Jaakkola and Alexander (2014) include resource contributions in the conceptualization of CEBs and define them as "voluntary resource contributions that have a brand or firm focus but go beyond what is fundamental to transactions, occur in interactions between the focal object and/or other actors, and result from motivational drivers" (p. 248). In the work of Jaakkola and Alexander (2014), resources involve knowledge, skills, labor, experience, relationships, and time. Based on this work, Harmeling *et al.* (2017) describe customer engagement as "voluntary resource contribution to a firm's marketing function, going beyond financial patronage" (p. 316). They further divide customer-owned resources (that are contributed to marketing functions) into network assets, persuasion capital, knowledge stores, and creativity.

Resource investment is the act of expending resources to gain advantages. Hollebeek *et al.* (2016) highlight resource investment in their discussion of CEBs, which involve "motivationally driven, volitional investment of focal operant resources (including cognitive, emotional, behavioral, and social knowledge and skills) and operand resources (e.g., equipment) into brand interactions in service systems." Operand resources are tangible and physical resources, such as raw materials (Constantin and Lusch, 1994) that need "some action to be performed on them to have value" (Vargo and Lusch, 2011, p. 184). Operant resources, such as knowledge and expertise, produce effects by acting on operand resources and other operant resources (Constantin and Lusch, 1994).

Some other research discusses resources and CEBs within the service-dominant (S-D) logic (Vargo and Lusch, 2004), which is deemed as a meta-framework supporting engagement research (Brodie *et al.*, 2011; Hollebeek *et al.*, 2016; Jaakkola and Alexander, 2014). This logic articulates that value creation is realized through the process of one party employing resources (e.g., competencies) to benefit the other party (Vargo and Lusch, 2004, 2008). The notion of resources (especially knowledge and skills) plays a crucial role in the S-D logic (Vargo and Lusch, 2004; 2011). Moreover, this logic states that value is co-created by integrators (e.g., customers) through the integration of resources (Vargo and Lusch, 2004), which is critical for the development of customer engagement (Hollebeek *et al.*, 2016).

We believe that resource integration involves both investing one's own resources and utilizing the other party's resources. *Resource investment* refers to expending one's own resources, with the expectation of achieving benefits. We use "investment" as opposed to "expenditure" because investment implies that the act of spending resources is motivated by customers' goals and expectations of a payoff. *Resource utilization* involves making use of company-furnished resources (such as employees) to serve both customers' and companies' purposes. In the context of resource investment and resource utilization, we next examine employee–customer engagement theories.

Employee–Customer Engagement Theories

Customer engagement and employee engagement are driven by motivational forces based on attitudinal constructs such as satisfaction (Anderson *et al.*, 2000; Harter *et al.*, 2002), commitment (Keiningham *et al.*, 2015), and identification (Homburg *et al.*, 2009) (see Figure 5.4). Earlier research is rooted in the *service-profit chain* (SPC) paradigm in which the employee's effort is considered an input to customer satisfaction and customer satisfaction is considered an input to customer loyalty as well as the firm's financial outcomes (e.g., Kamakura *et al.*, 2002). The SPC model (Heskett *et al.*, 1994, see Figure 5.5) provides an integrative framework for understanding how a firm's operational investments into service quality are related to customer perceptions and behaviors and how these translate into profit. It holds the view that satisfied employees are more productive and provide better service quality and value than less-satisfied employees, thus leading to higher customer satisfaction. While the original framework (Heskett *et al.*, 1994) with its variants (e.g., Return on Quality framework, Rust *et al.*, 1995) has proven to be useful, the SPC paradigm is somewhat limiting in terms of understanding engagement as it is based on the systems approach that is generally mechanistic in nature rather than organic.

Recently, Hogreve *et al.* (2017) using meta-analytic studies revisited the SPC model and tested the extended SPC model (see Figure 5.6). They challenged the sufficiency of the original SPC model on three grounds. First, the original SPC model suggests that internal service quality primarily enhances employee satisfaction and only indirectly influences employee retention and productivity, external service quality, and firm profitability. Hogreve *et al.* (2017) argue that higher levels of internal service quality increase employee dependence through higher costs of leaving and also because it fosters reciprocal behavior. Internal service quality also enables service

Figure 5.4 Customer engagement and employee engagement are driven by motivational forces based on attitudinal constructs such as satisfaction, commitment, and identification.

Figure 5.5: Original Service-Profit Chain (SPC) Model (Heskett *et al.*, 1994)

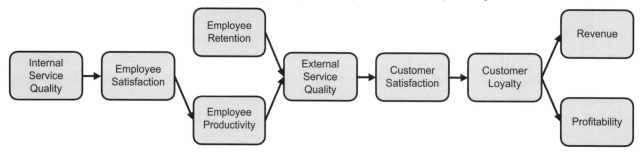

Figure 5.6: Extended Service Profit Chain (SPC) Model (Hogreve *et al.* 2017)

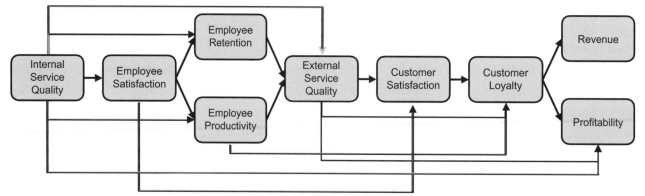

Adapted from Jens Hogreve, Anja Iseke, Klaus Derfuss, and Tonnjes Eller (2017), The Service-Profit Chain: A Meta-Analytic Test of a Comprehensive Theoretical Framework, *Journal of Marketing* 81, May 41–61.

employees to acquire skills and knowledge to better serve customers, thus increasing their productivity. Further, because customers infer service quality also from organizational service image, and not just from the service encounter, internal service quality also directly impacts external service quality. Finally, improvements in internal service quality help reduce costs and increase service efficiency, primarily by way of improved task performance and discretionary citizenship behavior, which then improves firm profitability. These additional roles and benefits of internal service quality are consistent with the literature on *service climate framework* (Schneider *et al.*, 1998), which posits that employee perceptions of management support and facilitation of service performance lead to favorable customer responses. Similar to the SPC model that has been assessed at both individual and business-unit levels, service climate can potentially be studied at both levels, albeit prior research has focused more at the business-unit level.

Second, the original SPC model posits that external service quality is a key determinant of customer intentions and behavior, with a focus on service outcomes rather than service encounters. Hogreve *et al.* (2017) argue that emotional contagion and reciprocity account for additional effects during the service encounter. Through emotional contagion, employee satisfaction directly enhances customer satisfaction through the flow of emotions (Hennig-Thurau *et al.*, 2006). The *emotional contagion framework* has been utilized to explain the correspondence between employee affect and customer response (e.g., Pugh, 2001; Brown and Lam, 2008). It operates at the individual level focusing on affect transfer in the context of employee–customer interactions in limited service encounters. Further, employee productivity, characterized by competence and customer orientation, also directly impacts customer loyalty. Competent and reliable service encounter engenders trust and relational bond and customers reciprocate by demonstrating loyalty (Gremler and Gwinner, 2000).

Third, the original SPC model implies that to optimize firms' financial performance, firms should maximize external service quality and customer satisfaction. However, Hogreve *et al.* (2017) argue that while customer satisfaction is important, customers also develop loyalty with firms through identification (Bhattacharya and Sen, 2003). Exceptional service quality helps build attractive social identities and thus customers are motivated to remain loyal. This is consistent with the findings of Homburg *et al.*, (2009) who found strong support for the social identity-based constructs that complement the conventional satisfaction-based SPC model. They provided evidence that employee identification with the company is associated with stronger customer–company identification mediated by customer orientation and this results in higher customer's willingness to pay and subsequently the financial performance of the firm. Further, firm profitability is also enhanced by improving the return on service quality (Rust *et al.*, 2002). Finally, because service quality requires investments in service equipment and personnel, its impact on profitability depends on whether or not the benefits exceed the cost. This is consistent with the return-on-quality framework (Rust *et al.*, 1995) that addresses the cost issues of implementing external service quality, a critical issue that was starkly missing from the original SPC framework.

Generalized exchange theory (GET; Bearman, 1997; Marshall, 1998) provides an alternative to social exchange theory (Bagozzi, 1975) specific to dyadic relationships by examining indirect, reciprocal exchange relationships among three or more exchange partners. GET focuses on "a chain of indirect, univocal, reciprocal transfers among at least three actors" (Marshall, 1998, p. 274). In generalized exchange, "there is no one-to-one correspondence between what two actors directly give to and receive from each other. A's giving to B is not reciprocated by B's giving to A, but by C's giving to A, where C is the third party" (Takahashi, 2000, p. 1106). Based on organizational support theory, the indirect, reciprocal model of generalized exchange works in the following sequence: first, an employee who is highly satisfied with his job (because of actions of the employer/firm) could reciprocate indirectly by satisfying the firm's customers; second, if the customer feels satisfied, she or he will reciprocate indirectly to the employer/firm by revealing purchase intentions; and finally, if the employer/firm is satisfied by customer responses, the firm will reciprocate to the employees such that they are more satisfied. Evanschitzky *et al.* (2011a) empirically demonstrate this effect by showing that the effect of owner–franchisee satisfaction on customer satisfaction is mediated by employee satisfaction, that is, owners who are satisfied have a positive multiplier effect on customer loyalty through both satisfied employees and satisfied customers. Further, employee satisfaction has a double-positive effect on customer satisfaction, such that improving employee satisfaction not only increases customer satisfaction but also nearly doubles the impact of customer satisfaction on customer purchase intention.

Moderators of Employee-Customer Engagement

In their meta-analysis, Brown and Lam (2008) found several contextual factors that moderate employee satisfaction → customer satisfaction and employee satisfaction → service quality. Both relationships were substantially stronger in services performed on people as compared to services performed on people's possessions. The same was true for studies conducted at the organizational level as compared to the individual level and also when employee satisfaction was measured globally as compared to

when it was measured by facet. These findings imply that employee job satisfaction is critical to attain positive customer responses in personal services due to strong emotional contagion effect. Further, a strong service climate (Schneider *et al.*, 1998), which operates at the group/organizational level, is more powerful in positively impacting customer responses due to interdependence effects whereby employees feed off of one another's positive affect, creating synergy effects. Managerial policies that clarify role expectations for employees and a service climate that provides support for employees are important.

Hogreve *et al.* (2017) in their meta-analytic study found that intangibility of services was a significant moderator between internal service quality and employee satisfaction. In highly intangible services where it is difficult for customers to evaluate, management makes a strong commitment to service quality as the service employee personifies the service attempting to reduce any ambiguity (Bebko, 2000). The second moderator tested by Hogreve *et al.* (2017) was co-production. They found that the effect of internal service quality on employee satisfaction was more pronounced in services that required customer co-production. As co-production can be demanding on service employees, internal service quality that supports employee development, co-production culture, and reward and recognition creates more satisfied employees. Kumar and Pansari (2016) examined the moderating effect of a firm's business type (B2B versus B2C, and manufacturing versus services) on employee engagement and its effects on customer engagement and firm financial performance. The effect becomes stronger for service-oriented firms and B2B firms.

Marketing scholars have long acknowledged the importance of managing customers and employees to enhance sales and revenues (e.g., Evanschitzky *et al.*, 2011b). It is important that firms treat both their customers and employees well; however, what happens when the firm's actions toward one stakeholder is inconsistent with the other stakeholder? Does consistency in firm activities directed at its customers and its employees affect the firm's long-term value? Groening *et al.* (2016) argued that a firm's activities directed at one stakeholder group may become more informative in the eyes of the investors when they are consistent with the firm's activities directed at another stakeholder group. More specifically, a firm's achievements/lapses directed at its customers (employees) are more informative to investors' valuation (i.e., carries more weight) if the firm also garners achievements/lapses directed at its employees (customers). In contrast, inconsistent activities directed at customers and employees provide mixed-signals and are likely to be discounted by investors. Support from customers and employees are *jointly* valuable to the firm as they are complimentary, and how the firm manages complex relationships between these two critical stakeholders is part of the recipe for competitive advantage. Therefore, engaging customers and customers should not be viewed as a zero-sum game; rather, there is a symbiotic and a mutually reinforcing association when the interests of both stakeholders are satisfied (Groening *et al.*, 2016).

EMPLOYEE–CUSTOMER ENGAGEMENT STRATEGIES

Kumar and Pansari (2016) suggest several strategies for firms that are at different levels of employee engagement and customer engagement. Based on their empirical study capturing data from employees and customers in two time frames, they demonstrated that high engagement scores led to improvement in firm performance. The authors

argue that the time for a new strategic orientation that encapsulates both customer and employee engagement is now as previous emphasis on market orientation and its impact on performance has faded over time, Specific engagement strategies are relevant for firms at different levels in the engagement scores.

High–High (High CE and High EE) Segment

In this type of firm, the employees perform to the best of their ability to deliver the organizational values to customers. The profits of such firms are expected to be higher than the profits of other firms in the industry that do not engage both customers and employees. Engaged employees help improve firm profit through reduced cost and increased efficiencies (Kumar and Pansari, 2015). Similarly, customers contribute through purchases and incentivized referrals, social media influence, and customer feedback and knowledge (Kumar, 2013). Interestingly, they found that employee engagement contributes to firm performance, both, directly and indirectly through customer engagement. Such firms need to focus on retaining their existing employees and customers to reap the long-term benefits of engagement.

High–Low (High CE and Low EE) Segment

These firms allocate maximum resources to engage their customers by increasing their customer purchase, extracting value on their referrals, maximizing their influence, and exploiting their feedback and knowledge. While profit-making potential is high for these firms, their costs due to higher rates of employee attrition and disengagement may compromise such potential. Especially, where companies invest a lot of money in employee training and development, employees who are disengaged tend to quit the company eventually ending up poaching valuable clients (Kumar and Pansari, 2015). Employers need to focus on increasing their employee satisfaction by allocating resources and strategies that foster greater job/supervisor satisfaction as well as employee identification and commitment.

Low–High (Low CE and High EE) Segment

In this category, firms typically focus on their employees but not on their customers. These firms typically cannot compete in the marketplace toward sustained performance. Customer relationship marketing (CRM) managers need to identify specific facets of engagement where customers are not fully leveraged, i.e., in purchase, incentivized referral, influence, and knowledge domains. Accordingly, targeted approach, specific to engagement domain performance, can be adopted by examining customers' past purchase and non-purchase behavior, and introducing or doubling up strategies that further incentivizes customers.

Low–Low (Low CE and Low EE) Segment

Firms in this segment are often not operating at optimum profitability, and therefore, allocating resources, first, toward customer engagement might be a good starting point. This is because high customer engagement will initiate the profit cycle, which can then be reinvested into employee engagement over time. Here again, firms should adopt targeted approach toward identifying specific aspects of low engagement, both customers and employees, and then putting appropriate structures and processes in place to motivate them. These firms need to develop new strategic orientation *vis-à-vis* customers and employees, namely "engagement orientation". However, firms need to be cognizant of the caveat that the consequences of engagement structures/strategies are realized in the long term rather than in the short term (Evanschitzky *et al.*, 2011b).

EMPLOYEE ENGAGEMENT SCOREBOARD

The scorecard is composed of a number of items used to measure the individual employee engagement components (based on a 1–5 scale, with '1' being lowest and '5' being highest). A company's overall employee engagement is directly influenced by the components of employee engagement, i.e., employee satisfaction, employee identification, employee commitment, employee loyalty, and employee performance (see Figure 5.7). Employees with low satisfaction scores often exhibit poor work quality and an increasing likelihood of absenteeism. Managers can help boost their satisfaction levels by rearranging their work duties and responsibilities that better match their skill sets and interests and develop new incentives for higher performance. However, when employees are satisfied, it is still possible for them to operate with lower levels of identification toward the company they work for. Such employees do not share the organizational culture and values that define the company with repercussions on extra-role citizenship behaviors. Managers can help promote employee identification by re-aligning and reinforcing organizational culture with its employees. The presence of employee satisfaction and identification still does not guarantee employee commitment as they are not emotionally connected with the organization. Managers need to periodically review different incentives mechanisms that exceed their competition's offerings to employees, so as to curb attrition and enhance employee commitment. Ensuring employee loyalty is a valuable asset to the company and managers can develop this asset by empowering employees for personal and career growth and providing opportunities for family members. Employee performance gaps need to alert managers that regular training programs, mentorship programs, and performance

Figure 5.7: Employee Engagement Scorecard

THE EMPLOYEE ENGAGEMENT SCORECARD

For companies to get the most out of employee engagement, they need to understand their current HR strategies and the effects of those strategies on employees. Each of the items in the five bulleted lists represents an area in which employees can rate their experience with the organization on a scale of 1 to 5; the minimum possible score on the scorecard is 20, and the maximum is 100.

	EMPLOYEE SATISFACTION	EMPLOYEE IDENTIFICATION	EMPLOYEE COMMITMENT	EMPLOYEE LOYALTY	EMPLOYEE PERFORMANCE	
Number of items:	5	7	3	3	2	
Items used to measure the concept	• Receives recognition for a job • Feels close to people at work • Feels good about working at this company • Feels secure about job • Believes that the management is concerned about employees	• Proud to tell others about employment • Feels a sense of ownership • Feels a sense of pride • Views the success of the brand as his own • Treats organization like family • Says "we" rather than "they" • Feels like it's a personal compliment when the brand is praised	• Commitment to deliver the brand promise increases along with knowledge of the brand • Very committed to delivering the brand promise • Feels like the organization has a great deal of personal meaning	• Content to spend the rest of her or his career in this organization • Does not have intention to change to another organization • Intention to stay is driven by competency in delivering the brand promise	• Performance in the last appraisal exceeded expectations • Believes there is increased opportunity for improved performance in this organization	
						TOTAL
Minimum score:	5	7	3	3	2	**20**
Maximum score:	25	35	15	15	10	**100**

Adapted from V. Kumar and Anita Pansari (2015), Measuring the Benefits of Employee Engagement, *MIT Sloan Management Review* 56(4): 67–72.

incentives can go long ways in enhancing employee performance, and if not adequately addressed can negatively affect the company's bottom line.

KEY TAKEAWAYS

- Relationship criteria, namely, descriptive, instrumental, and normative collectively capture the full gamut of firm stakeholder relationships pertaining to employees and customers. The descriptive criterion describes, and sometimes explains, firm characteristics and behaviors. The instrumental criterion identifies connections between firm actions taken to manage stakeholders and firm objectives. The normative criterion interprets the moral guidelines and obligations of the firm toward stakeholders. In general, relationship quality is mainly characterized by trust, commitment, satisfaction, and organizational identification.

- For employees as internal stakeholders, the primary relationship criteria are descriptive and instrumental, while the secondary relationship criterion is normative. The foundational pillars of stakeholder relationship quality for employees are based on managerial competence-based trust, identification-based trust, and benevolence-based trust. The effectiveness of relationship quality for employees is characterized by two dimensions: management activities and communication effectiveness.

- For customers as external (proximal) stakeholders, the primary relationship criterion is instrumental, while the secondary relationship criterion is normative. The foundational pillars of stakeholder relationship quality for customers are based on technical competence-based trust and benevolence-based trust. The effectiveness of relationship quality for customers is characterized by two dimensions: (1) tangibility and reliability (i.e., technical competence-based trust) and (2) responsiveness, assurance, and empathy (i.e., benevolence-based trust).

- Employee engagement involves investment of personal resources (e.g., physical, emotional, cognitive resources) and utilization of firm-provided resources (e.g. job tasks, job environment). Effective resource integration brings about emotional connection and employee engagement.

- Customer engagement involves resource investment and resource utilization. Operant resources include cognitive, emotional, behavioral, and social knowledge and skills, and operand resources include tangible and physical resources. Effective resource integration brings both customer–firm–peer resources together and customer engagement behavior.

- Earlier models of the service-profit chain (SPC) view that satisfied employees are more productive and provide better service quality, which then leads to higher customer satisfaction, stronger loyalty, and firm outcomes.

- In the recently modified SPC framework, the role of internal service quality is accentuated with additional roles and benefits such that employee perceptions of management support and facilitation of service performance lead to favorable customer responses. The role of external service quality is also expanded with a focus on service outcomes (loyalty) rather than service encounters only. Further, employee productivity also directly impacts customer loyalty, among others.

- Employee job satisfaction is critical to attain positive customer responses in personal services performed on people (versus goods) (see Figure 5.8). For intangible services difficult to evaluate, firms invest more on internal service quality as employee satisfaction helps reduce customer ambiguity. Also,

Figure 5.8 Employee job satisfaction is critical to attain positive customer responses in personal services performed on people.

as customer co-production can be demanding on service employees, internal service quality supporting employee development creates satisfied customers.

- Firms characterized by high employee/high customer engagement are expected to post higher than average profits in the industry. Firms characterized by low employee/high customer engagement have high profit potential from the customer side; however, employee attrition and disengagement may compromise such potential.

- Firms characterized by high employee/low customer engagement focus on employees but not customers, and as such typically they cannot compete in the marketplace. Firms characterized by low employee/low customer engagement do not operate at optimum profitability. Such firms need to first allocate resources toward building customer engagement, initiate the profit cycle before re-investing into building employee engagement.

EXERCISES

Questions

1. Explain the concept of stakeholder criteria as applied to firm–stakeholder relationships. Discuss the three types of stakeholder criterion: (1) descriptive criterion, (2) instrumental criterion, and (3) normative criterion.

2. What is relationship quality? What are the essential foundational pillars upon which companies can build quality relationships with their customers? Which foundational pillar is particularly important in customer–company relationship and why?

3. Discuss (1) the primary and secondary relationship criteria and (2) pillars of stakeholder relationship quality relevant for employees. Comment on the following statement: "Relationship quality with internal stakeholders (i.e., employees) should be built on managerial competence-based trust, identification-based trust, and benevolence-based trust".

4. Discuss (1) the primary and secondary relationship criteria and (2) pillars of stakeholder relationship quality relevant for customers. Comment on the following statement: "Relationship quality with external proximal stakeholders (i.e., customers) should be built on technical competence-based trust and benevolence-based trust".

5. Discuss the concept of employee and customer engagement from a resource integration (i.e., resource investment and resource utilization) perspective. How does this perspective align with the S-D logic?

6. In the extended service profit chain (SPC) model, discuss the additional roles of internal service quality in a firm's profitability. Explain the additional mechanisms in the extended SPC model that influence customer satisfaction and loyalty.

7. "While customer satisfaction is necessary for a company's financial performance, it may not be sufficient". Discuss this statement in light of the complementary role of customer–company identification.

Group Discussion

1. A private financial services company ABC scores very high on customer engagement. Customers are highly engaged in both purchase and non-purchase behaviors and the company extracts maximum value on their referrals, influencing power and knowledge capabilities. However, ABC scores very low on employee engagement and regularly incurs expenses on re-training employees due to high attrition.

As a small group, discuss the immediate steps you would take to increase employee engagement. The employee engagement scorecard is a valuable tool consisting of scores on individual dimensions: employee satisfaction, employee identification, employee commitment, employee loyalty, and employee performance. What specific strategies will you recommend to ABC if the scores are low on (a) satisfaction, (b) identification, and (c) commitment?

2. A public financial services company XYZ scores very high on employee engagement. As a public undertaking, the company has heavily invested in several employee engagement programs such as job security, job rotation, employee (re)training and skill-set upgrade programs, mentorship programs, organizational culture, and most importantly performance incentive and reward structures. However, customers are not engaged nearly enough in either purchase (e.g., cross-selling and up-selling) or non-purchase behaviors (e.g., referrals, influence, and knowledge contribution). While such combinations are not commonplace, XYZ cannot compete in the marketplace toward sustained performance.

As a small group, discuss the immediate steps you would take to increase customer engagement. What specific strategies will you recommend to XYZ if customers are low on (a) customer lifetime value (including cross-selling and up-selling), (b) customer referral value, (c) customer influence value, and (d) customer knowledge value?

HBS and Ivey Cases

- AnswerDash (9-516-106)

- Re-inventing Best Buy (9-716-455)

- Chase Sapphire (9-518-024)

- Laurs & Bridz (9B18A004)

CASE QUESTIONS

AnswerDash

1. How can the concept of stakeholder criteria be applied to firm–stakeholder relationships for AnswerDash?

2. What are the essential foundational pillars upon which AnswerDash can build quality relationships with its customers? Which foundational pillar is particularly important in this context and why?

3. How should AnswerDash build relationship quality with internal stakeholders (i.e., employees)? In this respect, discuss the roles of managerial competence-based trust, identification-based trust, and benevolence-based trust.

4. In the case of AnswerDash, discuss employee and customer engagement from a resource integration (i.e., resource investment and resource utilization) perspective.

5. In the extended service profit chain (SPC) model, discuss the additional roles of internal service quality in AnswerDash's profitability. Explain the additional mechanisms in the extended SPC model that influence customer satisfaction and loyalty.

6. Discuss the immediate steps AnswerDash should take to increase employee engagement. How can AnswerDash make use of the employee engagement scorecard to evaluate employee satisfaction, employee identification, employee commitment, employee loyalty, and employee performance?

Re-inventing Best Buy

1. What are the essential foundational pillars upon which Best Buy can build quality relationships with its customers? Which foundational pillar is particularly important in this context and why?

2. How should Best Buy build relationship quality with external proximal stakeholders (i.e., customers)? In this respect, discuss the roles of technical competence-based trust and benevolence-based trust.

3. In the extended service profit chain (SPC) model, discuss the additional roles of internal service

quality in Best Buy's profitability. Explain the additional mechanisms in the extended SPC model that influence customer satisfaction and loyalty.

4. Discuss the complementary roles of customer–company identification in determining Best Buy's financial performance.

5. Discuss the immediate steps Best Buy should take to increase customer engagement. What specific strategies will you recommend to Best Buy if customers are low on (a) customer lifetime value, (b) customer referral value, (c) customer influence value, and (d) customer knowledge value?

Chase Sapphire

1. How can the concept of stakeholder criteria be applied to firm–stakeholder relationships for JPMorgan?

2. What are the essential foundational pillars upon which JPMorgan can build quality relationships with its customers? Which foundational pillar is particularly important in this context and why?

3. How should JPMorgan build relationship quality with internal stakeholders (i.e., employees)? In this respect, discuss the roles of managerial competence-based trust, identification-based trust, and benevolence-based trust.

4. How should JPMorgan build relationship quality with external proximal stakeholders (i.e., customers)? In this respect, discuss the roles of technical competence-based trust and benevolence-based trust.

5. Discuss the complementary roles of customer–company identification in determining JPMorgan's financial performance.

6. Discuss the immediate steps JPMorgan should take to increase employee engagement. How can JPMorgan make use of the employee engagement scorecard to evaluate employee satisfaction,

employee identification, employee commitment, employee loyalty, and employee performance?

Laurs & Bridz

1. How can the concept of stakeholder criteria be applied to firm–stakeholder relationships for Laurs & Bridz?

2. What are the essential foundational pillars upon which Laurs & Bridz can build quality relationships with its customers? Which foundational pillar is particularly important in this context and why?

3. How should Laurs & Bridz build relationship quality with internal stakeholders (i.e., employees)? In this respect, discuss the roles of managerial competence-based trust, identification-based trust, and benevolence-based trust.

4. In the extended service profit chain (SPC) model, discuss the additional roles of internal service quality in Laurs & Bridz's profitability. Explain the additional mechanisms in the extended SPC model that influence customer satisfaction and loyalty.

5. Discuss the immediate steps Laurs & Bridz should take to increase employee engagement. How can Laurs & Bridz make use of the employee engagement scorecard to evaluate employee satisfaction, employee identification, employee commitment, employee loyalty, and employee performance?

REFERENCES

Adams, J.S. (1965), Inequity in Social Exchange, in L. Berkowitz (Ed.), *Advances in Experimental Social Psychology*. New York, NY: Academic Press Inc.

Anderson, E.W., C. Fornell, and V. Mittal (2000), Strengthening the Satisfaction-Profit Chain, *Journal of Service Research* 3(2): 107–120.

Bagozzi, R.P. (1975), Marketing as Exchange, *Journal of Marketing* 39(4): 32–39.

Bakker, Arnold B. and Evangelia Demerouti (2007), The Job Demands-Resources Model: State of the Art, *Journal of Managerial Psychology* 22(3): 309–328.

Barney, J.B., and W. Hesterly (1996), Organizational Economics: Understanding the Relationships between Organizations and Economic Analysis, in S.R. Clegg, W.R. Nord, and C. Hardy (Eds.), *Handbook of Organization Studies* (pp. 115–147). London: Sage Publications.

Bearman, P. (1997), Generalized Exchange, *American Journal of Sociology* 102(5): 1383–1415.

Bebko, C.P. (2000), Service Intangibility and Its Impact on Consumer Expectations of Service Quality, *Journal of Services Marketing* 14(1): 9–27.

Berman, S.L., A.C. Wicks, S. Kotha, and T.M. Jones (1999), Does Stakeholder Orientation Matter? The Relationship between Stakeholder Management Models and Firm Financial Performance, *Academy of Management Journal* 42(5): 488–506.

Bhattacharya, C.B. and S. Sen (2003), Consumer-Company Identification: A Framework for Understanding Consumers' Relationships with Companies, *Journal of Marketing* 67: 76–88.

Bowden, Jana Lay-Hwa (2009), The Process of Customer Engagement: A Conceptual Framework, *Journal of Marketing Theory and Practice* 17(1): 63–74.

Brickson, S.L. (2005), Organizational Identity Orientation: Forging a Link between Organizational Identity and Organization's Relations with Stakeholders, *Administrative Science Quarterly* 50(4): 576–609.

Brickson, S.L. (2007), Organizational Identity Orientation: The Genesis of the Role of the Firm and Distinct Forms of Social Value, *Academy of Management Review* 32(3): 864–888.

Brodie, Roderick J., Linda D. Hollebeek, Biljana Juric, and Ana Ilic (2011), Customer Engagement: Conceptual Domain, Fundamental Propositions, and Implications for Research, *Journal of Service Research* 14(3): 252–271.

Brown, S.P. and S.K. Lam (2008), A Meta-Analysis of Relationships Linking Employee Satisfaction to Customer Responses, *Journal of Retailing* 84(3): 243–255.

Choi, J. and H. Wang (2009), Stakeholder Relations and the Persistence of Corporate Financial Performance, *Strategic Management Journal* 30: 895–907.

Christian, Michael S., Adela S. Garza, and Jerel E. Slaughter (2011), Work Engagement: A Quantitative Review and Test of its Relations with Task and Contextual Performance, *Personnel Psychology* 64(1): 89–136.

Clarkson, M.B.E. (1995), A Stakeholder Framework for Analyzing and Evaluating Corporate Social Performance, *Academy of Management Review* 27: 42–56.

Colquitt, J.A., D.E. Conlon, M.J. Wesson, C.O.L.H. Porter, and K.Y. Ng (2001), Justice at the Millennium: A Meta-Analytic Review of 25 years of Organizational Justice Research, *Journal of Applied Psychology* 86(3): 425–445.

Constantin, James A. and Robert F. Lusch (1994), *Understanding Resource Management.* Oxford, OH: The Planning Forum.

Day, G.S. (1994), The Capabilities of Market-Driven Organizations, *Journal of Marketing* 58(4): 37–52.

De Wulf, K., G. Odekerken-Schröder, and D. Iacobucci (2001), Investments in Consumer Relationships: A Cross-Country and Cross-Industry Exploration, *Journal of Marketing* 65(October): 33–50.

DiMaggio, P., and W. Powell (1983), The Iron Cage Revisited: Institutional Isomorphism and Collective Rationality in Organizational Fields, *American Sociological Review* 48: 147–160.

Donaldson, T. and L.E. Preston (1995), The Stakeholder Theory of the Corporation: Concepts, Evidence, and Implications, *Academy of Management Review* 20(1): 65–91.

Dutton, J.E., J.M. Dukerich, and C.V. Harquail (1994), Organizational Images and Member Identification, *Administrative Science Quarterly* 39(2): 239–263.

Eldor, Liat, and Itzhak Harpaz (2016), A Process Model of Employee Engagement: The Learning Climate and its Relationship with Extra-Role Performance Behaviors, *Journal of Organizational Behavior* 37: 213–235.

Evan, W.M. and R.E. Freeman (1984), A Stakeholder Theory of the Modern Corporation: Kantian Capitalism, in T. Beauchamp and N. Bowie (Eds.), *Ethical Theory in Business* (pp. 75–93). Englewood Cliffs, NJ: Prentice-Hall.

Evanschitzky, H., C. Groening, V. Mittal, and M. Wunderlich (2011a), How Employer and Employee Satisfaction Affect Customer Satisfaction: An Application to Franchise Services, *Journal of Service Research* 14(2): 136–148.

Evanschitzky, H., F.V. Wangenheim, N.V. Wunderlich (2011b), Perils of Managing the Service Profit Chain: The Role of Time Lags and Feedback Loops, *Journal of Retailing* 88(3): 356–366.

Fassin, Y. (2009), The Stakeholder Model Refined, *Journal of Business Ethics* 84(1): 113–135.

Freeman, R.E. (1999), Divergent Stakeholder Theory, *Academy of Management Review* 24: 233–236.

Freeman, R.E. and W.M. Evan (1990), Corporate Governance: A Stakeholder Interpretation, *The Journal of Behavioral Economics* 19: 337–359.

Freeman, R.E., J.S. Harrison, A.C. Wicks, B.L. Parmar, and S. De Colle (2010), *Stakeholder Theory: The State of the Art*. Cambridge, UK: Cambridge University Press.

Friedman A.L. and S. Miles (2006), *Stakeholders: Theory and Practice*. Oxford: Oxford University Press.

Frooman, J. (1999), Stakeholder Influence Strategies, *Academy of Management Review* 24: 191–205.

Garbarino, E. and M.S. Johnson (1999), The Different Roles of Satisfaction, Trust, and Commitment in Customer Relationships, *Journal of Marketing* 63(April): 70–87.

Gremler, D.D. and K.P. Gwinner (2000), Customer-Employee Rapport in Service Relationships, *Journal of Service Research* 3(1): 82–104.

Griffith, D.A. (2010), Understanding Multi-Level Institutional Convergence Effects on International Market Segments and Global Marketing Strategy, *Journal of World Business* 45: 59–67.

Groening, C., V. Mittal, Y.A. Zhang (2016), Cross-Validation of Customer and Employee Signals and Firm Valuation, *Journal of Marketing Research* 53(1): 61–76.

Harmeling, Colleen M., Jordan W. Moffett, Mark J. Arnold, and Brad D. Carlson (2017), Toward a Theory of Customer Engagement Marketing, *Journal of the Academy of Marketing Science* 45(3): 312–335.

Harter, J.K., F.L. Schmidt, and T.L. Hayes (2002), Business-Unit-Level Relationship between Employee Satisfaction, Employee Engagement, and business Outcomes: A Meta-Analysis, *Journal of Applied Psychology* 87(2): 268–279.

Hennig-Thurau, T., M. Groth, M. Paul, and D.D. Gremler (2006), Are All Smiles Created equal? How Emotional Contagion and Emotional Labor Affect Service Relationships, *Journal of Marketing* 70: 58–73.

Hennig-Thurau, T., K.P. Gwinner, and D.D. Gremler (2002), Understanding Relationship Marketing Outcomes: An Integration of Relational Benefits and Relationship Quality, *Journal of Service Research* 4(3): 230–247.

Heskett, J.L., T.O. Jones, G.W. Loveman, W. Earl Sasser Jr., and L.A. Schlesinger (1994), Putting the Service-Profit Chain to Work, *Harvard Business Review* 72(2): 164–174.

Hill, C.W.L., and T.M. Jones (1992), Stakeholder-Agency Theory, *Journal of Management Studies* 29: 131–154.

Hillman, A.J. and G.D. Keim (2001), Shareholder Value, Stakeholder Management, and Social Issues: What's the Bottom Line? *Strategic Management Journal* 22: 125–139.

Hodson, R. (2004), Organizational Trustworthiness: Findings from the Population of Organizational Ethnographies, *Organization Science* 15(4): 432–445.

Hogreve, Jens, Anja Iseke, Klaus Derfuss, and Tonnjes, Eller (2017), The Service-Profit Chain: A Meta-Analytic Test of a Comprehensive Theoretical Framework, *Journal of Marketing* 81: 41–61.

Hollebeek, Linda D., Jodie Conduit, and Roderick J. Brodie (2016), Strategic Drivers, Anticipated and Unanticipated Outcomes of Customer Engagement, *Journal of Marketing Management* 32(5–6): 393–398.

Homburg, C., J. Wieseke, and W.D. Hoyer (2009), Social Identity and the Service-Profit Chain, *Journal of Marketing* 73(2): 38–54.

Jaakkola, Elina and Matthew Alexander (2014), The Role of Customer Engagement Behavior in Value Co-creation: A Service System Perspective, *Journal of Service Research* 17(3): 247–61.

Jensen, J. and W. Meckling (1976), Theory of the Firm: Managerial Behavior, Agency Cost and Ownership Structure, *Journal of Financial Economics* 3: 305–360.

Jones, T.M. and A.C. Wicks (1999), Convergent Stakeholder Theory, *Academy of Management Review* 24(2): 206–221.

Kahn, William A. (1990), Psychological Conditions of Personal Engagement and Disengagement at Work, *Academy of Management Journal* 33(4): 692–724.

Kamakura, W.A., V. Mittal, F. de Rosa, and J.A. Mazzon (2002), Assessing the Service-Profit Chain, *Marketing Science* 21(3): 294–317.

Keiningham, T.L., C.M. Frennea, L. Aksoy, A. Buoye, V. Mittal (2015), A Five-Component Customer Commitment Model: Implications for Repurchase Intentions in Goods and Services Industries, *Journal of Service Research* 18(4): 433–450.

Kogut, B. and U. Zander (1992), Knowledge of the Firm, Combinative Capabilities, and the Replication of Technology, *Organization Science* 3(3): 383–397.

Kostova, T. and S. Zaheer (1999), Organizational Legitimacy under Conditions of Complexity: The Case of the Multinational Enterprise, *Academy of Management Review* 24(1): 64–81.

Kumar, V. (2013), *Profitable Customer Engagement: Concepts, Metrics, and Strategies*. New Delhi: Sage Publications.

Kumar, V. and A. Pansari (2015), Measuring the Benefits of Employee Engagement, *MIT Sloan Management Review* 56(4): 67–72.

Kumar, V. and A. Pansari (2016), Competitive Advantage through Engagement, *Journal of Marketing Research* 53: 497–514.

Kumar, V., Lerzan Aksoy, Bas Donkers, Rajkumar Venkatesan, Thorsten Wiesel, and Sebastian Tillmanns (2010), Undervalued or Overvalued Customers: Capturing Total Customer Engagement Value, *Journal of Service Research* 13(3): 297–310.

Kumar, N., L.K. Scheer, and J.B.E.M. Steenkamp (1995), The Effects of Supplier Fairness on Vulnerable Resellers, *Journal of Marketing Research* 32(1): 54–65.

Lewicki, R.J. and B.B. Bunker (1996), Developing and Maintaining Trust In Work Relationships, in R.M. Kramer and T.R. Tyler (Eds.), *Trust in Organizations Frontiers of Theory and Research* (pp. 114–139). Thousand Oaks, CA: Sage.

Lewis, J.D. and A. Weigert (1985), Trust as Social Reality, *Social Forces* 63: 967–985.

Litz, R. A. (1996), A Resource-Based View of the Socially Responsible Firm: Stakeholder Interdependence, Ethical Awareness, and Issue Responsiveness as Strategic Assets, *Journal of Business Ethics* 15(12): 1355–1363.

Madhavan, R. and R. Grover (1998), From Embedded Knowledge to Embodied Knowledge: New Product Development as Knowledge Management, *Journal of Marketing* 62(4): 1–4.

Madhok, A. (2006), Opportunism, Trust and Knowledge: The Management of Firm Value and the Value of Firm Management, in R. Bachmann and A. Zaheer (Eds.), *Handbook on Trust* (pp. 107–123). Cheltenham: Edward Elgar.

Marshall, K.P (1998), Generalized Exchange and Public Policy: An Illustration of Support for Public Schools, *Journal of Public Policy and Marketing* 17(2): 274–286.

Maslach, Christina, Wilmar B. Schaufeli, and Michael P. Leiter (2001), Job Burnout, *Annual Review of Psychology* 52(1): 397–422.

Mayer, R.C., J.H. Davis, and F.D. Schoorman (1995), An Integration Model of Organizational Trust, *Academy of Management Review* 20: 709–735.

Meyer, J.P., N.J. Allen, and C.A. Smith (1993), Commitment to Organizations and Occupations: Extension and Test of a Three-Component Conceptualization, *Journal of Applied Psychology* 78(4): 538–551.

Mitchell, R.K., B.R. Agle, and D.J. Wood (1997), Toward a Theory of Stakeholder Identification and Salience: Defining the Principle of Who and What Really Counts, *Academy of Management Review* 22(4): 853–886.

Moorman, C., G. Zaltman, and R. Deshpande (1992), Relationships between Providers and Users of Market Research: The Dynamics of Trust Within and Between Organizations, *Journal of Marketing Research* 29(August): 314–328.

Morgan, R.M. and S.D. Hunt (1994), The Commitment-Trust Theory of Relationship Marketing, *Journal of Marketing* 58(3): 20–38.

North, D. (1990), *Institutions, Institutional Change, and Economic Performance*. Cambridge University Press.

North, D. (2005), Institutions and the Performance of Economies over Time, *Handbook of New Institutional Economics*. Springer.

Palmatier, R.W., L.K. Scheer, M.B. Houston, K.R. Evans, and S. Gopalakrishna (2007), Use of Relationship Marketing Programs in Building Customer-Salesperson and Customer-Firm Relationships: Differential Influences on Financial Outcomes, *International Journal of Research in Marketing* 24: 210–223.

Pansari, Anita and V. Kumar (2017), Customer Engagement: The Construct, Antecedents, and Consequences, *Journal of the Academy of Marketing Science* 45(3): 294–311.

Parasuraman, A., V.A. Zeithaml, and L.L. Berry (1991), Refinement and Reassessment of the SERVQUAL Scale, *Journal of Retailing* 67(4): 420–450.

Parasuraman, A., V.A. Zeithaml, and L.L. Berry (1995), A Conceptual Model of Service Quality and its Implications for Future Research, *Journal of Marketing* 49: 41–50.

Pfeffer, J. and G. Salancik (1978), *The External Control of Organizations: A Resource Dependency Perspective*. New York, NY: Harper & Row.

Pirson, M. and D. Malhotra (2011), Foundations of Organizational Trust: What Matters to Different Stakeholders? *Organization Science* 22(4): 1087–1104.

Preston, L.E. and H.J. Sapienza (1990), Stakeholder Management and Corporate Performance, *Journal of Behavioral Economics* 19: 361–375.

Pugh, D.S. (2001), Service with a Smile: Emotional Contagion in the Service Encounter, *Academy of Management Journal* 44(5): 1018–1027.

Roberts, K., S. Varki, and R. Brodie (2003), Measuring the Quality of Relationships in Consumer Services: An Empirical Study, *European Journal of Marketing* 37(1): 169–196.

Rousseau, D.M., S.B. Sitkin, R.S. Burt, and C. Camerer (1998), Not So Different After All: A Cross-Discipline View of Trust, *Academy of Management Review* 23(3): 393–404.

Rowley, T.J. (1997), Moving Beyond Dyadic Ties: A Network Theory of Stakeholder Influences, *Academy of Management Review* 22(4): 887–910.

Rust, R.T., C. Moorman, and P.R. Dickson (2002), Getting Return on Quality: Revenue Expansion, Cost Reduction, or Both? *Journal of Marketing* 66: 7–24.

Rust, R.T., A.J. Zahorik, and T.L. Keiningham (1995), Return on Quality (ROQ): Making Service Quality Financially Accountable, *Journal of Marketing* 59: 58–70.

Schaufeli, Wilmar B., Marisa Salanova, Vicente González-Romá, and Arnold B. Bakker (2002), The Measurement of Engagement and Burnout: A Two Sample Confirmatory Factor Analytic Approach, *Journal of Happiness Studies* 3(1): 71–92.

Schneider, B., S.S. White, M.C. Paul (1998), Linking Service Climate and Customer Perceptions of Service Quality: Test of a Causal Model, *Journal of Applied Psychology* 83(2): 150–163.

Schoorman, F.D., R.C. Mayer, and J.H. Davis (2007), An Integrative Model of Organizational Trust: Past, Present, and Future, *Academy of Management Review* 32(2): 344–354.

Shankman, N.A. (1999), Reframing the Debate between Agency and Stakeholder Theories of the Firm, *Journal of Business Ethics* 19: 319–334.

Sheth, J.N. and A. Parvatiyar (1995), Relationship Marketing in Consumer Markets: Antecedents and Consequences, *Journal of the Academy of Marketing Science* 23(3): 255–271.

Sirgy, J.M. (2002), Measuring Corporate Performance by Building on the Stakeholders' Model of Business Ethics, *Journal of Business Ethics* 35: 143–162.

Sitkin, S.B. and N.L. Roth (1993), Explaining the Limited Effectiveness of Legalistic 'Remedies' for Trust/Distrust, *Organization Science* 4(3): 367–392.

Tajfel, H. and J.C. Turner (1986), *The Social Identity Theory of Intergroup Behavior.* Chicago, IL: Nelson-Hall.

Takahashi, N. (2000), The Emergence of Generalized Exchange, *American Journal of Sociology* 105(4): 1105–1134.

Van Doorn, Jenny, Katherine N. Lemon, Vikas Mittal, Stephan Nass, Doreen Pick, Peter Pirner, and Peter C. Verhoef (2010), Customer Engagement Behavior: Theoretical Foundations and Research Directions, *Journal of Service Research* 13(3): 253–266.

Vargo, Stephen L. and Robert F. Lusch (2004), Evolving to a New Dominant Logic for Marketing, *Journal of Marketing* 68(1): 1–17.

Vargo, Stephen L. and Robert F. Lusch (2008), Service-Dominant Logic: Continuing the Evolution, *Journal of the Academy of Marketing Science* 36(1): 1–10.

Vargo, Stephen L. and Robert F. Lusch (2011) It's All B2B… and Beyond: Toward a Systems

Perspective of the Market, *Industrial Marketing Management* 40(2): 181–187.

Vermillion, L.J., W.M. Lassar, and R.D. Winsor (2002), The Hunt-Vitell General Theory of Marketing Ethics: Can It Enhance our Understanding of Principal-Agent Relationships in Channels of Distribution? *Journal of Business Ethics* 41, 3(December): 267–285.

Verona, G. (1999), A Resource-Based View of Product Development, *Academy of Management Review* 24(1): 132–142.

Vivek, Shiri D., Sharon E. Beatty, and Robert M. Morgan (2012), Customer Engagement: Exploring Customer Relationships beyond Purchase, *Journal of Marketing Theory and Practice* 20(2): 122–146.

Waddock, S.A. and S.B. Graves (1997), The Corporate Social Performance-Financial Performance Link, *Strategic Management Journal* 18(4): 303–319.

Williamson, O.E. (1991), Strategizing, Economizing, and Economic Organization, *Strategic Management Journal* 12: 75–94.

Zaheer, A., B. McEvily, and V. Perrone (1998), Does Trust Matter? Exploring the Effects of Interorganizational and Interpersonal Trust on Performance, *Organization Science* 9(2): 141–159.

Customer Relationship Marketing: Analytical Models and Strategies

OVERVIEW

In Chapter 6, first we discuss customer relationship marketing (CRM)-based analytical models, both for purchase and non-purchase customer behavior. Various models are discussed including traditional metrics such as recency–frequency–monetary value (RFM) model, share of wallet (SOW) model, and past customer value (PCV) model, as well as contemporary models based on customer lifetime value (CLV) concepts. CLV is an advanced forward-looking metric and several variations of the family of CLV models are briefly discussed, including model formulation, estimation, and key merits and demerits. Next, we provide models for customer engagement including customer referral value (CRV), customer influence value (CIV), and customer knowledge value (CKV). Finally, we discuss strategies for maximizing CLV, segmentation strategies, extending CLV to customer engagement value, and linking customer equity to shareholder value. At the end of the chapter, we provide key takeaways and conclude with discussion questions and HBS and Ivey cases. But first, to give a flavor of CRM analytical models, we provide some real-life vignettes.

OPENING VIGNETTES

Vignette 1: Traditionally, the airline industry rewarded customers based on the miles flown. That is, each customer regardless of their profitability potential with the company would get equal reward such as 1000 points for 1000 miles. Now airlines are increasingly striving to satisfy different customers to different extent by varying the level of rewards and customer experience with the firm. Virgin Airlines (see Figure 6.1) provides royal service to its first class passengers, starting with chauffeur-driven car service to the airport, to exclusive access to Virgin's business lounge with varied services ranging from beauty treatment, dining to golf driving ranges, and in-flight massage therapy.

Figure 6.1: Beyond points for miles flown, Virgin Airlines provides royal service to its first class passengers.

Vignette 2: Sprint fired 1000 of their 53 million customers for calling their call center too frequently. An average Sprint customer spends about $55 per month, of which $24 is profit for the firm. However, it cost $2 to $3 per minute to have a customer talk with a customer service representative and if that customer talks for more than eight to 12 minutes per month, Sprint will lose money on that customer. These types of customers are a drain on the company's resources and Sprint viewed them as misfits. Hence, the company got rid of these customers. Based on past customer value (PCV), which has been a traditional method of customer valuation, it made economic sense. However, when examined from a CLV perspective did the company make the right decision? What if a customer fired had a low CLV but high size of unused wallet (SUW) making it an overall moderately high future value? In the extreme case of low CLV and low SUW, is Sprint (slated to merge with T-Mobile) still justified in firing such customers given the potential of inviting the wrath of other customers including new customers and negative publicity? These are questions to ponder.

INTRODUCTION: MEASURING CUSTOMER VALUE

Creating and communicating perceived value to customers depends on the right amounts of resource allocation by firms that would enable them to match customer perceptions of value. This requires firms to identify and ascertain the value that customers provide to the firm. Similar to customers deriving value from products and services offered, firms, too, derive value from their customers. Kumar and Reinartz (2012) define this value from the customer as "the economic value of the customer relationship to the firm — expressed on the basis of contribution margin or net profit" (p. 4).

Various metrics are available for measuring the value of the customer, and in implementing the customer relationship marketing (CRM) strategies. Some traditional metrics are Recency–Frequency–Monetary value (RFM), Share of Wallet (SOW), Past Customer Value (PCV), and tenure and duration. These existing metrics have several limitations and they do not link the value of a customer to future profitability. In contrast, Customer Lifetime Value (CLV) is an advanced metric that is widely gaining popularity across all sectors and industries. The forward-looking CLV metric considers the future value of a customer to the firm, and aids in designing and implementing marketing strategies for the present, thus maximizing profitability (Gupta *et al.*, 2006). Kumar and Reinartz (2016) advocate for the use of forward-looking CLV metrics of customer valuation. It is the future value in terms of CLV metric that will help firms to treat each customer differently according to her or his contribution. The sum total of lifetime value of all customers of the firm represents the customer equity of the firm. Reinartz and Kumar (2003) discuss drivers of CLV and classify into two types: (1) relationship exchange characteristics and (2) customer heterogeneity. Exchange characteristics include the set of variables that describe relationship activities, whereas heterogeneity refers to demographic and psychographic variations. While big data allows

historical information (e.g., sales revenue, marketing spending) to predict future behavior, there are several challenges, and as such firms are increasingly relying on forward-looking metrics as opposed to relying on insights from past value contribution. In the next section, drawing from the work of Kumar and Reinartz (2016), we briefly discuss the traditional CRM models as well as the contemporary CLV-based models.

TRADITIONAL CRM MODELS

RFM Approach

Based on the assumption that past purchase behavior of customers better predict their future purchases than demographic data, recency, frequency, and monetary (RFM) scoring models have been used in marketing for over four decades. Historically, the initial applications were in B2C contexts: direct marketing, insurance, banking, telecommunications, etc. Basically, the customers are ranked based on their R, F, and M score. Recent purchasers, frequent purchasers, and big spenders on average receive higher scores. The higher the score, the more profitable is the customer, which is expected to continue in the future. A basic ranking, within parent cell ranking, or weighted cell ranking can be used. The RFM approach is built on the assumption that the "right" customer in the future looks a lot like the "right" customer in the past.

In basic RFM, the customers are scored on each factor separately. That is, the customers are ranked based on the recency of their purchases and then split into subgroups (e.g., quintiles). As a result, there could be five quintiles where the top quintile represents the 20% that has made the most recent purchases. The procedure is then repeated for frequency and total money spent and reveals $5 \times 5 \times 5 = 125$ cells from highest to lowest ranking. In within parent cell ranking, the cells are grouped based on recency just as it is for the basic approach. However, each group is then sub-grouped based on frequency (rather than separately). Each of the resulting 25 cells is finally ranked by monetary value. This approach requires more sorting than the former. In weighted cell ranking, weights are assigned to the metrics and sorted accordingly. These weights can be equal; however, an often used weight scheme is: (3*R) + (2*F) + (1*M). The specific weights used depend on the data and specific application. For example, based on the response rate, M may turn out to be the most important factor in some cases.

Share of Wallet

Share of wallet (SOW) refers to the share of a company of a customer's expenditure for a given offering category (see Figure 6.2). Although market share has been shown to uniquely impact the financial performance of the firms based on their strategy types (Uslay *et al.*, 2010), and market share and share of wallet are linked, targeted efforts to increase the share of large wallet customers can have more direct and positive impact on the bottom line. For example, major casinos "comp" their high rollers (or "whales") with the hope to attract them to stay in their location whenever they

visit, i.e., they hope to attract close to 100% share of gambling wallet. In other cases, firms target much smaller shares. The data is typically acquired through primary surveys, which is then combined with other predictors of behavior in a database (behavioral and demographic variables) and share of wallet is then modeled as the dependent variable.

$$\text{Share of Wallet: } \frac{S_j}{\sum_{j=1}^{J} S_j},$$

where S is the actual sales to the focal customer, J refers to firm in category, and the denominator represents the value of sales made by all firms to the focal customer.

Past Customer Value

The simple logic behind the past customer value (PCV) approach is that history is the best predictor of future performance. The model uses extrapolation on previous transactions of a customer (i.e., past profits) to predict the customer's future value. Time value of money is used to adjust previous contributions,

Figure 6.2: Share of wallet (SOW), referring to the share of a company of a customer's expenditure for a given offering category, is a traditional CRM model.

and calculate past customer value (PCV) for each customer. It can be calculated as:

$$\text{PCV:} \sum_{t=1}^{T} GC_{it}{}^{*}(1 + d)^{t},$$

where i is the customer, d is the applicable discount rate, T is the number of periods prior to the current period, and GC_{it} is the gross contribution of the transaction of customer i in time t.

CONTEMPORARY CLV-BASED MODELS

Aggregate Approach

According to this approach, the average lifetime value of a customer is derived from the lifetime value of a cohort, or segment, or even a firm. This is also known as the top-down approach, and the estimation of CLV can be accomplished by identifying and measuring the factors that drive CLV. Three approaches are available for computing the average CLV. In the first approach, the sum of lifetime values of all the customers is calculated (Gupta *et al.*, 2004). This value is referred to as the customer equity of a firm and is calculated as follows:

$$CE = \sum_{i=1}^{I} \sum_{t=1}^{T} CM_{it} \left(\frac{1}{1 + \delta} \right)^{t},$$

where CE = customer equity of the customer base (sum of individual lifetime values),
CM = average gross contribution margin in time period t, (after considering marketing costs),
δ = discount rate,
i = customer index,
t = time period, and
T = the number of time periods for which CE is being estimated.

In the second approach, the average CLV of a customer is calculated from the lifetime value of a cohort or customer segment (Berger and Nasr, 1998).

The average CLV of a customer in the first cohort can then be expressed as:

$$CLV_1 = \sum_{t=1}^{T} \left[\frac{(GC - M)}{(1 + d)^{t}} r^{t} \right] - A,$$

where
r = rate of retention,
d = discount rate or the cost of capital for the firm,
t = time period,
T = the number of time periods considered for estimating CE,
GC = the average gross contribution,
M = marketing cost per customer, and
A = the average acquisition cost per customer

In the third approach, customer equity of the firm is first calculated as the sum of return on acquisition, return on retention, and return on add-on selling (Blattberg *et al.*, 2001). Following this, average CLV can then be calculated by dividing CE by the number of customers, and is expressed as follows:

$$CE(t) = \sum_{i=0}^{I} \left[N_{i,t} a_{i,t} (S_{i,t} - C_{i,t}) - N_{i,t} B_{i,a,t} \right.$$

$$+ \sum_{k=1}^{\infty} N_{i,t} a_{i,t} \left\{ \pi_{j=1}^{k} P_{j,t+k} \right\} (S_{i,t+k} - C_{i,t+k}$$

$$\left. - B_{i,r,t+k} - B_{i,Ao,t+k}) \left\{ \frac{1}{1 + d} \right\}^{k} \right]$$

$$CE(t) = \sum_{k=0}^{t} CE(t - k),$$

where,
CE (t) = the customer equity value for customers acquired at time t,
$N_{i,t}$ = the number of potential customers at time t for segment i,
$a_{i,t}$ = the acquisition probabilities at time t for segment i,
i,t = the retention probability at time t for a customer in segment i,
$B_{i,a,t}$ = the marketing cost per prospect (N) for acquiring customers at time t for segment i,

$B_{i,r,t}$ = the marketing in time period t for retained customers for segment i,

$B_{i,Ao,t}$ = the marketing costs in time period t for add-on selling for segment i,

d = discount rate,

$S_{i,t}$ = sales of the product/services offered by the firm at time t for segment i,

$C_{i,t}$ = cost of goods at time t for segment i,

I = the number of segments,

i = the segment designation, and

t_0 = the initial time period.

One of the important applications of computing average CLV is to evaluate competitor firms (Gupta and Lehmann, 2005). In the absence of competitors' customer-level data, firms can deduce information from published financial reports about approximate gross contribution margin, marketing, and advertising spending by competing firms to arrive at reasonable estimates of average CLV for competitors. Such an exercise would help the firm to know the profitability of the competitors' customers. The average CLV approach can also be used for evaluating the market value of the firm. It has been demonstrated that for high-growth companies, aggregate CLV of a firm or customer equity may be used as a surrogate measure of a firm's market value. However, average CLV has limited use as a metric for allocation of resources across customers. This is because the average CLV metric does not capture customer-level variations in CLV, which is the basis for developing customer-specific strategies. Also, calculating the aggregate CLV does not allow corrective measures to be implemented at the segment-level or individual customer level. Hence, it is necessary to calculate the CLV of individual customers in order to design individual-level strategies.

Individual Approach

Customer lifetime value (CLV), at an individual level, is calculated as the sum of cumulated cash flows — discounted using the weighted average cost of capital (WACC) — of a customer over her or his entire lifetime with the company (Kumar, 2007). It is a function of the predicted contribution margin, the propensity for a customer to continue in the relationship, and the marketing resources allocated to the customer. It is important to note that WACC is one of the measures that represents the discount factor used to compute CLV. There are other measures of discount factor (e.g., Tbills rate) that can be used to compute CLV. In its general form, CLV can be expressed as:

$$CLV_i = \sum_{t=1}^{T} \frac{(\text{Future Contribution Margin}_{it} - \text{Future Cost}_{it})}{(1 + d)^t},$$

where,

i = customer index,

t = time index,

T = the number of time periods considered for estimating CLV, and

d = discount rate.

The CLV literature provides various approaches through which individual-level CLV can be calculated (see Figure 6.3). In terms of the time horizon, studies have used an arbitrary time horizon (Reinartz and Kumar, 2003), a boundless time horizon (Fader *et al.*, 2005; Gupta *et al.*, 2004), and an infinite/unbound time horizon if the contribution margins and retention rates are constant over a period of time (Gupta and Lehmann, 2003). Studies have also computed CLV in a contractual setting (Braun and Schweidel, 2011; Fader and Hardie, 2010) and a non-contractual setting (Reinartz and Kumar, 2003).

Estimating Models Independently (Venkatesan and Kumar, 2004)

Model form:

$$CLV_{it} = \sum_{t=1}^{T_i} \frac{GC_{it}}{(1 + r)^{t/f_i}} - \sum_{l=1}^{n} \frac{\sum_m MC_{i.m.l}}{(1 + r)^l},$$

where,

$GC_{i,t}$ = gross contribution from customer i in purchase occasion t,

Figure 6.3: The Customer Lifetime Value (CLV) literature provides various approaches through which individual-level CLV can be calculated.

$MC_{i,m,l}$ = marketing cost, for customer i in communication channel m in time period l,

f_i (or frequency) = 12/expinti (where expinti is the expected inter-purchase time for customer i),

r = discount rate, n = number of years to forecast, and

T_i = number of purchases made by customer i.

Venkatesan and Kumar (2004) use a generalized gamma distribution to model inter-purchase time and employ panel-data regression to model the contribution margin. Several antecedents such as supplier-specific factors and customer characteristics are modeled to explain purchase frequency and contribution margin. The key merits of this model include: (1) accounting for customers to return to the firm after a temporary dormancy in a relationship, and (2) aiding in resource allocation decisions on marketing communication channels. The key limitations include not accounting for competitive responses and consumers' brand switching behavior.

Estimating Models Simultaneously (Venkatesan et al., 2007)

Model form: Likelihood function:

$$L = \prod_{i=1}^{n} \prod_{j=1}^{J_i} \sum_{k=1}^{K} \phi_{ijk} \big[f_k(t_{ij}|\alpha_k, \lambda_{ijk}, \gamma_k)$$
$$\times \, p\big(\Delta Q_{ij}|\delta_{i,k}, \delta_k^*, \sigma_k^2\big)\big]^{c_{ij}} \, S_k\big(t_{ij}|\alpha_k, \lambda_{ijk}, \gamma_k\big)^{(1-c_{ij})}$$

where, $f(t_{ij}|\alpha, \lambda, \gamma)$ = the density function for the generalized gamma distribution,

$S(t_{ij}|\alpha, \lambda, \gamma)$ = the survival function for the generalized gamma distribution,

$p(\Delta Q|\delta, \delta^*, \sigma^2)$ = the density function for purchase quantity,

c_{ij} = the censoring indicator, where $c_{ij} = 1$ if the jth inter-purchase time for the ith customer is not right-censored, and

$c_{ij} = 0$ if the jth inter-purchase time for the ith customer is right-censored.

Simultaneous modeling of purchase frequency, marketing cost, and gross contribution solves the issues of endogeneity and heterogeneity (Venkatesan *et al.*, 2007). These authors use the Bayesian decision theory to model the three parameters simultaneously to address the uncertainty in customer response to marketing actions. Several applications in B2C settings including winning back lost customers have utilized this methodology (see Boatwright *et al.*, 2003; Kumar *et al.*, 2015). The key merits of this model include (1) accounting for endogeneity and heterogeneity, and (2) providing more accurate results than independent estimation. The key limitations are that the model development and estimation are complex.

Brand Switching Approach (Rust et al., 2004)

Model form:

$$\text{CLV} = \sum_{t=0}^{T_{ij}} \frac{1}{(1 + d_i)^{\frac{t}{f_i}}} V_{ijt} \times \pi_{ijt} \times B_{ijt},$$

where,

T_{ij} = number of purchases customer i makes during the specified time period,

d_i = firm j's discount rate,

f_i = average number of purchases customer i makes in a unit time (e.g., per year),

V_{ijt} = customer i's expected purchase volume of brand j in purchase t,

π_{ijt} = expected contribution margin per unit of brand j from customer i in purchase t, and

B_{ijt} = probability that customer i buys brand j in purchase t.

Rust *et al.* (2004) model acquisition and retention of customers in the context of brand switching by collecting information on the brand purchased in the previous purchase occasion, the probability of purchasing a different brand, and individual-specific CE driver ratings from the customers. They then model individual-level utilities to find brand switching probability using Markov switching matrix. Customer's future expected contribution for each brand is computed by multiplying the probability by the contribution per purchase. The summation of expected contribution over time produces the CLV for the customer, adjusting for the time value of money. The key merits of this model include: (1) using it when the firm has a cross-sectional and longitudinal database, and (2) accounting for all types of marketing expenditures and accommodating competition. The key limitations are that the sample selection can play an important role in the accuracy of the metric and the model often relies heavily on survey-based data, thus leading to an increase in sampling cost and survey biases.

Monte Carlo Simulation Algorithm (Rust et al., 2011)

Model form:

$$p\left(\prod_{it}, \text{Pur}_{it},\ X_{it} \right) = p\left(\prod_{it} | \text{pur}_{it} = 1, X_{it} \right)$$
$$\times\ p(\text{pur}_{it} = 1 | X_{it}) \times p(X_{it}),$$

where,

Pur_{it} is the indicator of purchase and is equal to 1 if customer i purchases from the firm in time t, and 0 otherwise.

Rust *et al.* (2011) present a simulation model that accurately predicts future customer profitability and performs better than existing methods. In this model, the profitability of a customer is measured in terms of total profits and net present value (NPV) of profits. Customer predictions are captured by the propensity of the customer to purchase in each future time period and the associated profit generated in conjunction with marketing costs. The key merits of this model include: (1) a better predictive power over simpler competing models, and (2) better understanding of customer profitability and firm value. The key limitations are that it cannot be used in a lost-for-good setting as well as its heavy reliance on long purchase histories.

Customer Migration Model (Dwyer, 1997)

Model form:

$$\text{CE} = \sum_{t=0}^{T} \frac{MM_t C_t P_t}{(1 + d)^t},$$

where,

MMt is a matrix that contains the probabilities of customers moving from one segment to another at time t,

C_t is a vector containing the number of customers in each segment at time t, and

P_t is the profit from each segment at time t.

In Dwyer's (1997) model, customer behavior can be predicted on historical probabilities of purchase depending on recency and the current recency state in which the customer is located. Segmentation variables include RFM metric and demographic variables. The key merit of this model is that it considers probabilistic nature of customer purchases. The key limitation is that it can be used only in limited business settings.

Deterministic Model (Jain and Singh, 2002)

Model form:

$$CLV = \sum_{i=1}^{N} \frac{(R_i - C_i)}{(1 + d)^{i=0.5,}}$$

where,

i = the period of cash flow from customer transaction,
R_i = revenue from the customer in period i,
C_i = total cost of generating the revenue R_i in period i, and
N = the total number of periods of projected life of the customer under consideration.

These models focus on inputs and outputs and are used to study firm actions such as customer acquisition, retention, customer profitability, cross-buying behavior, and product return behavior (Reinartz and Kumar, 2002; Kumar and Reinartz, 2016). Other related models assume a constant gross contribution margin and marketing costs (Berger and Nasr, 1998). The key merits of this model include (1) having higher predictive accuracy, and (2) aiding in firm-level strategy development. The key limitations include (1) requiring huge amounts of individual customer data, (2) not considering the relationship between model parameters, (3) it is descriptive, but not prescriptive, and therefore less helpful in managerial decision-making, and (4) it does not account for competition.

Probabilistic Model (Dreze and Bonfrer, 2009)

Model form:

$$CLV_\tau = \frac{(1 + d)^\tau}{(1 + d)^\tau - p(\tau)} A(\tau),$$

where,

τ = a fixed time interval between contacts,
$A(\tau)$ = expected surplus from communications following the interval, and
$p(\tau)$ = probability of retention given that interval.

In this model by Dreze and Bonfrer (2009), the observed behavior is the result of an underlying stochastic process governed by latent behavioral characteristics, which is individual-specific. This type of model attempts to explain and predict observed behavior and not explain differences in observed behavior. The key merits of this model include (1) using it when the firm does not have longitudinal database, and (2) the identification of sub-drivers aids in better resource allocation. The key limitations include (1) assuming purchase volume and inter-purchase time to be exogenous, (2) calling for frequent updating of the model, and (3) placing heavy reliance on data and less reliance on managerial insight.

Structural Model (Sunder et al., 2016)

Model form:

$$U_{it} = \sum_{j=1}^{J} \left[\Psi_{it} \ln (1 + q_{ijt}) \right] + \lambda_i \ln \left[y_{it} - \sum_{j=1}^{J} (P_{jt} q_{ijt}) \right],$$

where,

U_{it} = overall utility from consumption by consumer i at time t,
y_{ijt} = baseline utility,
y_{it} = unobserved budget allocation within category by consumer i at time t,
P_{jt} = price of brand j at time t, and
q_{ijt} = quantity of brand j consumed by consumer i at time t. The q_{ijt} can then be used in the assessment of CLV.

Sunder *et al.* (2016) model multiple discreteness (i.e., consumers purchasing more than one brand in one purchase occasion) in a structural model while accounting for variety-seeking behavior in assessing customer CLV. The key merits of this model include

(1) how it is based on theoretical underpinnings of consumer behavior, (2) accounting for various salient aspects of consumer behavior (e.g., multiple discreteness, budgeting, etc.), which cannot be addressed by other methods, and (3) aiding in accurate out of sample prediction and managerial policy simulations. The key limitations are that the model development and estimation is very complex and relies heavily on across and within variation in customer purchases.

A PRIMER ON CUSTOMER LIFETIME VALUE (CLV)

A main advantage of CLV approach is that it not only incorporates future expected value of a customer but also the probability of that customer remaining active in future periods. In contrast with the former methods, CLV enables optimal allocation of resources at the individual customer level.

Segment-wise Calculation of CLV

In the simplest sense, if we assign (assume) a value to the revenue generated by a customer and the cost of serving that customer, we can derive the margin that the customer contributes to the bottom line of the firm in a given time frame (typically a year).

$$\text{CLV} = \sum_{t=1}^{T} \frac{(p_t - c_t)r_t}{(1 + d)^t} - \text{AC},$$

where,

T is the time horizon for the calculations,

p_t is the price paid by the customer at time t,

c_t is the cost of serving the customer at time t,

r_t is the probability of customer repeat purchase at time t,

d is the discount rate or cost of capital for the firm,

and AC is the customer acquisition cost.

Let's consider the case of a subscription magazine targeting college students. Assume that the average subscription lasts four years, the annual margin per subscriber is $12, annual retention rate as 90%, subscriber acquisition cost is $20, and the interest rate is 5%. Using the above formula, the estimated lifetime value of a subscriber would be merely $18.30.

However, let's assume that the magazine has a loyal following that extends beyond college years. In this case, we can assume that the margin (M) is fixed over time, and we can simplify the CLV formula by assuming the life cycle is infinite (i.e., N→∞). Thus, the basic customer lifetime value equation for infinite economic life becomes

$$\text{CLV} = \sum_{t=0}^{\infty} \frac{mr^t}{(1 + d)^t} = m\frac{r}{1 - r + d} - \text{AC}.$$

In this scenario, the CLV per subscriber of the magazine is significantly higher $72–$20 = $52. Assuming an infinite life-time cycle and constant retention rate, we can compute margin multiples. For example, with 95% retention and 5% discount rate, CLV is 9.5 times the margin per customer whereas with 65% retention and 12.5% discount rate it is only 1.37 times the margin.

It has been estimated that a 5% increase in customer retention improves profitability by 25%–100%! Given the prominence of *r* in the above equation, it is not hard to imagine how this dramatic effect comes about. Some (but not all) retained customers may pay price premiums, buy more, generate positive word-of-mouth (WOM), and enable cost savings (may cost less to serve and decrease overall acquisition costs). For example, Harrah's reported that its loyalty program improved its share of gambling wallet from 36% to 53%; it also increased slot revenue 12% by using its CRM database to redesign the casino floor. In the process, it also increased its occupancy rates, and revenue from top-tier guests (Young and Stepanek, 2003).

The margin (m) has been found to be relatively stable over time (Gupta and Lehmann, 2005). However, we can also incorporate a growth rate to the equation (assuming 1 + i is larger than r(1 + g)):

$$CLV = m\,\frac{r}{1 + i - r(1 + g)}.$$

Instead of an infinite life, the expected lifetime of the customer (i.e., $1/(1 - r)$) may also be used for estimating CLV. For example, with 90% retention rate, the expected lifetime is 10 years. Although, simple and straightforward, it has been shown that the expected lifetime approach overestimates CLV (Gupta *et al.*, 2006).

Advanced Measurement of CLV

The CLV models presented above make several simplifying assumptions. For example, the retention rate is constant and applies equally to the customer groups. However, in many cases retention probability changes drastically from customer (segment) to customer (segment) and should not be averaged across customers (see Figure 6.4). Generally speaking, making the models more realistic means making them more complex. For example, when we account for

return on acquisition, return on retention, and return on add-on selling, we observe (Blattberg *et al.*, 2001)

$$CE_{(t)} = \sum_{i=0}^{I}$$

$$\left[\begin{array}{l} N_{i,t}\alpha_{i,t}(S_{i,t} - c_{i,t}) - N_{i,t}B_{i,\alpha,t} + \sum_{k=1}^{\infty} N_{i,t}\alpha_{i,t}\left(\prod_{j=1}^{k}\rho_{j,t+k}\right) \\ (S_{i,t+k} - c_{i,t+k} - B_{i,r,t+k} - B_{i,AO,t+k})\left(\dfrac{1}{1+d}\right)^k \end{array} \right]$$

where,

$CE_{(t)}$ is the customer equity value for customer acquired at time t,

$N_{i,t}$ is the number of potential customers at time t for segment i,

$\alpha_{i,t}$ is the acquisition probability at time t for segment i,

$\rho_{i,t}$ is the retention probability at time t for a customer in segment i,

$B_{i,\alpha,t}$ is the marketing cost per prospect (N) for acquiring customer at time t, segment i,

$B_{i,r,t}$ is the marketing in time period t for retained customers for segment i,

$B_{i,AO,t}$ is the marketing costs in time period t for add-on selling for segment i,

d is the discount rate,

$S_{i,t}$ is the sales of the product/services offered by the firm at time t for segment i,

$C_{i,t}$ is the cost of goods at time t for segment i,

I is the number of segments,

J is the segment designation, and

t_0 is the initial time period.

The average CLV can then be calculated by dividing CE by the total number of customers. Average CLV metric is useful to evaluate competitors (good estimates of competitor CLVs can be calculated based on publicly available data), and can also be used as a proxy of firms' market valuation for high growth companies. However, it does not render itself for one-to-one marketing approaches at the individual level (Gupta and Lehmann, 2008).

Figure 6.4: Segment-wise calculation of CLV can be done to assess the contribution of various segments.

CUSTOMER LIFETIME VALUE

Individual CLV Calculation

The calculation of CLV includes determining the (time-adjusted) future contribution margin, future costs, and customer retention. In the following section, we discuss the components and the method of calculating contribution margin and future costs. Expressed in general form, CLV is

$$CLV_i = \sum_{t=1}^{T} \frac{(\text{Future Contribution Margin}_{it} - \text{Future Cost}_{it})}{(1+d)^t},$$

where,

i = customer index,

t = time index,

T = forecast horizon, and

d = discount rate.

In contrast with contractual setting where prediction of the customer retention metric is emphasized, the focus is on predicting future customer behavior and contribution margin in non-contractual settings (where customer defection rates are significantly higher) (Reinartz and Kumar, 2000).

P(Active) refers to the probability that a customer continues to purchase from the firm in the future. This is calculated at the unique individual level in contrast with the aggregate retention rate. The Net Present Value (NPV) of Expected Gross Contribution (EGC) (Reinartz and Kumar, 2003) can be calculated as follows:

$$\text{NPV of EGC}_{it} = \sum_{n=t+1}^{t+x} P(Active)_{in} \times \frac{\text{AMGC}_{it}}{(1+d)^n},$$

where,

AMGC_{it} is average gross contribution margin in period t based on all prior purchases,

i is the customer index,

t is the period for which NPV is being estimated,

n is the number of periods beyond t,

d is the discount rate, and

$P(Active)_{in}$ is the probability that customer i is active in period n.

As an example, let's use the example of a customer who spends $60, $100, $110, $190, and most recently $210 on her or his cable bundle package, respectively. Assuming an average gross contribution margin of 50%, a discount rate of 12% per annum, and the probability of her remaining active is 50% for the next month and 35% for the month after that, we can calculate the NPV of EGC of the customer as follows:

$$AMGC = (60 + 100 + 110 + 190 + 210)/5$$
$$= \$134.$$

$$\text{NPV of EGC} = 0.5 \times \frac{134}{(1+0.01)^1} + 0.3 \frac{134}{(1+0.01)^2}$$
$$= \$105.7445.$$

P(Active) is calculated based on frequency and time between purchases. That is

$$P(Active) = \left(\frac{T}{N}\right)^n,$$

where,

n is the number of purchases made during the observation period,

T is the time between first and last purchase,

N is the time between first and focal period for prediction.

For example, consider the following purchase schedule by three customers:

If we want to estimate P(Active) for week 10

$$P(Active)_{\text{Ali}} = \left(\frac{5}{10}\right)^2 = 0.25$$

$$P(Active)_{\text{Ben}} = \left(\frac{5}{9}\right)^2 = 0.31.$$

$$P(Active)_{\text{Charlize}} = \left(\frac{6}{10}\right)^5 = 0.08.$$

Based on previous purchase frequency patterns of Ali and Ben, it would not be unlikely for them to make a purchase during week 10. However, Charlize, who was previously the most active, has not purchased in a while and is not likely to purchase in the future. Ali is about three times more likely to remain an active customer than Charlize. The basic equation to calculate P(Active) can certainly be improved and customized to serve a particular context better.

Marketing cost usually leads the market response (sales and profits). Therefore, assuming that marketing costs take place at the beginning of a period and that gross contribution is observed at the end of a period, CLV formula can be stated as:

$$CLV_i = \sum_{n=t+1}^{t+x} P(Active)_{in} \times \frac{AMGC_{it}}{(1+d)^n} - \sum_{n=1}^{x} M_{in} \times \left(\frac{1}{1+d}\right)^{n-1} - AC.$$

Assumptions of the model include that when a customer defects, he/she does not return (customers that return after defection are treated as a new customer by the model). This also called the "lost for good" scenario. Naturally, this is not necessarily true in the real world, and the model underestimates CLV. To incorporate the possibility of a customer coming back and enable a second life-time value, predicted frequency can be included in the CLV model (Venkatesan and Kumar, 2004):

$$CLV_i = \sum_{y=1}^{T_i} \frac{CM_{i,y}}{\underbrace{(1+r)^y}_{frequency_i}} - \sum_{l=1}^{n} \frac{\sum_m c_{i,m,l} \times x_{i,m,l}}{(1+d)^{l-1}},$$

where,

CLV_i is the lifetime value of customer i,

$CM_{i,y}$ is the predicted contribution margin from customer I in purchase occasion y,

d is the discount rate,

$c_{i,m,l}$ is the unit marketing cost for customer i in channel m in year l,

$x_{i,m,l}$ is the number of contacts to customer i in channel m in year l,

frequency is the predicted purchase frequency for customer i,

n is the number of years to forecast, and

T_i is the predicted number of purchases by customer i until the end of planning period.

MODELS OF CUSTOMER ENGAGEMENT

With an increase in the size of databases and its availability in real time, customer engagement analytics provide an opportunity to capture such dynamic data that appear in online settings. The emergence of social media — the "group of Internet-based applications that build on the ideological and technological foundations of Web 2.0 and that allow the creation and exchange of User-Generated Content" forms an important part of customer–firm relationship.

Customer Referrals

Kumar, Peterson, and Leone (2007) showed that customers who were behaviorally less loyal had a stronger impact on referring new customers when compared to behaviorally loyal customers. They also showed that the referral process brought in customers without excessive marketing expenditure and who would, otherwise, not have positively responded to traditional marketing programs (see Figure 6.5). Customer referral value (CRV) is a metric that captures the monetary value of a customer associated with the future profits given by each refereed prospect, discounted to the present value. Many companies offer incentives to the referring customer, or both the referring customer and customers who have been referred. In such case, a referral is a firm-incentivized recommendation from a current referring customer to a prospect, or referred customer. Referral programs offer

Figure 6.5: The referral process may bring in customers without excessive marketing expenditure and who would, otherwise, not have positively responded to traditional marketing programs.

different types of incentives including free service, free products, credit, points, vouchers, gifts, discounts, or cash. Ryu and Feick (2007) found that when a reward was extended to both prospects and referred customers, customers were more likely to make referrals to stronger ties in the network; however, when only the referred customers received incentives, the referrals were made to weak ties in the network. Either ways, referrals allow firms to acquire new customers for lower acquisition costs (compared to traditional methods) with the added benefit of a lifetime source of new revenue stream.

The study by Schmitt *et al.* (2011) found that customers acquired through incentivized referral programs were more valuable to the company than customers acquired through traditional methods. From data obtained from a financial services firm, customer samples acquired through both methods were compared for their individual contribution margin and loyalty data for a period of 33 months after the referral program rollout. On contribution margin, the study found an increased profitability of about 25% of customers acquired through referrals compared to their counterparts, and this difference was highest during the initial period but gradually disappeared toward the tail end of the

cycle. Further, the contribution margin differential was enough to cover all the costs associated with the referral program. On customer loyalty, the study found referred customers were 18% less likely to leave and the higher retention rate remained high for the entire time period. Thus, referred customers are more valuable to the firm as a result of higher contribution margin and greater loyalty. This study found that over a six-year period, referred customers had a higher CLV by 25% compared to the CLV of those acquired by traditional methods. In short, the higher contribution margin and greater loyalty combined with lower acquisition costs, yields higher profits for companies.

Referral Seeding Strategies

Hinz *et al.* (2011) studied which seeding strategy is the best in terms of referrals generated in the social network, i.e., friends, family, and co-workers. They examined the level of connectivity measured by the "degree centrality" scale, which takes higher values for people with more connections and lower values for those with fewer connections. They also examined the type of connectivity measured by the "betweenness centrality" scale, which takes higher values for people with more unique connections and lower values with fewer unique connections to others. They identified three groups of customers: (1) "hubs," individuals with many connections, (2) "fringes," individuals with fewer connections, and (3) "bridges," people with unique connections. Hubs are conducive to high-degree seeding strategies when the initial marketing message (seed) is communicated, whereas fringes are given low-degree seeding. High-betweenness seeding strategy is used when the seed is communicated to bridges. These authors, through an online social networking platform, found that high-degree seeding increased the probability of successful referrals by 53% and high-betweenness seeding by 39%, as compared to random sampling. In contrast, low-degree seeding significantly lowered the probability of successful referrals by 81% as compared to random seeding. This suggests that high-degree seeding and bridge seeding strategy are most effective, particularly when the referrer is incentivized, albeit, the high-degree strategy is more pragmatic.

Measurement of CRV

CRV has two components: (1) discounted value of customers who joined because of the referral and (2) discounted value of customers who would join anyway regardless of the referral (see Figure 6.6). The first component relates to referred customers, who would not have joined otherwise, and includes both savings in customer acquisition and the revenue

Figure 6.6: Customer Lifetime and Referral Value Metrics

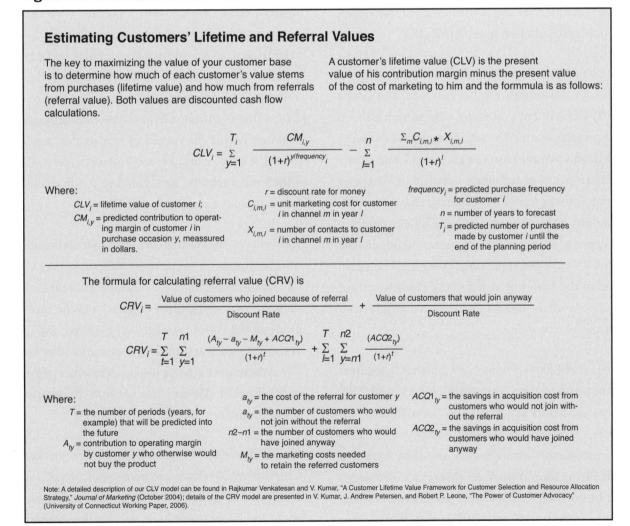

Estimating Customers' Lifetime and Referral Values

The key to maximizing the value of your customer base is to determine how much of each customer's value stems from purchases (lifetime value) and how much from referrals (referral value). Both values are discounted cash flow calculations.

A customer's lifetime value (CLV) is the present value of his contribution margin minus the present value of the cost of marketing to him and the formmula is as follows:

$$CLV_i = \sum_{y=1}^{T_i} \frac{CM_{i,y}}{(1+r)^{y/frequency_i}} - \sum_{l=1}^{n} \frac{\Sigma_m C_{i,m,l} \star X_{i,m,l}}{(1+r)^l}$$

Where:

CLV_i = lifetime value of customer i;

$CM_{i,y}$ = predicted contribution to operating margin of customer i in purchase occasion y, meassured in dollars.

r = discount rate for money

$C_{i,m,l}$ = unit marketing cost for customer i in channel m in year l

$X_{i,m,l}$ = number of contacts to customer i in channel m in year l

$frequency_i$ = predicted purchase frequency for customer i

n = number of years to forecast

T_i = predicted number of purchases made by customer i until the end of the planning period

The formula for calculating referral value (CRV) is

$$CRV_i = \frac{\text{Value of customers who joined because of referral}}{\text{Discount Rate}} + \frac{\text{Value of customers that would join anyway}}{\text{Discount Rate}}$$

$$CRV_i = \sum_{t=1}^{T} \sum_{y=1}^{n1} \frac{(A_{ty} - a_{ty} - M_{ty} + ACQ1_{ty})}{(1+r)^t} + \sum_{l=1}^{T} \sum_{y=n1}^{n2} \frac{(ACQ2_{ty})}{(1+r)^t}$$

Where:

T = the number of periods (years, for example) that will be predicted into the future

A_{ty} = contribution to operating margin by customer y who otherwise would not buy the product

a_{ty} = the cost of the referral for customer y

a_{ty} = the number of customers who would not join without the referral

$n2–n1$ = the number of customers who would have joined anyway

M_{ty} = the marketing costs needed to retain the referred customers

$ACQ1_{ty}$ = the savings in acquisition cost from customers who would not join without the referral

$ACQ2_{ty}$ = the savings in acquisition cost from customers who would have joined anyway

Note: A detailed description of our CLV model can be found in Rajkumar Venkatesan and V. Kumar, "A Customer Lifetime Value Framework for Customer Selection and Resource Allocation Strategy," *Journal of Marketing* (October 2004); details of the CRV model are presented in V. Kumar, J. Andrew Petersen, and Robert P. Leone, "The Power of Customer Advocacy" (University of Connecticut Working Paper, 2006).

Adapted from V. Kumar, J.A. Petersen, and R.P. Leone (2007), How Valuable is Word of Mouth? *Harvard Business Review* 85(10): 139–146.

generated from their future purchases. The referring customer takes credit for all future transactions of the referred customer. Here the exact time of the referral is critical as it determines the time period for proper discounting of the future value. It is important to know the number of referrals made in a year and the cost of referrals due to incentive programs in place. For customers who would have joined the company anyway, it is sufficient to include only the savings in acquisition costs. Thus, acquisition savings are included in the calculation for both group of customers; however, they contribute differently to the referring customer's CRV. It is also possible to add indirect referrals wherein the referred customer in turn provides referrals to other and becomes referring customer. As the CRV of the firm increases, the original referrer can also be credited in terms of her or his contribution to the firm's CRV.

The challenge is linking high CLV customers with high CRV customers. Kumar, Peterson, and Leone (2007) showed that customers who score highly on CLV measure are not the same customers who score highly on CRV measure. In fact, their data shows that the top 30% of customers based on CLV have no overlap with the top 30% of customers based on CRV. Therefore, only focusing on high CLV customers at the expense of high CRV customers might alienate high CRV customers, not only losing their potential value to the firm but also driving them to spread negative word-of-mouth (WOM) that will further damage the firm value.

Kumar *et al.* (2007) propose a 2 × 2 matrix to segment customers based on low and high CLV and CRV scores. The four segments are (1) Affluents, (2) Misers, (3) Advocates, and (4) Champions. Affluents are customers with high CLV but they have low CRV, Firms should work on marketing campaigns that build their CRV. Misers are customers that are low in both CLV and CRV, in that, they neither make a lot of purchases, nor do they refer many new customers. Firms can communicate product information to increase their purchase activities without much investment. Advocates are high on CRV but low on CLV, which means they are active in spreading information to other customers. Firms can offer increased perceived product value to such customers with the hopes of increasing their CLV. Finally, champions are high on both CLV and CRV and represent the best customers of the firm (See Figure 6.7).

Customer Influence

Social media is present in different forms including online interaction (e.g., blogs, Twitter), online collaboration (e.g., social bookmarking, Pinterest), multimedia (e.g., video sharing, YouTube), entertainment (e.g., music sharing, Pandora), and reviews (e.g., user forums, Yahoo). These services are popular on Facebook and Twitter. Customer influence value (CIV) is the monetary gain or loss realized by a firm that is attributable to a customer (influence), through her or his spread of positive or negative WOM. It is based on customer influence effect (CIE), which measures the net spread and influence of a message from a particular individual.

CIV relies on the effect of each customer's influence on other customers, i.e., customer influence effect (CIE. CIE is determined by (1) whether there is a connection between two users, (2) if there is, was the receiver aware of the WOM message being spread, and (3) if yes, did the receiver spread the message to other users? CIE is therefore the net spread of an instance of WOM and is also related to user data, network characteristics, content, and user appeal (Kumar, 2013).

Kumar *et al.* (2013) measure CIV by first measuring CIE. How WOM flows across a network of individuals is assessed by individual-specific data and metadata about the information itself, such as the category to

Figure 6.7: Customer Value Matrix Based on Customer Lifetime Value (CLV) and Customer Referral Value (CRV) Scores

The Customer Value Matrix

When we segmented the customers in our telecom sample according to their lifetime values and referral values, it was easy to see which customers needed to be encouraged to buy more and which should be nudged to make more recommendations.

Average CRV after one year

	LOW	**HIGH**
HIGH (Average CLV after one year)	**AFFLUENTS** 29% of customers CLV = $1,219 CRV = $49	**CHAMPIONS** 21% of customers CLV = $370 CRV = $590
LOW	**MISERS** 21% of customers CLV = $130 CRV = $64	**ADVOCATES** 29% of customers CLV = $180 CRV = $670

Note: Cutoff points for the low and high CLVs and CRVs were set at the median value for both measures.

Adapted from V. Kumar, J.A. Petersen, and R.P. Leone (2007), How Valuable is Word of Mouth? *Harvard Business Review* 85(10): 139–146.

which it belongs. They measure the stickiness index (SI) defined as an array of the degree to which a user or an instance of WOM is specific to each category of topics. That is, it refers to how specific the user is to a particular category of words, based on the association of words between each other and with other words used by all users globally. It is based on semantic linkages of word-level interactions to understand the context of words and the probable association between the array of words given a global association across word clouds. It is the match between a user's SI and WOM instance, which indicates the degree of stickiness. For instance, if user A sends 50 tweets to user B, and if 25 tweets are about ice creams and related topics (milkshakes, desserts), then the stickiness index (SI) of user A is 0.5. The compatibility of the users determines the attractiveness of the message and helps determine the number of social media users actively discussing a specific topic. The authors also computed

the influencing ratio, defined as the relative influence of multiple individuals in the network referring the product to a particular referral. If a person has been influenced by many individuals, the influence of each individual on that person is determined through the CIE metric.

Kumar *et al.* (2013) provide an illustration of how to compute CIV. Assuming that the influencer has an equal effect on each of the influencer he/she influences and that the CLV is observed, then using Hubbell's influence measure, the CIE can be computed as follows:

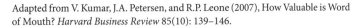

$$CIE_j = \omega_j + \sum_i k_{j \to i} \times CIE_i,$$

where CIE_j is the CIE of a user j, ω is the degree of spread (number of messages posted), $k_{j \to k}$ is the Hubbell's influence of j on i.

In the illustration taken from Kumar *et al.* (2013) (see Figure 6.8), assume Alexa influences Bob and Carol and Bob influences Carol and David. To compute the CIV for Alexa, we need to consider the CLV and CIV for both Bob and Carol. Since Carol is influenced by both Bob and Alexa, the CLV and the CIV of Carol will be equally divided between Alexa and Bob. That is, the CIV of Alexa is the same as the complete CLV and CIV of Bob and half the CLV and CIV of Carol. The illustration in the Table provides how CIV is computed using Hubbell's influence methodology.

Customer Knowledge

Kumar (2013) defines customer knowledge value (CKV) as the monetary value attributed to a customer by a firm due to the profit generated by implementing an idea, suggestion, or feedback from that customer. This can include collaboration with the firm, in which case customer collaborator value (CCV) can be computed. Customers offer firms preferences in the knowledge development process that allow them

to innovate with new product and service offerings. Customer feedback can be obtained through onsite surveys, online surveys, traditional market research channels including personal/telephone surveys, focus groups, etc. Particularly, important is the role of negative feedback option in integrating with other feedback data. Negative feedback gives a sense of credibility to the existing positive reviews, can help potential customers in making their purchase decisions, and allows firms the opportunity to make improvements in their customer service.

Customers often vary in their willingness and ability to participate in co-creation tasks and therefore, firms are interested in pre-selection mechanisms to identify the right segments. Customer selection models such as scoring models that incorporate drivers of customer willingness and ability to co-create in an online environment are often helpful (Hoyer *et al.*, 2010). Suitable pre-selection models that screen millions of ideas are useful similar to clickstream data in the online purchase funnel. Often, brand community

Figure 6.8: Customer Influence Value Metrics

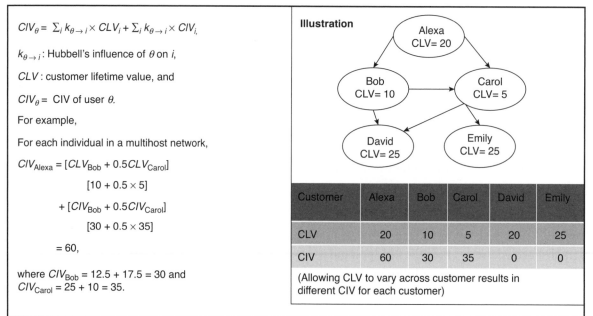

$CIV_\theta = \Sigma_i \, k_{\theta \to i} \times CLV_i + \Sigma_i \, k_{\theta \to i} \times CIV_i$,

$k_{\theta \to i}$: Hubbell's influence of θ on i,

CLV: customer lifetime value, and

CIV_θ = CIV of user θ.

For example,

For each individual in a multihost network,

$CIV_{Alexa} = [CLV_{Bob} + 0.5 CLV_{Carol}]$

$[10 + 0.5 \times 5]$

$+ [CIV_{Bob} + 0.5 CIV_{Carol}]$

$[30 + 0.5 \times 35]$

$= 60$,

where $CIV_{Bob} = 12.5 + 17.5 = 30$ and $CIV_{Carol} = 25 + 10 = 35$.

Illustration

Customer	Alexa	Bob	Carol	David	Emily
CLV	20	10	5	20	25
CIV	60	30	35	0	0

(Allowing CLV to vary across customer results in different CIV for each customer)

Adapted from V. Kumar, V. Bhaskaran, R. Mirchandani, and M. Shah (2013), Creating a Measurable Social Media Marketing Strategy: Increasing the Value and ROI of Intangibles and Tangibles for Hokey Pokey, *Marketing Science* 32(2): 194–212.

members indicate strong interest in the product and possess extensive product knowledge and are willing to engage by contributing their expertise. Tracking a customer's knowledge/expertise, which is often correlated with CLV, is valuable in assessing CKV up to a point as very high levels of CLV might denote high satisfaction and therefore little incentive to provide feedback, i.e., inverted U-shaped relationship (Kumar *et al.*, 2010). Not just expertise, but willingness to provide feedback is also important. Sometimes, valuable knowledge components related to products modification and service recovery can be extracted from defected customers who might also contribute to CKV. Also, the level of connectedness of customers to other customers and (prospects) can provide the capability to better assimilate information from their networks thereby enhancing their KBV (Kumar *et al.*, 2010).

DEVELOPING AND IMPLEMENTING CRM STRATEGIES

Strategies for Maximizing Customer Lifetime Value (CLV)

Customer Acquisition

Here a fundamental issue in customer acquisition is in identifying the probability of a customer being acquired. Villanueva *et al.* (2008) showed that market channels influence the customer acquisition process and the value that newly acquired customers bring to the firm. These authors delineated two functions: (1) the value-generating function linking the newly acquired customers' contributions to the firm's equity growth, and (2) the acquisition response function linking the number of acquisitions to marketing spending by the firm. They found that marketing-induced customers add short-term value; however, WOM customers add nearly twice as much long-term value to the firm. WOM referrals and the source of

such referrals certainly impact the prospect's purchase likelihood. Von Wangenheim and Bayon (2007) found that customer satisfaction influenced the number of WOM referrals, which in turn had an impact on customer acquisition. Kumar and Reinartz (2016) list a host of questions that have been delved into by scholars:

- How likely are prospects to respond to acquisition promotion initiated by firms?

- How do marketing variables such as shipping fee, WOM referral, and promotion depth, influence prospects' response behavior?

- How much profit or value will acquisition campaign bring to companies?

- How many new customers can we acquire and how long will they stay with the company?

Customer Retention

Monitoring a customer's purchase and attitudinal behavior is pivotal in understanding when a firm should actively pursue a retention strategy *vis-à-vis* a customer. Tracking loyal customers' purchase data who are profitable coupled with shifts in attitude over time is critical to developing retention strategies. This is important, more so, as firms want to minimize defecting customers who leave the company due to unmet needs and can potentially hurt brand and firm value through negative WOM. Several statistical modeling and estimation procedures (Markov chain, Bayesian estimation) allow for measuring customer's future value and profitability based on prior transaction data, thus enabling firms to determine how much to spend on a customer. One practical strategy for retaining customers is to nurture their cross-buying behavior. Research shows that cross-buying customers extend the duration of their relationship with the firm (Reinartz and Kumar, 2003), increase their purchase frequency (Reinartz et al. 2008), and contribute to higher profit (Kumar et al., 2008). However, greater customer cross-buying does not always result in higher customer profitability. Shah *et al.* (2012) find that customer cross-buying is not necessarily profitable for all customers of the firm and can adversely affect a firm's bottom line. Some important questions that have been looked into include:

- What is the lifetime duration of the customer?

- How much will the customer spend, and will it be in multiple product categories?

- What will firms do in order to retain a customer who is worth retaining?

Customer Churn

Customers who are likely to churn exhibit symptoms of their dissatisfaction such as fewer frequency, longer time between purchases, and lower response to marketing stimulus. Customer churn and switching behavior is relevant in a contractual setting and research shows several factors contributing toward churn, including customer status, cross-sensitive classifiers, price sensitivity, and switching behavior, etc. (e.g., Danaher, 2002). Kumar and Reinartz (2016) list critical questions related to customer churn that have been addressed including:

- Can churn be predicted and when can firms intervene to prevent customers from churning?

- How much should be spent on churn prevention?

Customer Win Back

When customers churn, it does not mean the end of the customer life cycle. Firms can still win lost customers back and give them a second life. While lost customers are familiar with the product, winning back is not easy as they often are dissatisfied with the products/services, which made them leave in the first place. Stauss and Friege (1999) provide a framework for regaining lost customers. Not all customers are worthy of win back; rather, firms should focus on the second lifetime value, segment them on this basis, and evaluate customers in each segment to

determine why they defected. Generally, lowering reacquisition price to buy-back is an optimal strategy. Kumar *et al.* (2015) found that the lost customers' first lifetime experiences and behaviors, reason for defection, and the nature of the win back offer made to lost customers are associated with the likelihood of customer reacquisition and their second lifetime duration and profitability. Some critical questions studied (Kumar and Reinartz, 2016) include:

- How should firms approach customers to win them back?

- What elements should firms focus to get back lost customers?

Customer Segmentation Strategies using CLV and Size of Unused Wallet (SUW)

Kumar *et al.* (2009) propose a customer-centric framework (as opposed to product-centric) to maximizing firm profitability using relationship marketing strategy following a reverse direction approach compared to the conventional approach. In the conventional approach, customer acquisition starts with innovation of high-quality product and services designed to meet high levels of customer satisfaction for all customers. Higher levels of satisfaction lead to higher levels of loyalty (retention), which then leads to higher levels of profits. The satisfaction–loyalty–profitability framework employs backward-looking metrics for current customers only and the links in each part of the framework are weak and therefore does not guarantee profitability. In the reverse logic framework (RLF) (discussed in chapter 2) the starting point is future customer value, or customer profitability, measured by CLV. Before selectively choosing to up-sell and cross-sell, firms should assess individual customer CLV and accordingly implement a customized loyalty/experience plan for customers based on their profitability potential. The idea is that rewarding the most profitable customers, at the expense of less profitable or unprofitable customers, will increase their retention rate. In addition, acquisition of future customers is based on a matching profile of the current profitable customers.

While CLV is useful to evaluate the future profitability of the customer, it does not provide information on the overall profit potential of the customer. Kumar *et al.* (2009) propose that to maximize the profitability of each customer with the firm, it is useful to evaluate CLV together with the customer's size of unused wallet (SUW). SUW represents the incremental profit potential of the customer obtained (or inferred) from marketing intelligence and information archival systems. Three levels of CLV (low, medium, and high) crossed with two levels of SUW (low and high) lead to six customer segments.

Segments 1 and 2 (in Figure 6.9) represent high CLV customers who generate disproportionately high profitability to the firm (80:20 rule based on Pareto Principle). However, segment 1 customers are low in SUW who spend most of their entire share of wallet with the firm. With such customers, the firm strategy should focus on nurturing the relationship by offering special rewards and privileges through loyalty programs. Segment 2 represents high CLV customers with high SUW meaning these are customers with high net worth and therefore the focus should be on defending the relationships from competition. Defending or augmenting strategies could use up-selling/cross-selling. However, if such customers do not respond favorably to firm's marketing efforts, the firm should increase the incentives offered to these high CLV customers by an amount that is equivalent to the cost of acquiring a new high CLV customer.

Segments 3 and 4 (in Figure 6.9) represent medium CLV customers who generate profitability but not as high as high CLV customers, although they represent the largest number of customers (50%). Segment 3 customers do not have much room to grow their business with the firm and therefore the firm must sustain the current level of spending and at the same time limiting their marketing efforts.

Figure 6.9: Customer Segmentation Using Customer Lifetime Value (CLV) and SUW

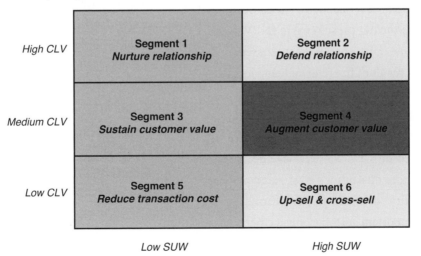

Adapted from V. Kumar, Ilaria Dalla Pozza, J. Andrew Petersen, and Denish Shah (2009), Reversing the Logic: The Path to Profitability through Relationship Marketing, *Journal of Interactive Marketing* 2: 147–156.

Segment 4 customers are moderate CLV and high SUW showing a promise for up-sell and cross-sell initiatives. If they do not respond favorably to firm's marketing efforts, the firm should reduce its marketing effort and instead, focus on deriving profits from every transaction.

Segments 5 and 6 (in Figure 6.9) represent low CLV who do not generate profit for the firm; instead they are a drain on company's resources. Segment 5 customers are not preferred by firms and some might even fire these customers based on either past value or future value of customers. This, however, might have unintended consequences of negative word-of-mouth (WOM) effect that might draw the wrath of current customers and future prospects. However, customers in segment 6, with low CLV but high SUW, might be a good target for up-sell and cross-sell.

Extending CLV to Customer Engagement Value

Customers acquired through referrals are both less expensive and more valuable than those acquired through traditional methods (Schmitt *et al.*, 2011). While customers acquired are more valuable in the short-term, referred customers are twice as valuable in the long-term (Villanueva *et al.*, 2008). Customer referral value (CRV) is the net present value (NPV) of the future profits of new customers who purchased the firm offerings as a result of the referral behavior of the current customer incentivized by firm-referral programs. CRV is an interesting concept as it allows the firm to save on acquisition cost as well as maximize profits based on CLV. Models have been developed that captures customer's past referral behavior and behavioral drivers of CRV (Kumar *et al.*, 2007). The next important customer engagement value is derived from valuing customer influences, or customer influence value (CIV). Specifically,

the influence by WOM propagation and network evolution with every instance of WOM is captured by CIV. CIV takes into account the net spread, i.e., customer influence effect (CIE) of positive and negative information, and computes the monetary gain or loss realized by the firm attributable to a customer.

Valuing customer knowledge contribution is an important engagement outcome measured by customer knowledge value (CKV). Customers add value to the firm by participating in reviewing products and providing valuable feedback for product solutions and/or new product development. Further, they add value by providing support services and knowledge information. CKV, therefore, is conceptualized as value since the customer adds to the firm through her or his feedback (Kumar *et al.*, 2010). Kumar (2013) explains feedback response strategy design and implementation based on whether the feedback is positive/negative and whether the feedback warrants immediate/long-term action by the firm. For instance, KLM started the "KLM Surprise" campaign (positive/immediate) to track how happiness spreads surprising travelers with unique gifts based on their social networking profiles. On the negative feedback, Netflix is a good example. Netflix got negative feedback after changing their pricing model (negative/immediate), which caused the firm to revert to the initial plan. Starbucks initiated the "My Starbucks Idea" combining social media and feedback mechanism followed by Starbucks "Ideas in Action" where employees talk about how ideas were implemented. On the negative side, Canadian Broadcasting Corporation (CBC) reversed its decision to remove the holiday track *Baby It's Cold Outside* (a classic duet from 1944) after sparking several headlines and vigorous debates on social media.

Linking Customer Equity to Shareholder Value

The links between CLV and shareholder value become more obvious once the focus of the marketing manager shifts from expense and revenue to investment and assets (Ramaswami *et al.*, 2009). Customers respond to marketing activities through their attitudinal metrics (satisfaction, loyalty), behavioral metrics (choice, loyalty, CLV), and engagement metrics (CRV, CIV, and CKV), which in turn boost firm value. These improvements are expected to lead to higher brand and customer equity, and increase sales, market share, cash flow, return on investment (ROI), and ultimately the value of the firm as measured by market capitalization (shareholder value) (Rust *et al.*, 2004).

Customer equity represents the total lifetime values of all customers of the firm. While customer satisfaction has been linked to higher firm value in terms of immediate cash flows and future growth options, customer equity can also be used as a method of firm valuation especially in the long-term (Gupta *et al.*, 2004). Kumar and Shah (2009) proposed a framework linking customer engagement and cash flow with the stock price of the firm, i.e., market capitalization. For instance, these authors implemented CLV-based strategies and empirically demonstrated that increases in stock price for B2B and B2C firms were 32.8 % and 57.6%, respectively in a nine-month period.

Figure 6.10 shows that value is created to and from customers. Firms engage in long-term customer relationships only when customer perceived value (i.e., value to customers) and firm value (i.e., value from customers) are aligned. The alignment is an evolutionary process that takes into account changing customer and competitive factors, which then impacts changes in resource allocation and marketing activities.

Figure 6.10: Aligning Customer Perceived Value and Firm Value

Ensuring Value Alignment: An Organizing Framework

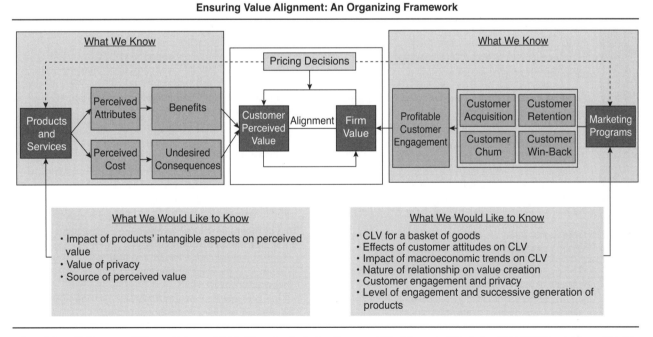

Adapted from V. Kumar and Werner Reinartz (2016), "Creating Enduring Customer Value", *Journal of Marketing* AMA/MSI Special Issue, Vol. 80, November, pp. 36–68.

Strategies for Maximizing Relationship Equity: Role of Qualitative Research

Information about customer lifetime value (CLV) can be limited and misleading indicator of the status and potential of a customer relationship. CLV models and CRM strategies do very little to ascertain relationship realities and strengthen relationship bonds. Fournier and Avery (2011) through qualitative studies (critical incident interviews, case studies) and large sample surveys identified three important ways in which the current CRM strategies fail and how they can turn current practice into opportunities to develop strong relationship equity with customers (see Figure 6.11).

First, companies forget that their relationships are not just with consumers but people who have deep relational needs which current CRM models are not adequately designed to capture and decode. Most current CRM systems monitor their customers' purchase histories (e.g., RFM approach) and project future customer lifetime value (CLV) (e.g., CLV models); however, they fail to take into account what individual consumers are feeling and what makes them tick. Unfortunately, CRM models are unable to find meaning by assembling micro-information into abstract wholes that would help managers decode how the brand fits in the person's life. Beyond purchase and demographic data, it is the individual context (e.g., people's needs and expectations, broader emotional wellbeing, customer experience) that significantly shapes a person's brand relationships and companies need to allocate resources to gain such insights.

Figure 6.11: A New Spotlight on Customer Relationship Marketing (CRM): Putting the "R" Back in CRM

SHINING A NEW SPOTLIGHT ON RELATIONSHIPS

Companies can maximize the value of their customer relationships by redefining how they think about customer value and how they measure it. Shifting some aspects of current practices can open significant new opportunities in the future.

CURRENT PRACTICE	OPPORTUNITY
From managing customers as economic assets...	**To understanding customers as people**
• From data and information...	• To context and meaning
• From knowledge...	• To understanding
• From data systems that collect individual customer transactions and behavioral traits...	• To representatives who respond to the whole person through careful listening, empathic understanding and a grounded appreciation of people and their lives
From a focus on building loyal relationships with highest-value customers...	**To the comprehensive management of relationships across the entire spectrum**
• From segmenting based on purchase patterns...	• To segmenting based on relationship benefits, contracts and rules
• From executing brand loyalty programs...	• To engaging a full range of relationship programs dedicated to different relationship goals
• From a single-minded focus on reducing costs to serve and enhancing revenues from individual customers...	• To variable strategies that focus on different rules to create profitable engagements
• From allocating resources to the most profitable customers and away from all others...	• To allocating resources against relationship types providing strategic value
From a one-sided, opportunistic relationship philosophy...	**To a perspective that recognizes the contributing roles companies and customers play**
• From taking the credit for relationship successes...	• To accepting blame for relationship failures
• From a focus on customers' actions when diagnosing the causes of unprofitable relationships...	• To decoding the company,s behavioral signals and the roles these actions play
• From narrow specification of the company's formal CRM outreach activities as relationship signals...	• To an appreciation that with every company interaction, relationship equity is created or destroyed
• From viewing customers as good versus bad investments...	• To a more nuanced view of relationships as optimized/under-delivered, healthy/stress laden or positive/negative in tone
• From alienating or firing bad customers....	• To renegotiating and repairing bad relationships to increase their value

Adapted from Susan Fournier and Jill Avery (2011), "Putting the "Relationship" Back Into CRM, *MIT Sloan Management Review*, spring, pp. 63–72.

Companies can employ ethnographic studies and in-depth interviews that can uncover the rules of engagement to decode how the brand fits in with customer's life.

Second, Fournier and Avery (2011) point out that current CRM strategies are relationship outcome-focused based on costs and lifetime values. Instead, marketers should also focus on inputs that create customer value by carefully examining the portfolio of brand relationships among customers on the basis of emotional versus utilitarian needs and strong and deep versus weak and superficial ties. They identified 18 different types of brand relationships that offer profit potential although most companies focus on loyal "brand marriages." The key is to understand norms governing each relationship contract for each segment and cost/benefit calculus in pursuing them. For instance, although "best friendships" and "marriages" occupy similar emotional space, they follow different rules of engagement. Marriages are built on commitment, love, and fidelity whereas best friendships are built on intimacy and reciprocity. Companies can create an inventory of relationships by using perceptual mapping to plot prominent brand relationship types within brands and categories. The goal is to identify relationship patterns across consumers to segment them on relationship types.

Third, Fournier and Avery (2011) emphasize companies take responsibilities that are two-way rather than one-sided. Instead of taking credit for relationship successes, companies should accept blame for relationship failures. Instead of focusing on customer's actions when diagnosing unprofitable relationships, companies should decode their behavioral signals and the roles they play in customers engaging in opportunistic behaviors. For instance, Best Buy found that its policies encouraged bad customer behavior; customers returning products only to buy the same items at lower used-product prices. Instead of putting the blame on customers, Best Buy revamped its sales promotion strategies that were fixated on deals and revised return policies to make it harder for people to game the system. Interestingly, the authors found that companies that crack down on these troublesome customers are the very customers the company worked so hard to get through its CRM programs, a phenomenon called the "best customer trap." These customers are created when companies reward good customers with discounts and special treatment and permit them to break rules; over time when expectations increase, they are often more costly to serve. Here, companies must codify, by relationship types, which rules are fixed and which ones may be nice to have but are less consequential to the relationship. To assess relationship health and performance, companies need to monthly or annually track studies on relationship motives, benefits, and rules of engagement.

KEY TAKEAWAYS

- Firms derive value from customers defined as the economic value of the customer relationship to the firm expressed on the basis of contribution margin or net profit.

- Traditional CRM models include the recency, frequency, and monetary (RFM) approach, share of wallet (SOW) approach, and past customer value (PCV) approach. While useful, these employ backward-looking metrics and do not link the value of a customer to future lifetime profitability.

- Contemporary CRM models use customer lifetime value (CLV) approach at the aggregate and individual levels. At the aggregate level, CLV can be measured for all customers, also termed customer equity; for all customers within a segment; for all customers calculated as sum of return on acquisition, return on retention, and return on add-on selling. At the individual level, CLV is computed as the sum of cumulated cash flows over the entire lifetime, discounted using the weighted cost of capital.

- CLV models are now highly complex using specialized estimation methods such as independent versus simultaneous estimation, brand switching models using Markov switching probabilities, Monte Carlo simulation algorithm, customer migration model, deterministic model, probabilistic model, and structural model.

- Customer referral value (CRV) is a metric that captures the monetary value of a customer associated with the future profits given by each refereed prospect, discounted to the present value. Referral programs offer incentives including free service, free products, credit, points, vouchers, gifts, discount, or cash.

- Customers acquired through incentivized referral program are more valuable to the firm (e.g., contribution margin, loyalty, and CLV) than those acquired through traditional methods.

- Referral seeding strategies using hubs (high degree centrality) are effective for initial marketing message; fringes (low-degree centrality) are given low-degree seeding; bridges (people with unique connections) are given high-betweenness seeding strategy.

- Firms save on acquisition cost and discounted value of customers of referrals who would not have joined otherwise, except for referrals. Firms save on acquisition cost of customers only who would have joined the firm anyways, regardless of referral.

- High CLV customers are not necessarily high CRV customers also. Thus, firms should work on marketing campaigns to build CRV for customers with High CLV/Low CRV (Affluents). Firms should work on increasing perceived product value to customers with High CRV/Low CLV

(Advocates). High CLV/High CRV represent the "best customers" (Champions). The real challenge is for firms to target Low CLV/Low CRV customers (Misers).

- Marketing-induced customers add short-term value but WOM-induced customers add twice as much long-term value in customer acquisition strategies. Tracking loyal customers' purchase data with shifts in attitudinal data over time is critical to developing retention strategies. Retention strategy can be employed by nurturing cross-buying as these customers extend the duration of their relationship with the firm and increase their purchase frequency. However, cross-buying does not always result in higher customer profitability.

- Firms need to understand customer churn behavior, its causes and outcomes, and how it can be predicted in advance. Even with churn, some customers might be worth bringing back. Not all customers are worthy of win back. Firms should focus on second customer lifetime value (SCLV).

- While CLV is useful to evaluate the future profitability of a customer, it does not provide information on the overall profit potential of the customer. Thus, CLV should be used with customer's size of unused wallet (SUW), defined as the incremental profit potential of a customer. Several specific strategies based on segments arising out of CLV and SUW combinations can be developed. For instance, customers with High CLV/High SUW represents high net worth individuals and thus firms should use defending/augmenting strategy. However, customers with Low CLV/Low SUW are bad customers for firms and subject to being fired based on past and future value.

- Firms should develop an integrated customer valuation strategy that links CLV, CRV, CIV, CKV, and SUW with traditional metrics for each individual customer, customer segment, and entire market.

- Customer equity represents the total lifetime values of all customers of the firm and can be used as a method of firm valuation especially in the long-term.

- CRM strategies, while effective, also have limitations. Customers are people with deep relational needs and firms need to decode to find how the brand fits in the person's life. Relational norms peculiar to each specific type of relationship needs to be identified and profiled. Firms should also view this relationship as two-sided and take responsibility for relationship failure or bad customer behavior.

EXERCISES

Questions

1. Explain conceptually the following traditional CRM metrics and their computational methodology: (a) recency-frequency-monetary (RFM); (b) share of wallet (SOW) approach; and (c) past customer value (PCV).

2. Explain conceptually the following contemporary CRM metrics and their computational methodology: (a) aggregate approach (using CLV and customer equity methods) and (b) individual approach (using CLV method). Discuss how the average CLV approach at the aggregate level can be used as a surrogate measure of a firm's market value.

3. What are the strengths and limitations of using CLV models with (a) independent estimation and (b) simultaneous estimation? Explain how the simultaneous estimation model (Venkatesan *et al.*, 2007) is used to win back lost customers.

4. Explain conceptually the following CLV-based models and their computational methodology: (a) Monte Carlo simulation algorithm; (b) customer migration model; (c) deterministic model; (d) probabilistic model; and (e) structural model.

5. Explain the following concepts: (a) customer referral value (CRV); (b) customer influence value (CIV); and (c) customer knowledge value (CKV).

6. Comment on the following statement: "Customers acquired through incentivized referral programs are more valuable to the company than customers acquired through traditional methods."

7. Research shows that high CRV customers are not necessarily high CLV customers. What can companies do to convert them into high CLV customers?

8. Explain how marketers compute customer influence effect (CIE) and customer influence value (CIV).

9. Explain customer selection models used to identify customers for their collaborative potential with companies through idea generation, feedback, knowledge development, and co-creation value.

10. Discuss some marketing strategies that companies can use to (a) maximize customer acquisition; (b) maximize customer retention; (c) minimize customer churn; and (d) maximize customer win back. How can customer churn be predicted? Are all customers worthy of win-back strategy (and why)?

11. Comment on the following statement: "Customers respond to marketing activities through their attitudinal metrics (satisfaction, loyalty), behavioral metrics (choice, loyalty, CLV), and engagement metrics (CRV, CIV, and CKV), which in turn, leads to customer equity and shareholder value."

12. While CRM-based models are highly useful, there is also a place for qualitative research (e.g., ethnographic studies, in-depth interviews). Make a strong case for qualitative research in understanding customer–brand relationships. Should (and how can) companies foster different types and levels of customer–brand relationships instead of just focusing on loyal brand relationships?

Group Discussion

1. Joanne is a typical customer of a telecommunications company. The monthly subscription or the base gross contribution margin is $40. At the end of September, the company wants to know the value Joanne is likely to provide to the company in the next three months (October, November, and December). Her transaction details are as follows: monthly purchase amount for the three months (October to December) are $20, $10, and $10, respectively; profit margin are 20%, 20%, and 20%, respectively; marketing cost are $5, $7, and $7, respectively. Further, Joanne's probability of buying additional services (e.g., text messaging, upgraded data plan, etc.) is 0.55, 0.50, and 0.40, respectively.

   As a small group, discuss the steps involved in the calculation of CLV and compute the CLV of Joanne at the end of each subsequent month. Assume an annual discount rate of 12% or 1% monthly.

2. John is a typical customer of a telecommunications company. His semi-annual data related to referral behavior are as follows: total number of referrals per period (n_2) is 4; marketing cost per period (M_{ty}) is $18; average gross margin (A_{ty}) is $98; cost of referral ($a_{ty}$) is $40; acquisition cost savings ($ACQ1_{ty}$ and $ACQ2_{ty}$) is $5; number of customers who joined because of the referral (n_1) is 2; number of customers who would have joined anyway (n_2-n_1) is 2; and yearly discount rate (r) is 15%.

   As a small group, discuss the steps involved in the calculation of CRV and compute the CRV of John for one year?

HBS and Ivey Cases

- AnswerDash (9-516-106)
- Reinventing Best Buy (9-716-455)

- Chase Sapphire (9-518-024)
- Laurs & Bridz (9B18A004)

CASE QUESTIONS

AnswerDash

1. How can AnswerDash make use of the following traditional CRM metrics: (a) recency-frequency-monetary (RFM); (b) share of wallet (SOW); and (c) past customer value (PCV)?

2. How can AnswerDash make use of the following contemporary CRM metrics and their computational methodology: (a) aggregate approach (using CLV and customer equity methods) and (b) individual approach (using CLV method)?

3. Should AnswerDash use the following CLV-based models and their computational methodology: (a) Monte Carlo simulation algorithm; (b) customer migration model; (c) deterministic model; (d) probabilistic model; and (e) structural model? Defend your reasoning.

4. How can AnswerDash make use of the following concepts: (a) customer referral value (CRV); (b) customer influence value (CIV); and (c) customer knowledge value (CKV)?

5. Explain how AnswerDash can make use of customer selection models to identify customers for their collaborative potential through idea generation, feedback, knowledge development, and co-creation value.

6. Discuss some marketing strategies that AnswerDash can use to (a) maximize customer acquisition; (b) maximize customer retention; (c) minimize customer churn; and (d) maximize customer win back. How can it predict customer churn? Are all customers worthy of win-back strategy (and why)?

Reinventing Best Buy

1. Explain how Best Buy can make use of the simultaneous estimation model (Venkatesan *et al.*, 2007) to win back lost customers. How can Best Buy maximize the second customer lifetime value (SCLV) of its win-back customers?

2. Research shows that high CRV customers are not necessarily high CLV customers. What can Best Buy do to convert them into high CLV customers?

3. Draw the following graphical model for Best Buy. "Customers respond to marketing activities through their attitudinal metrics (satisfaction, loyalty), behavioral metrics (choice, loyalty, CLV), and engagement metrics (CRV, CIV, and CKV), which in turn leads to customer equity and shareholder value."

4. How can Best Buy make use of qualitative research in understanding customer–brand relationships? Should (and how can) it foster different types and levels of customer–brand relationships instead of just focusing on loyal brand relationships?

5. Explain how Best Buy can make use of customer selection models to identify customers for their collaborative potential through idea generation, feedback, knowledge development, and co-creation value.

6. Discuss some marketing strategies that Best Buy can use to (a) maximize customer acquisition; (b) maximize customer retention; (c) minimize customer churn; and (d) maximize customer win back. How can it predict customer churn? Are all customers worthy of win-back strategy (and why)?

Chase Sapphire

1. How can JPMorgan make use of the following traditional CRM metrics: (a) recency-frequency-monetary (RFM); (b) share of wallet (SOW); and (c) past customer value (PCV)?

2. How can JPMorgan make use of the following contemporary CRM metrics and their computational methodology: (a) aggregate approach (using CLV and customer equity methods) and (b) individual approach (using CLV method)?

3. Explain how JPMorgan can make use of the simultaneous estimation model (Venkatesan *et al.*, 2007) to win back lost customers. How can JPMorgan maximize the second customer lifetime value (SCLV) of its win-back customers?

4. Should JPMorgan acquire customers through incentivized referral programs or through traditional methods? Why?

5. Explain how JPMorgan can make use of customer selection models to identify customers for their collaborative potential through idea generation, feedback, knowledge development, and co-creation value.

6. Discuss some marketing strategies that JPMorgan can use to (a) maximize customer acquisition; (b) maximize customer retention; (c) minimize customer churn; and (d) maximize customer win back. How can it predict customer churn? Are all customers worthy of win-back strategy (and why)?

7. Discuss some marketing strategies that JPMorgan can use toward its customers who are (a) high on customer lifetime value (CLV) and high on size of unused wallet (SUW); and (b) low on customer lifetime value (CLV) and low on size of unused wallet (SUW).

Laurs & Bridz

1. Explain how Laurs & Bridz can make use of the simultaneous estimation model (Venkatesan *et al.*, 2007) to win back lost customers. How can Laurs & Bridz maximize the second customer lifetime value (SCLV) of its win-back customers?

2. Should Laurs & Bridz use the following CLV-based models and their computational methodology: (a) Monte Carlo simulation algorithm; (b) customer

migration model; (c) deterministic model; (d) probabilistic model; and (e) structural model? Defend your reasoning.

3. How can Laurs & Bridz make use of the following concepts: (a) customer referral value (CRV); (b) customer influence value (CIV); and (c) customer knowledge value (CKV)?

4. Should Laurs & Bridz acquire customers through incentivized referral programs or through traditional methods? Why?

5. Explain how Laurs & Bridz can make use of customer selection models to identify customers for their collaborative potential through idea generation, feedback, knowledge development, and co-creation value.

6. Discuss some marketing strategies that Laurs & Bridz can use to (a) maximize customer acquisition; (b) maximize customer retention; (c) minimize customer churn; and (d) maximize customer win back. How can it predict customer churn? Are all customers worthy of win-back strategy (and why)?

7. Draw the following graphical model for Laurs & Bridz. "Customers respond to marketing activities through their attitudinal metrics (satisfaction, loyalty), behavioral metrics (choice, loyalty, CLV), and engagement metrics (CRV, CIV, and CKV), which in turn leads to customer equity and shareholder value."

REFERENCES

Berger, P.D. and N.I. Nasr (1998), Customer Lifetime Value: Marketing Models and Applications, *Journal of Interactive Marketing* 12(1): 17–30.

Blattberg, R.C., G. Getz, and J.S. Thomas (2001), *Customer Equity: Building and Managing Relationships as Valuable Assets*. Boston, MA: Harvard Business Publishing.

Boatwright, P., S. Borle, and J. Kadane (2003), A Model of the Joint Distribution of Purchase Quantity and Timing, *Journal of the American Statistical Association* 98(463): 564–572.

Braun, M. and D.A. Schweidel (2011), Modeling Customer Lifetimes with Multiple Causes of Churn, *Marketing Science* 30(5): 881–902.

Danaher, P.J. (2002), Optimal Pricing of New Subscription Services: Analysis of a Market Experiment, *Marketing Science* 21(2): 119–138.

Dreze, X. and A. Bonfrer (2009), Moving from Customer Lifetime Value to Customer Equity, *Quantitative Marketing and Economics* 7(3): 289–320.

Dwyer, R.F. (1997), Customer Lifetime Valuation to Support Marketing Decision Making, *Journal of Interactive Marketing* 11(4): 6–13.

Fader, P.S. and B. GS Hardie (2010), Customer-Base Valuation in a Contractual Setting: The Perils of Ignoring Heterogeneity, *Marketing Science* 29(1): 85–93.

Fader, P.S., B.G.S. Hardie, and K.L. Lee (2005), 'Counting Your Customers' the Easy Way: An Alternative to the Pareto/NBD Model, *Marketing Science* 24(2): 275–284.

Fournier, S. and J. Avery (2011), Putting the 'Relationship' Back Into CRM, *MIT Sloan Management Review* (spring): 63–72.

Gupta, S. and D.R. Lehmann (2003), Customers as Assets, *Journal of Interactive Marketing* 17(1): 9–24.

Gupta, S., D. Hanssens, and J. A. Stuart (2004), Valuing Customers, *Journal of Marketing Research* 41: 7–18.

Gupta, S., D. Hanssens, B. Hardie, W. Kahn, V. Kumar, N. Lin, et al. (2006), Modeling Customer Lifetime Value, *Journal of Service Research* 9(2): 139–155.

Gupta, S. and D.R. Lehmann (2005), *Managing Customers as Investments: The Strategic Value of Customers in the Long-Run.* Upper Saddle River, NJ: Wharton School Publishing.

Gupta, S. and D.R. Lehmann (2008), Models of Customer Value, in *Handbook of Marketing Decision Models* (pp. 255–290). New York, NY: Springer Science + Business Media.

Hinz, O., B. Skiera, C. Barrot, and J.U. Becker (2011), Seeding Strategies for Viral Marketing: An Empirical Comparison, *Journal of Marketing* 75(6): 55–71.

Hoyer, W.D., R. Chandy, M. Dorotic, M. Krafft, and S.S. Singh (2010), Consumer Co-Creation in New Product Development, *Journal of Service Research* 13(3): 283–296.

Jain, D. and S. S. Singh (2002), Customer Lifetime Value Research in Marketing: A Review and Future Directions, *Journal of Interactive Marketing* 16(2): 34–46.

Kumar, V. (2007), Customer Lifetime Value — The Path to Profitability, *Foundations and Trends in Marketing* 2(1): 1–96.

Kumar, V. (2013), *Profitable Customer Engagement: Concepts, Metrics, and Strategies.* New Delhi: Sage Publications.

Kumar, V. and D. Shah (2009), Expanding the Role of Marketing: From Customer Equity to Market Capitalization, *Journal of Marketing* 73: 119–136.

Kumar, V. and R. Mirchandani (2013), Increasing the ROI of Social Media Marketing, *MIT Sloan Management Review* 54(1): 55–61.

Kumar, V. and W. Reinartz (2012), *Customer Relationship Management: Concept, Strategy, and Tools.* Heidelberg, Germany: Springer.

Kumar, V. and W. Reinartz (2016), Creating Enduring Customer Value, *Journal of Marketing* 80: 36–68.

Kumar, V., M. George, and J. Pancras (2008), Cross-Buying in Retailing: Drivers and Consequences, *Journal of Retailing* 84(1): 15–27.

Kumar, V., M. George, and R.P. Leone (2007), How Valuable is Word-of-Mouth? *Harvard Business Review* 85(10): 139–146.

Kumar, V., I.D. Pozza, J.A. Petersen, and D. Shah (2009), Reversing the Logic: The Path to Profitability through Relationship Marketing, *Journal of Interactive Marketing* 2: 147–156.

Kumar, V., J.A. Petersen, and R.P. Leone (2007), How Valuable is Word of Mouth? *Harvard Business Review* 85(10): 139–146.

Kumar, V., Lerzan Aksoy, Bas Donkers, Rajkumar Venkatesan, Thorsten Wiesel, and Sebastian Tillmanns (2010), Undervalued or Overvalued Customers: Capturing Total Customer Engagement Value, *Journal of Service Research* 13(3): 297–310.

Kumar, V., V. Bhaskaran, R. Mirchandani, and M. Shah (2013), Creating a Measurable Social Media Marketing Strategy: Increasing the Value and ROI of Intangibles and Tangibles for Hokey Pokey, *Marketing Science* 32(2): 194–212.

Kumar, V., Y. Bhagwat, and X. Zhang (2015), Regaining 'Lost' Customers: The Predictive Power of First-Lifetime Behavior, the Reason for Defection, and the Nature of the win-Back Offer, *Journal of Marketing* 79: 34–55.

Ramaswami, S.N., R.K. Srivastava, and M. Bhargava (2009), Market-based Capabilities and Financial Performance of Firms: Insights into Marketing's Contribution to Firm Value, *Journal of the Academy of Marketing Science* 37: 97–116.

Reinartz, W. and V. Kumar (2000), On the Profitability of Long-Life Customers in a Non-Contractual Setting: An Empirical Investigation and Implications for Marketing, *Journal of Marketing* 64: 17–35.

Reinartz, W. and V. Kumar (2002), The Mismanagement of Customer Loyalty, *Harvard Business Review* 80(7): 86–94.

Reinartz, W. and V. Kumar (2003), The Impact of Customer Relationship Characteristics on Profitable Lifetime Duration, *Journal of Marketing* 67: 77–99.

Reinartz, W., S. Thomas, and G. Bascoul (2008), Investigating Cross-Buying and Customer Loyalty, *Journal of Interactive Marketing* 22(1): 5–20.

Rust, R.T., K.N. Lemon, and V.A. Zeithaml (2004), Return on Marketing: Using Customer Equity to Focus Marketing Strategy, *Journal of Marketing* 68: 109–127.

Rust, R.T., V. Kumar, and R. Venkatesan (2011), Will the Frog Change into a Prince? Predicting Future Customer Profitability, *International Journal of Research in Marketing* 28(4): 281–294.

Ryu, G. and L. Feick (2007), A Penny for Your Thoughts: Referral Reward Programs and Referral Likelihood, *Journal of Marketing* 71(1): 84–94.

Schmitt, P., B. Skiera, and C. Van den Bulte (2011), Referral Programs and Customer Value, *Journal of Marketing* 75(1): 46–59.

Shah, D., V. Kumar, Y. Qu, and S. Chen (2012), Unprofitable Cross-Buying: Evidence from Consumer and Business Markets, *Journal of Marketing* 76: 78–95.

Stauss, B. and C. Friege (1999), Regaining Service Customers: Costs and Benefits of Regain Management, *Journal of Service Research* 1(4): 347–361.

Sunder, S., V. Kumar, and Y. Zhao (2016), Measuring the Lifetime Value of a Customer in the Consumer Packaged goods (CPG) Industry, *Journal of Marketing Research* 53: 901–921.

Uslay, C., A. Altintig, and R.D. Winsor (2010), An Empirical Examination of the 'Rule of Three': Strategy Implications for Top Management, Marketers, and Investors, *Journal of Marketing* 74: 20–39.

Venkatesan, R. and V. Kumar (2004), A Customer Lifetime Value Framework for Customer Selection and Resource Allocation Strategy, *Journal of Marketing* 68: 106–125.

Venkatesan, R., V. Kumar, and T. Bohling (2007), Optimal Customer Relationship Management using Bayesian Decision Theory: An Application for Customer Selection, *Journal of Marketing Research* 44: 579–594.

Villanueva, J., S. Yoo, and D.M. Hanssens (2008), The Impact of Marketing-Induced versus Word-of-Mouth Customer Acquisition on Customer Equity Growth, *Journal of Marketing Research* 45: 48–59.

Von Wangenheim, F. and T. Bayon (2007), The Chain from Customer Satisfaction vis Word-of-Mouth Referrals to New Customer Acquisition, *Journal of the Academy of Marketing Science* 35(2): 233–249.

Young M.L. and M. Stepanek (2003), Trends: Loyalty Programs, *CIO Insights*, December 1.

07

Building B2C Relationships: Brand Equity and Customer– Brand Relationship

OVERVIEW

In Chapter 7, first we discuss brand equity from the firm's perspective followed by customer-based brand equity (CBBE) — its definition and dimensions, namely brand awareness, brand association, perceived quality, and brand loyalty. Subsequently, we present the integrative brand equity model and examine brand equity creation from the relationship marketing perspective. Four factors are examined: (1) customer-based brand equity (CBBE) factors, (2) market signaling factors, (3) brand identity factors, and (4) consumer–brand relationship factors. At the end of the chapter, we provide key takeaways and conclude with discussion questions and HBS and Ivey cases. But first, to give a flavor of customer relationship marketing (CRM) and brand equity, we provide some real-life vignettes.

OPENING VIGNETTES

Vignette 1: In the early years of Apple, its brand had high internal brand strength characterized by employees' brand commitment and brand citizenship behavior, reflecting an organizational culture of creativity and innovation. However, at the time its attitudes and behaviors of highly brand-committed employees were not reflected on the external market, partly because of Microsoft's dominance, thus impacting Apple's present and future brand equity development at that time. This situation of high internal brand strength and low external brand strength often represents the starting point for companies creating brand equity. Lots have happened since then. In 2018, Apple had the highest brand equity of $182.8 billion (Forbes, 2018) as a result of balancing internal and external brand strength (see Figure 7.1).

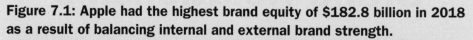

Figure 7.1: Apple had the highest brand equity of $182.8 billion in 2018 as a result of balancing internal and external brand strength.

Vignette 2: According to J.D. Power's Initial Quality Study, Hyundai was the fastest growing car maker in the US between 2000 and 2005 and was ahead of Toyota, lagging behind only Lexus and Porsche. Hyundai's new crossover SUV, Veracruz, was an attractive product and claimed to be better than Lexus although was priced $10K cheaper. However, between 2005 and 2007, Hyundai's sales growth flattened while the sales of Toyota soared in the same period. What happened? A market research experimental study showed that branding played a key role in consumer perception and decision-making process. For instance, a car model with Toyota logo had a commanding 92% "intent to purchase"; however, the same product with Hyundai logo dropped to 52% and without the Hyundai logo (i.e., no logo at all) rose to 71%. Subsequently, Hyundai renewed their ad and spent around $400 million on new branding initiatives. Hyundai successfully targeted its loyal segment pursuing them with customer-centric value-based proposition as they moved up the value chain including luxury segment. Typically, Hyundai loyal and value-based customers upgraded and bought Hyundai Genesis at the luxury market rather than Mercedes Benz E-Class (Kumar, 2013). Hyundai built its brand equity over time by developing long-term customer–brand relationship.

INTRODUCTION: DEFINITION AND DIMENSIONS OF BRAND EQUITY

Brand equity is such a complex concept that its conceptualizations in the literature are diverse, fragmented, and inconclusive (Christodoulides and de Chernatony, 2010) (see Figure 7.2). Winters (1991) notes that one will get various answers to what brand equity means and a similar statement comes from Berthon *et al.* (2001) suggesting that brand equity is a difficult concept to grasp in part due to its definitional problems. Despite the fact that there is no single definition for brand equity, there is an agreement among scholars that brand equity represents the added value endowed by the brand to the product (Farquhar, 1989).

However, Berthon *et al.* (2001) questioned the usefulness and validity of this definition, because it confuses who the beneficiaries of brand equity are. A review of the brand equity literature reveals that there are two main perspectives of brand equity. Some researchers define brand equity considering the financial perspective, which is more useful in financial accounting (e.g., Simon and Sullivan, 1993). Other definitions consider consumer perspective and call it consumer-based brand equity

(CBBE) (e.g., Aaker, 1991; Erdem and Swait, 1998; Keller, 1993). Consequently, Berthon *et al.* (2001) suggested that brand equity should be bifurcated into organizational brand equity and customer-brand equity, depending on the focal beneficiary in the discussion. In a recent literature review by Christodoulides and de Chernatony (2010), firm-based brand equity (FBBE) and consumer-based brand equity (CBBE) were distinguished, wherein the former is about the financial value added to the business by brand equity and the latter focuses on the market share and profitability of the brand. Some scholars have attempted to integrate the two facets of brand equity, providing a holistic view of the brand equity concept (e.g., Burmann *et al.*, 2009; Wang *et al.*, 2008). However, CBBE has received more popularity as it is the driving force behind firm performance, which is reflected by FBBE. In this respect, one of the most used definitions of CBBE is "the differential effect of brand knowledge on consumer response to the marketing of the brand" (Keller, 1993). In this chapter, we will focus primarily on CBBE. However, we first provide a brief discussion on FBBE and then start our discussion on CBBE.

Figure 7.2: Brand equity is a complex concept and its conceptualizations in the literature are diverse, fragmented, and inconclusive.

Firm-Based Brand Equity

Studies on FBBE measure the added value of the brand due to its significant impact of firms' market performance. This stream of studies also examines the antecedents and consequences of brand equity at the aggregated level. The first attempt in this research stream focused on objective indicators that are easily accessible to firms such as cash flows, revenues, and market shares. For example, Simon and Sullivan (1993) analyzed brand equity from the company's performance in the financial market. Specifically, they derived the value of brand equity by subtracting the value of tangible assets from the total value of the company and observing the changes caused by brand equity antecedents such as current and past advertising, age of the brand, order of entry, and current and past advertising share. Similar ideas were implemented in the study by Ailawadi *et al.* (2003), where brand equity was reflected by a brand's direct impact on sales and its moderating impact on price–sales relationship. In other words, Ailawadi *et al.* (2003) measured the positive influence on the revenue of a branded product. Another alternative was proposed by Srinivasan *et al.* (2005), where brand equity was assessed by the incremental probability to choose the branded product compared to a base product. Similar to Srinivasan *et al.* (2005), Sriram *et al.* (2007) used the incremental utility to purchase the branded product as the proxy for brand equity, controlling for a bunch of market, and marketing-mix variances.

From above discussion, it is not hard to see that brand equity is not a concept that can be measured directly with a simple survey (despite Park and Srinivasan (1994) who provided a potential survey to use). An indirect approach to measure brand equity requires scholars to identify the antecedents and consequences of brand equity. The consequences of brand equity are agreed upon by most scholars, as the definition is built upon its consequences, i.e., differentiated effect caused by the brand. However, the literature seems to remain diverse and fragmented about the sources of brand equity. For example, Mahajan *et al.* (1994) proposed three sources of brand equity: (1) enhanced performance and/or marketing efficiency associated with the brand, (2) longevity of the brand due to its loyal consumer base and distribution relationships, and (3) carryover potential to other brands and markets of the acquiring firm. Besides these attribute-based and non-attribute-based sources, Srinivasan *et al.* (2005) proposed to include brand awareness because their focus was at the individual customer level. Stepping further, Raggio and Leone (2006) borrowed from CBBE and considered brand knowledge and brand image as the sources of brand equity.

Some scholars consider marketing efforts and other firm-controllable factors as the origins of brand equity. Yoo *et al.* (2000) provided one of the early influential work from this viewpoint. In the study, they examined the impact of marketing efforts on different dimensions of brand equity and showed the positive impact of price, store image, distribution intensity, advertising expenses, and the frequency of sales promotion on three CBBE dimensions (i.e., perceived quality, brand loyalty, brand association/brand awareness). Specifically, they revealed that price, store image, distribution intensity, and advertising expenses improve perceived quality of the branded product, while sales promotions reduced it; that the distribution intensity and advertising expense result in brand loyalty; and that store image and advertising enhance brand awareness and brand association, while sales promotion lessens it. Buil *et al.* (2013) further examined the impact of advertising and promotions on brand equity. Different from Yoo *et al.* (2000), they believed CBBE dimensions are not in parallel but in a hierarchical model, where attitudes and norms influence intentions and intentions in turn affect behavior. As a result, their model considers positive influence of brand awareness on brand association and perceived quality and positive influence of brand association and perceived quality on brand loyalty. Consistent with Yoo *et al.* (2000), their empirical results showed positive impact of advertising expenses on perceived quality, brand awareness, and brand association, and negative impact of sales promotions. In addition, their result revealed that individuals' attitudes toward the advertisement also have positive impacts as advertising does and that non-monetary promotions have positive impact on brand association and perceived quality, opposite to monetary promotions. From the preceding review, it can be observed that CBBE has become an essential part of brand equity. Thus, the following section will elaborate on CBBE.

Customer-Based Brand Equity

Customer-based brand equity (CBBE) is widely accepted as the added value endowed by the brand to the product, and it is not difficult to look at the effect from the consumer's perspective. Several definitions of CBBE have been propounded by scholars. One of the first definitions of brand equity was proposed by Farquhar (1989) who defined it as "the added value with which a given brand endows a product." Many researchers have defined brand equity similar to Farquhar's (1989) definition (Aaker, 1991; Keller, 1993; Pappu *et al.*, 2005; Yoo and Donthu, 2001). For instance, Aaker (1991) defines brand equity as "a set of assets and liabilities linked to a brand, its name and symbol that add to or subtract from the value provided by a product or service to a firm and/or that firm's customers." Keller (1993) defined CBBE as "the differential effect of brand knowledge on consumer response to the marketing of the brand" (p. 2), where he emphasizes the core role of brand knowledge as a brand node in memory to which a variety of associations are linked. Specifically, he decomposes brand knowledge into brand awareness and brand image based on the associative network memory

model: brand awareness relates to the strength of the brand node in memory and reflects consumers' ability to identify the brand under different conditions, and brand image describes the perception about the brand as reflected by the brand association held in memory. In other words, brand knowledge denotes consumers' recognition and perception of the brand.

Similar ideas were adapted by Leonard (2000) in his discussion of service brand equity, where brand awareness and brand image represent customers' recognition and perception of the brand correspondingly. His service brand equity model, against the common inclination to associate branding with goods, suggests that branding is associated with the company in the service context, and thus brand meaning, primarily coming from the experience with the company, has a disproportionately large impact on brand equity than brand awareness, which largely originates from controlled communications of the company, because customers' experiences are the total product of the service company.

Different from Keller (1993) analyzing the cognitive processing of a brand name, Aaker (1996, 2009) conceptualized brand equity from its values brought to the company and its consumers and proposed four dimensions for brand equity: (1) brand awareness, (2) brand association, (3) perceived quality, and (4) brand loyalty. These dimensions could be approximately considered as specific facets of brand awareness and brand association in Keller's (1993) model. Specifically, name awareness is a specific facet of brand awareness, while brand loyalty, perceived quality, and other brand associations are three facets of brand association.

These two theories became the building blocks of brand equity for subsequent researchers. Using Aaker's (1991) and Keller's (1993) conceptualization, Cobb-Walgren *et al.* (1995) were among the early pioneers to measure CBBE. They modeled (1) *brand awareness*, (2) *brand association*, (3) *perceived quality*, and (4) *brand loyalty* as the four dimensions of brand equity. In later empirical studies (e.g., Pappu *et al.*, 2005), these four dimensions were validated as the four main constructs for brand equity.[1] We discuss these four dimensions of brand equity next.

1. **Brand Awareness**: Keller (1993) defined brand awareness as made up of brand recognition and brand recall and believed brand awareness influences customers' decision-making through learning advantages, consideration advantages, and choice advantages. Based on Keller (1993), brand recognition is "the consumer's ability to discriminate the brand as having been seen or heard previously," whereas, brand recall is "the consumer's ability to retrieve the brand when given the product category, the needs fulfilled by the category, or some other types of probe as a cue." Aaker (1996) classified brand awareness into four levels: (1) mere recognition, (2) recall, (3) top-of-mind, and (4) brand dominance. Further, brand awareness may have two main aspects: (1) depth and (2) breadth. While the former is the ease with which consumers recall or recognize a brand, the latter comes from the scope of the circumstances that the brand hits consumer's mind (Hoeffler and Keller, 2002).

2. **Brand Association**: Brand association is defined as "the meaning of the brand for the consumers" consisting of three components: (1) attributes, (2) benefits, and (3) attitudes (Keller, 1993). Associations consist of all thoughts, feelings, perceptions, images, experiences, beliefs, and attitudes toward a brand. Brand associations can induce pleasant feelings and attitudes in consumers' minds. In particular, brand experience is defined as "subjective, internal consumer responses (sensations, feelings, and cognitions) and behavioral responses evoked by brand-related stimuli that are part of a brand's design and identity, packaging, communications, and environments" (Brakus *et al.*, 2009, p. 53). Customers tend to form certain brand perceptions when they experience a brand in terms of various brand stimuli like name, logos, color, packaging, and advertisements. Brand experience does not presume a motivational state nor constitutes an evaluative state and thus varies from other motivational and emotional constructs like brand involvement and attachment (Zaichkowsky, 1985, Park *et al.*, 2010). It is also distinct from attitudinal concepts such as brand evaluation (Fishbein and Ajzen, 1975). It primarily comprises four facets where the *affective facet* captures emotions; *intellectual facet* corresponds to brand's capability to stimulate thinking, both analytical and imaginative thinking; *sensory facet* relates to esthetic and sensory qualities that appeal to the senses; and *behavioral facet* corresponds to actions and bodily experiences with a brand (Zarantonello and Schmitt, 2010; Nysveen *et al.*, 2013).

3. **Perceived Quality**: Zeithaml (1988) defined perceived quality as "the consumer's judgment about a product's overall excellence or superiority." It is not the same as actual quality and is an overall valuation that looks like the consumer's attitude toward the product (Zeithaml, 1988). Perceived quality helps improve the brand's capacity to charge a premium price or extend itself through differentiating it from the competitors. Rindova *et al.* (2005) refer to "perceived quality" as a dimension of technical efficacy — a judgment of the quality of the firm's output. Similar to Rindova *et al.* (2005), we conceptualize perceived quality in a much broader framework. Using the

---

1 Notably, some studies (e.g., Yoo and Donthu 2001) reported that brand awareness and brand association could be hardly distinguished, and thus they suggested a three-dimension scale.

Love and Kraatz's (2009) framework, technical efficacy characterizes a firm's ability to fulfill stakeholders' material needs and is coupled with consequences and tangible organizational outputs, e.g., producing superior products and services (for customers) or delivering superior financial results (for investors). While existing studies have emphasized "perceived quality" of products/services as a distinct dimension of firm reputation among customers, we propose that "product and service efficacy" is a broader concept that not only embodies perceived quality but also the sacrifice made in terms of money, time, and effort, that is perceived value (Cronin *et al.*, 2000). A firm that employs high-quality inputs and productive assets to turn out quality products/services will correspondingly charge premium price (Rindova *et al.*, 2005), and all these serve as resource signals of product and service efficacy. Further, the benefits of "product and service efficacy" reside not only in the functional and aesthetic domains but also in the relational benefits reaped during the exchange process. Indeed, in support of our contention, there is growing evidence that customers not only desire to maximize equity and valued benefits vis-à-vis product and service quality but also to engage in meaningful relationships with companies (Ahearne *et al.*, 2005; Bhattacharya and Sen, 2003).

4. ***Brand Loyalty:*** Aaker (1991) defined brand loyalty as "the attachment that a customer has to a brand." Some researchers have used the behavioral perspective for brand loyalty. For example, Oliver (1997, p. 392) defined brand loyalty as "a deeply held commitment to rebuy or repatronize a preferred product or service consistently in the future, despite situational influences and marketing efforts having potential to cause switching behavior." Pappu *et al.* (2005) and Yoo and Donthu (2001) considered the attitudinal approach and defined brand loyalty as "the tendency to be loyal to a

brand." Brand loyalty is just as complex as brand equity due to its diverse meanings and controversial definitions. For example, Fournier and Yao (1997) revealed the diverse nature of brand loyalty, despite it representing a powerful bond between the consumer and the brand. Specifically, they identified three types of loyalties for brands and used three metaphors, (1) marital commitment, (2) falling in love, and (3) adolescent best friendship, to describe these different loyalties. In his work, Aaker (1996, 2009) particularly emphasized brand loyalty as the core dimension of brand equity, because loyalty is tightly associated with the brand name and brings substantial revenues for the company and results in the differentiated effect of brand knowledge on consumers. From the definition of brand loyalty, i.e., biased attitudinal and behavioral preference toward a brand (Dick and Basu, 1994; Jacoby and Chestnut, 1978), it is not hard to see that brand loyalty and brand equity share a large overlap. In fact, brand loyalty was repeatedly validated to be the core dimension of brand equity (Pappu *et al.*, 2005; Yoo and Donthu, 2001).

Both Aaker's (1996, 2009) and Keller's (1993) work on brand equity focused on consumers' cognitive processes for brand equity, rooted deeply in cognitive psychology. An alternative approach is to consider the brand as a market signal in the market with imperfect and asymmetrical information (Erdem and Swait, 1998). Specifically, the content, clarity, and credibility of a brand are signals that increase perceived quality and reduce information costs and the risks perceived by consumers, and these effects are the differential effects of brand knowledge (in Keller's (1993) term) or the added values endowed by the brand (the consensus about brand equity) (see Figure 7.3). In this view, the emphasis of the brand is its credible information provided to consumers rather than the content or the clarity. Thus, brand trust, the confident expectations

Figure 7.3: Customer-based brand equity (CBBE) is the added value endowed by the brand to the product.

of the brand's reliability and intentions (Delgado-Ballester *et al.*, 2003), is a critical antecedent for brand equity (Delgado-Ballester and Munuera-Alemán, 2005). On the other hand, brand trust is a significant antecedent of relationship commitment (Hess and Story, 2005) as well as brand loyalty (Delgado-Ballester and Munuera-Aleman, 2001; Kim *et al.* 2008; Morgan and Hunt, 1994), serving as the cornerstone for the customer–brand relationship (Fournier, 1998). The customer–brand relationship depicts the connections and bonds between consumers and the brand, including relevant concepts such as brand attachment, brand passion, brand romance, brand relationship orientation, brand commitment, brand love, and so on (Fetscherin and Heinrich, 2015). Different from the discussion on brand equity, studies on consumer–brand relationship were limited to strong, positive relationships between consumers and the brand. For example, Fournier (1998) identified 15 types of consumer–brand relationships (see Table 7.1), and only two or three of them (i.e., committed partnerships, kinships, and dependencies) that would be considered brand equity has been established.

Finally, brand identity is included in the discussion of brand equity, representing the uniqueness of the brand association in Keller's (1993) model (Keller, 2001). Brand identity, the guiding positioning of the brand, influences the firms' integrated marketing communications (IMC) strategies, which in turn contributes to build the brand value, or brand equity (Madhavaram *et al.*, 2005). da Silveira *et al.* (2013) further expanded brand identity into a dynamic concept that is mutually impacted by the firms' brand management strategies and consumers' responses. This shift in the conceptualization of brand identity also calls for an integrated, identity-based view of brand equity, which is introduced in the following section.

Integrative Brand Equity

Despite the substantial body of brand equity models, Burmann *et al.* (2009) criticize that most brand equity models lack a sufficiently rigorous theoretical basis, and they build their models on the market-based

Table 7.1: Types of Consumer–Brand Relationships

A TYPOLOGY OF CONSUMER–BRAND RELATIONSHIP FORMS		
Relationship form	**Definition**	**Case examples**
Arranged marriages	Non-voluntary union imposed by preferences of third party. Intended for long-term, exclusive commitment, although at low levels of affective attachment.	Karen's adoption of her ex-husband's preferred brands (e.g., Mop 'n Glo, Palmolive, Hellman's): Jean's use of Murphy's Oil soap as per manufacturer recommendation.
Casual friends/buddies	Friendship low in affect and intimacy, characterized by infrequent or sporadic engagement, and few expectations for reciprocity or reward.	Karen and her household cleaning brands.
Marriages of convenience	Long-term, committed relationship precipitated by environmental influence versus deliberate choice, and governed by satisficing rules.	Vicki's switch to southern regional Friend's Baked Beans brand from favored B&M brand left behind in the northeast.
Committed partnerships	Long-term, voluntarily imposed, socially supported union high in love, intimacy, trust, and a commitment to stay together despite adverse circumstances. Adherence to exclusivity rules expected.	Jean and virtually all her cooking, cleaning, and household appliance brands; Karen and Gatorade.
Best friendships	Voluntary union based on reciprocity principle, the endurance of which is ensured through continued provision of positive rewards. Characterized by revelation of true self, honesty, and intimacy. Congruity in partner images and personal interests common.	Karen and Reebok running shoes; Karen and Coke Classic; Vicki and Ivory.
Compartmentalized friendships	Highly specialized, situationally confined, enduring friendships characterized by lower intimacy than other friendship forms but higher socioemotional rewards and interdependence. Easy entry and exit attained.	Vicki and her stable of perfumes.
Kinships	Non-voluntary union with lineage ties.	Vicki's brand preference for Tetley tea or Karen's for Ban, Joy, and Miracle Whip, all of which were inherited from their mothers.
Rebounds/avoidance-driven relationships	Union precipitated by desire to move away from prior or available partner, as opposed to attraction to chosen partner per se.	Karen's use of Comet, Gateway, and Success Rice.
Childhood friendships	Infrequently engaged, affectively laden relation reminiscent of earlier times. Yields comfort and security of past self.	Vicki's Nestle's Quik and Friendly's ice cream; Jean's use of Estée Lauder, which evokes memories of her mother.
Courtships	Interim relationship state on the road to committed partnership contract.	Vicki and her Musk scent brands during initial trial period.
Dependencies	Obsessive, highly emotional, selfish attractions cemented by feeling that the other is irreplaceable. Separation from other yields anxiety. High tolerance of other's transgressions results.	Karen and Mary Kay; Vicki and Soft 'n Dry

(continued)

Table 7.1 Types of Consumer–Brand Relationships (*continued*)

A TYPOLOGY OF CONSUMER–BRAND RELATIONSHIP FORMS		
Flings	Short-term, time-bounded engagements of high emotional reward, but devoid of commitment and reciprocity demands.	Vicki's trial size shampoo brands.
Enmities	Intensely involving relationship characterized by negative affect and desire to avoid or inflict pain on the other.	Karen and her husband's brands, post-divorce; Karen and Diet Coke; Jean and her other-recommended-but-rejected brands (e.g., Jif peanut butter, Kohler stainless steel sinks).
Secret affairs	Highly emotive, privately held relationship considered risky if exposed to others.	Karen and the Tootsie Pops she sneaks at work.
Enslavements	Non-voluntary union governed entirely by desires of the relationship partner. Involves negative feelings but persists because of circumstances.	Karen uses Southern Bell and Cable Vision because she has no other choice.

Reproduced from Fournier (1998).

and competence-based view of the firm and the brand identity philosophy of branding. They argue that brand identity precedes and is the basis of brand image, which is one of the cornerstones of CBBE, and thus active management of the brand is only possible through the management of brand identity. In this identity-based model of brand equity, Burmann *et al.* (2009) defined brand equity as "a present and future valuation derived from internal and external brand-induced performance, including psychological brand equity, behavioral brand equity, and financial brand equity." The integration of the model incorporates internal and external perspectives and behavioral and financial determinants (see Figure 7.4).

Burmann *et al.* (2009) further focused on brand strength (i.e., psychological and behavioral brand equity), considering it as the ground for financial brand equity and future potential brand equity. Different from previous studies on CBBE or FBBE, they also considered the behavioral significance of a brand for internal stakeholders (i.e., employees), because all sources of brand identity are based on the decisions and actions of its employees. Coincidently, the term "part-time marketers"

(Gummesson, 1991), referring to those employees outside of marketing or sales, emphasizes the major indirect influence on the customer-brand experience.

Specifically, employees' brand commitment and brand citizenship behaviors are two primary components of *internal brand strength*, because they represent employees' psychological (attitudinal) and behavioral aspects of internal brand equity. Employees' brand commitment is the psychological attachment of employees to the brand, influencing their willingness to exert extra efforts toward reaching brand goals. Brand citizenship behaviors, on the other hand, describe a number of generic employee behavior that enhances brand identity, including helping behavior, organizational compliance, individual initiative, sportsmanship, organizational loyalty, self-development, and civic virtue (cf. Podsakoff *et al.*, 2000). Burmann and Zeplin (2005) argued that employees' brand commitment is the key driver for employees' brand citizenship behaviors and identified three drivers of employees' brand commitment: (1) compliance, (2) identification, and (3) internalization with brand identity.

Figure 7.4: Identity-Based Brand Equity Model

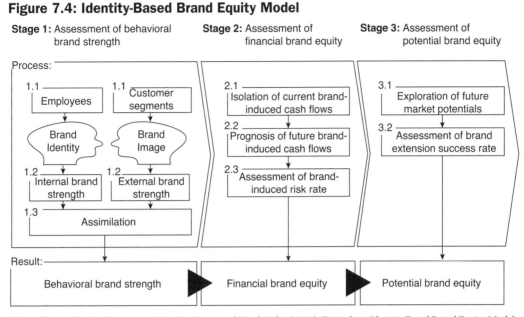

Adapted from Christoph Burmann, Marc Jost-Benz, and Nicola Riley (2009), Towards an Identity-Based Brand Equity Model, *Journal of Business Research* 62: 390–397.

Burmann *et al.* (2009) categorized *external brand strength* into knowledge-, benefit-, and preference-oriented measures, depending on the primary reasoning for brand strength. Knowledge-oriented measures consider brand strength as the quantity and quality of brand associations, or in other words, whether and what consumers will link the brand to. Obviously, brand awareness is a typical measure in this category. Benefit-oriented measures believe that brand strength comes from the benefit that a brand can provide to customers, and thus the (1) brand benefit uniqueness, (2) perceived brand quality, and (3) brand benefit clarity are three measures in this category. Preference-oriented measures focus on the comparative advantages of the brand compared to other brands or non-branded products, and thus it includes brand sympathy and brand trust.

Further, Burmann *et al.* (2009) apply the balance theory (Heider, 1958) to examine the success of the long-term system of the brand. Specifically, the internal and external brand strengths should be assimilated so that the brand achieves the same level of attitudes and behaviors from its employees and

customers. Moreover, they suggest that the force to maintain the balance of the system originates from the employee side and is translated to the consumers' side during the interaction between consumers and employees. That is because employees receive more exposure to the brand, and thus they are more easily influenced by the brand identity (i.e., the mere exposure effect, cf. Obermiller, 1985).

The behavioral brand strength influences financial brand equity of the firm through current cash flows, future cash flows, and risk rate applied to the discounted brand-induced cash flow model. After adjusting current cash flow by means of residual-oriented cash flow approach, the prognosis of future brand-induced cash flows represents the second stage of the financial brand equity assessment. This is an important step as it allows for both internal and external brand strength to evolve over time and be assimilated. A comprehensive brand equity measurement reflects not only the current development of a brand but also future opportunities. In the final stage, the financial and potential brand equities are synthesized into total brand equity.

Brand Equity Creation from Relationship Marketing (RM) Perspective

The preceding review has included most contemporary models and thoughts on brand equity, and it can be concluded that brand equity is largely driven by consumers' perceptions and reactions to the brand and, therefore, could be managed by strategically developing a brand identity within the company and conveying such a brand identity via employee–customer interactions and marketing-mix stimuli. From these ideas about brand equity, it is not hard to see that relationship marketing (Gronroos, 1994) could play a significant role. In fact, the central concept in brand equity, brand loyalty,[2] is exactly the desired outcome of relationship marketing from the firm's perspective. In this sense, building brand equity is to enhance the brand loyalty or to achieve a strong customer–brand relationship, consistent with the philosophy of relationship marketing (see Figure 7.5).

Our earlier review has revealed at least four sets of factors that contribute to customers' loyalty to the brand: (1) CBBE factors, (2) market signaling factors,

(3) brand identity factors, and (4) customer-brand relationship factors. Thus, the following section will review how to create, maintain, and enhance brand loyalty via these sets of factors, integrating the philosophies of relationship marketing and contemporary studies in the brand equity literature.

Customer-Based Brand Equity

Built on the traditional hierarchy of effects model, Buil *et al.* (2013) proposed that *brand awareness* is the cornerstone that leads to the formation of attitudes toward the brand (i.e., *perceived quality* and *brand association*), which in turn results in attitudinal loyalty (i.e., *brand loyalty*). Similarly, Oliver (1999) proposed that consumers first become loyal in a cognitive sense, then later in an affective sense, still later in a conative manner (i.e., intention), and finally in a behavioral manner. Empirical results (e.g., Buil *et al.*, 2013; Yoo *et al.*, 2000) reveal that brand loyalty is indirectly impacted by almost all marketing-mix strategies including price, distribution, and promotions. In this process, brand awareness, perceived quality, and brand association serve as mediating constructs.

Figure 7.5: Building brand equity is to enhance the brand loyalty or to achieve a strong customer—brand relationship

---

2 Some scholars focus on the "true" brand loyalty, emphasizing the central role of brand commitment (e.g., Amine 1998; Kim *et al.*, 2008), but such an argument is not popular in the field and prone to a cognitive-only view. Thus, this review still uses brand loyalty in a more general meaning including either attitudinal or behavioral loyalty.

For example, Yoo *et al.* (2000) showed that price, distribution, and advertisement enhance consumers' awareness of the brand, increase perceived quality about the branded product, and enrich meaning associated with the brand.

Among these factors influencing brand loyalty, the most significant one should be advertising. This is consistent with the view in relationship marketing that the customer–brand relationship starts from communication (Grönroos, 2004). In fact, Grönroos (2004) noted that integrated marketing communication (IMC) is an important part of a relationship marketing strategy. He further stated that if relationship marketing is to be successful, an integration of all marketing communications messages (e.g., traditional media, digital media, social media) is needed to support the establishment, maintenance, and enhancement of relationships with customers (and other stakeholders). Coincidentally, Madhavaram *et al.* (2005) conducted a study specifically on IMC strategies and brand equity. In their study, IMC strategies generated brand equity contacts, information-bearing experience that a customer or prospect has with the brand, which influence brand equity. They specifically considered the synergy and effectiveness of IMC and validated their antecedent role for brand equity.

Market Signaling

Market signaling views brand equity from the market perspective, suggesting that brand names are in fact the market signals assuring consumers in the asymmetric market environment. The focal construct in this stream, brand trust, is also a key antecedent of the relationship development (e.g., Hess and Story, 2005; Morgan and Hunt, 1994). Trust is conceptualized as including the element of risk or vulnerability, and defined as the psychological willingness of a party to be vulnerable to the actions of another based on positive expectations regarding the other party's motivations and/or behavior (Mayer *et al.*, 1995). Specifically, Morgan and Hunt (1994) put relationship commitment and trust as two key mediating variables for relationship marketing, because they encourage marketers to work at preserving relationship investments by co-operating with exchange partners, resist attractive short-term alternatives for long-term benefits of staying with exchange partners, and view potentially high-risk actions as being prudent due to the belief that their partners will not act opportunistically. Similarly, Delgado-Ballester and Munuera-Aleman (2001) posited that trust is a key factor that differentiates relationships from transactions.

Although brand loyalty is not exactly brand commitment per se as some have argued (Amine, 1998), they are, however, interchangeably used in past studies (e.g., Hess and Story, 2005) because brand commitment is the attitudinal loyalty to the brand. Thus, the trust–commitment link could be a potential approach to enhance brand equity. In fact, Chaudhuri and Holbrook (2001) revealed that brand trust and brand affect are two drivers for brand loyalty, which in turn impacts market share and relative price.

While studies on customer–brand trust have identified several antecedents of this construct, three characteristics of the trustee (described in chapter 5) that explain a large portion of trustworthiness are: (1) ability, i.e., skills, competencies, and characteristics enabling a firm to effectively perform in a specific domain; (2) benevolence, i.e., extent to which a trustee is believed to want to do good to the trustor, aside from an egocentric motive; and (3) integrity (the trustor's perception that the trustee adheres to a set of principles — personal and moral integrity that is deemed acceptable to the trustor) (Mayer *et al.*, 1995; Schoorman *et al.*, 2007). The ability-based trustworthiness is driven by "technical efficacy"

(Love and Kraatz, 2009), namely "product and service efficacy" and "market prominence," which in the terminology of CBBE is perceived quality of the brand. Similarly, the benevolence- and integrity-based trustworthiness is driven by "organizational character" and "symbolic conformity" (Love and Kraatz, 2009).

Doney and Cannon (1997) examined the nature of trust and argued that trust is developed through a series of cognitive processes: calculative, prediction, capability, intentionality, and transference (described in chapter 5). Specifically, trust can be built upon: (1) the larger cost of cheating the partner (calculative); (2) the ability to forecast the behavior of the partner (prediction); (3) the determination of the partner's ability to meet its obligation (capability); (4) the intention of the partner in the exchange (intentionality); and (5) the testimony of a trusted third party (transference). Notably, these processes have no sequential order, and multiple processes could be involved at the same time. For example, the frequent contact with the salesperson could provide better prediction for the salesperson's behavior, enable to interpret the salesperson's intention to consider the buyer's benefits, and even infer a greater cost of cheating due to the effort invested in the communication. Different from Doney and Cannon (1997), Hess and Story (2005) proposed that trust is developed based on a series of satisfactory performance in the interactions. Specifically, they distinguished brand attributes from product or service attributes and suggested that the former is brand trust and the latter is satisfaction. Also, they proposed that brand trust leads to both personal and functional connection while satisfaction merely results in functional connection. These two connections lead to brand commitment and are reflected by the outcomes. In addition, they suggest that brand characteristics, consumer characteristics, the performance of the product, and firm responsiveness could moderate the relationship formation. For example, certain product categories, such as automobile

and other high involvement categories, naturally involve more relational aspects and thus relationship is more likely to establish.

Despite Doney and Cannon's (1997) and Hess and Story's (2005) work suggesting that brand trust is developed through interactions (transactions), customer–company interface is not the only interaction that a customer could engage in brand-relevant activities. Brand community denotes specialized bound community based on a structured set of social relations among admirers of a brand (Muniz and O'Guinn, 2001), and such a bound community could be extended to include consumers' relationship with possessed branded product and with marketing agents (McAlexander *et al.*, 2002). In other words, brand community includes consumer–brand, consumer–product, consumer–marketer, and consumer–consumer interactions under a specific brand. From earlier discussions, brand community could serve to establish brand trust, which in turn leads to brand loyalty. Social media-based brand community is selected to illustrate the implications of brand community in the development of brand trust and brand loyalty.

Casaló *et al.* (2007) investigated free software communities due to its great development in recent years and the existence of alternatives contrasting the effects of the brand community. The authors argued that free software communities are clear instances of brand community because they satisfy three core components of a brand community: consciousness of kind, rituals and traditions, and sense of moral responsibility (Muniz and O'Guinn, 2001). In the study, the authors argued that the participation in a brand community increases brand trust in two ways. First, the members can increase their knowledge regarding the brand and its product in the interaction with other community members. Such a familiarity reduces the uncertainty of using the branded product, and thus it increases brand trust. Second, the member can perceive that the brand is concerned about their needs and desires in their participation toward developing new products and services in the brand community. Such a perception of the good intention of the brand helps to increase brand trust. The authors also examined the sequential impact of brand trust on brand loyalty as well as the direct impact from brand community participation to brand loyalty, and significant results were achieved in all proposed links.

Similar to Casaló *et al.* (2007), Laroche *et al.* (2012) also built their model upon the three core components of the brand community, but they treated community engagement as one of value creation practices of brand community which leads to brand trust. In addition to community engagement, Laroche *et al.* (2012) also considered social networking, impression management, and brand use as three other value creation practices. Following a similar logic, the authors argued that brand trust is developed in these value creation practices as a result of information dissemination. In other words, brand trust is developed due to the information passed among members reducing uncertainty and information asymmetry. Also, they argued that these practices offer members more value from the brand community, which evokes the calculative process of trust. In their empirical study on social media-based brand community, they found that only impression management and brand use significantly lead to brand trust. In other words, creating favorable impressions of the brand and helping other members to use the brand could lead to brand trust. The authors explained the result by suggesting that the effect of practices in social media-based brand communities may not have evolved enough to significantly affect brand loyalty.

Another study on social media-based brand community comes from Pentina *et al.* (2013), where the focus is on the perceived personality match in the consumer–brand interaction. Specifically, they applied the social identity theory (Tajfel, 2010) to argue that the perceived similarity in the personality will make members associate themselves with this in-group. Perceiving the similarity and being in the group could enhance the prediction and the intentionality of the trust-building process (Doney and Cannon, 1997).

However, not all voices are positive toward brand trust and relationship building. Lantieri and Chiagouris (2009) discussed the macro trends of the decline of trust and criticized the pseudo-relationship building activities. The authors commented that many efforts to build relationship with consumers have stopped short of satisfying consumers expectations — customer relationship marketing (CRM) efforts seem one-sided, merely providing a way for the company to gather information about their customers or to make misguided sales pitches without giving the consumer something both relevant and valuable in return. Even in cases where consumers trust a brand, any relationship or emotional connection may not go farther than that.

Brand Identity

As previously introduced, brand identity is a strategic tool in the creation of brand equity (Aaker, 1996; Burmann *et al.*, 2009; Keller, 2001). Notably, da Silveira *et al.* (2013) conceptualized brand identity as dynamic and emanating from brand managers and consumers. Specifically, they suggest that brand identity is a dynamic process to which brand managers and consumers contribute (see Figure 7.6). Firms display organizational identity through strategies, processes, structures, and activities. Marketing managers contribute via marketing and communication strategies and actions, and consumers contribute through building their individual and collective identities as well. They suggest that brand identity originates from brand managers and further developed through mutually influencing inputs from managers and consumers.

Figure 7.6: Brand identity is a dynamic process to which brand managers and consumers contribute

Companies have organizational identity. The scholarly work of Shelley Brickson (2005, 2007) draws attention to the distinction between two essential orientations of organizational identity: (1) *individualistic organizational identity* and (2) *collectivist organizational identity*. Individualistic organizational identity focuses on whether or not the firm is driven to succeed in comparison to others. Here, efficiency in maximizing organizational interests is valued in relationships with external stakeholders. By contrast, in a collectivist organizational identity, the locus of organizational self-definition is the larger group of generalized stakeholders, and the focal firm is seen as contributing to their collective welfare. Here, the relationship is neither meant to maximize efficiency nor meant to foster permanent and strong dyadic ties, but rather to advance a common overarching goal, referred to as an ideological psychological contract. A firm's individualistic organizational identity (Brickson, 2007) is built on technical competence-based trust and managerial competence-based trust, such as perceived quality of products and services, financial performance, and market prominence. Similarly, a firm's collectivist

organizational identity (Brickson, 2007) is built on integrity- and benevolence-based trust, such as social and environmental responsibility (Agarwal *et al.*, 2015).

Customers also possess identity and seek customer–company identification. Customer–company identification represents an overlap between a customer's sense of self and sense of an organization (Bhattacharya and Sen, 2003). Recent work by Johnson *et al.* (2012) and Wolter and Cronin (2015) links cognitive and affective aspects of organizational identification to motivations of self-uncertainty and self-enhancement in customers. With respect to cognitive customer-company identification, self-uncertainty originates from self-categorization theory in which an individual uses identification with an organization as a means to reduce subjective uncertainty by taking on the characteristics of the social identity prototype (Hogg and Terry, 2000). This cognitive overlap between a customer's self-concept and her or his perception of the company is driven by a comparison of the company's values with the personal values of the individual. By considering their conceptual overlap, customers receive confidence and control of their social situation and this appeals to customers' need for self-continuity as they are drawn toward companies who share similar identities that deeply matter to them and are relatively stable — i.e., central and enduring (Albert and Whetten, 1985; Bhattacharya and Sen, 2003; Whetten, 2006).

With respect to affective customer–company identification, it stems from social identity theory and the need for self-enhancement — i.e., motivation to maintain or enhance the positivity, or decrease the negativity of the self (Reid and Hogg, 2005; Bhattacharya and Sen, 2003). Affective identification allows customers to bask in the reflected glory of an organization's successes offering them increased status and positive self-concept. Unlike cognitive identification that manifests itself in cognitive appraisal, affective identification results in customers' evaluating ones' selves against the perceived identity of an organization, manifested in positive emotional response. That is, the process of self-enhancement is manifested directly in how the customer feels about an organization rather than how a customer thinks about an organization (Wolter and Cronin, 2015).

Ghodeswar (2008) suggested that brand identity includes a core and extended identity. The core identity should remain constant as the brand moves to new markets or develops new products and broadly focus on product attributes, service, user profile, store ambience, and product performance. The extended identity, on the other hand, should provide brand texture and completeness and focus on brand personality, relationship, and strong symbolic association, similar to the brand association dimension of CBBE. Ruzzier and de Chernatony's (2013) study on the brand identity development of Slovenia provides an excellent example to illustrate this process. Specifically, borrowing from

brand identity models, they considered vision, values, personality, and distinguishing preference as key aspects and added mission and benefits. Specifically, mission and vision provide a clear sense of direction, because the former pertains to the reason for the existence of the entity and the latter seeks to bring about an improved environment by identifying a societally beneficial purpose that a welcomed set of values can help achieve. Values and personality contribute to the differentiation as the former drives the behavior and the style of interaction between stakeholders and the latter includes peoples' main traits and their main ways of life. Distinguishing preferences and benefits specify the uniqueness of the branding place as the former includes a place's attraction or attributes and the latter refers to the rewards perceived to be offered by the place.

Customer-Brand Relationship

Finally, brand equity and customer relationship marketing in reality overlap as they represent two critical sources of intangible, market-based assets that can be leveraged into superior financial performance (Srivastava *et al.*, 1998). However, brand equity fundamentally represents the differential effect of brand knowledge on customer response and is therefore a "product-centered" concept (Rust *et al.*, 2004). Palmatier (2008) argues that although relationship marketing and branding activities focus on building customer loyalty and financial performance, branding primarily focuses on "products" with extensions to the firm, whereas relationship marketing primarily focuses on "relationships" with extensions to the firm. This distinction is clear at the core level of products versus relationships; however, it gets murky at the firm level. In other words, Palmatier (2008) argues that at the firm level it is difficult to parse out brand equity and relational equity that contribute to customer equity, which represents the total lifetime value of all customers of the firm.

KEY TAKEAWAYS

- Firm-based brand equity (FBBE) is found by subtracting the value of tangible assets from the total value of the firm. Alternatively, FBBE is assessed by the incremental probability to choose the branded product compared to a base product.

- Consumer-based brand equity (CBBE) is the differential effect of brand knowledge on consumer response to the marketing of the brand and reflects the added value endowed by the brand to the product.

- CBBE consists of four dimensions: brand awareness, brand association, perceived quality, and brand loyalty. Brand awareness can be classified as brand recognition, brand recall, top-of-mind, and brand dominance. Brand association is defined as the meaning of the brand consisting of attributes, benefits, and attitudes. Collectively it includes all thoughts, feelings, perceptions, images, experiences, beliefs, and attitudes toward a brand. Perceived quality reflects the technical efficacy (superiority) of the products and services linked with a brand. Brand loyalty shares both attitudinal and behavioral components reflecting attachment and commitment to re-patronize.

- Integrative brand equity is the present and future valuation derived from internal and external brand-induced performance, including psychological brand equity, behavioral brand equity, and financial brand equity. Internal brand strength is characterized by employee brand commitment and brand citizenship behavior. External brand strength is characterized by knowledge-based (e.g., quality/quantity of brand associations), benefit-based (e.g., uniqueness, quality, and clarity), and preference-based measures (e.g., brand sympathy and trust).

- Customer loyalty (i.e., customer retention), a central concept of brand equity, is the desired outcome of customer relationship marketing.

- The hierarchy-of-effects model suggests that customers first become loyal to a brand in a cognitive sense (brand awareness), then in an affective sense (perceived quality/brand association/attitudinal loyalty), followed by conative sense (behavioral intention) and then behavioral sense (behavioral loyalty). Integrated market communication (IMC) is an important relationship marketing tool that managers can use to build brand equity and customer retention.

- Brand names are market signals assuring customers in asymmetric market environment that they can trust the brand and therefore invest in long-term relationship with customers. In this context, trust–commitment pillar of relationship marketing is a potential approach to enhance brand equity.

- Trust is developed through a series of cognitive processes including calculative trust, prediction, capability, intentionality, and transference. Three facets of brand trust include ability, benevolence, and integrity. Relationship building opportunities with customers exist not just at exchange levels but at engagement levels beyond purchase, including brand community engagement.

- Brand identity is a strategic tool in the creation of brand equity and hence long-term customer relationship. Marketing managers contribute toward building brand identity in two ways: (1) individualistic organizational identity based on technical and managerial-competence based trust such as quality of products/services, financial performance, and market prominence; and (2) collectivistic organizational identity based on integrity and benevolent-based trust such as CSR-related activities.

- Customers also possess identity and seek customer–company identification to meet their need for self-continuity and self-enhancement. Over time, customer identification with companies builds long-term relationships.

- Both brand equity and relational equity contribute to customer equity at the firm level, i.e., total lifetime value of all customers of the firm.

EXERCISES

Questions

1. Define customer-based brand equity and firm-based brand equity. Despite the fact that both approaches recognize the added value endowed by the brand, what are some fundamental differences between them?

2. Explain the four dimensions of customer-based brand equity: (a) brand awareness; (b) brand association; (c) perceived quality; and (d) brand loyalty.

3. What are the components of internal brand strength (for employees) and external brand strength (for customers) in generating behavioral brand strength? How is behavioral brand strength converted into financial brand equity?

4. Comment on the following statement: "The central concept in brand equity is brand loyalty, the desired outcome of relationship marketing from the firm's perspective. In this sense, building brand equity is to enhance brand loyalty and a strong customer-brand relationship".

5. Discuss how the trust–commitment theory of relationship marketing can be a potential approach to building brand equity among customers. Explain the market signaling function of brand equity through the different processes of customer–brand trust development.

6. Brand identity is a strategic tool in the creation of brand equity. Explain how companies project their individualistic and collectivist organizational identity to customers.

7. Similar to how companies project their identity with customers through marketing and communication strategies, customers also identify with companies. Discuss the underlying motivations and psychological mechanisms involved in customer–company identification.

8. While branding focuses on "products," relationship marketing focuses on "relationships" with extensions to the firm. Explain how the former, i.e., brand equity and the latter, i.e., relational equity contribute to customer equity, representing the lifetime value of all customers of the firm.

Group Discussion

1. A private mobile phone company ABC has a segment of customers that score *low* on customer lifetime value (CLV) metrics but *high* on customer-brand value (CBV) metrics. CLV is measured based on forward-looking metrics discussed in Chapter 6. CBV is measured by aggregating and averaging customer scores on eight components: (1) brand awareness, (2) brand image, (3) brand trust, (4) brand affect, (5) brand purchase intention, (6) brand loyalty, (7) premium price behavior, and (8) brand advocacy. These customers have high brand value but are not expected to remain loyal to the brand.

    As a small group, discuss specific strategies to align CLV and CBV potential for customers in this segment. How can marketers successfully link customer-based brand equity (CBBE), market signaling, and brand identity with growth in CLV performance?

2. A private mobile phone company XYZ has a segment of customers that score *high* on customer lifetime value (CLV) metrics but *low* on customer brand value (CBV) metrics. As noted earlier, CLV is measured based on forward-looking metrics discussed in Chapter 6. CBV is measured by aggregating and averaging customer scores on eight components: (1) brand awareness, (2) brand image, (3) brand trust, (4) brand affect, (5) brand purchase intention,

(6) brand loyalty, (7) premium price behavior, and (8) brand advocacy. These customers have potential with the company in the future, but do not consider the brand to be of high value. That is, their brand-related awareness, knowledge, attitude, purchase intention, and brand behavior are not strong.

As a small group, discuss specific strategies to align CLV and CBV potential for customers in this segment. How can marketers successfully build "brand management" and "engagement strategies" to push these customers into true loyalists as they have a good profitability potential? How will branding strategies change to maximize CLV as these customers progress through (a) acquisition stage, (b) retention stage, and (c) attrition stage of the customer lifecycle?

HBS and Ivey Cases

- AnswerDash (9-516-106)

- Re-inventing Best Buy (9-716-455)

- Chase Sapphire (9-518-024)

- Laurs & Bridz (9B18A004)

CASE QUESTIONS

AnswerDash

1. Which approach should AnswerDash use to evaluate brand equity: customer-based brand equity or firm-based brand equity? Why?

2. In the context of AnswerDash, what are the components of internal brand strength (for employees) and external brand strength (for customers) in generating behavioral brand strength? How can AnswerDash convert behavioral brand strength into financial brand equity?

3. How can AnswerDash build brand equity and foster brand loyalty? Should AnswerDash emphasize more on brand awareness, perceived quality, or brand association? Why?

4. Explain how AnswerDash can project its individualistic and collectivist organizational identity to customers to develop a desired brand identity.

5. How can AnswerDash foster brand equity and relational equity to build customer equity, representing the lifetime value of all customers of the firm?

6. What specific strategies would you recommend to AnswerDash to align customer lifetime value (CLV) and customer brand value (CBV) potential for its customers? How can it successfully link customer-based brand equity, market signaling, and brand identity with growth in CLV performance?

Reinventing Best Buy

1. In the context of Best Buy, discuss the four dimensions of customer-based brand equity: (a) brand awareness; (b) brand association; (c) perceived quality; and (d) brand loyalty.

2. How can Best Buy build brand equity and foster brand loyalty? Should Best Buy emphasize more on brand awareness, perceived quality, or brand association? Why?

3. Discuss how Best Buy can make use of the trust-commitment theory of relationship marketing to build brand equity among customers. Which aspects of firm-specific trust should Best Buy emphasize more toward its customers: ability, benevolence, or integrity? Why?

4. What underlying motivations and psychological mechanisms can Best Buy employ to foster customer–company identification?

5. How can Best Buy foster brand equity and relational equity to build customer equity, representing the lifetime value of all customers of the firm?

6. What specific strategies would you recommend to Best Buy to align customer lifetime value (CLV) and customer brand value (CBV) potential for its customers? How can it successfully link customer-based brand equity, market signaling, and brand identity with growth in CLV performance?

7. How can Best Buy successfully build "brand management" and "customer engagement" strategies to push customers high on CLV ratings but low on CBV ratings into true loyalists as they have a good profitability potential? How will branding strategies change to maximize customer lifetime value (CLV) as these customers progress through (a) acquisition stage, (b) retention stage, and (c) attrition stage of the customer lifecycle?

8. How can Best Buy successfully build "brand management" and "customer engagement" strategies to push customers low on CLV ratings but high on CBV ratings into true loyalists as they are not expected to remain loyal to the brand? How will branding strategies change to maximize customer lifetime value (CLV) as these customers progress through (a) acquisition stage, (b) retention stage, and (c) attrition stage of the customer lifecycle?

Chase Sapphire

1. In the context of JPMorgan, what are the components of internal brand strength (for employees) and external brand strength (for customers) in generating behavioral brand strength? How can JPMorgan convert behavioral brand strength into financial brand equity?

2. Discuss how JPMorgan can make use of the trust–commitment theory of relationship marketing to build brand equity among customers? Which aspects of firm-specific trust should JPMorgan emphasize more toward its customers: ability, benevolence, or integrity? Why?

3. Explain how JPMorgan can project its individualistic and collectivist organizational identity to customers to develop a desired brand identity.

4. How can JPMorgan foster brand equity and relational equity to build customer equity, representing the lifetime value of all customers of the firm?

5. What specific strategies would you recommend to JPMorgan to align customer lifetime value (CLV) and customer brand value (CBV) potential for its customers? How can it successfully link customer-based brand equity, market signaling, and brand identity with growth in CLV performance?

6. How can JPMorgan successfully build "brand management" and "customer engagement" strategies to push customers high on CLV ratings but low on CBV ratings into true loyalists as they have a good profitability potential? How will branding strategies change to maximize customer lifetime value (CLV) as these customers progress through (a) acquisition stage, (b) retention stage, and (c) attrition stage of the customer lifecycle?

7. How can JPMorgan successfully build "brand management" and "customer engagement" strategies to push customers low on CLV ratings but high on CBV ratings into true loyalists as they are not expected to remain loyal to the brand? How will branding strategies change to maximize customer lifetime value (CLV) as these customers progress through (a) acquisition stage, (b) retention stage, and (c) attrition stage of the customer lifecycle?

Laurs & Bridz

1. Which approach should Laurs & Bridz use to evaluate brand equity: customer-based brand equity or firm-based brand equity? Why?

2. In the context of Laurs & Bridz, what are the components of internal brand strength (for employees) and external brand strength (for customers) in generating behavioral brand strength? How can Laurs & Bridz convert behavioral brand strength into financial brand equity?

3. How can Laurs & Bridz build brand equity and foster brand loyalty? Should Laurs & Bridz emphasize more on brand awareness, perceived quality, or brand association? Why?

4. How can Laurs & Bridz foster brand equity and relational equity to build customer equity, representing the lifetime value of all customers of the firm?

5. What specific strategies would you recommend to Laurs & Bridz to align customer lifetime value (CLV) and customer brand value (CBV) potential for its customers? How can it successfully link customer-based brand equity, market signaling, and brand identity with growth in CLV performance?

6. How can Laurs & Bridz successfully build "brand management" and "customer engagement" strategies to push customers high on CLV ratings but low on CBV ratings into true loyalists as they have a good profitability potential? How will branding strategies change to maximize customer lifetime value (CLV) as these customers progress through (a) acquisition stage, (b) retention stage, and (c) attrition stage of the customer lifecycle?

7. How can Laurs & Bridz successfully build "brand management" and "customer engagement" strategies to push customers low on CLV ratings but high on CBV ratings into true loyalists as they are not expected to remain loyal to the brand? How will branding strategies change to maximize customer lifetime value (CLV) as these customers progress through (a) acquisition stage, (b) retention stage, and (c) attrition stage of the customer lifecycle?

REFERENCES

Aaker, D.A. (1991), *Managing Brand Equity: Capitalizing on the Value of a Brand Name*. New York, NY: The Free Press.

Aaker, D.A. (1996), Measuring Brand Equity across Products and Markets, *California Management Review* 38(3): 102–120.

Aaker, David A. (2009), *Managing Brand Equity*, Simon and Schuster, New York, NY.

Ahearne, M., C.B. Bhattacharya, and T. Gruen (2005), Antecedents and Consequences of Customer-Company Identification: Expanding the Role of Relationship Marketing, *Journal of Applied Psychology* 90(May): 574–585.

Agarwal, J., O. Osiyevskyy, and P.M. Feldman (2015), Corporate Reputation Measurement: Alternative Factor Structures, Nomological Validity, and Organizational Outcomes, *Journal of Business Ethics* 130(2): 485–506.

Ailawadi, K.L., D.R. Lehmann, and S.A. Neslin (2003), Revenue Premium as an Outcome Measure of Brand Equity, *Journal of Marketing* 67(4): 1–17.

Albert, S. and D.A. Whetten (1985), Organizational Identity, *Research in Organizational Behavior* 7: 263–295.

Amine, A. (1998), Consumers' True Brand Loyalty: The Central Role of Commitment, *Journal of Strategic Marketing* 6(4): 305–319.

Berthon, P.R., N. Capon, J.M. Hulbert, M. Murgolo-Poore, J. Napoli, L. Pitt, and S. Keating (2001), Organizational and Customer Perspectives on Brand Equity: Issues for Managers and Researchers, in *ANZMAC*, Auckland, NZ

Bhattacharya, C.B. and S. Sen (2003), Consumer-Company Identification: A Framework for Understanding Consumers' Relationships with Companies, *Journal of Marketing* 67(2): 76–88.

Brakus, J.J., B.H. Schmitt, and L. Zarantonello (2009), Brand Experience: What Is It? How Is

It Measured? Does It Affect Loyalty? *Journal of Marketing* 73: 52–68.

Brickson, S.L. (2005), Organizational Identity Orientation: Forging a Link between Organizational Identity and Organizations' Relations with Stakeholders, *Administrative Science Quarterly* 50(4): 576–609.

Brickson, S.L. (2007), Organizational Identity Orientation: The Genesis of the Role of the Firm and Distinct Forms of Social Value, *Academy of Management Review* 32(3): 864–888.

Buil, I., L. de Chernatony, and E. Martínez (2013), Examining the Role of Advertising and Sales Promotions in Brand Equity Creation, *Journal of Business Research* 66(1): 115–122.

Burmann, C., M. Jost-Benz, and N. Riley (2009), Towards an Identity-Based Brand Equity Model, *Journal of Business Research* 62(3): 390–397.

Burmann, C. and S. Zeplin (2005), Building Brand Commitment: A Behavioral Approach to Internal Brand Management, *Journal of Brand Management* 12(4): 279–300.

Casaló, L., C. Flavián, and M. Guinalíu (2007), The Impact of Participation in Virtual Brand Communities on Consumer Trust and Loyalty: The Case of Free Software, *Online Information Review* 31(6): 775–792.

Chaudhuri, A and M.B. Holbrook (2001), The Chain of Effects from Brand Trust and Brand Affect to Brand Performance: The Role of Brand Loyalty, *Journal of Marketing* 65(2): 81–93.

Christodoulides, G. and L. de Chernatony (2010), Consumer-Based Brand Equity Conceptualization and Measurement: A Literature Review, *International Journal of Market Research* 52(1): 43.

Cobb-Walgren, C.J., C.A. Ruble, and N. Donthu (1995), Brand Equity, Brand Preference, and Purchase Intent, *Journal of Advertising* 24: 25–40.

Cronin, J.J. Jr., M.K. Brady, and G.T.M. Hult (2000), Assessing the Effects of Quality, Value, and Customer Satisfaction on Consumer Behavioral Intentions in Service Environments. *Journal of Retailing* 76(2): 193–218.

da Silveira, C., C. Lages, and C. Simões (2013), Reconceptualizing Brand Identity in a Dynamic Environment, *Journal of Business Research* 66(1): 28–36.

Delgado-Ballester, E. and J. Luis Munuera-Aleman (2001), Brand Trust in the Context of Consumer Loyalty, *European Journal of Marketing* 35(11/12): 1238–1258.

Delgado-Ballester, E. and J.L. Munuera-Alemán (2005), Does Brand Trust Matter to Brand Equity?, *Journal of Product and Brand Management* 14(3): 187–196.

Delgado-Ballester, E., J.L. Munuera-Aleman, and M.J. Yague-Guillen (2003), Development and Validation of a Brand Trust Scale, *International Journal of Market Research* 45(1): 35–56.

Dick, A.S. and K. Basu (1994), Customer Loyalty: Toward an Integrated Conceptual Framework, *Journal of the Academy of Marketing Science* 22(2): 99–113.

Doney, P.M. and J.P. Cannon (1997), An Examination of the Nature of Trust in Buyer-Seller Relationships, *Journal of Marketing* 61(2): 35.

Erdem, T. and J. Swait (1998), Brand Equity as a Signaling Phenomenon, *Journal of Consumer Psychology* 7(2): 131–157.

Farquhar, P.H. (1989), Managing Brand Equity, *Marketing Research* 1(3): 24–33.

Fetscherin, M. and D. Heinrich (2015), Consumer Brand Relationships Research : A Bibliometric Citation Meta-Analysis, *Journal of Business Research* 68(2): 380–390.

Fishbein, M. and I. Ajzen (1975), *Belief, Attitude, Intention, and Behavior: An Introduction to Theory and Research.* Reading. M: Addison-Wesley.

Forbes (2018), The World's Most Valuable Brands 2018, by Kurt Badenhausen, May 23, 2018 https://www.forbes.com/sites/kurtbadenhausen/2018/05/23/the-worlds-most-valuable-brands-2018

Fournier, S. (1998), Consumers and Their Brands: Developing Relationship Theory in Consumer Research, *Journal of Consumer Research* 24(4): 343–353.

Fournier, S. and J.L. Yao (1997), Reviving Brand Loyalty: A Reconceptualization within the Framework of Consumer-Brand Relationships, *International Journal of Research in Marketing* 14(5): 451–472.

Ghodeswar, B.M. (2008), Building Brand Identity in Competitive Markets: A Conceptual Model, *Journal of Product and Brand Management* 17(1): 4–12.

Gronroos, C. (1994), From Marketing Mix to Relationship Marketing: Towards a Paradigm Shift in Marketing, *Asia-Australia Marketing Journal* 2(1): 9–29.

Grönroos, C. (2004), The Relationship Marketing Process: Communication, Interaction, Dialogue, Value, *Journal of Business and Industrial Marketing* 19(2): 99–113.

Gummesson, E. (1991), Marketing-Orientation Revisited: The Crucial Role of the Part-Time Marketer, *European Journal of Marketing* 25(2): 60.

Heider, F. (1958), *The Psychology of Interpersonal Relations, American Sociological Review.* Hoboken, NJ: John Wiley & Sons Inc.

Hess, J. and J. Story (2005), Trust-Based Commitment: Multidimensional Consumer-Brand Relationships, *Journal of Consumer Marketing* 22(6): 313–322.

Hoeffler, S. and K.L. Keller (2002), Building Brand Equity through Corporate Societal Marketing, *Journal of Public Policy & Marketing* 21(1): 78–89.

Hogg, M.A. and D.J. Terry (2000), Social Identity and Self-Categorization Processes in Organizational Contexts, *Academy of Management Review* 25: 121–140.

Jacoby, J. and R. Chestnut (1978), *Brand Loyalty: Measurement and Management.* New York, NY: Wiley, John Wiley & Sons Incorporated.

Johnson, M.D., F.P. Morgeson, and D.R. Hekman (2012), Cognitive and Affective Identification: Exploring the Links between Different Forms of Social Identification and Personality with Work Attitudes and Behavior, *Journal of Organizational Behavior* 33: 1142–1167.

Keller, K.L. (1993), Conceptualizing and Measuring and Managing Customer-Based Equity, *Journal of Marketing* 57(1): 1–22.

Keller, K.L. (2001), Building Customer-Based Brand Equity, *Marketing Management* 10(2): 14–19.

Kim, J., J.D. Morris, and J. Swait (2008), Antecedents of True Brand Loyalty, *Journal of Advertising* 37(2): 99–117.

Ruzzier, M.K. and L. de Chernatony (2013), Developing and Applying a Place Brand Identity Model: The Case of Slovenia, *Journal of Business Research* 66(1): 45–52.

Kumar, V. (2013), *Profitable Customer Engagement: Concepts, Metrics, and Strategies.* Sage Publication, New Delhi, India.

Lantieri, T. and L. Chiagouris (2009), Brand Trust in an Age without Trust: Expert Opinions, *Journal of Consumer Marketing* 26(2): 78–86.

Laroche, M., M.R. Habibi, M.O. Richard, and R. Sankaranarayanan (2012), The Effects of Social Media Based Brand Communities on Brand Community Markers, Value Creation Practices, Brand Trust and Brand Loyalty, *Computers in Human Behavior* 28(5): 1755–1767.

Leonard, L (2000), Cultivating Service Brand Equity, *Journal of the Academy of Marketing Science* 28(1): 128–137.

Love, E.G. and M. Kraatz (2009), Character, Conformity, or the Bottom Line? How and Why Downsizing Affected Corporate Reputation, *Academy of Management Journal* 52(2): 314–335.

Madhavaram, S., V. Badrinarayanan, and R.E. McDonald (2005), Integrated Marketing Communication (IMC) and Brand Identity as Critical Components of Brand Equity Strategy: A Conceptual Framework and Research Propositions, *Journal of Advertising* 34(4): 69–80.

Mahajan, V., V.R. Rao, and R.K. Srivastava (1994), An Approach to Assess the Importance of Brand Equity in Acquisition Decisions, *Journal of Product Innovation Management* 11(3): 221–235.

Mayer, R.C., J.H. Davis, and F.D. Schoorman (1995), An Integration Model of Organizational Trust, *Academy of Management Review* 20: 709–735.

McAlexander, J.H., J.W. Schouten, and H.F. Koenig (2002), Building Brand Community, *Journal of Marketing* 66(1): 38–54.

Morgan, R.M. and S.D. Hunt (1994), The Commitment-Trust Theory of Relationship Marketing, *Journal of Marketing* 58(3): 20.

Muniz, A.M. and T.C. O'Guinn (2001), Brand Community, *Journal of Consumer Research* 27(4): 412–432.

Nysveen, H., P.E. Pedersen, and S. Skard (2013), Brand Experiences in Service Organizations: Exploring the Individual Effects of Brand Experience Dimensions, *Journal of Brand Management* 20(5): 404–423.

Obermiller, C. (1985), Varieties of Mere Exposure: The Effects of Processing Style and Repetition on Affective Response, *Journal of Consumer Research* 12(1): 17.

Oliver, R.L. (1997), *Satisfaction: A Behavioral Perspective on the Consumer*. New York, NY: Irwin/McGraw-Hill.

Oliver, R.L. (1999), Whence Consumer Loyalty?, *Journal of Marketing* 63(May): 33–44.

Palmatier, Robert W. (2008), *Relationship Marketing*. Cambridge, MA: Marketing Science Institute.

Pappu, R., P.G. Quester, and R.W. Cooksey (2005), Consumer-Based Brand Equity: Improving the Measurement—Empirical Evidence, *Journal of Product & Brand Management* 14(3): 143–154.

Park, C., D.J. MacInnis, J. Priester, A.B. Eisingerich, and D. Iacobucci (2010), Brand Attachment and Brand Attitude Strength: Conceptual and Empirical Differentiation of Two Critical Brand Equity Drivers, *Journal of Marketing* 74(6): 1–17.

Park, C.S. and V. Srinivasan (1994), A Survey-Based Method for Measuring and Understanding Brand Equity and Its Extendibility, *Journal of Marketing Research* 31(2): 271.

Pentina, I., L. Zhang, and O. Basmanova (2013), Antecedents and Consequences of Trust in a Social Media Brand: A Cross-Cultural Study of Twitter, *Computers in Human Behavior* 29(4): 1546–1555.

Podsakoff, P.M., S.B. Mackenzie, J.B. Paine, and D.G. Bachrach (2000), OCB Organizational Citizenship Behaviors : A Critical Review of the Theoretical and Future Research, *Journal of Management* 26(3): 513–563.

Raggio, R.D. and R.P. Leone (2006), The Theoretical Separation of Brand Equity and Brand Value: Managerial Implications for Strategic Planning, *Journal of Brand Management* 14(5): 380–395.

Reid, S.A. and M.A. Hogg (2005), Uncertainty Reduction, Self-Enhancement, and Ingroup Identification, *Personality and Social Psychology Bulletin* 31: 804–817.

Rindova, V.P., I.O. Williamson, A.P. Petkova, and J.M. Sever (2005), Being Good or Being Known: An Empirical Examination of the Dimensions, Antecedents, and Consequences of Organizational Reputation, *Academy of Management Journal* 48(6): 1033–1049.

Rust, R.T., K.N. Lemon, and V.A. Zeithaml (2004), Return on Marketing: Using Customer Equity to Focus Marketing Strategy, *Journal of Marketing* 68: 109–127.

Schoorman, F.D., R.C. Mayer, and J.H. Davis (2007), An Integrative Model of Organizational Trust: Past, Present, and Future, *Academy of Management Review* 32(2): 344–354.

Simon, C.J. and M.W. Sullivan (1993), The Measurement and Determinants of Brand Equity: A Financial Approach, *Marketing Science* 12(1): 28–52.

Srinivasan, V., C.S. Park, and D.R. Chang (2005), An Approach to the Measurement, Analysis, and Prediction of Brand Equity and Its Sources, *Management Science* 51(9): 1433–1448.

Sriram, S, S. Balachander, and M.U. Kalwani (2007), Monitoring the Dynamics of Brand Equity Using Store-Level Data, *Journal of Marketing* 71(2): 61–78.

Srivastava, R.K., T.A. Shervani, and L. Fahey (1998), Market-Based assets and Shareholder Value: A Framework for Analysis, *Journal of Marketing* 62: 2–18.

Tajfel, H. (2010), *Social Identity and Intergroup Relations*. Cambridge University Press, New York, NY.

Wang, H., Y. Wei, and C. Yu (2008), Global Brand Equity Model: Combining Customer-Based with Product-Market Outcome Approaches, *Journal of Product & Brand Management* 17(5): 305–316.

Whetten, D.A. (2006), Albert and Whetten Revisited: Strengthening the Concept of Organizational Identity, *Journal of Management Inquiry* 15: 219–234.

Winters, L.C. (1991), Brand Equity Measures: Some Recent Advances, *Marketing Research* 3(4): 70–73.

Wolter, J.S. and J.J. Cronin (2015), Re-Conceptualizing Cognitive and Affective Customer–Company Identification: The Role of Self-Motives and Different Customer-Based Outcomes, *Journal of the Academy of Marketing Science*, 44(3): 397–413.

Yoo, B. and N. Donthu (2001), Developing and Validating a Multidimensional Consumer-Based Brand Equity Scale, *Journal of Business Research* 52(1): 1–14.

Yoo, B. and N. Donthu, and S. Lee (2000), An Examination of Selected Marketing Mix Elements and Brand Equity, *Journal of the Academy of Marketing Science* 28(2): 195–211.

Zaichkowsky, J.L. (1985), Measuring the Involvement Construct, *Journal of Consumer Research* 12(3): 341–352.

Zarantonello, L. and B.H. Schmitt (2010), Using the Brand Experience Scale to Profile Consumers and Predict Consumer Behaviour, *Journal of Brand Management* 17(7): 532-540.

Zeithaml, V. (1988), Consumer perceptions of Price, Quality, and Value: A Means-End Model and Synthesis of Evidence, *Journal of Marketing* 52: 2–22.

08

Building B2C Relationships: Corporate Reputation and Customer–Brand Relationship

OVERVIEW

In Chapter 8, we first discuss the linkage between customer–brand relationship and corporate reputation. We conceptualize customer-based corporate reputation as a second-order abstract construct (reputation-as-assessment, generalized favorability) consisting of first-order asset constructs (reputation-as-asset constructs denoted by perceived value, market prominence, and societal ethicality) and argue for the primacy of halo effect in customers' perceptions of firm reputation. Based on this conceptualization, we then discuss the interrelationship between corporate reputation and customer relationship marketing (CRM). Next, we discuss an identity-based symbolic-instrumental framework of customer-based reputation explaining how customer–brand congruity, brand prominence, and customer–company identification affect perceptions of corporate reputation. At the end of the chapter, we provide key takeaways and conclude with discussion questions and HBS and Ivey cases. But first, to give a flavor of CRM and corporate reputation, we provide some real-life vignettes.

OPENING VIGNETTES

Vignette 1: The multinational company General Electric (GE) has garnered a reputation as a well-run organization. As a corporate brand, GE has moved its focus from customer comfort and convenience (We Bring Good Things to Life) to a more future-oriented positioning (Imagination at Work) that promises creative and innovative products. At the product level, one of GE's former product brands, NBC (now owned by Comcast), distinguished itself from the competition with the promise of compelling "must-see" programming. In doing so, GE established legitimacy through corporate reputation, relevancy through corporate brand, and differentiation through product brand (Ettenson and Knowles, 2008). However, in recent times GE is in doldrums as its profitability and brand value have collapsed significantly even though its reputation is relatively quite high (Top 10 in 2014 Fortune's World's Most Admired Companies).

Vignette 2: Samsung's brand purpose "We Exist to Inspire the World, Create the Future" has earned the company the third spot (84.4 points) in the 2016 US RepTrak reputation ranking (see Figure 8.1). Samsung's Galaxy products have rendered it as one of the "top tech" companies focused on relentless innovation with a strong brand expressiveness and brand strength (82.8 points). In contrast, Nike's brand purpose "We Exist to Inspire the Athlete Within Us All" was ranked #41 (77.9 points) in the same ranking. Although strong, there is a scope for improvement in Nike's performance across the dimensions of reputation, namely, performance, product/services, innovation, workplace, governance, citizenship, and leadership. Nike communicates often across multiple touchpoints but lacks authenticity and consistency in its corporate brand narrative (Reputation Institute Report). Does strong brand necessarily equate with good reputation?

Figure 8.1: Samsung's brand purpose "We Exist to Inspire the World, Create the Future" has earned the company high spots in reputation rankings.

INTRODUCTION

In an earlier chapter on brand equity (Chapter 7), we discussed customer-based brand equity, its definition and dimensions, namely brand awareness, brand association, perceived quality, and brand loyalty. We also presented an integrative brand equity model explaining brand equity creation from the relationship marketing perspective. In recent years, however, corporate scandals have brought the "reputation imperative" to the forefront. Interest in corporate reputation has never been higher, and we see this renewed emphasis on protecting and enhancing reputation in the growing number of reputation rankings published in popular business press. This raises an important question: how is brand related to corporate reputation and how does corporate reputation influence customer–brand relationship?

To answer the first question, it is important to realize that brand and corporate reputation are not the same concept. Brand is a "customer-centric" concept that focuses on what a product/service or the firm has promised to its customers, whereas reputation is a "company-centric" concept that focuses on the credibility and respect that a firm has among a broad set of stakeholders such as employees, investors, regulators, communities, as well as customers (Ettenson and Knowles, 2008). While both are intangible assets, reputation is a necessary pre-condition for people's willingness to do business with a company when stakeholders perceive the firm as reliable, honest, accountable, responsible, and quality conscious. These aspects of reputation generate legitimacy for the company in an industry pointing toward parity, but it doesn't create relevancy and points of differentiation that sets it apart from its competitors. Legitimacy implies the basic minimum level of adherence to social norm and expectations, necessary to gain the firm's social license to operate in a particular context. However, legitimacy should be considered a minimum accountability threshold to

reach; once exceeded, it does not help a company to stand out from its comparison (i.e., reference) group in the stakeholders' minds (Deephouse and Carter, 2005; King and Whetten, 2008). Hence, every firm must have three crucial qualities to sustain strong customer–brand relationships — (1) legitimacy, (2) relevancy, and (3) differentiation (Ettenson and Knowles, 2008). We start our discussion first with a conceptualization of corporate reputation.

CONCEPTUALIZING CORPORATE REPUTATION

Over the past decade, several scholars have attempted to reconcile varying definitions of corporate reputation, albeit without much success (Barnett *et al.*, 2006; Devers *et al.*, 2009; Fischer and Reuber, 2007; Walker, 2010; Lange *et al.*, 2011) (see Figure 8.2). Several definitions have been proposed. For instance, summarizing a substantive body of marketing literature, Gotsi and

Figure 8.2: Scholars have attempted to reconcile varying definitions of corporate reputation, although without much success.

Wilson (2001) proposed the following integrative view (p. 29): "A corporate reputation is a stakeholder's overall evaluation of a company over time. This evaluation is based on the stakeholder's direct experience with the company, and other forms of communication and symbolism that provides information about the firm's actions and/or comparison with the actions of other leading rivals" (here, the emphasis is on the way the reputation is formed over time). An earlier influential work by Herbig and Milewicz (1995) stressed the importance of consistency of corporate actions in reputation judgments: "Reputation is the estimation of the consistency over time of an attribute of an entity…This estimation is based on the entity's willingness and ability repeatedly to perform an activity in a similar fashion" (p. 5). Arguably the most notable at its time was the review done by Barnett *et al.* (2006), suggesting that the definitional landscape of corporate reputation primarily consists of three distinct clusters of meaning: (1) reputation as an awareness, (2) reputation as an assessment, and (3) reputation as an asset (i.e., some attribute of value). The later influential review by Lange *et al.* (2011) argued that corporate reputation should be defined as "familiarity with the organization, beliefs about what to expect from the organization in the future, and impressions about the organization's favorability" (p. 153). They found similar clusters as that of Barnett *et al.* (2006), labeling the three conceptual clusters as (1) "being known" (i.e., awareness construct), (2) "being known for something" (i.e., asset construct), and (3) "generalized favorability" (i.e., assessment construct).

Drawing from Lange *et al.* (2011) and Barnett *et al.* (2006), Agarwal *et al.* (2018) attempted to integrate the three definitional clusters within a conceptual framework. *Reputation-as-Awareness* is the stakeholders' collective perceptual representation reflecting broad visibility of the firm, regardless of judgment or evaluation, reflecting that stakeholders know and recognize the company (i.e., "being known"). In addition to recognition, reputation-as-awareness also reflects the perceived prominence of the company in its industry, or the extent to which it stands out relative to competition in the stakeholders' minds. However, stakeholders also form judgments about particular aspects of an organization's activities. This piecemeal evaluation is reflected in a set of *Reputation-as-Asset* dimensions, formally defined as judgments of particular attributes or characteristics of the firm (i.e., being known for something: e.g., reputation for quality or reputation for financial performance) with respect to the firm's ability to create value in a particular domain of activity based on past behavior. Finally, firms are also evaluated by stakeholders as a holistic entity (versus piecemeal evaluations), which is reflected in *Reputation-as-Assessment*.

At a broad level, these differing perspectives can be reconciled and integrated within a conceptual framework by examining its theoretical and operational definitions (Bagozzi, 2011). Agarwal *et al.* (2018) adopt an integration of the three differing perspectives around the definition of corporate reputation offered by Fombrun (2012), defined as "a *collective assessment* of a company's *attractiveness* to a *specific group of stakeholders* relative to a *reference group of companies* with which the company competes for resources" (p. 100, italicized for added emphasis). Consistent with Fombrun's (2012) definition of corporate reputation, Agarwal *et al.* (2018) model corporate reputation as a superordinate multi-dimensional construct integrating the three definitional perspectives (i.e., awareness, asset and assessment) within a unified conceptual framework. Specifically, they suggest that for customers-as-stakeholders, corporate reputation has two levels, the aggregate second-order construct (generalized favorability) that triggers a "halo effect" on individual first-order reputational dimensions. At the second-order level, reputation is an "assessment" construct of generalized favorability, i.e., affective judgment reflecting a company's overall attractiveness to its customers. In addition to second-order "generalized favorability," corporate reputation construct includes specific first-order dimensions. Each dimension represents a piecemeal evaluative judgment of a specific aspect of the firm's past history and future actions (i.e., "being known for something").

Generalized Favorability

At the second-order "assessment" level, reputation triggers a "halo effect," transcending any specific aspect of an organization's past or future due to common variance (Jarvis *et al.*, 2003). In other words, in addition to particular attributes of corporate reputation (such as reputation for innovativeness, or reputation for customer orientation), customers also form a generalized, global evaluation of a company ("halo effect," or generalized favorability in the case of reputation), which implicitly triggers the evaluation of all individual dimensions (Agarwal *et al.*, 2015). However, the reputational "halo effect" does not stem from prior financial performance only. Rather, it is formed as a result of processing of the company's past history and current signals regarding its likely future behaviors, to inform judgments of the firm's "overall appeal" when compared to other leading rivals. A firm's reputation is largely influenced by the corporate images that stakeholders receive every day manifested by the company's behavior, communication, and symbolism (Gotsi and Wilson, 2001). These images are transient perceptions or impressions of a company associated with a particular event or action, while reputation "implies a more lasting, cumulative, and global assessment rendered over a longer time period" (Gioia *et al.*, 2000, p. 66). Individual corporate images get aggregated in the stakeholders' cognitive processes, resulting in the formation of the "halo effect," i.e., generalized favorability judgment.

Once formed and entrenched in stakeholders' minds, this "assessment" construct of reputation embodies and

reflects perceptions of the firm's core identity, i.e., central, distinctive, and enduring traits based on the identity the company hopes to project to stakeholders through strategically crafted projected image of itself, but often refracted and filtered through third parties, resulting in perceived image, i.e., externally perceived self-view (Foreman *et al.*, 2012). Over time, it gets chronically activated via evaluative conditioning (Gawronski and Bodenhausen, 2006) through repeated identities and signals from the environment that characterize the company's corporate identity (Rindova *et al.*, 2005).

A firm can project both individualistic corporate identity and collectivist corporate identity (Brickson, 2005, 2007), the former focusing on whether or not the firm is driven to succeed compared to its rivals and demonstrate efficiency in maximizing corporate interests; the latter focusing on the collective welfare of generalized stakeholders. The basis of such identities is, however, based on corporate trust (Mayer *et al.*, 1995; Schoorman *et al.*, 2007). Love and Kraatz (2009) call it the "corporate character" of a firm, in that stakeholders ascribe positive reputations to firms that appear to possess desirable character traits of trustworthiness. This is because people tend to anthropomorphize organizations as conscious actors and are concerned about their suitability as exchange partners. Customers view signals and actions as occasions for attributing traits to the organization and tend to admire firms that possess character traits of trustworthiness, credibility, and transparency as opposed to opportunism, as they become the basis for projecting a firm's future behavior. This view is consistent with previous operationalizations of the firm's reputation, reflecting the firm's emotional appeal, "generalized favorability," sympathy, credibility, fairness; see Figure 8.3.

Product and Service Efficacy

Technical efficacy characterizes a firm's ability to fulfill stakeholders' material needs and is coupled

Figure 8.3: Customer Perception of Corporate Reputation: Assessment and Asset Constructs

Adapted from Agarwal, J., M. Stackhouse, and O. Osiyevskyy (2018), I Love That Company: Look How Ethical, Prominent, and Efficacious It Is: A Triadic Organizational Reputation (TOR) Scale, *Journal of Business Ethics* 153(3): 889–910.

with consequences and tangible corporate outputs (Love and Kraatz, 2009), for example, producing superior products and services for customers. A technical efficacy logic implies that reputational change reduces to change in performance directly relevant to stakeholders (i.e., instrumental logic: how does this affect me personally?) While existing studies have emphasized "perceived quality" of products/services as a distinct dimension of corporate reputation among customers, Agarwal *et al.* (2018) propose that "perceived value" is a broader concept that not only embodies perceived quality but also the sacrifice made in terms of money, time, and effort (i.e., value for the money). Further, the benefits of "perceived value" reside not only in the functional and esthetic domains, but also in the relational benefits reaped during the exchange process (Ahearne *et al.*, 2005; Bhattacharya and Sen, 2003). This view is consistent with prior research and may be reconciled with some dimensions of corporate reputation (e.g., quality of products/services, customer orientation, value for money, competence; see Figure 8.3).

Market Prominence

Agarwal *et al.* (2018) partition the technical efficacy explanation of corporate reputation into two distinct dimensions: *Perceived Value* and *Market Prominence* for customers-as-stakeholders; the former reflecting customer-centric view and the latter competitor-centric view. This partitioning reflects the fundamental distinction between perceived quality and prominence — i.e., stakeholder's evaluation of the company's absolute and relative performance, respectively; a distinction that should not be ignored, in lieu of our definition of corporate reputation (e.g., Rindova *et al.*, 2005). They define the second dimension of corporate reputation ("market prominence") as reflecting the degree of the firm's shared evaluative judgment among customers and the extent to which it stands out *vis-à-vis* its competitors — i.e., reference group-centric evaluative judgment. This aspect of technical efficacy logic implies that firm actions may themselves affect reputation, because of their inherent implications for performance change. This view is consistent with prior research and may be reconciled with some dimensions of corporate reputation (e.g., leadership/vision; see Figure 8.3).

Societal Ethicality

Symbolic conformity refers to a firm's reputation tied to meeting socially constructed standards within the cultural system that it is embedded in (Love and Kraatz, 2009), and the firm does so by adopting culture-specific and context-specific structures and practices that are locally appropriate and culturally desirable. That is, stakeholders confer good reputations not only on firms that are able to fulfill their financial and performance obligations, but also on firms that exemplify cultural fitness and conformity to local norms. This perspective draws from neo-institutional theory (DiMaggio and Powell, 1983; Scott, 2001), which holds that organizations, embedded within broader institutional environment, adopt structures and practices embodying normative values and cultural beliefs of stakeholders in response to field-level pressures to gain legitimacy and support. This view is also consistent with prior research and may be reconciled with the dimensions of corporate reputation in prior literature: e.g., in Figure 8.3 the dimensions of social and environmental responsibility and good employer/workplace environment reflect the "symbolic conformity" of a firm in the customers' minds and can be broadly captured as "societal ethicality."

Corporate Reputation and Customer Relationship Marketing (CRM)

Customer–brand relationships can be examined at both the second-order and first-order levels of corporate reputation (see Figure 8.4). At the higher generalized level, a customer's perception of reputation is seen through the lens of "organizational character." Customers ascribe good reputation to companies that have demonstrated trustworthiness and integrity as part of their "core" values. It takes time for companies to build reputational stock and this image is often enduring in the minds of customers. This means that past "conduct" that is consistent and perceived to be predictable in customers' minds becomes the basis for the formation and development of the company's "organizational character". However, once reputation-as-character is embedded in customers' cognitions as a higher-order concept, it is used as a quick proxy and heuristic ("halo effect") to activate reputation-as-conduct

Figure 8.4: Customer–brand relationships can be examined at both the second-order and first-order levels of corporate reputation.

in the areas of perceptions of product and service efficacy, societal ethicality, and market prominence. When information is scarce, the "halo effect" becomes an important signal of the firm's future behavior. A positive evaluation of a firm's character during crisis also serves as a buffer sustaining long-term customer–brand relationships, brand equity, and firm value. That is, a strong "organizational character" is often quite resilient in acting as a buffer against sporadic negative information leveled against the company. Managers should therefore build and protect the integrity of the company's accumulated "reputational capital" — i.e., its organizational character — as it significantly influences its dimension-based reputations.

Although related (in particular through the common influence of the second-order "halo effect" of generalized favorability), the three dimensions (i.e., product and service efficacy, market prominence, and societal ethicality) are to a large extent independent, allowing a company to have favorable reputation in one area and unfavorable in another. This independence of dimensions explains the seeming "paradoxes" like that of Goldman Sachs Group (a global investment bank), one of a few American major companies having simultaneously the best and worst reputation. On the one hand, the company is rightly considered one of the best banking companies in the US, having favorable technical efficiency reputation (high on market prominence and product and service efficacy), manifested in the "best investment bank" award, and having "the best brand name in business." On the other hand, after the global financial crisis of 2008 the company manifested all the negative sentiments about Wall Street firms (i.e., unfavorable societal ethicality reputation).

The impressive financial performance of Goldman Sachs Group corroborates Agarwal *et al.*'s (2018) empirical finding revealing disproportionately high weight assigned to product and service efficacy facet

of corporate reputation. This suggests that managers should allocate resources, first and foremost, on product and service efficacy, as this particular dimension captures most of the variance in reputation for customers-as-stakeholders. Compromising on either product/service value or customer relationship aspects of the exchange process will undermine corporate reputation. It is the relational exchange process at multiple touchpoints that customers directly experience and remember which puts a face on the company's reputation. Trying to consistently allocate resources on societal ethicality and market prominence, which are more diffused to broader generalized stakeholders and has long-term implications, at the expense of compromising the immediate product and service efficacy is not only damaging to the reputational asset, but may raise serious questions on the "organizational character" of the firm.

Agarwal *et al.*'s (2018) conceptualization of corporate reputation is consistent with those scholars espousing the identity theory in explaining corporate reputation. Identity theory tells us that companies, over time, develop features that are central, enduring, and distinctive and that are contextualized in a system of beliefs and values (Albert and Whetten, 1985; Fombrun, 2012). At the same time, it has also been acknowledged that customers identify with companies in an active, selective, and volitional way that satisfies their self-definitional needs of self-continuity, self-distinctiveness, and self-enhancement (Bhattacharya and Sen, 2003). This has *three* implications. First, driven to satisfy the "need for self-continuity," customers are motivated to maintain a stable and consistent sense of self, both over time and across situations and are drawn toward companies whose central identities are relatively stable and enduring. For customers-as-stakeholders, this is primarily reflected in predictable and consistent instrumental and relational benefits that maximize their "perceived value." Second, customers also have a "need for self-distinctiveness" that is satisfied in relationships with firms that reflect "market prominence." Companies, not just customers, as social actors also compete with motives and drives, such as a desire for status and distinctiveness, and customers ascribe favorable reputation to firms when their need for self-distinctiveness maps on to corporate drive toward market prominence (Highhouse *et al.*, 2009). Third, the local cultural context provides an avenue for customer's self to be expressed and aligned with that of the organization as shared collective values that are often socially constructed standards. Herein, customers' "need for self-enhancement" is satisfied — and so is the company's corresponding desire for approval — when firms display "societal ethicality" that aligns with stakeholders' higher-order needs rendering them legitimacy and in return support for symbolic conformity (Deephouse and Carter, 2005). In the next section, we present and explain an identity-based symbolic-instrumental framework of customers' perceptions of corporate reputation.

Symbolic-Instrumental Framework of Customers' Perceptions of Corporate Reputation

According to social identity theory (Tajfel and Turner, 1979, 1986), individuals derive identity not only from personal identity (i.e., that related to a person's individual sense of self), but also from social identity (i.e., that related to groups to which a person belongs or is affiliated). Findings indicate that people can identify with organizations even when they are not formal group members (e.g., Scott and Lane, 2000), such as consumers who can identify with the companies they patronize (Bhattacharya and Sen, 2003; Ahearne *et al.*, 2005; Einwiller *et al.*, 2006). The identity perspective on customer–brand relationships has evolved to be an important research stream in marketing literature at both the brand and corporate levels (Bhattacharya and Sen, 2003; Brown and Dacin, 1997; Escalas and

Bettman, 2005). Customer–company identification is defined as the extent to which consumers perceive themselves as sharing the same self-definitional attributes with the company. Customers identify with companies in an active, selective, and volitional way that satisfies at least one of their three self-definitional needs stated earlier in this chapter: (1) need for self-continuity, (2) need for self-distinctiveness, and (3) need for self-enhancement (Bhattacharya and Sen, 2003). Customers find a company's identity attractive when it is similar to their own identity, as it allows them to focus on self-relevant information inherent in company identities (i.e., self-knowledge) and to authentically express their traits and values by enacting valued identities (i.e., self-expression).

Driven to satisfy the *need for self-continuity*, customers are motivated to maintain a stable and consistent sense of self, both over time and across situations (Kunda, 1999). This desire to see one's self as being consistent over time (also known as self-verification and self-affirmation) is powerful and often triggered by a perceived threat to the integrity of the self, which results in the individual seeking confirmation and stability about the self (Ashforth *et al.*, 2008). Research indicates that individuals are capable of manipulating the immediate environment by selecting interaction partners that provide self-confirming feedback to support their sense of consistency and stability in the self (Stets and Harrod, 2004). Thus, customers are drawn toward companies who share similar identities that deeply matter to them and are relatively stable — i.e., central and enduring (Albert and Whetton, 1985; Whetten, 2006). Even when organizations change their identity, they often reframe the meaning of existing identity labels so as to preserve a sense of connection with the past thus providing a sense of continuity (Corley *et al.*, 2006; Gioia *et al.*, 2000; Rousseau, 1998). Thus, *identity similarity* makes the brand identity more attractive, consequently motivating customers to identify with the brand.

Self-brand congruity, defined as the perceived similarity of personality between the self and the brand along attributes (Aaker, 1997), reflects the notion of identity similarity that Bhattacharya and Sen (2003) conceptualize as an important antecedent to consumer–company identification. This notion is consistent with research on person–organization fit (Cable and DeRue, 2002). Rousseau (1998) distinguishes between situated identification and deep structure identification, in that the former involves a sense of belongingness to the collective triggered by situational cues, whereas the latter involves a more fundamental connection between the individual and the collective, that includes altered self-schemas giving a strong sense of self-collective congruence (see also Riketta *et al.*, 2006). The formation of company identification involving self-brand congruity is likely preceded by episodes of emulation of the corporate identity where one changes to become more similar to the collective (Pratt, 1998), thus necessitating a bottom-up process of consumer–company identification. The bottom-up process addresses the thoughts, feelings, and actions a consumer uses to negotiate the boundaries between the self and the company (Ashforth *et al.*, 2008; Mayhew, 2007) in a self-defining manner to become more similar to the collective. Self-brand congruity serves a strong motivational influence in establishing a deep structure identification that is inherently stable and enduring.

Therefore, customers with high self-brand congruity find the brand identity more attractive because it offers a sense of continuity or consistency of self-concept fulfilling higher-order needs (Agustin and Singh, 2005; Dukerich *et al.*, 2002), which in turn induces them to identify more with the brand. The likelihood that these needs will be met by competitors is low since brand personality representing brand imagery associations is a point of difference rather than a point of parity among brands (Keller, 2008), which intuitively is not easily substitutable by congruity with another brand (Lam *et al.*, 2012, 2013). Thus, self-brand congruity serves to meet higher-level symbolic goals validating their unique motives underlying the need for similarity and continuity.[1] That is, customers with higher levels of customer–brand congruity tend to have higher levels of customer–company identification.

While self-brand congruity is a reflection of similarity in personality dimensions between the customer and the brand, the self is embedded in a larger socio-cultural and institutional context. That is, the local cultural context provides an avenue for self-brand congruity to be expressed and aligned with firms as shared collective values that are often socially constructed standards and categories (Staw and Epstein, 2000). Over time, stakeholders and companies come to share understandings and expectations about the structures and practices that are locally appropriate and culturally desirable. Customers confer good reputations on firms that exemplify cultural stipulations of which they are part of and penalize firms that fail to conform to and display cultural fitness (Love and Kraatz, 2009). Likewise, similar to customers, organizations as social actors compete with motives, drives, and intentions also display goals of self-presentation, namely, desire for approval (Highhouse *et al.*, 2009; Whetten *et al.*, 2009). Such cultural fitness, by adopting structures and practices in response to field-level pressures, renders firm legitimacy and support in return for this conformity (Deephouse and Carter, 2005; Love and Kraatz, 2009). That is, customers with higher levels of customer–brand congruity tend to have positive perceptions of corporate reputation.

At the same time, customers also have a need to distinguish themselves from others in social contexts and this *need for self-distinctiveness* creates a tension

---

1 It should be noted that consumer–brand identification is both cognitive and affective in nature and is a gestalt construct at a higher level of abstraction, distinct from the less abstract self-brand congruity.

with the need for similarity. Brewer's optimal distinctiveness theory (Brewer, 1991) suggests that by adopting opposing social identities, people try to satisfy both needs for assimilation and differentiation. Distinctiveness, relative to competition, thus is an important corporate characteristic that motivates customers to identify with a company as it satisfies their need for self-distinctiveness. Furthermore, the *need for self-enhancement* motivates customers to both maintain and grow their positive self-esteem by positively differentiating their in-group from a comparison out-group (Ashforth, 2001; Haslam and Ellemers, 2005).

We argue that company identification acts in a top-down process of influencing customers particularly through corporate prestige and distinctiveness that is germane to corporate attachment (Dutton *et al.*, 1994; Smidts *et al.*, 2001; Ashforth *et al.*, 2008). That is, self-categorization is triggered often by situational cues (i.e., brand prominence) and the individual enacts a de-personalized social identity thus implicitly regarding identification as situated rather than deep (Mayhew, 2007; Rousseau, 1998). Brand prominence signals consumers that the brand will meet instrumental goals thus validating their self-knowledge and motives underlying the needs for self-distinctiveness and self-enhancement. Brand prominence can be conceptualized as a need fulfilling mechanism for instrumental or lower-order needs in a market-based exchange (Agustin and Singh, 2005) since competitors with parity or superior performance can imitate market prominence over time. The demands of the institutional environment push firms to become increasingly similar over time, not differentiated (DiMaggio and Powell, 1983). Need gratification theory suggests that brand prominence as a lower-order need will be temporally satisfied and that consumers will eventually place more emphasis on higher-order symbolic needs (Lam *et al.*, 2013). In short, customers with higher

levels of brand prominence perception have higher levels of customer-company identification.

Corporate reputation is valuable in reducing uncertainties and information asymmetries (and thus market uncertainties) in the minds of stakeholders. From an economics perspective, strategic firm choices reveal their true attributes thus signaling to customers to assess relevant firm attributes in their construction of corporate reputation. From an institutional perspective, uncertainty is reduced through exchange of information among diverse actors in the corporate field (e.g., institutional intermediaries, high-status actors) making some firms more salient and central, and thus more prominent, in the stakeholders' mind (Rindova *et al.*, 2005; King and Whetton, 2008). In marketing literature, the cognitive and affective aspects of brand prominence have been studied by measuring the frequency and ease with which brand-related thoughts come to mind (Park *et al.*, 2010). Brand prominence as an antecedent of corporate reputation embodies both strategic signals of competing firms and the collective knowledge about and recognition of a firm in its corporate field. Prominence garnered by expert intermediaries and through affiliation with high-status actors, who use specialized knowledge and rigorous scrutiny, implicitly assumes opinions of perceived quality that is disseminated across stakeholders. Customers reciprocate to institutional influences by their purchase behavior and the aggregate of these choices makes the firm more widely recognized (Rindova *et al.*, 2005).

Not just customers, but companies as social actors compete with motives, drives, and intentions (Whetten *et al.*, 2009) and display goals of self-presentation, namely, desire for status (see Figure 8.5). While, identities are concerned with the question, "what are we as an organization?" reputation is concerned with the question, "what do stakeholders

Figure 8.5: Not just customers, but companies as social actors display goals of self-presentation, namely, desire for status.

actually think of the organization?" Consumers' need for distinctiveness and impressiveness maps on to the corporate motive of status seeking (i.e., prominence) from its constituents (Highhouse *et al.*, 2009). Consumers ascribe reputation to firms based on their ability to fulfill material needs and performance (i.e., technical efficacy, Love and Kraatz, 2009) to which they are obligated to society. Brand prominence exemplified by perceived quality and collective recognition, therefore, influences customer-based corporate reputation.

Pratt (1998) notes that many of the motivations for individuals to identify with an organization touch on fairly basic human needs, most prominently the needs of safety, affiliation, and uncertainty reduction. Psychological safety and trust are at the heart of self-consistency and self-efficacy motives (Erez and Earley, 1993) and threats from out-group members increase identification with in-group members (Haslam and Ellemers, 2005). Further, people are meaning seekers and the process of identifying with collectives helps reduce uncertainty associated with interacting in

new environments, especially in corporate contexts (Weick, 1995). Both from an economics perspective and institutional theory perspective, corporate reputation is a powerful intangible asset in reducing uncertainties and information asymmetries in the minds of stakeholders. From an economics perspective, strategic firm choices reveal their true attributes thus signaling to customers to assess relevant firm attributes in their construction of corporate reputation. From an institutional perspective, uncertainty is reduced through exchange of information among diverse actors in the corporate field (e.g., institutional intermediaries, high-status actors) making some firms more salient and central, and thus more prominent, in the stakeholders' mind (Rindova *et al.*, 2005; King and Whetton, 2008). Thus, consumers create a sense of order in their world by reducing uncertainty and building trust through the deeper meanings provided by the collectives they associate with.

Corporate reputations are judgments about a firm made by stakeholders (e.g., customers) that are rooted in perceptions of corporate identity and impressions of its image, often activated by triggering events from a firm's more visible actions (Barnett *et al.*, 2006). As stated earlier, both individualistic and collectivist corporate identities (Brickson, 2005, 2007) are based on customers' levels of firm-specific trust. Individualistic corporate identity that is rooted in ability-based trust (Mayer *et al.*, 1995; Schoorman *et al.*, 2007) results in corporate reputation seen from the lens of an instrumental perspective, whereas the collectivist corporate identity built on benevolence-based and integrity-based trust (Mayer *et al.*, 1995; Schoorman *et al.*, 2007) is seen from a normative lens, albeit acknowledging the firm's implicit pursuit of value creation. Highhouse *et al.* (2009) describes these two components of corporate reputation as impressiveness (i.e., regarded as having prominence) and respectability (i.e., regarded as having honor and integrity). This viewpoint also reconciles perspectives on reputation that emphasize efficiency and character (Love and Kraatz, 2009) and reliability and trustworthiness (Fombrun, 1996). Therefore, customers with higher levels of customer–company identification will have higher levels of customer-based corporate reputation.

KEY TAKEAWAYS

- Brand and branding is a "customer-centric" concept that focuses on what a product/service or the firm has promised to its customers, whereas reputation is a "company-centric" concept that focuses on the credibility and respect that a firm has among a broad set of stakeholders. While branding creates relevancy and differentiation, reputation provides legitimacy to a firm granting social license to operate in society.

- Corporate reputation is a collective assessment of a company's attractiveness to a specific group of stakeholders relative to a reference group of companies with which the company competes for resources. At the global level, reputation is generalized favorability reflecting the firm's emotional appeal and organizational character (i.e., reputation-as-character). At the dimensional level, reputation is multi-faceted comprising of product and service efficacy, market prominence, and societal ethicality for customer-as-stakeholders (i.e., reputation-as-conduct).

- For customers, organizational character is best reflected in product and service efficacy (perceived value including relational value) experienced at multiple touchpoints in relational exchanges, which puts a face on the company's reputation.

- Perceived product and service efficacy facet of corporate reputation satisfies customers' need for self-continuity; market prominence facet satisfies customers' need for distinctiveness; and societal ethicality satisfies customers' need for self-enhancement.

- Self-brand congruity is an important antecedent to customer–company identification and serves to meet higher-level symbolic goals. Customers confer good reputations on firms that exemplify cultural stipulations of which they are part of and penalize firms that fail to conform to and display cultural fitness.

- Customers have a need for distinctiveness and brand prominence act as powerful signals that the brand will meet their instrumental goals thus validating their motives underlying the needs for self-distinctiveness and self-enhancement. Brand prominence as an antecedent of corporate reputation embodies both strategic signals of competing firms and the collective knowledge about and recognition of a firm in its corporate field.

- Corporate reputation is a powerful intangible asset in reducing uncertainties and information asymmetries in the minds of customers (Figure 8.6). Strategic firm choices reveal their true attributes thus signaling to customers to assess relevant firm attributes in their construction of corporate reputation. Uncertainty is also reduced through exchange of information among diverse actors in the corporate field making some firms more salient and central, and thus more prominent, in customers' mind.

- Companies that project their corporate identity from an individualistic perspective (product/service efficacy, financial performance) are seen by customers as rooted in ability-based trust, whereas companies that project their corporate identity from a collectivist perspective (CSR, environment, consumer welfare) are seen by customers from the normative lens rooted in benevolence-based and integrity-based trust. While both are important, it is the "organizational character" that customers use as quick proxy for corporate reputation.

EXERCISES

Questions

1. Comment on the following statement: "Brand is a 'customer-centric' concept that focuses on what a product/service or the firm has promised to its customers, whereas reputation is a 'company-centric' concept that focuses on the credibility and respect that a firm has among a broad set of stakeholders".

2. While reputation provides a firm legitimacy to reach a minimum accountability threshold, it is relevancy and differentiation that provides brand equity and competitive advantage. Do you agree with this statement and why?

3. While there are several definitions of corporate reputation, three facets of reputation emerge as common threads: (a) reputation-as-awareness; (b) reputation-as-asset; and (c) reputation-as-assessment. Explain each of these facets of reputation with real-life examples.

Figure 8.6: Corporate reputation is a powerful intangible asset in reducing uncertainties and information asymmetries in the minds of customers.

4. Customers evaluate a company's reputation based on its overall organizational character. At the same time customers also evaluate reputation at the dimensional level, namely, product and service efficacy, societal ethicality, and market prominence. Explain how customers integrate multiple evaluations of reputation and the role of "halo effect" in reputation judgments of companies. Where should marketers allocate maximum resources to enhance and protect reputational capital for customers-as-stakeholders?

5. Is it possible for a company to have a strong brand name (e.g., superior product quality, cutting-edge innovation) and, yet, a poor reputation? If so, explain this paradox. How can marketers resolve this paradox? Explain using a real-life example.

6. Explain how (a) "product and service efficacy" dimension of corporate reputation satisfies customers' need for self-continuity; (b) "market prominence" dimension satisfies customers' need for self-distinctiveness; and (c) "societal ethicality" dimension satisfies customers' need for self-enhancement?

7. Customers with a high level of self-brand congruity find the brand identity of a company attractive, consequently leading to strong customer–company relationship. Explain the psychological motivations underlying this relationship. What can marketers do to enhance and protect it?

8. Customers have opposing needs: need for conformity as well as need for distinctiveness, which creates a tension. Similarly, companies also have seemingly opposing desires: desire for approval (i.e., cultural fitness) as well as desire for prestige (i.e., technical fitness). Explain these conflicting needs and desires for customers and companies, respectively. What can marketers do to resolve such conflicts?

Group Discussion

1. According to Reputation Institute (2016) RepTrak publication, Google leads across most reputation dimensions in Canada. These dimensional scores are — product/services (80.5), innovation (82.1), workplace (80.6), governance (77.5), citizenship (76.0), leadership (79.9), and performance (81.5). It is the *third* best ranked company in Canada with a score of 79.9 (after Lego and Porter Airlines) and ranks *first* in all dimensions except product/services. It also leads across the three dimensions focused on CSR, namely, (1) governance, (2) citizenship, and (3) leadership (CSR Index of 78.1 versus 70.7 for Canada50 average).

   As a small group, discuss Google Canada's reputation in terms of its (a) organizational character and (b) dimensions, namely, product and service efficacy, market prominence, and societal ethicality? Do customers care for high CSR performance when the company is not the best in product and services? How important is organizational character of the company as measured by esteem, feeling, trust, and admiration? How does Google Canada's reputation score impact (a) customer purchase behavior; (b) customer engagement behavior; and (c) customer response to corporate crisis?

2. Facebook has had a tumultuous time in the recent past from accusations of influencing the outcome of the US Presidential election to the alleged exploitation of up to millions of personal profiles by partner, Cambridge Analytica. Can customers trust Facebook? Based on Reputation Institute's latest 2018 RepTrak study, only 38.5% of the world's population trusts any large company to do the right thing. Most companies have suffered a setback on the key measures that impact reputation. Facebook, in particular, experienced a significant drop in reputation (score of 60.5 in 2018), both in emotional connection and in several

key dimensions of reputation. Facebook has been especially vulnerable in the areas of citizenship and governance that align with ethics and CSR. Further, data also show that behavioral support for Facebook (e.g., customer engagement behavior) is on a downward trend.

As a small group, discuss how Facebook's drop in corporate reputation will impact the company's brand value and brand equity. With a weakened "organizational character," what should Facebook do to reverse the trend and regain trust and customer–company relationship? How closely is the reputation of Facebook linked with the reputation of its CEO, Mark Zuckerberg? Does Facebook have sufficient historical "reputational capital" to ride out the current crisis?

HBS and Ivey Cases

- AnswerDash (9-516-106)

- Re-inventing Best Buy (9-716-455)

- Chase Sapphire (9-518-024)

- Laurs & Bridz (9B18A004)

CASE QUESTIONS

AnswerDash

1. How can AnswerDash enhance its corporate reputation by building credibility and respect that it has among a broad set of stakeholders?

2. Should AnswerDash stress its reputation or brand relevancy and differentiation to build brand equity and competitive advantage? Why?

3. What dimensions should AnswerDash emphasize: product and service efficacy, societal ethicality, or market prominence? Where should it allocate maximum resources to enhance and protect reputational capital for customers-as-stakeholders?

4. Explain how can AnswerDash do the following: (a) emphasize product and service efficacy dimension of corporate reputation to satisfy customers' need for self-continuity; (b) emphasize market prominence dimension to satisfy customers' need for self-distinctiveness; and (c) emphasize societal ethicality' dimension to satisfy customers' need for self-enhancement.

5. Customers have opposing needs: need for conformity as well as need for distinctiveness, which creates a tension. Similarly, companies also have seemingly opposing desires: desire for approval (i.e., cultural fitness) as well as desire for prestige (i.e., technical fitness). Explain these conflicting needs and desires for customers and companies, respectively. What can AnswerDash do to resolve such conflicts?

6. Discuss AnswerDash's reputation in terms of its (a) organizational character and (b) dimensions, namely, product and service efficacy, market prominence, and societal ethicality. How important is organizational character of the company as measured by esteem, feeling, trust, and admiration?

Re-inventing Best Buy

1. Should Best Buy stress its reputation or brand relevancy and differentiation to build brand equity and competitive advantage? Why?

2. What dimensions should Best Buy emphasize: product and service efficacy, societal ethicality, or market prominence? Where should it allocate maximum resources to enhance and protect reputational capital for customers-as-stakeholders?

3. Explain the psychological motivations underlying customer-company relationship. What can Best Buy do to enhance and protect it?

4. Customers have opposing needs: need for conformity as well as need for distinctiveness, which creates a tension. Similarly, companies

also have seemingly opposing desires: desire for approval (i.e., cultural fitness) as well as desire for prestige (i.e., technical fitness). Explain these conflicting needs and desires for customers and companies, respectively. What can Best Buy do to resolve such conflicts?

5. Discuss Best Buy's reputation in terms of its (a) organizational character and (b) dimensions, namely, product and service efficacy, market prominence, and societal ethicality. How important is organizational character of the company as measured by esteem, feeling, trust, and admiration?

6. Discuss how Best Buy's corporate reputation impacts the company's brand value and brand equity. What should it do to strengthen its reputation and enhance trust and customer–company relationship?

Chase Sapphire

1. How can JPMorgan enhance its corporate reputation by building credibility and respect that it has among a broad set of stakeholders?

2. With respect to JPMorgan, explain each of these facets of reputation: (a) reputation-as-awareness; (b) reputation-as-asset; and (c) reputation-as-assessment. Which facet(s) should JPMorgan put more emphasis to build its reputation? Why?

3. What dimensions should JPMorgan emphasize: product and service efficacy, societal ethicality, or market prominence? Where should it allocate maximum resources to enhance and protect reputational capital for customers-as-stakeholders?

4. Explain how can JPMorgan do the following: (a) emphasize product and service efficacy dimension of corporate reputation to satisfy customers' need for self-continuity; (b) emphasize market prominence dimension to satisfy customers' need for self-distinctiveness; and (c) emphasize societal

ethicality' dimension to satisfy customers' need for self-enhancement?

5. Explain the psychological motivations underlying customer–company relationship? What can JPMorgan do to enhance and protect it?

6. Customers have opposing needs: need for conformity as well as need for distinctiveness, which creates a tension. Similarly, companies also have seemingly opposing desires: desire for approval (i.e., cultural fitness) as well as desire for prestige (i.e., technical fitness). Explain these conflicting needs and desires for customers and companies, respectively. What can JPMorgan do to resolve such conflicts?

Laurs & Bridz

1. How can Laurs & Bridz enhance its corporate reputation by building credibility and respect that it has among a broad set of stakeholders?

2. Should Laurs & Bridz stress its reputation or brand relevancy and differentiation to build brand equity and competitive advantage?

3. With respect to Laurs & Bridz, explain each of these facets of reputation: (a) reputation-as-awareness; (b) reputation-as-asset; and (c) reputation-as-assessment. Which facet(s) should Laurs & Bridz put more emphasis to build its reputation? Why?

4. Customers have opposing needs: need for conformity as well as need for distinctiveness, which creates a tension. Similarly, companies also have seemingly opposing desires: desire for approval (i.e., cultural fitness) as well as desire for prestige (i.e., technical fitness). Explain these conflicting needs and desires for customers and companies, respectively. What can Laurs & Bridz do to resolve such conflicts?

5. Discuss Laurs & Bridz's reputation in terms of its (a) organizational character and (b) dimensions,

namely, product and service efficacy, market prominence, and societal ethicality. How important is organizational character of the company as measured by esteem, feeling, trust, and admiration?

6. Discuss how Laurs & Bridz's corporate reputation impacts the company's brand value and brand equity. What should it do to strengthen its reputation and enhance trust and customer–company relationship?

REFERENCES

Aaker, J.L. (1997), Dimensions of Brand Personality, *Journal of Marketing Research* 34(3): 347–356.

Agarwal, J., M. Stackhouse, and O. Osiyevskyy (2018), I Love That Company: Look How Ethical, Prominent, and Efficacious It Is: A Triadic Organizational Reputation (TOR) Scale, *Journal of Business Ethics* 153(3): 889–910.

Agarwal, J., O. Osiyevskyy, and P.M. Feldman (2015), Corporate Reputation Measurement: Alternative Factor Structures, Nomological Validity, and Organizational Outcomes, *Journal of Business Ethics* 130(2): 485–506.

Agustin, C. and J. Singh (2005), Curvilinear Effects of Consumer Loyalty Determinants in Relational Exchanges, *Journal of Marketing Research* 52: 96–108.

Ahearne, M., C.B. Bhattacharya, and T. Gruen (2005), Antecedents and Consequences of Customer-Company Identification: Expanding the Role of Relationship Marketing, *Journal of Applied Psychology* 90(May): 574–585.

Albert, S. and D.A. Whetten (1985), Organizational Identity, in L.L. Cummings and B.M. Staw (Eds.), *Research in Organizational Behavior*. Greenwich: JAI Press Inc.

Ashforth, B.E. (2001), *Role Transitions in Organizational Life: An Identity-Based Perspective*. Mahwah, NJ: Erlbaum.

Ashforth, B.E., S.H. Harrison, and K.G. Corley (2008), Identification in Organizations: An Examination of Four Fundamental Questions, *Journal of Management* 34(3): 325–374.

Bagozzi, R.P. (2011), Measurement and Meaning in Information Systems and Organizational Research: Methodological and Philosophical Foundations, *MIS Quarterly* 35(2): 261–292.

Barnett, M.L., J.M. Jermier, and B.A. Lafferty (2006), Corporate Reputation: The Definitional Landscape, *Corporate Reputation Review* 9(1): 26–38.

Bhattacharya, C.B. and S. Sen (2003), Consumer-Company Identification: A Framework for Understanding Consumers' Relationships with Companies, *Journal of Marketing* 67(2): 76–88.

Brewer, M.B. (1991), The Social Self: On Being the Same and Different at the Same Time, *Personality and Social Psychology Bulletin* 17: 475–482.

Brickson, S.L. (2005), Organizational Identity Orientation: Forging a Link between Organizational Identity and Organizations' Relations with Stakeholders, *Administrative Science Quarterly* 50(4): 576–609.

Brickson, S.L. (2007), Organizational Identity Orientation: The Genesis of the Role of the Firm and Distinct Forms of Social Value, *Academy of Management Review* 32(3): 864–888.

Brown, T.J. and P.A. Dacin (1997), The Company and the Product: Corporate Associations and Consumer Product Responses, *Journal of Marketing* 61: 68–84.

Cable, D.M. and D.S. DeRue (2002), The Convergent and Discriminant Validity of Subjective Fit Perceptions, *Journal of Applied Psychology* 87: 875–884.

Corley, K.G., C.V. Harquail, M.G. Pratt, M.A. Glynn, C.M. Fiol, and M.J. Hatch (2006), Guiding Organizational Identity through Aged Adolescence, *Journal of Management Inquiry* 15: 85–99.

Deephouse, D. L. and S.M. Carter (2005), An Examination of Differences between Organizational Legitimacy and Organizational Reputation, *Journal of Management Studies* 42(2): 329–360.

Devers, C.E., T. Dewett, Y. Mishina, and C.A. Belsito (2009), A General Theory of Organizational Stigma, *Organization Science* 20: 154–171.

DiMaggio, P.J. and W.W. Powell (1983), The Iron Cage Revisited: Institutional Isomorphism and Collective Rationality in Organizational Fields, *American Sociological Review* 48: 147–160.

Dukerich, J.M., B.R. Golden, and S.M. Shortell (2002), Beauty is in the Eye of the Beholder: The Impact of Organizational Identification, Identity, and Image on the Cooperative Behaviors of Physicians, *Administrative Science Quarterly* 47: 507–533.

Dutton, J.E., J.M. Dukerich, and C.V. Harquail (1994), Organizational Images and Member Identification, *Administrative Science Quarterly* 39: 239–263.

Einwiller, S.A., A. Fedorikhin, A.R. Johnson, and M.A. Kamins (2006), Enough is Enough! When Identification no Longer Prevents Negative Corporate Associations, *Journal of the Academy of Marketing Science* 34: 185–194.

Erez, M. and P.C. Earley (1993), *Culture, Self-Identity, and Work*. New York: Oxford University Press.

Escalas, J.E. and J.R. Bettman (2005), Self-Construal, Reference Groups, and Brand Meaning, *Journal of Consumer Research* 32: 378–389.

Ettenson, R. and J. Knowles (2008), Don't Confuse Reputation with Brand, *MIT Sloan Management Review* 49(2): 19–21.

Fischer, E. and R. Reuber (2007), The Good, the Bad, and the Unfamiliar: The Challenges of Reputation Formation Facing New Firms. *Entrepreneurship Theory and Practice* 31(1): 53–75.

Fombrun, C.J. (1996), *Reputation: Realizing Value from the Corporate Image*. Boston: Harvard Business School Press.

Fombrun, C.J. (2012), The Building Blocks of Corporate Reputation: Definitions, Antecedents, Consequences, in M.L. Barnett and T.G. Pollock (Eds.), *The Oxford Handbook of Corporate Reputation* (pp. 94–113), Oxford University Press, Oxford, UK.

Foreman, P.O., D.A. Whetten, and A. Mackey (2012), An Identity-Based View of Reputation, Image, and Legitimacy: Clarifications and Distinctions among Related Constructs, in Michael L. Barnett and Timothy G. Pollock (Eds.), *The Oxford Handbook of Corporate Reputation* (pp. 179–200). Oxford University Press, Oxford, UK.

Gawronski, B. and G.V. Bodenhausen (2006), Associative and Propositional Processes in Evaluation: An Integrative Review of Implicit and Explicit Attitude Change, *Psychological Bulletin* 132(5): 692.

Gioia, D.A., M. Schultz, and K.G. Corley (2000), Organizational Identity, Image, and Adaptive Instability, *Academy of Management Review* 25(1): 63–81.

Gotsi, M. and A.M. Wilson (2001), Corporate Reputation: Seeking a Definition, *Corporate Communications: An International Journal* 6(1): 24–30.

Haslam, S.A. and N. Ellemers (2005), Social Identity in Industrial and Organizational Psychology: Concepts, Controversies and Contributions, *International Review of Industrial and Organizational Psychology* 20: 39–118.

Herbig, P. and J. Milewicz (1995), The Relationship of Reputation and Credibility to Brand Success, *Journal of Consumer Marketing* 12(4): 5–10.

Highhouse, S., M.E. Brooks, and G. Gregarus (2009), An Organizational Impression Management Perspective on the Formation of Corporate

Reputations, *Journal of Management* 35(6): 1481–1493.

Jarvis C.B., S.B. Mackenzie and P.M. Podsakoff (2003), A Critical Review of Construct Indicators and Measurement Model Misspecification in Marketing and Consumer Research, *Journal of Consumer Research* 30(2): 199–218.

Keller, K.L. (2008), *Strategic Brand Management: Building, Measuring, and Managing Brand Equity* (3rd ed.). Upper Saddle River: Pearson/Prentice Hall.

King, B.G. and D.A. Whetten (2008), Rethinking the Relationship between Reputation and Legitimacy: A Social Actor Conceptualization, *Corporate Reputation Review* 11(3): 192–207.

Kunda, Z. (1999), *Social Cognition: Making Sense of People*. Cambridge, MA: The MIT Press.

Lam, S. K., M. Ahearne, and N. Schillewaert (2012), A Multinational Examination of the Symbolic–Instrumental Framework of Consumer–Brand Identification, *Journal of International Business Studies* 43(3): 306–331.

Lam, S.K., M. Ahearne, R. Mullins, B. Hayati, and N. Schillewaert (2013), Exploring the Dynamics of Antecedents to Consumer-Brand Identification with a New Brand, *Journal of the Academy of Marketing Science* 41: 234–252.

Lange, D., P.M. Lee and Y. Dai (2011), Organizational Reputation: A Review. *Journal of Management* 37(1): 153–184.

Love, E.G. and M. Kraatz (2009), Character, Conformity, or the Bottom Line? How and Why Downsizing Affected Corporate Reputation, *Academy of Management Journal* 52(2): 314–335.

Mayer, R.C., J.H. Davis, and F.D. Schoorman (1995), An Integration Model of Organizational Trust, *Academy of Management Review* 20: 709–735.

Mayhew, M.G. (2007), *Identity and Identification in Organizational Contexts: Towards an Interactionist Perspective*, Unpublished Doctoral Dissertation University of Queensland.

Park, C.W., D.J. MacInnis, J.R. Priester, A.B. Eisingerich, and D. Iacobucci (2010), Brand Attachment and Brand Attitude Strength: Conceptual and Empirical Differentiation of Two Critical Brand Equity Drivers, *Journal of Marketing* 74: 1–17.

Pratt, M.G. (1998), To Be or Not To Be? Central Questions in Organizational Identification, in D.A. Whetten and P.C. Godfrey (Eds.), Identity in Organizations: Building Theory Through Conversations (pp. 171–207). Thousand Oaks, CA: Sage.

Riketta, M., R. van Dick, and D.M. Rousseau (2006), Employee Attachment in the Short and Long Run: Antecedents and Consequences of Situated and Deep-Structure Identification, *Zeitschrift für Personalpsychologie* 5(3): 85–93.

Rindova, V.P., I.O. Williamson, A.P. Petkova, and J.M. Sever (2005), Being Good or Being Known: An Empirical Examination of the Dimensions, Antecedents, and Consequences of Organizational Reputation, *Academy of Management Journal* 48(6): 1033–1049.

Rousseau, D.M. (1998), Why Workers Still Identify with Organizations, *Journal of Organizational Behavior* 19: 217–233.

Schoorman, F.D., R.C. Mayer, and J.H. Davis (2007), An Integrative Model of Organizational Trust: Past, Present, and Future, *Academy of Management Review* 32(2): 344–354.

Scott, W.R. (2001), *Institutions and Organizations*. (2nd ed.). Thousand Oaks, CA: Sage.

Scott, S.G. and V.R. Lane (2000), A Stakeholder Approach to Organizational Identity, *Academy of Management Review* 25(1): 43–62.

Smidts, A., A.T.H. Pruyn, and C.B.M. van Riel (2001), The Impact of Employee Communication and Perceived External Prestige on Organizational Identification, *Academy of Management Journal* 44: 1051–1062.

Staw, B.M. and L.D. Epstein (2000), What Bandwagons Bring: Effects of Popular Management Techniques on Corporate Performance, Reputation, and CEO Pay, *Administrative Sciences Quarterly* 45: 523–556.

Stets, J.E. and M.M. Harrod (2004), Verification across Multiple Identities: The Role of Status, *Social Psychology Quarterly* 67(2): 155–171.

Tajfel, H. and J.C. Turner (1979), *An Integrative Theory of Intergroup Conflict.* Monteray, CA: Brooks/ Cole.

Tajfel, H. and J.C. Turner (1986), *The Social Identity Theory of Intergroup Behavior.* Chicago, IL: Nelson-Hall.

Walker, K. (2010), A Systematic Review of the Corporate Reputation Literature: Definition, Measurement, and Theory, *Corporate Reputation Review* 12(4): 357–387.

Weick, K.E. (1995), *Sensemaking in Organizations.* Thousand Oaks, CA: Sage.

Whetten, D.A. (2006), Albert Whetten Revisited: Strengthening the Concept of Organizational Identity, *Journal of Management Inquiry* 15: 219–234.

Whetten, D.A., T. Felin, and B.G. King (2009), The Practice of Theory Borrowing in Organizational Studies: Current Issues and Future Directions, *Journal of Management* 35: 537–563.

09

Ethical Foundations of Customer Relationship Marketing

OVERVIEW

In Chapter 9, we first discuss positive ethics using the popular Hunt and Vitell (1986) framework, followed by a detailed discussion of normative ethics in marketing, examining consequences-based ethical theories, duty-based ethics, contract-based morality, and virtue-based ethics. In particular, we provide a detailed discussion on justice-based theories and moral foundations theories that help explain justifying how a particular ethical standard might apply to a given marketing practice and articulating the reasons for upholding such an ideal. In the wake of growing expectations of stakeholders for firms to engage in social/political issues and motivate change, we examine a framework of company moral authority in the marketplace. Finally, we discuss the case of digital marketing and privacy as seen from the customers' lens of ethical theories. At the end of this chapter, we provide key takeaways and conclude with discussion questions and HBS and Ivey cases. But first, to give a flavor of customer relationship marketing (CRM) and ethics, we provide some real-life vignettes.

OPENING VIGNETTES

Vignette 1: In 2018, Delta released a statement explaining their decision to discontinue a travel discount for National Rifle Association (NRA) members by stating that the "decision reflects the airline's neutral status in the current national debate over gun control amid recent school shootings. Out of respect for our customers and employees on both sides, Delta has taken this action to refrain from entering this debate and focus on its business". In a retaliatory move to punish the airline for taking this stance, Georgia state legislators eliminated a proposed tax break that would have benefited Delta. Industry observers note that while the decision to take a public stance on either side of the political debate carries considerable risk, staying neutral may no longer be an option (see Figure 9.1).

Figure 9.1: Companies like Delta Airlines are finding that they can no longer remain neutral on national ethical issues like gun control.

Vignette 2: In the absence of a dedicated privacy right, federal regulators have been reluctant to enforce privacy protections across companies and government entities. Questions surrounding whether and how the federal government ought to intervene remains a challenge for the Federal Trade Commission (FTC). The FTC applies two legal frameworks: (1) the Notice and Choice model composed of fair information practice principles (FIPP) and (2) the Harms-Based model that looks at whether physical/economic harm results to consumers from corporate misuse of personal information. Should marketers go beyond the legal framework and consider the ethical ramifications of information privacy as seen by customers? Can privacy protection be used as a strategy for a firm's competitive advantage in a marketplace rife with technology and data collection at multiple customer touchpoints?

INTRODUCTION

Ethics in marketing has a rich history dating back 50 years with the early emphasis characterized by descriptive and anecdotal approach. The descriptive criterion of the stakeholder framework describes, and sometimes explains, an actor's view of what the firm actually *is* vis-à-vis stakeholders, as well as the mechanisms through which different views come into being (Donaldson and Preston, 1995; Jones and Wicks, 1999). In short, descriptive justification mirrors the observed reality of firms and reveals what firms actually do.

Today, research in marketing ethics approaches in a positive and empirical manner uncovering empirical patterns in a network of relationships involving ethical constructs. Positive ethics describes and explains what actually seems to occur in morally charged situations based on observation or data. It is here that the instrumental criterion identifying connections between actions taken to manage stakeholders and firm objectives is adopted (Jones and Wicks, 1999). Several review articles taking inventory of research in marketing ethics (Nill and Schribrowsky, 2007; Schlegelmilch and Oberseder, 2009) point to the dominance of positive ethics in marketing, including popular models such as Hunt and Vitell (1986) model of ethical decision-making, which have been empirically tested.

Despite the preponderance of positive ethics approach to tackling ethical issues in marketing, firms, institutions, and stakeholders today continue to exhibit ethical (and legal) lapses in decisions that have widespread repercussions. For instance, there seems to be a growing litany of companies that have recently transgressed and failed to demonstrate moral grounding, including Apple (i.e., supply chain issues), Facebook (i.e., privacy and data protection), Volkswagen (VW) (i.e., engine tampering), and the list goes on. What seems to be missing is normative ethics. There is clearly a need for a normative ethics in conjunction with the positive ethics as the two are symbiotically intertwined as seen in the stakeholder theory, which accounts for the normative criterion as well. The normative criterion interprets moral guidelines and obligations of the firm toward its stakeholders (Evan and Freeman, 1984). The normative justification elevates the principle of fairness and justice to a higher level and moves away from "economic contracts" as captured under instrumental justification to "social contracts," though in the pursuit of value creation (Freeman, 1999).

THE HUNT-VITELL (H-V) THEORY OF MARKETING ETHICS

The original Hunt-Vitell (H-V) theory of marketing ethics has been used frequently in marketing explaining a wide variety of ethical/moral phenomena. The model was conceptualized to provide a general theory of ethical decision-making process that draws on both the deontological and teleological ethical traditions in moral philosophy. The revised model is argued to be a *general* theory of ethical decision-making, not just of *marketing* ethics, incorporating multiple ethical perspectives and concepts.

The H-V theory addresses the situation in which individuals confront problems that are perceived as having ethical content. This is an important first step. The next step is identifying possible alternatives or actions (fewer than the universe of potential alternatives) that might be taken to resolve the ethical problem. Once the individual perceives the set of alternatives, two kinds of evaluations take place: deontological and teleological. In the deontological evaluation (DE) process, people evaluate the inherent rightness or wrongness of each alternative's behavior by comparing them to a set of pre-determined deontological norms. These norms are personal values or rules of moral behavior ranging from general beliefs (e.g., honesty, stealing, and cheating) to issue-specific beliefs (e.g., deceptive advertising and product safety). Donaldson and Dunfee (1994) discuss the integrative social contracts theory and the deontological norms of "hyper-norms" and "local norms." Local norms are context specific and community-based, whereas hyper-norms are universal norms that represent "principles so fundamental to human existence that . . . we would expect them to be reflected in a convergence of religious, philosophical, and cultural beliefs" (Donaldson and Dunfee, 1994, p. 265). By contrast, teleological evaluation (TE) process focuses on four constructs: (1) the perceived consequences of each alternative for various stakeholder groups, (2) the probability that each consequence will occur to each stakeholder group, (3) the desirability or undesirability of each consequence, and (4) the importance of each stakeholder group (see Figure 9.2).

The H-V theory proposes that the teleological evaluation (TE) process is influenced by the desirability and probability of consequences, as well as the importance of stakeholders. That is, the teleological evaluation (TE) process for an alternative K, with regard to stakeholders 1, 2, 3, . . . m, who have differing importance weights (IW) is

$$TE_K = \sum_{n=1}^{n=m} [IW_1 \times PosCon_1 \times P_{Pos}]$$
$$- [IW_1 \times NegCon_1 \times P_{Neg}]$$
$$+ [IW_2 \times PosCon_2 \times P_{Pos}]$$
$$- [IW_2 \times NegCon_2 \times P_{Neg}] + ...$$

where IW_1 = importance of stakeholder 1; $PosCon_1$ = positive consequences on stakeholder 1; $NegCon_1$ = negative consequences on stakeholder 1; P_{Pos} = probability of positive consequences occurring; and P_{Neg} = probability of negative consequences occurring.

Figure 9.2: Hunt-Vitell Model of Marketing Ethics

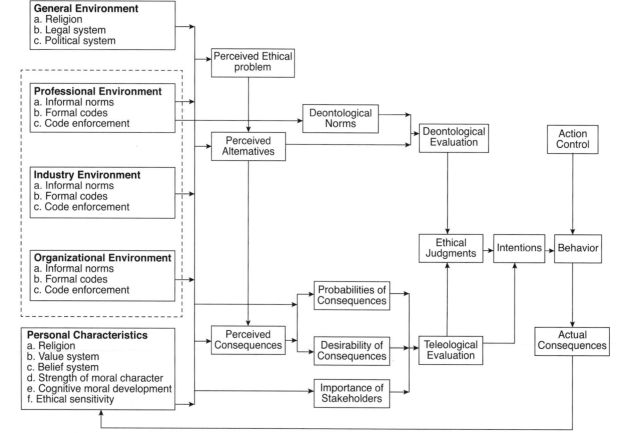

Reproduced from Shelby D. Hunt and Scott J. Vitell (1993), "The General Theory of Marketing Ethics: A Retrospective and Revision" in *Ethics in Marketing*, edited by N. C. Smith and J. A. Quelch (pp. 775–784), Homewood, IL: Richard D. Irwin.

An individual's ethical judgments are a function of the person's deontological evaluation (DE), i.e., applying norms of behavior to each of the alternatives and teleological evaluation (TE) representing an evaluation of the sum total of goodness versus badness likely to be provided by each alternative for all relevant stakeholders. The information processing rules will differ across different people's personal moral codes. The H-V theory proposes that ethical judgments will sometimes differ from intentions because TE also directly affects intentions. While people may perceive a particular alternative as the most ethical, they may intend to choose another alternative because of certain preferred consequences. Action control in the model is the extent to which an individual actually exerts control in the enactment of an intention in a particular situation.

After behavior is enacted, an evaluation of the actual consequences of the alternative selected engenders learning, which provides feedback to "personal characteristics." Several personal characteristics that often influence specific aspects of the ethical decision-making process are identified. These are (1) religion, such that highly religious people would have more clearly defined deontological norms and such norms would play a stronger role in ethical judgments; (2) individual's value system; (3) individual's belief system, for instance, to the extent one believes that all people are motivated solely by self-interest and opportunism, this belief will likely influence unethical behavior; (4) strength of moral character such as virtuous moral character (i.e., virtues of perseverance, courage, integrity, and compassion); (5) cognitive moral development; and (6) ethical sensitivity.

Finally, environmental influences, including cultural environment, industry environment, professional environment, and organizational environment, are important antecedents to the decision-making process. For instance, all industries, professional associations, and organizations have complex sets of norms, some of which are formalized in codes, but most of which are informal norms communicated in day-to-day interactions. These norms form a framework by which individuals are socialized into their respective organizations, professions, and industries.

NORMATIVE MARKETING ETHICS

The foundation of normative marketing ethics draws primarily from philosophy but sometimes from law and religion (see Figure 9.3). A normative definition of ethical marketing that involves an ideal to which the marketers should aspire is, *ethical marketing* which refers to the practices that emphasize transparent, trustworthy, and responsible personal and/or organizational marketing policies and actions that exhibit integrity, as well as fairness to consumers and other stakeholders (Murphy *et al.*, 2017, p. 5). Laczniak and Murphy (2019) discuss four types of normative ethical theories: (1) consequentialism, (2) duty-based ethics, (3) contract-based morality, and (4) virtue ethics. They are highlighted to remind marketing analysts that these normative frameworks have very different formulations and ethical implications.

Figure 9.3: Normative marketing ethics frameworks draw primarily from philosophy but sometimes from law and religion.

Consequences-based ethical theories (Bentham, 1984; Mill, 1979) state that a marketing decision is ethical or unethical based exclusively on its *outcome*. That is, if a decision results in more good consequences than bad ones, it is ethical. The major consequences-based ethical paradigm is utilitarianism (act and rule utilitarianism), which stipulates that the greatest good should be done for the greatest number of individuals. Act utilitarianism is after the fact where a company changes its policies only when significant pushback occurs whereas rule utilitarianism follows a principle before examining the consequences. These models of marketing ethics fall in line with the Hunt-Vitell framework discussed earlier.

Deontology/Duty-based ethics (Bowie, 1999; Kant, 1981) stipulates that intentions and motivations, not consequences, are what should drive ethical decision making. Kant posits three formulations of categorical imperative. The first is the "universality principle", which advocates that there are universal laws that should apply to all people in all situations (e.g., never bribe). The second variant of the categorical imperative is to "treat people always as ends and never as means merely" (e.g., the dignity of all persons). The third is the "moral community" formulation, which argues for fairness in a society — adopting rules as if an individual does not know her or his role in any dispute.

Laczniak and Murphy (2019) point out that several scholars have advanced duty-based theoretical premises in their marketing writings. For instance, decades ago, Laczniak (1983) applied Ross' (1930) *prima facie* (at first sight/self-evident) *duties* to marketing questions. Therein, six major duties from Ross with implications for marketing are discussed. An extensive application of duty-based thinking in marketing scholarship is Laczniak and Murphy (2006), which formulates seven normative basic perspectives for ethical and socially responsible marketing. They are (1) ethical marketing puts

people first; (2) ethical responsibility exceeds legal requirements; (3) ethical marketing considers intent, means, and ends; (4) ethical marketers try to inspire moral imagination; (5) ethical marketers embrace core values; (6) ethical marketers accept the stakeholder concept; and (7) ethical marketers embrace a process of moral reasoning (Laczniak and Murphy, 2011).

Contract-based morality (Rawls, 1971) posits two principles — (1) the liberty and justice principles that are never to be violated. The "liberty principle" implies that consumers and other stakeholders have the right to be equitably treated by all other stakeholders while (2) the "difference principle" suggests that disadvantaged parties be granted pathways to improve their position in society when public policies about markets are formulated (Laczniak, 1983). Laczniak and Murphy (2008) applied the difference principle focusing on normative ideals such as justice in market exchange, fairness within the supply channel, and more emphasis on vulnerable consumer segments. Rawls also introduced the *veil of ignorance*, a thought experiment that fair-minded individuals would use to create the rules of morality to be formulated as if they did not know their position in society. For business applications, Donaldson and Dunfee (1999) developed a business-centric theory of social contracts with two important principles: (1) "moral free space" that allows for a degree of relativity in developing the rules, and (2) "hyper-norms" that are universal in scope such as fundamental religious, cultural, philosophical, and legal norms.

Ethics of virtue (Aristotle, 1962; MacIntyre, 1984) is another foundation of normative marketing ethics. Unlike utilitarianism and duty-based ethics that focus on the decision-making process, ethics virtue focuses on the decider (manager), and not the decision. It is the person and the quality of her or his character that are most important in ethics, not simply an analysis of the decision to be made. Virtues are good habits that must be practiced and are learned by witnessing and imitating the behavior of admirable mentors and role models. In marketing, Williams and Murphy (1990) were the first to indicate that the ethics of virtue holds promise for guiding behavior of marketers. Later, Murphy (1999) proposed five virtues as being central to marketing — (1) integrity, (2) trust, (3) fairness, (4) respect, and (5) empathy — and discussed how these applied to managers from several countries and companies. Another refinement of virtue ethics in marketing focused on applying this normative theory to "relationship marketing" (Murphy et al., 2007). Herein, the three stages of relationship marketing — (1) establishing, (2) sustaining, and (3) reinforcing — were paired with three corresponding virtues of trust, commitment, and diligence.

NORMATIVE IDEALS: JUSTICE-BASED THEORIES

There is vast potential to examine customer–brand relationship transpiring at the exchange level from the justice framework (see Figure 9.4). The mature field of organizational justice offers us a repository of justice-related theories with ethical underpinnings, which can be cross-fertilized to better understand customer–brand relationships. Several justice theories have been applied to successfully explain people's evaluations of the procedures and outcomes received from various organizational authorities. Among these theories are social exchange model of justice, group-value model of justice, instrumental model of justice, and heuristic model of justice. However, the justice literature largely remains fragmented and there is a need to unify these theoretical mechanisms to understand customer–brand and company relationships under the umbrella of an integrative framework.

Companies endeavoring to develop meaningful and quality relationships with customers signify a strategic shift from the traditional approach of simply offering tangible goods to an approach based on the creation of intangible customer value acquired through customer–company relationships. In general, scholars overwhelmingly agree that it is trust that differentiates transactional from relational exchanges and is critical for relationship development and maintenance (Atuahene-Gima and Li, 2002; Garbarino and Johnson, 1999; Morgan and Hunt, 1994; Palmatier *et al.*, 2006; Palmatier, 2008; Schoorman *et al.*, 2007).

Figure 9.4: The justice framework offers great potential to examine customer–brand relationship transpiring at the exchange level.

While the importance of firm-specific trust has been well-documented in relationship marketing literature (e.g., Atuahene-Gima and Li, 2002; Sirdeshmukh *et al.*, 2002), trust's origins in justice models in customer–company relationships has been largely ignored.

With the exception of social exchange theory (e.g., Bagozzi, 1974; Blau, 1964; Morgan and Hunt, 1994), all other models of organizational justice have played a virtually non-existent role in explaining customer–frontline employee interaction. While the social exchange model of justice is a seminal theory entailing reciprocity norms, one of its key limitations has been its pre-dominant reliance on the resource-based view of justice (Tyler, 1994), which prescribes that customers are motivated to maximize equity and valued benefits in the long term. The relational-based view of justice, namely, the group-value model links concerns about justice to concerns about social bonds that exist between people and organizations. Social standing — both inclusion and intragroup status — is related to "pride" of being associated with a group and "respect," which reflects one's status within the group and involves treatment with dignity to every member of the group (Tyler and Blader, 2003). We believe other justice models can add to our understanding of customer–brand relationship at the exchange level such as instrumental and heuristic models of justice. The instrumental model of justice posits that self-serving biases in people motivates them to regulate procedures in place which serve instrumental roles in achieving desirable outcomes (Thibaut and Walker, 1975; Tyler, 1994). The heuristic model of justice posits that people use fairness information to make judgments regarding trustworthiness in order to reduce feelings of uncertainty or when outcome judgments are unavailable or difficult to judge (Van den Bos et al., 1998). While satisfaction and trust are foundational in marketing exchanges, moral norms arising out of various justice models can

further strengthen customer–brand relationships — a promising area worthy of future research.

Justice theorists often focus on three major issues: (1) how people respond to the outcomes they receive, (2) how they react to the procedures with which these outcomes are obtained, and (3) how they react to treatment received as procedures are enacted. The first issue involves *distributive justice* or the perceived fairness of the outcomes an exchange partner receives (Adams, 1965; Tyler, 1994). Distributive justice is based on the principles of equity and equality, in which a favorable evaluation depends on the perceived equality between inputs and outcomes compared to a point of past reference. The second issue involves *procedural justice* — which refers to the fairness and the quality of the decision-making process. Individuals view procedures as fair when the control of the procedures is vested in them and when they can exercise process control thereby influencing changes in organizational policies, they find objectionable (Leventhal, 1980; Tyler, 1994). The third issue, related to procedural justice, is *interactional justice* — which refers to the treatment people receive as procedures are enacted, including the disclosure of information and provision of explanations of decisions taken by authorities (Cohen-Charash and Spector, 2001). We use these three dimensions of justice to build each of the four theoretical models of justice (i.e., (1) social exchange model of justice, (2) group-value model of justice, (3) instrumental model of justice, and (4) heuristic model of justice) next.

Social Exchange Model of Justice

Social exchange theory proposes that the behaviors of parties in an exchange relationship can be explained through social interactions entailing repeated exchanges, future obligations, and an expectation that each party will fulfill her or his obligations in the long-run (Blau, 1964). Obligations are diffuse and ill-defined, and exchanges occur based on long-term relationship without concern for direct and immediate compensation as in an economic exchange (Konovsky, 2000). Consequently, trust becomes important in social exchange, and is defined as confident, positive expectations regarding a trustee's conduct, motives, and intentions in situations entailing risk (Colquitt and Rodell, 2011).

Research in organizational justice has shown that both procedural justice and interactional justice have a strong effect on attitude toward institutions and organizational trust (i.e., system-related evaluation as opposed to event-based evaluation; Ambrose *et al.*, 2007; Cropanzano *et al.*, 2001; Moorman and Byrne, 2005; Rupp and Cropanzano, 2002). Institutional evaluations of firm-specific trust require a long-term perspective regarding the fairness rules that govern the exchange relationship and it is procedural and interactional justice that provide the basis for such assessments. Further, while organizational research suggests that distributive justice better predicts attitude toward specific events (as compared to system-related evaluations; Ambrose *et al.*, 2007; Cropanzano *et al.*, 2001), meta-analytic studies by Colquitt *et al.* (2001) and Cohen-Charash and Spector (2001) found mixed results suggesting that distributive justice also predicted trust in organizations (Aryee *et al.*, 2002).

In keeping with the social exchange model of justice, customers' trust in a firm is based on their perceptions of distributive justice, procedural justice, and interactional justice. While the enactment of justice during relational exchanges occurs at the customer-frontline employee interface, customer trust in frontline employees directly influences firm-specific trust explained through affect transfer and inferential reasoning (Sirdeshmukh *et al.*, 2002). Because customer–frontline employees act as agents of the firm, the principle that apparently prescribes and controls the behavior of agents, greater customer trust in them will likely lead to higher levels of firm-specific trust (Bergen *et al.*, 1992).

Group-Value Model of Justice

As an alternative view of procedural justice, Lind and Tyler (1988) proposed the group-value model, which purports that procedural justice informs people about their social connection to groups and group authorities. According to the group-value model, people value relationships with groups because they are a means of fulfilling self-definitional needs and they provide information about self-validation (Dutton *et al.*, 1994). Social categorization in a group is evaluated according to three relational concerns, namely, (1) *trust*, (2) *neutrality*, and (3) *social standing* (Tyler, 1989; Tyler and Blader, 2003; Tyler *et al.*, 1996). Although the group-value model was later relabeled the "relational model" (Tyler, 1994) with a shift away from the label of trust to trustworthiness, we use trust in the conventional sense as employees' positive expectations about the motives of decision-making authorities as demonstrated primarily by their benevolence and integrity, but also by their competence. Neutrality involves assessment of the degree to which the decision-making procedures are unbiased, honest, and fact-driven. Social standing — both inclusion and intragroup status — is related to pride of being associated with a group and respect which reflects one's status within the group and involves treatment with dignity to every member of the group (Tyler and Blader, 2003; Blader and Tyler, 2009). Thus, according to the group-value model, individuals look to three judgments, namely, (1) trust, (2) neutrality, and (3) standing, as signals of how much they are valued by their groups.

The essence of neutrality is captured by procedural justice (i.e., the fairness and quality of the decision-making process; Leventhal, 1980; Tyler, 1994). By the same token, social standing is captured by interactional justice (i.e., the treatment and respect people receive as procedures are enacted and the disclosure of information and explanation; Cohen-Charash and Spector, 2001; Tyler and Blader, 2003).

Both neutrality and standing are therefore linked with procedural and interactional justice in organizations and contain elements of social identity. In the group-value model, organizational identification is an important proximal mediator between justice perceptions and organizational citizenship behavior (Moorman and Byrne, 2005).

Customer–company encounters are venues in which customers participate in identity-related activities, which help in the formation and maintenance of their identity. Positive relational exchanges generated by relational-based justice enactments help confirm customer–company identification (Arnett *et al.*, 2003) defined as the cognitive connection between the definition of a company and the definition a customer applies to him- or herself (Bergami and Bagozzi, 2000; Bhattacharya and Sen, 2003). These enactments of justice engender a sense of respect and self-esteem that helps customers affirm their identity salience and thus identification toward the company (Ahearne *et al.*, 2005; Bhattacharya and Sen, 2003). Thus, procedural justice, interactional justice, and trust are direct antecedents of customer–company identification.

Instrumental Model of Justice

The instrumental model of justice links evaluations of decision-making authorities to judgments of direct and indirect control over the outcomes of allocation procedures. Individuals view procedures as fair when control is vested to them and are more likely to prefer procedures that maximize the favorability of their personal outcomes (Thibaut and Walker, 1975; Tyler, 1994). The assumption behind the instrumental theory is that self-serving and egocentric biases toward favorable outcomes lead individuals to believe that opportunity for voice allows decision makers to see the "rightness" of their claims, thereby giving them greater consideration (Shapiro and

Brett, 2005). That is, the need for distributive justice motivates people to exercise voice through which they provide facts to mitigate biases in decision-making (i.e., procedural justice) and present their needs to be heard and understood (i.e., interactional justice). Input to decision is valued as it provides the next best alternative to outcome control and is seen as instrumental in trying to achieve desirable outcomes. Thus, people tend to report greater levels of procedural and interactional justice when they perceive that authorities have been receptive and responsive to their expressed views regardless of outcome favorability. Further, the notion of control over procedural justice, which has the potential to forestall opportunism and influence personal outcome in the exchange process also generates perceptions of trustworthiness (Smith and Barclay, 1997). Thus, outcome favorability helps regulate the procedures in place and customers' sense of procedural justice and interactional justice serve instrumental roles in trying to attain desirable outcomes and firm-specific trust.

Heuristic Model of Justice

The fairness heuristic theory focuses on the cognitive processing of fairness information under the conditions of uncertainty, namely fear of exploitation or rejection by group authorities (Lind *et al.*, 2001; Van den Bos and Lind, 2002; Van den Bos *et al.*, 1997, 1998). There are two mechanisms at play here. First, individuals who give up some control to organizational decision-making authorities seek to obtain information related to the decision makers' trustworthiness in order to reduce feelings of uncertainty. People often do not have information on trustworthiness of authorities and in such cases their reactions to an outcome are strongly affected by procedural fairness information (Van den Bos *et al.*, 1998). Justice perceptions can be formed more quickly and easily than trustworthiness since adherence to rules that are frequently encountered are easier to interpret. Procedural justice provides reassurance to people that they need not fear exploitation or rejection by the organization and that they can approach their relationship in a less defensive manner. Hence, people examine information related to procedural fairness and use this as a heuristic to make judgments on trustworthiness — i.e., both procedural justice and interactional justice accorded to them serve their functional role of a heuristic (or proxy) as antecedents to trust (Van den Bos *et al.*, 1998).

Second, when information on procedural justice is available before outcome judgments or when outcome judgments are difficult to judge (with confidence), people tend to use available knowledge about procedural and interactional justice as heuristics to judge the fairness of the outcomes. Van den Bos *et al.* (1997) found support for the reasoning that what people judge to be fair is more strongly affected by information that is available earlier (i.e., primacy effect) and they argue that in most situations procedural information is available earlier than outcome information. Lind *et al.* (2001) by manipulating the timing of fairness-relevant experiences found similar primacy effect on fairness judgments and a moderation of this effect by group identification. Furthermore, Van den Bos *et al.* (1998) argue that sometimes outcome fairness is difficult to judge when social comparison information is missing, an assumption that distributive justice theories emphasize. They found that in such instances, individuals would initially use procedural and interactional justice as proxies and later incorporate outcome information if and when additional information is available. Procedural and interactional justice serve their role of a heuristic (proxy) that strongly affects people's outcome fairness judgments, also known as the fair process effect. Hence, in the heuristic model of justice, both procedural justice and interactional justice will influence distributive justice and trust.

MORAL FOUNDATIONS THEORY

Moral foundations theory (MFT) (Haidt and Graham, 2007; Haidt and Joseph, 2004), grounded in evolutionary theory, identifies five moral domains involving systems of values, psychological mechanisms, and social norms that motivate attitudes and behavior: (1) harm/care, (2) fairness/reciprocity, (3) in-group/loyalty, (4) authority/respect, and (5) purity/sanctity (see Figure 9.5). Harm/care originated from suffering, distress, and children's neediness, and is characterized today by empathy, caring, and kindness (virtues), as well as compassion (emotion). Fairness/reciprocity originated to curb cheating and is characterized today by egalitarianism, social justice, and trustworthiness (virtues), as well as gratitude (positive emotion) and guilt (negative emotion). In-group/loyalty originated from a threat or challenge to a group, characterized today by loyalty, patriotism, and self-sacrifice (virtues) as well as group pride and rage at traitors (emotions). Authority/respect originated from indicators of dominance or submission, and is characterized today by respect for one's elders, obedience, and deference (virtues), as well as fear (emotions). Finally, purity/sanctity originated from the need to avoid

Figure 9.5: Moral foundations theory (MFT) identifies five moral domains and principles involving systems of values, psychological mechanisms, and social norms that motivate attitudes and behavior.

waste products and pathogens, and is characterized today by temperance, chastity, piety, and cleanliness (virtues), as well as disgust (emotion).

While all five foundations (Harm and Care, Fairness and Reciprocity, In-group and Loyalty, Authority and Respect, and Purity and Sanctity) are rooted in anthropological and evolutionary accounts of morality, the first two are commonly construed as the *individualizing* foundations because they — in their ties to the human concern with caring and protecting vulnerable individuals from harm and for fairness, reciprocity, and justice — focus on the rights and welfare of individuals (i.e., the "ethic of autonomy"). The latter three foundations, tied to the "ethics of community and divinity," are, on the other hand, construed as the *binding* foundations because they emphasize in-group loyalty, obedience to authority, and shared rituals of purity and decency, as instruments of group-binding and group-strengthening. In short, the individualizing dimension is concerned with protecting individuals' rights and treating them fairly whereas the binding foundation is centered on preserving the group as a whole (Haidt and Graham, 2007). At the individual level, although most people are concerned about each of the five moral domains, they prioritize them differently (Haidt, 2013). For example, liberals tend to prioritize the so-called individuating moral foundations that focus on protecting others from harm (scoring highly on measures of harm/care) and upholding the rights of the self and others (scoring highly on fairness/reciprocity) (Graham *et al.*, 2011). In contrast, conservatives tend to prioritize the so-called binding moral foundations, prioritizing in-group/loyalty, authority/respect, and maintaining ideological and physical purity/sanctity (Graham *et al.*, 2011; Haidt and Graham, 2007).

From a customer–company relationship perspective, individual-orientation on moral foundations needs to be examined in terms of their levels of fit with organizational orientation on moral foundations. Baskentli *et al.* (2019) study how customers respond differently to companies based on each entity's orientation on moral foundations. They chose seven domains based on the Kinder, Lydenberg, and Domini (KLD) classification: (1) employee relations (e.g., safe and healthy working environment), (2) human rights (e.g., basic rights and freedoms of all human beings, (3) diversity (e.g., gender, age, sex, and ethnicity), (4) community issues (e.g., educational initiatives, volunteer programs, and charitable giving), (5) corporate governance (e.g., transparency and governance framework), (6) environment (e.g., use of recycled materials, and renewable energy), and (7) product (e.g., innovative, safe, and quality products). To explore such inter-domain differences in customer reactions to corporate social responsibility (CSR), these authors focus on the individual- vs. group-orientation of CSR domains, which pertain to whether a CSR domain is perceived as focusing on protecting and enhancing the welfare of individuals or groups. For instance, the domain of human rights addresses the welfare of each and every individual human being, and as such the domain of human rights is more likely to be perceived as higher on individual-orientation. In contrast, the domain of community focuses on strengthening and enhancing the welfare of groups (i.e., communities), and is thus likely to be perceived as higher on group-orientation. Baskentli *et al.* (2019) find that the congruence between customers' moral foundations and firm-level CSR domains elicits greater positive reactions to a company engaged in CSR. That is, customers with individualizing moral concerns react more positively to firm CSR domains perceived as more individual oriented; similarly, customers with binding moral concern react more positively with firm CSR domains perceived as more group-oriented.

Much of the extant literature on ethics and morality in marketing and customer–brand relationships is grounded on gaining insight on the morality of the individual and how the individual's view of morality influences the way the individual interacts in the marketplace. Morality has been studied with respect to moral values of an individual in the context of moral philosophy (Hunt and Vitell, 1986), moral virtues (Murphy, 1999), moral identity (Reed *et al.*, 2007), moral awareness and attentiveness (Reynolds, 2008), moral evaluations (Olson *et al.*, 2016), and moral emotions (McGraw *et al.*, 2012; Chan *et al.*, 2014). However, morality of organizations and entities is an under-studied area of research. Hoppner and Vadakkepatt (2019) present a conceptual framework delineating moral authority of entities (as opposed to individuals) in the marketplace and how corporate entities can take a public stand on controversial issues (as opposed to staying neutral) to effect positive changes, not just for the entity, but for society in general.

MORAL AUTHORITY IN THE MARKETPLACE

Historically, business entities have sought to remain silent on moral issues preferring to not risk alienating customers. However, times have changed and today, there is mounting pressure and expectations from stakeholders that business entities should be active participants in society, rather than just profit-maximizing entities. Firms that cave into this pressure do so at their own peril. Developed using a contingency approach (e.g., Ferrell and Gresham, 1985; Jones, 1991) Hoppner and Vadakkepatt (2019) advance a conceptual framework that explains how an entity will encounter moral situations that will require a decision to be made regarding whether to take a stance and that its decision and effects will be contingent upon a multitude of factors existing at multiple levels (i.e., entity-level factors, industry-level factors, and societal-level factors). The conceptual framework is given in Figure 9.6.

Taking a Stance

A sociopolitical stance refers to publicly adopting a position with respect to a social or political issue. Business entities must first decide *if* they are going to exert their moral authority to take a stance, when faced with a moral issue. Needless to say, the possession of

Figure 9.6: A Framework of Moral Authority in the Marketplace

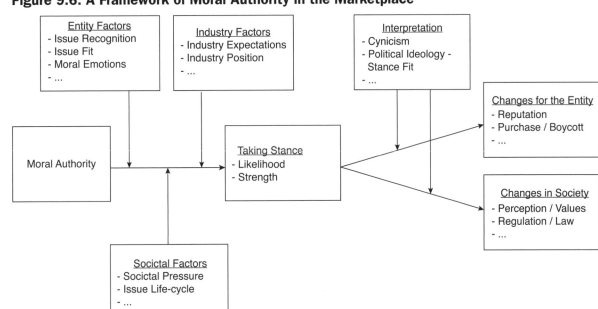

Adapted from Jessica J. Hoppner and Gautham Vadakkepatt (2019), Examining Moral Authority in the Marketplace: A conceptualization and Framework, *Journal of Business Research* 95: 417–427.

moral authority does not require an entity to use it. It is used only when the firm recognizes that something is morally wrong (i.e., when "what is" does not align with "what should be"), and is motivated to change the situation (i.e., to take a stance). The probability of publicly adopting a position refers to the likelihood of taking a stance. Taking a stance is an important decision because it indicates that the entity has formally entered into the conversation regarding the sociopolitical issue. Once an entity decides to take a stance, they must then decide *how* they are going to take a stand. The strength of stance refers to the degree of commitment toward the stance ranging from a weak stance (e.g., condoning or condemning) to a strong stance (e.g., investing resources).

Moderating Factors Influencing the Moral Authority and Taking a Stance Relationship

As noted earlier, the likelihood that a business entity exercises its moral authority to take a stance and the strength of its stance is contingent on three categories of factors: (1) entity-level factors, (2) industry-level factors, and (3) societal-level factors. We now elaborate on each of these three categories of factors and develop propositions related to representative constructs within each category.

Entity-Level Factors: Entity-level factors refer to the characteristics of an entity that are at least partially under its control and can influence entity behavior. The three entity-level factors focused on here are issue recognition, issue fit, and moral emotions. *First*, in order to behave morally, an individual must first be aware that a situation can be viewed through a moral lens (Rest, 1986). Moral awareness refers to this ability to determine that a situation contains moral content and could/should be considered from a moral viewpoint. When moral awareness is lacking, it is unlikely that a situation will be viewed as a moral problem. Issue recognition is defined as an entity's

ability to determine an issue or situation as causing moral harm to others and ascribing importance to these issues. If an entity (i.e., firm) has greater issue recognition, the firm will have greater motivation to exert their moral authority to take a stance in efforts to address a situation they view as a moral problem. *Second*, sociopolitical issues vary in their relevance and importance to firms and its stakeholders. Against this backdrop, issue fit refers to the perceived link between the entity's image, positioning, and target market and the issue's image and stakeholders it impacts. The extent of the fit between an entity and an issue will influence whether moral authority is exerted to take a stance, where the greater the fit, the greater the positive impact of moral authority on likelihood to take a stance. If there is a high fit, a stance is more likely to be viewed as authentic, morally grounded, and therefore well received by its stakeholders. *Third*, moral emotions (Haidt, 2003) refer to emotions that are felt by an individual in response to a moral violation and include, among other emotions, moral distress, moral disgust, and moral outrage. Moral emotions are not driven by self-interest; rather, linked to the interest or welfare either of society as a whole or in part. Stronger the moral emotions elicited by a situation, the greater the likelihood that a firm will exercise its moral authority to take a stance attempting to alleviate or, at least, minimize the harm caused by the situation.

Industry-Level Factors: Hoppner and Vadakkepatt (2019) discuss industry-level factors, which refer to the characteristics or events occurring in the industry that can influence the behavior of the entity and other members of the industry. The two industry-level factors they focus on are industry expectations and industry position. Regarding industry expectations, industries vary in the saliency of moral issues. Accordingly, industries have varying expectations to remedy the problems in the marketplace, generated by the consumption of its products and otherwise.

High-expectation industries are where moral issues are more salient and/or of greater concern and more likely to engage in sociopolitical stances, whereas low-expectation industries are where moral issues are seemingly less of a concern and/or less salient and firms are less likely to take a stance. Industry position is another factor. Firms within an industry can choose to position themselves as a leader or a follower with regard to moral issues and events. A leader position refers to when an entity is one of the first to take a stance on an issue on its own accord, whereas a follower position, on the other hand, refers to a situation when a firm is a late adopter of a sociopolitical stance and is typically taking a stance in response to demands from its stakeholders and/or to follow the lead of another entity in the marketplace. Being a leader, while it accrues first-mover advantage, also carries risk.

Societal-Level Factors: Societal-level factors refer to the macroeconomic events occurring in society that are outside the control of the firm or the industry but can influence behavior in the marketplace. The two societal-level factors focused on here are social pressure and issue life cycle. Regarding social pressure, a firm can take a stance when confronted with social pressure, i.e., pressure or attention for an issue brought onto by stakeholders in society. This pressure can be short-term (e.g., viral social media campaigns) or more long-term (e.g., grassroots efforts). Given that firms are dependent on different stakeholders for resources needed for its existence, threat of withholding these resources is an effective method that stakeholders can use to get them to exercise their moral authority to take a stance. Moreover, social pressure can also have implications for the strength of the stance taken. As social pressure mounts, firms exercising their moral authority are more apt to take stronger stances as uncertainty is removed regarding the stakeholders' viewpoint on the issue and an unequivocal stance will be needed to placate stakeholders. Regarding

issue lifecycle, it can be argued that sociopolitical issues and movements also have lifecycles, similar to products. Specifically, issue life cycle reflects the acceptance of social movement in a society, whereas industry position reflects the relative position of the business entity within an industry with regard to a sociopolitical issue. For example, a sociopolitical issue might be in the late stages of the issue life cycle (e.g., equal pay for women), but a firm is taking a leader position on that sociopolitical issue within an industry (e.g., Starbucks).

Impact of Taking a Stance: Firms are often motivated to take a stance on sociopolitical issues to effect change reflective of their definition of morality. Regardless of intent, taking a stance can result in either positive and/or negative changes for the entity and in society. *First*, the effect of firms taking a stance can be either positive or negative. Findings from the CSR literature suggest that sociopolitical stances can positively impact financial performance due to increased access to resources from supported stakeholders (e.g., Waddock and Graves, 1997), easier time recruiting employees (e.g., Turban and Greening, 1997) and attracting socially conscious customers (e.g., Hillman and Keim, 2001). Equally important, taking a stance could act as a proxy for advertising, increasing overall demand for the firm's products, increased customer–company identification and trust (Bhattacharya and Sen, 2003; Lichtenstein *et al.*, 2004). However, there may be a negative impact as well. It has long been perceived that it is better for firms to not engage in sociopolitical issues as for each group that supports a stance, there is another group that opposes it (McDonnell, 2016). With a divided marketplace, it is almost guaranteed that by taking a stance, some stakeholders will be antagonized, potentially leading to detrimental financial and non-financial effects. *Second*, arguably, the intent behind taking a stance is to effect changes in society via the values and perceptions held or the laws and regulations enforced. When firms take stances, it can help to legitimize the issue and add momentum to the associated movements. Beyond legitimizing an issue, the stances of firms may encourage legislators in government to pass or retract laws in line with the sociopolitical issues being supported.

Moderating Factors Influencing the Impact of Taking a Stance

First, cynicism defined as an attitude characterized by feelings of disillusionment and distrust of other people, groups, and/or institutions (Detert *et al.*, 2008) have been linked to negative outcomes (e.g., Skarmeas and Leonidou, 2013). Cynics frequently question the motives of others. Cynics are more likely to question the authenticity and/or credibility of firms taking a stance, and particularly their motives — whether the motive was to truly drive change or was to acquire self-serving benefits (i.e., increased profits or greater entity visibility). *Second,* the fit between political ideology and stance is important. Political ideology can be defined as a set of ideas, beliefs, and principles reflecting an individual's view on policies and how society should be governed (Ball and Dagger, 2006). Prior research has shown that conservatives have a strong tendency for status quo in both the personal and sociopolitical domains, cherish individualism, and are more resistant to change in comparison to liberals (Jost *et al.*, 2003). Some scholars have even extended this generalization to argue that conservatives are more motivated by loss prevention while liberals are more motivated by a gains framework (Janoff-Bulman, 2009). These differences in sociopolitical viewpoints have significant implications for how political ideology moderates the relationship between a stance and its consequences. Specifically, it suggests that the impact of a business entity's sociopolitical stance is moderated by the fit of the stance with the political ideology of the stakeholders.

DIGITAL MARKETING AND PRIVACY: AN ETHICAL PERSPECTIVE

The growth of big data and the corresponding privacy issues associated are hallmarks of the 21st century. Marketers risk being on the wrong side of [ethical] history with their unreflective approach to the exploitation of consumers' information. Recent marketing ethics scholarship has examined controversial tactics such as online behavioral targeting. This strategy "has the technological potential to violate consumers' privacy rights to an unprecedented degree . . . and is often nontransparent and deceptive" (Nill and Aalberts, 2014, p. 126). In a review article on the current state of privacy scholarship in marketing and related disciplines, Martin and Murphy (2017) propose transcending narrow disciplinary perspectives toward a more multi-dimensional approach to studying privacy. In the future, we see the need for companies like *Facebook* and *Google* to go beyond the narrow utilitarian calculus of monetizing consumer data to one highlighting greater transparency. Scholars should draw on normative or behavioral decision theories to understand more fully the notion of "informed consumer choice" and reasonable expectations for corporate use of personal information. Marketers seem to have done little investigation into the question of to what extent consumers have the ethical right to control the use of their personal information by sellers.

Although previous research has acknowledged the existence of multiple stakeholders, technology has brought about new types of relationships that exist between things, i.e., the Internet of Things and between customers and digital devices (electronic commerce, e.g., Amazon; mobile commerce, e.g., mobile apps, QR codes; social commerce, e.g., Instagram, Pinterest, and Facebook). Innovations in technology such as artificial intelligent agents,

Google Glass, big data are increasingly facilitating the development of advanced insights into every aspect of the customer journey. For example, about two-thirds of today's new cars have sensors and communications systems that send and receive data, offering potential for carmakers to find out more about how drivers use their vehicles. Digital and social media revolution has strengthened the importance of customer engagement behavior wherein customers participate beyond purchase in firms' offerings or activities, thus generating a wealth of data (Van Doorn *et al.*, 2010). Mobile marketing through location-based services such as GPS including geo-fencing and geo-conquesting allow marketers to target promotions to customers as they enter a proximal radius of the marketer's brick-and-mortar location and close competitor's location, respectively (Fong et al., 2015). Such data collection system raises serious ethical concerns about privacy, security, ownership, control, trust, fraud, misrepresentation, and the extent to which primary relationships can and should be capitalized upon (Malhotra *et al.*, 2004).

Martin and Murphy (2017) discuss several ethical frameworks that shed light on privacy over and above legal frameworks such as the Notice and Choice model composed of fair information practice principles (FIPP) and Harms-Based Model adopted by the Federal Trade Commission (FTC). The key questions boil down to: (1) should a company be allowed to acquire and store information about individuals without their knowledge or consent, and (2) should a company be allowed to disclose information about individuals to other parties without their knowledge or consent? For instance, social contract theory accounts for exchange purpose, risks, and potential harm and FIPP incorporates the tenets of social contract theory and firms are fulfilling their obligations of notice and choice. However, missing are dimensions of information sharing and security and how consumers perceive fairness. Marketers need to look at distributive

and procedural justice from the customers' perspective. Distributive justice in the form of customer outcomes as a result of risking privacy include customized offering, personalization value, streamlined customer–firm interactions, access to free services, and financial compensation. While customers value these outcomes and are willing to provide their information, they also experience feelings of vulnerability in relinquishing personal information (Awad and Krishnan, 2006). On procedural justice, customers desire privacy policies that are less complex and straightforward in helping them understand how their information is captured, used, protected, and shared.

As long as companies compete in markets where privacy protections can be differentiated and are valued by customers, privacy as a strategy toward firms' competitive advantage is a viable option (Martin and Murphy, 2017). Firms need to provide baseline protection to avoid complete erosion of privacy-based customer utility; beyond which, firms can target different segments with varying preferences for privacy under conditions of market heterogeneity. Strong privacy management provides customers with positive brand experience, greater loyalty, and stronger customer–brand relationships; all this toward greater firm competitive advantage. Martin and Murphy (2017) offer the following tenets as *best practices for privacy as strategy*:

1. Firms that prioritize data privacy in an authentic way will experience positive performance, including favorable market response, customer loyalty, and engagement benefits;

2. Firms that involve their customers in the information privacy dialogue will experience positive performance;

3. Firms that implement privacy promoting practices will experience positive performance under the condition that they align data privacy practices across all aspects of the firm;

4. Firms that focus on what they do right with respect to data privacy will experience positive performance;

5. Firms that commit to data privacy practices over the long-term will experience positive performance; and

6. Firms that embody these privacy practices as strategy tenets will experience heightened customer trust.

KEY TAKEAWAYS

- According to the H-V model, an individual's ethical judgment is a function of deontological and teleological evaluations, representing an evaluation of the sum of the total goodness vs. badness likely to be provided by each alternative for all relevant stakeholders. The revised model is argued to be a general theory of ethical decision-making, not just of marketing ethics, incorporating multiple ethics' perspectives including descriptive, positive, and normative ethics.

- Ethical marketing refers to the practices that emphasize transparent, trustworthy, and responsible personal and/or organizational marketing policies and actions that exhibit integrity, as well as fairness to customers and other stakeholders (see Figure 9.7).

- Consequences-based ethical theories state that a marketing decision is ethical or unethical based exclusively on its outcome. Deontology or duty-based ethics states that intentions and motivations, not consequences, are what should drive ethical decision-making.

- Normative tenets for ethical and socially responsible marketing include putting people first; exceeding legal requirements; considering intent, means, and ends; inspiring moral imagination; embracing core values; accepting the stakeholder concept; and embracing a process of moral reasoning.

Figure 9.7: Ethical marketing refers to the practices that emphasize all of these qualities.

RELIABILITY   INTEGRITY   TRANSPARENCY

HONESTY   CORE VALUES   COMMITMENT

SOCIAL RESPONSIBILITY   TRUST   CONNECTION

- Contract-based morality is based on the principles of liberty and justice. A business-centric theory of integrative social contract emphasizes two principles: (1) moral free space for developing rules and (2) hyper-norms with universal rules.

- Virtue-based ethics focuses on the character traits of the decision-maker as opposed to the decision-making process. Several virtues are central to building good customer–company relationships including integrity, trustworthiness, fairness, respect, and empathy.

- In general, three aspects of justice theories can be applied to customer–company relationships: distributive justice (i.e., perceived fairness of the outcome), procedural justice (fairness and the quality of the decision-making process), and interactional justice (quality of treatment people received including information disclosure and explanations received).

- During customer–employee interactions, customers form firm-specific trust based on perceptions of distributive justice, procedural justice, and interactional justice (social exchange model).

- During customer–employee interactions, customers form customer–company identification based on perceptions of procedural justice (i.e., neutrality and unbiased decision-making), interactional justice (i.e., social standing including pride and respect), and firm-specific trust (group-value model).

- During customer–employee interactions, customers form firm-specific trust based on whether or not they are able to exercise voice to mitigate biases in decision-making and present their needs to be heard. Such motivation is guided by self-interest toward outcome favorability (instrumental model).

- During customer–employee interactions, when customers do not have information on firm trustworthiness, their reactions to outcomes are impacted by procedural justice. Further, when outcome judgments are difficult to assess with confidence, customers use procedural and interactional justice as proxies (heuristic model).

- Individualizing moral foundations emphasize pillars of harm/care and fairness/reciprocity whereas binding moral foundations emphasize in-group/loyalty, authority/respect, and purity/sanctity. These moral pillars have implications on how customers perceive firms' activities/strategies including product/service efficacy, market prominence, and CSR initiatives, among others.

- Firms are often motivated to take a stance on sociopolitical issues to effect change in society but also itself in a positive way. Accordingly, they are increasingly engaging in taking a stance toward social/political issues, which can be rewarding (e.g., proxy for advertising, increased identification, and trust leading to increased financial performance) but also risky (e.g., divided segments with opposing reactions leading to decreased financial performance). Customers see moral authority of firms and their willingness to take a stand based on several firm, industry, and societal factors.

- Given an explosion of data collection, data storage and usage, and data sharing at various customer touchpoints in the entire customers' journey (pre-purchase, purchase, and post-purchase), understanding ethical foundations and frameworks from the customers' perspective (not just legal which sets a minimum threshold) is critical.

- Marketers should examine information privacy from multiple ethical viewpoints and adopt the best practices to leverage privacy as a strategy. Best practices can include prioritizing of privacy, involving customers in dialogs, implementing "good" and "right" privacy promoting practices, committing to long-term privacy practice, and embodying privacy as part of firm strategy.

EXERCISES

Questions

1. Explain the concept of positive ethics in marketing. The Hunt-Vitell (H-V) theory of marketing ethics is based on positive ethics wherein an individual makes an ethical judgment based on deontological and teleological evaluation. Discuss the concept of deontological and teleological evaluation and how ethical judgments are formed. Do ethical judgments always predict intention and behavior in a consistent way? Why or why not?

2. Explain the concept of normative ethics in marketing. Discuss the four types of normative ethical theories: (a) consequence-based ethics; (b) duty-based ethics; (c) contract-based morality; and (d) virtue-based ethics.

3. Virtue ethics (integrity, trust, fairness, respect, and empathy) is central to marketing at various customer touchpoints. Explain how virtue ethics is related to the fundamental axioms of relationship marketing. How do virtue ethics change across different stages of the relationship lifecycle?

4. Explain the concept of (a) distributive justice; (b) procedural justice; and (c) interactional justice. How can marketers apply justice-based theories toward customers at transactional and relational exchange levels?

5. Discuss the following models of justice relevant for customers' relationships with companies: (a) social exchange model of justice; (b) group-value model of justice; (c) instrumental model of justice; and (d) heuristic model of justice. Which model of justice is more relevant at the customer–frontline employee interface and under what conditions?

6. Explain the five moral domains in the moral foundations theory: (a) harm and care; (b) fairness and reciprocity; (c) in-group and loyalty; (d) authority and respect; and (e) purity and sanctity. Discuss how customers' tendencies toward individualizing moral foundation (i.e., ethic of autonomy) and binding moral foundation (i.e., ethics of community and divinity) affect their perceptions of companies individualistic versus collectivistic identities.

7. Discuss whether firms should exercise their moral authority over controversial moral and political issues in society. What factors should firms consider seriously before deciding to take a stance? Does taking a stance always help the firm or society in general? When can it backfire and negatively affect customer–company relationship?

8. With digital and social media revolution, customers' information privacy has never been more at stake than now. The fundamental questions are: (a) should a firm be allowed to acquire and store information about customers without their knowledge or consent? and (b) should a firm be allowed to disclose information about customers to other parties without their knowledge or consent? Discuss these questions using the lens of normative ethical theories.

9. In markets where privacy protection is differentiated and is valued by customers, can companies use privacy as a "strategic tool" for competitive advantage? Discuss the pros and cons. What are the best practices for privacy as strategy?

Group Discussion

1. In 2015, the United States Environmental Protection Agency (EPA) issued a notice of violation of the Clean Air Act to German automaker, Volkswagen (VW) when it was found that the company intentionally programmed its diesel engines to activate their emissions controls only during lab emissions testing. As a result, VW passed the lab tests but emitted up to 40 times more nitrogen oxide. Regulators in multiple countries began to

investigate VW and its stock price fell in value by a third in the days immediately after the news. VW spent 16.2 billion euros in rectifying the issue.

As a small group, using the H-V model of marketing ethics, discuss the ethical steps in the decision process leading up to the judgment and the ensuing crisis. Given customers are an important stakeholder group and the very high probability of negative consequences, why do you think there was disconnect between ethical judgment and intention/behavior? Would the application of normative theories (e.g., virtue-based ethics) by VW executives have made any difference at all? How can VW regain its public trust?

2. In the current society that we live, it is a challenge to sustain a business with conservative values. This can be very limiting especially when the company attempts to accommodate all stakeholders. This is what happened to Chick-Fil-A when (in 2012) Dan Cathy, president and CEO, expressed his opinion on gay issues publicly emphasizing family values and biblical values. As a company, they pride themselves in community service (Chick-Fil-A created a Foundation) and uphold a very high standard of honor, dignity, and respect for every person. Cathy's strong dedication to his family and biblical values caused controversy although he knew it was not a popular stance to take with all stakeholders. This resulted in a battle between the left and the right, two groups in the United States that have never been more polarized.

As a small group, discuss Chick-Fil-A's taking a public stance from the following ethical theories: (a) consequence-based ethics, (b) duty-based ethics, (c) contract-based ethics, and (d) virtue-based ethics. Some might argue that it is better not to take a stance, especially with a polarized customer base as customer–company relationships (and profitability) are at stake. What is your position and why?

HBS and Ivey Cases

- AnswerDash (9-516-106)

- Reinventing Best Buy (9-716-455)

- Chase Sapphire (9-518-024)

- Laurs & Bridz (9B18A004)

CASE QUESTIONS

AnswerDash

1. Which of the four types of normative ethical theories should AnswerDash adopt: (a) consequence-based ethics; (b) duty-based ethics; (c) contract-based morality; and (d) virtue-based ethics? Why?

2. Show how virtue ethics (integrity, trust, fairness, respect, and empathy) is central to AnswerDash's marketing at various customer touchpoints.

3. How can AnswerDash apply justice-based theories (distributive justice; procedural justice; and interactional justice) toward customers at transactional and relational exchange levels?

4. Discuss how customers' tendencies toward individualizing moral foundation (i.e., ethic of autonomy) and binding moral foundation (i.e., ethics of community and divinity) affect their perceptions of AnswerDash's individualistic versus collectivistic identities?

5. Discuss whether AnswerDash should exercise its moral authority over controversial moral and political issues in society? What factors should it consider seriously before deciding to take a stance? What risks are involved in taking a stance?

6. In markets where privacy protection is differentiated and is valued by customers, can AnswerDash use privacy as a "strategic tool" for competitive advantage? Discuss the pros and cons.

Reinventing Best Buy

1. How would you apply the Hunt-Vitell (H-V) theory of marketing ethics to explain customers' evaluations of Best Buy's ethical judgment?

2. Which of the four types of normative ethical theories should Best Buy adopt: (a) consequence-based ethics; (b) duty-based ethics; (c) contract-based morality; and (d) virtue-based ethics? Why?

3. Show how virtue ethics (integrity, trust, fairness, respect, and empathy) is central to Best Buy's marketing at various customer touchpoints.

4. How can Best Buy apply justice-based theories (distributive justice, procedural justice, and interactional justice) toward customers at transactional and relational exchange levels?

5. Which model of justice (social exchange model of justice, group-value model of justice, instrumental model of justice, or heuristic model of justice) is more relevant for Best Buy at the customer–frontline employee interface and under what conditions?

6. Discuss how customers' tendencies toward individualizing moral foundation (i.e., ethic of autonomy) and binding moral foundation (i.e., ethics of community and divinity) affect their perceptions of Best Buy's individualistic versus collectivistic identities?

7. Discuss whether Best Buy should exercise its moral authority over controversial moral and political issues in society? What factors should it consider seriously before deciding to take a stance? What risks are involved in taking a stance?

8. Discuss if Best Buy were to take a public stance against abortion based on the following ethical theories: (a) consequence-based ethics, (b) duty-based ethics, (c) contract-based ethics, and (d) virtue-based ethics? Some might argue that it

is better not to take a stance, especially with a polarized customer base as customer–company relationships (and profitability) are at stake. What is your position and why?

Chase Sapphire

1. Show how virtue ethics (integrity, trust, fairness, respect, and empathy) is central to JPMorgan's marketing at various customer touchpoints.

2. How can JPMorgan apply justice-based theories (distributive justice; procedural justice; and interactional justice) toward customers at transactional and relational exchange levels?

3. Which model of justice (social exchange model of justice, group-value model of justice, instrumental model of justice, or heuristic model of justice) is more relevant for JPMorgan at the customer–frontline employee interface and under what conditions?

4. Discuss how customers' tendencies toward individualizing moral foundation (i.e., ethic of autonomy) and binding moral foundation (i.e., ethics of community and divinity) affect their perceptions of JPMorgan's individualistic versus collectivistic identities?

5. Discuss whether JPMorgan should exercise its moral authority over controversial moral and political issues in society? What factors should it consider seriously before deciding to take a stance? What risks are involved in taking a stance?

6. How should JPMorgan address customers' information privacy issues? What privacy issues are important? Discuss these questions using the lens of normative ethical theories?

7. In markets where privacy protection is differentiated and is valued by customers, can JPMorgan use privacy as a "strategic tool" for competitive advantage? Discuss the pros and cons.

Laurs & Bridz

1. Which of the four types of normative ethical theories should Laurs & Bridz adopt: (a) consequence-based ethics; (b) duty-based ethics; (c) contract-based morality; and (d) virtue-based ethics? Why?

2. Show how virtue ethics (integrity, trust, fairness, respect, and empathy) is central to Laurs & Bridz's marketing at various customer touchpoints.

3. How can Laurs & Bridz apply justice-based theories (distributive justice, procedural justice, and interactional justice) toward customers at transactional and relational exchange levels?

4. Which model of justice (social exchange model of justice, group-value model of justice, instrumental model of justice, or heuristic model of justice) is more relevant for Laurs & Bridz at the customer–frontline employee interface and under what conditions?

5. Discuss how customers' tendencies toward individualizing moral foundation (i.e., ethic of autonomy) and binding moral foundation (i.e., ethics of community and divinity) affect their perceptions of Laurs & Bridz's individualistic versus collectivistic identities?

6. Discuss whether Laurs & Bridz should exercise its moral authority over controversial moral and political issues in society. What factors should it consider seriously before deciding to take a stance? What risks are involved in taking a stance?

7. How should Laurs & Bridz address customers' information privacy issues? What privacy issues are important? Discuss these questions using the lens of normative ethical theories.

REFERENCES

Adams, J.S. (1965), Inequity in Social Exchange, in L. Berkowitz (Ed.), *Advances in Experimental Social Psychology* (vol. 2, pp. 267–299). New York, NY: Academic Press.

Ahearne, M., C.B. Bhattacharya, and T. Gruen (2005), Antecedents and Consequences of Customer-Company Identification: Expanding the Role of Relationship Marketing, *Journal of Applied Psychology* 90(May): 574–585.

Ambrose, M.L., R.L. Hess, and S. Ganesan (2007), The Relationship between Justice and Attitudes: An Examination of Justice Effects on Event and System-Related Attitudes, *Organizational Behavior and Human Decision Processes* 103: 21–36.

Aristotle (1962), *Nicomachean Ethics*. New York, NY: Macmillan.

Arnett, D.B., S.D. German, and S.D. Hunt (2003), The Identity Salience Model of Relationship Marketing Success: The Case of Nonprofit Marketing, *Journal of Marketing* 67: 89–105.

Aryee, S., P.S. Budhwar, and Z.X. Chen (2002), Trust as a Mediator of the Relationship between Organizational Justice and Work Outcomes: Test of a Social Exchange Model, *Journal of Organizational Behavior* 23: 267–285.

Atuahene-Gima, K. and H. Li (2002), When Does Trust Matter? Antecedents and Contingent Effects of Supervisee Trust on Performance in Selling New Products in China and the United States, *Journal of Marketing* 66(July): 61–81.

Awad, N.F. and M.S. Krishnan (2006), The Personalization Privacy Paradox: An Empirical Evaluation of Information Transparency and the Willingness to be Profiled Online for Personalization, *MIS Quarterly* 30: 13–28.

Bagozzi, R.P. (1974), Marketing as an Organized Behavioral System of Exchange, *Journal of the Academy of Marketing Science* 23(4): 272–277.

Ball, T. and R. Dagger (2005), *Political Ideologies and the Democratic Ideal*. New York, NY: Pearson Longman.

Baskentli, S., S. Sen, S. Du, and C.B. Bhattacharya (2019), Consumer Reactions to Corporate Social Responsibility: The Role of CSR Domains, *Journal of Business Research* 95: 502–513.

Bentham, J. (1984), *An Introduction to the Principles of Morals and Legislation*. New York, NY: Hafner Publishing.

Bergami, M. and R.P. Bagozzi (2000), Self-Categorization, Affective Commitment and Group Self-Esteem as Distinct Aspects of Social Identity in the Organization, *British Journal of Social Psychology* 39(December): 555–577.

Bergen, M., S. Dutta, and O.C. Walker Jr. (1992), Agency Relationships in Marketing: A Review of the Implications and Applications of Agency and Related Theories, *Journal of Marketing* 56(July): 1–24.

Bhattacharya, C.B. and S. Sen (2003), Consumer-Company Identification: A Framework for Understanding Consumers' Relationships with Companies, *Journal of Marketing* 67(2): 76–88.

Blader, S.L. and T.R. Tyler (2009), Testing and Extending the Group Engagement Model: Linkages between Social Identity, Procedural Justice, Economic Outcomes, and Extra-role Behavior, *Journal of Applied Psychology* 94(2): 445–464.

Blau, P.M. (1964), *Exchange and Power in Social Life*. New York, NY: John Wiley and Sons.

Bowie, N. (1999), *Business Ethics: A Kantian*. Perspective, Malden, MA: Blackwell.

Chan, C., L. Van Bowen, E.B. Andrade, and D. Ariely (2014), Moral Violations Reduce Oral Consumption, *Journal of Consumer Psychology* 24(3): 381–386.

Cohen-Charash, Y. and P.E. Spector (2001), The Role of Justice in Organizations: A Meta-Analysis, *Organizational Behavior and Human Decision Processes* 86: 278–321.

Colquitt, J.A., D.E. Conlon, M.J. Wesson, C.O. Porter, and K.Y. Ng (2001), Justice at the Millennium: A Meta-Analytic Review of 25 years of Organizational Justice Research, *Journal of Applied Psychology* 86: 425–445.

Colquitt, J.A. and J.B. Rodell (2011), Justice, Trust, and Trustworthiness: A Longitudinal Analysis Integrating Three Theoretical Perspectives, *Academy of Management Journal* 54(6): 1183–1206.

Cropanzano, R., Z.S. Byrne, D.R. Bobocel, and D.R. Rupp (2001), Moral Virtues, Fairness Heuristics, Social Entities, and Other Denizens of Organizational Justice, *Journal of Vocational Behavior* 58: 164–209.

Detert, J.R., L.K. Trevino, and V.L. Sweitzer (2008), Moral Disengagement in Ethical Decision Making: A Study of Antecedents and Outcomes, *Journal of Applied Psychology* 93(2): 374–391.

Donaldson, T. and T. Dunfee (1994), Towards a Unified Conception of Business Ethics: Integrative Social Contracts Theory, *Academy of Management Review* 19(April): 252–284.

Donaldson, T. and T. Dunfee (1999), *Ties that Bind: A Social Contracts Approach to Business Ethics*. Boston, MA: Harvard Business School Press.

Donaldson, T. and L.E. Preston (1995), The Stakeholder Theory of the Corporation: Concepts, Evidence, and Implications, *Academy of Management Review* 20(1): 65–91.

Dutton, J.E., J.M. Dukerich, and C.V. Harquail (1994), Organizational Images and Member Identification, *Administrative Science Quarterly* 39(June): 239–263.

Evan, W.M. and R.E. Freeman (1984), A Stakeholder Theory of the Modern Corporation: Kantian Capitalism, in T. Beauchamp and N. Bowie (Eds.), *Ethical Theory in Business* (pp. 75–93). Englewood Cliffs, NJ: Prentice-Hall.

Ferrell, O.C. and L.G. Gresham (1985), A Contingency Framework for Understanding Ethical Decision Making in Marketing, *Journal of Marketing* 49(3): 87–96.

Fong, N.M., Z. Fang, and X. Luo (2015), Geo-Conquesting: Competitive Locational Targeting of Mobile Promotions, *Journal of Marketing Research* 52: 726–735.

Freeman, R.E. (1999), Divergent Stakeholder Theory, *Academy of Management Review* 24: 233–236.

Garbarino, E. and M.S. Johnson (1999), The Different Roles of Satisfaction, Trust, and Commitment in Customer Relationships, *Journal of Marketing* 63(April): 70–87.

Graham, J., B.A. Nosek, J. Haidt, R. Iyer, S. Koleva, and P.H. Ditto (2011), Mapping the Moral Domain, *Journal of Personality and Social Psychology* 101(2): 366–385.

Haidt, J. (2003), The Moral Emotions, in R.J. Davidson, K.R. Scherer, and H.H. Goldsmith (Eds.), *Handbook of Affective Sciences* (pp. 852–870). Oxford: Oxford University Press.

Haidt, J. (2013), Moral Psychology for the Twenty-First Century, *Journal of Moral Education* 42(3): 281–297.

Haidt, J. and J. Graham (2007), When Morality Opposes Justice: Conservatives have Moral Intuitions that Liberals may not Recognize, *Social Justice Research* 20(1): 98–116.

Haidt, J. and C. Joseph (2004), Intuitive Ethics: How Innately Prepared Intuitions Generate Culturally Variable Virtues, *Daedalus* 133(4): 55–66.

Hillman, A. and G. Keim (2001), Shareholder Value, Stakeholder Management, and Social Issues: What's the Bottom Line? *Strategic Management Journal* 22(2): 125–139.

Hoppner, J.J. and G.G. Vadakkepatt (2019), Examining Moral Authority in the Marketplace: A Conceptualization and Framework, *Journal of Business Research* 95: 417–427.

Hunt, S.D. and S.J. Vitell (1986), A General Theory of Marketing Ethics, *Journal of Macromarketing* 6(Spring): 5–15.

Hunt, S. D. and S. J. Vitell (1993), The General Theory of Marketing Ethics: A Retrospective and Revision, in *Ethics in Marketing*, edited by N.C. Smith and J.A. Quelch (pp. 775–784), Homewood, IL: Richard D. Irwin.

Janoff-Bulman, R. (2009), To Provide or Protect: Motivational Bases of Political Liberalism and Conservatism, *Psychological Inquiry* 20(2–3): 120–128.

Jones, T.M. (1991), Ethical Decision Making by Individuals in Organizations: An Issue Contingent Model, *Academy of Management Review* 16(2): 366–395.

Jones, T.M. and A.C. Wicks (1999), Convergent Stakeholder Theory, *Academy of Management Review* 24(2): 206–221.

Jost, J.T., J. Glaser, A.W. Kruglanski, and F.J. Sulloway (2003), Political Conservatism as Motivated Social Contagion, *Psychological Bulletin* 129(3): 339–375.

Kant, I. (1981), *Grounding for the Metaphysics of Morals*. Indianapolis, IN: Hackett.

Konovsky, M.A. (2000), Understanding Procedural Justice and its Impact on Business Organizations, *Journal of Management* 26(3): 489–511.

Laczniak, G.R. (1983), Frameworks for Analyzing Marketing Ethics, *Journal of Macromarketing* 3(1): 7–18.

Laczniak, G.R. and P.E. Murphy (2006), Normative Perspectives for Ethical and Socially Responsible Marketing, *Journal of Macromarketing* 26(2): 154–177.

Laczniak, G.R. and P.E. Murphy (2008), Distributive Justice: Pressing Questions, Emerging Directions and the Promise of a Rawlsian Analysis, *Journal of Macromarketing* 18(March): 511.

Laczniak, G.R. and P.E. Murphy (2011), Ethical Marketing and Marketing Strategy, in R.A. Peterson and R.A. Kerin (Eds.), *Marketing Strategy* (pp. 72–83, vol. 1), Wiley International Encyclopedia of Marketing, West Sussex, UK: John Wiley.

Laczniak, G.R. and P.E. Murphy (2019), The Role of Normative Marketing Ethics, *Journal of Business Research* 95: 401–407.

Leventhal, G.S. (1980), What Should be done with Equity Theory? New Approaches to the Study of Fairness in Social Relationships, in K. Gergen, M. Greenberg, and R. Willis (Eds.), *Social Exchange: Advances in Theory and Research* (pp. 27–55). New York, NY: Plenum Press.

Lichtenstein, D.R., M.E. Drumwright, and M.B. Bridgette (2004), The Effect of Corporate Social Responsibility on Customer Donations to Corporate-Supported Nonprofits, *Journal of Marketing* 68(4): 16–32.

Lind, A.E., L. Kray, and L. Thompson (2001), Primacy Effects in Justice Judgments: Testing Predictions from Fairness Heuristic Theory, *Organizational Behavior and Human Decision Processes* 85(2): 189–210.

Lind, A.E. and T.R. Tyler (1988), *The Social Psychology of Procedural Justice*. New York, NY: Plenum.

MacIntyre, A. (1984), *After Virtue*. (2nd ed.). Notre Dame, IN: U. of Notre Dame Press.

Malhotra, N.K., S.S. Kim, and J. Agarwal (2004), Internet Users' Information Privacy Concerns: The Construct, the Scale, and a Causal Model, *Information Systems Research* 15: 336–355.

Martin, K.D. and P.E. Murphy (2017), The Role of Data Privacy in Marketing, *Journal of the Academy of Marketing Science* 45(2): 135–155.

McDonnell, M. (2016), Radical Repertoires: The Incidence and Impact of corporate-Sponsored Social Activism, *Organization Science* 27(1): 53–71.

McGraw, A.P., J.A. Schwartz, and P.E. Tetlock (2012), From the Commercial to the Communal: Reframing Taboo Trade-offs in Religious and Pharmaceutical Marketing, *Journal of Consumer Research* 39(1): 157–173.

Mill, J.S. (1979), *Utilitarianism*. Indianapolis, IN: Hackett Publishing Company.

Moorman, R.H., and Z.S. Byrne (2005), How Does Organizational Justice Affect Organizational Citizenship Behavior?, in J. Greenberg and J.A. Colquitt (Eds.), *Handbook of Organizational Justice* (pp. 355–380). Mahwah, NJ: Lawrence Erlbaum Associates.

Morgan, R.M. and S.D. Hunt (1994), The Commitment-Trust Theory of Relationship Marketing, *Journal of Marketing* 58(3): 20–38.

Murphy, P.E. (1999), Character and Virtue Ethics in International Marketing: An Agenda for Managers, Educators, and Researchers, *Journal of Business Ethics* 18(1): 107–124.

Murphy, P.E., G.R. Laczniak, and F. Harris (2017), *Ethics in Marketing: International Cases and Perspectives*, 2nd edition, London: Routledge.

Murphy, P.E., G.R. Laczniak, and G. Wood (2007), An Ethical Basis for Relationship Marketing: A Virtue Ethics Perspective, *European Journal of Marketing* 41(1/2): 37–57.

Nill, A. and R.J. Aalberts (2014), Legal and Ethical Challenges of Online Behavioral Targeting in Advertising, *Journal of Current Issues and Research in Advertising* 35: 126–146.

Nill, A. and J.A. Schibrowsky (2007), Research on Marketing Ethics: A Systematic Review of the Literature, *Journal of Macromarketing* 27(3): 256–273.

Olson, J.G., B. McFerran, A.C. Morales, and D.W. Dahl (2016), Wealth and Welfare: Divergent Moral Reactions to Ethical Consumer Choices, *Journal of Consumer Research* 42(6): 879–896.

Palmatier, R.W. (2008), Interfirm Relational Drivers of Customer Value, *Journal of Marketing* 72(July): 76–89.

Palmatier, Robert W., Rajiv P. Dant, Dhruv Grewal, and Kenneth R. Evans (2006), Factors Influencing the Effectiveness of Relationship Marketing: A Meta-Analysis, *Journal of Marketing* 70: 136–153.

Rawls, J. (1971), *A Theory of Justice*. Cambridge, MA: Harvard University Press.

Reed, A. II, K. Aquino, and E. Levy (2007), Moral Identity and Judgments of Charitable Behaviors, *Journal of Marketing* 71(1): 178–193.

Rest, J.R. (1986), *Moral Development: Advances in Research and Theory*. New York, NY: Praeger.

Reynolds, S.J. (2008), Moral Attentiveness: Who Pays Attention to the Moral Aspects of Life? *Journal of Applied Psychology* 93(5): 1027–1041.

Ross, W.D. (1930), *The Right and the Good*. Oxford, UK: Clarendon Press.

Rupp, D.E., and R. Cropanzano (2002), The Mediating Effects of Social Exchange Relationships in Predicting Workplace Outcomes from Multi-foci Organizational Justice, *Organizational Behavior and Human Decision Processes* 89: 925–946.

Schlegelmilch, B.D. and M. Oberseder (2009), Half a Century of Marketing Ethics: Shifting Perspectives and Emerging Trends, *Journal of Business Ethics* 93(1): 1–19.

Schoorman, F.D., R.C. Mayer, and J.H. Davis (2007), An Integrative Model of Organizational Trust: Past, Present, and Future, *Academy of Management Review* 32(2): 344–354.

Shapiro, D.L. and J.M. Brett (2005), What is the Role of Control in Organizational Justice?, in J. Greenberg and J.A. Colquitt (Eds.), *Handbook of Organizational Justice* (pp. 155–177). Mahwah, NJ: Lawrence Erlbaum Associates.

Sirdeshmukh, D., J. Singh, and B. Sabol (2002), Consumer Trust, Value, and Loyalty in Relational

Exchanges, *Journal of Marketing* 66(January): 15–37.

Skarmeas, D. and C.N. Leonidou (2013), When Consumers Doubt, Watch Out! The Role of CSR Skepticism, *Journal of Business Research* 66(2): 1831–1838.

Smith, B.J. and D.W. Barclay (1997), The Effects of Organizational Differences and Trust on the Effectiveness of Selling Partnerships, *Journal of Marketing* 61(January): 3–21.

Thibaut, J. and L. Walker (1975), *Procedural Justice: A Psychological Analysis*. Hillsdale, NJ: Erlbaum.

Turban, D. and D. Greening (1997), Corporate Social Performance and Organizational Attractiveness to Prospective Employees, *Academy of Management Journal* 40(3): 658–672.

Tyler, T.R. (1989), The Psychology of Procedural Justice: A Test of the Group Value Model, *Journal of Personality and Social Psychology* 57(November): 830–838.

Tyler, T.R. (1994), Psychological Models of the Justice Motive: Antecedents of Distributive and Procedural Justice, *Journal of Personality and Social Psychology* 67(November): 850–863.

Tyler, T.R., and S.L. Blader (2003), The Group Engagement Model: Procedural Justice, Social Identity, and Cooperative Behavior, *Personality and Social Psychology Review* 7(4): 349–361.

Tyler, T.R., P. Degoey, and H. Smith (1996), Understanding Why the Justice of Group Procedures Matters: A Test of the Psychological Dynamics of the Group-Value Model, *Journal of Personality and Social Psychology* 70(May): 913–930.

Van den Bos, K. and E.A. Lind (2002), Uncertainty Management by Means of Fairness Judgments, in M.P. Zanna (Ed.), *Advances in Experimental Social Psychology* (pp. 1–60). San Diego, CA: Academic Press.

Van den Bos, K., R. Vermunt, and H.A.M. Wilke (1997), Procedural and Distributive Justice: What is Fair Depends More on What Comes First than on What Comes Next, *Journal of Personality and Social Psychology* 72(January): 95–104.

Van den Bos, K., H.A.M. Wilke, and E.A. Lind (1998), When do we Need Procedural Fairness? The Role of Trust in Authority, *Journal of Personality and Social Psychology* 75(6): 1449–1458.

Van Doorn, Jenny, Katherine N. Lemon, Vikas Mittal, Stephan Nass, Doreen Pick, Peter Pirner, and Peter C. Verhoef (2010), Customer Engagement Behavior: Theoretical Foundations and Research Directions, *Journal of Service Research* 13(3): 253–266.

Waddock, S.A. and S.B. Graves (1997), The Corporate Social Performance-Financial Performance Link, *Strategic Management Journal* 18(4): 303–319.

Williams, O.F. and P.E. Murphy (1990), The Ethics of Virtue: A Moral Theory for Marketing, *Journal of Macromarketing* 10(1): 19–29.

Customer Relationship Marketing: Digital Marketing and Social Media

OVERVIEW

In Chapter 10, we examine the intricate relationship between digital and social media marketing and customer–brand relationship. First, we discuss how digital technologies are changing marketing strategies by way of search engine advertising, mobile marketing, and the Internet of Things (IoT), followed by a framework of digital marketing that links the five 'C's: (1) customers, (2) collaborators, (3) competitors, (4) context, and the (5) company. The next part of this chapter relates to social media marketing and relationship marketing. We discuss social media marketing followed by two frameworks of social media: (1) contingency framework of social commerce and (2) the functional blocks framework. We then discuss and provide an assessment of the critical issues in the implementation of social media marketing. In particular, we discuss seven functions: (1) identity function, (2) conversation function, (3) sharing function, (4) presence function, (5) relationship function, (6) reputation function, and (7) group function. Finally, we summarize the seven steps to social media success for firms (Kumar and Mirchandani, 2012). At the end of the chapter, we provide key takeaways and conclude with discussion questions and HBS and Ivey cases. But first, to give a flavor of customer relationship marketing (CRM) in an age of digital technologies and social media, we provide some real-life vignettes.

OPENING VIGNETTES

Vignette 1: Google provides daily statistics of the number of impressions, number of clicks, click-through rate (CTR), conversion rate, cost-per-click (CPC), total cost, average position, and quality scores, among others. Among these metrics, position, CTR, and conversion rate exert the most impact on acquisition costs. As the search ad moves up to the top of the result page, the CTR is higher. As technology and online business models evolve, Google has been embedding prices of searched products directly in its organic search, which provides customers the option of bypassing websites with higher prices (see Figure 10.1). From the customers' perspective, do these options cut down customers' search time and the number of website visits? From the firms' perspective, should companies opt-in or not?

Figure 10.1: Google has been at the forefront of adopting digital technologies to facilitate customer relationship marketing.

Vignette 2: Digital technologies enable firms to wrap their core products and services with digital services. They allow versioning of products and services, especially information products, and provide opportunities for networked products as in Internet of Things (IoT). How do these technology wraps affect customer engagement and privacy concerns surrounding data capture by firms?

Vignette 3: Members of Apple Support Community can become top participants in an area of specialty on Leaderboards by helping their fellow community members. Apple allows engaged customers to learn more about Apple products and to share their knowledge with the community. Apple has provision for customers to post a new question and find answers, solve problems, and highlight helpful responses. Customers can earn points, levels, and rewards by exploring and participating in the Apple Support Community while having a fun experience. This helps active customers grow their reputation and also get rewarded in the community. Further, customers in their product or technology specialty can reach specialty status which other customers can know based on their showcased profile.

INTRODUCTION: DIGITAL MARKETING AND RELATIONSHIP MARKETING

The concept of digital marketing has undergone evolution over the years from what was described as marketing of products and services using digital channels to an all-encompassing term that describes the process of using digital technologies to acquire customers and build customer preferences, promote brands, retain brands, and increase sales. Digital marketing has been a hot topic among scholars and practitioners in the recent decade as the internet becomes an essential part of everyone's life. Kannan and Li (2017) define digital marketing as "An adaptive, technology-enabled process by which firms collaborate with customers and partners to jointly create, communicate, deliver, and sustain value for all stakeholders" (p. 23). In other words, digital marketing emphasizes the impact of information technology on the market environment, the practices of market research and marketing strategies, and the creation of values for the customers and the firm. Specifically, digital technologies reduce information asymmetries between customers and sellers in significant ways, providing more touchpoints for the interactions between different parties of stakeholders (Edelman, 2010).

In this section, we will review digital technologies that have changed, are changing, and will continue to change the practice of marketing strategies and how companies plan to develop strong relationships with their digital-networked customers. Specifically, we select search engine advertising, mobile marketing, and the Internet of Things (IoT) to discuss the impact of technologies on marketing. This selection represents the "mature" technology (i.e., search engine advertising), the "rising star" technology (i.e., mobile marketing), and the "future trends" technology (i.e., the Internet of Things), providing an extensive observation for the impact of technologies on marketing.

SEARCH ENGINE ADVERTISING

Search engine could be the most important way for users to find needed information on the Internet. Firms contact online users largely with the help of these search engines, and thus search engine could be the most important advertising channel in the digital age. Past studies have shown that being displayed in search engine results generates a better outcome for firms compared to other online and offline channels, such as emails and offline advertising (Chan *et al.*, 2011; Dinner *et al.*, 2014; Wiesel *et al.*, 2010).

Particularly, the display position in the search results is an important indicator of the effectiveness of the sponsored links. Agarwal *et al.* (2011) revealed that the position of the advertisement has significant impact on the click-through rate (CTR), and that the higher ranking in specific keyword searches also increases the turnover rate and revenue. Similar conclusions were drawn by Rutz *et al.* (2012) in an exploration of the antecedents of conversion rate. Specifically, they found that a higher position contributes more to the increase in the conversion rate than in clicks (65% versus 35%). Again, Narayanan and Kalyanam (2015) noted the importance of the position of the advertisement: the causal effect at top position as a proportion of the baseline CTR is 20.6%, in comparison to 10.7%, 16.7%, and 19.5% at third, sixth, and seventh positions, respectively.

However, the investment in search engine advertising could be tricky. The results for a given keyword search provided by search engines are composited by organic (natural) and sponsored (paid) results: the former is ranked in the order of the relevancy to the search query and the latter is allocated to advertisers through a competitive auction. While sponsored links seem to be an easy (costly) way to get displayed to users, it remains critical to improve the ranking in organic results. Katona and Sarvary (2009) showed that the top organic sites do not have many needs to bid for sponsored links. Coincidently, Berman and Katona (2013) suggested that high-quality sites have an advantage in the organic results and thus the main value of search engine optimization (SEO) is the tool to avoid the potentially hefty payments for sponsored links in their investigation of the budget allocation between improving the ranking of organic results and sponsored results. Also, Yang and Ghose (2010) concluded that the presence of organic listings is associated with a higher probability of click-throughs on paid ads, and vice versa. All these findings point to the fact that it is necessary to invest in improving the relevancy of the website to searched keywords to get a better display position in the organic results and/or spend the budget smartly to win auctions for certain keyword results. Desai *et al.* (2014) shed more light on the keyword selection by investigating whether to bid for the search for own site or the competitors' site. Applying game theory, they suggested bidding on competitors' site often leads to a prisoner's dilemma, which benefits the search engine but harms both the company and its competitor. Still, firms should buy their own brand name in response to potential threats from their competitors.

Search engine advertising, while effective, is merely a channel to communicate with consumers online (see Figure 10.2), and thus merely focusing on its outcome is insufficient. Xu *et al.* (2012) argued that online advertisements could indirectly increase the probabilities of subsequent clicks through other formats of advertisements, which in turn contribute to the final conversion. For example, display advertisements have a low direct effect on purchase conversions, but they indirectly stimulate subsequent visits through other online advertisement formats, such as search advertisements. In this sense, there is a need to assess the performance of these online ads in a multiple channel basis. Li and Kannan (2013) investigated the spillover effects across online marketing channels. They revealed that firm-initiated channels, such as emails and paid display advertisements, have strong spillover effects compared to customer-initiated channels such as search and direct visit. In addition, traditional marketing channels, such as TV advertising, also have an impact on the online searches, increasing the frequency and the specificity (Joo *et al.*, 2014, 2016). Liaukonyte *et al.* (2015) showed that a TV ad promotes a higher level of website visits and sales and that such an impact works best for an action-focus content.

Figure 10.2: Search engine advertising is an effective channel to communicate with consumers online.

MOBILE MARKETING

The quick adoption of the mobile phone and the smartphone has raised the attention of marketing scholars and practitioners. Lamberton and Stephen (2016) identified the use of mobile marketing as one of the emerging research topics on digital, social media, and mobile marketing field. Mobile devices have four important characteristics different from other channels: (1) location-specificity, (2) portability, (3) wireless, and (4) personal (Shankar *et al.*, 2010; Shankar and Balasubramanian, 2009). These characteristics make mobile marketing different from traditional mass marketing in three aspects: (1) its scope of audience is that users opt-in to receive communication; (2) its messages should be precise and short to fit in the visual space on the phone; and (3) it allows marketers to deliver location-sensitive messages and to measure and track responses at a relatively low cost (Shankar and Balasubramanian, 2009). Shankar *et al.* (2010) further suggested that mobile phone is not merely a gadget but also a cultural object as a part of everyday traditions and practices. They noted the use of mobile phone for communication, entertainment, information search, socializing, and conducting transactions as a "mobile lifestyle" (p. 112). As a result, mobile users are resisting mobile marketing communications based on an online survey of mobile phone users conducted by Watson *et al.* (2013).

However, the same survey also reported that consumers indicate a more positive attitude towards mobile marketing when they have more control through opt-in and opt-out options. In this sense, the need to opt-in has a critical role in the success of mobile marketing. Barwise and Strong (2002) examined permission-based mobile advertising (PBMA) and concluded that explicit permission is essential for the acceptance and customer satisfaction about marketing messages. Kumar *et al.* (2014) attempted to model the consumers' opt-in and opt-out behaviors. They identified two types of users that are less likely to opt-in for mobile marketing: "second nature surfers" and "voluminous variety" (p. 407). Specifically, "second nature surfers" are frequent mobile users and online shoppers. They have no children or just started a family and like music, job search, online auctions, and social networking. "Voluminous variety" is a group of people who are heavy online users, either child centric or pursuing personal hobbies such as news, sports, and travel. In addition, they suggested that over-marketing could lead to opt-outs from the communication. In this sense, marketers need to find an optimal amount of communication on mobile

devices. Krafft *et al.* (2017) analyzed factors that influence consumers' decision to grant permission to firms from their cost-benefit perspective. Specifically, they identified personal relevance, entertainment, incentive, lottery, and consumer information control as benefits and registration costs, intrusiveness, and privacy concerns as costs. The results in their study showed that personal relevance, entertainment, monetary incentives, consumers' information control, privacy concerns, and intrusiveness are the most significant reasons impacting customers' likelihood to grant permission for mobile marketing.

Privacy is one of the major concerns in the digital era (Agarwal and Karahanna, 2014). Specifically, privacy concerns are about the amount of individual-specific data possessed by others relative to the value of benefits received, whether the individual has control over personal information as manifested by the existence of voice or exit, and consumers' own awareness of organizational information privacy practices (Malhotra *et al.*, 2004). Bergström (2015) revealed that different people could have different concerns about different online activities. For example, age has a positive impact on concerns for misuse when searching for information while trust in other people has a negative impact. Internet use, trust in other people, and attitudes toward surveillance have negative impact on concerns when handling emails. When using debit cards, gender, internet use, experience of internet, political opinion could have an impact on privacy concerns. These privacy concerns, along with the type of information, impact consumers' trusting beliefs and risk beliefs, both of which in turn impact consumers' behavioral intentions (Malhotra *et al.*, 2004). Martin and Murphy (2017) summarized three factors that help to assure privacy concerns: trust, personalization, and control. Trust is the cornerstone for privacy concerns, and it has positive impacts on consumers' willingness to disclose, purchase, clickthrough, and advertising acceptance, along with numerous indirect impacts such as via consumer vulnerability. Personalization could help to overcome privacy concerns by increasing consumers' engagement, but it potentially raises more concerns on privacy when data collection is not explicitly granted. Lastly, providing controls to opt out is an effective approach to suppress a spectrum of data privacy vulnerabilities and to promote trust and reduce emotional violation.

INTERNET OF THINGS

If search engine represents a mature channel in the digital world, mobile marketing is in the growth period, and the Internet of Things (IoT) is just slowly getting through its introduction period. But its bright future has drawn a lot of attention of marketers and scholars. It is estimated that the combined market of IoT will grow to about \$520 billion in 2021[1] (Columbus, 2018). Beyond its greater potential in the market value, IoT will impact the information available to supply chain partners and the supply chain operations, because it provides more accurate and real-time visibility into the flow of materials and products. Moreover, service industries can benefit from the adoption of IoT through enhancing services (and revenues) and becoming leaders in the markets (Lee and Lee, 2015).

IoT is a new technology paradigm envisioned as a global network of machines and devices capable of interacting with each other (Lee and Lee, 2015, p. 431) (see Figure 10.3). Ng and Wakenshaw (2017) identified IoT as "a system of uniquely identifiable and connected constituents (termed as Internet-connected constituents) capable of virtual representation and virtual accessibility leading to an Internet-like structure for remote locating, sensing, and/or operating the constituents with real-time data/

information flows between them, thus resulting in the system as a whole being able to be augmented to achieve a greater variety of outcomes in a dynamic and agile manner" (p. 6). In plain language, IoT connects products, processes, and services (Saarikko *et al.*, 2017). Specifically, the characteristics of IoT can be conceptualized as the liquification and density of information resources, digital materiality, assemblage, and as the modules, transactions, and service in the service system. These characteristics imply two levels of capability sets of IoT. At a micro-level, IoT provides real-time data and information flow with its capability of virtual representation and accessibility for remote locating, sensing, and operating. At a macro-level, IoT and its applications (e.g., smart homes and cities) allow for a greater variety of outcomes to be achieved (Ng and Wakenshaw, 2017).

While the potential impact of IoT is significant, its business applications currently remain in an exploratory phase. Lee and Lee (2015) identified three categories of applications: monitoring and control, big data and business analytics, and information sharing and collaboration. Specifically, the monitoring and control systems with IoT collect various data about the production, allowing managers and automated controllers to track real-time performance anywhere and anytime. The smart home is a typical example for this application — it allows users to check the status of their home and set up schedules to make automatic adjustments. The big data and business analytics become possible with the numerous information made available by IoT. Analyzing such information helps to discover and resolve business issues, such as changes in consumer behavior and market conditions, to increase customer satisfaction, and to provide value-added services to customers. For example, the adoption of wearable gadgets allows health care providers to collect information about the

---

1   In an earlier forecast, Gartner (2015) merely estimated a market of 50 billion by the year 2020.

patient's everyday behavior and health status, creating opportunities for the provider to offer prevention services. The connectiveness of objects also allows information sharing and collaboration that occur between people, between people and things, and even between things. The information sharing and collaboration enhance situational awareness and avoid information delay and distortion in the supply chain management, and they also enable more interactions with customers using highly relevant information, increasing customer engagement, customer satisfaction, and higher revenue.

Ng and Wakenshaw (2017) argue that the era of digital connectivity is converting goods into fluid, which are dynamically reconfigurable, engaging service offerings that can incorporate customization for customers. In addition, they suggest that firms can achieve the scalability through standardization of the core components that exhibit low variety and simultaneously provide customers the personalization in the peripheral components with high variety, which could vary in cross-section and change over time. In other words, the product sold by firms is a vehicle not only fulfilling basic functions but also allowing customized functions that are attached to it. Similar thoughts were discussed by Saarikko *et al.* (2017): they concluded that complementing a product with services provides a clear and tangible means of highlighting the long-term value of a product over its competition. In addition, they emphasized the tremendous opportunity for value creation in the adoption of IoT. Specifically, IoT provides opportunities to support customers to fulfill their actual needs rather than assumed needs, and thus it serves as a solid base for long-term relationships.

Figure 10.3: Internet of Things (IoT) is a new technology paradigm envisioned as a global network of machines and devices capable of interacting with each other.

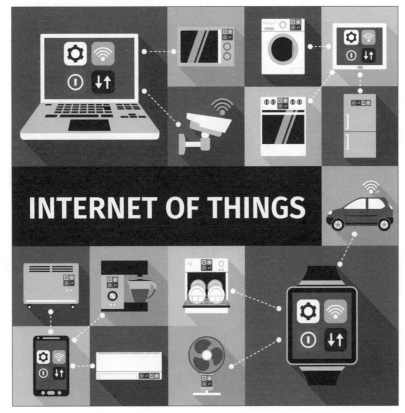

DIGITAL MARKETING: A FRAMEWORK

The American Marketing Association (AMA) definition of marketing can be adapted to digital marketing as "activities, institutions, and processes facilitated by digital technologies for creating, communicating, delivering, and exchanging value for customers and other stakeholders (see Figure 10.4)." As previously noted, Kannan and Li (2017) define digital marketing as "An adaptive, technology-enabled process by which firms collaborate with customers and partners to jointly create, communicate, deliver, and sustain value for all stakeholders." These authors propose a conceptual framework that delineates how digital technologies interact with the five 'C's: (1) customers, (2) collaborators, (3) competitors, (4) context, and (5) company as well as the interface among these elements. In particular, these authors discuss institutions and structures that emerge from these interactions — platforms and two-sided markets, search engines, social media, and user-generated content (UGC), emerging consumer behavior, and contextual interactions (Figure 10.5).

The decision journey, especially consideration and evaluation, for a customer in a digital environment is fairly compressed focusing on search engines, online reviews, and recommendations relative to offline journey. Consumer behavior spans across digital and traditional offline environments, and the effectiveness of each environment depends on several factors including perceived risk and utilitarian/hedonic product type. Then is the role of digital technologies in the facilitation of social media and user-generated content (UGC) (e.g., word-of-mouth (WOM), online reviews, ratings, and social media interactions). For instance, Toubia and Stephen (2013) demonstrate two motivations behind customers' contribution to social media: (1) intrinsic utility and (2) image utility. The emergence of

Figure 10.4: Digital marketing encompasses activities, institutions, and processes facilitated by digital technologies for creating, communicating, delivering, and exchanging value for customers as well as other stakeholders.

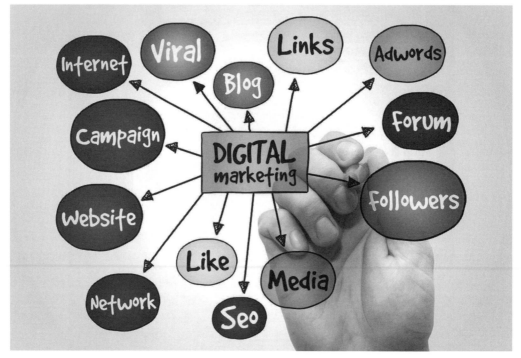

platforms — for customer-to-customer interactions, customer–seller interactions, and those that leverage two-sided markets — connects firms to its markets using digital technologies. These platforms are third-party entities that connect individual buyers with individual sellers (eBay), customers with many sellers (Amazon, Alibaba), firms, and the crowd (Kickstarter), etc. Firms also have to contend with search engines as both collaborators and platforms compete with other firms for customers. Digital technologies also interact with different contexts of geography, privacy, regulation, and piracy.

According to Kannan and Li (2017), digital technologies augment the core product with digital services (e.g., automobiles with GPS systems), help networking of products to release the dormant value inherent in the product (e.g., housing and automobiles dormant values released through rental markets such as Airbnb and Uber), and morph products into

digital services (e.g., software, music, video). Such personalization and customization enabled by digital technologies influence pricing strategies (dynamic pricing, freemium products), promotion strategies (Netflix recommendation system, location-based mobile promotion), and channel strategies (omni-channel and multi-channel).

Digital technologies create outcomes that enhance value for customers and for firms (Figure 10.5). Firms can leverage the interactions of digital technologies with the environment and with its own marketing research and marketing strategies. Value for customers as a result of digital technologies is created in the form of value equity, brand equity, relationship equity (Rust *et al.*, 2004), and customer satisfaction; value for each customer is created by acquisition, retention, and profitability, i.e., CLV concept and for the market in the form of customer equity; and firm value is created as a result of sales, profit, and growth rate.

Figure 10.5: A Framework of Digital Marketing

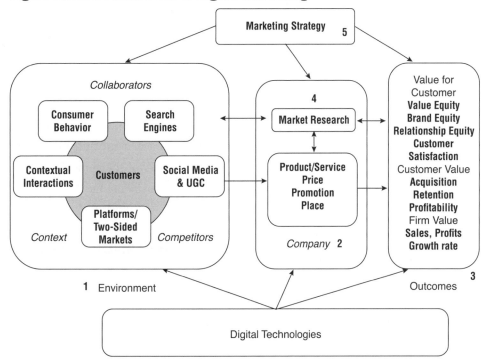

Adapted from P.K. Kannan and Hongshuang 'Alice' Li (2017), Digital Marketing: A Framework, Review, and Research Agenda, *International Journal of Research in Marketing*, 34: 22–45.

SOCIAL MEDIA MARKETING AND RELATIONSHIP MARKETING

Internet has become a part of our life. It is estimated that over 51% of the world population (approximately 3.8 billion people) uses the internet (International Telecommunication Union, 2018). Social media has become a daily channel for people to read and discuss things happening in their life, in the city, in the country, and even in the world. It was reported that nearly two-thirds of Americans used social networking sites in 2015. A more direct example of the usage of social media is Donald Trump, the US President, who posted 5139 tweets during his 2016 presidential campaign and 2568 tweets during the first year of his presidency. Due to such popularity, social media is the new and the most important channel for firms to conduct their marketing strategies and to achieve their marketing goals.

Interviewing and surveying experts of social media marketing, Felix *et al.* (2017) developed a holistic framework for strategic social media marketing with four central dimensions: (1) scope, (2) culture, (3) structure, and (4) governance. Particularly, they proposed that "social media marketing is an interdisciplinary and cross-functional concept that uses social media (often in combination with other communications channels) to achieve organizational goals by creating value for stakeholders. On a strategic level, social media marketing covers an organization's decisions about social media marketing scope (ranging from defenders to explorers), culture (ranging from conservatism to modernism), structure (ranging from hierarchies to networks), and governance (ranging from autocracy to anarchy)" (p. 123). They advocated that firms should focus on building a relationship with customers, employees, communities, and other stakeholders to take advantage of social media marketing.

However, developing a relationship with consumers on the social media platforms is not as simple as it sounds. Fournier and Avery (2011) described marketers on the social web as "the party crashers" because social media is not a new media channel for the communication about the marketers' brands but for people and their conversations. Conversely, users take advantage of these customer-empowering platforms to criticize companies and brands, which are inherently interesting, shareable, and that travel fast and far. This counter effect is a result of an equal, if not greater, say about the brand and its behaviors. Further, Fournier and Avery (2011) suggested that the era of social media marketing is the age of the social collective, the age of transparency, the age of criticism, and the age of parody. These new themes require strategies different from those in the traditional marketing channels, such as the shift of the goal from brand building to brand protection, the transition of the focus from strategic planning to executional excellence, and the adjustment of the emphasis from brand differentiation to brand resonance. In other words, born in the interactions among end users, social media features democratized communications taking away the power from those in marketing and public relations and giving it to individual customers and the community. This democratization in the communication requires managers to better understand what social media is and what it provides to individual users. Thus, the next section will cover a brief introduction of the definition and the history of social media, as well as things that users do on social media.

UNDERSTANDING SOCIAL MEDIA

When talking about social media, people often are referring to websites such as Facebook, Instagram, LinkedIn, Twitter, YouTube, and so on. These impressions about social media give us a hint of what the term "social media" refers to: it has something to do with the internet, it involves social interactions among people, and it exchanges information generated by the users. Formally, Kaplan and Haenlein (2010) defined social media as "a group of Internet-based applications that build on the ideological and technological foundations of Web 2.0, and that allow the creation and exchange of User Generated Content" (p. 61) (see Figure 10.6). Further, Kaplan and Haenlein (2010) explain that Web 2.0 represents a set of basic functionalities that enable people to interact with the website (e.g., Adobe Flash), and to publish (e.g., RSS) and retrieve data (e.g., AJAX) from the website, and that User Generated Content (UGC) are, as its literal meaning indicates, the various forms of media content that are publicly available and created by end users. More specifically, UGC has to (1) be published publicly to a selected group of people or everyone on social networking sites, (2) show a certain amount of creative effort, and (3) be created outside of professional routines or practice. In this sense, social media includes social network sites (e.g., Facebook, Twitter, LinkedIn,

etc.), which (a) promotes interpersonal contacts and encourages weak ties and user-generated content sites (e.g., Instagram, YouTube, Wikipedia, etc.); (b) supports creativity, foreground cultural activity and promotes the exchange of amateur or professional content, trading and marketing sites (e.g., eBays, Groupon, Craigslist, etc.); (c) aims at exchanging or selling products, and social network games (e.g., FarmVille, SimCity Social, Clash Royale, etc.); and (d) is distributed primarily through social networks and features multiplayer and asynchronous gameplay mechanics.

This is not (not even close to) an exhaustive list for the types of social media available, and it is meaningless to sharply delineate various types of social media platforms because the blurry boundaries among these categories and sites provide various functions to their users. For example, Facebook encourages users to post creative contents such as photos and posts and implement social games into its platform to enable its users to play together, making it not only a social

Figure 10.6: Social media are a group of Internet-based applications that allow the creation and exchange of User Generated Content.

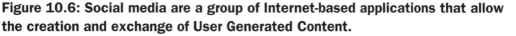

network site but also user-generated content site and a social network game platform. Fundamentally, these moves aim at carving out and appropriating one or more specific niches in the continuous battle to dominate a segment of online sociality, because social media were initially developed for the online interactions of a specific niche community (van Dijck, 2013). In other words, the need for connectedness bred these social media platforms and drove people to use these social media. Thus, the dynamic evolution in the social media world makes it hard to clearly classify the categories and types of websites and its provided services. In the next section, we provide two social media frameworks that help explain the mechanisms and underlying motivations: (1) contingency framework of social commerce by Yadav *et al.* (2013) and (2) honeycomb framework by Kietzmann *et al.* (2011).

SOCIAL COMMERCE: A CONTINGENCY FRAMEWORK

Yadav *et al.* (2013) define "social commerce as exchange-related activities that occur in, or are influenced by, an individual's social network in computer-mediated social environments, where the activities correspond to the need recognition, pre-purchase, purchase, and post-purchase stages of a focal exchange" (p. 312). Two important tenets of this definition are: (1) the scope of exchange-related activities includes both online/offline activities consumers engage in before, during, and after a transaction along with corresponding firms' initiatives to facilitate those activities and (2) social media occurs in a subset of computer-mediated environment, or computer-mediated social environment, which is a dynamic distributed network, potentially global in scope, and which has substantial social content. For instance, Facebook, Twitter, and Pinterest are global computer-mediated environments with social characteristics.

The motivations for firms' presence and initiatives in social commerce are to collect market information from consumers' posts, to foster conversations between consumers, to organize consumer-generated creative content, and to contribute to ongoing conversations. The availability of firm social commerce platforms and firm-specific initiatives spurs customer attention and stimulation of demand for the brand, information search including online reviews, immediate or delayed purchase, and sharing of consumption experience. Yadav *et al.* (2013) organize the framework to discuss the value-creation potential of social commerce spanning the four stages of customer decision-making process: (1) need recognition, (2) pre-purchase, (3) purchase, and (4) post-purchase (Figure 10.7).

Need Recognition: Social media platforms play an important role in influencing and determining customer-perceived needs. There are several informational social signals that influence perceived needs including purchases made, products liked or pinned, places visited by friends, etc. Further, normative interpersonal influences that are value-expressive as well as utilitarian in nature also motivate customers to conform to their peers. Yadav *et al.* (2013) discuss several product characteristics that might moderate including how conspicuous is the consumption, publicly versus privately consumed products, luxury versus necessities, etc. Platform characteristic such as tie strength between communicators is also important in generating awareness. For instance, Facebook and blogging communities are characterized by stronger links compared to Twitter and Pinterest that have weaker links.

Pre-Purchase: Social commerce activities such as customer-generated content are perceived more trustworthy compared to marketer-generated content, and as such customer reviews, ratings, and recommendations carry diagnostic information for information search, consideration set, and product

Figure 10.7: A Contingency Framework of Social Commerce

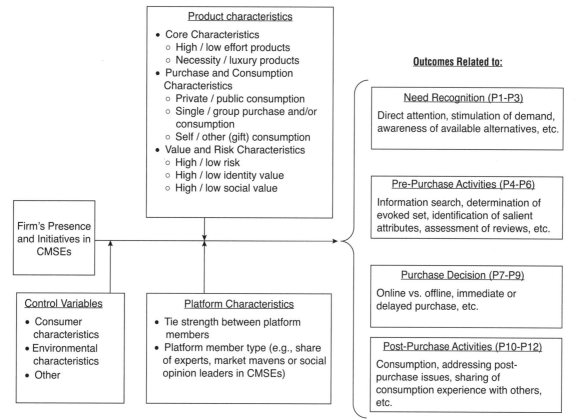

Adapted from M.S. Yadav, K. de Valck, T. Hennig-Thurau, D.L. Hoffman, and M. Spann (2013), Social Commerce: A Contingency Framework for Assessing Marketing Potential, *Journal of Interactive Marketing*, 27 pp. 311–323.

and attribute comparison. However, depending on the levels of perceived risk, customers will turn to experts for higher performance risk (e.g., blogs, videos), to social opinion leaders for higher psychological/social risk (e.g., Facebook, Twitter), and market mavens for higher financial risk (e.g., discussion forums, review platforms).

Purchase: Social media platforms allow customers to make important purchase decisions such as product choice, retailer choice, timing of the purchase, and terms and conditions of purchase. For instance, timing of purchase is critical in cases where dynamic pricing models are utilized by marketers based on available capacity, predicted demand, and actual booking such as in the airline industry. Similarly, marketers provide live chat applications for customers to share information to their social network at the point of purchase and receive instant feedback.

Post-Purchase: Customers share their post-purchase experiences such as satisfaction/dissatisfaction with other customers using ratings, reviews, recommendations, tweets, blog posts, and like buttons. They engage in such activities to help others, bond with others, and express pride with a view to construct their social identity, relevant more for brands with high identity value. Further, there is greater proclivity to share when customers see a fit between a social group and its brand character narrative (Kozinets *et al.*, 2010).

SOCIAL MEDIA: FUNCTIONAL BLOCS FRAMEWORK

Kietzmann *et al.* (2011) provide a honeycomb framework to classify different social media activities by analyzing the users' needs engaging in diverse social media. Specifically, the framework includes seven functional blocks: (1) identity, (2) conversations, (3) sharing, (4) presence, (5) relationship, (6) reputation, and (7) groups. In other words, users reveal personal information portraying themselves in certain ways (i.e., identity function), start conversations with other users (i.e., communication function), exchange contents that interest them and their peers (i.e., sharing function), indicate their current status and accessibility (i.e., presence function), build relationships with other users (i.e., relationship function), recognize the standing of others (i.e., reputation function), and form communities and groups (i.e., group function). In addition, Kietzmann *et al.* (2011) provide a four 'C' guideline for social media marketing, suggesting that the managers should first recognize and understand the social media landscape, then develop strategies that are congruent with, or suited to, different social media functionality as well as the goal of the firm, and finally act as a curator of social media interaction and content and chase for information about social media activities in the execution of the social media marketing plans.

This framework provides an avenue to assess the critical issues in social media marketing with its clear classification of diverse functions, which provides a consensus for the goals to achieve (Figure 10.8). The following section will elaborate on the most-discussed topics in social media marketing in accordance with the functions/goals they serve.

CRITICAL ISSUES IN THE IMPLEMENTATION OF SOCIAL MEDIA MARKETING

Identity Function: Brand Personality

Formally, identity functional block is defined as the extent to which users reveal their identities in a social media setting (Kietzmann *et al.*, 2011, p. 243), including conscious and unconscious self-disclosure of personal information, such as name, gender, age, thoughts, feelings, preferences and so on. These self-disclosures do not merely provide basic information about the user but also reveal her or his personality. Recent studies revealed that users tend

Figure 10.8: A Functional Blocs Framework of Social Media

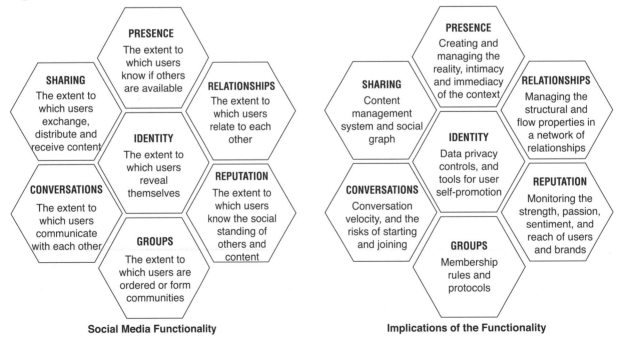

Adapted from Jan H. Kietzmann, Kristopher Hermkens, Ian P. McCarthy, and Bruno S. Silvestre (2011), Social Media? Get Serious! Understanding the Functional Building Blocks of Social Media, *Business Horizons*, Indiana University, 54, pp. 241–251.

to extend their offline personality into the domains of social media (Back *et al.*, 2010; Golbeck *et al.*, 2011; Gosling *et al.*, 2011; Qiu *et al.*, 2012). Golbeck *et al.* (2011) attempted to use Facebook posts and other information available (e.g., number of friends connected, activities, relationship status, etc.) on the users' Facebook page to predict their personality at an acceptable level (correlation varies among .48 to .65). Also, Gosling *et al.* (2011) investigated the connection between users' behavior (e.g., viewing pages, commenting others' page, adding photos, etc.) on Facebook and their personality, and they concluded that the activities on Facebook can help to predict the offline personality of a user. Moreover, Back *et al.* (2010) found that the personality revealed in the users' social network profile (i.e., Facebook and schülerVZ) is their actual personality rather than the ideal personality. Finally, Qiu *et al.* (2012) showed that a user's personality could be correctly judged by unfamiliar raters based on the microblogs (tweets in their study) of the user, especially the neuroticism and the agreeableness dimension of the Big Five personality dimensions.

When participating in social media, firms do not get more power than normal social media users do due to the nature of social media. The fact that everyone is viewed as a normal user makes social media a good platform for firms to achieve brand anthropomorphism or the attribution of a human form, human characteristics, or human behavior to the brand. Brand anthropomorphism has been considered as an effective approach to build brand trust (Hudson *et al.*, 2016). In her fundamental work, Fournier (1998) suggested that the consumer–brand relationship is built upon the consideration that the brand act as human in the relationship with its everyday execution of marketing plans and tactics. Specifically, the anthropomorphic process increases the credibility of a non-human agent by increasing perceived controllability of the agent's

behavior (Waytz *et al.*, 2014). In this sense, firms disclose their information about themselves, their brands, and their products, and interact with other users like normal users, and their information and activities on social media could convey their brand personality as well.

Brand personality is the cornerstone in the development of customer–brand relationship on social media (Gretry *et al.*, 2017) because of its positive impact on consumers' willingness to interact with the company (Schoenbachler and Gordon, 2002). But brand personality is not a novel concept to managers nor scholars: brand personality, as a strong indicator of brand identity, helps to establish a stronger customer–brand relationship, which in turn positively impacts consumers' affective, attitudinal, and behavioral responses to the brand (Eisend and Stokburger-Sauer, 2013; Freling and Forbes, 2005; Louis and Lombart, 2010; Malär *et al.*, 2011; Plummer, 2000; Radler, 2018). Particularly, this positive impact of brand personality occurs when consumers perceive the self-image congruence or the match between their self-concept and the personality of the product, the brand, or the firm (Kressmann *et al.*, 2006; Liu *et al.*, 2012), because the self-image congruence results in a greater tendency toward emotional attachment to the brand. Moreover, certain brand personal traits also have positive effects on consumers' responses. For example, Sung and Kim (2010) reported that sincerity and ruggedness dimensions are more related to brand trust while excitement and sophistication have more impact on brand affect. Along the same lines, Freling *et al.* (2011) suggested that the favorability, originality, and clarity of the brand personality appeal dimensions have positive influence on consumers' purchase intention.

The perceptions of brand personality are formed and influenced by consumers' contacts with the brand, including direct association (e.g., brand's user imagery) and indirect inference (e.g., product category associations) (Plummer, 2000). In this sense, brand personality was traditionally considered to be built and developed under heavy, consistent marketing communications, such as advertisements (Eisend and Stokburger-Sauer, 2013). On social media platforms, firms have more opportunities to interact with their target customers and users, and thus it seems logical to assume that firms are more likely to develop a brand personality on the social media platform. Yet, few studies have investigated what impact social media has on the development of brand personality or how brand personality is built and shaped in the context of social media. The only exception is Killian and McManus's (2015) work, which offered managerial guidelines to integrate social media with other communication channels. In their work, four themes were extracted from interviewing experts about the cross-platform integration: (1) consistency, (2) customization, (3) commitment, and (4) caution. Particularly, they suggested that the activities and communications on social media should be consistent with the essence of the brand, and thus employees who are responsible to manage the brands' social presences should receive detailed guideline and proper training about the essence of the brand. Similar opinions were expressed by experts in the Felix *et al.* (2017) study as the anarchy governance of social media marketing. Specifically, an expert in their in-depth interview suggested that "The company should have something like social media guidelines that determine certain basic principles and make non-compliant behavior punishable" and that "If one strives for an open and transparent service organization, this [training] restores the service employee's freedom, and they can be 'themselves' in their work."

Conversation Function: Customer Engagement

Conversation functional block is defined as the extent to which users communicate with other users in a social media setting (Kietzmann *et al.*, 2011, p. 244), including asymmetric communications such as blogs and tweets, and symmetric ones like instant messages and forum posts. Communicating on social media does not merely provide an extra channel for customers to get in touch with firms but also encourages more customer engagement behaviors other than purchase in their interaction with other customers or users (Brodie *et al.*, 2011; van Doorn *et al.*, 2010; Sashi, 2012; Sawhney *et al.*, 2005). Customer engagement has become a new perspective for customer-centric marketing strategies and a step closer to relationship marketing (Verhoef *et al.*, 2010). As discussed in Chapter 4, Brodie *et al.* (2011) suggest that "customer engagement (CE) is a psychological state that occurs by virtue of interactive, co-creative customer experience with a focal agent/object in focal service relationship. It occurs under a specific set of context dependent conditions generating differing CE levels; and exists as a dynamic, iterative process within service relationships that cocreate value. CE plays a central role in a nomological network governing service relationships in which other relational concepts (e.g., involvement, loyalty) are antecedents and/or consequences in iterative CE processes. It is a multidimensional concept subject to a context- and/or stakeholder-specific expression of relevant cognitive, emotional and/or behavioral dimensions" (p. 260). This definition implies that customer engagement is the most desired status in customer–brand relationship.

Social media or the Internet in general is a great platform to get customers engaged because of its unprecedented reach and interactive nature. Specifically, communications on social media are not constrained by physical proximity, allowing firms to reach a large customer base more frequently at a lower cost. Also, the flexibility to switch between the synchronous and asynchronous communication provides more freedom to participate in the conversations, which increases the persistence and the commitment of customers to engage with the company (Sawhney *et al.*, 2005). As discussed in Chapter 2, van Doorn *et al.* (2010) suggested three types of antecedents for customer engagement: (1) customer-based, (2) firm-based, and (3) context-based factors. Specifically, customer-based factors include customers' attitudes formed in the transactions and contacts with the firm, such as satisfaction, trust, identity, consumption goal, resources, and perceived cost/benefit. Firm-based factors refer to the firm's marketing efforts and outcomes such as brand characteristics, firm reputation, firm size/diversification, firm information usage and processes, and industry. Context-based factors consist of environmental factors such as political, economic, social, and technological aspects (PEST). In parallel, Sashi (2012) suggested a circular framework for the process to build the customer engagement, including connection, interaction, satisfaction, retention, commitment, advocacy, and engagement. In this framework, customer engagement requires affective and calculative commitment between seller and customers and only occurs when strong emotional bonds are established.

At the same time, firms have to assess customer engagement with certain measures. As discussed in Chapters 2 and 6, Kumar *et al.* (2010) proposed the idea of customer engagement value (CEV) defined as the creation of value by customers for firms. CEV occurs through an elaborate mechanism relative to purchase transactions and is composed of customer lifetime value, customer referral value, customer influencer value, and customer knowledge value. Specifically, Kumar *et al.* (2010) discuss behavioral, attitudinal, and network metrics for these four components as well as interactions among these four components. Alternatively, Peters *et al.* (2013) proposed a social media metric with four interrelated elements: (1) motives, (2) content, (3) network structure, and (4) social roles and interactions. In this model,

motives measure the intellectual, social, and cultural value that motivates the usage of social media. Content depicts the quality, valence, and the volume of messages sent on social media. Network structure describes the size, connections, distributions, and segmentation of the social network. Social roles and interaction assess interactions occurred on social media, such as sharing, gaming, expressing, and networking. With this framework, the authors provided nine guidelines for social media metrics and dashboards:

1. transition from control to influence;

2. shift from states and means to processes and distribution;

3. shift from convergence to divergence;

4. shift from quantity to quality;

5. leverage transparency and feedback-loop on metrics;

6. balance the metrics;

7. cover general to specific;

8. shift from urgency to importance; and

9. balance theory and pragmatism.

Despite these frameworks and guidelines, it seems most firms are not as successful as expected in engaging their customers on social media (Fournier and Avery, 2011; Schultz and Peltier, 2013). Schultz and Peltier (2013) criticized the use of short-term benefits to attract customer engagement was no different from sales promotion. Further, the blurry definition of customer engagement results in a lack of a clear goal in developing social media marketing plans. But more importantly, the nature of social media contributes largely to the failures of these attempts to engage customers: social media provides an equal say to consumers and thus everyone — yet no one — is the audience on social media. Fournier and Avery (2011) used the term "open source branding" to depict social media communications, implicating participatory, collaborative, and socially linked behaviors, whereby consumers serve as creators and disseminators of branded content.

As a result, these differences require more efforts to understand customers or users on social media, without taking anything for granted. For example, a recent study by Gretry *et al.* (2017) revealed a mixed impact of informal style of communication, challenging the intuition and the common practice on social media. Specifically, they revealed that social media users adapt role theory in their interactions on social media, which means they expect firms to behave properly in accordance with their roles in the interaction. In this sense, informal style of communication is not appropriate in the conversation with customers unfamiliar with the brand, and thus it could reduce the perceived trust of the brand. Also, hedonic versus utilitarian consumptions are impacted differently by figurative and assertive language (Kronrod and Danziger, 2013; Kronrod *et al.*, 2012). Hedonic products are more suitable for assertive and figurative languages due to higher compliance, while utilitarian products are more suitable for non-assertive and literal languages. These findings suggest that firms should be cautious about the style and content communicated on social media.

In addition, social media marketing needs the effort of everyone in the firm. Similar to the notion of "part-time marketer" in relationship marketing, social media marketing requires the participation of all employees regardless of their positions in the firm. Felix *et al.* (2017) reported that such a decentralized, dissolved, and cross-functional network structure is more advocated by experts and specialists in both their interviews and surveys.

Sharing Function: Crisis Management

Sharing functional block is defined as the extent to which users exchange, distribute, and receive content (Kietzmann *et al.*, 2011, p. 245). Sharing is another essential reason for users to gather on social media — "social" literally implies that the exchanges between users are crucial. This feature, as well as the greater say of normal users, makes social media an evil when negative news about the firm occurs because bad news travels faster than good news, more so on social media. United Airlines learned a costly lesson from social media in 2017, which resulted in an instant vanishing of $250 million stock value in a single day, not to mention a significant drop in customer reputation right after the incident (Czarnecki, 2017).[2]

The United Airlines case illustrates how an incident becomes a storm of public relation crisis for even a giant in the industry. Benoit (2018) examined this case and two phases in United's attempt to repair its image. The first statement attempted to downplay the offense, relying mainly on differentiation and mortification, and the second one appeared to emerge grudgingly, using mortification and corrective action. Specifically, the first statement attempted to differentiate the incident by stating "re-accommodating" rather than violently remove a passenger off the airplane. On the other hand, United confessed its wrongdoing and committed corrective actions in its second attempt. For instance, the CEO apologized multiple times in different channels to the victim as well as other passengers on board, and took the corrective actions, revising the overbooking policy to prevent the recurrence of similar episodes within few days. The author suggested that one of the implications from the incident is that the rapid rise of social media is a fundamental element of the crisis communication

---

2   The crisis started from an attempt to substitute four flight crew members for passengers already seated on United Airlines flight 3411 traveling from Chicago, Illinois, to Louisville, Kentucky. Three passengers accepted travel vouchers but no one else volunteered to leave the airplane. Then, Chicago security personnel physically removed a passenger, David Dao, from the flight. The process was taped by multiple

situation: social media provides the instantaneous distribution of incriminating pictures, videos, and other accusatory messages, and persuasive attacks or criticisms are an important component in the social media environment.

This challenge on crisis management from social media comes from the real-time communications on social media as an active platform for stakeholders to express their opinions and share others' as well. Gruber *et al.* (2015) discussed the role of leaders in a crisis and suggested several tips for crisis management and leadership on social media. Specifically, it is virtually impossible for more mainstream communication tactics due to the reach and speed of social media and thus crisis management activities are largely reactive in nature. In this case, sensemaking, the attempt to create order of what has occurred, provides a context for understanding what has happened is a critical initial step. Also, the leader should demonstrate a capacity to recover from a downturn, and resiliency is effortful because of the emotional toll that cries can take. Finally, the authors suggest that a social media plan should be developed before the crisis hits in addition to the presence and engagement on social media on normal days.

Presence Function: The "Like" Button

Presence functional block is defined as the extent to which users can know if other users are accessible (Kietzmann *et al.*, 2011, p. 245). It also includes "mere virtual presence" to other users, or cases that ones' activities or preferences are introduced to other users via the recommender system (Naylor *et al.*, 2012). One of the well-known mere virtual presence is

Facebook's "Like" button, where the user endorses her or his likeness or support to certain content or user, and which is described as an "easy way to let people know that you enjoy it without leaving a comment." The presence of the other users in the "like" button of a brand potentially changes its perception (Naylor *et al.*, 2012). We elaborate the details next.

In their studies, Naylor *et al.* (2012) applied the literature from reference groups to argue that mere virtual presence of the brand could have an impact on customers' attitude toward the brand, despite social impact theory which does not support. Specifically, the authors suggested the inferred commonality effect, which is the increase in their trust and favorability toward a similar reviewer inferring a shared taste and preference. They then extended that in the case of a mere virtual presence such as the "like" button, even without any persuasive intent or information provided, the users could potentially observe a demographic similarity. On the contrary, dissimilar presence could result in negative adjustments of preference for users. In the case where presented users are a mix of similar and dissimilar users, or that presented users could not be properly identified, the mere virtual presence still achieves a positive impact on the user's perception because the user might (1) focus on similar users only, or (2) anchor on the self to infer that ambiguous others are like them. In short, the presence of other users has a positive impact on brand perception except when dissimilar users only are presented. This work suggests that managers should attempt to manipulate their displayed mere virtual presence in response to target customer demographics by employing emerging tracking and targeting tools

---

passengers on the flight and posted on social media. The most influential one, from Audra Bridges, was shared more than 87,000 times and viewed 6.8 million times in merely 24 hours (Marotti and Zumbach, 2017). On the same day, United CEO Oscar Munoz issued a statement in which he apologized for having "re-accommodated" four passengers, including Dao, but an internal letter he sent quickly went public reaffirming his support for the employees while describing Dao as "disruptive and belligerent" (Czarnecki, 2017). United suffered a huge backlash as public opinion went sour. Its stock price dropped, vanishing $250 million market value at the end of the next day, and boycotts were called among social media users across the US, China, and Vietnam (Czarnecki, 2017). Under pressure, Munoz issued a second apology and committed a revision of United's overbooking policy a few days later. Still, 40% of millennials in the US said they would either no longer fly on United or avoid giving it their business (Passy, 2017).

provided by social media platforms. When such tools are not applicable, alternative strategies should be designed based on the fan base and the target customers. Firms should reveal its fan base when the fan base is homogeneous and similar to the target audience or when the fan base is heterogeneous but includes a target audience. Conversely, maintaining the ambiguity of the fan base is a better strategy when the fan base has no relevance to the target audience.

Relationship Function: Social Customer Relationship Marketing (CRM)

Reputation functional block is defined as the extent to which users can be related to other users (Kietzmann *et al.*, 2011, p. 246). To firms, the integration of social media and customer relationship management, in other words social CRM, has emerged as a trending topic (Heller Baird and Parasnis, 2011; Trainor *et al.*, 2014). Different from traditional customer relationship management, social CRM recognizes the role of the business is to facilitate collaborative experiences and dialogues that customers value rather than to manage customers. In other words, social CRM focuses on incorporating both customer transactions and customer interactions.

As an integrated concept, social CRM is composed of CRM and social media dimensions (Malthouse *et al.*, 2013). The authors further decomposed CRM dimension into three components (i.e., (1) relationship initiation, (2) maintenance, and (3) termination) like traditional CRM, and they analyzed social media dimension according to the level of customers' engagement on social media. In other words, these two dimensions result in a two (social media engagement: low vs. high) by three (CRM stage: acquisition, retention, termination) comparison. In their discussion, CRM with low customer engagement is pretty close to traditional CRM, except firms gain more ability to generate insights about customers' characteristics. On the other hand, CRM with high

customer engagement is a different story: firms lose control over the message to which its customers are exposed. Due to this phenomenon, acquisition cannot be isolated from retention: a message or promotion intended to acquire new customers will be soon spread to existing customers, which could potentially result in existing customers leaving. In this sense, sophisticated CRM strategies balancing the retention and acquisition activities no longer work on customers highly engaged with the company on social media. This change requires coordination across acquisition and retention silos. Moreover, these highly engaged customers could make trouble using their say on social media, spreading negative word-of-month or comments, when being divested by the firm.

In response to the challenges and complexities in social CRM, Malthouse *et al.* (2013) suggest that managers should focus on multiple forms of value (i.e., customer engagement value and its variants, cf. Kumar *et al.*, 2010) and engage content in their design of social CRM strategies. In the execution stage, attention should be paid to the use of cutting-edge data and information technology and in revolutionizing the employees' mindset. The latter point coincides with previous discussions on encouraging all employees to participate in the social media marketing with proper training, sufficient guidelines, and greater autonomy. The former point (explained next), however, is worth more elaboration due to the great potential and impact of "big data" for social CRM and marketing decisions.

The information technology has evolved so fast that firms now have plenty of data about its customers' behaviors collected from social media as well as other online approaches. "Big data" is the term to describe the high-volume (usually over 1 TB) information asset. Besides its volume, big data is also associated with high variety, high velocity, questionable veracity, and yet low value (Gandomi and Haider, 2015). Specifically, high variety refers to the numerous types of information gathered in big data, such as numbers, text, images, audio and video, and most of them are unstructured or semi-structured for machine analysis. High velocity means the unprecedented rate of data generated and required speed at which the data should be analyzed and acted upon. Veracity represents the unreliability inherent in some sources of data. Low value does not mean big data is less valuable to firms, but that the value density in big data is low in contrast to its volume.

Given these features of big data, big data analytic tools were developed for the analysis of specific types of data, including text analytics, audio analytics, video analytics, social media analytics, and predictive analytics (for more details, cf. Gandomi and Haider, 2015). The adoption and application of these tools and traditional marketing analytic tools results in different strategic options varying in the degree of complexity and knowledge types, leading to different levels of new product success (Xu *et al.*, 2016). Specifically, a high adoption and application of both big data analytic tools and traditional marketing analytic tools, featuring high complexity and more customized knowledge, gives firms the highest level of new product success. The traditional tools contribute to innovation and new ideas, and the big data tools enable firms to make decisions quickly in a dynamic environment. On the contrary, the use of either method alone limits knowledge generation in both the short term and the long term.

Reputation Function: eWOM

Reputation functional block is defined as the extent to which users identify the standing of others, including themselves, in a social media setting (Kietzmann *et al.*, 2011, p. 247). For companies and their brands, electronic word-of-mouth (eWOM) has attracted the most attention since social media emerged. In their pioneering work, Hennig-Thurau *et al.* (2004) defined eWOM as "any positive or negative statement made by

potential, actual, or former customers about a product or company, which is made available to a multitude of people and institutions via the Internet" (p. 39). Alternatively, eWOM can be simply put as WOM on social media.

WOM has been one of the most important indicators of a company's market performance for decades. It is more influential on behavior than other marketer-controlled sources because of the source reliability and the flexibility of interpersonal communication (Buttle, 1998). Ample evidence also shows that negative WOM has even more powerful impact than positive WOM (e.g., East *et al.*, 2007, 2008; Richins, 1983). eWOM receives much attention due to the significance of WOM, and social media provides customers a place to share their opinions on and experiences with goods and services with a multitude of other consumers. A greater voice of customers on social media makes their opinions (i.e., eWOM) important to firms. In particular, Hung and Li (2007) found that eWOM provides information for other customers to learn about product and persuasion knowledge, which in turn leads to behavior outcomes such as customers' consideration and consumer reflexivity. Also, Erkan and Evans (2016) found that eWOM information, if adopted, positively impacts customers' behavioral intentions, such as purchase. Particularly, they applied the reasoned action theory, which postulates that behavioral intentions are decided by attitude and subjective norms, to explain the impact of eWOM information: adopted eWOM information shapes customers' attitude and thus influences on behavioral intentions.

What kind of eWOM information could be adopted or trusted by customers? Many factors have been considered and examined by scholars. For example, Erkan and Evans (2016) considered information quality, information credibility, customers' needs of information, and customers' attitude toward information as four antecedents of information usefulness, which antecedes the information adoption. Teng *et al.* (2014), on the other hand, examined the impact of argument quality, source credibility, source attractiveness, source perception, and source style of eWOM message on information acceptance. Doh and Hwang (2009) included customers' involvement with the product as well as their prior knowledge about the product as moderators on the impact of eWOM. Park and Lee (2009) analyzed how the direction of eWOM, website reputation, the type of product impacts the effect of eWOM. Hussain *et al.* (2017) considered the impact of eWOM source credibility and perceived risk on the adoption of eWOM. At this point, it seems the literature has failed to reach a definitive answer for this question.

Another important question is, what motivates customers to engage in eWOM? Customer satisfaction, customer loyalty, quality, customers' commitment, customers' trust, and perceived value are for sure relevant as the antecedents of WOM (de Matos et al., 2008). In addition, Chu and Kim (2011) provide a list of customers' individual characteristics that determine customers' engagement in eWOM, including three social media-specific characteristics: (1) tie strength with their contacts, (2) homophily of their contacts, and (3) trust in their contacts. Further, they also provide one personal characteristic, customers' susceptibility to interpersonal influence. Specifically, customers' tie or bond with their contacts is positively related to their engagement: a strong tie could potentially impact directly on customers' decisions, while a weak tie could also facilitate their information-seeking behavior and allow the dissemination and spread of eWOM among the users. Homophily refers to the homogeneity level of the group the users interact with. As mentioned earlier, the perception of shared commonalities of the reviewer is positively relevant to the trust toward and preference to the reviewers' comment, and as such a higher level of homophily results in a higher level of engagement

of the users in eWOM. Trust plays a vital role in information exchange and knowledge integration, as it allows individuals to justify and evaluate their decision to provide or attain more useful information. In this sense, a higher trust in social media increases the users' engagement in eWOM. Lastly, customers' susceptibility to interpersonal influences, including the normative and informational influences, determines the power of WOM in general, including eWOM.

Group Function: Brand Community

Group functional block is defined as the extent to which users can form communities and sub communities (Kietzmann *et al.*, 2011, p. 247). In business practices, brand communities on social media are one of the most important avenues to build brand equity, a topic discussed earlier in chapter 7. Besides brand equity, brand community also serves as an effective tool to engage customers in the value co-creation (Hajli *et al.*, 2017; Healy and McDonagh, 2013). The co-creation of value reflects the current trend of a service-dominant logic in marketing (Vargo and Lusch, 2004), which highlights the value-creation process involving the customer as a co-creator of value (Payne *et al.*, 2008). Specifically, value co-creation could be realized in the forms of customers' emotional engagement through advertising and promotional activities, customers' self-service to solve a problem, customers' participation as a part of service experience, and the co-design of products.

Among these forms of value co-creation, brand community is a significant vehicle to achieve the co-design of products. Particularly, brand community offers a valuable source for the development of new and innovative products (Füller *et al.*, 2008). Members in a brand community have a strong interest in the product and the brand, and they also have extensive product knowledge and engage in product-related discussions. These characteristics enable them to solve problems and to generate new product ideas as a valuable source for innovation. More generally, brand community facilitates the value co-creation process allowing for more and various interactions between the firm and customers and among customers. Tynan *et al.* (2010) conducted a case study about luxury brands to examine the impact of brand community on value-co-creation. Specifically, the constellation of individuals in these communities includes customers and experts with a variety of knowledge base: from contemporary art to fabric material. In this sense, brand communities inspire luxury brand designer and provide insights to maintain topicality and relevance for the brand. On the other hand, activities and experiences in brand communities, such as interactions with high status individuals of the company (e.g., luxury brand owner and designer) and exclusive events, offer members privileged access to information and social capital among members in their peer group. These experiences from brand communities enhance the exclusivity and prestige of the brand, because they are literally what money cannot buy.

The development of brand communities cannot be achieved without the marketers' efforts to facilitate the characteristics of brand community: consciousness of kind, shared rituals and traditions, and a sense of moral responsibility (Muniz and O'Guinn, 2001). McAlexander *et al.* (2002) observed the building of Jeep's brand community with these efforts during their fieldwork at Jamborees and Camp Jeep brand fests, events for the brand owner and potential owners engaging in brand consumption and the celebration thereof. Specifically, marketers created the context in which owner interaction occurs, such as ritual storytelling facilitated by barbecues and roundtable discussions. They also took an active role in establishing the shared rituals, traditions, and meanings that foster consciousness of kind, such as exhibits about the history of Jeep and informative booklets about the techniques and tips of off-road driving. Finally,

"tread lightly", aiming at protecting the environment and preserving access to off-high-way trails, was largely promoted as a cornerstone value for the community throughout the events. Kilambi *et al.* (2013) provided specific guidelines for marketers to establish the brand community. They argued that the very first step is to develop a strong brand identity for themselves and for their implied audiences. Once the brand identity is established, constitutive marketing is implemented and iterated. Constitutive marketing includes firms' communication with messages imbued with myths, articulating ideological framework, brand personality, character traits, and cultural meaning and members responses assume the role and expectations to be empowered as a brand community with those who engage in the same act. For example, the emergence of Apple community is a calculated exercise in constitutive marketing: its founding myth ("we hope that we are as creative, inventive and free as Steve Jobs and Steve Wozniak.") and its "1984" television ad, "Think Different" campaign, and "Get a Mac" campaign. Constitutive rhetoric provides members with narratives to inhabit as subjects and motivates them to experience and insert "narrativized" members-as-agents into the world.

SEVEN STEPS TO SOCIAL MEDIA SUCCESS

Kumar and Mirchandani (2012) explained the seven-step framework for social media marketing (see Figure 10.9):

- Step 1: Monitor the conversations — It starts with monitoring brand-related conversations unfolding in social media platforms across customers, influencers, and brands.

- Step 2: Identify influential individuals — Firms can identify influencers who have the potential to spread the firm's message.

Figure 10.9: Social Media Success: A Seven-Step Framework

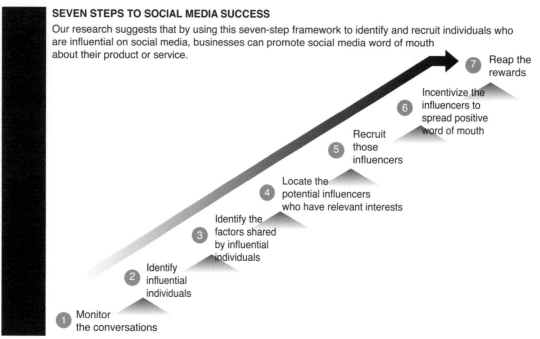

Adapted from V. Kumar and R. Mirchandani (2012), *Increasing the ROI of Social Media Marketing* MIT Sloan Management Review 54(1): 54–61.

- Step 3: Identify the factors shared by influential individuals — Firms can create profile on influencers to be able to locate and encourage them to spread the firm's products and services. Engagement of influencers can be captured using Customer Influence Effect (CIE) metric consisting of message spread, influence, and social impact.

- Step 4: Locate influential individuals who have interests relevant to the campaign — The firm needs to identify those social media influencers who also show interest in the firm's products and services. This can be captured by Stickiness Index (SI), which measures the degree of WOM generated by a particular user on a given topic (e.g., product category).

- Step 5: Recruit influential individuals who have interests relevant to the campaign to talk about company's product or service — the firm enlists these influencers to spread positive WOM. This can be achieved by developing interactive online content and designing strategies to engage the recruits in a way that can be tracked and measured.

- Step 6: Incentivize those influencers to spread positive WOM about the product or service — The firm can incentivize recruited influencers (e.g., discounts, recognition) to create a buzz to retain current customers and attract prospects.

- Step 7: Reap the rewards from increasingly effective social media campaigns — Firms can accurately measure the performance of their social media campaigns by using the above steps. Strategies can be refined as firms are able to link social media with product and brand growth.

KEY TAKEAWAYS

- Digital marketing is an adaptive, technology-enabled process by which firms collaborate with customers and partners to jointly create, communicate, deliver, and sustain value for all stakeholders.

- Search engine display results and display position generate better outcome for firms (e.g., click-through rate, conversion rate, revenue). The main value of search engine optimization (SEO) lies in organic results with high relevancy rather than paid results.

- Mobile devices have four important characteristics different from other channels: (1) location-specificity, (2) portability, (3) wireless, and (4) personal. While mobile phones are used for communication, entertainment, information search, socializing, and conducting transactions as characteristic of a mobile lifestyle, customers prefer mobile marketing when they are given more control such as permission-based mobile advertising. Marketers need to understand the benefits/costs of mobile marketing, particularly the case of information privacy, from customers' perspective and not just the firms' perspective.

- Internet of Things (IoT) is a new technology paradigm envisioned as a global network of machines and devices capable of interacting with each other. Its applications are on the rise in monitoring and control, big data and business analytics, and information sharing and collaboration among customers, objects, and firms, creating new opportunities for value creation and long-term customer–company relationships.

- Digital technologies with the emergence of several platforms augment the core product with digital services (e.g., cars with GPS), help networking of products to release dormant value inherent in products (e.g., Airbnb), and morph products into digital services (software).

- Digital technologies enable personalization and customization of marketing-mix strategies in the areas of pricing (e.g., dynamic pricing), promotion (e.g., location-based mobile promotion), and channel (omni-channel).

- Digital technologies create value for customers in the form of customer satisfaction, value equity, brand equity, and relationship equity.

- The era of social media marketing is marked by the social collective, transparency, criticism, power shift, and democratization. Marketers need to focus not just on brand building but brand protection, not just on strategic planning but execution, and not just on brand differentiation but on brand resonance.

- Social media is a group of Internet-based applications that builds on the ideological and technological foundations of Web 2.0, and that allows for the creation and exchange of User Generated Content. It includes social network sites, user-generated content sites, trading and marketing sites, and social network games. Yet, it is meaningless to sharply delineate various types of social media platforms because the boundaries among these categories and sites are blurry, providing various functions to their users.

- Social commerce is defined as exchange-related activities that occur in, or are influenced by, an individual's social network in computer-mediated social environment, where the activities correspond to the need recognition, pre-purchase, purchase, and post-purchase stages of a focal exchange.

- Value creation in social media in the need recognition stage is through informational social influences and normative interpersonal influences. In the pre-purchase stage, value creation is through customer-generated content (e.g., reviews, ratings, recommendations) as these are considered more trustworthy than marketer-generated content. In the purchase stage, value creation in social media platforms corresponds to choice and timing of purchase, critical in some industries (e.g., airlines), where dynamic pricing models are time-sensitive and sensitive to capacity utilization. In the post-purchase stage, value creation corresponds with sharing customers' post-purchase experiences with a view to express their social identity and to bond with one another.

- Social media has seven functional blocks to satisfy the users' needs: (1) identity, (2) conversation, (3) sharing, (4) presence, (5) relationship, (6) reputation, and (7) group. The marketer should first recognize and understand the social media landscape, then develop strategies that are congruent with, or suited to, different social media functionality, as well as the goal of the firm. Finally, the marketer should act as a curator of social media interaction and content and chase for information about social media activities in the execution of the social media marketing plans.

- The fact that everyone is viewed as a normal user makes social media a good platform for firms to achieve brand anthropomorphism, an effective approach to build brand trust. In addition, the information disclosed by firms about themselves, their brands, and their products and their interaction with other users on social media could convey their brand personality.

- Brand personality is the cornerstone in the development of consumer–brand relationship on social media because of its positive impact on consumers' willingness to interact with the company.

- The assessment of customer engagement considers customer lifetime value, customer referral value, customer influencer value, and customer knowledge value. Guidelines for marketers on the social media assessment include: (1) transition from control to influence; (2) shift from states and means to processes and distribution; (3) shift from convergence to divergence; (4) shift from quantity to quality; (5) leverage transparency and feedback-loop on metrics; (6) balance the metrics; (7) cover general to specific; (8) shift from urgency to importance; and (9) balance theory and pragmatism.

- CRM with high customer engagement on social media is different because firms lose control over the message to which its customers are exposed. As a result, acquisition cannot be isolated from retention, and thus the co-ordination across acquisition and retention silos becomes essential. Marketers should focus on multiple forms of value, engaging content in their design of social CRM strategies and paying attention to the use of cutting-edge data and information technology, revolutionizing employees' mindset in the execution.

- Brand community facilitates the value co-creation process allowing more and various interactions between the firm and consumers and among consumers (see Figure 10.10). The development of brand communities cannot be achieved without marketers' efforts to facilitate the characteristics

Figure 10.10: Brand community facilitates the value co-creation process by facilitating interactions between the firm and consumers and among consumers.

of brand community: consciousness of kind, shared rituals and traditions, and a sense of moral responsibility.

EXERCISES

Questions

1. Define digital marketing. How has the nature and scope of digital marketing changed over the years from simply marketing of products and services using digital channels?

2. Discuss the importance of "display position" and "relevancy" in search engine advertising. Discuss the advantages and disadvantages of organic versus sponsored results. Explain the spill-over effects of online ads across multiple channels.

3. What is mobile marketing and what are its main characteristics? Discuss permission-based mobile advertising (PBMA) and the critical role of "customer control" in influencing customers to grant permission to marketers. What are customer-related factors that facilitate PBMA?

4. Comment on the following statement: "If search engine is in the mature stage, mobile marketing is in the growth stage, then Internet of Things (IoT) is in the introductory stage." What is IoT and what are its main characteristics and capabilities? What are its current and future applications in marketing and how will it impact the relationship marketing paradigm?

5. Explain how digital technologies interact with customers by way of (a) search engines; (b) social media and user-generated content; (c) platforms/two-sided markets; (d) contextual interactions; and (e) consumer behavior. How do digital technologies enhance value for customers and for the firm?

6. Discuss how social media marketing builds customer relationships by way of scope, culture, structure, and governance. Explain why marketers should focus more on brand protection (versus brand building) and brand resonance (vs. brand differentiation) in their social media marketing strategy.

7. Discuss the following roles of social media as classified in the honeycomb framework: (a) identity function; (b) conversation function; (c) sharing function, (d) presence function; (e) relationship function; (f) reputation function; and (g) group function? How can marketers use each of these customer and user needs to build stronger relationships?

8. Firms need to identify and recruit individuals who are influential on social media about the company's products and services. Explain the seven-step framework to successful social media marketing.

Group Discussion

1. Netflix uses an online recommendation system that focuses on highlighting specific products (shows and movies) that may be of interest to customers. These recommendation systems are either based on similarity of a focal customer to other customers (collaborative filtering), attributes of previously viewed products (content filtering), or mixtures of both (hybrid filtering). Making use of individual-level browsing, rating, and purchase data among others, Netflix tailors recommendations to increase the relevance of its offerings. Such personalized communication and online recommendation system fosters customer engagement behaviors in the form of purchases, feedback, word-of-mouth, and referrals.

As a small group, discuss how Netflix digital technologies interact with customer via search engines and social media/user-generated content. How does Netflix create value for customers through its online recommendation system, and in return, how does it create value for the company?

2. Facebook is among the largest online social networks in the world. With 2.3 billion monthly active users around the world (as of 2018), Facebook is an important tool to connect customers with brands, other customers, and online communities. Their mission is empowering people, enabling community building, and connecting the world. Facebook also offers targeted advertising opportunities and encourages people to exchange online information related to products and services.

As a small group, discuss the following different motives/user needs in customer engagement with Facebook: (a) identity function; (b) conversation function; (c) sharing function, (d) presence function; (e) relationship function; (f) reputation function; and (g) group function. Suggest ways for Facebook to design and deliver successful social media marketing strategies.

HBS and Ivey Cases

- AnswerDash (9-516-106)
- Re-inventing Best Buy (9-716-455)
- Chase Sapphire (9-518-024)
- Laurs & Bridz (9B18A004)

CASE QUESTIONS

AnswerDash

1. Discuss the nature and scope of digital marketing practiced by AnswerDash. Is it simply marketing of products and services using digital channels? Does AnswerDash augment its core product with digital services or morph its core product into digital services?

2. How can AnswerDash make use of "display position" and "relevancy" in search engine

advertising? Discuss the advantages and disadvantages of organic versus sponsored results for AnswerDash.

3. How do digital technologies enhance value for customers and for AnswerDash?

4. How can AnswerDash make use of social media marketing to build customer relationships by way of scope, culture, structure, and governance? Explain why it should focus more on brand protection (vs. brand building) and brand resonance (vs. brand differentiation) in its social media marketing strategy.

5. How can AnswerDash make use of the following roles of social media as classified in the honeycomb framework: (a) identity function; (b) conversation function; (c) sharing function, (d) presence function; (e) relationship function; (f) reputation function; and (g) group function? How can it use each of these customer and user needs to build stronger relationships?

6. Discuss the following different motives/user needs in customer engagement with AnswerDash: (a) identity function; (b) conversation function; (c) sharing function, (d) presence function; (e) relationship function; (f) reputation function; and (g) group function? Suggest ways for AnswerDash to design and deliver successful social media marketing strategies?

Re-inventing Best Buy

1. Discuss the nature and scope of digital marketing practiced by Best Buy. Is it simply marketing of products and services using digital channels?

2. How can Best Buy make use of "display position" and "relevancy" in search engine advertising? Discuss the advantages and disadvantages of organic versus sponsored results for Best Buy.

3. What is Internet of Things (IoT) and how can Best Buy make use of IoT to strengthen its relationship marketing platform?

4. How do digital technologies enhance value for customers and for Best Buy? Discuss how Best Buy can personalize and customize its marketing-mix strategies for its customers using digital technologies.

5. How can Best Buy make use of the following roles of social media as classified in the honeycomb framework: (a) identity function; (b) conversation function; (c) sharing function, (d) presence function; (e) relationship function; (f) reputation function; and (g) group function? How can it use each of these customer and user needs to build stronger relationships?

6. How can Best Buy identify and recruit individuals who are influential on social media about the company's products and services?

7. Discuss the following different motives/user needs in customer engagement with Best Buy: (a) identity function; (b) conversation function; (c) sharing function, (d) presence function; (e) relationship function; (f) reputation function; and (g) group function. Suggest ways for Best Buy to design and deliver successful social media marketing strategies?

Chase Sapphire

1. Discuss the nature and scope of digital marketing practiced by JPMorgan. Is it simply marketing of products and services using digital channels?

2. How can JPMorgan make use of permission-based mobile advertising (PBMA) and what is the critical role of "customer control" in influencing customers to grant it permission?

3. What is Internet of Things (IoT) and how can JPMorgan make use of IoT to strengthen its relationship marketing platform?

4. How do digital technologies enhance value for customers and for JPMorgan? How can JPMorgan use user-generated content in social media (i.e., reviews, ratings, and recommendations) to maximize customer value?

5. How can JPMorgan make use of social media marketing to build customer relationships by way of scope, culture, structure, and governance? Explain why it should focus more on brand protection (vs. brand building) and brand resonance (vs. brand differentiation) in its social media marketing strategy.

6. How can JPMorgan make use of the following roles of social media as classified in the honeycomb framework: (a) identity function; (b) conversation function; (c) sharing function, (d) presence function; (e) relationship function; (f) reputation function; and (g) group function? How can it use each of these customer and user needs to build stronger relationships?

7. Discuss the following different motives/user needs in customer engagement with JPMorgan: (a) identity function; (b) conversation function; (c) sharing function, (d) presence function; (e) relationship function; (f) reputation function; and (g) group function. Suggest ways for JPMorgan to design and deliver successful social media marketing strategies.

Laurs & Bridz

1. How can Laurs & Bridz make use of permission-based mobile advertising (PBMA) and what is the critical role of "customer control" in influencing customers to grant it permission?

2. What is Internet of Things (IoT) and how can Laurs & Bridz make use of IoT to strengthen its relationship marketing platform?

3. How do digital technologies enhance value for customers and for Laurs & Bridz?

4. How can Laurs & Bridz make use of social media marketing to build customer relationships by way of scope, culture, structure, and governance? Explain why it should focus more on brand protection (vs. brand building) and brand resonance (vs. brand differentiation) in its social media marketing strategy.

5. How can Laurs & Bridz make use of the following roles of social media as classified in the honeycomb framework: (a) identity function; (b) conversation function; (c) sharing function, (d) presence function; (e) relationship function; (f) reputation function; and (g) group function? How can it use each of these customer and user needs to build stronger relationships?

6. How can Laurs & Bridz identify and recruit individuals who are influential on social media about the company's products and services?

REFERENCES

Agarwal, Ashish, Kartik Hosanagar, and Michael D. Smith (2011), Location, Location, Location: An Analysis of Profitability of Position in Online Advertising Markets, *Journal of Marketing Research* 48(6): 1057–1073.

Agarwal, Ritu and Elena Karahanna (2014), Management Information Systems Research Center, University of Minnesota, *MIS Quarterly* 24(4): 665–694.

Back, Mitja D., Juliane M. Stopfer, Simine Vazire, Sam Gaddis, Stefan C. Schmukle, Boris Egloff, and Samuel D. Gosling (2010), Facebook Profiles Reflect Actual Personality, Not Self-idealization, *Psychological Science* 21(3): 372–374.

Barwise, Patrick and Colin Strong (2002), Permission-Based Mobile Advertising, *Journal of Interactive Marketing* 16(1): 14–24.

Benoit, William (2018), Crisis and Image Repair at United Airlines: Fly the Unfriendly Skies, *Journal of International Crisis and Risk Communication Research* 1(1): 11–26.

Bergström, Annika (2015), Online Privacy Concerns: A Broad Approach to Understanding the Concerns of Different Groups for Different Uses, *Computers in Human Behavior* 53: 419–426.

Berman, Ron and Zsolt Katona (2013), The Role of Search Engine Optimization in Search Marketing, *Marketing Science* 32(4): 644–651.

Brodie, Roderick J, Linda D Hollebeek, Biljana Jurić, and Ana Ilić (2011), Customer Engagement, *Journal of Service Research* 14(3): 252–271.

Buttle, Francis A (1998), Word of Mouth: Understanding and Managing Referral Marketing, *Journal of Strategic Marketing* 6(3): 241–254.

Chan, Tat Y., Chunhua Wu, and Ying Xie (2011), Measuring the Lifetime Value of Customers Acquired from Google Search Advertising, *Marketing Science* 30(5): 837–850.

Chu, Shu-Chuan and Yoojung Kim (2011), Determinants of Consumer Engagement in Electronic Word-of-Mouth (eWOM) in Social Networking Sites, *International Journal of Advertising* 30(1): 47–75.

Columbus, Louis (2018), IoT Market Predicted to Double By 2021, Reaching $520B, *Forbes*, https://www.forbes.com/sites/louiscolumbus/2018/08/16/iot-market-predicted-to-double-by-2021-reaching-520b.

Czarnecki, Sean (2017), Timeline of a Crisis: United Airlines, *PR Week*, https://www.prweek.com/article/1435619/timeline-crisis-united-airlines.

de Matos, Celso Augusto, Carlos Alberto, and Vargas Rossi (2008), Word-of-Mouth Communications in Marketing: A Meta-Analytic Review of the Antecedents and Moderators, *Journal of the Academy of Marketing Science* 36(4): 578–596.

Desai, Preyas S., Woochoel Shin, and Richard Staelin (2014), The Company That You Keep: When to Buy a Competitor's Keyword, *Marketing Science* 33(4): 485–508.

Dinner, Isaac M., Harald J. Heerde Van, and Scott A. Neslin (2014), Driving Online and Offline Sales: The Cross-Channel Effects of Traditional, Online Display, and Paid Search Advertising, *Journal of Marketing Research* 51(5): 527–545.

Doh, Sun-Jae and Jang-Sun Hwang (2009), How Consumers Evaluate eWOM (Electronic Word-of-Mouth) Messages, *CyberPsychology & Behavior* 12(2): 193–197.

East, Robert, Kathy Hammond, and Malcolm Wright (2007), The Relative Incidence of Positive and Negative Word of Mouth: A Multi-Category Study, *International Journal of Research in Marketing* 24(2): 175–184.

East, Robert, Kathy Hammond, and Wendy Lomax (2008), Measuring the Impact of Positive and Negative Word of Mouth on Brand Purchase Probability, *International Journal of Research in Marketing* 25(3): 215–224.

Edelman, David C (2010), Branding in the Digital Age, *Harvard Business Review* 88(12): 62–69.

Eisend, Martin and Nicola E Stokburger-Sauer (2013), Brand Personality: A Meta-Analytic Review of Antecedents and Consequences, *Marketing Letters* 24(3): 205–216.

Erkan, Ismail and Chris Evans (2016), The Influence of eWOM in Social Media on Consumers' Purchase Intentions: An Extended Approach to Information Adoption, *Computers in Human Behavior* 61: 47–55.

Felix, Reto, Philipp A. Rauschnabel, and Chris Hinsch (2017), Elements of Strategic Social Media Marketing: A Holistic Framework, *Journal of Business Research* 70: 118–126.

Fournier, Susan (1998), Consumers and Their Brands: Developing Relationship Theory in Consumer Research, *Journal of Consumer Research* 24(4): 343–353.

Fournier, Susan and Jill Avery (2011), The Uninvited Brand, *Business Horizons* 54(3): 193–207.

Freling, Traci H, Jody L. Crosno, and David H Henard (2011), Brand Personality Appeal: Conceptualization and Empirical Validation, *Journal of the Academy of Marketing Science* 39(3): 392–406.

Freling, Traci H, and Lukas P. Forbes (2005), An Empirical Analysis of the Brand Personality Effect, *Journal of Product & Brand Management* 14(7): 404–413.

Füller, Johann, Kurt Matzler, and Melanie Hoppe (2008), Brand Community Members as a Source of Innovation, *Journal of Product Innovation Management* 25(6): 608–619.

Gandomi, Amir and Murtaza Haider (2015), Beyond the Hype: Big Data Concepts, Methods, and Analytics, *International Journal of Information Management* 35(2): 137–144.

Gartner (2015), Gartner Says 6.4 Billion Connected Things Will Be in Use in 2016, Up 30 Percent From 2015, https://www.gartner.com/en/newsroom/press-releases/2015-11-10-gartner-says-6-billion-connected-things-will-be-in-use-in-2016-up-30-percent-from-2015.

Golbeck, Jennifer, Cristina Robles, and Karen Turner (2011), Predicting Personality with Social Media, in *Proceedings of the 2011 Annual Conference Extended Abstracts on Human Factors in Computing Systems-CHI EA '11*, New York, NY: ACM Press: 253.

Gosling, Samuel D., Adam A Augustine, Simine Vazire, Nicholas Holtzman, and Sam Gaddis (2011), Manifestations of Personality in Online Social Networks: Self-Reported Facebook-Related Behaviors and Observable Profile Information, *CyberPsychology, Behavior, and Social Networking* 14(9): 483–488.

Gretry, Anaïs, Csilla Horváth, Nina Belei, and Allard C.R. van Riel (2017), 'Don't Pretend to be my Friend!' When an Informal Brand Communication Style Backfires on Social Media, *Journal of Business Research* 74: 77–89.

Gruber, Daniel A., Ryan E. Smerek, Melissa C. Thomas-Hunt, and Erika H. James (2015), The Real-Time Power of Twitter: Crisis Management and Leadership in an Age of Social Media, *Business Horizons* 58(2): 163–172.

Hajli, Nick, Mohana Shanmugam, Savvas Papagiannidis, Debra Zahay, and Marie-Odile Richard (2017), Branding Co-creation with Members of Online Brand Communities, *Journal of Business Research* 70: 136–144.

Healy, Jason C., and Pierre McDonagh (2013), Consumer Roles in Brand Culture and Value Co-creation in Virtual Communities, *Journal of Business Research* 66(9): 1528–1540.

Heller Baird, Carolyn and Gautam Parasnis (2011), From Social Media to Social Customer Relationship Management, *Strategy & Leadership* 39(5): 30–37.

Hennig-Thurau, Thorsten, Kevin P. Gwinner, Gianfranco Walsh, and Dwayne D. Gremler (2004), Electronic Word-of-Mouth via Consumer-Opinion Platforms: What Motivates Consumers to Articulate themselves on the Internet?, *Journal of Interactive Marketing* 18(1): 38–52.

Hudson, Simon, Li Huang, Martin S. Roth, and Thomas J. Madden (2016), The Influence of Social Media Interactions on Consumer–Brand Relationships: A Three-Country Study of Brand Perceptions and Marketing Behaviors, *International Journal of Research in Marketing* 33(1): 27–41.

Hung, Kineta H., and Stella Yiyan Li (2007), The Influence of eWOM on Virtual Consumer Communities: Social Capital, Consumer Learning, and Behavioral Outcomes, *Journal of Advertising Research* 47(4): 485–495.

Hussain, Safdar, Wasim Ahmed, Rana Muhammad Sohail Jafar, Ambar Rabnawaz, and Yang Jianzhou (2017), eWOM Source Credibility, Perceived Risk and Food Product Customer's Information Adoption, *Computers in Human Behavior* 66: 96–102.

International Telecommunication Union (2018), Key ICT Indicators for Developed and Developing Countries and the World [Data file], https://www.itu.int/en/ITU-D/Statistics/Documents/statistics/2018/ITU_Key_2005-2018_ICT_data_with LDCs_rev27Nov2018.xls.

Joo, Mingyu, Kenneth C. Wilbur, Bo Cowgill, and Yi Zhu (2014), Television Advertising and Online Search, *Management Science* 60(1): 56–73.

Joo, Mingyu, Kenneth C. Wilbur, and Yi Zhu (2016), Effects of TV Advertising on Keyword Search, *International Journal of Research in Marketing* 33(3): 508–523.

Kannan, P.K. and Hongshuang "Alice" Li (2017), Digital Marketing: A Framework, Review and Research Agenda, *International Journal of Research in Marketing* 34(1): 22–45.

Kaplan, Andreas M. and Michael Haenlein (2010), Users of the World, Unite! The Challenges and Opportunities of Social Media, *Business Horizons* 53(1): 59–68.

Katona, Zsolt and Miklos Sarvary (2009), The Race for Sponsored Links: Bidding Patterns for Search Advertising, *Marketing Science* 29(2): 199–215.

Kietzmann, Jan H., Kristopher Hermkens, Ian P. McCarthy, and Bruno S. Silvestre (2011), Social Media? Get Serious! Understanding the Functional Building Blocks of Social Media, *Business Horizons* 54(3): 241–251.

Kilambi, Ana, Michel Laroche, and Marie-Odile Richard (2013), Constitutive Marketing Towards Understanding Brand Community Formation, *International Journal of Advertising* 45(1): 45–64.

Killian, Ginger and Kristy McManus (2015), A Marketing Communications Approach for the Digital Era: Managerial Guidelines for Social Media Integration, *Business Horizons* 58(5): 539–549.

Kozinets, R.V., K. de Valck, A.C. Wojnicki, and S.J.S. Wilner (2010), Networked Narratives: Understanding Word-of-Mouth Marketing in Online Communities, *Journal of Marketing* 74(2): 71–89.

Krafft, Manfred, Christine M. Arden, and Peter C. Verhoef (2017), Permission Marketing and Privacy Concerns—Why Do Customers (Not) Grant Permissions?, *Journal of Interactive Marketing* 39: 39–54.

Kressmann, Frank, M. Joseph Sirgy, Andreas Herrmann, Frank Huber, Stephanie Huber, and Dong Jin Lee (2006), Direct and Indirect Effects of Self-Image Congruence on Brand Loyalty, *Journal of Business Research* 59(9): 955–964.

Kronrod, Ann and Shai Danziger (2013), 'Wii Will Rock You!' The Use and Effect of Figurative Language in Consumer Reviews of Hedonic and Utilitarian Consumption, *Journal of Consumer Research* 40(4): 726–739.

Kronrod, Ann, Amir Grinstein, and Luc Wathieu (2012), Enjoy! Hedonic Consumption and Compliance with Assertive Messages, *Journal of Consumer Research* 39(1): 51–61.

Kumar, V, Lerzan Aksoy, Bas Donkers, Rajkumar Venkatesan, Thorsten Wiesel, and Sebastian Tillmanns (2010), Undervalued or Overvalued Customers: Capturing Total Customer Engagement Value, *Journal of Service Research* 13(3): 297–310.

Kumar, V. and R. Mirchandani (2012), Increasing the ROI of Social Media Marketing, *MIT Sloan Management Review* 54(1): 55–61.

Kumar, V., XI (Alan) Zhang, and Anita Luo (2014), Modeling Customer Opt-In and Opt-Out in a Permission-Based Marketing Context, *Journal of Marketing Research* 51(4): 403–419.

Lamberton, Cait and Andrew T. Stephen (2016), A Thematic Exploration of Digital, Social Media, and Mobile Marketing: Research Evolution from 2000 to 2015 and an Agenda for Future Inquiry, *Journal of Marketing* 80(6): 146–172.

Lee, In and Kyoochun Lee (2015), The Internet of Things (IoT): Applications, Investments, and Challenges for Enterprises, *Business Horizons* 58(4): 431–440.

Li, Hongshuang (Alice) and P.K. Kannan (2013), Attributing Conversions in a Multichannel Online Marketing Environment: An Empirical Model and a Field Experiment, *Journal of Marketing Research* 51(1): 40–56.

Liaukonyte, Jura, Thales Teixeira, and Kenneth C. Wilbur (2015), Television Advertising and Online Shopping, *Marketing Science* 34(3): 311–330.

Liu, Fang, Jianyao Li, Dick Mizerski, and Huangting Soh (2012), Self-Congruity, Brand Attitude, and Brand Loyalty: A Study on Luxury Brands, *European Journal of Marketing* (T. Abimbola, Ed.), 46(7/8): 922–937.

Louis, Didier and Cindy Lombart (2010), Impact of Brand Personality on Three Major Relational Consequences (Trust, Attachment, and Commitment to the Brand), *Journal of Product and Brand Management* 19(2): 114–130.

Malär, Lucia, Harley Krohmer, Wayne D Hoyer, and Bettina Nyffenegger (2011), Emotional Brand Attachment and Brand Personality: The Relative Importance of the Actual and the Ideal Self, *Journal of Marketing* 75(4): 35–52.

Malhotra, Naresh K., Sung S. Kim, and James Agarwal (2004), Internet Users' Information Privacy Concerns (IUIPC): The Construct, the Scale, and a Causal Model, *Information Systems Research* 15(4): 336–355.

Malthouse, Edward C, Michael Haenlein, Bernd Skiera, Egbert Wege, and Michael Zhang (2013), Managing Customer Relationships in the Social

Media Era: Introducing the Social CRM House, *Journal of Interactive Marketing* 27(4): 270–280.

Marotti, Ally and Lauren Zumbach (2017), Video Shows United Airlines' Passenger Dragged off Plane, *Chicago Tribune*, Chicago.

Martin, Kelly D. and Patrick E. Murphy (2017), The Role of Data Privacy in Marketing, *Journal of the Academy of Marketing Science* 45(2): 135–155.

McAlexander, James H., John W Schouten, and Harold F Koenig (2002), Building Brand Community, *Journal of Marketing* 66(1): 38–54.

Muniz, Albert M. and Thomas C. O'Guinn (2001), Brand Community, *Journal of Consumer Research*, 27(4): 412–432.

Narayanan, Sridhar and Kirthi Kalyanam (2015), Position Effects in Search Advertising and their Moderators: A Regression Discontinuity Approach, *Marketing Science* 34(3): 388–407.

Naylor, Rebecca Walker, Cait Poynor Lamberton, and Patricia M West (2012), Beyond the 'Like' Button: The Impact of Mere Virtual Presence on Brand Evaluations and Purchase Intentions in Social Media Settings, *Journal of Marketing* 76(6): 105–120.

Ng, Irene C.L. and Susan Y.L. Wakenshaw (2017), The Internet-of-Things: Review and Research Directions, *International Journal of Research in Marketing* 34(1): 3–21.

Park, Cheol and Thae Min Lee (2009), Information Direction, Website Reputation and eWOM Effect: A Moderating Role of Product Type, *Journal of Business Research* 62(1): 61–67.

Passy, Jacob (2017), Survey: Nearly half of Young Americans Say they Won't Fly United Anymore, *Market Watch*, https://www.marketwatch.com/story/nearly-half-of-young-americans-wont-fly-united-anymore-2017-04-21.

Payne, Adrian F, Kaj Storbacka, and Pennie Frow (2008), Managing the Co-creation of Value, *Journal of the Academy of Marketing Science* 36(1): 83–96.

Peters, Kay, Yubo Chen, Andreas M Kaplan, Björn Ognibeni, and Koen Pauwels (2013), Social Media Metrics—A Framework and Guidelines for Managing Social Media, *Journal of Interactive Marketing* 27(4): 281–298.

Plummer, Joseph T. (2000), How Personality Makes a Difference, *Journal of Advertising Research* 40(6): 79–83.

Qiu, Lin, Han Lin, Jonathan Ramsay, and Fang Yang (2012), You are What you Tweet: Personality Expression and Perception on Twitter, *Journal of Research in Personality* 46(6): 710–718.

Radler, Viktoria Maria (2018), 20 Years of Brand Personality: A Bibliometric Review and Research Agenda, *Journal of Brand Management* 25(4): 370–383.

Richins, Marsha L. (1983), Negative Word-of-Mouth by Dissatisfied Consumers: A Pilot Study, *Journal of Marketing* 47(1): 68.

Rust, R., K. Lemon, and D. Narayandas (2004), Customer Equity Management, Prentice Hall, New Jersey, USA.

Rutz, Oliver J., Randolph E. Bucklin, and Garrett P. Sonnier (2012), A Latent Instrumental Variables Approach to Modeling Keyword Conversion in Paid Search Advertising, *Journal of Marketing Research* 49(3): 306–319.

Saarikko, Ted, Ulrika H. Westergren, and Tomas Blomquist (2017), The Internet of Things: Are you Ready for What's Coming?, *Business Horizons* 60(5): 667–676.

Sashi, C.M. (2012), Customer Engagement, Buyer-Seller Relationships, and Social Media, *Management Decision* 50(2): 253–272.

Sawhney, Mohanbir, Gianmario Verona, and Emanuela Prandelli (2005), Collaborating to Create: The Internet as a Platform for Customer Engagement in Product Innovation, *Journal of Interactive Marketing* 19(4): 4–17.

Schoenbachler, Denise D. and Geoffrey L. Gordon (2002), Trust and Customer Willingness to Provide Information in Database-Driven Relationship Marketing, *Journal of Interactive Marketing* 16(3): 2–16.

Schultz, Don E. and James Jimmy Peltier (2013), Social Media's Slippery Slope: Challenges, Opportunities and Future Research Directions, *Journal of Research in Interactive Marketing* 7(2): 86–99.

Shankar, Venkatesh and Sridhar Balasubramanian (2009), Mobile Marketing: A Synthesis and Prognosis, *Journal of Interactive Marketing* 23(2): 118–129.

Shankar, Venkatesh, Alladi Venkatesh, Charles Hofacker, and Prasad Naik (2010), Mobile Marketing in the Retailing Environment: Current Insights and Future Research Avenues, *Journal of Interactive Marketing* 24(2): 111–120.

Sung, Yongjun and Jooyoung Kim (2010), Effects of Brand Personality on Brand Trust and Brand Affect, *Psychology and Marketing* 27(7): 639–661.

Teng, Shasha, Kok Wei Khong, Wei Wei Goh, and Alain Yee Loong Chong (2014), Examining the Antecedents of Persuasive eWOM Messages in Social Media, *Online Information Review* (D. David Stuart, Ed.), 38(6): 746–768.

Trainor, Kevin J., James (Mick) Andzulis, Adam Rapp, and Raj Agnihotri (2014), Social Media Technology Usage and Customer Relationship Performance: A Capabilities-Based Examination of Social CRM, *Journal of Business Research* 67(6): 1201–1208.

Toubia, Oliver and Andrew T. Stephen (2013), Intrinsic vs. Image-Related Utility in Social Media: Why do People Contribute Content to Twitter? *Marketing Science* 32(3): 368–392.

Tynan, Caroline, Sally Mckechnie, and Celine Chhuon (2010), Co-creating Value for Luxury Brands, *Journal of Business Research* 63: 1156–1163.

van Dijck, Jose (2013), *The Culture of Connectivity: A Critical History of Social Media.* Oxford University Press, Oxford, UK.

van Doorn, Jenny, Katherine N Lemon, Vikas Mittal, Stephan Nass, Doreén Pick, Peter Pirner, and Peter C Verhoef (2010), Customer Engagement Behavior: Theoretical Foundations and Research Directions, *Journal of Service Research* 13(3): 253–66.

Vargo, Stephen L. and Robert F. Lusch (2004), Evolving to a New Dominant Logic for Marketing, *Journal of Marketing* 68(1): 1–17.

Verhoef, Peter C, Werner J Reinartz, and Manfred Krafft (2010), Customer Engagement as a New Perspective in Customer Management, *Journal of Service Research* 13(3): 247–252.

Watson, Catherine, Jeff McCarthy, and Jennifer Rowley (2013), Consumer Attitudes towards Mobile Marketing in the Smart Phone Era, *International Journal of Information Management* 33(5): 840–849.

Waytz, Adam, Joy Heafner, and Nicholas Epley (2014), The Mind in the Machine: Anthropomorphism Increases Trust in an Autonomous Vehicle, *Journal of Experimental Social Psychology* 52: 113–117.

Wiesel, Thorsten, Koen Pauwels, and Joep Arts (2010), Practice Prize Paper—Marketing's Profit Impact: Quantifying Online and Off-line Funnel Progression, *Marketing Science* 30(4): 604–611.

Xu, Lizhen, Jason A. Duan, and Andrew B. Whinston (2012), Path to Purchase: A Mutually Exciting Point Process Model for Online Advertising and Conversion, *Management Science* 60(6): 1,392–1,412.

Xu, Zhenning, Gary L. Frankwick, and Edward Ramirez (2016), Effects of Big Data Analytics and Traditional Marketing Analytics on New Product Success: A Knowledge Fusion Perspective, *Journal of Business Research* 69(5): 1,562–1,566.

Yadav, M.S., K. de Valck, T. Hennig-Thurau, D.L. Hoffman, and M. Spann (2013), Social Commerce: A Contingency Framework for Assessing Marketing Potential, *Journal of Interactive Marketing* 27: 311–323.

Yang, Sha and Anindya Ghose (2010), Analyzing the Relationship between Organic and Sponsored Search Advertising: Positive, Negative or Zero Interdependence?, *Marketing* Science 29(4): 602–623.

11

Future of Customer Relationship Marketing: New Directions for Research

OVERVIEW

In Chapter 11, we discuss several important research directions that are promising as a result of big data revolution, availability of computing power, and emerging models of estimating customer lifetime value (CLV), both transaction/engagement-based B2C activities. We also discuss some unintended consequences (dark side) of customer–brand relationships including forms of dis-identification and privacy related issues. In particular, we provide a discussion on the role of ethics in general, and normative ethics in particular, in building customer relationship marketing (CRM). Finally, we provide a brief discussion on some challenges and research opportunities facing B2B relationship marketing. At the end of the chapter, we provide key takeaways and conclude with discussion questions and HBS and Ivey cases. But first, to give a flavor of CRM and future research trends, we provide some real-life vignettes.

OPENING VIGNETTES

Vignette 1: American Express uses a multi-tier loyalty program for its customers to induce greater loyalty and retention (see Figure 11.1). Some of its customers are the "best" customers and are classified as Gold members. This causes an upward shift in their expectations: "I am a Gold member, so I am entitled to receive excellent service." However, a potential discrepancy between perceived performance and expectations may have a strong negative effect on customer satisfaction, i.e., "satisfaction trap." How does American Express handle rising expectations from its best customers?

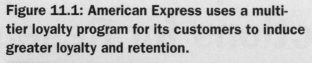

Figure 11.1: American Express uses a multi-tier loyalty program for its customers to induce greater loyalty and retention.

Vignette 2: Significant research has been done on online ratings, reviews, and social media interactions and the data has been related to company sales, brand performance, and stock market returns, including the impact of social influence on ratings and reviews. There are several areas still un-explored. How can data on social interactions, reviews, and ratings be used for designing new products and services (see Figure 11.2)? How can firms actively monitor and manage social media toward positive brand image and reputation? While sentiment analysis is used to capture valence information (number of stars or likes), future research should look at semantic analysis of user-generated content.

Figure 11.2: How can data on online social interactions, reviews, and ratings be used for designing new products and services?

INTRODUCTION

In the past two decades, research on customer relationship marketing (CRM) has proliferated and matured in terms of new customer-based CRM theories, models, and frameworks. Advances have been made in both purchase-based loyalty programs capturing customer lifetime value (CLV) but more recently in customer engagement strategies (customer referral value [CRV], customer influence value [CIV], and customer knowledge value [CKV]). Sophisticated models and metrics to determine customer value and customer equity have evolved. Understanding the need for a holistic approach to CRM, employee engagement strategies have been linked with customer engagement strategies as well. At the same time, customer-based relationship marketing strategies need to be designed and implemented in the context of other critical stakeholders — hence, the need for a stakeholder-focused approach to relationship marketing. In particular, understanding B2B relationships is critical with the growth of emerging markets, disruptive technology, and a power shift in buyer–supplier relationships.

In a digitally connected world, placing more emphasis on a broad set of stakeholders, in simultaneously addressing their multiple interests, is absolutely critical for building superior customer–brand relationship, than merely taking a myopic market-driven approach. Notably, with recent advances in digital technologies and access to big data, CRM strategies now can be customized in the deepest and widest sense ever possible. Yet, several areas of concerns still exist and there remains more work to be done. With new opportunities in the digital and social media realm, come new sets of problems and pitfalls; hence, the time for marketers to fully understand and appreciate ethical theories, particularly, normative ethics from the customers' perspective is now. Understanding and implementing ethics of the highest order at every conceivable touchpoint in the customers' journey is not only the "right" thing to do, it is also the "smart" thing to do, making a strong "business case" for ethics.

In this chapter, we discuss critical research issues and questions surrounding CRM that are interesting, but more importantly relevant for scholars and practitioners, going forward. These include static versus dynamic view of relationship; financial versus engagement outcomes; engagement strategies and relationship stages; digital and social media strategies; unintended consequences of relationship marketing strategies; multiple facets of customer–company identification; role of normative ethics in relationship marketing; modeling new types of costs in customers' value perception especially considering the role of privacy; and challenges and opportunities in B2B relationship marketing. We discuss each of these next.

STATIC VERSUS DYNAMIC VIEWS OF RELATIONSHIP

One of the research issues is whether the relationship lifecycle view matches reality. Lewicki *et al.* (2006) argue that previous studies have been "static" and that longitudinal examinations of individual relationships remain noticeably absent. Most frameworks note that relationships begin with an *exploratory* or *identifying stage*, marked by limited confidence in the partner's ability and trustworthiness, as well as a willingness to explore the relationship because customers perceive value when perceived benefits outweigh undesired consequences for the focal partner's offering but also relative to competitive offerings. When initial experiences are positive and produce both desired outcomes and experiential evidence of trustworthiness, relationships grow during the *expansion* or *developing stage*. This growth includes an escalation of reciprocated transactions and increased affective attachment, as demonstrated in variables such as trust, commitment, and satisfaction. When the relationship continues to the developing phase, the partners obtain increased benefits and greater inter-dependence, and then reach a *maturity, commitment*, or *maintaining stage*. Their calculative trust is replaced by knowledge-based (Rousseau *et al.*, 1998) and affective-based trust that leads to long-term commitments to the relationship. However, research also suggests that previously successful relationships can enter a *negative* or *terminating stage* in which trust and commitment decline over time (Dwyer *et al.*, 1987; Jap and Ganesan, 2000). Grayson and Ambler (1999) test the link between relational constructs and performance outcomes moderated by relationship duration and find support for their expectations of a "dark side" of long-term relationships.

Palmatier (2008) and later Palmatier *et al.* (2013) propose a dynamic framework of studying relationship trajectories over time. Some scholars have started addressing this issue by using latent growth curve modeling to study the time-varying trajectories of constructs (Bollen and Curran, 2006; Palmatier *et al.*, 2013). Latent growth curve analysis investigates the developmental or growth process of constructs by modeling the level, velocity, and acceleration factors (latent growth parameters) that explain the observed growth trajectories. The study by Palmatier *et al.* (2007) shows that trust increases during the first six years, but commitment peaks at about year four and then starts to decay. Trust and commitment appear dynamically linked, such that the initial level of trust positively influences the initial level of commitment, but the velocity of trust also positively influences the velocity of commitment. The effect of the initial level of commitment on sales growth is not significant; only the velocity and acceleration of commitment exert significant positive effects on exchange performance (e.g., sales growth). The study also found that low levels of initial trust and/or commitment in a relationship may be overcome by higher levels of velocity and/or acceleration. In a later study, Palmatier *et al.* (2013) provide theoretical and empirical evidence

for a dynamic model of relationship marketing validating that commitment velocity influences sales performance, beyond the impact of the static level of commitment. They also found that while trust, communication, and investment capabilities influence commitment velocity, it is the investment capabilities that drive commitment velocity through continual exploration and exploitation of opportunities.

Therefore, cross-sectional studies that typically employ levels rather than velocity and acceleration of relational constructs fail to capture the dynamic effects and can also mislead researchers. Future scholars should capture information on relationship dynamics (i.e., velocity and acceleration) as they are more diagnostic than static lifecycle information (i.e., levels). In this sense, there is a critical need to study relationship-based constructs using causal research design (as opposed to survey designs) and latent growth modeling methods. For instance, the customer satisfaction-loyalty link in relationship frameworks studied through satisfaction and attitudinal surveys has traditionally suffered from common method variance bias. High correlation between satisfaction-loyalty is a spurious predictor of future customer loyalty with the firm. Studies have shown that several exogenous factors have contributed more to the variance in loyalty than satisfaction, including relationship duration and prior usage (Bolton and Lemon, 1999) and customer knowledge about competitive alternatives (Capraro *et al.*, 2003), among others. Palmatier (and his colleagues) have certainly set the trend in this important research direction.

FINANCIAL VERSUS ENGAGEMENT OUTCOMES

The most common metrics, sales-based outcome measures take many forms, including annual sales growth, sales diversity (number of different products and services sold to a customer), sales volatility (variability in sales over time), and share of wallet (SOW) (sales penetration for a specific customer). Some sales-based metrics are relevant only for a portfolio of customers, such as the number of new customers generated or retention and churn rates (firm's ability to retain existing customers). Then there are profitability-based outcome measures, which include price premiums (e.g., percentage a customer will pay to deal with a seller with which it has a strong relationship) and reduced selling costs. However, aggregate measures of performance best encapsulate the diverse mechanisms by which RM affects performance. Customer lifetime value (CLV)-based measures capture the broad range of potential performance enhancing relational behaviors because it discounts future cash flows and selling costs and thereby indicates the customer's present value (i.e., both sales and profit effects). While popular, its calculations are sensitive to assumptions (margins, future growth rates, allocation of costs). Palmatier (2008) discusses another aggregate outcome measure, return on investment (ROI), well suited for evaluating specific marketing programs. Based on an earlier study (Palmatier *et al.*, 2006), the author finds mixed results of ROI when social, structural, and financial RM programs are implemented. Specifically, social programs generate positive returns, structural programs break even in the first year, and financial programs fail to generate positive returns in the short term. Finally, Palmatier (2008) discusses that knowledge-based outcomes, while not a true financial measure, may represent an important outcome of strong customer–seller relationships. Customers often provide insights into new markets, help firms uncover new product opportunities, enable them to beta test and refine new product concepts, and accelerate the adoption of new product launches. However, linking RM investments in current customers to different future customers often represents an insurmountable problem. Knowledge-based outcomes, such as number of patents, time

to market, and new product success rate, also may provide insights into some relational benefits not captured in financial measures. Measuring knowledge-based outcomes may be especially important for firms implementing innovation-based strategies. CKV-based metrics are still in an infancy stage, and marketers need to develop reliable and valid metrics for CKV, and how these metrics relate with CLV, CRV, and CIV. For instance, Kumar *et al.* (2010) argue that CKV is often correlated with CLV but might the inverted U-shaped relationship hold true? These and other CKV-related research questions need to be studied.

ENGAGEMENT STRATEGIES AND RELATIONSHIP STAGES

Venkatesan *et al.* (2018) discuss a few research opportunities of interest and relevance for managers to be able to extract full value from customers. First, during acquisition stage, most of the research has focused on CLV of a potential customer (Kumar *et al.*, 2010). However, relatively little research has looked at leveraging CIV and CKV of potential customers. How can firms identify potential customers with large social networks and high degree of influence and what are the best methods of acquiring them (see Figure 11.3)? How can firms identify and predict the future CKV of lead users before adoption and the best methods of acquiring them? Second, during growth stage, much research has looked at extracting higher value from customers by way of cross-selling and up-selling to current customers (Kumar *et al.*, 2008). What is relatively unknown is what role does customer experience play in motivating customers to influence prospects directly through referrals or indirectly through sharing recommendations through social networks (i.e., CRV and CIV)? Would the portfolio of products used to cross-sell and up-sell be different when the firm is trying to increase

CLV versus CRV and CIV? Third, during retention stage, most research has focused on retention and churn models (e.g., Neslin *et al.*, 2006). What is less known is what motivates staying customers to share their experiences through word-of-mouth (CRV) and influence (CIV)? Under what conditions, can CIV offer greater value to the firm even when their CLV is not as profitable? For instance, a current Gmail customer may not be profitable to Google but may create same-side and cross-side network effects. Finally, during win-back stage, some research has examined the types of win-back offers to customers based on their second customer lifetime value (SCLV) (Kumar *et al.*, 2015). However, little is known about the relative importance of CKV, CRV, and CIV that firms should evaluate for win-back customers. Since SCLV is the sole focus in win-back strategy, how important is second customer referral value (SCRV) and second customer influence value (SCIV)? Answers to these research questions will help marketers to accurately allocate resources in the right value generation stream and optimize total lifetime value of customers and consequently improve return on investment (ROI).

DIGITAL AND SOCIAL MEDIA STRATEGIES

Prior to the big data era, companies have been collecting CRM related information about their customers through membership cards, browser cookies, and click stream analysis. With the advent of social media, companies can now access disparate and huge data on their customers and their social networks. There is a growing need to conduct empirical research that seeks to measure the impact of social commerce across decision-making phases (i.e., need recognition, pre-purchase, purchase, and post-purchase) and across social media platforms (e.g., Facebook, Twitter, Pinterest). Yadav *et al.* (2013) discusses several research avenues. First, scholars need to provide compelling evidence for the potential of social commerce beyond non-computer mediated approaches. There is a growing demand from managers for "numbers" that will provide justifying the allocation of financial resources. The value of social information, beyond other information source, needs to be ascertained parsing out online versus offline effects and multiple sources of social information. Second, given the differences in content

Figure 11.3: How can firms identify potential customers with large social networks and high degree of influence and what are the best methods of acquiring them?

and functionality across social media platforms, scholars need to set up experimental studies to examine inter-platform differences (Facebook, Twitter), social transaction differences, and their impact on sales revenue. Third, the interaction of social network sites (SNS) and stage of customer journey needs to be explicated. For instance, does social information acquired from Facebook increase the likelihood of purchase from Facebook commerce site? Finally, there is a need to develop a reliable and valid "social transaction" metric that links firm revenues to computer-mediated social network environments. Further, the ability to process unstructured data can be used in predictive analytic models estimating CLV or responses to marketing activities (Malthouse *et al.*, 2013). For instance, variables can be extracted from social media content to flag an interest, emotion, or attitude of a customer for segmentation strategy or predictive modeling.

UNINTENDED CONSEQUENCES OF RELATIONSHIP MARKETING STRATEGIES

Customer Expectations/Entitlement

If a firm explicitly acknowledges to some of its customers that they are the "best" customer by classifying them as priority and privileged customers, this may cause an upward shift in their expectations. Based on expectation confirmation theory (Oliver, 1980), customer satisfaction is a function of the potential discrepancy between perceived performance and expectation, which has a strong negative effect on customer satisfaction, i.e., the "satisfaction trap." High-tier customers are prone to this satisfaction trap more as a negative incident has a substantial detrimental impact on satisfaction relative to low-tier customers (Von Wangenheim and Bayón, 2007). Such high standing customers feel a sense of entitlement and demand services commensurate with their

standing (Wetzel *et al.*, 2014). In practice, it may be hard to circumvent such increased expectations of high-tier customers. Conversely, the effect of a positive critical incident is stronger for low-tier customers than for high-tier customers. Over time, depending on customer's profitability track record, customers may also change their tier membership, getting promoted to a higher tier or demoted to a lower tier. A drop in reward is more damaging to the customer–firm relationship than a corresponding increase based on Prospect theory (Kahneman and Tversky, 1979) wherein customers are more sensitive to losses than to gains of similar magnitude. So, when customers experience upgrades, followed by downgrades, increased expectations are shattered by losses leading to lower trust, commitment, loyalty, and engagement behavior (Van Berlo *et al.*, 2014; Wagner *et al.*, 2009). The negative effect is particularly strong with an external locus of causality, rather than with an internal or situation locus, as the customer may blame the firm for the demotion and consider the demotion as unfair or due to opportunistic behavior of the firm (Van Berlo *et al.*, 2014).

Customer Heterogeneity

What about customers of a firm where customers in the higher tiers receive discretionary preferential treatment in an attempt to stimulate desired engagement behaviors? A customer may observe these differential treatments and compare the way she/he is treated with reciprocity norms, with how other customers are treated, and with norms based on input–outcome ratios (Steinhoff and Palmatier, 2015). Preferential treatment may delight one customer but enrage or embarrass another and the effect depends on the degree of justification, imposition, visibility, and surprise. In general, customers prefer preferential treatments that are justified, imposed by the firm, visible to other customers, and a surprise to the recipients. However, a substantial proportion of customers may feel embarrassed if the preferential treatment is visible and if the imposed treatment creates a disadvantage for other customers (Butori and De Bruyn, 2013). In addition, Steinhoff and Palmatier (2015) find significant "bystander" effects: the relationships with low-tier customers who observe others' preferential treatment are harmed considerably. Therefore, accommodating such customer heterogeneities is a major challenge in the design and management of loyalty programs.

Customer Reactance

Some customers have a higher propensity to provide false information to marketers or engage in negative response as a result of highly personalized and marketing messages they believe violate their privacy (Martin and Murphy, 2017; Tucker, 2014) (see Figure 11.4). The literature on information privacy shows that, in general, customers are willing to provide personal information in exchange for customized offerings and personalization value as a quid pro quo (Schumann *et al.*, 2014). However, there is also a parallel privacy paradox, which suggests that customers also experience feelings of vulnerability,

while valuing marketer-initiated benefits, and in extreme forms can trigger psychological reactance manifested as communication avoidance, information falsification, and derogatory word-of-mouth (White *et al.*, 2008). Customers who perceive power imbalance related to firm's privacy practices are more likely to manifest reactance. Firms can mitigate customer reactance effect by transferring greater control to customers and providing increased data transparency to them (Martin *et al.*, 2017).

MULTIPLE FACETS OF CUSTOMER– COMPANY IDENTIFICATION

Identification

According to social identity theory (Tajfel and Turner, 1979, 1986), individuals derive identity not only from personal identity (i.e., that related to a person's individual sense of self), but also social identity (i.e., that related to groups to which a person belongs or is affiliated). The theory purports that social identity can be derived from groups to which one explicitly

Figure 11.4: Some customers have a higher propensity to engage in negative response as a result of highly personalized and marketing messages they believe violate their privacy

belongs, as well as groups that the individual perceives a sense of affiliation with or similarity to, even when the individual has no contact with specific group members (Brewer, 1991). Most research examining organizational identification has done so in formal membership contexts (Bergami and Bagozzi, 2000; Bhattacharya *et al.*, 1995) and a sizeable amount of this research has focused specifically on employees' identification with the organizations they work for (Ashforth and Mael, 1989; Bergami and Bagozzi, 2000; Dutton *et al.*, 1994; Kreiner and Ashforth, 2004). More recent findings indicate that people can identify with organizations even when they are not formal group members (e.g., Pratt, 2000; Scott and Lane, 2000), such as customers who can identify with the companies they patronize (Ahearne *et al.*, 2005; Bhattacharya and Sen, 2003; Einwiller *et al.*, 2006). Certainly, marketers have successfully used loyalty-based reward programs, cross-selling/up-selling, and engagement strategies to extract the full value of identified customers.

However, qualitatively distinct customer–company identification experiences can arise (see Elsbach, 1999; Kreiner and Ashforth, 2004; for similar notions in the employee–organization domain), and that customer connections with companies can be more complex and varied than current consumer identification models can account for. While extant research conceptualizes customer identification as a one-dimensional continuum from low to high (Ahearne *et al.*, 1995; Einwiller *et al.*, 2006), a two-dimensional model wherein customers can experience either low or high identification (i.e., a sense of connection with the organization and viewing the organization's identity as reflecting her or his own identity) and either low or high dis-identification (i.e., a sense of separation from the organization and viewing the organization's identity as not reflecting her or his own identity) is possible. This can result in four distinct consumer identification experiences:

1. identification (high identification/low dis-identification),

2. dis-identification (low identification/high dis-identification),

3. ambivalent identification (high identification/high dis-identification), and

4. neutral identification (low identification/low dis-identification).

Since most research in customer relationship marketing (CRM) relates to identification, we will only focus on dis-identification, ambivalent identification, and neutral identification next as areas for future research.

Dis-identification

Consider the experience of dis-identification whereby a customer actively separates her or his identity from the company and experiences a negative relational categorization of the self and the firm (Elsbach and Bhattacharya, 2001). As a result, identification and dis-identification are often negatively correlated, but are not viewed as being at opposite ends of a one-dimensional scale (e.g., Elsbach, 1999; Kreiner and Ashforth, 2004). Dis-identification may occur, e.g., because the customer's own identity is at odds with the company's identity, values, or practices. For example, a customer may dis-identify with The Gap Inc. after hearing about sweatshop labor practices — something that the customer wishes to separate the self from.

Theoretical support for the notion of consumer dis-identification experiences is found in social identity theory, which proposes that people strive to maintain a positive social identity and that when a social identity becomes viewed negatively, individuals will attempt to restore positive identity, sometimes by physically or psychologically distancing the self from that group (Tajfel and Turner, 1979; Jackson *et al.*, 1996). Thus, demonstrating who one is *not* may also be a way of maintaining a positive and distinctive social identity (Brewer, 1991). Further support for dis-identification lies in Heider's (1958) balance theory, which suggests that individuals can maintain both connections and separations between themselves and social objects to achieve self-concept balance. Thus, while consumers sometimes achieve balance in terms of how they see themselves by identifying with companies, dis-identification can be a means of maintaining consistency (Elsbach, 1999). Further, the self-regulatory system can be motivated by either a desired or undesired end state (see Crowe and Higgins, 1997). Thus, consumer dis-identification is conceptualized as an avoidance orientation grounded in avoiding undesired outcomes. Current CRM models can integrate CLV and CIV concepts with dis-identified customers and whether or not it is profitable to use win-back strategies. Not all customers are worthy of win-back; rather, firms should focus on the second lifetime value, segment them on this basis, and evaluate customers in each segment to determine why they dis-identify.

Ambivalent Identification

Although not empirically examined in the customer context, ambivalent identification toward companies occurs when an individual simultaneously identifies and dis-identifies with an organization (Elsbach, 1999). Given the complexity of modern organizations, it is quite possible to identify with one aspect of the organization while dis-identifying with another (Kreiner and Ashforth, 2004). Consider a customer who identifies with Walmart's support of local charities, but simultaneously dis-identifies with Walmart because its practices often have adverse effects on local economies. It is also possible to simultaneously identify and dis-identify with the same aspect of the company. Consider a consumer who identifies with Walmart's cost-cutting strategy as it leads to superior efficiency in services, but dis-identifies with this practice because it contributes to inferior product quality.

As noted earlier, social identity theory proposes that individuals are motivated to maintain positive views of themselves and their social identities (Tajfel and Turner, 1979). One implication of this is that people will often reinforce positive aspects of their social groups, while simultaneously dissociating from negative aspects of their social groups (Jackson *et al.*, 1996; Snyder *et al.*, 1986; Tajfel and Turner, 1979). Ambivalent attitudes have also been demonstrated in research on social groups (Costarelli and Palmonari, 2003; Jost and Burgess, 2000), employee-organizational identification (Kreiner and Ashforth, 2004; Pratt, 2000), and consumer emotions (Otnes *et al.*, 1997). The evidence from these related literatures supports our suggestion that ambivalent identification experiences may also arise between consumers and the companies they patronize. How can firms use customer engagement strategies to motivate ambivalent customers in becoming effective referrals and influencers? Can firms effectively use loyalty programs, cross-selling, up-selling, and incentivized referrals to sway ambivalent customers toward identified customers?

Neutral Identification

Neutral identification involves being low in both identification and dis-identification with regard to an organization (Elsbach, 1999; Kreiner and Ashforth, 2004). Rather than being a midpoint on a one-dimensional scale, neutral identification represents low dis-identification and low identification. Take, for example, a customer who feels neither a strong connection nor disconnection toward a company. Given that social identity theory suggests that individuals are motivated to either reinforce or downplay group associations depending on their ability to confer a positive social identity (Tajfel and Turner, 1979), it seems likely that group associations that have no self-relevant social identity implications for the individual will result in neutral identification. Indeed, neutral identification has been observed in the employee–organizational literature (Kreiner and Ashforth, 2004). It has also been forwarded that neutral identification with a company can be a state of self-definition in its own right (Dukerich *et al.*, 1998; Elsbach, 1999), such that one can define the self by neither strongly identifying nor dis-identifying with the company. Drawing from past research then, we propose that customers may also experience neutral identification regarding the companies they patronize. These customers need an extra dose of motivation and CLV strategies can be effectively leveraged into customer engagement strategies to extract customer engagement value (i.e., CRV, CIV, and CKV). Both customer equity and relational equity of this segment that remains untapped could be harnessed.

ROLE OF NORMATIVE ETHICS IN RELATIONSHIP MARKETING

Since Murphy *et al.*'s (2007) commentary over a decade ago regarding relationship marketing and virtue ethics, customers now have fewer interactions with brick and mortar stores. Online marketing has greatly influenced buyer–seller relationships. The virtue of trust is still central to moving customers from a transaction-oriented mindset to a more relational one. The Edelman Trust Barometer recently revealed that trust in institutions has declined broadly in the United States. Over 80% of consumers say that trust is important but only 28% believe that companies are more trustworthy today than in the past (Stephens, 2018). With this backdrop, Laczniak and Murphy (2019) advocate that firms (and scholars) return to the virtue of trust, a promise that has been the bedrock of relationship marketing for some time (Gundlach and Murphy, 1993; Morgan and Hunt, 1994; Garbarino and Johnson, 1999). Besides building trust, other virtues, like transparency and integrity, need further clarification so that their benefits to brand success are more fully understood.

An important question relates to the norm generation of how ethics is (or should be) defined and how ethical values that are relevant for marketers should be generated. What does it really mean to act ethically in a marketing context? Several approaches can be examined on how norms are generated including Murphy's (1999) virtue ethics, integrative social contract theory (Dunfee *et al.*, 1999), Kant's three formulations of the categorical imperative (Bowie, 1999), communicative approach such as dialogic idealism (Nill, 2003), and Laczniak and Murphy's normative framework based on seven integrated perspectives. Relationship marketers should identify and accept the authentic norms of the communities they are embedded in, as long as these norms are compatible with hyper-norms and follow the spirit of the overall macrosocial contract (Dunfee *et al.*, 1999). However, the concept of hyper-norms has been criticized for its difficulty in justifying and interpreting what these norms are and in providing practical guidance to managers. Similarly, deontological approaches such as Kantian categorical imperative have been criticized for being too abstract to provide practical guidance or too strict to consider complex situations.

Relationship marketing scholars need to identify the full spectrum of marketing-relevant hyper-norms applicable in all customer–brand relational touchpoints and explore the antecedents of authentic and legitimate norms prevalent in each community, especially in the global marketplace where there is drive to transfer such norms. For instance, should firms get involved in taking a moral stand in a political/social discourse? Not all moral stances are equal and diverse issues with varying likelihood and strength will elicit a myriad of stakeholder reactions; hence, there is a need for relationship marketing scholars to develop a conceptual taxonomy of stances that will inform marketers of various pathways to positively impact both business and society. A related pertinent research question remains: how can companies minimize political backlash when taking a stance as invariably there is bound to be both positive and negative reactions from a divided marketplace? Further, research indicates that individuals with liberal political ideology tend to prioritize individuating moral foundations of harm/care and fairness/reciprocity and justice each focusing on protecting vulnerable individuals and their rights and welfare, respectively. In contrast, conservatives tend to prioritize binding moral foundations of in-group/loyalty, authority and respect, and purity/sanctity. We see a promising blend of research in marketing originating from political ideology (Ball and Dagger, 2005) and moral foundations theory (Haidt and Graham, 2007) that influence customers in their market and non-market choices.

MODELING NEW TYPES OF COSTS IN CUSTOMER'S VALUE PERCEPTION: CASE FOR PRIVACY

Palmatier (2008) points out that extant research focuses mostly on the seller's relationship marketing benefits and costs. Firms derive value from their customers defined as "the economic value of the customer relationship to the firm — expressed on the basis of contribution margin or net profit" (p. 4). Various metrics are available for measuring the value of the customer and in implementing the CRM strategies. These include backward-looking metrics such as Recency--Frequency–Monetary value (RFM), Share of Wallet (SOW), and Past Customer Value (PCV) and forward-looking metrics such as Customer Lifetime Value (CLV), Customer Referral Value (CRV), Customer Influence Value (CIV), and Customer Knowledge Value (CKV).

However, more research should focus on customer's relationship marketing benefits and costs, and the concept of customer value as seen by customers (see Figure 11.5). Kumar and Reinartz (2016) define

perceived value as customers' net valuation of the perceived benefits accrued from an offering that is based on the costs they are willing to give up for the needs they are seeking to satisfy. Customers choose actions that, ceteris paribus, maximize the desired consequences and minimize undesired consequences. Perceived attributes are aggregated by customers into abstract benefits and there is a long tradition of preference measurement in marketing that uses compositional and decompositional models (Green and Srinivasan, 1978, 1990; Holbrook, 1981; Rao, 2014; Agarwal *et al.*, 2015). However, this mapping process is considered only for the offering's attributes but has overlooked monetary and non-monetary cost aspects such as price, transaction costs, risks, and privacy. For instance, while customers' needs and costs on customer perceptions of value have been studied from tangible product aspects, the intangible aspects of network effect on perceived value is largely underexplored. Besides price modeled much in marketing analytical models, there is a large set of transaction costs, learning costs, maintenance and life cycle cost not considered in existing models. Especially, in the context of digitization (Google, Facebook), customers pay not in monetary costs but in terms of personal information they are willing to give up in the exchange. Privacy is becoming so important that some customers are willing to pay to preserve privacy (Rust *et al.*, 2002). A more comprehensive treatment of the value of privacy is required both in online and offline context and the trade-off between privacy and willingness to pay. Further, given increasing levels of customer engagement behaviors, what is the role of customer engagement in customer privacy issues, in that will greater engagement lower the sensitivity to privacy? How can normative ethical theory inform what firms should be doing to exceed customer privacy expectations, especially in the absence of a strong legal framework (Martin and Murphy, 2017)? While

Figure 11.5: More research should focus on customer's relationship marketing benefits and costs and the concept of customer value as seen by customers.

most marketers are not looking for idealism, but for strategies and systems that work, an understanding of ethical theories and tenets is helpful to better structure ethical questions (Nill, 2003).

Martin and Murphy (2017) caution against taking a narrow utilitarian calculus of monetizing customer data in favor of a comprehensive and multidimensional approach that offers customers greater control, privacy, and transparency. According to them, several unanswered research questions still remain: How can normative ethical theory pave the way for what organizations should be doing to exceed consumer privacy expectations? How might we better understand consumer preference and choice related to organizational use of their information? How might we capture cross-cultural and cross-national variation of privacy concerns across stakeholder groups? And how can we understand firm recovery strategies to reengage customers after massive privacy failure? (Martin and Murphy, 2017, pp. 152). Future research can draw from a plethora

of ethical theories, e.g., consequence-based, duty-based, contract-based, and virtue-based theories to address each of these complex and fast-moving dynamic issues confronting customers at various relational touchpoints. The normative analysis of ethical behavior in marketing can focus on outcomes, intentions, agreed to conventions, the character of the manager or any combination thereof. When several ethical perspectives are applied to complicated marketing situations, the investigation becomes deep and multifarious.

CHALLENGES AND NEW RESEARCH OPPORTUNITIES IN B2B RELATIONSHIP MARKETING

There is potential for customer engagement in B2B relationships. Using a Delphi approach, Griffin *et al.* (2013) identified three themes in B2B innovation: (1) improving the understanding of B2B customer needs and customer involvement in new products;

(2) innovating in B2B beyond the lab; and (3) the role of marketing in B2B innovation. B2B customers can be engaged in a timely and cost-effective way while at the same time protecting sensitive information (Noordhoff *et al.*, 2011). While, Hoffman, Kopalle, and Novak (2010) have developed a scale to identify customers who are likely to be good sources of information, there is a need to develop measures of customer engagement value in B2B markets. Given the critical role of strategic alliances in B2B relationships, customer (partner) selection and valuation using the Lead User approach (Von Hippel, 2005) is highly relevant in generating breakthrough innovations. Future relationship efficacy in B2B markets depends on the concept of open innovation (Chesbrough, 2003) — innovation outside the firm — where risks and rewards of innovation are shared with key stakeholders. The role of marketing in B2B innovation or new product development (NPD) process needs to become more prominent by researching and removing existing barriers such as functional power structures and time-to-market pressures (Lilien, 2016).

In the same vein, Grewal *et al.* (2015) conducted a Delphi study that identified four research challenges in B2B buying: (1) the increasing importance and growth of emerging markets; (2) the changing landscape of B2B buying; (3) the increasing sophistication of sellers; and (4) the impact of changes in technology. Given the wide institutional differences in developed versus emerging markets and, in particular, the nature of governments and the influence of political ties on business processes in emerging markets, Grewal *et al.* (2015) identify several areas of research opportunities. How do firms with dominant informal relationships with other firms in emerging economies buy? How can sellers from emerging economies, traditionally competing on cost, now selling to buyers in new and developed markets transition from cost-based competition to value-based competition? On the flip side, how can

sellers from developed markets selling to buyers in emerging markets adapt in terms of relationship transition? Similarly, given that the buyer–seller interdependence has increased, the nature of the buying process and buying relationship has also changed and evolved into different types, including routinized exchange relationships, transactional buying operations, and organic buying relationships. More research on the antecedents and boundary conditions of these specialized buyer relationships is warranted. As buyer power increases, suppliers are increasingly expected to co-create value for buyers forcing them to be creative in adopting a "value mindset" that reflects the sellers' grasp of the buyer's ability to realize maximum value (DeLeon and Chatterjee, 2017). Finally, emerging advances in digital information technologies and digital manufacturing technologies are having disruptive effects in buyer–seller relationships, buying processes, and value co-creation. These disruptions, like a double-edged sword, also provide a spawning ground for new and fresh research ideas in B2B relationships.

KEY TAKEAWAYS

- The nature and type of trust changes as customers progress through different stages in their relationships with companies. There is a need for studying the dynamic nature of customer relationships in terms of velocity and acceleration of relational constructs (not just static levels) over the lifecycle stages and their impact on sales growth.

- The full spectrum of financial and engagement outcome metrics needs to be evaluated. Typical financial outcomes include sales-based (e.g., sales growth, sales diversity, sales volatility) and profitability-based metrics (e.g., price premiums, reduced selling costs). Typical engagement outcomes include CLV metrics (e.g., CLV-based models); however, more research is warranted for CRV, CIV, and CKV metrics.

- More research is needed to find out how firms can best leverage different types of customer engagement values: CLV, CRV, CIV, and CKV in different combinations and at different lifecycle stages, namely, acquisition, growth, retention, and win-back.

- There is a growing need to conduct empirical research that seeks to measure the impact of social commerce across decision-making phases — i.e., need recognition, pre-purchase, purchase, and post-purchase and across various social media platforms — e.g., Facebook, Twitter, Pinterest.

- While multi-tier loyalty programs are valuable, there may be unintended consequences of relationship marketing strategies such as, changing customer expectation/entitlement, customer heterogeneity, and customer reactance as a result of too much personalization. There is also a need for research on how firms can trade-off loyalty/engagement programs with segments of dis-identification: dis-identified customers, ambivalent customer, and neutral customers and the types of strategies most effective for each of these segments.

- Despite the preponderance of positive ethics approach to tackling ethical issues in marketing, firms today continue to exhibit ethical (and legal) lapses in decisions that have widespread repercussions. Relationship marketers should identify and practice the authentic norms and hypernorms of the communities they are embedded in, as long as these norms are compatible with hypernorms and follow the spirit of the overall macrosocial contract. Future research can draw from a plethora of ethical theories, e.g., consequence-based, duty-based, contract-based, and virtue-based theories to address each of these complex and fast-moving dynamic issues confronting customers at various relational touchpoints.

- Customers' scope of costs in their assessment of value is changing driven by shifting cost-benefit calculus. In particular, information privacy and how it represents a new type of cost in customer relationships with companies is important. Ethics as seen by customers, not just marketers, is critical for building customer–company relationship.

- Understanding and implementing ethics of the highest order at every conceivable touchpoint in the customers' journey is not only the "right" thing to do, it is the "smart" thing to do, making a strong "business case" for ethics. In this respect, customer relationship marketing has a bright future but several important research issues need to be addressed (see Figure 11.6).

- Understanding customer engagement in B2B markets is highly relevant for good information; hence, customer selection and valuation is critical for breakthrough innovation. Open innovation involving external stakeholder, notwithstanding costs and risks, is crucial for future relationship efficacy in B2B markets. Herein, the role of marketing cannot be overemphasized enough.

- B2B relationship marketing presents several research opportunities: given the growth in emerging markets and increasing interdependence in buyer–seller relationships, how do buyer–seller relationships evolve and adapt? Disruptive technology and an increasing pressure for sellers to adopt a value mindset provide, both, challenges and opportunities in B2B relationships.

Figure 11.6: Customer relationship marketing has a bright future but several important research issues need to be addressed.

EXERCISES

Questions

1. As customer–company relationships grow, the nature of trust changes from calculative-based trust in the exploratory stage, to knowledge-based trust in the growth stage, to affective-based trust in the maturity stage leading up to commitment. However, in several cases, the relationship enters a terminating stage in which trust and commitment declines. Discuss why this happens and what factors contribute toward the decline.

2. Research has shown that the effect of the initial level of commitment on sales growth is not significant; however, the velocity and acceleration of commitment on sales growth is. Similarly, low levels of trust and commitment may be overcome by higher levels of velocity and acceleration of the same. Discuss the need for a dynamic model of relationship marketing (as opposed to a static model) and explain the process mechanisms.

3. There are several outcome metrics used by marketers in assessing the efficacy of customer relationship marketing. These include (a) sales-based metrics (e.g., sales growth, share of wallet); (b) profitability-based metrics (e.g., price premium, selling cost); (c) aggregate-based metrics (e.g., CLV, ROI); and (d) engagement-based metrics (e.g., CKV, CIV). Discuss the pros and cons of each type of outcome metric and under what conditions is one type more suitable than the other.

4. There remain several unanswered questions relating customer relationship stage (acquisition, growth, retention, and win-back) and type of customer lifecycle value (e.g., CLV, CRV, CIV, and CKV). Draw up a list of important research questions linking lifecycle value type with relationship stage that has potential for new insights for marketers.

5. There remain several unanswered questions relating customer decision-making stage (need recognition, pre-purchase, purchase, and post-purchase) and type of social media platforms (e.g., Facebook, Twitter, LinkedIn, Pinterest). Draw up a list of important research questions linking platform type with decision-making stage that has potential for new insights for marketers.

6. There are several unintended consequences (dark side) of customer relationship marketing strategies that can backfire as a result of (a) customer expectations and entitlement; (b) customer heterogeneity; and (c) customer reactance. Explain each of these mechanisms, how they work, and what should marketers do to minimize such unintended consequences. Are there other types of unintended consequences that marketers need to be cognizant about and be prepared for?

7. Explain the following facets of customer–company identification: (a) identification; (b) dis-identification; (c) ambivalent identification; and (d) neutral identification. Discuss what type of marketing program (e.g., loyalty program, cross-selling, up-selling, incentivized referrals) is most appropriate to sway the following customers toward identified customers: (a) dis-identified customers; (b) ambivalent customers; (c) neutral customers.

8. Comment on the following statement: "Relationship marketing needs to identify the full spectrum of marketing-relevant hyper-norms applicable in all customer-brand relational touchpoints and explore the antecedents of authentic and legitimate norms prevalent in each community".

9. Explain perceived value as seen by customers and companies in relationship marketing. Explain how customer perception of value has changed in recent times, particularly the changing nature of relationship costs (e.g., transaction cost, learning cost, maintenance and lifecycle cost) in the value equation.

10. Marketers need to broaden their ethical toolkit (beyond narrow utilitarian calculus) and see relationship marketing from the customers' perspective in a way that offers them greater control, privacy, and transparency. Provide your personal ethical perspective on this thought and give reasons why you agree or disagree.

11. Comment on the following statement: "The role of marketing in B2B innovation and new product development needs to become more prominent." What barriers need to be removed for this to happen?

12. Emerging technologies such as digital information technologies and digital manufacturing technologies are having a disruptive effect on buyer–seller relationships. Explain in what ways is it affecting B2B relationships and what emerging challenges and opportunities do you see in this process.

Group Discussion

1. ABC Inc. has adopted the latest research on customer relationship marketing (provided by Palmatier, 2008), which validates that important information is not captured in the stage of lifecycle as in the trajectory or relationship dynamics (i.e., velocity and acceleration). It is the trajectory of trust that influences outcomes through its effect on commitment. Further, it is not all doom and gloom if customer trust and commitment are at low levels. Rather, low levels of customer trust and commitment may be overcome by higher levels of velocity and acceleration.

As a small group, discuss how ABC Inc. can integrate relationship dynamics into its relationship marketing strategy. Discuss why it is critical that ABC Inc. focus on "growing" rather than "maintaining" relationship with its customers. Offer strategic advice to ABC Inc. on what are some "best practices" to grow the relationship with customers.

2. Consider a customer who identifies with Walmart's support of local charities and sustainable practices, but simultaneously dis-identifies with Walmart because its practices often have adverse effects on local economies. It is also possible to simultaneously identify and dis-identify with the same aspect of the company. Consider another customer who identifies with Walmart's cost-cutting strategy as it leads to superior efficiency in services, but dis-identifies with this practice because it contributes to inferior product quality.

As a small group, discuss the psychological mechanisms that motivate customers toward ambivalent identification. Are ambivalent customers "neutral" in their identification with Walmart. Discuss what marketing program (e.g., loyalty program, cross-selling, up-selling, incentivized referrals) should Walmart adopt to sway customers with ambivalent identification toward full identification. How can Walmart convert ambivalent customers to become high influencers and referrals?

HBS and Ivey Cases

- AnswerDash (9-516-106)
- Reinventing Best Buy (9-716-455)
- Chase Sapphire (9-518-024)
- Laurs & Bridz (9B18A004)

CASE QUESTIONS

AnswerDash

1. Discuss the need for AnswerDash to adopt a dynamic model of relationship marketing (as opposed to a static model) and explain the process mechanisms.

2. There are several outcome metrics used to assess the efficacy of customer relationship marketing.

These include (a) sales-based metrics (e.g., sales growth, share of wallet); (b) profitability-based metrics (e.g., price premium, selling cost); (c) aggregate-based metrics (e.g., CLV, ROI); and (d) engagement-based metrics (e.g., CKV, CIV). Discuss the pros and cons of each type of outcome metric and under what conditions is one type more suitable than others for AnswerDash.

3. Identify the unintended consequences (dark side) of customer relationship marketing strategies that can backfire as a result of (a) customer expectations and entitlement; (b) customer heterogeneity; and (c) customer reactance. Explain each of these mechanisms, how they work, and what should AnswerDash do to minimize such unintended consequences.

4. Discuss what type of marketing program (e.g., loyalty program, cross-selling, up-selling, incentivized referrals) is most appropriate for AnswerDash to sway the following customers toward identified customers: (a) dis-identified customers; (b) ambivalent customers; (c) neutral customers.

5. Explain perceived value of a relationship with AnswerDash as seen by customers in relationship marketing Explain how customer perception of value has changed in recent times, particularly the changing nature of relationship costs (e.g., transaction cost, learning cost, maintenance and lifecycle cost) in the value equation

6. How can AnswerDash broaden its ethical toolkit (beyond narrow utilitarian calculus) and see relationship marketing from the customers' perspective in a way that offers them greater control, privacy, and transparency?

7. Emerging technologies such as digital information technologies (AI, machine learning) are having a disruptive effect on buyer–seller relationships. Explain in what ways is it affecting AnswerDash's

relationships with partners and customers and what emerging challenges and opportunities do you see in this process.

Reinventing Best Buy

1. How would you characterize the nature of trust in customer–company relationships for Best Buy: calculative-based trust in the exploratory stage, knowledge-based trust in the growth stage, or affective-based trust in the maturity stage leading up to commitment? What can Best Buy do to prevent the relationships from entering a terminating stage in which trust and commitment declines?

2. There remain several unanswered questions relating customer decision-making stage (need recognition, pre-purchase, purchase, and post-purchase) and type of social media platforms (e.g., Facebook, Twitter, LinkedIn, Pinterest). Draw up a list of important research questions linking platform type with decision-making stage that has potential for new insights for Best Buy.

3. Identify the unintended consequences (dark side) of customer relationship marketing strategies that can backfire as a result of (a) customer expectations and entitlement; (b) customer heterogeneity; and (c) customer reactance. Explain each of these mechanisms, how they work, and what should Best Buy do to minimize such unintended consequences.

4. Discuss what type of marketing program (e.g., loyalty program, cross-selling, up-selling, incentivized referrals) is most appropriate for Best Buy to sway the following customers toward identified customers: (a) dis-identified customers; (b) ambivalent customers; (c) neutral customers.

5. Explain perceived value of a relationship with Best Buy as seen by customers in relationship marketing. Explain how customer perception of value has changed in recent times, particularly the changing nature of relationship costs (e.g., transaction cost,

learning cost, maintenance and lifecycle cost) in the value equation.

6. How can Best Buy broaden its ethical toolkit (beyond narrow utilitarian calculus) and see relationship marketing from the customers' perspective in a way that offers them greater control, privacy, and transparency?

7. Discuss how Best Buy can integrate relationship dynamics into its relationship marketing strategy. Discuss why it is critical that Best Buy focus on "growing" rather than "maintaining" relationship with its customers.

Chase Sapphire

1. How would you characterize the nature of trust in customer–company relationships for JPMorgan: calculative-based trust in the exploratory stage, knowledge-based trust in the growth stage, or affective-based trust in the maturity stage leading up to commitment? What can JPMorgan do to prevent the relationships from entering a terminating stage in which trust and commitment declines?

2. Discuss the need for JPMorgan to adopt a dynamic model of relationship marketing (as opposed to a static model) and explain the process mechanisms.

3. There are several outcome metrics used to assess the efficacy of customer relationship marketing. These include (a) sales-based metrics (e.g., sales growth, share of wallet); (b) profitability-based metrics (e.g., price premium, selling cost); (c) aggregate-based metrics (e.g., CLV, ROI); and (d) engagement-based metrics (e.g., CKV, CIV). Discuss the pros and cons of each type of outcome metric and under what conditions is one type more suitable than others for JPMorgan.

4. There remain several unanswered questions relating customer decision-making stage (need recognition, pre-purchase, purchase, and post-purchase) and type of social media platforms (e.g.,

Facebook, Twitter, LinkedIn, Pinterest). Draw up a list of important research questions linking platform type with decision-making stage that has potential for new insights for JPMorgan.

5. Identify the unintended consequences (dark side) of customer relationship marketing strategies that can backfire as a result of (a) customer expectations and entitlement; (b) customer heterogeneity; and (c) customer reactance. Explain each of these mechanisms, how they work, and what should JPMorgan do to minimize such unintended consequences.

6. Discuss what type of marketing program (e.g., loyalty program, cross-selling, up-selling, incentivized referrals) is most appropriate for JPMorgan to sway the following customers toward identified customers: (a) dis-identified customers; (b) ambivalent customers; (c) neutral customers.

7. Explain perceived value of a relationship with JPMorgan as seen by customers in relationship marketing. Explain how customer perception of value has changed in recent times, particularly the changing nature of relationship costs (e.g., transaction cost, learning cost, maintenance and lifecycle cost) in the value equation.

8. How can JPMorgan broaden its ethical toolkit (beyond narrow utilitarian calculus) and see relationship marketing from the customers' perspective in a way that offers them greater control, privacy, and transparency?

9. Discuss how JPMorgan can integrate relationship dynamics into its relationship marketing strategy. Discuss why it is critical that JPMorgan focus on "growing" rather than "maintaining" relationship with its customers.

10. Discuss what marketing program (e.g., loyalty program, cross-selling, up-selling, incentivized referrals) and communications program (e.g.,

advertising strategy, positioning strategy, PR strategy) should JPMorgan adopt to sway customers with ambivalent identification toward full identification. How can JPMorgan convert ambivalent customers to become high influencers and referrals?

Laurs & Bridz

1. How would you characterize the nature of trust in customer–company relationships for Laurs & Bridz: calculative-based trust in the exploratory stage, knowledge-based trust in the growth stage, or affective-based trust in the maturity stage leading up to commitment? What can Laurs & Bridz do to prevent the relationships from entering a terminating stage in which trust and commitment declines?

2. Discuss the need for Laurs & Bridz to adopt a dynamic model of relationship marketing (as opposed to a static model) and explain the process mechanisms.

3. There are several outcome metrics used to assess the efficacy of customer relationship marketing. These include (a) sales-based metrics (e.g., sales growth, share of wallet); (b) profitability-based metrics (e.g., price premium, selling cost); (c) aggregate-based metrics (e.g., CLV, ROI); and (d) engagement-based metrics (e.g., CKV, CIV). Discuss the pros and cons of each type of outcome metric and under what conditions is one type more suitable than others for Laurs & Bridz.

4. Identify the unintended consequences (dark side) of customer relationship marketing strategies that can backfire as a result of (a) customer expectations and entitlement; (b) customer heterogeneity; and (c) customer reactance. Explain each of these mechanisms, how they work, and what should Laurs & Bridz do to minimize such un-intended consequences.

5. Discuss what type of marketing program (e.g., loyalty program, cross-selling, up-selling, incentivized referrals) is most appropriate for Laurs & Bridz to sway the following customers toward identified customers: (a) dis-identified customers; (b) ambivalent customers; (c) neutral customers.

6. Explain perceived value of a relationship with Laurs & Bridz as seen by customers in relationship marketing. Explain how customer perception of value has changed in recent times, particularly the changing nature of relationship costs (e.g., transaction cost, learning cost, maintenance and lifecycle cost) in the value equation.

7. Discuss how Laurs & Bridz can integrate relationship dynamics into its relationship marketing strategy. Discuss why it is critical that Laurs & Bridz focus on "growing" rather than "maintaining" relationship with its customers.

8. Discuss what marketing program (e.g., loyalty program, cross-selling, up-selling, incentivized referrals) and communications program (e.g., advertising strategy, positioning strategy, PR strategy) should Laurs & Bridz adopt to sway customers with ambivalent identification toward full identification. How can Laurs & Bridz convert ambivalent customers to become high influencers and referrals?

REFERENCES

Agarwal, J., W.S. DeSarbo, N.K. Malhotra, and V.R. Rao (2015), An Interdisciplinary Review of the Research in Conjoint Analysis: Recent Developments and Directions for Future Research, *Customer Needs and Solutions*, 2(1): 19–40.

Ahearne, M.C., C.B. Bhattacharya, and T. Gruen (2005), Antecedents and Consequences of Customer-Company Identification: Expanding the Role of Relationship Marketing, *Journal of Applied Psychology* 90: 574–585.

Ashforth, B.E. and F. Mael (1989), Social Identity Theory and the Organization, *Academy of Management Review* 14: 20–40.

Ball, T. and R. Dagger (2005), *Political Ideologies and the Democratic Ideal.* New York: Pearson Longman.

Bergami, M. and R.P. Bagozzi (2000), Self-Categorization, Affective Commitment and Group Self-Esteem as Distinct Aspects of Social Identity in the Organization, *British Journal of Social Psychology* 39: 555–577.

Bhattacharya, C.B., H. Rao, and M.A. Glynn (1995), Understanding the Bond of Identification: An Investigation of its Correlates among Art Museum Members, *Journal of Marketing* 59: 46–57.

Bhattacharya, C.B. and S. Sen (2003), Consumer-Company Identification: A Framework for Understanding Consumers' Relationships with Companies, *Journal of Marketing* 67: 76–88.

Bollen, Kenneth A. and Patrick J. Curran (2006), *Latent Curve Models: A Structural Equation Perspective,* Hoboken, NJ: John Wiley & Sons.

Bolton, Ruth N. and Katherine N. Lemon (1999), A Dynamic Model of Customers' Usage of Services: Usage as an Antecedent and Consequence of Satisfaction, *Journal of Marketing Research,* 36: 171–199.

Bowie, N. (1999), *Business Ethics: A Kantian Perspective,* Malden, MA: Blackwell.

Brewer, M.B. (1991), The Social Self: On Being the Same and Different at the Same Time, *Personality and Social Psychology Bulletin* 17: 475–482.

Butori, R. and A. De Bruyn (2013), So You Want To Delight Your Customers: The Perils of Ignoring Heterogeneity in Customer Evaluations of Discretionary Preferential Treatments, *International Journal of Research in Marketing* 30: 358–367.

Capraro, Anthony J., Susan Broniarczyk, and Rajendra Srivastava (2003), Factors Influencing the Likelihood of Customer Defection: The Role of Customer Knowledge, *Journal of the Academy of Marketing Science* 31(2):164–176.

Chesbrough, H.W. (2003), *Open Innovation: The New Imperative for Creating and Profiting from Technology.* Boston: Harvard Business School Press.

Costarelli, S. and A. Palmonari (2003), Ingroup Ambivalence and Experienced Affect: The Moderating Role of Social Identification, *European Journal of Social Psychology* 33(6): 813–821.

Crowe, E. and E.T. Higgins (1997), Regulatory Focus and Strategic Inclinations: Promotion and Prevention in Decision-Making, *Organizational Behavior and Human Decision Processes* 69: 117–132.

DeLeon, A.J. and S.C. Chatterjee (2017), B2B Relationship Calculus: Quantifying Resource Effects in Service-Dominant Logic, *Journal of the Academy of Marketing Science* 45: 402–427.

Dukerich, J.M., R. Kramer, and J. McLean Parks (1998), The Dark Side of Organizational Identification, in David A. Whetten and Paul C. Godfrey (Eds.), *Identity in Organizations: Building Theory Through Conversations,* Thousand Oaks: Sage.

Dunfee, T.W., N.C. Smith, and W.T. Ross Jr. (1999), Social Contracts and Marketing Ethics, *Journal of Marketing* 63: 14–32.

Dutton, J.E., Dukerich, J.M., and C.V. Harquail (1994), Organizational Images and Member Identification, *Administrative Science Quarterly* 39: 239–263.

Dwyer, Robert F., Paul H. Schurr, and Sejo Oh (1987), Developing Buyer-Seller Relationships, *Journal of Marketing* 51(2): 11–27.

Einwiller, S.A., A. Fedorikhin, A.R. Johnson, and M.A. Kamins (2006), Enough is Enough! When Identification No Longer Prevents Negative

Corporate Associations, *Journal of the Academy of Marketing Science* 34: 185–194.

Elsbach, K. (1999), An Expanded Model of Organizational Identification, *Research in Organizational Behavior* 21: 163–200.

Elsbach, K. and C.B. Bhattacharya (2001), Defining Who You Are by What You're Not: Organizational Disidentification and the National Rifle Association, *Organization Science* 12: 393–413.

Garbarino, E. and M.S. Johnson (1999), The Different Roles of Satisfaction, Trust, and Commitment in Customer Relationships, *Journal of Marketing* 63: 70–87.

Grayson, Kent and Tim Ambler (1999), The Dark Side of Long-Term Relationships in Marketing Services, *Journal of Marketing Research* 36: 132–141.

Green PE, Srinivasan V. (1978), Conjoint Analysis in Consumer Research: Issues and Outlook, *Journal of Consumer Research*, 5(2): 103–123.

Green PE, Srinivasan V. (1990), Conjoint Analysis in Marketing: New Developments with Implications for Research and Practice, *Journal of Marketing*, 54(4): 3–19.

Grewal, R., G.L. Lilien, S. Bharadwaj, P. Jindal, U. Kayande, R.F. Lusch, *et al.* (2015), Business-to-Business (B2B) Buying: Challenges and Opportunities, *Customer Needs and Solutions* 2: 192–208.

Griffin, A., B.W. Josephson, G.L. Lilien, F. Wiersema, B. Bayus, R. Chandy, *et al.* (2013), Marketing's Role in Innovation in Business-to-Business Firms: Status, Issues, and Research Agenda, *Marketing Letters* 24(2): 323–337.

Gundlach, G.T. and P.E. Murphy (1993), Ethical and Legal Foundations of Relational Marketing Exchange, *Journal of Marketing* 57(4): 35–46.

Haidt, J. and J. Graham (2007), When Morality Opposes Justice: Conservatives Have Moral Intuitions that Liberals May Not Recognize, *Social Justice Research* 20(1): 98–116.

Heider, F. (1958), *The Psychology of Interpersonal Relations*, New York: Wiley.

Hoffman, D.L., P.K. Kopalle, and T.P. Novak (2010), The "Right" Consumers for Better Concepts: Identifying Consumers High in Emergent Nature to Develop New Product Concepts, *Journal of Marketing Research* 47(5): 854–865.

Holbrook, M.B. (1981), Integrating Compositional and Decompositional Analyses to Represent the Intervening Role of Perceptions in Evaluative Judgments, *Journal of Marketing Research*, 18(February): 13–28.

Jackson, L.A., L.A. Sullivan, R. Harnish, and C.N. Hodge (1996), Achieving Positive Social Identity: Social Mobility, Social Creativity, and Permeability of Group Boundaries, *Journal of Personality and Social Psychology* 70: 241–254.

Jap, Sandy D. and Shankar Ganesan (2000), Control Mechanisms and the Relationship Life Cycle: Implications for Safeguarding Specific Investments and Developing Commitment, *Journal of Marketing Research* 37: 227–245.

Jost, J.T. and D. Burgess (2000), Attitudinal Ambivalence and the Conflict between Group and System Justification Motives in Low Status Groups, *Personality and Social Psychology Bulletin* 26: 293–305.

Kahneman, D. and A. Tversky (1979), Prospect Theory: An Analysis of Decision under Risk, *Econometrica* 47(2): 263–292.

Kreiner, G.E. and B.E. Ashforth (2004), Evidence Toward an Expanded Model of Organizational Identification, *Journal of Organizational Behavior* 25: 1–27.

Kumar, V., Lerzan Aksoy, Bas Donkers, Rajkumar Venkatesan, Thorsten Wiesel, and Sebastian Tillmanns (2010), Undervalued or Over-valued Customers: Capturing Total Customer

Engagement Value, *Journal of Service Research* 13(3): 297–310.

Kumar, V., Y. Bhagwat, and X. Zhang (2015), Regaining 'Lost' Customers: The predictive Power of First-Lifetime Behavior, the Reason for Defection, and the Nature of the win-Back Offer, *Journal of Marketing* 79: 34–55.

Kumar, V., J.A. Petersen, and R.P. Leone (2010), Driving Profitability by Driving Customer Referrals: Who, When, and How, *Journal of Marketing* 74(5): 1–17.

Kumar, V. and W. Reinartz (2016), Creating Enduring Customer Value, *Journal of Marketing* 80: 36–68.

Kumar, V. M. George, and J. Pancras (2008), Cross-Buying in Retailing: Drivers and Consequences, *Journal of Retailing* 84(1): 15–27.

Laczniak, Gene R. and Patrick E. Murphy (2019), The Role of Normative Marketing Ethics, *Journal of Business Research* 95: 401–407.

Lewicki, Roy. J., Edward C. Tomlinson, and Nicole Gillespie (2006), Models of Interpersonal Trust Development: Theoretical Approaches, Empirical Evidence, and Future Directions, *Journal of Management* 32: 991–1022.

Lilien, G.L. (2016), The B2B Knowledge Gap, *International Journal of Research in Marketing* 33: 543–556.

Malthouse, Edward C., Michael Haenlein, Bernd Skiera, Egbert Wege, and Michael Zhang (2013), Managing Customer Relationships in the Social Media Era: Introducing the Social CRM House, *Journal of Interactive Marketing* 27(4): 270–280.

Martin, K.D., A. Borah, and R.W. Palmatier (2017), Data Privacy: Effects on Customer and Firm Performance, *Journal of Marketing* 81(1): 36–58.

Martin, Kelly D. and Patrick E. Murphy (2017), The Role of Data Privacy in Marketing, *Journal of the Academy of Marketing Science* 45(2): 135–155.

Morgan, R.M. and S.D. Hunt (1994), The Commitment-Trust Theory of Relationship Marketing, *Journal of Marketing* 58: 20–38.

Murphy, P.E. (1999), Character and Virtue Ethics in International Marketing: An Agenda for Managers, Educators, and Researchers, *Journal of Business Ethics* 18(1): 107–124.

Murphy, P.E., G.R. Laczniak, and G. Wood (2007), An Ethical Basis for Relationship Marketing: A Virtue Ethics Perspective, *European Journal of Marketing* 41(1/2): 37–57.

Neslin, S.A., S. Gupta, W. Kamakura, J. Lu, and C.H. Mason (2006), Defection Detection: Measuring and Understanding the Predictive Accuracy of Customer Churn Models, *Journal of Marketing Research*, 43(2): 204–211.

Nill, A. (2003), Global Marketing Ethics: A Communicative Approach, *Journal of Macromarketing* 23(2): 90–104.

Noordhoff, C.S., K. Kriakopoulos, C. Moorman, P. Pauwels, B.G.C. Dellaert (2011), The Bright Side and Dark Side of Embedded Ties in Business-to-Business Innovation, *Journal of Marketing* 75(5): 34–52.

Oliver, R.L. (1980), A Cognitive Model of the Antecedents and Consequences of Satisfaction Decisions, *Journal of Marketing Research* 17(4): 460–469.

Otnes, C.O., T.M. Lowrey, and L.J. Shrum (1997), Toward an Understanding of Consumer Ambivalence, *Journal of Consumer Research* 24: 80–93.

Palmatier, Robert W. (2008), *Relationship Marketing*, Cambridge: Marketing Science Institute.

Palmatier, Robert W., Rajiv P. Dant, Dhruv Grewal, and Mark B. Houston (2007), *Relationship Marketing Dynamics* (pp. 1–37). Seattle: University of Washington Working Paper 1.

Palmatier, Robert W., Srinath Gopala Krishna, and Mark B. Houston (2006), Returns on Business-to-Business Relationship Marketing Investments:

Strategies for Leveraging Profits, *Marketing Science* 25: 477–493.

Palmatier, Robert W., Mark B. Houston, Rajiv P. Dant, and Dhruv Grewal (2013), Relationship Velocity: Toward a Theory of Relationship Dynamics, *Journal of Marketing* 77: 13–30.

Pratt, M.G. (2000), The Good, the Bad, and the Ambivalent: Managing Identification among Amway Distributors, *Administrative Science Quarterly* 45: 456–493.

Rao V. R. (2014), *Applied Conjoint Analysis*. Springer, New York.

Rousseau, Denise M., Sim B. Sitkin, Ronald S. Burt, Colin Camerer (1998), Not So Different after All: A Cross-Discipline View of Trust, *Academy of Management Review* 23(3): 392–404.

Rust, R. T., P.K. Kannan, and N. Peng (2002), The Customer Economics of Internet Privacy, *Journal of the Academy of Marketing Science* 30(4): 451–460.

Schumann, J.H., F.V. Wangenheim, and N. Groene (2014), Targeted Online Advertising Reciprocity Appeals to Increase Acceptance among Users of Free Web Services, *Journal of Marketing* 78: 59–75.

Scott, S.G. and V.R. Lane (2000), A Stakeholder Approach to Organizational Identity, *Academy of Management Review* 25: 43–62.

Snyder, C.R, M.A. Lassegard, and C.E. Ford (1986), Distancing after Group Success and Failure: Basking in Reflected Glory and Cutting off Reflected Failure, *Journal of Personality and Social Psychology* 51: 382–388.

Steinhoff, L. and R.W. Palmatier (2015), Understanding Loyalty Program Effectiveness: Managing Target and Bystander Effects, *Journal of the Academy of Marketing Science* 44(1): 88–107.

Stephens, M. (2018), Trust is Vital in Trade, *South Bend Tribune* April 6, A7–A8.

Tajfel, H. and J.C. Turner (1979), *An Integrative Theory of Intergroup Conflict,* Monterey, CA: Brooks/Cole.

Tajfel, H. and J.C. Turner (1986), *The Social Identity Theory of Intergroup Behavior,* Chicago, IL: Nelson-Hall.

Tucker, C.E. (2014), Social Networks, Personalized Advertising and Privacy Controls, *Journal of Marketing Research* 51(5): 546–562.

Van Berlo, G., J. Bloemer, and V. Blazevic (2014), Customer Demotion in Hierarchical Loyalty Programs, *The Service Industries Journal* 34(11): 922–937.

Venkatesan, Rajkumar, J. Andrew Petersen, and Leandro Guissoni (2018), Measuring and Managing Customer Engagement Value through the Customer Journey, in Robert W. Palmatier, V. Kumar, and Colleen M. Harmeling (Eds.), *Customer Engagement Marketing* (pp. 53–74). Palgrave Macmillan, Springer Nature, London, UK.

Von Hippel, E. (2005), *Democratizing Innovation,* Cambridge: MIT Free Press.

Von Wangenheim, F. and T. Bayon (2007), Behavioral Consequences of Overbooking Service Capacity, *Journal of Marketing* 71: 36–47.

Wagner, T., T. Hennig-Thurau, and T. Rudolph (2009), Does Customer Demotion Jeopardize Loyalty? *Journal of Marketing* 73(3): 69–85.

Wetzel, H.A., M. Hammerschmidt, and A.R. Zablah (2014), Gratitude versus Entitlement: A Dual Process Model of the Profitability Implications of Customer Prioritization, *Journal of Marketing* 78(2): 1–19.

White, T.B., D.L. Zahay, H. Thorbjornsen, and S. Shavitt (2008), Getting Too Personal: Reactance to Highly Personalized Email Solicitations, *Marketing Letters* 19: 40–50.

Yadav, M.S., K. de Valck, T. Hennig-Thurau, D.L. Hoffman, and M. Spann (2013), Social Commerce: A Contingency Framework for Assessing Marketing Potential, *Journal of Interactive Marketing* 27: 311–323.

Subject Index

A

ability, 139
ability-based trust, 209, 235–236
ability-based trustworthiness, 209
absorptive capacity, 68
advertising expenses, 200–201
affective facet, 202
aggressive selling, 24
alliance coordination, 67–68, 91, 92
alliance learning, 67, 68, 92
alliance scanning, 67–68, 91, 92
ambivalent identification, 13, 317, 318, 324, 325, 328
American Marketing Association (AMA), 4, 107, 280
associative learning, 111, 112, 124, 125, 127
authority/respect, 255, 256, 263

B

backward-looking metrics, 34, 184, 189, 320
balance theory, 207, 289, 298, 318
B2B relationship marketing, 14, 43, 51, 55, 80, 309, 311, 321, 323
B2C customers, 13
behavioral antecedents, 78
behavioral facet, 202
benefit-oriented measures, 207
benevolence, 9, 75, 91, 139, 144, 209, 214, 216, 217, 253
benevolence-based trust, 140, 141, 143, 153, 154, 155, 156, 157, 212
betweenness centrality, 178
big data analytic tools, 293
brand, 14, 235
    association, 37, 197, 200–202, 204, 207–208, 213–216, 218, 225
    awareness, 10, 22, 126, 197, 200–202, 207–208, 214–216, 225
    community, 12, 36, 182, 210–211, 214, 294–295, 298
    identity, 10, 197, 204, 206–208, 211–213, 214–218, 231–232, 237, 287, 295
    loyalty, 2, 10, 24, 44, 188, 197, 200–204, 208–211, 214–216, 218, 225
    name, 106–107, 201, 203, 209, 214, 230, 237, 276

    personality, 12, 213, 232, 286–288, 295, 298
    prominence, 11, 223, 233–235
    strength, 10, 14–16, 198, 206–207, 214–218, 224
    switching, 171–172, 190
    trust, 203–204, 207–211, 214–215, 287, 298
brand equity, 7, 10, 14–16, 36, 43, 197–211, 213–218, 225, 230, 236, 238–240, 281, 294, 297
    creation from relationship marketing perspective, 10, 197, 208, 225
    customer-based brand equity, 10, 197, 201, 204, 208, 215–218, 225
    firm-based brand equity, 200, 214, 216, 217
    integrative brand equity, 10, 197, 204, 214, 225
branding, 23, 87, 198, 201, 206, 213, 215–218, 235, 289
brand-owned touch points, 38
business-centric theory of social contracts, 250
business-to-business (B2B) marketers, 54
    vs. B2C markets, 8, 55, 90
business-to-business (B2B) marketing, 28, 54, 55
    vs. B2C markets, 8, 55, 90
business-to-business (B2B) relational dynamics, 14
business-to-business (B2B) relationships, 13–14, 31, 53, 66, 71, 72, 76, 118, 311, 321–323, 325
business-to-consumer (B2C) markets vs. B2B markets, 8, 66, 78, 84, 90, 322, 323
business-to-customer (B2C) relationships, 29, 59, 112, 118, 197, 223
    by stimulating non-purchase behavior, 112–123
    by stimulating purchase behavior, 107–112
buyer financial based values, 82, 83, 93
buyer satisfaction, 73, 91
buyer-seller channel relationships, 71–80, 93
buyer-seller relationships, 26
    relationship dynamics in, 8, 51, 58, 71–79, 312, 325, 327–328
    service dominant (S-D) logic in, 7, 8, 9, 14, 21, 27–28, 44–45, 63, 80, 92, 94, 112, 114, 125, 147
    value creation in, 5–6, 14, 28–29, 33, 37, 60, 82–83, 112, 114, 137–138, 140–141, 143, 147, 187, 211, 235, 247, 279, 297
buyer-seller satisfaction, in channel relationships, 73
buyer-supplier relationships, 73, 84, 93, 95, 311
"bystander" effects, 316

Company Index

Name Index